Diana

AN EXTRAORDINARY LIFE

Diana
An Extraordinary Life

PHOENIX ILLUSTRATED

BORN TO BE ROYAL

The Royal Family weren't strangers to Diana, nor she to them. Her father had been equerry to the Queen, and she herself was a playmate of Prince Andrew and Prince Edward on their Sandringham holidays

I t looked like just another investiture. Those who were to receive awards from the Queen, given in the New Year's Honours List, arrived at Buckingham Palace and were shepherded into line by royal officials.

But 24 February 1981 was to be no ordinary occasion of this sort. This, as the delighted visitors learned at first hand, was the day the engagement of Prince Charles was going to be announced, after years of speculation.

When the news broke officially, excitement was instant. Anticipation flared up like a forest fire. Everyone at the Palace, outside in London, throughout Britain and around the world wanted to know who was the lucky girl the Prince had chosen to be his bride and future Queen.

The answer, Lady Diana Frances Spencer, 19, youngest daughter of the 8th Earl Spencer of Althorp House, meant little at first. Diana was a shy, demure unknown, suddenly thrust into stardom. Just how significant and universal that stardom was to become no one, not even Diana herself, could yet realize, or even imagine.

Prince Charles had been dubbed the world's most eligible bachelor for many years. He was still a toddler of only three, in 1951, when the press began marrying him off.

When, later, Charles had the chance to think about it for himself, he said he would prefer to marry 'someone British' and once unwarily suggested that 30 might be a good age for him to wed. Speculation surged on regardless, and bookies actually offered odds on who the girl might be.

In reality, Charles' choice was very limited. A royal princess would be hard to come by as a wife, since most potential candidates were either too young, or they were Catholics. By law, no royal in the line of succession to the throne can marry, or be, a Catholic. Charles' future wife also had to be capable of taking on royal public duties and interesting herself in the royals' traditional charity work.

NO EASY CHOICE FOR CHARLES

Charles' wife had to have an unblemished past. That was no mean requirement after the 'permissive society' which arrived in the 1960s. Charles, in fact, had to give up one of his girlfriends, Davina Sheffield, after her former lover came out of the woodwork to reveal that they had lived together.

Right Diana in her highly-sprung pram in the early 1960s. Her earliest memory was of 'the smell of the warm plastic' of the pram's hood as she was wheeled around by a succession of nannies. **Left** This sketch of Diana, aged 4, was executed in November 1965 by Madame Pawlikovska, a family friend.

Charles, who had been very much in love, was heartbroken, but such was royal duty. Camilla Shand, who as Camilla Parker-Bowles was to play such a major role in Charles' later life, was turned down for similar reasons after they met in 1971.

Lady Diana, fortunately, had the necessary clean slate. She was very young for her nineteen years and had always kept her admirers at a distance. She also appeared suitable in many other ways. Diana had no career ambitions, except for marriage and motherhood. She was pretty. She was healthy. She seemed dutiful and came from an important and well-founded aristocratic family.

Perhaps most vital of all, Diana appeared on the royal scene just as Charles was coming under pressure to make up his mind and get married. His

> *" I never got any O-levels – always too busy. Brain the size of a pea, I've got."*
> LADY DIANA SPENCER

father, Prince Philip, was particularly concerned that his eldest son should fulfil his dynastic duty and produce future heirs to the throne. At 32, Charles was at an age when he might be expected to settle down. If he did not hurry up, Philip and others in the royal circle argued, the age gap between him and the virginal, fertile wife that he needed would become ridiculously large. As it was, Diana was nearly thirteen years younger than Charles. Later, though, both Charles and Diana dismissed the age gap as 'unimportant'.

Diana, then, seemed the right girl in the right place at the right time. But she had an added advantage not given to Charles' other girlfriends: the Royal Family already knew her.

Lady Diana Frances Spencer was born on 1 July 1961 at Park House on the Queen's Sandringham estate. Her father, Edward John Spencer, then Viscount Althorp, was heir to the 7th Earl Spencer and related to the Dukes of Marlborough. British wartime Prime Minister Winston Spencer Churchill came from the Marlborough family.

Viscount Althorp, who became 8th Earl Spencer in 1975, came from a long line of royal officials and

Above and left Diana's father, Earl Spencer, was a skilful amateur photographer and, especially in the years following his separation from the children's mother, he took countless pictures of the children as they grew up. The picture above was taken at Althorp, the family home. The picture on the left was taken in 1968 and shows Diana and her younger brother Charles, the present Earl Spencer, whose affection for her is obvious.

- Aged nearly 21, Prince Charles is invested as Prince of Wales at Caernavon Castle, **right**, on 1 July, Diana's 8th birthday
- Neil Armstrong becomes the first man to set foot on the Moon
- John Wayne wins a Best Actor Oscar for *True Grit*
- Richard Nixon takes oath as President of the United States
- Paul and Linda McCartney marry
- Kray twins sentenced to life imprisonment
- General de Gaulle resigns as President of France
- Edward Kennedy and Mary Jo Kopechne in car accident at Chappaquidick; she drowns

Above left Diana in 1970, during a summer holiday at Itchenor in Sussex. The 'shy Di' look is already evident. **Left** Park House, Sandringham, a 10-bedroomed house where Diana lived until 1975, when her father became 8th Earl Spencer. **Below** He and the four children then moved to Althorp, Northamptonshire, the Spencers' ancestral seat.

advisers. He had himself been equerry, an officer in the Royal Household, to both King George VI and Queen Elizabeth II. Both Diana's grandmothers were ladies-in-waiting and personal friends of the Queen Mother. Diana's mother, who married 'Johnny Spencer' in 1954, was the former Honourable Frances Ruth Burke Roche, daughter of the 4th Baron Fermoy, an Irish nobleman.

THE SPENCER CHILDREN

Diana was the fourth of the Spencers' five children and the youngest daughter. The eldest was Lady Sarah, now Lady Sarah McCorquodale, born in 1955. She was followed in 1957 by Lady Jane, who later married Sir Robert Fellowes, the Queen's Private Secretary. Next came a son, John, who died a short while after his birth in 1960. Charles, the present and 9th Earl Spencer, arrived three years after Diana, in 1964.

The young Spencer family grew up to enjoy the country life, with its county shows, race meetings and opportunities for horseriding and other sports in the beautiful green open spaces of Norfolk. Diana had her own pony and kept a pet guinea pig called Peanuts. Sadly, though, happy family life was

shattered in 1967 when Diana's mother left her father to be with Peter Shand Kydd, the wallpaper millionaire. There followed a painful divorce in 1969, so painful that afterwards Frances Shand Kydd would never talk about it. Diana's father was given custody of the children. He, too, remarried, in 1976. His second wife was Raine, Countess of Dartmouth and the daughter of Barbara Cartland, the prolific romantic novelist.

PLAYING WITH THE PRINCES

Meanwhile, Diana had made friends with the Queen's two younger sons, Princes Andrew and Edward. When the Royal Family was in residence at nearby Sandringham, the three children, close in age, made quite a mischievous crew. For Diana, Prince Charles stood in as the admired elder brother

Above Diana's impishness comes shining through in this cheerful shot of her wielding a croquet mallet while on holiday in the summer of 1970. **Left** Diana's father with, from left, Sarah, Charles, Jane and Diana. **Below** From an early age Diana had a love of dressing up, often borrowing her older sisters' clothes for the purpose and wearing them with panache.

that she had never had, though he was probably far too grown-up to take part in their fun.

Charles is supposed to have seen Diana for the first time when she was still in her cradle. It seems that the Prince was among the local gentry who came to pay their respects, in 1961, soon after Diana's birth. Being so much older, though, Charles is unlikely to have paid much attention to the little girl who later romped around with his brothers.

Diana grew to be 5ft 10½ins tall, with a fine figure and, well into teenage, a rather plump face. Like other girls of her aristocratic class, she was not

The Private Princess Child of a broken home

Diana was, unfortunately, an example of the damage that a broken home can cause in later life. She was only six when, according to a Spencer family servant, her mother Frances 'just wasn't there any more'.

Frances, then Viscountess Althorp, has denied that she left so abruptly. Instead, she asserts, she tried to let her children down lightly and prepare them for the day she left their father. The Althorps divorced two years later when Diana was eight.

Diana never fully got over it. At times, she showed she loved her mother, telephoned her regularly and accompanied her on shopping trips. At other times, mother and daughter quarrelled and there were periods when they did not speak to each other.

Lacking confidence

Diana was very close to her father, who brought his children up after their mother left. Even so, Diana grew up with many signs of the damage the divorce had done. Diana was unusually shy. She was immature. She lacked self-confidence. Like her sister Sarah, she suffered eating disorders. She also found it hard to trust people, perhaps in case they let her down.

Diana also craved love and when she felt confident enough to give it, as she did with her children, she tended to swamp and overwhelm people. She was also over-romantic, expecting the roses-round-the-door and happy-ever-after package that few marriages are ever likely to offer.

To an extent, the adulation Diana received from her millions of admirers went some way towards recompensing her for what she had lost. But when her own marriage ended, it was brought sharply home to her that this was too often the fate of those who come from broken homes. Divorce can be a vicious circle.

Had she lived, her main aim in life would have been to ensure that her sons did not suffer as she had.

Right Diana with her mother, Frances, at the wedding of her brother, Charles, on 16 September 1989 at St. Mary's Church, Brington, in Northamptonshire.

Above Diana's parents, Edward John, Viscount Althorp and the Honourable Frances Roche, on their wedding day in 1954. She was 12 years his junior.
Right Diana with her stepmother, Raine, outside Claridge's during a shopping trip on 8 May 1996.

IN CONTEXT TAKE OFF
1980

- Space shuttle *Columbia*, **right**, takes off for the first time
- Robert Runcie becomes Archbishop of Canterbury
- John Lennon is murdered outside his New York home
- Ronald Reagan, former film star, elected President of the United States
- Bjorn Borg wins men's singles at Wimbledon for the 5th successive time

expected to be especially academic. At school, which she left with no 'O' levels, her main interest seemed to be younger children, with whom she had a remarkable rapport. She knew instinctively how to deal with youngsters on their own terms, a valuable talent for a future Princess of Wales.

Diana was less happy when she was sent to a finishing school in Switzerland in 1977. She missed her family. She also missed Prince Andrew, on whom she had a teenage 'crush'. At her boarding school in Kent, Diana had kept a photograph of Andrew above her bed and, it appears, had girlish dreams of marrying him one day.

MEETING CHARLES AGAIN

Back in England after only six weeks at the finishing school, she was introduced – or rather re-introduced – to Prince Charles by her sister Sarah. The meeting took place in a field near Sandringham and Charles was impressed: he thought Diana 'a splendid 16-year-old'. However, regarding her as still a child, he probably thought little more of it.

Around this time, Lady Sarah herself was the centre of wedding speculation as Charles approached his 30th birthday. Sarah, though, was not in love with Charles and in any case baulked at the public life that would be hers if she married into the Royal Family. The speculation fizzled out, but two years later, it started up again. This time, the Spencer girl in question was Diana.

Diana's teenage years were years of great change. Holidays were spent with one or other of her parents, generally in the country. She is seen here, **above and centre right**, in the west of Scotland, where her mother, Frances, had moved to a 1000-acre estate with new husband Peter Shand Kydd. Soufflé the pony was a great comfort to Diana. As she moved into her mid-teens, **bottom right**, she hankered for the bright lights of London. After finishing school she moved into a flat in Kensington, supporting herself by working with children, **opposite page**.

invitation, this time to stay at Balmoral while the royals were there on summer holiday.

The beautiful surroundings of the Scottish Highlands gave them plenty of opportunity for long walks. They talked, did some salmon fishing and discovered a new and deeper friendship. Soon, Charles was looking at Diana with new eyes. He was touched when she told him that he needed somebody to look after him. It was only a matter of time before Charles got the idea that the 'somebody' was Diana herself.

After everyone returned to London, Charles made several telephone calls to Diana's Kensington flat, which had been bought with funds bequeathed

> ## "It's wrong, you are lonely; you should be with somebody to look after you."
> DIANA TO CHARLES, JULY 1980

by her maternal grandmother. She shared the flat with several girl friends. A number of secret meetings followed at the homes of friends Charles knew he could trust to be discreet. Realising the need for discretion as she did, Diana was not surprised by these precautions and told her flatmates not to reveal anything of what was happening. Like good friends, they never uttered a word.

Word, nevertheless, got out. The press got wind

By then, she was an even more 'splendid' 18-year-old, with a warm, sympathetic personality and striking good looks. Charles now began to take her seriously. In 1979, he and Diana danced together at a ball given by the Duke of Richmond. It was quite obvious that they were interested in each other.

Later that same summer, Diana was invited to spend yachting week at Cowes, on the Isle of Wight, with the Royal Family. The budding romance very nearly ended then and there when Diana sneaked up on Charles while swimming and overturned his windsurfer. Charles was thoroughly soaked, but fortunately his sense of humour came to the rescue, and the romance proceeded.

Before long, Diana was becoming a fixture in the royals' social life. In 1980, she received another

IN THE NEWS

Charles to marry Lady Diana Spencer

Following the announcement of the engagement of Lady Diana Spencer to Prince Charles, the Daily Star quoted Diana as telling her father, 'I can give all my love to the Royal Family. I can give all my love to everybody. I have so much love to give'. The paper also revealed how Charles had asked Earl Spencer for his daughter's hand in marriage. According to the Earl, the Prince telephoned his London flat and said 'Can I marry your daughter? I have asked her and, very surprisingly, she has said yes.' And the Earl replied, 'I am delighted. Well done!'

A DAILY STAR CELEBRATION ISSUE

of Charles' new romance and for the first time, Diana was besieged by reporters and photographers. Diana, who was shy and blushed easily, was unused to such avid interest. She tried to cope, but before long, press interest became so overwhelming that her mother had to make a direct appeal to the press to leave her daughter alone, or at least treat her with more consideration.

Meanwhile, Buckingham Palace was busy issuing official denials of a romance. Even so, behind the scenes, Charles was being urged to make a decision, partly because if he did not, then Diana's own position might be compromised.

Charles was a thoughtful, considerate man and knew better than anyone else the pressures that would come Diana's way if she married him. He proposed to Diana in a fit setting – a candlelit dinner – but made sure she knew what she would be taking on: not just him, but the Royal Family and, in a way, the whole country.

> **"I asked her to think it over, in case it would be too awful."**
> PRINCE CHARLES, AFTER PROPOSING

Some time before, Diana had planned a holiday in Australia with her mother. Charles told her to go and while she was there, think it over. Diana had no need for that. She never had any doubts, so much so that she did not spend the planned twelve days in Australia, but returned to England early.

DELIGHT AT THE NEWS

The engagement of Prince Charles and Diana was announced a few days after her return, and the popular reception was ecstatic.

The Royal Family was said to be 'delighted', the Queen and Prince Philip 'thrilled'. Charles, who had once been a rather solitary figure, spending evenings alone in his apartments, suddenly acquired a new zest.

All this confirmed to the British public what they most wanted to know: the forthcoming marriage between the Prince of Wales and Lady Diana Spencer was deemed to be a love match.

Left and below Once news of her romance with Charles became public, Diana got her first taste of press pursuit. She was waylaid by photographers outside her flat and on her way to and from the kindergarten where she worked.
Right On 24 February 1981 the engagement was announced and a photocall was held in the gardens of Buckingham Palace.

❧ Protocol ❧

ROLE OF A QUEEN CONSORT

Prince Charles was not choosing a wife only for himself. He was also choosing a future Queen Consort. A Queen Consort becomes Queen through marriage, whereas a Queen-Regnant or reigning Queen, like Elizabeth II, inherits the throne in her own right. A Queen Consort nevertheless has big responsibilities. She is the mother of the heir to the throne. She represents the caring aspect of monarchy. So Lady Diana had a lot to live up to. As a role model she might have looked to Queen Elizabeth, the Queen Mother, seen **right** *with the future George VI.*

THE ROYAL SUCCESSION &

Prince Charles and Diana, Princess of Wales are both descendants of King James I.

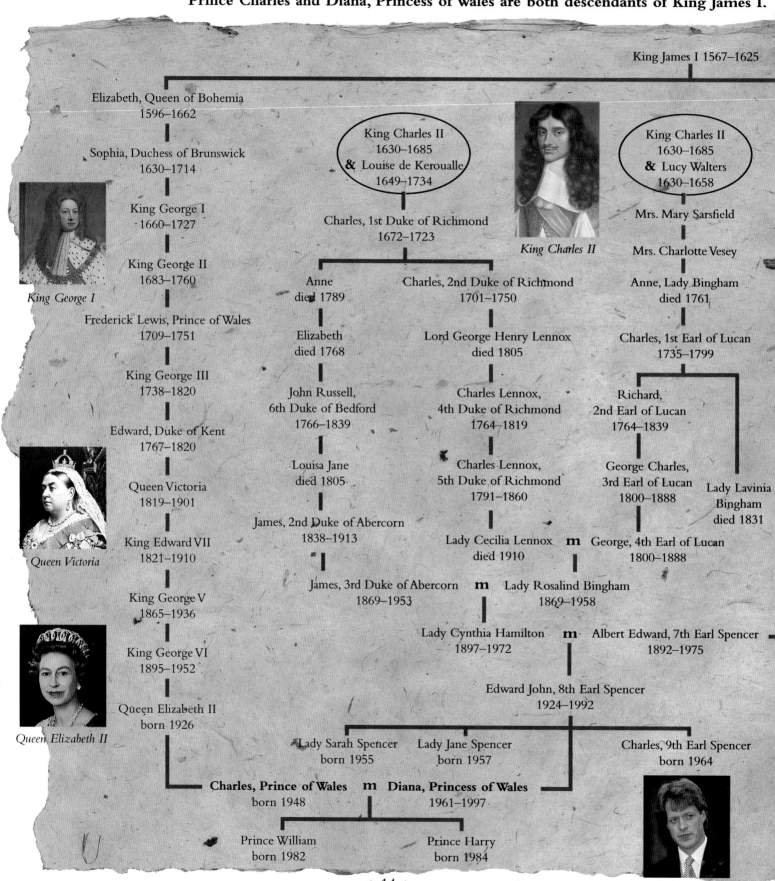

King James I 1567–1625

Elizabeth, Queen of Bohemia
1596–1662

King Charles II
1630–1685
& Louise de Keroualle
1649–1734

King Charles II
1630–1685
& Lucy Walters
1630–1658

King Charles II

Sophia, Duchess of Brunswick
1630–1714

Charles, 1st Duke of Richmond
1672–1723

Mrs. Mary Sarsfield

King George I
1660–1727

Mrs. Charlotte Vesey

King George I

King George II
1683–1760

Anne
died 1789

Charles, 2nd Duke of Richmond
1701–1750

Anne, Lady Bingham
died 1761

Frederick Lewis, Prince of Wales
1709–1751

Elizabeth
died 1768

Lord George Henry Lennox
died 1805

Charles, 1st Earl of Lucan
1735–1799

King George III
1738–1820

John Russell,
6th Duke of Bedford
1766–1839

Charles Lennox,
4th Duke of Richmond
1764–1819

Richard,
2nd Earl of Lucan
1764–1839

Edward, Duke of Kent
1767–1820

Louisa Jane
died 1805

Charles Lennox,
5th Duke of Richmond
1791–1860

George Charles,
3rd Earl of Lucan
1800–1888

Lady Lavinia
Bingham
died 1831

Queen Victoria

Queen Victoria
1819–1901

James, 2nd Duke of Abercorn
1838–1913

Lady Cecilia Lennox **m** George, 4th Earl of Lucan
died 1910   1800–1888

King Edward VII
1821–1910

James, 3rd Duke of Abercorn **m** Lady Rosalind Bingham
1869–1953   1869–1958

King George V
1865–1936

Lady Cynthia Hamilton **m** Albert Edward, 7th Earl Spencer
1897–1972   1892–1975

Queen Elizabeth II

King George VI
1895–1952

Edward John, 8th Earl Spencer
1924–1992

Queen Elizabeth II
born 1926

Lady Sarah Spencer
born 1955

Lady Jane Spencer
born 1957

Charles, 9th Earl Spencer
born 1964

Charles, Prince of Wales m Diana, Princess of Wales
born 1948   1961–1997

Prince William
born 1982

Prince Harry
born 1984

9th Earl Spencer

THE SPENCER FAMILY TREE

Men and women of the Spencer family have been loyal servants to a long line of monarchs.

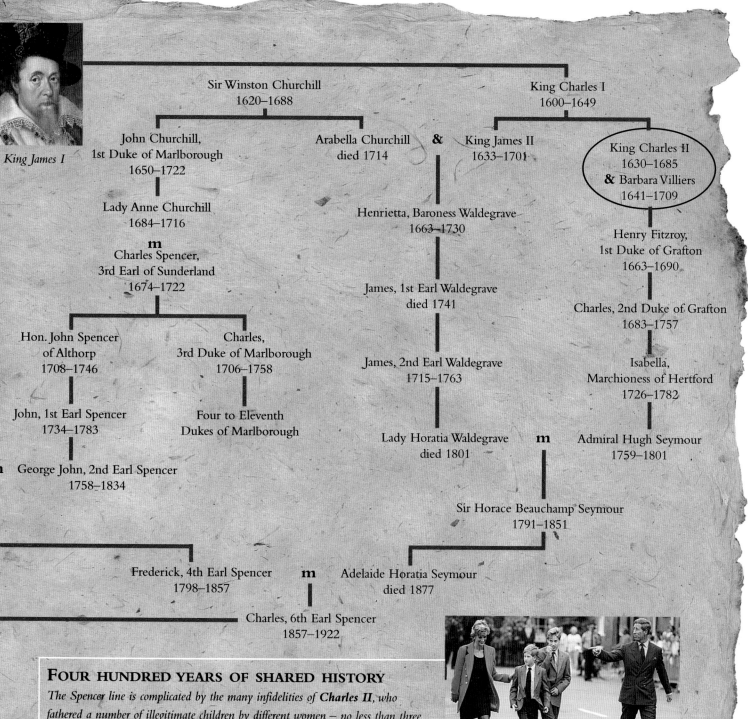

King James I

Sir Winston Churchill
1620–1688

King Charles I
1600–1649

John Churchill,
1st Duke of Marlborough
1650–1722

Arabella Churchill
died 1714

&

King James II
1633–1701

King Charles II
1630–1685
& Barbara Villiers
1641–1709

Lady Anne Churchill
1684–1716

Henrietta, Baroness Waldegrave
1663–1730

Henry Fitzroy,
1st Duke of Grafton
1663–1690

m

Charles Spencer,
3rd Earl of Sunderland
1674–1722

James, 1st Earl Waldegrave
died 1741

Charles, 2nd Duke of Grafton
1683–1757

Hon. John Spencer
of Althorp
1708–1746

Charles,
3rd Duke of Marlborough
1706–1758

James, 2nd Earl Waldegrave
1715–1763

Isabella,
Marchioness of Hertford
1726–1782

John, 1st Earl Spencer
1734–1783

Four to Eleventh
Dukes of Marlborough

Lady Horatia Waldegrave
died 1801

m

Admiral Hugh Seymour
1759–1801

George John, 2nd Earl Spencer
1758–1834

Sir Horace Beauchamp Seymour
1791–1851

Frederick, 4th Earl Spencer
1798–1857

m

Adelaide Horatia Seymour
died 1877

Charles, 6th Earl Spencer
1857–1922

FOUR HUNDRED YEARS OF SHARED HISTORY

*The Spencer line is complicated by the many infidelities of **Charles II**, who fathered a number of illegitimate children by different women – no less than three of his offspring were ancestors of **Diana**. **Prince Charles** is not descended from Charles II but shares with Diana a common ancestor in **King James I**, the first Stuart king and grandfather of Charles II. The Stuart dynasty ended after the death of James II's younger daughter, the childless Queen Anne. The throne passed to the descendants of King James I's daughter, **Elizabeth, Queen of Bohemia**. These were the Hanoverians. The line of succession of British monarchs is shown at far left. Latest in the line of succession is Prince William, **seen right** with his brother Harry and his parents.*

Glamorous Gowns

Diana in evening wear was the fairytale princess come to life. After dark was the time she made her most glamorous fashion statements and wooed her adoring public

Evening dresses gave Diana her best opportunities for making a really grand impact, and to dazzle at galas, balls, dinners and other events. Her height gave designers plenty of opportunity to use interesting materials. Her beautiful blonde hair and glowing complexion enabled her to carry off many different colours. In fact, there seemed to be no style, colour or neckline which failed to make her look just fabulous.

Before Diana, the royals' wardrobes, including their evening dresses, had not been much to write home about. But once Diana came on the scene, the fashion world sat up and took notice. Here was a great chance to promote British fashion, and Diana, with her shapely size 10 figure, was the best possible model – royal, beautiful and stylish. Diana's

Left Looking stunning in Catherine Walker's beaded gown and bolero jacket in November, 1989. There was a huge difference in fashion sense between the schoolgirlish Lady Diana Spencer – seen, **right**, in the notorious black taffeta dress by the Emmanuels (see *In the News*, page 23) with Monaco's Princess Grace – and the stylish Princess of Wales, in a Catherine Walker creation in July 1988, **far right**.

own early taste in evening dresses had been rather little-girlish: lots of frills, furbelows, full skirts, puff sleeves and gauzy materials. This, in fact, was the sort of evening wear favoured by the Sloane Rangers, a group of young, well-born socialites, to which she belonged.

However, when she became a royal princess, her Sloane outfits would no longer do. High fashion had to be the order of the day in future, though it was high fashion with a particular royal difference.

Because royals like Diana were very much on show during evening engagements, dresses had to be comfortable and easy to move in. Diana was tall for a woman, and she often had to bend forward to shake hands with the people standing in line to be presented to her. So, designers had to be careful with slim skirts. They had to avoid making them too tight on the hips so that she could be photographed from behind without looking ungainly.

> " *She was always much more modern than…fashionable…she had her own style.* "
> JOSEPH ETTEDGUI

A skirt that was stretched too tightly over the royal posterior would not do.

Designers had to be careful about the fronts of Diana's evening dresses, too. She could not show too much cleavage, so very low necklines were out. At the same time, she had to avoid looking swaddled by a too-high neckline, unless this was integral to the whole design.

One high neckline that did work well was that on the superb red dress she wore in Australia in 1985 (see page 23). The gown featured wide built-up shoulders, with a bodice and skirt that tapered down to the ankles, almost coming to a point, creating an 'inverted triangle' in outline.

Being tall and very slim, Diana looked terrific. The straight-across shoulder-to-shoulder neckline, relieved by a small 'keyhole' in the centre, was an essential feature of the dress' triangular shape.

Conversely, Diana often favoured off-the-shoulder evening gowns, some of them underarm-to-underarm styles, playing safe with one shoulder

Two evening guises for the youthful Diana. **1** Sweet but sophisticated in a figure-revealing, sparkled gown. **2** In 1981, romantic but more fussy with a puff-sleeved, full-skirted dress by Belville Sassoon.

3 Dancing with Charles in 1985, she wears an off-the-shoulder, full-skirted ballgown in electric blue, created by Bruce Oldfield. **4** Diana had no fear of drama, as this striking, froth-skirted evening dress by Murray Arbeid shows. A bold colour statement was made by wearing one long black and one long red glove. Diana wore the gown to the première of the film *The Mission*, in October 1986.

5 Diana wears a Catherine Walker gown and scarf at a 1988 gala performance of *Miss Saigon* in London. The swathed dress is suitably theatrical, with pleats reminiscent of an ancient Greek costume. **6** Diana wore this Christina Stambolina figure-hugger in July 1993, at the Serpentine Gallery, on the evening that Charles admitted adultery in a television interview.

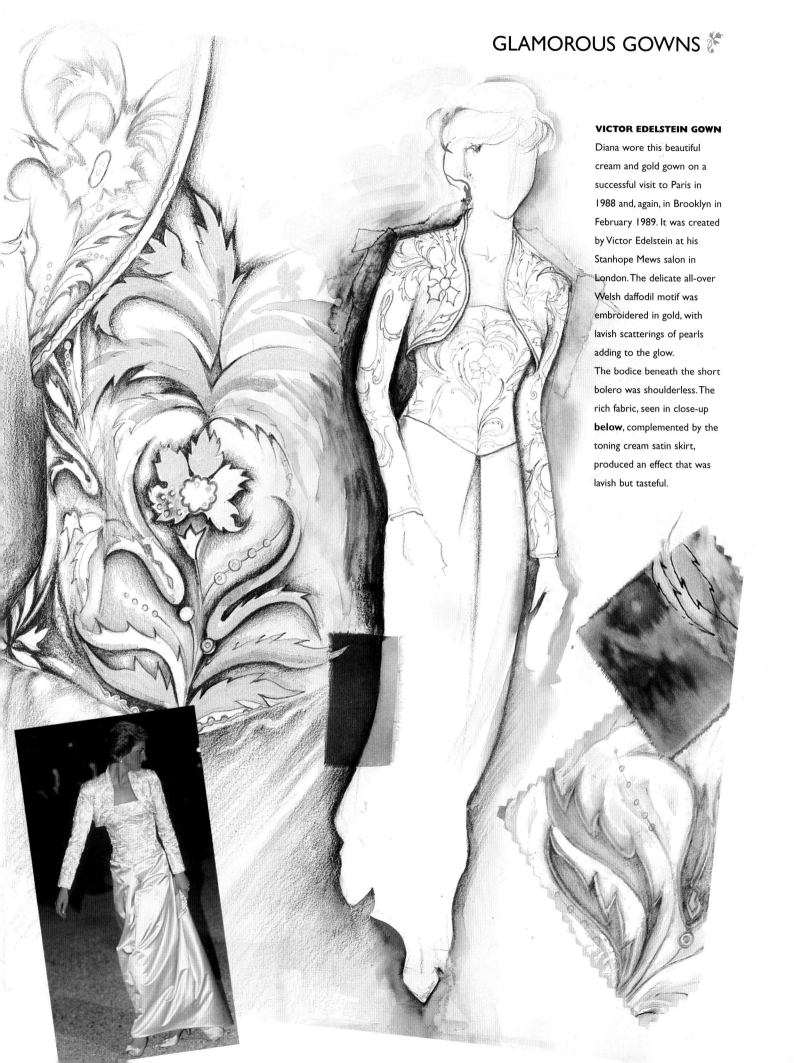

VICTOR EDELSTEIN GOWN

Diana wore this beautiful cream and gold gown on a successful visit to Paris in 1988 and, again, in Brooklyn in February 1989. It was created by Victor Edelstein at his Stanhope Mews salon in London. The delicate all-over Welsh daffodil motif was embroidered in gold, with lavish scatterings of pearls adding to the glow. The bodice beneath the short bolero was shoulderless. The rich fabric, seen in close-up **below**, complemented by the toning cream satin skirt, produced an effect that was lavish but tasteful.

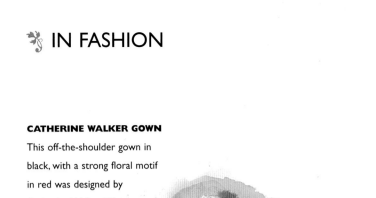

CATHERINE WALKER GOWN

This off-the-shoulder gown in black, with a strong floral motif in red was designed by Catherine Walker. Diana wore it at a British Embassy dinner held in Paris, France in November 1988, on the occasion of her five-day visit with Prince Charles. The entire trip was a notable sartorial success and this gown drew the catchy headline 'French Dressing!' in at least one English magazine.

Left The modest touches of jewellery – earrings but no necklace and just a simple pearl bracelet – help make the impact of this floor-length Catherine Walker gown even greater.

Below, left and right Diana wore this eye-catching oriental brocaded top by Catherine Walker as part of two different dresses. Even a princess with a wardrobe worth £1 million knew how to economize.

strap. Very early on, Diana learned a hard lesson about strapless evening gowns. On her first evening appearance, at Goldsmith's Hall in the City of London, on 9 March 1981, shortly after her engagement, she wore a very low-cut black taffeta dress designed by David and Elizabeth Emmanuel. The Emmanuels later went on to design Diana's wedding dress. Diana was a bit plumper then than she later became – by about two dress sizes, in fact – and she showed rather more bosom than she might have wished. When she realised the effect it had created, she burst into tears and cried on the shoulder of Princess Grace of Monaco. Princess Grace, the former film star and an older woman well versed in the business of elegant public appearances, gave Diana some useful advice about evening dresses and she never made the same mistake again.

Diana knew now that, for respectability's sake, she could not afford to make her bust too prominent. So, she turned to other ways of revealing her shapely shoulders without giving too much away.

> *"At the very beginning she didn't care about clothes, but gradually she grew to enjoy fashion."*
> BRUCE OLDFIELD

She did not, however, give up shoulderless evening gowns altogether. She compromised in, for example, the off-the-shoulder gown she wore in 1987 to the Cannes Film Festival: this had a high underarm-to-underarm top of pleated fabric. It was elegant, but showed nothing untoward.

Another example was the red wide-necklined dress by Victor Edelstein, which Diana wore to a gala dinner during the Washington trip in October 1990. The neckline came to a point just above her cleavage, but the bodice itself was loose over the bust, while her waist was emphasized just the same by transverse pleating.

Another important point Diana learned was that, to keep her public happy, the most interesting part of her evening dresses should be the top half, from the waist up. When seated in the royal box at the opera or the cinema, or at the dinner table, the skirt, however beautiful or interesting, would be

hidden from members of the audience, who would inevitably want to stare at her. This was one reason why the bodices of Diana's evening gowns were often elaborate, with plenty of beading, brocade and, in one instance, a dramatic stand-up collar.

One good example of clever royal evening dress design was a gown with a long-sleeved, round-necked top, heavily embroidered with crimson and lilac flowers (see page 21). The top ended with three patterned bands under the bust. With it, Diana wore a plain straight lilac skirt which keyed in with the flowers. So, when she was sitting down, what people saw of Diana was the elaborate top with an above-the-waist glimpse of the lilac skirt.

Another skirt she wore with the same top achieved the same effect another way. This was a fuller skirt in a lighter, shinier lilac with a deep horizontal ruched band stretching from under the bust·

> ### "She'd say, 'I need a dress for this party tomorrow night. Can you make me something?'"
> #### David Sassoon

to the hips. Only a woman with a slim waist and hipline like Diana could get away with it, but get away with it she did.

There were times, of course, when Diana tired of having skirts which played second fiddle to her tops. Even so, 'top interest' had to be maintained. One ingenious answer was to design an evening dress with a plain black underarm-to-underarm bodice which stretched down to her hips (see page 18). Below that was a great froth of filmy red skirt, the bottom edged with a thin line of black. With this, Diana wore one long black glove reaching several inches above her elbow and one long red glove. So the colour statement was made, even when the skirt was hidden.

The skirt itself was unusual – short in the front and long at the back. With it, Diana wore black tights and plain black shoes. The whole ensemble was stunning, but observed another vital royal rule for dressing: never reveal too much knee, or at least, not inadvertently.

In the last years of her life, Diana often wore day

1 This short evening dress, worn to a Hong Kong gala evening at the Barbican in London, in 1991, has a Chinese lantern-style bodice in wine red velvet. **2** Indian intricacy. Diana's top for this Catherine Walker evening dress, worn during her tour of India with Charles in 1992, reproduces a traditional Indian decorative pattern.

3 Bruce Oldfield, an ex-Barnardo's boy, designed masses of silver lamé pleating into this covered-up V-necked dress from 1989. **4** This straightforward off-the-shoulder dress in lilac, with a full skirt, was worn to the ballet in Auckland in April 1983. The dress was designed by Donald Campbell for Diana's trip to New Zealand.

5 Ultra feminine: all pink puffs and pearls by Catherine Walker. One of Diana's more obviously elaborate gowns, worn to the Guildhall in 1985, it had had the sleeves lengthened. **6** Worn in June 1993 to an outdoor sculpture exhibition at London's Serpentine Gallery, this black sophisticated number, with cross-over straps, shows off Diana's back artfully.

Diana delighted the Australians in 1985 with this stunning Bruce Oldfield evening gown, **left**, that only a truly slender woman could wear. Apart from its dazzling colour, the genius of this dress was its elegant line and the way the built-up shoulders created an inverted triangle effect.

suits with skirts above the knee, but that was the fashion of the time, and she had great knees, anyway. Royal protocol had it, though, that no dress should be worn which ran the risk of giving spectators a glimpse of knee to which they had no right. The red and black evening dress followed this rule quite cleverly, providing plenty of fullness in the front, even though the skirt length came only just below the knee. That way, Diana could walk, dance and sit down while remaining confident that her knees remained out of sight.

Freedom of movement

When it came to functions where there would be dancing, Diana's evening dresses had to be designed so that she could move freely while still looking elegant. Charles and Diana danced quite energetically at some evening engagements, but her dresses did not revert to the very full skirts she wore at the start of her marriage. Instead, the dresses had their skirts 'relaxed' a little to give freedom of movement on the dance floor.

Diana wearing evening dress was always a fine sight to see. She stuck to the royal rules for proper dressing. She rarely overdid her outfits. She used her natural assets – her height, her slim figure and her blonde colouring – to the utmost. No wonder she became a royal fashion icon and, with increasing sophistication and assurance, taught millions of women around the world about taste and style.

IN THE NEWS

A mistake she never repeated

The press were out in force when Lady Diana went to London's Goldsmith's Hall soon after her engagement in 1981. They didn't miss a thing, and inevitably made much of a tentative glimpse of Diana's bust that they – and she – never expected. Headline writers had a field day with lines like 'What a boob!'.

Diana, of course, was mortified. This was her first real experience of public life in the glare of the cameras. Her first experience, too, of how minutely the press would be observing her every movement, and just how unforgiving the media could be.

The Italian Tour

Throughout her life, Diana became increasingly accomplished at the art of royal tours. Her visit, with Charles, to Italy in 1985 was one of the most successful and most warmly received

Italy in springtime. A charming prince, a beautiful princess. A country with many historic fascinations. A warm-hearted people keen to greet the royal visitors in the emotional fashion shown only by Italians. These were the ingredients for success that characterized Charles and Diana's tour of Italy, which took place between 19 April and 5 May 1985.

Like many nations which have shed their monarchs, the Italians have a keen interest in foreign royalty. They were delighted by Charles and entranced by Diana and expressed their welcome in typically generous style. 'Ciao, Carlo!' ('Hi, Charles!') they yelled from the crowd. And 'Che bella!' ('What a beauty!') they murmured to Diana. Both Charles and Diana were at times confronted by a forest of hands to be grasped and shaken in greeting.

The tour began on Friday, 19 April, in an off-shore part of Italy, the Mediterranean island of Sardinia. Here, the royal couple's VC-10 touched down to a welcome so enthusiastic that the waiting masses nearly destroyed the crowd control barriers. A group of children managed to burst through, but failed to reach Charles and Diana before they

Above There was never a shortage of Italians crowding round to meet, greet and shake hands with Diana.
Right Charles and Diana's ride in a gondola in Venice lasted only four minutes, but it was watched with interest all the way. It was to round off a perfect tour on the royal couple's last day, 5 May.

Above Arriving at La Spezia on *Britannia*, Diana matched Charles' naval uniform with a jaunty sailor-style hat.

stepped into their car and were whisked away.

There was a folk dancing display, which Diana thought '*magnifico*', before the Prince and Princess boarded the royal yacht *Britannia* which sailed into La Spezia, the Italian naval port near Genoa. The frigate *Ajax* escorted them in and, to signal their arrival, fired a 21-gun salute in their honour. The couple watched a demonstration by helicopters and anti-submarine craft. Diana evidently did not want to miss a thing. Charles was about to go off alone to view top secret NATO missile operations, but Diana insisted on coming along, too.

At the opera

The mood was cultured that evening, when Charles and Diana went to the opera to see a performance of Puccini's *Turandot* (see *In the News*).

On Sunday, 21 April, they attended morning service at the All Saints Episcopalian Church in Milan, then lunched with friends of the Royal Family, Prince and Princess Borromeo, on the privately-owned island of Isola Bella on Lake Maggiore. That evening, it was Charles and Diana's turn to play host. At the Italian Government Hospitality House, the Prefettura, they gave a reception for members of the media appointed to accompany their tour.

Prince Charles, a keen opera fan, had loved the performance of *Turandot* and even greater thrills awaited him on Monday, 22 April, when he and Diana drove to the Church of Santa Maria delle Grazie in Milan to view Leonardo da Vinci's great

IN THE NEWS

Diana causes upset over dress

The dress worn by Diana to the performance of Turandot, on 20 April 1985, a pink evening gown created by one of Diana's favourite fashion designers, Victor Edelstein. It caused grumbles from the audience because it had been seen several times before. One Italian socialite, the Marchesa Francesca Patrizi, was reported as saying that Diana looked like a 'charming shopgirl'. For the rest of her trip Diana went out of her way to wear new outfits, many of them created by British designers.

New outfit to silence critics

Diana replies with elegance

From AMIT ROY in Milan

THE Princess of Wales answered the fashion critics on her Italian tour by wearing an elegant new outfit yesterday.

She turned up in Milan to see restoration work on Leonardo da Vinci's Last Supper in a costume that many cheek lightweight summer suit.

The grey check patterning and outfit. The jacket, with camera had a V-shaped neckline and buttoning back and the skirt was tight.

Upset

The three-button suit — worn as a dress — is by her favourite designer, Bruce Oldfield.

The hemline was notably shorter than the Princess usually wears.

Until yesterday Diana had puzzled fashion drive into Europe. All out-fit on what had been billed a British fashion drive into Europe. All what she wore out by newspaper reporters that her wardrobe for the trade trip was costing about £80,000, but it is known that she has brought seven to Italy and will be on view for a glimpse of the tour programme sits for a glimpse of the royal couple and yesterday, in every royal couple, the crowds were growing.

Daily the crowds were growing the Princess, in every royal couple's delight, walkabout, to the chants of "Diana! Diana!"

Diana yesterday: Shimmering check
Picture: JAMES GRAY

Turn to Page 2, Col. 4

masterpiece *The Last Supper*, a fresco he finished around 1497. At the time Charles and Diana were there, the fresco was being extensively restored. The couple realised at once what a mammoth task this was, describing it as 'traumatically overwhelming'.

Afterwards, Charles and Diana stopped off at Cascina Costa to tour the Agusto helicopter factory before flying to Florence to stay at the Villa la Pistra, the home of the famous British art historian Sir Harold Acton.

Florence, a great cultural centre crammed with wonderful sights, was well worth the three days Charles and Diana spent there. The Italian sun was, happily, shining, creating a stunning panorama of the city as the couple viewed it from high up, at the

> **"I really must go and see the original drawings [of 'The Last Supper']…in Windsor Castle."**
> PRINCE CHARLES

Church of St. Miniato. The church itself was interesting to explore, with its ancient crypt and monastery, but Diana could not resist the lure of the tourist shop sited there. In a minor shopping spree, she bought a piggy bank for three-year-old Prince William, a 23-herb liqueur, a ceramic pot and, for herself, a kilo of honey.

Diana forgot, though, that royals never carry any money while on tour. One of her detectives had to

Above Diana's Victor Edelstein evening gown, worn for the opera, was lovely, but fashion followers in the audience were disappointed that the Princess chose not to surprise them with an outfit that they had not seen before.

Left Diana loved shopping and could not resist a tourist shop at a church and monastery in Florence. The monks, led by Monsignor Aldinucci, seen here with Charles and Diana, made her a gift of her 'purchases' when she realized that, as royal protocol demands, she had no money.

try paying the 54,500 lire (£20) she had spent, but did not have enough. Monsignor Aldinucci, who was accompanying the royal couple, came to the rescue. Diana's purchases he said, were gifts from himself and his priests. Diana blushed, though whether from pleasure or relief, no one knew.

Viewing art treasures

Like many visitors before and since, Charles and Diana found Florence somewhat overwhelming, with its rich heritage of statues, paintings, frescoes and churches. One big highlight was Botticelli's renowned painting of *Venus rising from the Sea*, in the Uffizzi, which Charles and Diana viewed on the afternoon of 24 April, after lunching at the Palazzo Medici Riccardi. They spent some time at the world-famous gallery, exploring many of its rooms, which contain priceless gems of art from the Renaissance and other periods.

Everywhere Charles and Diana went, the crowds gathered to greet them. People crammed balconies, hung out of windows, even climbed walls to get a glimpse of their illustrious visitors. After all the

> ## "We must come back here one day and do this privately."
> PRINCE CHARLES

excitements of the day, 24 April ended with a private dinner in the company of the Marchese and Marchesa Pucci. The Pucci name was world famous for elegant fashion design and with Diana by now well-established as a world-class fashion icon, the talk was lively and well-informed.

By this time, Charles and Diana had been 'on the go' for almost a week, so the morning of Thursday, 25 April was set aside as time off. The break was brief. Charles and Diana spent a few hours after breakfast exploring the splendid gardens at the Villa la Pietre, but then had to leave for Livorno, where they were due to rejoin the royal yacht *Britannia*. On the way, they toyed with the idea of making a detour to see the Leaning Tower of Pisa, but resisted the temptation and carried on to Livorno.

Once the royal couple was aboard, *Britannia* sailed south towards Civitavecchia. Next day, a

Right Diana in animated conversation with Francesco Cossiga, President of the Italian Senate. Later in 1985, he succeeded Sandro Pertini as President of Italy.

Above *Venus rising from the Sea* by Botticelli delighted Charles and Diana when they viewed it in the famous Uffizzi gallery in Florence on 24 April.

week into their tour, Charles and Diana were in Rome, the Italian capital.

The couple undertook separate engagements that first day in Rome, Friday, 26 April. Charles called on Francesco Cossiga, President of the Italian Senate and afterwards went on to the Chamber of Deputies at the Palazzo Montecitorio. Diana, meanwhile, visited the leukaemia ward of a Rome hospital and despite her few words of Italian, managed to spread her usual cheer among the nurses and patients. She herself was, however, saddened by the suffering she witnessed.

In the late afternoon, the Prince and Princess joined forces once more to visit the United Nations Food and Agricultural Organisation building and 'Boys' Town', the Citta dei Ragazzi, on the outskirts of Rome.

Next day, 27 April, Charles and Diana went

sightseeing. However, when they reached the Forum, the great meeting place of ancient Rome, the crowds which had massed to see them pressed in from all sides and the visit became an unofficial 'walkabout'. Charles had a deep interest in archeology, and had been looking forward to seeing the Forum excavations. Thoroughly frustrated, he had to give up. He hoped that things would be better at the Pantheon, another ancient site in Rome, but again the crowds closed in. People were everywhere, ignoring the ancient wonders to concentrate on the Prince and Princess of Wales.

Charmed by the president

Though disappointed to have the glory that was Rome denied them, the couple were charmed by the President of Italy, Sandro Pertini. He was well over eighty, but had lost none of his Latin charm. Knight-errant style, the old man kissed Diana's hand and told her how lovely she was.

Sunday, 28 April, was one of the more gruelling days of Charles and Diana's Italian tour. They attended a ceremony at the Anzio beach-head, some twenty miles south of Rome. In January 1944, Anzio had been a hell on earth where 24,000 British and American troops were killed or injured, attempting to consolidate a beachhead in Nazi-dominated territory. Charles, with his acute sense

Above Diana, soberly dressed for the occasion, visits the Allied war cemetery at Anzio, south of Rome, on Sunday, 28 April.
Left Charles explains to Diana how the ancient Greek amphitheatre at Syracuse, Sicily, would have been used. They visited it towards the end of their tour, on 30 April.

IN CONTEXT 1985

MINERS CAPITULATE

- The year-long miners' strike, **right**, ends in Britain, a crushing blow to the union movement
- The film *Out of Africa* wins an Oscar for Best Picture
- DNA fingerprinting developed for use in criminal investigations
- Rock Hudson dies of AIDS
- Bob Geldof organizes 'Live Aid' concerts for Ethiopia Famine Relief
- Bradford football stadium fire: 40 die in the blaze
- The Greenpeace ship *Rainbow Warrior* is blown up in Auckland Harbour, New Zealand by French agents
- Volcanic eruption in Colombia: two towns buried in mud, 20,000 die

Protocol

MEETING THE POPE

Pope John Paul was probably too tactful to express his opinion about the Queen's refusal to let Prince Charles attend Mass while in the Vatican. The reason for the veto was the Queen's position as Supreme Governor of the Protestant Church of England, a title Charles will inherit on becoming King. Because of this, the Queen was advised that it would not be proper for Charles to attend the Mass, a Catholic act of worship. Some senior churchmen in Britain and around the world – though not Robert Runcie, the Archbishop of Canterbury, seen **right** *with the Queen – would undoubtedly have taken offence.*

of history, and Diana with her natural sympathy for suffering, were greatly affected.

Later, they visited the nearby war cemetery, where they walked past the graves of men whose lives had been cut short in their prime. 'How young they were!' Diana kept on saying. She remained at the cemetery for 90 minutes, contemplating what might have been for all those youthful dead.

An audience with the Pope

That Sunday evening brought further frustrations. Charles and Diana had planned to hear Evensong at All Saints Anglican Church. But so many people, hoping to see the royal couple, had crammed into the narrow Via del Babulno leading to the church that they could not get through. Chief Inspector Colin Trimming, the royal bodyguard, took one look at the lack of crush barriers, and the inability of the Italian police to control the crowds and told Charles that Evensong was off.

At least Charles and Diana had a big day to look forward to. Whatever the delights and thrills they had experienced so far, their audience at the Vatican with Pope John Paul II, at 10.55am on Monday, 29 April, topped them all. Both Charles and Diana behaved like any other nervous visitors to the Vatican, at the prospect of meeting the imposing John Paul. Diana, in fact, looked worried. The

Right Enjoying every minute of their visit, Charles and Diana toured the Vatican after meeting the Pope. They are flanked by two of the Vatican's Swiss Guards.

Right Charles was nervous and Diana seemed terrified, but meeting Pope John Paul II, on Monday, 29 April, was the high point of the tour. Diana wore the long black dress and veil which is the correct costume for female visitors to the Vatican.

Above Charles and Diana, serenely relaxed, and scores of onlookers survey the famous St. Mark's Square in Venice on 5 May.

over two thousand years ago, audiences sat to watch plays performed on the open stage below by actors using huge masks to amplify their voices.

Wednesday, 1 May, was a long rest day, as Charles and Diana cruised the sparkling waters of the Mediterranean aboard *Britannia*. Diana sunbathed, Charles sketched. Lunch was taken *al fresco*, in the open air on deck.

Next day, it was back to official duty. *Britannia* put in at Trani, an ancient seaport on the Adriatic Sea. At Trani, the sun beat down, the temperature rose and a huge crush of excited and excitable spectators gathered. The pushing and shoving became so fierce that a five-year-old girl called Rosa got her hand caught in a barrier. Alerted by her crying, Charles ran to the barrier and lifted it so that Rosa could get her hand free. That was one

> *"She showed great compassion and understanding. She seemed very sad when she was told how the children needed treatment."*
>
> DR. LIDIO RUSSO, LEUKAEMIA SPECIALIST

actual audience was, of course, private, but no doubt the Pope, a very friendly man, made Charles and Diana feel at ease. They spent 45 minutes with him and emerged relaxed and smiling.

Fortunately, the Queen's controversial decision not to allow Charles to attend a private Mass with the Pope did not spoil the rest of the royal day. After lunch with Sir Mark Heath, British Ambassador at the Vatican, Charles and Diana were given a tour of this small enclave in the centre of Rome and thrilled to its many elegant buildings and beautiful treasures. They visited the Vatican museum, the famous Sistine Chapel with its ceiling painted by Michelangelo and St. Peter's Basilica.

Charles and Diana left Rome for Sicily the following day, 30 April, to visit a citrus fruit plantation near Catania. Then, it was on to Syracuse where they visited the Greek amphitheatre. This time, they got a good look at the ancient structure. They posed for photographs seated on the steps where

little girl who would never forget the gallantry of Prince 'Carlo' from England.

That afternoon, Charles and Diana visited St. Nicholas' Church at nearby Bari. This time, the Italian police had got their act together and the crowds were no problem.

Sensing the music

The same day, the Prince and Princess called in at the Istituto Provinciale Apicella, a school for deaf children at Morletta. The two of them thoroughly enjoyed themselves, playing with the children and watching the older ones give a gymnastic display. Despite the fact that the children could not hear the accompanying music, the gymnasts' precision and timing were perfect. Charles and Diana were most impressed.

A second day off at sea followed, on Friday, 3 May, as *Britannia* sailed from Bari to Venice. Charles was at his easel again. Diana improved her tan. And both took time out to play deck quoits. On

Sunday, 5 May, saw Charles and Diana attend the service at St. George's Anglican Church, then they embarked on another cruise, this time in that most romantic of crafts, a Venetian gondola.

The lucky gondoliers chosen to give the royal couple their four-minute ride, Mario de Pitta and his nephew Romano Magris, were openly thrilled at the honour. The gondola ride went ahead despite a light drizzle, which did nothing to dampen the enthusiasm of Venetians who massed by the score

> " *This has been a great honour for me.* "
> MARIO DE PITTA, GONDOLIER

along the short, 250-metre route.

The same afternoon, Prince William and Prince Harry arrived on an Andover of the Queen's Flight, to spend a few days cruising on *Britannia* with their parents. For Diana, who always missed her sons acutely when royal duty took her away from them, an exciting trip had ended in the best possible way.

On the evening of 5 May, the Wales family, now complete again, sailed away from Italy and its splendours. But even as they went, Charles and Diana, who had 17 days of wondrous sights to look back on, no doubt regaled their sons with tales of some of their most exciting experiences.

Saturday, 4 May, thousands of Italians lined the quay as *Britannia* docked at Riva dei Seti. Diana was up on the bridge taking pictures as the ship came in. The first of the many wonders of Venice the royal visitors saw was the Doges' Palace, where once the Doges, or Dukes, had controlled the vast, rich Venetian Empire. Next, they cruised along the length of the Grand Canal, Venice's main waterway. Venetians crowded around, waving, smiling and shouting greetings as Charles and Diana went by.

After lunch at the famous Cipriani restaurant on the island of Torcello, Charles and Diana made an unscheduled visit to a glass factory on Murano Island. By this time, the royal visit was drawing to its close. Charles and Diana spent their last evening in Italy dining at the Do Forni restaurant as honoured guests of the Mayor of Venice.

Above Charles and Diana are reunited with Princes William and Harry on board *Britannia* at the end of the Italian tour on Sunday, 5 May.

THE ROYAL WEDDING

In 1981, Britain's mood was transformed by Charles and Diana's wedding. Dreary winter had suddenly become spring with the announcement of the engagement in February. The wedding itself, on 29 July, seemed like high summer, despite the overcast skies

Royal engagements never last long. No sooner was the betrothal of Charles and Diana announced than plans were being made for the wedding. It was not just a simple matter of fixing a date. Members of the Royal Family had diaries crammed with engagements and all of them had to be consulted to find a day when they were all free, and in England, for the event. Not surprisingly, the date chosen, 29 July 1981, was close to the royals' summer break at Balmoral,

when they traditionally wound down their activities for a few weeks.

During the five-month engagement, though, it was royal business as usual, even for Charles. On 29 March, the Prince had to leave his new fiancée behind when he departed on a long-standing engagement, a five-week tour to Australasia, starting in New Zealand.

Diana was understandably upset, but she had plenty to cheer her up while Charles was away.

DIARY DATES
1981
3 March
Date of Charles and Diana's wedding announced
9 March
Diana with Charles at the Royal Opera House, Covent Garden
13 March
Diana at Sandown Park with Charles and Princess Margaret
27 March
Charles and Diana pay a formal visit to Cheltenham Police Station
29 March
Charles leaves for New Zealand and Australia on a five-week tour of four countries
22 May
Charles takes Diana to Tetbury, Gloucestershire, near Highgrove House, to meet the neighbours
June
Diana attends Ascot with the Royal Family
I July
Diana's 20th birthday
27 July
Diana moves into Clarence House, home of the Queen Mother
27 July
Pre-wedding dinner and ball at Buckingham Palace. Charles says goodbye to Camilla Parker-Bowles
28 July
Firework display in Hyde Park
29 July
The Royal Wedding
1 August
After two days at Broadlands, Charles and Diana fly to Gibraltar to start their honeymoon

Choosing her wedding dress and trousseau was just part of the fun. Other things were happening which did not come the way of ordinary brides. When Charles arrived 'down-under', he was confronted with a bevy of Diana lookalikes. Later, Diana expressed the view that lookalikes were 'vulgar', but there was no stopping the efforts to emulate her. Women besieged their hairdressers to get a Diana-style 'pageboy' cut. Blonde hair dye sold as never before. So did copies of Diana's low-heeled shoes, which she wore because of her height.

Inevitably, being suddenly pitched into the limelight affected the inexperienced Diana. She had a bad attack of wedding nerves and tried to call the whole thing off. But the fright passed and the wedding plans went forward. The first of Charles and Diana's 4000 wedding presents began to arrive. As

Previous page After the wedding, Diana soothed a nervous young bridesmaid under the watchful eye of the Queen. **Above** Diana travelled to St. Paul's as a commoner in the famous Glass Coach.

Above As Diana emerged from the Glass Coach, the wedding dress was at last revealed. **Left** The magnificent 25-foot-train was adjusted on the steps of St. Paul's Cathedral.

well as lavish gifts, such as a set of matching sapphire cuff links, brooch, bracelet and necklace from the Saudi Arabian royal family, there was a heart-shaped potato from a young schoolchild. Over a thousand presents were put on display at St. James' Palace and spectators flocked to view them.

The guest list, numbering 2650 people, was prepared but did not include Diana's step-grandmother, Barbara Cartland. Rumour had it that Princess Diana declined to invite the veteran romantic novelist, who was likely to turn up in her perennial shocking pink and overshadow the bride. St. Paul's Cathedral was chosen, instead of the traditional Westminster Abbey, because it was larger and able to accommodate all who were invited. St. Paul's also had better acoustics for the wedding music, which was to be performed by members of the Royal Opera House, Royal Philharmonic and English Chamber Orchestras, all companies of

> " *The most touching parting we've seen for a long time.* "
>
> **AIRPORT OFFICIALS,**
> **AS CHARLES LEFT FOR NEW ZEALAND**

which Charles was patron. The beautiful New Zealand opera star, soprano Kiri Te Kanawa, was invited to sing at the wedding service.

For the wedding dress, the traditional royal couturiers were passed over in favour of an unknown pair of young designers, David and Elizabeth Emmanuel, whom Diana had chosen. The Emmanuels, whose style was feminine and romantic, set to work in deepest secrecy.

Meanwhile, Diana was starting to feel her way in the world of royal engagements. Even though she had been close to the Royal Family since she was a child, she had much to learn. What was routine for Charles and the other royals was, to say the least, rather frightening for her.

Diana kept her head down too much. Her face tightened up when she knew the press cameras were on her. She blushed a lot.

In royal terms, Diana was a very raw recruit at this stage. In popular terms, people loved her all the more for her modest charm and lack of pretension.

CHRONICLE

The great day was going to be a public holiday and, as it approached, tourists poured in. The wedding was taking place at the height of the tourist season, and before long, London's hotels were bursting with visitors. One lucky American family managed to rent an apartment overlooking St. Paul's Cathedral. A television crew would be there to record their emotions as they savoured a once-in-a-lifetime view of the heir to the English throne emerging from the cathedral with his young bride.

Across the country, people prepared to celebrate with street parties. Bunting was hung across streets. In a return to an age-old form of merrymaking in England, bonfires were prepared so they could flare up in celebration on the wedding day.

On the wedding eve, 28 July, the guns of the King's Troop, the Royal Horse Artillery fired a salute in Hyde Park to mark the first marriage of a Prince of Wales for 118 years. This was followed by a big firework display. That evening, the Queen and Prince Philip gave a dinner party at Buckingham Palace for 40 relatives and friends of Charles and Diana. Among the guests was Lieutenant-Colonel Andrew Parker-Bowles, then commander of the

> " *Neither of us will ever forget the atmosphere. It was electric, almost unbelievable.* "
>
> PRINCE CHARLES

Blues and Royals Regiment of the Household Cavalry, which was to play its part in the brilliant pageantry of the wedding day as Sovereign's Escort. With him was his wife, Camilla.

On 29 July, the day dawned with no hint of sunshine. The streets approaching St. Paul's looked grey beneath overcast skies. Nothing, though, could dampen the enthusiasm of the crowds which crammed the route to wave flags, yell greetings, send up rousing cheers and generally display an emotion not seen in the capital since the Coronation of the Queen in 1953.

Around the world, almost a billion viewers were glued to TV screens. Some, in faraway time zones, sat up all night to take advantage of the satellite pictures and quadrophonic sound which linked them

IN THE NEWS

The most exciting event for decades

The press went overboard. The people were ecstatic. The marriage of Charles and Diana was the most thrilling royal event for decades. The most minute details became hot news – like Charles missing a step as he came down the stairs of St. Paul's Cathedral after a wedding rehearsal. Economically, Britain was having a hard time in 1981. As long as the royal wedding was in the news – and interest in it continued for a long time – it was the ideal tonic for a nation feeling depressed.

to London, half a world away.

All eyes were on Diana as she emerged that morning from the Glass Coach and climbed the red-carpeted steps of St. Paul's. The wedding dress, a frilled, romantic taffeta confection, was revealed at last. Its train was so long that it covered the steps behind her as she walked up to what she undoubtedly felt was her date with a dazzling destiny.

Charles, splendidly dressed in his naval No.1 ceremonial uniform, awaited his bride at the altar. She approached on the arm of her father, Earl Spencer. Diana was nervous. So was Charles. During the wedding ceremony she got his names in the wrong

Opposite page and above
Diana walked up the aisle on the arm of her father, who had still not entirely recovered from a stroke three years earlier, which almost killed him. **Left** Robert Runcie, Archbishop of Canterbury and Primate of All England, married Charles to his beautiful young bride.

> " *Do you want to feel my engagement ring? I'd better not lose it before Wednesday (29 July) or they won't know who I am.* "
>
> DIANA TO A BLIND WOMAN AT A PALACE GARDEN PARTY

order. Charles endowed her with all *her* worldy goods instead of *his*. Nobody minded. It simply added charm and a human touch to the solemnity of a great state occasion. The bride, though, did not promise to obey.

As Diana, now a Royal Highness, emerged on the arm of her new husband, the crowds outside the cathedral burst into deafening cheers. Their joy was almost tangible. Every inch of the ride back to Buckingham Palace, the royal couple were surrounded by a sea of Union Jacks, streamers, balloons and festive hats. Later, more crowds surged around the Palace as Charles and Diana appeared on the famous balcony for the expected kiss. At that, there were yet more roars of delight and approbation.

Spectators were still there in force to see Charles and Diana set off for Waterloo Station to catch a train to Broadlands, the Hampshire home of the Mountbatten family, where they were to spend the first days of their honeymoon. In this they were following in the footsteps of Charles' parents, who had begun their own married life at Broadlands, 34 years previously. The newlyweds spent two days in seclusion and Charles relaxed with some fishing on a renowned troutstream, the nearby River Test.

Right Charles and Diana retraced their steps down the aisle, as man and wife, to the delight of the 2000-strong congregation of family and friends. Diana was now Her Royal Highness the Princess of Wales, wife of the heir to the throne, and destined to be Charles' Queen Consort when, eventually, he becomes king.

Royal marriages are essentially family events, but as Charles is heir to the throne his marriage to Diana received the full panoply of a great state occasion. **Left** Crowds jammed the streets as the newlyweds drove from St. Paul's back to Buckingham Palace. **Right** Roars of delight greeted the couple's appearance on the balcony of the palace, where they sealed their happiest day with a public kiss.

⇜ Protocol ⇝

ENTER THE ROYAL LOVE MATCH

It was Queen Victoria who initiated the idea of royal couples marrying for love. In her day — she reigned from 1837 to 1901 — royal marriages were often arranged between two people from different countries who hardly knew each other. Worse, no one much cared whether they were compatible or wanted to marry. Victoria, who was madly in love with her own husband, Prince Albert, thought this was all wrong. Like any modern mother, she wanted her nine children to be happy. So, she decreed that her four sons and five daughters must at least like their prospective spouses, and vice versa. For the British public, it was a short step from 'like' to 'love', and so the idea of a royal love match became a must in the public consciousness.

The second part of the honeymoon was spent on board the royal yacht *Britannia*, which Charles and Diana joined at Gibraltar. The plan to embark at Gibraltar had caused problems for the King and Queen of Spain. They had been absent on the wedding day because of Spain's longstanding dispute with Britain over the Rock. Diana would later get to know King Juan Carlos and Queen Sofia well, but this was her first taste of the way royal arrangements can have political connotations.

Britannia set sail after an emotional farewell from 30,000 Gibraltarians, who lined the route to the dock to send the royal couple off in showers of confetti. In the two weeks that ensued, the yacht cruised to Algeria, then on to Tunisia, Sicily, the Greek islands and finally to Egypt. Free for a time from millions of eyes watching their every move and trying to lip-read their every word, Charles and Diana went snorkelling, scuba-diving, windsurfing and sunbathing. Ashore, they had beach barbecues

---

> " *Diana should get married in jeans, to give the industry a boost.* "
>
> A JEANS MANUFACTURER,
> INTERVIEWED ON RADIO

---

and, though boats full of eager cameramen and reporters were prowling the Mediterranean, they managed to elude them.

On the stopover in Egypt, President Anwar Sadat and his English-born wife Jihan came aboard *Britannia* for dinner. Then it was on through the Suez Canal to the Red Sea, where Charles and Diana went swimming, unaware that there was a 10-foot shark in the vicinity. The presence and size of the shark were revealed only when sailors on *Britannia* caught it.

The Sadats were there again when Charles and Diana arrived at Hurghada military airfield to board the RAF VC-10 which was to fly them to Scotland, where the third part of their honeymoon was to be spent with the Royal Family at Balmoral. The newlyweds were still there, in October, when President Sadat was assassinated and Charles had to leave to attend his funeral. Once again, Diana dis-

The Private Princess
Seeking happiness

Charles and Diana approached their marriage from two different directions which were destined never to meet.

At 20, Diana was rather immature. An incurable romantic,

Below Charles and Camilla soon after they met in 1971. Though each of them married other people, friends say their love remained constant.

she believed in a handsome prince who would whisk her away, like Snow White, to a life of fairytale happiness. Most young girls with such dreams usually get over them quite quickly. Not Diana. When the prince actually appeared and asked her to marry him, the dream became reality.

Charles' duty

It is possible that Prince Charles came to his marriage in a more pragmatic frame of mind. It seems likely that he never took entirely for granted the ideal of marrying for love. He and Diana were approaching the wedding in a somewhat different frame of mind. All else being equal, the marriage

could have worked and a truer love might have developed.

Their different characters, backgrounds and perceptions of marriage caused strains from the start. Diana proved too demanding for Charles to handle. Sources close to the Prince suggest that, although he and Camilla Parker-Bowles had agreed to end their affair to give his marriage a chance, Charles was soon fleeing back to Camilla for advice.

Diana, quite rightly, wanted her husband to herself. Charles felt he had been frogmarched into the marriage, especially by his forceful father Prince Philip. Diana and Charles were potentially two unhappy people.

covered that royal duty and public life could intrude both cruelly and suddenly on private royal time. It was a lesson that would be brought home to her time and again in future years.

Balmoral could not have been a greater contrast to the sun-soaked glamour of the Mediterranean. The Highland mists, the stark mountain vistas, and the quiet, staid country life of the royal estate were not features which greatly appealed to the new Princess of Wales. At heart Diana was a townie, fond of the bright lights and bustle and the air of something always happening which towns exude. Like the Duchess of York after her, she was somewhat daunted by the prospect of spending most of her honeymoon with her royal in-laws. Where ordinary

> *" Enjoy something like that? It was terrifying. Such a long walk up the aisle for a start. "*
> DIANA, ON THE WEDDING

couples craft their own life together, Balmoral taught Diana that she would have to live as the royals did. She would have to enjoy or try to enjoy their pastimes, follow their traditions – like attending the Braemar Games – and generally fit into long-established royal routines.

Later on, Diana came to dislike Balmoral, and ended up refusing to go there. For the moment, though, the new royal bride had to toe the royal line and, she realized, look as if she was enjoying herself.

She certainly managed to do so when, with Charles, she met the press by the River Dee, five miles from Balmoral and posed for photographs and questions. When asked how she was finding married life, Diana replied: 'I can highly recommend it'. Charles kissed her hand for the cameras. Both smiled and waved, as tradition required. After the photocall, they returned to Balmoral holding hands.

The honeymoon ended officially three months after the wedding, at the end of October. With the rest of the royals, HRH the Princess of Wales packed up at Balmoral and headed for London and her new, strictly timetabled, dutiful life of royal engagements and public appearances – and royal days that could last fifteen hours or more.

IN CONTEXT   THE ROYAL WEDDING YEAR
1981

- Iran releases American hostages after 444 days
- Sebastian Coe, **right**, claims world mile record
- Riots in Liverpool, Wolverhampton, Birmingham, Reading, Chester, Hull and Preston
- Gro Harlem Brundtland becomes Norway's first woman prime minister
- Natalie Wood, Hollywood film actress, drowns
- Peter Sutcliffe, the notorious 'Yorkshire Ripper', goes on trial
- Hosni Mubarek becomes President of Egypt

Carefree Casuals

Diana off-duty could appear in many guises: as a churchgoer, as a spectator, out shopping, or out with her children. Her main fashion aim when off-duty was to be unrecognizable

Three views of Diana as a spectator at the Guards' Polo Club, Smith's Lawn, Windsor, where Prince Charles often played polo. They show stages in her casual wear from summer 1983 (far right) to June 1985 (near right) and May 1988 with Prince William (main picture). The green dress (near right) was also worn at a polo match in Melbourne,

Like most women who have to dress up much of the time, Diana often used her off-duty moments to relax fashion-wise. She once compared dressing for public engagements to being a bride every day. Royal life as she saw it was that formal. It was also true that her high-fashion outfits for public appearances were meant to make her the centre of attention. Women eyed her for fashion points. Fashion pundits scrutinized her for hints of new trends. Men just admired her.

Relaxed approach

It was logical, then, that when she could dress to please herself on her days off, Diana frequently chose to appear so casual she could look positively sloppy: baggy trousers, blue jeans, sweatshirts, baseball caps, padded jackets, sometimes put together in unmatching colour schemes that were, as she intended, at odds with her fashion icon image.

With that, went little or no make-up and hair carelessly done or looking unbrushed. For Diana, this was the perfect disguise. What she wanted most of all was to look like any other young woman out shopping or taking her kids to the pictures.

To her satisfaction, she often went unrecognized. Diana dressed up to the nines was the image that most people had of her and what they expected to see. A young woman striding along in casuals, like dozens of others, must be someone else.

Quite apart from its value as camouflage, this transformation was not all that difficult for Diana. She seems to have had little personal interest in high fashion. It was too elaborate and too strict in its demands for a woman who liked free and easy styles and the informal life they typified.

Sloane Ranger

Normally, a young girl of 20, as Diana was when she got married, would have already developed a fashion sense of her own if she was ever going to have one. Diana did not do that. Early pictures of her give the impression that she slung on whatever clothes were to hand, with not much thought for the look of the whole ensemble.

One of Diana's pre-engagement outfits, a shirt with rolled-up sleeves under a sleeveless sweater worn with a flimsy, transparent skirt was fairly typical of her wardrobe at the time.

A curious mixture of sporty and pretty, this was, of course, fashion of a kind: 'Sloane Ranger' fashion. Before she married, Diana was part of the Sloane Ranger set, which included Sarah Ferguson, who would later marry the Duke of York.

This group of girls – all well-born, with plenty of their parents' money and sometimes their own to spend – got their name from the Sloane Square and

> ## "I wish everyone would stop talking about my clothes."
> ### PRINCESS DIANA

Sloane Street areas of fashionable Knightsbridge in London. This is where they congregated during the week, patronizing famous-name shops like Lagerfeld, Lacroix, Chanel, Valentino or Browns.

The Sloane 'uniform' was careless casuals by day, with an emphasis on velvet knickerbockers, and frilly, floral prints and full skirts by night. Essential Sloane Ranger gear included square silk scarves, soft suede loafers and anything with an Italian label.

Though most Sloanes stopped ranging in their twenties or when they married, Diana retained a

I Diana liked to retain her anonymity when out and about off-duty. This is a shot taken while she was out shopping in Knightsbridge in October 1994. Casuals were part of her disguise, though these two girls look as if they have rumbled her this time. Even so, no one really expected the glamorous Princess of Wales to be wearing drainpipe trousers, which suited Diana just fine.

2 Diana crossing the road with Prince Harry. Prince William was close behind on this informal shopping trip in Cirencester, near Highgrove, in September 1992. With or without her sons, Diana valued the times when she could be just another face in the street – yet another departure for royals which she initiated. Before Diana, royals never appeared dressed so casually and rarely mixed with crowds.

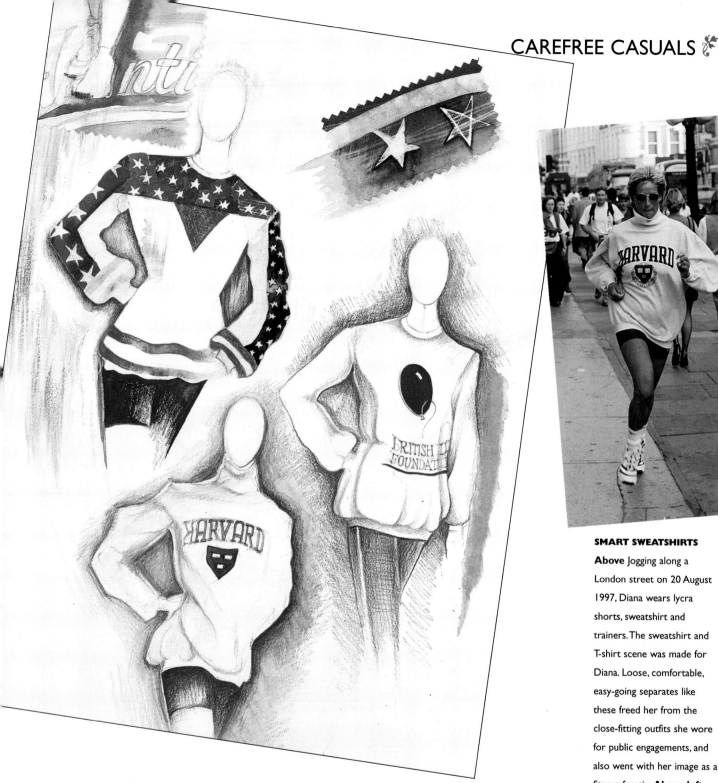

SMART SWEATSHIRTS

Above Jogging along a London street on 20 August 1997, Diana wears lycra shorts, sweatshirt and trainers. The sweatshirt and T-shirt scene was made for Diana. Loose, comfortable, easy-going separates like these freed her from the close-fitting outfits she wore for public engagements, and also went with her image as a fitness fanatic. **Above left, top and bottom** After her trips to the USA, Diana was often seen in American-style sweatshirts – the top one is a Virgin Airlines sweatshirt. **Above left, centre** The British Lung Foundation, of which Diana was patron, gave sweatshirts to Diana and her sons and benefited from invaluable publicity.

fondness for the style which persisted to the end of her life. The stunning £1 million wardrobe of high fashion wear which she acquired for her public life was never really her scene, however dazzling and glamorous she looked.

Diana was, after all, a rebel, challenging established royal practice on several fronts. Her casual wear, which so completely transformed her appearance, was, in its way, a protest against the straitjacket of high fashion which, as Princess of Wales, she was obliged to wear. Quite possibly, Diana would have been more content to dress in the quieter, classic fashion of the Queen, the Duchess of Kent or Princess Alexandra, none of whom ever made waves in the fashion world.

But not only was Diana a generation or more younger than these classic dressers, she also appeared on the scene at a time when the press and the public were longing for something more exciting from their royals. Over the centuries, the royals have been arbiters of fashion and have often been trend-setters. But in the 20th century they seem to have backed off from that role. So when Diana came along there was a vacancy for a good-looking, stylish trend-setter, with a sense of adventure and a taste for fun when it came to clothes.

Diana fitted the bill nicely and was seized on eagerly by newspaper editors, fashion commentators, women's magazines and the fashion world itself. And, in a sense, they made her what she was. By focusing on her clothes and her style to such a degree, they turned her into a fashion icon. And she had to dress the part year in, year out.

The irony is that the woman who was dubbed 'the greatest fashion icon of the century' was almost certainly more the creation of the media and her designers than of her own tastes. At heart, she was a casual and even unfashionable dresser.

Off-duty, Diana deliberately went for outfits as unlike high fashion as she could devise. The unco-ordinated colours and the odd style of the gear she wore while shopping in Cirencester around 1984 underlined the point: green sweater, red Puffa jacket, black trousers and brown calf-high boots.

> **"Clothes are for the job. They've got to be practical. Sometimes I can be a little outrageous, which is quite nice. But only sometimes."**
> PRINCESS DIANA

It is significant that after the divorce freed Diana from the obligation to dress to the ultimate for glittering public engagements, she reverted to the simpler style of her earlier years. Even when out in public, she wore unremarkable two-piece suits which were not a patch on the stunning daywear of her married days – and were not meant to be.

Naturally, though, Diana could not 'dress down' all the time when off-duty. She made semi-public appearances watching Prince Charles play polo at Smith's Lawn, near Windsor Castle, or attending yachting week at Cowes. The press, she knew, would be there to take pictures, so baseball cap and jeans would not do. Those pictures had been casually snapped in the street; Diana may not even have been aware the camera was on her. Accredited photographers

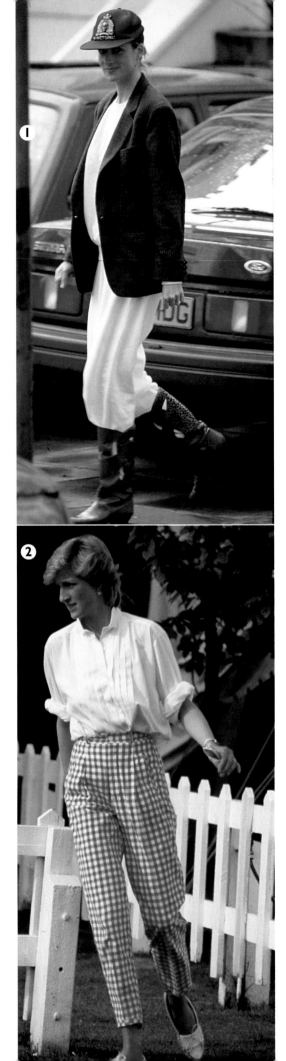

1 Diana could hardly get more casual than this. In this outfit of baggy tracksuit trousers, loose jacket, brown leather and fake fur cowboy boots and baseball cap, she even managed to hide the superb size 10 figure she worked hard to achieve. From the smile on her face, though, she was obviously happy like this. The picture was taken in summer 1988.

2 An earlier photograph of Diana at Highgrove in the summer of 1986. The check pants and slightly fussy loafers show that at this stage she was not yet ready to go the whole ultra-casual way. Just the same, the signs were still there of the sloppy shape of things to come. The Jan van Velden shirt was crisply pleated but the rolled-up sleeves were sending a different message.

were obviously an entirely different matter.

For these occasions, Diana chose smart casuals like the pleated skirt and big sweater she wore when arriving with Prince Harry at Aberdeen airport in 1986. Diana dressed the same way when she took William and Harry to school. At a polo match at Smith's Lawn, in 1984, she wore a long tunic blouse, with a wide belt at the waist and another pleated

> ## "My clothes are not my priority...fashion isn't my big thing at all."
> PRINCESS DIANA

skirt. That struck the balance Diana wanted between casual and smart.

Charles and Diana were pictured at another polo match in 1985, when they were on their second tour of Australia. But because this was part of an official visit, not just a day off at Windsor, Diana's clothes were that much more elaborate: white and green striped dress with crossover skirt and green belt.

Dressing for off-duty moments where the camera might snap her, or dressing appropriately so as not to steal the show at events where someone else was meant to be the star attraction was a fine art and one that Diana had undoubtedly mastered.

Above and left Diana had a great fondness for baseball caps, often wearing them to polo or on private shopping trips, and invariably sporting one when she drove her open-topped car. These caps were often presented to her by the armed services when she paid formal visits, or were given to her by American friends. William wears one too **(left)** on an informal shopping trip.

IN THE NEWS

All eyes on the new boy, and his mum

A child's first day at school can be a traumatic experience for a mother. For Diana it was doubly so. On 25 September, 1985, Prince William's first day at the £200-a-term Chepstow Villas nursery in Kensington brought the press out in force to headline the event.

The cameras were there to record a mother-son tussle as Diana, dressed for combat in easygoing casuals, had to hold back her overeager son. Diana often delivered William and picked him up in the afternoon, giving the other mothers a view of her extensive casual wardrobe.

Forever Young

Diana had a natural way with children that other royals did not even try to copy. It was not something that she had to learn and she used it tirelessly in efforts to improve children's lives

Princess Diana loved children – all children. She loved cuddling them, kissing them, talking to them, sharing their little secrets and just being with them. What was more, she knew how to communicate with children in their own terms. This is not an ability given to many people, and certainly not to public figures like royals who meet children with thousands looking on.

Nothing vanishes faster than dignity when an adult tries to connect with a child in a pseudo-childish way. That was never the case with Diana. She made her encounters with children appear entirely natural and relaxed. So much so that the children opened up and talked freely with her, instead of retreating into bashfulness as youngsters often do when confronted with important or glamorous strangers.

Some children felt so assured with Diana that they could be quite cheeky, knowing they would get away with it. When one little boy marched up to her and told her his mother had said she ought to give him a kiss, Diana replied: 'Well, then, I suppose you'd better have one.' And she promptly obliged.

It was this sort of instinctive response which was one of the secrets of Diana's success with

Left Princess Diana visiting a Hindu temple in north London in June 1997, where she was soon surrounded by children. **Below** She accepts a flower from a young fan.

Above Only Diana would talk to children in a swimming pool like this and not lose her dignity. She was on a visit to Ipswich, Suffolk in 1990. **Above right** On a visit to Australia in October 1996, the mother is pleased but the little boy's not quite sure what's going on, as he gets a royal pat on the head from the Princess of Wales.

children. They knew they never had to be in awe of her, as they would have been with a more obviously grand public personality. Diana was gracious, but not condescending. She could share laughs with children and get them talking, yet remain every inch a princess. It was a valuable talent.

A revolutionary approach

Diana's relaxed and easy grace enabled her to do things other royals rarely, if ever, risked. She could half-lie at the side of a swimming pool, talking to the children in the water without seeming awkward. When she was around children, she could take off her shoes and kneel down to get closer to them, and the youngsters, who thought fairytale princesses were just storybook characters, could believe Diana was the real thing.

This was a big revolution in royal behaviour. Though the public approved, others never got used to it, or wanted to. For example, court officials, whom the Queen once called 'more royal than we are' would go rigid with disapproval over what they saw as the antics of the Princess of Wales. In their opinion, royal conduct must never compromise

royal dignity. Diana's difficulties with those she later called 'the grey men' of the royal establishment stemmed partly from her hands-on approach to her job, and especially to children.

Prince Charles, too, used to get dismayed at Diana's public displays of emotion, even towards their sons. When she rushed up to them, arms outstretched to hug them, he became embarrassed.

> ## "She always loved babies."
> ### THE LATE EARL SPENCER ON DIANA

Charles was a loving, demonstrative father, who enjoyed romping about with William and Harry. He even allowed them to sit on him. But all that took place in private, at home. For Charles and the other royals, it was not for public consumption.

The traditional royal way of handling children, as experienced by Charles, was basically a hands-off business. This was not a matter of neglect. Nor did it mean a lack of interest in children. The role of wife and mother staying at home to raise a family simply did not feature in the life plans of royal or

Above Diana as she most liked to be – surrounded by children at Alice Springs during her tour of Australia with Prince Charles and William in 1983. **Left** In April 1983, on the same tour, Charles looks on as a little girl shows Diana her flag. Diana's interest was always genuine.

titled women. They had important social duties to fulfil. They were often involved in charity work. Consequently, royal or aristocratic girls were not brought up to change nappies, burp babies or pace the floor soothing fractious infants at teething time.

Nanny knows best

Royal mothers had barely given birth before their children were put in the charge of nurses whose job it was to bring them up. Many royal children, including Charles, were often closer to their nannies than they were to their parents, and knew them a great deal better. When small, the children, duly scrubbed clean, would meet their parents or, more often, just their mother, for about an hour at

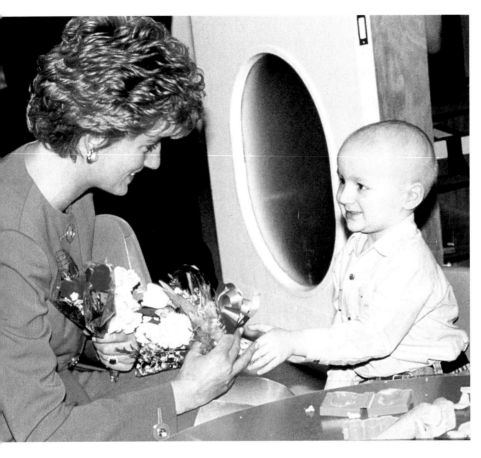

Left Diana on a hospital visit. Very young children, being naturally fearful of strangers, normally become solemn and wary when they meet one. Not with Diana, though. This child's smile shows instead pleasure and trust. **Right** A fond look and a hand-hold from Princess Diana. Children were likely to cherish such gestures for the rest of their lives. Diana would have been profoundly upset to see this disfigured boy, but her royal self-discipline never allowed her to show it openly.

teatime. Afterwards they were whisked back to the nursery, sooner rather than later if they misbehaved.

A royal mother's involvement with her children varied, depending on the level of her maternal instinct, but the demands of royal life and duty meant she was often away from home on other business. Prince Charles himself felt his mother had not been there for him often enough when he was a child because her duties as Queen took her away.

Diana's childhood

The aristocracy, into which Diana was born, dealt with children in much the same way. Diana's childhood experience paralleled Charles' except that her parents were divorced and her mother lost custody of the children. Diana felt rejected and unloved.

Brought up by a parade of nannies hired by her father, now a lone parent, Diana came to resent being palmed off like this when what she wanted was her own mother. Somewhere along the line, she resolved to break the cycle of absent parenthood so common among her class, and intended to become involved when she had her own children. Shortly

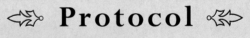

⌘ Protocol ⌘

HOW TO ADDRESS THE PRINCES

The rules for how to behave when meeting members of the Royal Family are not as inflexible as they are often made out to be. But most people choose to do the formal thing, even when the royals are young boys like Prince William and his brother Prince Harry.

The princes are called 'Sir'. On being introduced to them, men bow, women curtsy. William and Harry speak first, since royals initiate conversations — and end them, too. No one should sit down before they do.

Diana was well aware that her sons' lives would be filled with this kind of formality. So, she tried to give them as much ordinary boyish fun as she could, taking them to theme parks and the like.

At school, protocol is kept to a minimum, to make the princes' schooling as normal as possible. The other boys, certainly, call William and Harry by their ordinary names or whatever nickname they can get away with.

after Prince William was born in 1982, Diana announced she was going to bring him up herself.

For obvious reasons, that proved unrealistic, but she was determined to have as much to do with William's childhood as her public duties allowed. She saw as much of him as she could, and continued in the same fashion after Prince Henry was born. This, after all, was proof of something everyone had hailed when Diana became engaged to

> ## "It's all hard work and no pay."
> ### DIANA, ON REARING CHILDREN

Charles: her concern with the good old-fashioned domestic virtues.

In this, she was markedly different from most friends of her age and high birth who had their sights set elsewhere. They were more interested in doing the social round, having fun and, in some cases, following careers.

A career never entered Diana's head. Though the press dubbed her a 'working girl', when they found

she was helping a friend at the Young England Kindergarten, she was not really working there but doing what came naturally to her. A famous photograph (see p11) taken of the young Diana with two of her charges created a sensation because she had forgotten to put on a slip and the light shining through her thin skirt revealed her legs. What was ignored was something much more important: the trust and affection displayed by the children.

A talent for caring

Since then, virtually every picture taken of Diana with children has shown how much at ease they felt in her company. There was none of the slightly terrified awkwardness children often experience when confronted by famous and beautiful ladies, especially when a battery of cameras is likely to be popping all around them and everyone is staring.

When Diana became Princess of Wales, she saw a great opportunity to put her love of children to practical use. It was not long before she discovered the deprived, the underprivileged, the children of war-torn countries or those afflicted by disease. She

Above Diana in conference with a group of children at a Red Cross project at Panauti, Nepal, in March 1993. Language was rarely a barrier to her. Few other royals ever got as close to children in public as this, but Diana frequently did.

resolved to help them, and her royal position gave her the power to do so.

Royal ladies, who represent the feminine, caring side of monarchy, have traditionally concentrated their charity work on children. Diana, though, brought a new talent to this valuable work. Confronted with a handicapped child, or hearing a sad tale of squalid living conditions or the sufferings of children in war, her eyes would fill with tears. Facing a dying child in hospital, she would wave the cameras away to give the youngster space to talk quietly and privately. It became a well-known fact that after Diana had visited a hospital, the patients she saw, young or old, said they felt a lot better.

A brave face

What was less publicized was the effect that these encounters had on Diana. As she realized early on, working with children, especially sick children, could be harrowing. Royals could not afford to appear squeamish. It was one thing for Diana to show emotion over children, quite another for her to be seen to flinch at the often distressing sights they represented.

Fortunately, Diana's nerves were strong, and she knew the secret of communicating with children in these circumstances: ignore the burns, the missing

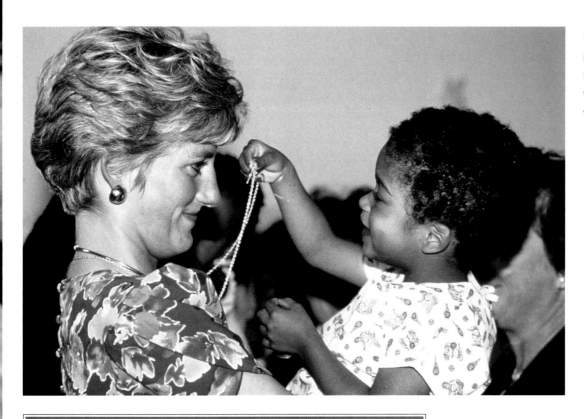

Left Not every girl gets to play with a princess's jewels. Diana brings a moment of fun into a child's life on a visit to Brazil in April 1991.

IN THE NEWS

Care and controversy

This was Diana as she most liked to be, bringing comfort to sick children, in this case a young cancer victim she met during her visit to Pakistan in 1996. This British newspaper made much of an innocent faux-pas on Diana's part: she had to be reminded to cover her head when a young patient recited a verse from the Koran, the 'bible' of Islam, the Muslim religion. There were other thorns in Diana's path, though. As a guest of her friends, Imran and Jemima Khan, Diana's visit to Pakistan was seen as a backdoor way for him to boost his political ambitions.

Opposite page Continents apart but the same warm response. **Far left** Diana gives a hug and a kiss to a boy on a visit to Chicago. **Near left** On the tour of India with Charles in 1992 this girl had an honoured seat on Diana's knee.

legs of landmine victims, the gaunt appearance of children with AIDS or cancer, and approach them simply as people who needed her interest, sympathy and a kind word or two to ease their pain. Over the years, Diana perfected this technique, until she could fearlessly confront the worst horrors that disease, deprivation or war could cause.

All the same, she knew that sympathy was not enough. Her contribution also had to be practical, and this was why she became patron of so many charities concerned with the plight of children. The Diana effect on these charities could be dramatic.

For instance, one of the first charities of which she became patron, while still engaged to Prince Charles, was the Malcolm Sargent Children's Cancer Fund. The Fund had been started, in 1968,

> ## "It's amazing how much happiness a small child brings to people."
> ### PRINCESS DIANA

by Sir Malcolm's manager, Sylvia Daley, working on her kitchen table. Once Diana became a patron, some 13 years later, the Fund was able to collect over £1 million a year for its various programmes. The Princess raised the Fund's profile by attending concerts and other functions.

The mother and baby charity Birthright was a fairly minor effort until Diana came along as patron in 1984. The £100,000 that Birthright had been giving to research projects soon shot up to £1 million a year for a much wider range of activities.

After that, Diana's name and involvement heightened public awareness about the ravages that

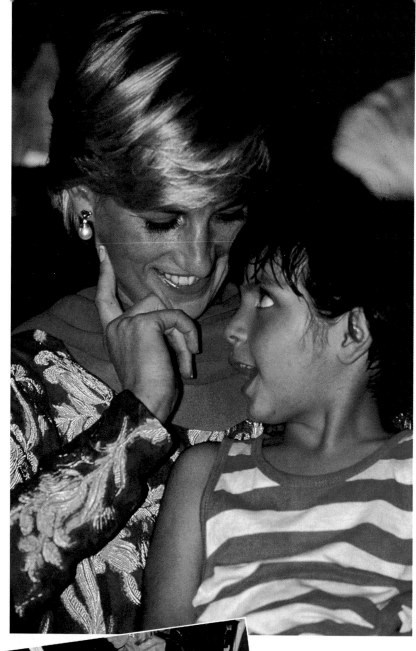

children suffered because of drugs, accidents, scarlet fever in pregnancy, meningitis and sexual abuse. She was not afraid, either, of controversial charity work. Her work for AIDS victims, both children and adults, was only one example.

The energy she put into the Child Accident Prevention Trust was hardly less, promoting the organization's vital message in speeches on television, at meetings and other functions. Diana was never a great public speaker: her voice was too small and her manner rather hesitant. But her strong commitment to children's causes and her real concern for their welfare came through every time.

How children saw her

Children, in their turn, were fascinated by Diana. Even as a figure on a TV screen or a picture in a newspaper, if that was all they knew of her, she made them aware of her empathy.

When she died so suddenly and violently on 31 August 1997, the shock felt by children was intense. Some wanted to give Diana whatever they possessed. Being children, it was little enough. But that was why so many of the tributes outside the royal palaces in London were written in a childish hand. And also why children gave up their teddy bears, their toys and their pocket money and left them with bunches of flowers to express their sorrow.

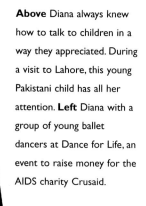

Above Diana always knew how to talk to children in a way they appreciated. During a visit to Lahore, this young Pakistani child has all her attention. **Left** Diana with a group of young ballet dancers at Dance for Life, an event to raise money for the AIDS charity Crusaid.

ALL IN GOOD TIME

After the excitement of the fairytale wedding and the three-month honeymoon, Diana started her new married life at the heart of the Royal Family, in the highly ordered and controlled world of Buckingham Palace. Adjusting to this new life would take time

Everyone who comes to Buckingham Palace has experienced it, the feeling that they have stepped into a time warp. Outside, beyond the railings in the Mall, sightseers bustle, cars drive by, the hum and buzz of the big city permeate the sedate tree-lined avenue, and the roar of traffic seeps through from busy, crowded Trafalgar Square, ten minutes' walk away. All that shuts off as the ceremonious atmosphere of the Palace asserts itself. Once through the front door, visitors are enveloped in hushed decorum, strict protocol and the terrifying thought that a member of the Royal Family might come round a corner and they will not know how to react.

When Diana became Her Royal Highness, The Princess of Wales all this was more familiar to her than it was to the occasional visitor. She had been around the Royal Family since she was a child. She knew how well ordered royal life had to be. But knowledge and experience can be two different

things. Even with all this behind her, to begin with Diana was intimidated by the environment that went with royal marriage.

Its keynote, she found, was formality. As her own public engagements later proved, Diana's style was much more informal and impulsive. For royals, emotion was under strict control. Yet giving love and displaying emotion were essential to Diana's being. Self-discipline and devotion to duty were the royal watchwords. Diana mastered the royal brand of discipline and duty, but interpreted it in her own way. She was not the sort to be stately or remote. Her heart was on her sleeve every time she encountered any suffering or deprivation. She was unable to hear a sad story dry-eyed.

A VERY DIFFERENT WORLD

A monarchy, of course, cannot be properly run on impulse. Its heavy responsibilities demand a disciplined approach. It was easier to be born into this rarified world than to marry into it. Overnight, it seemed, friends and relations had to curtsy to Diana. She took on a heavy programme of duties and obligations. She was shadowed everywhere by

Previous page Diana meets the people on her very first tour, to Wales in November 1981.
Above left Wales again. Diana looks to Charles for reassurance. **Above** Diana graciously accepts a bunch of flowers from a young wellwisher in Wales.
Left Lady Diana, in May 1981, on a walkabout in Tetbury, Gloucestershire.

bodyguards. Her days were strictly timetabled. As Diana herself afterwards put it, the business of being royal ensured that 'nothing happened naturally'. There were times when she felt the need to escape back to the real outside world.

Sometimes, at around 8.30 in the morning, she would jump into her car, drive down to nearby Knightsbridge and, taking the risk of parking on a double yellow line, dash into Harrods by a side door. There she sorted rapidly though the racks of clothes. Afterwards, rushing out with her purchases, she drove back to Buckingham Palace. The whole performance might take no more than 20 minutes.

The freedom to be an ordinary woman out shopping, however briefly, was important to Diana. When, later on, she determined that her sons should lead 'as normal a life as possible', a child's

> ## "It will take her a few years to learn the ropes."
> PRINCE PHILIP, ON DIANA

version of this was clearly what she had in mind.

However, the Royal Family, to which Diana belonged as the second lady in the land, had its own kind of normality. The royals moved as if on a circuit between their homes at Sandringham, Windsor Castle, Balmoral and Buckingham Palace. Public or state duties were carried out at Buckingham Palace. They attended the same sporting events year in year out – the Badminton Horse Trials, Ascot for the racing, Cowes on the Isle of Wight for the yachting, Balmoral for the shooting season. Other off-duty events included polo matches – Charles' particular passion – and hunting and fishing.

STRONG-MINDED REBEL

Diana found it hard to connect with that kind of life. Other royals were, basically, country people. Diana was much more of a 'townie'. She preferred the sunshine holiday spots of the Caribbean to the mists of Balmoral. She fell off a horse as a child and was a reluctant rider ever afterwards. Yet now, she belonged to a family that treasured horses. An animal-lover, she detested hunting and shooting. She could be a strong-minded rebel and would not be

❧ Protocol ❧

ROYALS AND PUBLIC LIFE

The busy public life royals lead today is not part of a long tradition. Before Prince Albert married Queen Victoria in 1840 and began modernizing the monarchy, people knew relatively little about their royals. In fact, in 1830, when Victoria's uncle William IV, **right**, became king, he rode around London introducing himself to his subjects.

Albert changed all that. He realized that the Royal Family had the influence and status to play a vital role in relieving poverty, helping the sick and unfortunate and so binding the people to the Royal Family in a new love and regard. From there, royal public duties burgeoned into the close personal involvement of today.

bent to fit the royal rules without a struggle.

As such, Diana caused problems for the court and the aides and officials of whom Charles once said ruefully 'we don't run them, they run us'. Later on, Diana would be depicted as a 'prisoner in the palace', a lively young woman worn down by royal routine and the stifling attentions of deferential, but manipulative courtiers. Though this was an exaggeration, there was some truth in it. Generally speaking, courtiers liked their royal masters and mistresses to be staid, quiet and pliable. They had their own, strict, view of proper royal behaviour and were not averse to reminding royals of it.

Some of them looked on the new Princess of Wales as a frisky young filly who needed to be broken, or at least, reined in. They never quite managed it. Though, in time, Diana calmed down from her early rebellious days, there was always the chance

> ## "It was as if Charles was married to them, not me, and they are so patronizing, it drives me mad."
>
> DIANA, ON CERTAIN PALACE COURTIERS

that she would do something spontaneous – like taking off her shoes in public, and, of course, kissing and cuddling children, old people or anyone else who engaged her sympathies.

Prince Charles, who was born to the royal routine, seems to have had some difficulty understanding Diana's need for the impulsive, emotional approach. There was, though, one area of their joint lives where their personal preferences met. As Prince of Wales, Charles had no dynastic function apart from waiting to succeed to the throne. Whatever else he did, whatever interests he took up, were *his* choice rather than roles laid down for him.

HIS MOTHER'S SHADOW

Charles also had to face the fact that as a husband, he was linked to his mother, the Queen, in a way no other married man had to be. For Diana, the Queen was the best of mothers-in-law; kindly, understanding, even a little indulgent at times. But the fact remained that Charles had to live in her shadow. What was more, the Queen had the monarch's right

Life with the Royal Family meant an unending round of private and public duty. **Above** Diana riding with the Queen – not a pursuit she enjoyed. **Near right** Diana with other members of the family at the Highland Games at Braemar, near Balmoral, and **far right** outside Sandringham Church at Christmas. **Below right** She plans her engagements with Anne Beckwith-Smith, her lady-in-waiting.

IN THE NEWS

Diana versus the 'Grey Men'

There was no way the young Diana could have commended herself to the old guard of royal courtiers after she married Prince Charles. The 'grey men', as Diana later called them in her controversial TV interview of 1995, reported in The Times, **right**, regarded her as a 'lightweight' and a 'featherhead'. They expected to remake Diana in the dutiful image of an ideal royal wife. They were in for a shock. Diana was too tough-minded for this treatment. She meant to be princess her way and refused to be patronized.

Princess tells of pain, depression, romance and the Palace enemy

What you don't know can hurt you.

DIARY DATES
1981
October
The last weeks of the Prince and Princess of Wales' honeymoon are spent with the Royal Family at Balmoral. The couple return to Buckingham Palace
November
Diana's first big public engagement, the tour of Wales.
Diana accompanies the Queen and members of the Royal Family to the State Opening of Parliament.
Announcement of Diana's first pregnancy
December
Diana falls down the stairs at Sandringham. The accident does not affect her unborn child. This was later said to be a suicide attempt.
Diana visits a primary school at Tetbury, near her home, Highgrove House
1982
February
Charles and Diana on holiday in the Bahamas. Diana snubs photographers at the airport by turning her back on them. However, papparazzi take sneak photographs of the 5-months pregnant princess as she relaxes on the beach
May
Charles and Diana move from Buckingham Palace to Kensington Palace. Barbara Barnes, 39, is appointed as the new nanny who will look after Diana's first child

to say how they should conduct their lives and bring up their children.

Though the Queen was too considerate to assert these rights in a hurtful way, Charles nevertheless longed for some freedom to manoeuvre and establish his own identity. An elusive quest when he was a bachelor, marriage enabled him to do it.

The first loosening of the bonds came in May 1982, when Charles and Diana moved from Buckingham Palace to apartments at Kensington Palace, where several other members of the Royal Family already lived. The next step came in 1988, when the Waleses transferred their offices from Buckingham Palace to St. James' Palace, except for their press people, who followed three years later.

The move from Buckingham Palace allowed

Charles and Diana to create a 'court' complementary to that of the Queen. The new arrangement suited Diana very well. The two palaces were not far apart and Diana often drove herself from Kensington Palace to St. James' Palace, entering by the Stable Yard. At St. James' Palace Diana had her own staff and offices, where conferences were held to hammer out her timetable of public duties.

Diana, a very tidy person, and something of a perfectionist when it came to arrangements, personally kept a diary called Season's Calendar, which divided her day into mornings, afternoons and evenings. Each section was filled not only with her daily engagements, but also with 'collar days' (the royal term for saints' days), the birthdays of other royals, Diana's appointments with her dentist, doctor or hairdresser, conferences with charity officials,

IN CONTEXT
1981-2
TORVILL AND DEAN TRIUMPH

- Jane Torvill and Christopher Dean, **right**, win European ice-dancing title
- US trade union leaders refused visas to visit communist Poland
- Guillotine abolished in France
- Second worst fall in London Stock Exchange history, on 23 September 1981, heralds start of slump
- Picasso's painting *Guernica* returns to Spain after 40 years in New York
- Aircraft crashes in Washington near the White House

Top left Diana in the royal procession at the State Opening of Parliament. **Above left** At a charity performance of *Private Lives*, in aid of the Royal Marsden Hospital's cancer appeal. **Above** Diana reviews a line of Chelsea pensioners on Founder's Day at the Royal Hospital. **Right** Diana with her sister, Sarah, at the Burghley Horse Trials.

her private lunch dates, weddings or christenings she meant to attend, private showings of new clothes – in fact anything and everything that might otherwise be forgotten in a very busy life.

This schedule was made much easier for Diana by the fact that it was based in surroundings of her own choice. Like every wife, Diana wanted to create her own home in her own style, and the two palaces gave her plenty of opportunity.

HOMELY ATMOSPHERE

Diana was fond of green, and at Kensington Palace she created for herself an eau-de-nil dressing room. The bathroom had mirrored walls, which optically increased its size. Elsewhere, the walls were painted in pale lemon and peach and the drawing room in yellow. Diana had her sitting room decorated in

> "*Being a princess is not all it's cracked up to be.*"
> PRINCESS DIANA

pale blue trellis wallpaper, with pink sofas, gilt mirrors and velvet bows over the pictures. Scattered here and there, she kept her ceramic 'pets' – rabbits, birds and her favourite animal, frogs.

Under Diana's direction, apartments eight and nine at Kensington Palace, linked in an L-shape, gained a distinctly homely atmosphere.

Later, St. James' Palace was redecorated. The walls were painted duck egg blue. New curtains in fashionable sacking-type material complemented furniture which was in an informal country style.

Diana never fully accepted some of the restrictions of her married life, especially the ever-present security guards. But the more congenial surroundings of her own home and workplace helped her cope with the demands of being royal.

As she herself said, the job was '30 per cent excitement and 70 per cent sheer slog', and there were times when the tedium of it all was mind-bending. Even so the 20-year-old who started out feeling crushed by the royal machine eventually turned herself into a professional who handled her job with skill and did it, if not in her own sweet time, then certainly in her own sweet way.

The Private Princess
The Camilla factor

Above The Parker-Bowles. Camilla flanked by her son Tom and daughter Laura, with husband Andrew in the background.

Diana apparently discovered on her honeymoon that Camilla Parker-Bowles was not just another of Charles' many friends, but someone much more dangerous: the soulmate which the thoughtful, often troubled prince needed.

As a result, Diana seemed determined to wage war in order to claim her man. But seeing off Camilla was not that easy.

Born on 17 July 1947, Camilla was the daughter of Major Bruce Shand and the Hon. Rosalind Cubitt. Through her mother, she was descended from a 14th-century king of Scotland and, ironically, from the last and most accomplished mistress of King Edward VII, Mrs. Alice Keppel.

Charles and Camilla met in 1971. Friends later revealed that their mutual attraction was instant. Charles, then 23, may have wanted to marry Camilla, but she was not the virginal bride he had to have. In 1973, Camilla married Andrew Parker-Bowles, an army officer, and had two children. Charles remained in Camilla's life and, not unusual in their social class, her husband accepted their friendship.

Diana, though, was not so willing. She had legal and moral rights on her side, offered youth and beauty and, through her children, continuity of Charles' royal line. But friends say she found the situation stressful and probably saw Camilla as one who shared aspects of Charles' past from which age and background excluded her. Camilla, moving more easily and confidently in the world Charles inhabited, must have seemed a powerful rival.

Main picture Diana in a Philip Somerville designed hat, attending the enthronement celebrations of Emperor Akihito of Japan, in Tokyo in 1990. Her pale blue gown, by Catherine Walker, was buttoned down the front, long and modest. **Left** Diana cut a dash in this drum majorette outfit by Catherine Walker with a hat by Graham Smith on an official visit to Sandhurst in 1987.

Special Occasions

Dress designers often get their inspiration from foreign cultures. This was useful for Princess Diana when her wardrobe on overseas tours had to compliment her hosts and, at times, take their sensibilities into account

There was a lot more to Diana's wardrobe than smart, trendsetting fashions, eye-catching hats or beautiful ball gowns. On overseas tours, there were cultural concerns to be addressed, and the subtle business of complimenting Charles and Diana's hosts by way of her wardrobe. In addition, designers had to bear in mind that an outfit was unlikely to be worn only once. Diana would almost certainly wish to wear it again later, probably with different accessories.

One clever choice of outfit, for example, was the white dress with large red dots which Diana wore during her tour of Japan in 1986. The dress was complemented by a matching red hat with the underside of its wide brim lined in white. Diana could not have chosen anything more appropriate for her first day in Japan. In effect, she was introducing herself to the Japanese by wearing their flag, or at least a version of it. The large red dots echoed the emblem of the Rising Sun, the symbol of Japan, and the significance of this was not lost on the royal couple's hosts. They were highly pleased.

It was on this same tour that the Japanese gave Diana a specially made kimono, the traditional dress of the country which is still worn on ceremonial occasions. The kimono was distinctly oversized, but politeness and diplomacy – a must for royals – had to prevail. Diana accepted the kimono as a token of Japanese friendship, as they intended.

By 1986, of course, Diana already knew very well what the rules were in such cases. On one of her very first public appearances as Princess of Wales, at the Braemar Games in Scotland in 1981, Diana joined in with the Royal Family's tradition of wearing tartan. For the occasion she wore a high-necked

> *"When I first arrived there were a lot of people to help me. It's now really my choice."*
> PRINCESS DIANA ON CHOOSING HER WARDROBE

woollen dress with a black velvet tam o'shanter.

Shortly afterwards, on her very first public engagement as Princess, her tour of Wales in November 1981, she wore a suit in the Welsh national colours of red and green. Diana's dark green pleated skirt was topped by a bright red jacket with dark green trimmings and she wore with it a wide-brimmed hat of the same colour.

Borrowed features

As time went on, wearing clothes that borrowed colours and other features from a host's culture or customs became a regular feature of Diana's wardrobe. Sometimes this was only subtly achieved, sometimes it was more straightforward. For instance, when Diana visited Sandhurst Military Academy in 1987, she wore a white 'drum majorette' two-piece suit trimmed with rows of gold braid. In 1991, during a Hong Kong gala evening at London's Barbican Centre, Diana appeared in a short crimson lace-skirted evening dress with a top made in outlined sections which resembled a Chinese lantern. The dress had originally been made for a tour of China, which had to be called off for political reasons at the last moment.

1 For Japan, 1986, Diana bought this white dress with large red dots as an off-the-peg number at Tatters, in Fulham Road, London. 2 This kimono was made specially for Diana and presented to her on her Japanese tour.

3 On a tour in September 1991 to Pakistan, a Muslim country, Diana covered her head with a locally made shawl as a mark of respect for Pakistani fashion and local traditions. 4 In Pakistan again, in May 1997, when Diana met her friends Imran and Jemima Khan. She is wearing an off-the-peg tunic and trousers that echo a style popular with many local women.

5 Demure Diana in tartan for the Braemar Gathering of September 1981. The picture, taken during her honeymoon, shows her wearing a dress designed by Caroline Charles. 6 Visiting Karnak, Luxor in Egypt, in May 1992, the princess wears a dress that echoes the colours of sun and sand that surround her. It was designed by Catherine Walker.

CATHERINE WALKER GOWN

Right and below This outfit was designed by Catherine Walker for Diana's visit to India in February 1992. The bolero top featured a flower and frond pattern, echoing designs often found in Muslim shrines. It was worn to a banquet in Delhi, held for the President of India.

CATHERINE WALKER TUNIC

Right and below This tunic was worn by Diana in February 1990 during a visit to Al Ain in the United Arab Emirates. The loose-fitting top and trousers were perfect for dining cross-legged on cushions, as is customary in the UAE. The outfit was created in 1986 for Diana's first trip to the Gulf.

①

②

1 At King Fahd's dinner in Riyadh, Saudi Arabia, in November 1986, Diana wore a black and white gown that picked up the colours of the robes worn by the men around her. The gown was designed by the Emmanuels, and with it Diana wore the Queen Mary tiara, given to her by the Queen on her marriage to Prince Charles.

2 Diana complimented her Pakistani hosts, the Chitral Scouts, in 1991 when she wore this gift, the scout uniform, during a visit to Lahore. Real maharajahs of the past would have outshone her in their elaborate, bejewelled, richly brocaded robes. But this modern version still managed to suggest the opulent magnificence of the luxury enjoyed by those wealthy men of the past.

The following year, 1990, Diana visited the Royal Hampshire Regiment, of which she was Colonel-in-Chief. This time, she did not bother with adaptations. Instead, she had a copy specially made of the Royal Hampshire's mess jacket and wore it with regulation white shirt, gold-buttoned white waistcoat and black bow tie.

Artistic licence

Another example of Diana adopting, rather than adapting, local dress came with her tour of Pakistan in 1991. Here, she went almost totally ethnic, with an outfit she wore in Lahore. Reminiscent of the luxurious robes worn by maharajahs and other potentates who had once ruled the Indian sub-continent, Diana's outfit featured a soft white cap with jewels and feathers ornamenting the front, and a top intricately embroidered with gold interlinked diamond-shapes that were emphasized by crimson, green and blue lozenges.

On such occasions, Diana was free to make her own fashion choices from the designs available, and her designers were free to use their artistic licence more or less as they pleased. The results were not always universally popular. Some officers at Sandhurst, for example, were said to be none too

> ## "She absolutely lit up the place... shimmering from head to toe."
> A MEMBER OF PARLIAMENT ON DIANA

happy to find their military uniform transformed into a fashion statement.

More than ruffled feathers could be caused, though, when Diana ventured into the more traditional cultures where the position of women was quite different from that in western countries. One area which posed 'tricky' problems was the Middle East, where women do not have equality with men as it is understood in the West, and there are strict rules about how they ought to dress.

In places like Muslim Kuwait or the United Arab Emirates, where Charles and Diana toured in 1989, female dress has to be modest and unrevealing. The idea is to prevent men other than a woman's husband finding her attractive, with all the possible consequences that might ensue from that.

At the most extreme, Muslim women are required to envelop themselves completely in long loose robes down to their ankles, cover their faces with a veil and so that even their hair will not be visible, shroud their heads in a scarf or a shawl.

Fortunately, Diana was not expected to comply fully, but despite the intense heat of the desert climate, she still had to be well and truly covered up. One outfit which Diana wore in Saudi Arabia fitted the bill admirably. She chose tight white trousers and a long lilac and white tunic. This was a much better choice than the long, heavy skirts worn by Margaret Thatcher, when Prime Minister, or the Queen on their own visits to the Muslim countries. Diana's outfit did not offend the sensibilities of her male hosts, and also preserved her modesty when it came to the traditional Muslim custom of sitting on the floor. Descended, like all Arabs, from desert nomads, the Saudis still made

> **"You should have seen some of those Arabs going ga-ga when they saw me on the Gulf tour."**
> DIANA, TO PRESS AFTER 1986 TOUR

ceremonial use of tents, with carpets laid on the bare sand, low tables and a mass of cushions to sit on. Diana's outfit enabled her to sit cross-legged and still look elegant.

Much later, in 1997, when Diana visited her friends Imran and Jemima Khan in Pakistan, another Muslim country, she wore the traditional 'shalwar kameez', a trousers-and-long-tunic outfit which served the same cultural purpose.

Not all Muslim countries, of course, are quite as strictly traditional as this. Egypt, for instance, is much more westernized and when Diana stopped off there on her honeymoon in 1981, she was able to wear her short skirts and no one minded.

Abstract inspiration

India, which has a large Muslim population and an even larger Hindu one, is also westernized, at least in the cities. Because dressing for modesty is not so strictly enforced there, this gave Catherine Walker, who designed a beautiful wardrobe for Diana's tour of India with Charles in 1992, the chance to try out something different in the traditional line. One of the strictest laws of Islam, the Muslim religion, is that no images of people or animals should be displayed. Though this is a severe restriction, it has inspired artists, sculptors and stonemasons to

> ## *"I do so like men in uniform."*
> ### PRINCESS DIANA

explore the beauties of abstract patterns, flower and leaf designs and geometric shapes. Catherine Walker, studying this characteristic Indian Muslim way with design, came across a lovely flower and frond pattern of the kind often seen in Muslim shrines, like the famous Taj Mahal.

Walker adapted it and used it to create a stunning evening top for Diana (see page 67), in which pearls and silver brocade sparkled out the pattern, while the bolero shape recalled the tasteful curved lines of Muslim architecture. This top was completed by a plain straight black skirt and Diana wore it with the Spencer family tiara.

This outfit, like all the others made as diplomatic fashion statements, was cleverly conceived to fit in with the rest of Diana's wardrobe. The trick was not only to create something which her hosts could identify as a compliment, but also to further Diana's image as a smart and elegant princess.

1 Opposite Diana wore this opulent glittering gown on the tour of the Gulf in March 1989. **1** Diana sometimes wore adventurous colour combinations. Here, purple and crimson were strikingly combined in this beautiful evening dress by Catherine Walker, which Diana wore during her visit to Thailand in 1988 for the celebrations of the King's 60th birthday. Diana wore silk flowers in her hair to complement the dress. The colours are typical of Thailand's exotic look.

2 In February 1990, Diana visited the men of the Royal Hampshire Regiment, in Germany. To their delight, she wore a replica mess jacket made by Gieves and Hawkes, the Saville Row tailors.

IN THE NEWS

Charles and Diana at Klondike hoe-down

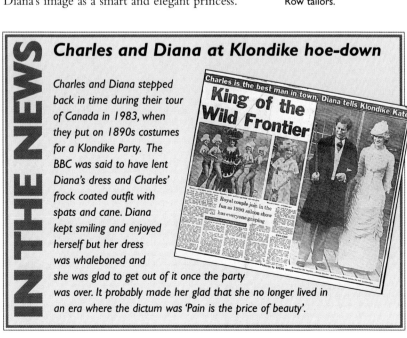

Charles and Diana stepped back in time during their tour of Canada in 1983, when they put on 1890s costumes for a Klondike Party. The BBC was said to have lent Diana's dress and Charles' frock coated outfit with spats and cane. Diana kept smiling and enjoyed herself but her dress was whaleboned and she was glad to get out of it once the party was over. It probably made her glad that she no longer lived in an era where the dictum was 'Pain is the price of beauty'.

Charles is the best man in town, Diana tells Klondike Kate

King of the Wild Frontier

Royal couple join in the fun as 1890 saloon show has everyone gasping

The People's Princess

VOGUE

JULY
£2.70

Happy Birthda

THE PRINCES

The Cover Girl

It was not long before magazines and newspapers discovered that with Diana on their covers or front pages, sales shot up by a fifth or more. This was how Diana became the world's greatest cover girl

Diana's early days as a member of the Royal Family gave little hint of her extraordinary future as a superstar cover girl. When the young, shy, nervous Lady Diana Spencer faced a battery of camera lenses, with photographers exhorting her to smile and give them a good picture, her jaw clamped and her smile, if any, became fixed. She looked at the ground, or hid behind her heavy fringe. She turned her back on the camera sometimes, put her head on one side or shrank down into her coat collar.

Request from the Queen

In her first few months as Princess of Wales, she became so unsettled at all the press attention that the Queen had to rescue her with an appeal for restraint. The onslaught cooled for a time, but it soon picked up speed again.

Diana never entirely got over her dislike of being photographed and especially of posing for press photographs, which she found embarrassing. Yet even she finally came to recognize that avid interest in the new Princess of Wales was as certain as tomorrow's sunrise. She was, after all, only the second such princess this century. Her predecessor, who became Queen Mary in 1910, had lived in a totally different era when it came to royal coverage. Attitudes then were more deferential and less intrusive and people had fewer opportunities to see any of the members of the Royal

Previous page This is how Diana appeared on the cover of *Vogue* in July 1994.
Left and below Diana, the world's most photographed woman appeared on thousands of magazine covers, both news and general interest titles.

Two pictures for the family album. Early photographic sessions with the young Waleses at home. **Above** with Prince William in 1982 and **above right** in Kensington Palace. These pictures show a slightly stiff formality, not evident in the press photographs of Diana on official duties during the same period.

Family on a daily basis in their newspapers.

The royals themselves had been different, too. They were less approachable and were held far more in awe than later became the case. Both as Princess of Wales and Queen, Mary was an awesome, majestic figure, not the sort a photographer would ask to say 'Cheese'.

Royal glamour girl

Between Queen Mary and Diana there had been only one or two royal glamour girls: possibly the most famous was Princess Margaret. But she had been young and newsworthy several years before the Queen opened the media floodgates with the TV programme *Royal Family*, in 1969. This allowed the public to see the Queen, Prince Philip and their children going about their daily lives as they had never been seen before, and created an appetite for more of the same, which was ready for mass feeding by the time Diana came on the scene.

Diana had it all: youth, beauty, breeding, personal appeal, warmth, status, instant fame and a great

future in the most highly regarded royal family in the world. In spite of herself, Diana's assets for the camera were also considerable. She had a flawless complexion, sparkling blue eyes, white teeth, and shining hair. She was marvellously photogenic.

What was more, the media was in just the right

> ## "Come on love, we're not going to take your teeth out!"
> PRESS CAMERAMAN TO LADY DIANA SPENCER

state of development to promote her to those dazzling heights, especially in their ever-increasing use of colour photography.

In the 1980s, magazines were using more colour than ever before. So were newspapers. The number of publications had burgeoned. Television coverage had expanded. In all, there had never been a greater opportunity for royals and other celebrities to be seen and recognized by so many millions of people. And in 1981, there was Diana, the perfect subject,

fully equipped and ready to lead the mass media into a new and very exciting age.

Diana's superstar cover girl status did not become a fact of media life overnight, of course. Contrary to popular belief, it was not impossible to take a bad picture of her in those early days. Diana discovered this for herself when she saw her engagement photographs. These told her that the camera, a merciless observer, had made her look fatter than she was because she was wearing a suit that bunched up round her waist and hips. Later on, slimmer, smoother lines characterized her wardrobe, giving a much slimmer look.

There was also the problem of the big nose. Though, fortunately, it did not spoil her profile, Diana's nose was very broad at the nostrils with a slight bend at the bridge. This was not a problem when Diana was photographed from a distance. Even from the side, her nose looked classically high-bridged and rather distinctive. The long lens, however, is a demanding master and in close-up, the

Above Diana faces the cameras – a task she became used to but never really liked. Diana's royal predecessor was the lively and very beautiful Princess Margaret, **inset above**.

nose could become obtrusive. Photographers took care, therefore, to film her at angles where her nose blended into the rest of her face. Several splendid full-face and three-quarter face shots resulted.

Mistakes with make-up

The face itself changed during Diana's apprenticeship as a top-flight photographic subject. Once she lost the plump face that went with her puppy fat, she acquired a classy, but fresh-faced look which the camera liked better. Like so many young girls, Diana had made mistakes with make-up. She wore heavy foundation, which tended to make her face mask-like. She applied too much rouge, which made her look flushed. And she borrowed the idea of blue eyeliner from Elizabeth Taylor, the film star. The dark-haired Taylor could get away with it. Fair-haired, fair-skinned Diana could not. On her, it looked very unnatural. She did better when she changed to subtler shades of brown or taupe, a brownish-grey eye shadow and

Previous page Typical of a snatched cover shot, Diana pauses, relaxed for the cameras, in one of her glittering evening gowns. **Above** A posed shot from a session with Lord Snowdon at Highgrove House. **Above right** On tour, the press captured Diana as the people's princess.

soft eyeliner – all of which made her eyes look both striking and large.

Diana also abandoned the heavy foundation and instead improved the glow of her complexion with make-up one shade lighter than her skin. The rouge which once made her colour seem far too high was replaced by a gold bronzer, which highlighted her face without making itself too evident.

In the mood

Though she worked hard to transform herself for the camera, Diana was not always in the mood to be photographed. This could be so even where photographers were officially accredited to one of her public engagements. Sometimes, it seems that she deliberately spoiled pictures by looking grumpy and po-faced, as she did when photographed with Charles during a private break in Hawaii in 1985. Pictures were taken, but not very widely published, which probably pleased Diana.

At other times, the lighting conditions under which the photographers had to work produced pictures which would never appear in print. They

❧ Protocol ❧

PHOTOS BY APPOINTMENT

When Diana died after the Paris car crash and a pack of paparazzi was thought to be responsible, there was some confusion between them and the newspaper and news agency staff photographers who take pictures of the Royal Family with Palace consent. These photographers are accredited by the Palace to record royal engagements or tours, or are invited to special photo-calls, such as the one, **below**, with Prince William. Royals, even the ever-patient Queen, have been known to shout at photographers if they get too close, even though they have the right to be there. The freelance paparazzi, however, are opportunists, snatching royal pictures as and when the chance presents itself.

FRAU
im Spiegel

1,60 DM · Nr. 33 6. 8. 1981 · Italien: 1000 L · Öster- C 8484
reich: 14,– ö. S. · Schweiz: 1,90 sfr Printed in Germa

**Die Hochzeit
von Charles
und Diana**

Auf vielen Farbseiten:
Die schönsten Fotos
vom Fest des Jahres

Curd Jürgens:
Meine Frau und ich
genießen jeden Tag,
der uns noch bleibt

Deutschlands
Sportlerinnen werden
immer hübscher

Neues TV-Traumpaar:
Rex Gildo
und Lena Valaitis

Prinz Charles u
Prinzessin Di

had to photograph Diana in all light conditions, showing a variety of expressions and gestures, from all angles and sometimes from awkward positions. This inevitably produced pictures that failed to make Diana easily or quickly recognizable. If the camera happened to catch an odd expression, or the light was not quite right, then photographs would be banished to the files, never to emerge again.

Posing problems

The great majority of photographs, of course, made Diana a delight to look at. Young, healthy, lively, interested in what she was doing and the people she was meeting. It was not a straightforward matter to capture her in this refreshing guise, but the photographers were greatly helped by the logistics of royal public engagements. Depending on the event and the time of day, engagements could last for several hours, with photographers present for much of the time, obtaining shot after shot of Diana. The time-scale was such that Diana was able to forget the photographers were there. That was when some of the best pictures of her were taken.

The difference between the posed press pictures, which Diana disliked, and photographs taken 'on the run', was very marked. When posing, Diana

Left The look initially associated with Lady Diana Spencer was the much vaunted 'Shy Di', splashed on to magazines and newspapers galore. **Inset left** Charles and Diana's tenth wedding anniversary in 1991 produced a fresh flood of royal interest in the media, allowing much reflection on the past decade, such as this *Sunday Express* feature.

Opposite page Diana, slightly stiff, caught 'on the run' by the press pack. **Inset** The Royal Wedding made magazine covers world-wide, such as *Frau im Spiegel* from Germany.

tended to stiffen up. Her eyes lost some of their sparkle. Her smile, once again, became fixed. She even looked rather furtive in some posed shots. However, when she was less conscious of the cameras during a public engagement, she looked very animated, and much more as if she was enjoying herself. It made a much prettier picture that way.

If only because there were more of them, pictures of Diana out and about, meeting ordinary people at public engagements, dominated the covers on which she appeared so frequently. Before long, it was possible to look over the stands at a newsagents and see perhaps 50 per cent of the magazines on sale, sometimes more, with Diana looking out of them. They were never there for long. Diana

> **"I used it as bedding for my children's hamsters."**
>
> DIANA ON A TABLOID NEWSPAPER

cover pictures were snapped up within hours, whether they appeared on women's magazines or lifestyle publications, which seemed a natural place for them, or on more specialized magazines which appeared to have no connection with royalty – photographic, computer, sports, political, even postage stamp and coin publications.

This was a publishing floodtide which did not please certain stuffier palace officials, and Diana apparently received a certain amount of criticism. The traditionalists disliked, first of all, the emphasis of make-up and also hairstyles involved in this kind of publicity. The Victorian idea was still prevalent at the palace that face-painting was somehow not

IN THE NEWS

They know it's all over

Any excuse was valid as long as newspapers and magazines could get Diana on their cover. She invariably boosted sales and might have been pictured on the cover of this German magazine of 17 November 1992 even without a special story attached. But Andrew Morton's book Diana: Her True Story *had just been published, revealing the scandal behind the fairytale marriage. 'Diana Final!' the headline read. 'It's all over with Charles!' Charles and Diana separated the following month.*

ladylike and not socially respectable. Royal ladies had used make-up before, but it was so light as to be almost invisible. Diana's outlined eyes went way beyond this subtlety. Royal ladies had also appeared on magazine covers before, notably the Queen Mother who, when young, had been one of the great beauties of her day. But that had been done

> "The press made Diana's life difficult, but she behaved very well... I wouldn't have done it myself at nineteen. I'd have collapsed!"
>
> HER FATHER, EARL SPENCER, ON THE PRE-ENGAGEMENT PURSUIT OF DIANA

tastefully, rarely and most often in the more muted, less dramatic black and white.

As far as the critics were concerned, the much bolder way in which Diana was displayed on covers equated the wife of the heir to the throne and a future Queen Consort with models, actresses, film and rock stars. Like all reactionaries who thought this way and wanted a return to the more sedate royal world of the past, Diana's critics were missing something which Diana had readily recognized. The new world of mass

Above right Diana pictured with Henry Kissinger at a benefit concert in 1995 in America, and **inset right** as she appeared in a picture taken the same evening, which was used on the memorial issue of *Time* magazine on 8 September 1997.

images, television sets, videos, the Internet and rapid technological advances in communications had no place in the ceremonious approach. Diana was not overfond of the camera, but she knew that royals could not afford to be left behind in the communications revolution.

Diana the superstar cover girl was, in a way, a product of that revolution and also a pioneer of it. Far from cheapening the royal image by making herself so accessible to the camera, she gave it a new, far more approachable persona. The fact that she made herself phenomenally popular by her other innovations, especially her tactile style of performing royal duties, made it that much easier for her to achieve her cover girl heights. The fact that she was probably the most loved of all royals, apart from the Queen Mother, did the rest.

BIRTH OF AN HEIR

Nurses at a hospital Diana was visiting late in October 1981 first noticed it: the extra warm glow of the young princess' complexion which, they guessed, meant she was pregnant. They were right

The birth of royal children has long been a cause for celebration, but the announcement on 5 November 1981 that Diana was expecting her first baby had a special joy to it. People were still basking in the afterglow of Charles and Diana's wedding, just over three months before. Diana had already become popular – she was loved, admired and regarded as the nation's new sweetheart. Already there was no doubt that Diana was a royal phenomenon. Within a very short time, she had acquired a countrywide club of devoted fans.

When out on public engagements, there were chants of 'We want Diana! We want Diana!' Those sections of the crowd who got Charles instead seemed openly disappointed. 'If I were you, I'd ask for your money back,' he told them ruefully. He apologized for not having enough wives to go round and suggested splitting Diana in two while he 'directed operations'. Charles' initial amusement

DIARY DATES

1982

21 June
Prince William born in Lindo Wing of St Mary's Hospital, Paddington, London

22 June
The Queen visits her third grandchild

22 June
Diana and William leave hospital

7 July
Intruder Michael Fagan gets into the Queen's bedroom at Buckingham Palace

4 August
Queen Mother's 82nd birthday

4 August
Prince William christened at Buckingham Palace

September
Diana represents the Royal Family at the funeral of Princess Grace of Monaco

November
Diana rides with the Queen to the State Opening of Parliament

22 December
Prince William, 6 months, appears before the cameras with his parents at Kensington Palace

December
William's first Christmas at Balmoral. But Diana is bored and returns to London.
Diana refuses to cooperate with press cameramen while skiing in Lichstenstein

1983
Rumours start about Diana's health

April
Diana insists on taking William on Australia tour

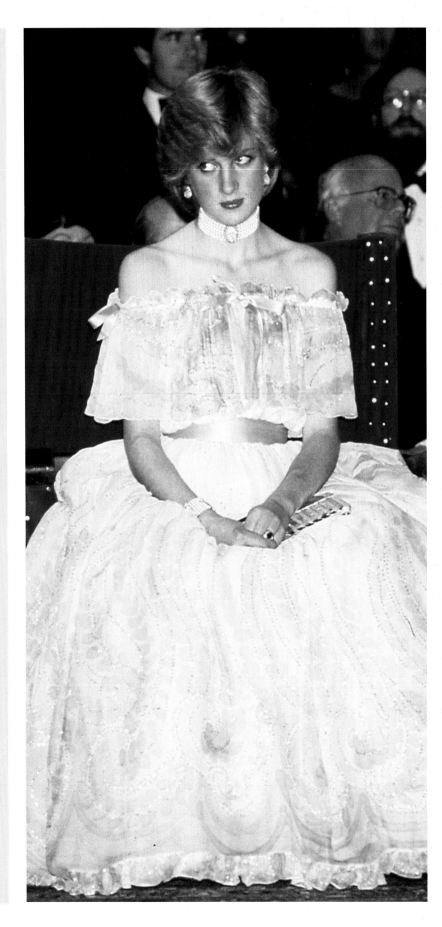

Previous page Charles and Diana show off William. **Left** Diana, the evening before her first pregnancy was made public. **Above** A pregnant Diana gets a helping hand from Charles.

was rumoured to have changed to chagrin, though and later, to resentment.

But in November 1981, it was all smiles and congratulations at the news of the royal baby, due to be born in the summer of 1982. A beloved princess, who so loved children, was going to have one of her own and produce an heir to the throne.

GETTING THE TIMING RIGHT

The actual announcement was held back until 5 November, to avoid a clash with the State Opening of Parliament by the Queen. Diana rode to the Opening with Princess Anne, in the Glass Coach which had carried her to her wedding. Her glowing appearance at this, her first full-dress state occasion, was noted by some commentators.

There was, though, some surprise that Diana was expecting a baby so soon. However, there was nothing unusual about a pregnancy in the first year

> ***"It was ridiculous to suggest that Diana would wait a year to start a family."***
> EARL SPENCER, DIANA'S FATHER

of a royal marriage. The Queen had given birth to Prince Charles within that time. Both Princess Alexandra and Princess Michael of Kent had given birth within the first year. What was different was the explicit nature of the announcement. When the Queen, then Princess Elizabeth, had been expecting in 1948, royal pregnancy was subject to a coy code. It was made known that she had cancelled all her engagements and she disappeared from public view until she got her waistline back after giving birth. This rather prudish procedure had changed by 1964 when both the Queen and Princess Margaret were seen in public heavily pregnant.

Diana had no qualms about appearing in the same state, but she proved, unfortunately, to be one of those mothers-to-be who was unwell in the first few months. Diana was sick all day at the start.

In true royal style, though, she insisted on carrying out her duties regardless, but appeared at engagements looking pale and wan. Before long, Diana had to give in and cancelled plans for five

Above The Queen and Diana watching polo. When the Queen was expecting Prince Charles in 1948 she withdrew from all public engagements. **Left** By 1964, when Prince Edward was due, no one was so coy. He is seen here in his pram.

IN CONTEXT *1982* THATCHER'S ELECTION TRIUMPH

- Argentina surrenders to end the Falklands War
- Margaret Thatcher, **right**, wins a second general election victory
- Italy defeats Germany in World Cup Final
- Princess Grace of Monaco killed in car crash
- Queen and Prince Philip meet US President Ronald Reagan
- Sally Ride, 32-year-old physicist, becomes first woman in space
- Israel invades Lebanon

CHRONICLE

engagements, including a visit to the Duchy of Cornwall, Charles' private estates. All day walkabouts, hard enough for royals when in full health, were ruled out until after Diana's baby was born. All Diana was allowed to do were those engagements which lasted only an hour or so.

In the temporary absence of the new princess from the public scene, attention, or rather speculation, concentrated upon peripherals. For a start, there was talk that Diana might be expecting twins. Twins had occurred in the Spencer family often

> **"It has been most harrowing...
> it was a particularly slow birth...
> a very worrying day."**
> EARL SPENCER, DIANA'S FATHER

enough to give the idea plausibility. Indeed, the wife of Diana's brother, the present Earl Spencer, would later give birth to twins.

It was suggested that Mabel Anderson, 55, Prince Charles' nanny, might look after the new royal baby. But the job went instead to 39-year-old Barbara Barnes, the daughter of a worker on the Earl of Leicester's estates. Miss Barnes was described as 'exceptionally firm with a great sense of humour' and an advocate of fresh air. Though this sounded like the formidable nannies of Victorian tradition, Barbara Barnes was in fact just the sort of modern-minded woman a modern-minded princess would want to have looking after her children.

Security guards were engaged and the Prince of Wales' staff worked flat out, coping with the flood of gifts which were already pouring in to the Palace several months before the baby was due.

A MODERN APPROACH

Press and public toyed with the idea that the royal cradle, made of cast-iron and decorated with organza and lace, would be brought out of mothballs and pressed into service again. The cradle, used by the Royal Family for a century, had once held the Queen, Princess Margaret and Prince Charles. Diana, however, was already putting into operation her own ideas about royal babies, their upbringing, their environment and much else. The nursery at

It's a boy!

The birth of Prince William on 21 June 1982 created as much excitement as the wedding of his parents 11 months before. Crowds massed outside St. Mary's Hospital, Paddington, London, where he was born. Charles was the focus of attention as a delighted new father and everyone, it seemed, wanted to shake his hand. No detail was too small for the press when it came to titbits of information about the new prince – his weight, eye and hair colour – all was revealed.

Left and above After early problems had passed, Diana did not mind appearing in public heavily pregnant. Meeting children (above) on a short walkabout still gave her much pleasure.

Above When pregnant, Diana still enjoyed turning out for glamorous evening engagements and, although her clothes may not have been as stylish as before, she still looked eyecatching. **Left** She baulked, however, at press cameras anxious to take yet more shots as she left for a holiday with Charles in the Bahamas, in 1982 when she was several months pregnant.

Highgrove House would be modern, well lit, delicately decorated in blue and gold and equipped with pretty furniture and easy-clean surfaces.

Diana did not, however, win the home-versus-hospital contest. For a long time, it had been traditional for royal children to be born at home. The Queen, for instance, had been born, in 1926, at her parents' London home, 17 Bruton Street. Her sister, Princess Margaret, was born at Glamis Castle in 1930, while Prince Charles came into the world in a maternity room at Buckingham Palace in 1948.

Diana, for once, wanted to follow royal tradition, but the Queen's gynaecologist, George Pinker, put his foot down. He insisted on the private Lindo Wing at St. Mary's Hospital, Paddington, a world-famous maternity unit equipped with all the latest

> ### "He's a doting Daddy and does everything perfectly."
> #### DIANA, ON CHARLES AND FATHERHOOD

technology. Both Princess Anne's children had been born there. Diana's baby would be the first child in direct line of succession to the throne to be born in hospital. Diana was obliged to concede, though her acquiescence may have been helped along by the fact that the nurses at the Lindo Wing were already adept at preserving the privacy of royal mothers. This was an especial relief to Diana, who knew how the press might complicate her life.

Despite, or maybe because of, her relatively brief appearances in public in the early days of her pregnancy, there was intense press interest in Diana, and this was not always in the best of taste. In February 1982, for instance, two photographers crawled through yards of dense undergrowth to take sneak shots of Diana, then five months pregnant, in her bikini while she was holidaying in the Bahamas.

LIVING WITH THE PRESS

After pictures of the Princess 'looking glum' had appeared in the press, Diana was reportedly shocked at speculation that the reason for her 'glumness' was because she and Charles had been arguing. As she was soon to learn, press pursuit, press speculation and some press guesses that came rather too near

the truth – like talk about her 'anorexic' appearance – were an occupational hazard of royal life.

Diana, though, created a few hazards of her own. She often drove herself down to Gloucestershire to oversee work carried out on Highgrove House. There was also the stress of moving to a new home in Kensington Palace five weeks before the birth, in May 1982. Two weeks before the birth, Diana danced at a fundraising ball at Broadlands in aid of the United World Colleges.

It may have been the dancing that did it. The baby was thought to be due on 1 July, Diana's 21st birthday, but at 4.30am on 21 June, her labour pains began. Prince Charles, with admirable prescience, had cancelled a polo match just in case this might happen. He was on hand, therefore, to help Diana into the back of a police Rover, and held her hand as they made the 10-minute drive to St. Mary's. Diana was so unprepared almost all she had with her was the green maternity dress she was wearing.

Labour lasted 16 hours and Diana had to be given a painkilling epidural before Prince William

The Private Princess Diana and eating disorders

The fact that Diana suffered from bulimia nervosa, a disease related to the slimmer's ailment, anorexia nervosa, remained unconfirmed until 1992 when it was revealed, along with her 'suicide attempts', by her friend James Gilbey. These were among the many startling revelations in the original edition of Andrew Morton's book *Diana: Her True Story*.

Long before this, though, there had been ongoing speculation as Diana lost weight far too rapidly, became thin and boney and, apparently, refused to eat properly.

Thought to be caused by stress, overwork, insecurity and an obsession with slimming, bulimia drove Diana to food binges followed by self-induced vomiting. On one occasion, at Windsor Castle, Diana was reportedly seen scoffing an entire rice pudding and bowls of custard. On another, she consumed a quantity of pork pies.

This was not the only incidence of slimming disease in the Spencer family. Diana's elder sister Sarah had been anorexic and, at one stage, got close to six stones.

Charles was doubtless aware of this and attempted to help by keeping an eye on Diana at mealtimes 'just to make sure she ate properly'. It was not an easy task. Bulimia also drove Diana to starve herself. While visiting Expo

Above *This was the dress that started rumours that Diana was anorexic. Its fullness made her look skinny and stick-like by contrast.*

'86 in Vancouver, she fainted, apparently from lack of sustenance. Later that year, during her tour of Japan with Charles, it was observed that she was living on one salad a day.

At this time, Charles and Diana's marriage difficulties were becoming acute.

In 1988, Diana's friend Carolyn Bartholomew apparently admitted threatening to reveal all to the press unless the Princess sought urgent medical attention. Diana gave in and went for help to a Guy's Hospital specialist, Dr Maurice Lipsedge.

In time, Diana's bulimia came under some control and in 1993 she was even able to joke about it.

Arthur Philip Louis, second in line to the throne, was born at 9.03pm on 21 June 1982. He weighed 7lbs 1½ozs and was given a baby tag marked 'Baby Wales'. Prince Charles was present during the birth and later praised his young wife's courage. The Prince nevertheless confessed to feeling 'overwhelmed by it all'. He was not even sure who William looked like and described him as 'sort of fairish with blue eyes'.

The Queen and Diana's parents, Earl Spencer and Mrs Shand Kydd, were in London for the birth, but other members of the Royal Family were

> *"You'll have to ask my wife.*
> *We're having a bit of an argument*
> *about that."*
> PRINCE CHARLES, ON THE BABY'S NAME

far away. The Queen Mother was about to fly off to an engagement when news of her third great-grandchild was brought to her at Heathrow Airport. Prince Andrew was serving with the Royal Navy in the Falkland Islands, where the brief 14-week war with Argentina had ended in British victory the week before. Princess Anne was in New Mexico. The news was flashed to the baby's new uncle and aunt.

Prince Charles emerged from St. Mary's at eleven in the morning, looking somewhat rumpled and stunned, to be greeted by a large crowd. Someone impudently demanded, 'give us another one!' The Prince laughed. 'Bloody hell!' Charles retorted, 'Give us a chance!'

GRANDPARENTS VISIT

As was customary, news of the royal birth was posted on a special ornate stand outside Buckingham Palace, where another crowd craned to read it. A 41-gun salute, for a boy, was fired in Hyde Park and at the Tower of London.

Next day, at 9.22am, Diana's mother visited her, then left to organize celebrations at her home in Scotland. The Queen arrived at 10.52am to find that Prince Charles had filled Diana's room with white roses. Diana's father, Earl Spencer, inspected his grandson, then left to celebrate with a beer. By

Above It was all smiles and congratulations for the delighted new father. Even the police holding back the crowds outside the hospital were enjoying themselves. They did not, however, prevent dozens of people extending their hands for Charles to shake. **Above right** The Queen, as keen as any grandmother to see her new grandchild, leaves the hospital after visiting the baby and her daughter-in-law. **Right** The crowds were still there outside the hospital when Diana insisted on going home, less than 24 hours after giving birth. Charles, holding the new baby, accompanied her to Kensington Palace.

Opposite page The happy royal parents with their first baby – one of the official pictures of Charles, Diana and Prince William. **Above** Barbara Barnes was engaged as William's nanny, although Diana wanted to look after her son herself as much as possible. **Left** Diana knew a few tricks to get William to perform for the camera.

the evening of 22 June, Diana was ready to go home. The usual stay was 48 hours, or as much as ten days, but Diana insisted on going home. At 6pm, she appeared with Charles outside St. Mary's, still wearing her green maternity dress, carrying their infant son in her arms. Not much could be seen of William, apart from a few wisps of fair hair and a glimpse of his newborn crumpled face.

Both Charles and Diana became completely absorbed in their baby son in the first few weeks of his life. Charles was said to be reading baby books and overseeing William at bath time. The royal parents coined a nickname, Wills, for their boy. Diana became almost besotted with her first child, playing with him, bathing him herself and worrying, like many mothers, that he might stop breathing.

QUASHING RUMOURS

Diana also had to put up with rumours that her marriage was 'unhappy', an idea which gained currency when Charles was away on an engagement and Diana gave a brunch to celebrate William's

> *"He hasn't got red hair, he's fair... he's got masses of beautiful blond hair."*
> DIANA, ON WILLIAM

arrival. Diana, however, insisted that 'marriage is wonderful', when opening an extension to the Royal School for the Blind as its president.

Prince William was christened, as royal tradition demanded, in the Music Room at Buckingham Palace on 4 August 1982. It was also the Queen Mother's 82nd birthday, which was why Charles and Diana chose the date. The baby prince, wearing the Royal Family christening robe of Honiton lace, was brought in by Barbara Barnes just before noon.

As Dr Robert Runcie, the Archbishop of Canterbury, performed the ceremony, sprinkling the royal infant with Jordan water, William let out three small cries. Later, when photographs were taken, he began howling loudly. Diana stuck her little finger in his mouth to quieten him. It was hardly like father, like son. When Prince Charles was christened, he slept through the whole thing.

❧ Protocol ❧

LINING UP FOR THE THRONE

The line of succession changes each time a child is born into the Royal Family. When Prince William arrived in 1982, he took his place as second in line after his father. His uncle, Prince Andrew, the Duke of York, dropped to third place. Andrew went down to fourth after Charles and Diana's second son, Prince Harry, was born in 1984. In the succession, boys have, so far, always taken precedence over girls, even if they are younger. However, Prince Charles has proposed a change that will give women equal rights. The lists below show the order of succession after Prince William was born in 1982, today, and if women were to have equal rights with men.

	1982		1997		Equal rights
1	Prince Charles	1	Prince Charles	1	Prince Charles
2	Prince William	2	Prince William	2	Prince William
3	Prince Andrew	3	Prince Harry	3	Prince Harry
4	Prince Edward	4	Prince Andrew	4	Princess Anne
5	Princess Anne	5	Princess Beatrice	5	Peter Phillips
6	Peter Phillips	6	Princess Eugenie	6	Zara Phillips
7	Zara Phillips	7	Prince Edward	7	Prince Andrew
8	Princess Margaret	8	Princess Anne	8	Princess Beatrice
9	Viscount Linley	9	Peter Phillips	9	Princess Eugenie
10	Sarah Chatto	10	Zara Phillips	10	Prince Edward

Peter and Zara Phillips are Princess Anne's children; Viscount Linley and Sarah Chatto are Princess Margaret's children; Princesses Beatrice and Eugenie are the children of Prince Andrew and Sarah Ferguson.

All Wrapped Up

In her early days as princess, Diana was not a natural hat and coat wearer but she soon graduated to the stylish, matching ensembles of her later royal years

When Diana became Princess of Wales, most women only wore formal outfits and hats for weddings and other dress-up family occasions. The Royal Family and some members of the aristocracy were becoming the last repository of elaborate daywear, hats included. When out on public engagements, the royals and their ladies-in-waiting were often wearing the only hats in sight. At the time of her marriage, Diana was

> *"Her main job is to be pretty and slim and wear a hat."*
> GERMAINE GREER

not a natural hat wearer, preferring the relaxed, informal styles of the day.

As a teenager, Diana was entirely comfortable with the casual everyday clothes scene. For her, as for most modern women, trousers and sweaters, or skirts and blouses were not only more practical, but fitted in with a new, faster-moving, more emancipated lifestyle. Consequently, she did not find it easy to adjust to the new, more formal royal approach to clothes.

During her 11 years as an active member of the Royal Family, from 1981 to 1992, Diana took some time to get to grips with the business of wearing hats and coats. In part, her early problems resulted

Above left Too much hair, too much hat, too much collar with this Bellville Sassoon coat and John Boyd hat Diana wore in Wales in 1982.
Near right Topped by a Gilly Forge hat, this Arabella Pollen coat swamped Diana's beautiful figure, though it kept her warm in Hamburg, Germany in November 1987. **Far right** This is better. A lovely matching pink check coat dress by Catherine Walker and a Philip Somerville hat with veil, worn in October 1990 at St. Paul's Cathedral.

from her longish, heavily-fringed hairstyle. It was designed for the hatless way of life of Diana's single days. Later, her hats and hairstyles worked better.

The point was made by a black broad-brimmed hat with ribbon round the crown, which Diana wore more than once, notably on her visit to Chesterfield in 1981. For a start, it was in a style that was far too old for a young girl like her, and forced her hair to sprout out from under the brim. Her fringe was pushed forward until her eyebrows practically disappeared from view.

Other hats, like the blue-grey cap with ostrich feather and veil, that was seen in 1982 when Diana visited University College Hospital in London,

> *"What I always noticed about her before we got married was her very good sense of style, which I appreciate."*
> PRINCE CHARLES

looked as if she had rummaged through her mother's wardrobe for something to wear. At 19 and 20, Diana looked a lot younger than her age and she had to mature before her hats stopped looking too old for her. Even at 24, in 1985, Diana still appeared so youthful that the swathed black and yellow hat made by Philip Somerville to match her black and yellow coat looked positively middle-aged.

Hat choice

With a total of some 75 hats to choose from, she was able to try out plenty of different styles – pill-boxes, small brims, wide brims, cap style with or without veils, flowers and feathers, boaters, high- and low-crowned hats and a hat which she wore in Japan in 1986 which was hardly there: it was just a white headband with a veil over her face.

Being the Princess of Wales, she was, of course, as much of a boost to British milliners as she was to British dress designers. John Boyd, for instance, had barely penetrated the world of royal millinery before Diana took a fancy to his small skull caps, and his way of solving the problem of keeping them in place: two built-in

1 Diana in a sweet little coat dress designed by Arabella Pollen and a John Boyd suede beret, worn in Wales, in November 1982.
2 Diana on Christmas Day in 1986, wearing a red veiled hat and caped coat.

3 Diana looking very smart in a matching three-piece outfit of colour-cued skirt, three-quarter coat by Bellville Sassoon and black-trimmed Frederick Cox hat. She wore this outfit in Hereford in 1985.
4 Hatless this time, in 1986, but the striking check coat makes a fashion statement without any help.

Left The veil is a bit overwhelming for the small tip-tilted hat created by John Boyd, one of Diana's favourite milliners, but the whole creation goes well with this Catherine Walker coat with black collar and cuffs. Diana wore the ensemble in 1982.

combs out of sight under the hat to anchor it to her hair.

However, even when the hats were young enough for her, some styles suited Diana better than others. She looked best in some of her broad-brimmed hats, but this style posed a problem. The royal rule was that hats should never obscure the royal face. Diana, who broke royal habits so often in other ways, did not always observe this one. The difficulty was sometimes solved by curling back the brim at the front, something which John Boyd did with the pink hat with self feather he designed for Diana to wear on her visit to Catania, Sicily, during her tour of Italy with Charles in 1985.

It was not a universal solution, though. A picture taken of Diana with the Queen Mother at Royal Ascot in 1981, before her wedding, shows the contrast between the old hand and the rookie. The Queen Mother, with decades of dressing for public view behind her, wore a large, but off-the-face pale blue hat. Diana wore a broad brim which made her face difficult to see.

She went on offering this obscured view from time to time, even after she married Charles. In 1987, Diana visited Caen, in northern France, and wore a red black-trimmed boater with a brim so

SASSOON COAT

This turquoise coat and matching hat, which Diana wore at Christmas 1981 and on other occasions, was ideal for a young princess and mother-to-be. Warm, pretty, with a fetching yoke and mandarin collar, the mauve flowers scattered over the coat gave it the right youthful look. The inset photograph shows Diana with her brother-in-law Prince Edward after the Christmas church service at St. George's Chapel, Windsor. Designed by Bellville Sassoon, this was one of the youthful Diana's forays into matching outfits which was exactly right – for her age, for unbulky smartness and for her developing pregnancy.

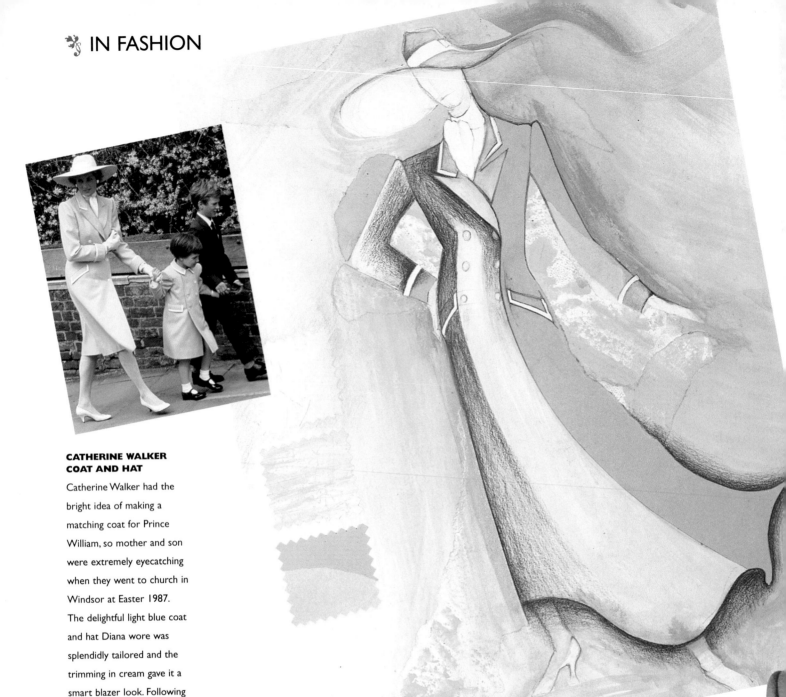

CATHERINE WALKER COAT AND HAT

Catherine Walker had the bright idea of making a matching coat for Prince William, so mother and son were extremely eyecatching when they went to church in Windsor at Easter 1987. The delightful light blue coat and hat Diana wore was splendidly tailored and the trimming in cream gave it a smart blazer look. Following media criticism, Diana and William were not seen again doing this fetching double act, even though at this young age William wouldn't have had much clothes sense, at least not enough to object to being dressed up to please grown ups! He wore the coat later. It's a pity, though, that Diana didn't wear more of this beautiful blue colour, which seemed to suit her so well.

wide that in some pictures, her eyes and half her nose disappeared beneath it. As fashion, it was splendid and the French adored Diana's flair and panache. But as royal headgear, it was not right.

This hat, worn with a matching red and black outfit, came from Diana's more sophisticated royal days and dealt with the problem of interference from her hair by enclosing it in a snood. On other occasions, though, Diana's hair often argued with her collar, so that a shorter cut which kept hair and collar apart was preferable for coats as well as hats.

Royals out on public engagements in autumn and winter spend more time than most people in the open air. Yet, they must avoid giving the impression of being bundled up in their coats to keep warm. They are expected to look smart and

unaffected by the cold. Shivering is out. Diana, however, felt the cold acutely, just as she suffered from that other climate extreme, excessive heat.

Defying the elements

Diana's answer was thermal underwear, and with the refreshing candour that marked her style in public, she was not shy of telling people about it. Thermals made a great difference. Even when she was pregnant with William and wore loose coats, such as the dark turquoise one with scattered pink flowers that she wore at Balmoral for Christmas 1982, thermals meant that the material did not have to be bulky, resulting in a better body-line. She looked a lot smarter at other times, too, when, for example, she wore a well-fitting tartan coat to tour

1 Diana wore a lot of these John Boyd skull cap hats, with or without trimmings in her early royal days.
2 This 'shako' style red hat looked a bit big on Diana.

3 This hat in peppermint green with black emphasis and large bow concealed Diana's face a bit too much for royal rules about hats. Royals are supposed to be easy to see but that wasn't the case when Diana wore this hat at Howe Barracks, Canterbury in 1994. **4** This is a cleverer way to wear a wide-brimmed hat. Diana wore this saucy 'inverted dish' hat at the Garter Ceremony in Windsor, in 1993, with a matching Catherine Walker suit.
Below left An upturned brim on a matching hat.

the College for Disabled Children at Froyle on a bitter winter's day in January 1989.

Diana's taste for far-too-fancy fashions – the sort of thing she wore in her early royal days – was also evident in some of the coats. For instance, the crimson ruffle-shouldered coat she wore in Liverpool in the spring of 1982 was just too much coat.

At that stage, of course, she was still in her experimental phase. She wore far too many frills and trimmings and, in Liverpool, a matching crimson hat with a self flower too many – over her right ear.

> ### "We don't make the price up out of a telephone book, you know, or go to Paris for a special feather."
> PHILIP SOMERVILLE, MILLINER

Another fussy coat from Diana's early days was a dark red Bellville Sassoon number, shot through with yellow and turquoise stitching and featuring a high-fringed collar and fringed hem. Diana wore it in London in 1981 soon after her first pregnancy was announced. She wore it again at Wrexham, Wales in 1982 when she chose a hat and bag to match the turquoise stitching.

Eventually, Diana left behind the fuss, the frills, and the over-emphasized collars, which marked her apprenticeship in the world of fashion. Then, she emerged smart, svelte and sophisticated.

IN THE NEWS

All wrapped up in Chanel

The red coat and matching hat which Diana wore when visiting Caen created a sensation in France. Not only for its marvellously vibrant colour, but also for its elegance and the fact that it was a French design: by Karl Lagerfeld. The French adored Diana's style and thought of her as almost French. In Britain the newspapers noted the compliment to France which Diana paid by wearing French rather than British fashion this time.

Ooh, c'est magnifique

The Team Player

Diana's function on state and other official occasions as a member of the Royal Family was much less 'starry' than her role as Princess of Wales and it proved to be very much more difficult

When Diana married Prince Charles, she joined a royal family like no other. It was the most prestigious royal family in the world. Its ancestry may not have been the most ancient, but its line was unbroken, except for a brief republican interlude in the mid-17th century, for over a thousand years. Members of this family had the weight of history behind them. Each one was a celebrity. Except for Prince Philip, whose upbringing was different, they were born to it.

Philip was, nevertheless, an extremely powerful influence. He did much to set the tone in the Royal Family. Strong-minded, formidable and a natural leader, he was actually more royal than the Queen. Born a prince of Greece in 1921, but not of Greek blood, Philip was descended from Danish and German royalty. Like the Queen, he was a great-great grandchild of Queen Victoria.

Philip had been married to the Queen for 34 years when Diana arrived on the scene. He had long felt it an honour to belong to the British Royal Family and gave his wife unswerving, even rock-like, support. Before him, the Queen Mother had done the same for his father-in-law, King George VI. Diana, in her turn, was expected to carry on the good work for Prince Charles.

Formidable in-laws

Though Diana was not the first Earl's daughter to marry into the Royal Family – the Queen Mother had done so in 1923 – this was a truly daunting battery of in-laws to acquire. With them, Diana

Above left Princess Diana attends the service for members of the Order of the Garter. The Queen, Prince Philip and Prince Charles are all members. So is the Queen Mother.

took on obligations and ceremonial duties over and above those which came her way as Princess of Wales. Diana's super-stardom in the rest of her royal life became irrelevant. When the Royal Family operated as a team, Diana became just another member of the cast.

The state and official royal occasions in which Diana was expected to take part were longstanding, set-piece affairs: Trooping the Colour was normally

Above From left, Princess Michael of Kent, the Duchess of York, Diana and the Duchess of Kent view the flypast with Prince Harry after the Trooping the Colour ceremony. **Left** The crowds outside Buckingham Palace watch the flypast, too.

Diana at the State Opening of Parliament. **Right** Sitting next to the Queen she was all smiles as she responded to the cheering crowds. **Far right** It was the same when she rode with Charles, who was wearing his Order of the Garter robes. **Left** But later, inside the House, she looked glum and bored when listening to the Queen's Speech, which was delivered in the chamber of the House of Lords.

celebrated in June on the Queen's official birthday, but there were also royal garden parties at Buckingham Palace, the State Opening of Parliament in October or November, the British Legion Festival of Remembrance at the Albert Hall in November, followed soon afterwards by the ceremony at the Cenotaph in Whitehall, London when the Queen and her family pay tribute to Britain's war dead. There were also the various ceremonies and receptions involved in state and official visits by foreign and Commonwealth heads of state, which occurred two or three times a year.

Diana might arouse the greatest press and public interest on occasions like these, but when the Royal

> ## "I have the best mother-in-law in the world."
> PRINCESS DIANA

Family operated as a team, the Queen was undisputed leading lady. The watchword was dignified serenity, gravity, pomp, circumstance and, sometimes, pageantry. None of this was a natural scene for a princess who was not always at ease with formality. The limelight of her own public work, which suited her better, got the adrenaline pumping and she swung into action in her own instinctive way.

State and official ceremonial, however, required a different approach. It had to be calm, somewhat aloof and needed a great deal of patience.

If Diana was bored, she was not supposed to show it. If something amused her, no one must know. If she felt unwell or something had upset her beforehand, it must never be apparent. Putting on an unruffled appearance proved difficult for Diana.

Bending the rules

To her credit, she usually managed to conceal any troubles or annoyances while appearing in public with the Royal Family, though the unvarying, olympic-class royal front which her in-laws had long ago perfected, was beyond her.

More subtly, though Diana sometimes contravened the rules of conduct for royals in public in a way not apparent to the casual observer or to the crowds, who were too excited to notice it in their excitement at seeing the Princess in the flesh.

But for the all-seeing, all scrutinizing press and photographers, who watched every expression, every piece of body language, and every tilt of the royal head, it was evident very early on that Diana was upstaging Charles. Friends let it be known that this hurt Charles a great deal. His charm and air of diffidence were genuine, but as heir to the throne, he was rather spoiled. Charles had never known any

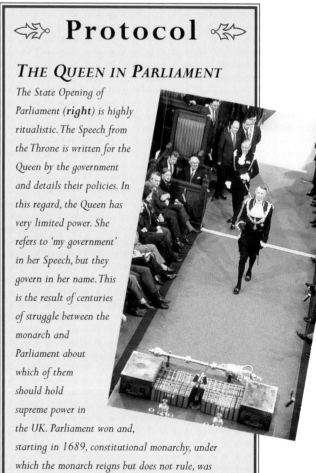

❧ Protocol ❧

THE QUEEN IN PARLIAMENT

The State Opening of Parliament (**right**) is highly ritualistic. The Speech from the Throne is written for the Queen by the government and details their policies. In this regard, the Queen has very limited power. She refers to 'my government' in her Speech, but they govern in her name. This is the result of centuries of struggle between the monarch and Parliament about which of them should hold supreme power in the UK. Parliament won and, starting in 1689, constitutional monarchy, under which the monarch reigns but does not rule, was achieved. Today the Queen's state duties, including the State Opening, are purely ceremonial.

Above The Duke and Duchess of York's wedding in 1986 received 'state occasion' treatment, just like Charles and Diana's wedding. Diana, standing next to Charles, fifth from the left, was in the front row at Westminster Abbey, but top billing naturally went to the newlyweds.

response but deference to his position. He had also worked and studied hard to be worthy of it. When he married Diana, it was expected that she would back him up in his onerous task. As far as the public show was concerned, this did not happen.

It appeared to many people that Charles was at first surprised, then put out, then angry to see Diana shoot up the royal popularity rankings and run away with all the publicity and attention. She was possibly too young to realize the effect this was having. In fact, as far as anyone, including Charles, could see, she was enjoying it enormously.

Snubbed by the Princess

In contrast to Diana, the Duchess of Kent and the Duchess of Gloucester, both of them untitled commoners when they married, had adapted successfully to royal public appearances and never once attempted to outdo their husbands. The Duchess of Gloucester was not even English, but the daughter of a Danish diplomat, yet she had taken to her unaccustomed royal position with both grace and charm. Diana was, or should have been, better

prepared than either of the duchesses. She had known the Royal Family since childhood. Their lives and their ways were familiar to her. Why, then, asked the royals, was she acting in this way?

Diana's sister-in-law, Princess Anne, did not bother to dwell on that question. She could be as formidable as her father, Prince Philip, and of all his

> **"One thing he wants to do is keep wearing the pants in the family."**
> SINCLAIR HILL, POLO FRIEND OF CHARLES

children, was most like him. The outspoken Anne did not take long to make her disapproval apparent. To her, Diana probably appeared as a mixture of film star, rock star, fashion model and airhead. Perhaps to Anne she seemed to lack solid royal virtues and Anne undoubtedly found Diana's emotional displays outlandish. Anne was also very defensive on behalf of her brother.

It was said that Anne coined her own nickname for Diana and it was not complimentary: the Dope.

Anne's irritation with Diana showed in New Mexico at the time of Prince William's birth. Asked by journalists what she thought of Diana's new son, she replied, grumpily: 'I didn't know she had one'. She did, of course.

Two years later, after Prince Harry arrived, Anne and her then husband Mark Phillips, were absent from the christening. It seemed a serious snub, and the excuse appeared worse than the crime. Anne and Mark had a prior engagement, shooting pheasant on their Gloucestershire estate with friends. Buckingham Palace put out an excuse about the shoot being pre-arranged so that Anne could not let her guests down, but no one was convinced.

Upsetting the Queen

Diana even managed to fall foul of her mother-in-law, a far less easy target than the irascible Anne. The Queen is a gentle, sympathetic, even soft-hearted woman, but even she has her limits. For instance, at the Braemar Gathering in 1981, during the last part of Charles and Diana's honeymoon, the newlyweds appeared to incur the Queen's wrath by laughing

Above State occasions, such as Trooping the Colour, are part and parcel of the Royal Family's official duties. They are expected not only to attend as required but to behave in an appropriate manner. Here the Queen Mother, the Duke and Duchess of Kent, Prince Charles and their guests, the Grand Duke and Duchess of Luxembourg, appear relaxed and in excellent spirits.
Left Diana, in contrast, rustles up a wry smile for the camera during the August 1995 VJ Day celebrations in The Mall, an occasion when her heart didn't seem to be wholeheartedly in the event.

Left The Cenotaph ceremony in November is a sad and solemn occasion. From left: The late King Olav of Norway, Diana, Princess Anne, the Duchess of York and the Queen Mother watch from a nearby balcony in London's Whitehall. Looking solemn is one thing but Diana seems thoroughly fed up. The Queen Mother's rather sad half-smile is much more appropriate.

IN THE NEWS

First time out

The press cameras were out in force and at the ready when Diana attended her first full-dress state occasion as Princess of Wales on 4 November 1982. It was almost like the royal wedding all over again – the Glass Coach, the tiara, the white dress and all. The event, the State Opening of Parliament by the Queen, tended to fade in importance compared to Diana's participation. Press and public attention were all focussed sharply on the new girl in the team.

Opposite page Diana looks miserable sitting next to Prince Charles at the Celebration of the 70th anniversary of the Armistice in the First World War in Paris, 1988. It was, quite simply, not the sort of event that appealed to her.

while the national anthem was being played. It was, in fact, Charles' fault. He made Diana giggle by whispering in her ear, then joined in. The Queen's steely glance was enough to silence both of them.

With Charles, the incident was a rare chink in the armour of decorum he had worn all his life. That could be forgiven once the initial royal annoyance had cooled. As for Diana, the kindest explanation was her youth and her inexperience, as

yet, with the business of royal public appearances. However, if the incident appeared like just a passing solecism, the Royal Family were soon disabused.

On 4 November 1981, the Queen and her family attended the State Opening of Parliament, an event of great importance with much pomp and pageantry, second only to a coronation.

More serious failings

Diana, however, did not seem to get into the right solemn spirit for it. She responded happily to the cheers from the crowds watching the royal procession on its way to the Houses of Parliament at Westminster. But once seated next to Prince Charles in the chamber of the House of Lords, she listened to the Queen's Speech looking thoroughly bored and disgruntled.

The next year, in November 1982, Diana rocked the boat again, this time much more seriously. She committed the gross impoliteness of being late for the Queen at the British Legion Festival of Remembrance at the Albert Hall, London. This was an event which the Royal Family attended every year without fail. Diana was expected to attend, too, but Charles arrived at the Albert Hall and announced she would not be coming. The chairs in

Above Charles dressed in naval uniform stands to attention and salutes at the Gulf War Parade in June 1991. Diana is at his side. At this time their formal separation was not far off, and they did not always look comfortable together when appearing in public.

the royal box were rearranged. The Queen arrived and sat down. Then, suddenly, Diana appeared with her bodyguard and, according to eyewitnesses, looked thoroughly fed up and disgruntled. By the end of the evening, though, the adoration of the

> **"I just don't like her. She may be doing all that charity work for Save the Children, but I can do it as well."**
>
> PRINCESS DIANA, ON PRINCESS ANNE

crowd had worked its magic on her. The audience, realizing Diana was there, applauded and she opened like a flower in the sunshine to all the acclaim. The development was not lost on Charles and his equally chagrined family. Diana had already introduced a sour note into the royal holiday at Balmoral the previous September by storming out, declaring herself bored and furious at her in-laws' patronizing attitude towards her. Now, there was this faux pas on an important date in the royal diary.

This was not all. Diana once again caused offence at the State Opening of Parliament in 1984. She attended the Opening looking, of course, extremely glamorous, but with a new hairstyle which gave a splendid view of her neck. The MPs goggled. Charles seemed unhappy and again the Queen was reported to be furious. The Opening was not meant to be a fashion show and the Queen reportedly viewed Diana's display as 'this bit of nonsense'.

Royal disquiet

Although the unfortunate incidents of 1981 and 1982 could be explained away as the stumbles of a royal novice, the Royal Family were widely rumoured to be seriously worried by 1984 when Diana still did not appear to know how to behave in public on state occasions. As time went on, and she became more and more difficult, these early worries seemed to be confirmed.

Reports of trouble in Charles and Diana's marriage were regularly denied. It is likely that the Royal Family were hoping against hope that the problems would pass, and that Diana would settle down and eventually handle the tedious, but still important, ceremonial part of her duties.

LIFE AT HIGHGROVE

For a royal country home, Highgrove House, near Tetbury, Gloucestershire, was relatively small. Even so, it was Charles' dream home. Unfortunately, Diana did not entirely share that dream

In 1980, when Charles was looking for a country home of his own, he wanted it to have plenty of farmland where he could put into practice his ideas on organic farming and non-artificial rearing of animals. At this time, of course, Charles was unmarried and could please himself.

Highgrove House, near the market town of Tetbury in Gloucestershire, fitted Charles' bill in several ways. His sister, Princess Anne, lived only eight miles away, at Gatcombe Park. Windsor Castle was not too far away. Neither were the polo fields at Cirencester Park, Cowdray Park and Smith's Lawn, Windsor. Playing polo was Charles' passion. Even more pertinently, Camilla Parker-Bowles and her husband Andrew also lived nearby.

Local estate agents had advertised Highgrove as 'a distinguished Georgian house comprising...four reception rooms, domestic quarters, nine bedrooms, six bathrooms, nursery wing and full central heating'. There were 350 acres of farmland, as well

Previous page Diana relaxes in the gardens at Highgrove. **Above** Charles at work, surrounded by the greenery he loves. At heart Charles is a countryman, according to his own description, and his garden is his pride and joy. **Right** Diana gives Harry a shoulder ride. **Opposite page** Charles, Harry and Diana have fun with a pet rabbit at Highgrove.

as extensive gardens and a beautiful view across country to Tetbury, with its prominent spire.

Much modernizing and landscaping would be needed, but with his interests in architecture and gardening, Charles hardly minded that. A deal was struck and the Duchy of Cornwall, Charles' estate, bought it for around £800,000 from Maurice Macmillan, son of the former Prime Minister.

Not long afterwards, when Charles became interested in the then Lady Diana Spencer, he took her to Highgrove to look the place over. At that stage, girls with marriage in mind are usually on their best behaviour. As far as is known, Diana had no objections to Highgrove, an opinion which would later change as she realized that the house, built at the end of the 18th century, was much more Charles' kind of place than hers.

It was certainly the sort of home a man like Prince Charles would fall in love with. Highgrove breathed history, with its centuries-old stone walls

and its classical interior. There was an ancient Roman road nearby. It had the air of belonging to the age of aristocratic country-house building two centuries ago. Highgrove provided the solitude and space for quiet contemplation that Charles valued.

EXPERT HELP

Enthusiastically, Charles set to work re-inventing Highgrove. He brought in experts like wild flower specialist Dr Miriam Rothschild, who ran the Royal Society for Nature Conservation – Charles was patron. He also called in Lady Mollie Salisbury, a friend and an experienced garden designer.

A wild flower garden was laid down, later to provide a pleasing vista of poppies, cornflowers and other plants. In the walled garden, with its box hedges and stone chip paths, Charles grew ten varieties of carrot, including a purple one, among the many vegetables which were all organically grown. Flowers to decorate and perfume Highgrove grew in a special greenhouse. Golden carp swam in the

> *" Highgrove sounds like something in Wimbledon. "*
> THE QUEEN, ON SEEING HIGHGROVE

pond, which was provided with a fountain. The hedge by the walled garden was later cut to intertwine the initials 'C' and 'D'.

Charles, assisted by a single gardener, did much of the work himself, including the digging, manuring and planting. According to Lady Salisbury, who called him 'a natural plantsman', Charles had a real talent for gardening, inherited from his grandparents, King George VI and Queen Elizabeth, the Queen Mother. He had always loved the beautifully kept gardens at the Royal Family homes and a garden all of his own was therapy.

Charles loved to sit in the patio garden doing paperwork, while the soothing sound of water flowed from a specially commissioned whale sculpture close to the beds of roses, which he had pruned. The avenue of yew trees, the woodland garden, the herds of sheep and Aberdeen Angus cattle which grazed in view of the house, the dry stone walls, the chickens scratching about in the

IN CONTEXT *1982-3*   IRA PUB BOMB ATROCITY

- Sixteen die in IRA bombing in Ulster village pub disco (**right**)
- USA invades Grenada
- Publication of the *Hitler Diaries*, which later turn out to be fakes
- Seve Ballesteros of Spain becomes US Masters golf champion
- US President Ronald Reagan advocates 'Star Wars' defence system
- £25 million stolen from Brinks Matt security van at London's Heathrow Airport

driveway and the surrounding fields comprised an idyllic setting. The company of his tenant farmers offered a valued chance to relax and talk the country talk Charles enjoyed.

Highgrove House itself was similarly remade. The terracotta hall had a new polished floor. Ionic columns graced the front of the house, which was also given a decorative balustrade. The furniture was mahogany. There were parquet floors, bowls of flowers from the plentiful gardens, a grandfather clock, soft flowery rugs, pink and yellow decor.

In the large German-style kitchen at the end of a long polished corridor, soft fruits were preserved in air-tight bottles or made into jam.

DIANA THE HOUSEWIFE

Here, too, Diana used to enjoy herself washing up, a chore to other women, but a rare treat for a princess who had grown up and as a married woman, now lived, surrounded by servants. Visitors

Opposite page Prince Charles, holding Prince Harry, and Diana with William, stand among the beautiful wild flowers that line the driveway to Highgrove House, which can be seen in the background. The beautiful gardens at Highgrove were designed to Charles' specification. **Left** Harry walks along the path by the swimming pool under his father's watchful eye. **Above** Harry peeks out over the doorway of the plastic garden house in the Highgrove gardens.

to Highgrove found Diana was a meticulous housewife. She was said to have hated it when William and Harry brought mud into the house, and did not, apparently, approve of Charles' chaotic private office, which those who saw it observed was cluttered up with papers and blue boxes full of state documents. By contrast, Diana's own pink bedroom, with its trellis wallpaper and lacy cushions never had a thing out of place.

As is traditional among royalty and the aristocracy, Charles and Diana had separate bedrooms. Charles was up early, at around 6.30am during weekends and other breaks spent at Highgrove. He would catch up on the latest farming news on the radio, then go for a walk or have a swim in the small swimming pool that was a gift from the army.

IN THE NEWS

20 million viewers watch TV interview

Sir Alastair Burnet's TV interview with Charles and Diana at Kensington Palace went out on the evening of 25 October 1985.

This was about a month before Diana walked out of Highgrove declaring herself bored, and returned to London. Charles stayed behind. The impression given in the TV interview, however, was one of a committed couple anxious to do their royal service. In fact, the disagreement over Highgrove reflected the state of their rocky relationship.

Daily Mail

The Charles and Diana hour rivets 20 million viewers

ARGUE? Everyone does... But WE don't!

Spy fear over RAF base

Breakfast included a poached egg before he went off for a day's hunting or a tour of the farms.

Diana, meanwhile, slept in until around seven, then breakfasted on grapefruit, a spoonful of wheatgerm, a couple of slices of wholemeal toast, live yoghurt and a cup of tea. She might spend the rest of the day cycling in the grounds, playing tennis on the £10,000 court Charles installed specially for her, picking flowers and fruit, having a swim, reading in one of the gardens or phoning friends.

THE ROYAL MENU

From time to time, Diana liked to do the cooking, though she confessed to being only 'average'. But whether prepared by herself or by her cook, meals at Highgrove were strong on healthy eating. The menu often featured avocado, kiwi fruit or fresh orange. Highgrove had its own version of shepherd's pie – made with organic vegetables, of course. It was called 'mince 'n' mash mush'.

Both Charles and Diana were careful eaters and rarely had red meat. Diana was fond of fish, which had to be meticulously filletted. Chicken, when served, had to be boned first. Highgrove was virtually self-sufficient in food, providing all the vegetables, eggs and butter for Charles and Diana's table. Charles was fussy about the Highgrove marmalade, which was made of quinces from the kitchen garden. He insisted it be made by methods used four centuries ago in the time of King Henry VIII. As far

> ## "Very therapeutic... and it's marvellous if you can see the effect."
> CHARLES, ON WORKING IN HIGHGROVE GARDENS

as is known, he did not order it served as it was then, as a delicacy to round off royal banquets.

Highgrove House was, of course, a marvellous place for the two young princes, offering every form of fun small boys most enjoy. There were pony rides, cycling tracks, a garden full of plastic slides and swings, a playhouse, hutches for pet rabbits and the thrill of watching a red Wessex helicopter land on the lawn to collect one or other of their parents and fly them to a public engagement. The princes and their mother were allowed into

the cockpit to be shown the instruments. William watched the signaller guiding in the helicopter so often that he was able to give the signals himself.

STRICT SECURITY

In some ways, however, the pervasive air of calm and peace at Highgrove was deceptive. Behind all its elegant loveliness was a mass of security devices and surveillance equipment. The stone cottages once inhabited by tenants on the estate became police listening posts. A footpath which originally ran through the garden had to be re-routed, although nothing could be done, apart from maximum alertness, about the proximity of the nearby main road.

Charles was used to security presence in all its forms. For him, guards and surveillance tended to blend in with the background. Diana was never able to get used to it and, sometimes, she felt caged in by it. She could not get accustomed, either, to the idea that as a royal, she could never be alone, whether at Kensington Palace, Highgrove or anywhere else.

There was also the presence in Highgrove House of a feature which underlined the heavy security

Top Definitely not a posed picture! Diana and the two young princes are seen looking in different directions. **Above** Prince William gives the salute, dressed in the uniform and the cap of the Parachute Regiment.

The Private Princess Separate interests

Talk of fairytale marriage and the royal love match put stars in the public's eyes, which obscured the many ways in which Charles and Diana differed from each other.

Charles seemed much older than his 32 years. Diana appeared a very young 20. He was serious-minded, rather professorial. He immersed himself in philosophies and history, appreciated classical music, opera, art and literature. She watched TV soaps, read romantic novels and enthused over pop and film stars.

Wives and husbands who are not quite on the same wavelength can still find common ground, but in this royal marriage, it proved difficult. Charles was said to be worried about the age gap between himself and Diana. He needed a soulmate, something Diana was perhaps too young to provide. Camilla was older and more mature, though. She was also a great deal more than simply a friend. She could share Charles' interests, knew how to listen to him and give him reassurance if he needed it.

What few understood about Charles was that a pretty face, like Diana's, appeared to be less vital to him than a good mind and a generous nature, like Camilla's.

Many observers believed it was Charles and Camilla, not Charles and Diana, who were made for each other.

Above *Charles enjoys his own company and is never happier than when sitting with a brush in hand, creating a watercolour of a landscape or one of the royal residences.*

Above left The garden at Highgrove was turned into a little boys' heaven by the slides, swings and climbing frames Charles and Diana provided for their sons.
Above Charles revelled in planting up areas himself. The work at Highgrove was done with his own hands, assisted by one gardener.

under which the heirs to the throne were obliged to live: a security room where they could shelter in case the house was attacked. The walls were lined with steel to protect against bombs and bullets. The doors and shutters had tight seals. There was a cache of weapons, food supplies and medical stores to last for months, and radio transmitters. The security room was proof against any onslaught short of a nuclear attack. It was never used, but Diana is said to have found its very existence disturbing.

Whatever else she enjoyed about Highgrove, and there were many aspects of it which appealed

> *" The business of riding scares the life out of me. I lost my nerve following an accident years ago. "*
>
> DIANA, ON NOT WANTING TO RELEARN TO RIDE AT HIGHGROVE

to her, the blanket of security tended to spoil it. By 1985, Diana was becoming disillusioned with this apparently idyllic yet, in reality, intimidating place.

Diana knew, of course, how close Camilla's home was to Highgrove. As early as 1983, it was being rumoured that Charles had decided to renew his acquaintanceship with Camilla and her husband, and that Diana was none too happy about it.

TIED TO HIGHGROVE

This appeared to be the reason behind Diana's reported efforts to leave Highgrove and move somewhere else, further away. Belton House in Lincolnshire was said to be considered as a possibility, but only briefly. The problem was that Highgrove House was not all that easy to leave. Other couples could live where they chose but, as royals, Charles and Diana did not have that freedom. They were tied to Highgrove by some of their own wedding presents. The wrought-iron front gates had been a gift from the people of Tetbury. The swimming pool had been purchased by soldiers who gave thousands of small donations.

It was, in any case, doubtful if Charles was serious about leaving a home which had absorbed so much of his own efforts. The gardens which had been recreated in the image of his environmental

Above Diana watches the boys from a doorstep. **Opposite page** Diana and the two boys play with Smokey, the Shetland pony. **Right** Charles strolls through the gardens. For him, Highgrove was a refreshing change from the bustle of London.

concerns were a treasure too precious to leave behind. William and Harry loved Highgrove, where their father gave them a lot of time and, among other treats, took them riding on farm tractors.

Diana seemed to be in a difficult situation. By 1985, she was already undertaking engagements on her own which the ever-scrutinizing press thought she could have done with Charles. Charles, though, did not seem comfortable in Diana's 'scene'. He was said not to be keen to attend a charity ball arranged by fashion designer Bruce Oldfield where the rock composer Jean-Michel Jarre and his film actress wife, Charlotte Rampling, were among the guests.

By the autumn of 1985, Diana seemed to friends to be disillusioned with Highgrove. She felt, apparently, that it was too small, and that she was cut off from her friends, who were different people to her husband's. This was when those friends, reportedly, became seriously worried about her.

❧ Protocol ❧

PRIVACY DISTURBED

*The Royal Family likes to be left alone to enjoy holidays at Balmoral, Sandringham or Windsor Castle. Essentially that means being left alone by the press and photographers, **right**.*

Charles and Diana, however, could not take the same freedom for granted at Highgrove House. Interest in Diana was so intense from the first that the temptation to snoop on the part of the press proved utterly irresistible.

Diana often felt besieged in her own home, fearing the long lenses that probed right inside Highgrove from the bushes in the surrounding gardens. In her early married days, she was said to be scared to go out of her front door.

The Wedding Dress

In the run-up to the wedding there was enormous speculation about Diana's wedding gown. On the day itself – 29 July 1981 – the dress became world-famous when it was finally revealed. It was soon the most copied wedding dress of all time

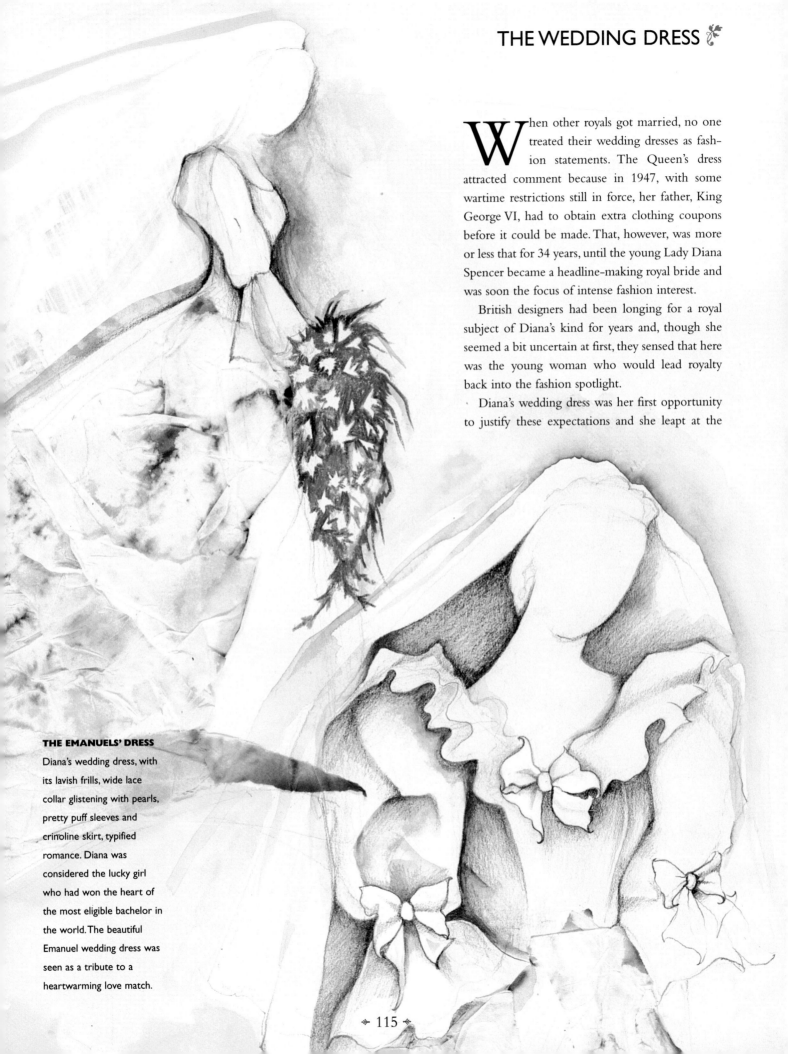

When other royals got married, no one treated their wedding dresses as fashion statements. The Queen's dress attracted comment because in 1947, with some wartime restrictions still in force, her father, King George VI, had to obtain extra clothing coupons before it could be made. That, however, was more or less that for 34 years, until the young Lady Diana Spencer became a headline-making royal bride and was soon the focus of intense fashion interest.

British designers had been longing for a royal subject of Diana's kind for years and, though she seemed a bit uncertain at first, they sensed that here was the young woman who would lead royalty back into the fashion spotlight.

Diana's wedding dress was her first opportunity to justify these expectations and she leapt at the

THE EMANUELS' DRESS

Diana's wedding dress, with its lavish frills, wide lace collar glistening with pearls, pretty puff sleeves and crinoline skirt, typified romance. Diana was considered the lucky girl who had won the heart of the most eligible bachelor in the world. The beautiful Emanuel wedding dress was seen as a tribute to a heartwarming love match.

THE TIARA

Above and right Diana wore the tiara and earrings which were one of the heirlooms belonging to her aristocratic family, the Spencers of Althorp. Fashioned from diamonds, the tiara was made in a beautiful leaf design with flower stems and leaves forming swirls and enclosing, at the front, the ideal motif for the occasion, a heart. The tiara and earrings, lent to Diana by her mother, Mrs Frances Shand Kydd, counted as the 'something borrowed', which brides traditionally wear. Diana's veil was plain.

chance. It was taken for granted that she would go to one of the long-established royal couturiers, Norman Hartnell or Hardy Amies, who had been providing tasteful styles for the royals since the days when the Queen Mother was Queen Consort. Diana, though, had her own ideas. She wanted something less mature than vintage Hartnell or Amies. Considering she was only 20, she was right.

Little-known designers

The designers Diana chose were David and Elizabeth Emanuel, a couple barely known until then outside the fashion world. The Emanuels had, however, already made some quiet progress in the wardrobes of the Duchess of Kent, Princess Michael and several show business personalities. They had first come to Diana's attention when she saw one of their blouses, a shell-pink chiffon creation with a high frilled neck. This was precisely the sort of feminine, romantic style which appealed to the young Diana, who liked high frilled necklines.

She also chose Emanuel for her first outing as Charles' fiancée in March 1981, wearing their off-the-shoulder evening gown, which revealed more

bust than she intended (see issue 1, page 17).

The fashion world being intensively competitive, the Emanuels had fixed a security lock to the door of their salon. It was just as well. As they set to work, the fashion world and fashion journalists buzzed with curiosity and anticipation.

> *"Lady Diana cried...shivered... and there were tears in her eyes."*
>
> NINA MISSESTZIS, SEAMSTRESS, WHEN DIANA PUT ON HER WEDDING DRESS

The secret was, of course, meticulously kept, but on the wedding day itself, the first glimpse was a teasing one. As Diana rode to St. Paul's Cathedral in the Glass Coach, all most people could see of the dress was a mass of creamy material piled high on the seats. As she stepped, or rather manoeuvred her way, out in front of the Cathedral, the dress was not fully revealed for some time.

The 25-foot train did not fully emerge until Diana was part of the way up the steps into St. Paul's. By the time it had disappeared through the door, Diana, on the arm of her father, Earl Spencer, was well into the three-and-a-half minute walk to the altar where Prince Charles was waiting.

Royal fashion icon

Diana had now staked her claim to be the next royal fashion icon before 700 million people watching on television world-wide and the privileged hundreds looking at the real thing from the street outside.

Diana's wedding dress was what later came to be widely recognized as pure Emanuel. She looked as if she had stepped straight from the pages of a fairy story book, or from one of those rich, glowing royal portraits which were fashioned to flatter by Renaissance artists. This was no flattery, though, Diana looked superb.

Made from heavy ivory taffeta woven and spun at Lullingstone, the only silk farm in England, the dress was romantic. Its shape recalled the days, over 150 years before, when wide crinolines were in fashion. The dress had all the romantic trimmings — bows, lace, big puffed sleeves, a tracery of flower-shaped lace along the hem and a wide deep lace collar which fluffed out over the shoulders. The

Top David and Elizabeth Emanuel were Diana's surprise choice to design her wedding dress. **Above** Diana loved the romantic, feminine Emanuel style, which was echoed in her wedding shoes with their heart-shaped motif. **Top left** The Emanuels are seen conferring with Diana at Kensington Palace, after the royal marriage, on designs and materials for more contributions to the Princess' wardrobe.

front of the bodice featured a panel of lace which reached down to merge with yet more lace encircling the waist.

'Something blue' was a blue bow, sewn to the waistband. A taffeta bow was placed where the two halves of the collar met, echoed by similar bows at the point where the full sleeves reached a veritable froth of lace looping around Diana's arms.

The lace was the traditional Honiton, made famous by the robe in which generations of royal infants were christened. Thousands of tiny mother

> ## "In 12 days time I shall no longer be me."
> DIANA, SHORTLY BEFORE HER WEDDING

of pearl sequins sparkled from the lace, the result of hours of toil with needles by Elizabeth Emanuel and her mother, who had not dared to farm the work out for fear of breaching the strict security.

For luck, Diana carried an 18-carat gold horseshoe made by jeweller, Douglas Buchanan, and for 'something borrowed' she wore the Spencer family tiara and earrings made of diamonds, which were lent to her by her mother, Mrs Frances Shand Kydd. Diana's veil was long and plain.

The wedding dress was greeted with great enthusiasm. It was taken for granted that other brides were waiting eagerly to wear something like

Above All the wedding finery was on display when the official wedding photographs were taken at Buckingham Palace. The bride, bridesmaids, pages and Charles and Andrew in their naval uniforms all contributed to a very pretty picture.

it at their own weddings, and artists and designers were busy making drawings from the television pictures. The first copy was seen in a shop window in London's West End within only five hours.

Falling out of royal favour

The Emanuels' creation was to influence wedding dress design for several years, and propelled them into the big time of fashion. It also enabled them, to the Princess' dismay, to get on the personal appearance and merchandising circuits. They fell out of royal favour because of this, but later, they were to design a stunning strapless evening gown with Christmas-like gold embroidery, which Diana wore to a film première in London in 1987.

The wedding dress was not, however, without its critics. One thing the Emanuels and Diana had apparently overlooked was the cramped space inside the Glass Coach. The dress emerged looking rather crumpled. Fortunately, once out of the Coach, the creases soon disappeared, but the cut of the bodice, which tended to bag over the bust, was not so easily disguised and attracted criticism.

Few people paid too much attention to these gripes, though. As far as the majority were concerned, the delectable Diana had become Charles' bride looking as a fairytale princess was expected to look, and thrilling everyone who saw her.

IN THE NEWS
Off-the-peg copies within hours

Diana's wedding dress filled pages and pages in the newspapers and magazines the day after the wedding. It seemed that women wanted to know every single detail, a natural reaction when the dress had been Britain's best kept secret for over five months.

The newspapers gave acres of space to pictures of the dress, the Emanuels' story of the making of the dress and the news of the off-the-peg copy that first appeared in a West End store within hours of the wedding.

BRIDESMAIDS' DRESSES

Diana's bridesmaids were dressed to look like miniatures of the new Princess, with similar puff sleeves, wide skirts and frilly lace collars. Each carried a bouquet and they were all crowned with circlets of flowers.

Touring the

Far East

Charles and Diana's tour of Indonesia and Hong Kong in 1989 was, unusually for a royal tour, arranged at the last minute. They had originally been meant to visit China until student protests in Beijing produced an international crisis

An unknown Chinese student who stood alone and defiant in front of government tanks in Tienanmen Square, Beijing on 4 June 1989 produced ripples of sympathy from around the world and did what few people have ever done: he changed the royal timetable and obliged Charles and Diana to cancel their projected tour of China.

The worldwide outrage at the brutal crushing of the student protest against lack of freedom in China did not, however, deny the Prince and Princess their taste of eastern promise. Indonesia, consisting of some 17,000 islands in southeast Asia, stood in very well for the abandoned Chinese tour. Linked to that were two days in Hong Kong which, it was felt, needed the reassurance of royal presence, however brief.

In 1984, Britain and China had agreed that the Crown Colony, under British rule since 1841, should revert to China when a 99-year lease ended in 1997. The Tienanmen Square massacre, in which hundreds were thought to have died and thousands were injured, had made the Hong Kong community, overwhelmingly Chinese, anxious about what awaited them when the People's Republic took over. A visit from the Prince and

Left Diana is pictured with Indonesian dancers, dressed in their traditional costumes. **Below** Throughout the East, garlanding visitors is a token of greeting and welcome.

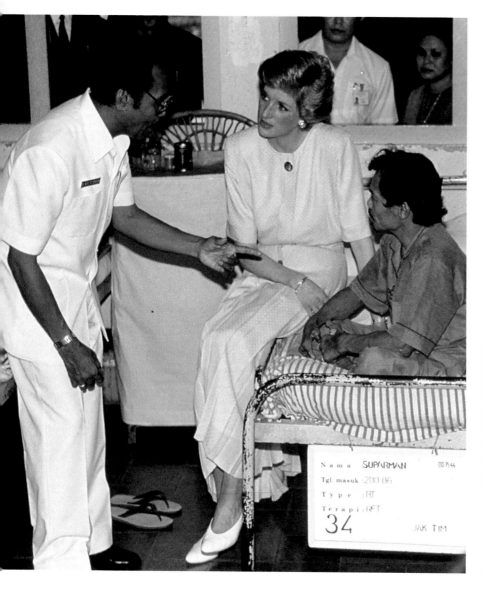

Above When Diana visited the Sitanala Hospital 15 miles from Jakarta, the Indonesian capital, she brought her sympathetic brand of comfort to patients suffering from leprosy, an horrific disease. **Above right** Diana tried her hand at bowls in the grounds of the hospital. It took her two tries but she scored well. **Opposite page** Charles and Diana enjoy some traditionally exotic Indonesian entertainment.

Princess of Wales would, for however long, provide some cheer. It would also show the communist Chinese that Hong Kong's history as part of the British Empire was something to be proud of and not lightly brought to an end.

The tour of both countries was to be crammed into a single week – 3 to 10 November 1989 – but Indonesia in particular had the advantage of providing much culture and history that was of great interest to both Charles and Diana.

An exotic note

For Charles, there was the fascination of a very ancient culture with all the age-old architecture that so fascinated him, as well as the chance to enquire further into an oriental religion,

Buddhism. For Diana, there was the Sitanala Leprosy Hospital near Jakarta, the Indonesian capital, where she would be able to bring comfort to those who engaged her greatest sympathy, the outcasts and pariahs shunned by society.

The tour started on an exotic note. Charles and Diana were due to fly in to Halim Airport, near Jakarta, in an RAF VC-10. The monsoon season had just started and, fearing that rain might spoil the royal arrival, the Indonesian President Thojib Suharto ordered his personal 'pawang', the official wizard called the Rain Mover, to dispose of some threatening thunderclouds. Heavy rain had drenched the Indonesian capital and on 3 November 1989, there were only two hours to go before Charles and Diana arrived. The pawangs,

IN THE NEWS

Diana is a hit in Hong Kong

Diana always created a big impression wherever she went. This newspaper headline in the Sun of 9 November, 1989 reflected the impact she made in Hong Kong, where the nervous inhabitants were cheered by the royal visit just after the Tienanmen Square massacre in Beijing in November 1989. As the headline KONG-QUEROR DI indicated, Diana captured many hearts and won much admiration in Hong Kong. Her beauty and elegance stunned everyone.

KONG-QUEROR DI

Radiant princess steals the hearts on a walkabout in old Hong Kong

whose magic is an integral part of official and other major events in Indonesia, had such a phenomenal success rate that, apart from the Pope the previous month, no state visit had ever been marred by rain. True to form, the rain stopped as the VC-10 appeared over Halim Airport and Charles and Diana stepped out under cloudless skies.

A group of Jakarta schoolchildren were there to give Diana a bouquet of orchids and jasmine. They placed a flower garland around Charles' neck. It was made of white jasmine and red roses, in the national colours of Indonesia.

Later, Charles and Diana were officially welcomed at the presidential palace, the Instana Merde. Charles, it appears, was suffering from jet lag and expressed fears that he might fall asleep, either on

the spot or next morning, when he was due to have another meeting with President Suharto.

Both Charles and Diana survived the jet lag, though, and were on duty as usual the next day, 4 November. Charles frequently took the opportunity to discuss national and international affairs with a country's rulers and especially the younger generation of future leaders. He regarded this as valuable training for his future role as king. Indonesia was no exception. But while he lunched with a group of Indonesians of his own generation – Charles was a few days away from his 41st birthday – Diana went out to the fringe of the jungle, 15 miles from Jakarta, to visit the leper hospital. She had specially asked to come, after hearing that there were as many as half a million Indonesians suffering from leprosy, a curable disease in the West.

An act of courage

It was certainly an act of courage on her part, despite the fact that she knew leprosy was not contagious, as many people believed. The disease, which destroys human tissue and causes horrific deformities, has been regarded with terror and loathing since Biblical times. Diana, however, entered the

Far left Charles and Diana examine with interest traditionally crafted Indonesian wares. **Left** Shaded by a large, elaborate Indonesian parasol from the excessive heat of the day, Diana greets crowds in her usual charming manner. **Right** Charles was fascinated by the ancient Buddhist temple of Borubadur where he climbed 120 steps to reach a 'magic' statue of Buddha and, maybe, make the traditional wish the figure was said to offer.

hospital wards unflinching and shook hands with the patients. This simple compassionate act was worth any amount of education aimed at dispelling fear and ignorance about leprosy. Diana stayed to talk with the patients, too, and her charm and smile remained to cheer their misery.

She found it harder to retain her composure when she moved onto the children's ward, but she spent some time there, sitting on the young patients' beds and chatting with them. She even

> ***"Women play such an important role in Indonesia, unlike many other Muslim countries."***
>
> DIANA, ON INDONESIAN WOMEN

joined in a game of bowls being played by some children outside the hospital. She made a mess of her first try, but scored well with the second.

The same evening, Charles and Diana got together to attend a reception at the British ambassador's residence, where an ice sculpture of the Tower of London was the centre of attraction. Unfortunately, the temperature had soared to 94

degrees Fahrenheit and the Tower began to look very sorry for itself as it slowly melted.

A full-scale presidential banquet followed where Diana, who rarely drank alcohol, refused the champagne. There was a display of traditional dancing and a bamboo band amused Charles with a local version of the march 'Colonel Bogie'.

The Buddhist temple

Next day, 5 November, Charles and Diana flew to Yogyakarta, where the prospect of seeing the world's oldest and largest Buddhist temple, the Borubadur, had Charles really excited. Built in around AD 750, it contained 504 statues of the Buddha, together with bell-shaped domes known as stupas and four miles of carvings depicting scenes from Buddha's life. Here, Charles' interest in archaeology and Buddhist philosophy came together, as he explored the ancient complex and climbed the 120 steps to the top of the temple. There, he touched the hand of a 'magic' statue of Buddha, which allowed him one wish. Charles never revealed what it was, or even if he had made one.

An ornate 18th-century Javanese palace, the Karaton, was the next visiting place for Charles and

Above A great mass of people gathered wherever Charles and Diana went. Here, eager sightseers crowd around the royal couple's car. **Right** In Hong Kong, Charles tries his hand at painting eyes on the model of the Chinese dragon, which features in festivals and entertainments.

Diana. The palace featured a Golden Pavilion scented by its surrounding banks of jasmine. A shadow puppet show, more exotic dancing and a concert by a traditional orchestra were staged to entertain the royal visitors. But the heat rather spoiled the visit. Diana, who tended to wilt when temperatures rose, tried to cool down by surreptitiously blowing at her face out of the corner of her mouth.

The rainforest

Charles spent the afternoon exploring the Wanagama Reafforestation Project, suitably clad in a safari suit. This, of course, catered for another of his many interests, ecology, and he spent some time in the new rainforest planted at Wanagama.

Diana, who by this time welcomed an opportunity to cool off, did not accompany her husband. But Charles brought her back a souvenir, some eucalyptus oil. For himself, he bought some honey from a roadside stall and for both of them, something very appropriate, a fan.

The Indonesian tour ended next day, on

❧ Protocol ❧

THE FORBIDDEN VISIT

Long before Charles and Diana visited Hong Kong in 1989, thousands of Vietnamese Boat People, right, refugees from the Communists, had been crowding into the colony. The exodus had begun in 1977, and by 1989, the Hong Kong authorities were preparing to repatriate some of the refugees, much against their will.

Their presence in Hong Kong represented an embarrassment at the time Charles and Diana arrived. Royals are supposed to avoid, or be kept out of, controversial political situations. The Boat People were a hot political issue. This is why Charles and Diana were not allowed to see them. The chance of their presence prompting demonstrations was considered too great.

6 November back in Jakarta. Diana visited the British school, then joined Charles to explore the Taman Mini theme park, where Indonesia's 27 provinces were all represented, giving visitors a short, but impressive taste of the country.

> **"It is impossible not to be impressed by the vigour and resourcefulness of the people."**
>
> CHARLES ON HONG KONG

Diana went on to a ladies' lunch where she was pleased to discover that Indonesian women were more emancipated than they were in other Muslim countries she had visited. Charles, meanwhile, had set himself the harder task of touring the slums at Orogol where 6000 barefoot inhabitants had only an horrendously polluted river for washing and drinking. Charles was pleased to bring them some relief as he opened a new British-built water purifying plant. The clean healthy water now on tap

was the first that the district of Orogol had seen.

That same evening, Charles and Diana flew on to Hong Kong for what could be only a fleeting visit. After landing, the Governor's launch ferried the royal couple to Queen's Pier, where a 21-gun salute was only part of the greeting. A traditional lion dance and a laser light show were also staged.

Meeting the Gurkhas

The following day, 7 November, Diana watched a first aid demonstration at a local youth branch of the Red Cross. Later, she moved on to visit *HMS Tamar*, a naval shore base. The royal yacht *Britannia* was berthed there at the same time. Nepalese children nearly smothered Diana in flowers as they placed five garlands over her head, one after the other. They were the young daughters of Gurkha officers stationed in Hong Kong.

Later on 7 November, Diana crossed to Sheh Wu Cham island to visit a drug addiction centre and meet some of the 200 young inmates being treated for heroin dependency. Rejoining Charles, Diana

Above Children always loved Diana. Here, on a walkabout on the last day of her tour, she is met by a hoard of Hong Kong children, all eager to touch the Princess. Diana, as usual, obliges, shaking as many hands as she can.

attended a gala concert given by the British Bach Choir to mark the opening of a new cultural centre on Kowloon. Though their time in Hong Kong was fast running out, and the extreme heat was oppressive, Diana managed to visit the Chak On estate, which housed 900 needy elderly people. She

> *"I would hardly be so tactless as to impart to you my views on the architectural design of this remarkable building."*
>
> CHARLES, ON OPENING THE HONG KONG CONVENTION AND EXHIBITION CENTRE

went as patron of Help the Aged, whose sister charity in Hong Kong, called Helping Hand, supported the estate.

The Hong Kong tour was over, it seemed, in a trice and it was time to move on again. But not in the same direction. On 8 November, after co-hosting a dinner on board *Britannia* for businessmen and politicians, Diana flew back to Britain.

Charles stayed on for a time to tour a herbal and natural medicine centre where he tasted Korean red ginseng and examined the chamois horns and the

Above This little boy had the thrill of his life when he met Diana and showed her his book during a visit to a youth branch of the Red Cross on 7 November in Hong Kong. **Left** After Diana returned to Britain on 8 November, Charles stayed in Hong Kong for two more days. Here he is seen visiting a herbal and natural medicine centre.

swallows' nests. A short while later, he boarded *Britannia* and sailed off for a private tour of islands in the South China Sea. Charles was making his own documentary on the environment for the BBC and he was keen to get on with the filming.

Compensations

There was, of course, regret that the Chinese tour had been cancelled. Still, there was a small compensation, at least for Charles. He visited the New Territories, the hinterland of Hong Kong, to view some high-rise housing, take tea with a Chinese lady, 78-year-old Mrs Tang Mok Ying, and call on the Second Battalion King Edward VII's Own Gurkha Rifles, whose Colonel-in-Chief he was.

Climbing Crest Hill to the army post at the top, Charles was able to look out across the border half a mile distant. Beyond it, all the way to the point where the mists blurred the horizon, lay the great expanse of the People's Republic of China.

MODEL PARENTS

Charles and Diana's second son, Prince Harry, was born two years after William. The couple were attentive and affectionate parents, but Diana's fun outings with the princes often perplexed the other royals

Diana's arrival on the royal scene had prompted more intrusive press coverage than ever, even before her engagement to Charles early in 1981. The first big press campaign, early in 1984, concerned her second pregnancy.

Every possible clue was probed. A happy and 'blooming' Diana, it was reported, had visited her gynaecologist, Mr George Pinker, twice within a few weeks. Buckingham Palace had denied all the rumours that a second baby was on the way, a surefire indication of a cover-up, as far as cynics were concerned. What was more, in June 1983, it had been announced that there would be no foreign tours for Diana in the early part of 1984.

The Palace's explanation was that the tours of 1983, to Australia and Canada, had been so hectic that the Princess was in need of a rest. The more inquisitive sections of the media discovered that the royal gynaecologist was returning from his holidays on 6 September. That day, Diana came down

to London from Scotland. This time, the absence of convenient explanations from Buckingham Palace seemed to confirm what everyone wanted to believe: that Diana was expecting again.

In September 1983, Diana was indeed pregnant for a second time. That month, at Balmoral, she was overheard telling the Queen and Princess Margaret the news. But sadly, within a week, Diana suffered a miscarriage. She was doubtless thankful that the melancholy event somehow slipped past media scrutiny and failed to make big headlines.

The beginning of 1984, however, brought the best possible compensation. Diana discovered she was expecting for a third time. The official announcement was made on 14 February 1984, but

> ## "I don't think I'm made for the production line, but it's all worth it in the end."
>
> DIANA, ON HAVING CHILDREN

speculation was rife until the last moment. Charles, for instance, was seen teasing and nudging Diana in public, as if the two of them had a delightful secret. The fact that the press were able to deduce that the secret was another pregnancy showed how minutely Charles and Diana were watched.

All the same, the announcement at least put paid to all the speculation, or rather sent it off in another direction. The gossips started tittle-tattling about whether Diana would have another boy or a girl.

AN EASIER BIRTH

Though all-day sickness again afflicted Diana for a time, this pregnancy was easier for her than the first and the birth of Prince Harry on 15 September 1984 was not nearly so arduous.

Diana went into labour at 7.30 that morning. Charles, once more in attendance, took her from Windsor to the Lindo Wing of St. Mary's Hospital, Paddington, along the M4 motorway. A police escort accompanied them. Prince Harry, described by his father as 'a thoroughly splendid chap', was born at 4.20 in the afternoon.

Charles telephoned the Queen and Prince Philip at Balmoral, Diana's father Earl Spencer and

IN THE NEWS

The press celebrate Harry's birth

The birth of Prince Harry on 15 September 1984 saw almost a repeat performance of the media excitement over Prince William's arrival two years earlier. However, the birth of Charles' heir – the next king – was bound to create a great deal more interest, and Harry, coming second, was the so-called 'spare'. Nevertheless, the new young prince made nationwide headlines as he joined what many people had already termed 'the next Royal Family'.

Opening page The official family photograph taken by Lord Snowdon to mark the christening of Prince Harry. Three generations of Windsors are seen in this picture. **Opposite page** Charles and Diana leave St. Mary's with the newly born Harry. **Left** Diana amuses a 13-month-old Harry with some puzzles. **Below** The two princes, in matching outfits, leave a plane of The Queen's Flight with Diana, at Aberdeen Airport in 1986.

DIARY DATES

1983
September
Diana has a miscarriage
1984
11-12 February
Diana in Norway to see *Carmen* performed by the London City Ballet, of which she was patron
14 February
Announcement of Diana's pregnancy
29 February
Charles and Diana attend concert by Genesis in aid of the Prince's Trust
3 April
Diana visits the Workface Centre, Glastonbury, Somerset
5 April
Diana visits the Burslem Factory of Royal Doulton Tableware at Stoke-on-Trent, Staffordshire
5 July
Charles and Diana at concert by Neil Diamond, in aid of the Prince's Trust
7 August
Charles visits Papua New Guinea
15 September
Birth of Prince Harry
10 November
Charles and Diana attend Service of Remembrance at the Guards' Chapel, Birdcage Walk, London
13 November
Diana visits the family centre of SENSE, the National Deaf-Blind and Rubella Association
29 November
Diana at reception in aid of Pre-School Playgroups Association
4 December
Diana visits the Royal School for the Blind at Leatherhead, Surrey

her mother Mrs Shand Kydd, in that order. Even at such an emotional moment as the birth of another son, the Prince of Wales managed to preserve the proper protocol. Diana's father, who was something of a showman, hoisted the Spencer family flag at Althorp House, his country home in Northamptonshire.

Once again, Diana insisted on being discharged quickly from hospital and appeared at the door of St. Mary's just over 22 hours after giving birth. Not long before, Charles had taken two-year-old Prince William, looking angelic in a smocked top, to meet his brother for the first time.

CHAMPAGNE CHARLIE

Charles drove Diana and their new son home to Kensington Palace. Having satisfied himself that all was well with both of them, he left in his Aston Martin to play polo at Smith's Lawn, Windsor. On arrival, there was an ad hoc party for him with champagne drunk out of paper cups, after which Charles spent an active hour or two playing an energetic few chukkas of polo.

Prince Henry Charles Albert David, to be

known, it was announced, as Prince Harry, was christened at Buckingham Palace on 21 December 1984, crying only once during the ceremony. Prince William, who was proving boisterous and easily bored by formal occasions, attempted to hijack the event by pulling faces, 'buzzing' the camera as the family pictures were being taken and generally making a play for all the attention. Thanks to him, the christening pictures were less set-piece than was traditional, with broad grins all round.

> **" An extraordinarily good baby, he sleeps marvellously, eats very well and doesn't wake us up too much in the middle of the night. "**
>
> DIANA, ON PRINCE HARRY

Though Harry was a 'good' baby, Charles and Diana soon discovered that having two children more than doubled the attention they required and the mayhem they caused. William, being older and already aware of who he was, could get rather imperious at times. Apparently, aged three and nicknamed Bill the Basher, he talked rather often about 'When I am King' and 'Grandma's castles'.

'You can't get past me,' he reputedly told Charles and Diana's staff, while deliberately blocking a doorway, on one occasion. 'I'm Prince William!' The staff joked him out of it – 'And I'm the Queen of the May!' they might retort.

Diana was not going to put up with any arrogance from her son. She proved a strict mother and on William's school sports day in 1990 smacked him in public for ignoring her when she called him.

NO SHORTAGE OF LOVE

However, even the most diligent gossips could not use this incident to launch a rumour that love was lacking in the Wales family. There was clearly a strong bond of love and affection between parents and sons. As if to make up to William for the public disgrace she had dealt him, but without diluting the lesson, Diana staged a big eighth birthday party for her elder son shortly afterwards. Later that year, the audience at Olympia, in London, were charmed to see William turn Diana's face towards him and

Protocol

NAMING NEW ROYALS

William and Harry followed a royal tradition by having four Christian names each. The first reflected their royal ancestry. William had the same name as four former kings of England, Harry the same name as eight.

William's other names are Arthur Philip Louis. Arthur recalls Prince Arthur, Duke of Connaught, Queen Victoria's third son. Philip was the name of William's paternal grandfather. Louis was a compliment to Prince Charles' beloved great-uncle Lord Louis Mountbatten, **above**.

Harry's other names, Charles Albert David, came, respectively, from his father, his great-grandfather King George VI, whose real name was Albert and from his great-uncle, King Edward VIII, later Duke of Windsor, whose real name was David.

Opposite page Three-year-old Harry leaves school in a goblin costume after he and fellow pupils staged a show. **Left** Diana with both boys in Spain in 1986. **Inset left** Prince Harry, dressed in full camouflage gear, meets the Gurkhas in March 1991. **Below** Prince William and Prince Harry ride in an open landau at the Trooping the Colour ceremony in 1989. Opposite them were Diana and the Queen Mother.

give her a big, smacking little-boy kiss.

Prince Harry, by contrast, seemed to be a quieter boy, rather more tractable than William. But with his brother, he was perfectly capable of taking over the Wales household at times. Harry proved a willing conspirator when William taught him how to stuff toys down the toilet. And their enthusiasm for the Teenage Mutant Ninja Turtles proved very occupying for Diana. Turtle models, books, toys, games – everything the fertile minds of the merchandisers could devise – cluttered the rooms at Kensington Palace. This was a pain for the meticulous Diana, but quite possibly she enjoyed the Turtle fad herself, because from the first she was a 'fun' mother.

Determined that her sons should have the same youthful fun as other boys freer to enjoy themselves, Diana took them to the circus, to theme parks,

The Private Princess
The state of the royal marriage

Many witnesses testified to the fact that Charles and Diana were a very close couple in the first two or three years of their marriage.

On holiday, for instance, they would stand by the edge of the sea with their arms around each other. Charles seemed extremely attentive. There were many pictures of Diana looking at her husband with the warm glow in her eyes and smile given only by a woman genuinely in love.

Rumours, nevertheless, had it otherwise. Before long, it was being whispered, Charles found Diana too demanding, temperamental and bossy. She apparently wanted more attention than he was able to give. Worse, or so the talk went, she misbehaved, threw tantrums and even flirted with other men to gain her husband's notice. Charles, according to his friends, was becoming worn down and despite his undoubted love for William and Harry, he wanted nothing more than to get away.

Above *Charles and Diana on holiday in Majorca in 1986, by which time the strains in the fairytale marriage were plain, even to the most casual royal observer.*

That, it was suggested, neatly accounted for Charles' frequent trips to Scotland and his sudden departure two days before the end of a holiday with Diana and the Spanish royal family in Majorca in 1986.

The official reason given for leaving Majorca so abruptly was Charles' fishing trip to Scotland. The gossips' reason was Camilla Parker-Bowles, whose relationship with Charles, it later emerged, had been renewed two or three years before.

Disneyland, the cinema or out to eat hamburgers. She was like any other young mum enjoying the company of her kids and giving them treats.

William and Harry were not, of course, ordinary boys and it was rumoured that Charles did not appreciate what Diana was trying to do. He told her, reportedly, that the fun outings and the attendant pictures and publicity were not commensurate with the boys' exalted position.

True or not, this made Charles look very stuffy. However, a stuffy father was never an apt description of the Prince. He delighted in his children and gave them big doses of affection. He said of them: 'When you have children of your own, you only

Above One of the boys' and, indeed, Diana's favourite days out was to the giant water splash at Thorpe Park. This outing, in April 1993, was enjoyed by all, including personal detectives and the public. **Left** William the pageboy walks out of church hand-in-hand with a bridesmaid at the wedding of Diana's best friend, Camilla Dunne and Rupert Soames in 1988.

then discover what fun they can be.'

Charles, though, was in the same unenviable position as most busy fathers, who would have liked to be there for their children, had work not interferred. When they were small, William and Harry were usually asleep by the time Charles returned home at around 6pm. He would sometimes find Diana sketching them as they slept, each cuddling a Snoopy dog toy. Diana was no great artist, but art experts found the sketches 'charming'.

> *"What you notice is how much she loves her boys."*
>
> FAIRGROUND LADY AT ALTON TOWERS
> AMUSEMENT PARK, ON DIANA

As and when he could, Charles did a great deal to make up for his frequent absences. He took Harry round the beautiful gardens at Highgrove House, explaining the flowers and plants to him. He would put Harry in the rear basket of his bicycle as he took both his sons riding. He played with them and indulged in those boisterous games peculiar to fathers and young boys.

Then, around 1988, when William was six and Harry four, Charles began spending more time away from his family. He was often in Scotland, 'on important business', Diana is reputed to have told William and Harry. Charles spoke to his sons on the phone quite regularly and wrote them affectionate letters, but it was not the same for the boys as their father's physical presence.

BROKEN ARM

They saw more of Charles when he broke his arm rather badly in a polo accident in the summer of 1990. But the media worked out that just after the accident, Charles and Diana did not see each other for 39 days. Charles, it seems, reappeared only for the boys' half-term holidays.

The rumour-mongering went even further than that. Friends of Charles revealed that at Highgrove, Charles wanted only one person to nurse his badly damaged arm back to health. Not Diana, though, or so the talk went. The nurse Charles chose was said to be his close friend, Camilla Parker-Bowles.

IN CONTEXT *1984* GELDOF LAUNCHES BAND AID

- US jazz bandleader Count Basie dies
- Fatal gas leak at Bhopal, India, kills 2000 people
- Bob Geldof pioneers Band Aid, the rock stars' charity appeal for Ethiopia, **right**
- Bishop Desmond Tutu of South Africa wins Nobel Peace Prize
- IRA bomb explodes at the Grand Hotel in Brighton, during the Conservative Party conference being held there
- US space shuttle *Discovery* returns from six-day maiden flight
- John de Lorean, failed car maker, acquitted of smuggling cocaine
- South African athlete Zola Budd given British citizenship and runs for Britain in the Los Angeles Olympics: collides with Mary Decker

Dressed for the day

Two-piece suits and day dresses are the staple of a working woman's wardrobe and Diana, a hard-working royal, owned a diverse collection of practical yet stylish outfits

As every businesswoman knows, the two-piece suit is a must for many purposes. It looks very smart and gives an efficient impression, yet need not lack the feminine touch.

As Princess of Wales, Diana was not, of course, a businesswoman in the usual sense. But she obviously appreciated the virtues of suits to give that 'neat ensemble' look. Suits also gave her plenty of opportunity to dress up their businesslike lines with pretty blouses, including her early favourite, the frilled-neck number.

Practical and comfortable

With day dresses, which included the coat dresses so well suited to the British climate, the formula was much the same: easy and comfortable to wear. The fuller skirts Diana wore early on let her off the problem posed later by straight or tight ones – how to make an elegant exit from cars on arrival at public engagements. But, even when her skirt-level rose above the knee, Diana soon became adept at following the advice of her grandmother, Ruth, Lady Fermoy: keep the knees together and swing out of the car seat by swivelling the hips.

As with the rest of her wardrobe, Diana went through a genesis before her daywear reached its elegant zenith. On her visit to Broadlands in Romsey, Hampshire in March 1981, Diana wore a leaf-green raw silk two-piece which, though pretty, typified her far-too-fancy style. Its full skirt

Opposite page On a visit to the Australian town of Macedon in 1985, Diana wore this stripy two-piece for a walkabout. **Right** Diana aired this pink and purple two-piece, with 'flying saucer' hat at Royal Ascot.

1 In her early days as a princess, Diana exhibited a fondness for fancy collars, like this wide, jagged-edged one. 2 Along the same lines was another early favourite, the frilled, pie crust collar. 3 If she wasn't wearing an eyecatching collar, then she often chose a pearl choker at her neck. 4 Yet another favourite from her younger days was this wide, ribbon-edged collar on a coat dress.

was pleated at the front. The V-necked jacket was belted with a cummerbund. With it, Diana wore one of the ruffle-necked blouses to which she took such a fancy after seeing an Emanuel outfit in that style. The effect was appealing, but messy and uncoordinated. Diana was not yet canny fashion-wise. Going for frills because they were feminine, she ended up looking overdressed.

More sophisticated

Diana remained that way for some time before the image makers got to work on her. The vast difference they made was most potently illustrated by the way Diana looked when she left hospital in 1984 after the birth of Prince Harry, compared to 1982 after Prince William was born. In only two years, the shy, slightly frumpy 20-year-old had become much more elegant and a royal professional who knew how to use style and colour.

The distinction between the two Dianas was also evident in her suits and daywear. For instance, the red 'Andy Pandy' outfit with sleeveless jacket and burgeoning striped red and white sleeves Diana wore to Ascot in June 1981, was not helped by the oversized bow round her neck.

The red and dark green suit Diana wore during her tour of Wales in October 1981, the first after her wedding, was a lot neater. But the belted jack-

et did nothing for an elegant line and the perilously perched matching hat, the red shoes (rather than dark green or black) and fussy tie at the front, conspired to do the same.

November 1981 was marked by a super-fussy appearance on the balcony overlooking the Cenotaph in Whitehall, London. Here, Diana sported too many details – wide frilled white collar, with

> ## "You don't think it's too tight? Good, then I'll buy it."
>
> DIANA TO HER BODYGUARD, WHEN BUYING AN OFF-THE-PEG DRESS

black ribbon bow, more frills at the cuffs, black feathers in her hat, plus a pearl choker.

Quite apart from the unnecessary detail, these outfits did little for the slim figure Diana had worked so hard to acquire. Her slim waist and hips were undetectable in loose or belted dresses which made the material bunch up and not just spoil the line, but eliminate it.

When the change came it was, surprisingly enough, only two months after the birth of Prince William in 1982 when, by rights, Diana should still have been working on getting her figure back. That August, she was pictured following Charles down

**CATHERINE WALKER
TWO-PIECE**

Right and below
Catherine Walker seems
consistently to have been
Diana's favourite designer.
This French-born fashion
designer runs The Chelsea
Design Company and
numbers some very well-
positioned women among
her clients. This floral two-
piece is perfect for the
summer.

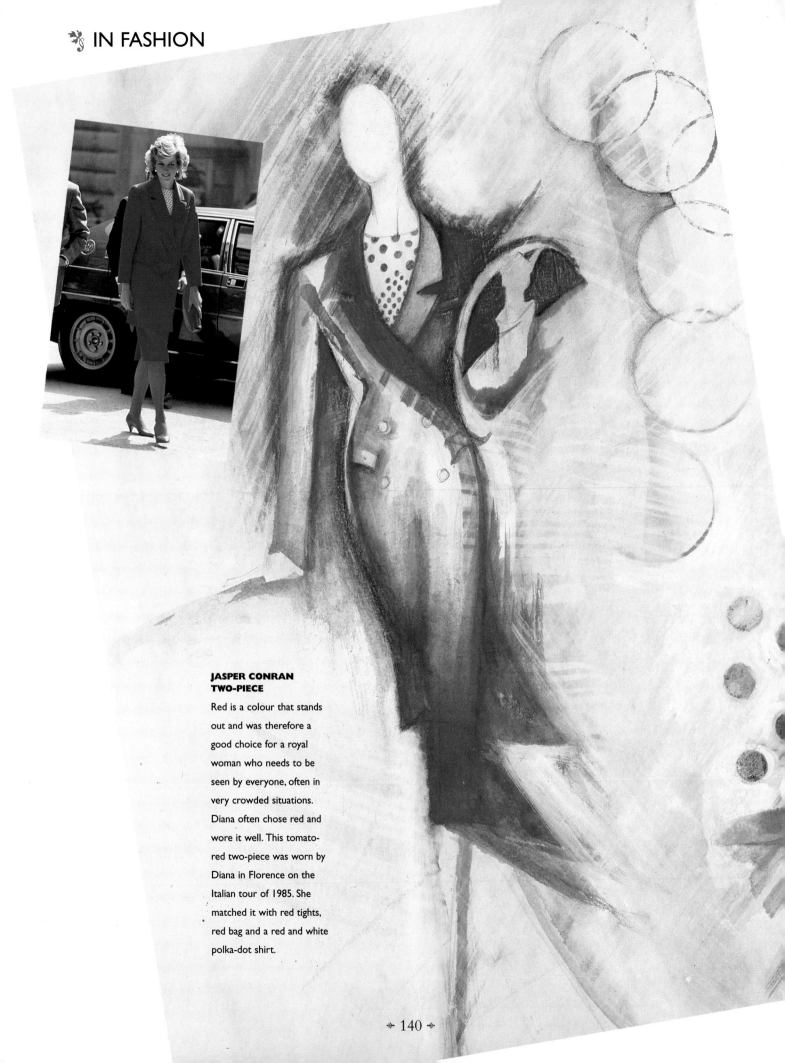

**JASPER CONRAN
TWO-PIECE**

Red is a colour that stands out and was therefore a good choice for a royal woman who needs to be seen by everyone, often in very crowded situations. Diana often chose red and wore it well. This tomato-red two-piece was worn by Diana in Florence on the Italian tour of 1985. She matched it with red tights, red bag and a red and white polka-dot shirt.

① ② ③ ④

aircraft steps at Heathrow wearing a smart, understated wine-coloured suit. The skirt was slim. The peplum jacket looked nicely sculptured, and though Diana wore it with a frilled blouse, she had suddenly grown up fashion-wise.

> **"The Princess has pared down her look. It is more minimal and polished than in the early days."**
> DAVID SASSOON, DESIGNER, ON DIANA

An example of her growing fashion sense was a delightful red coat dress which she wore in London in November 1982. It had large gathered sleeves, a mandarin collar, buttons down the front and a full calf-length skirt. The dark green side-fastening suit with shawl collar and light green piping, also worn in 1982, was another step in the right direction.

By 1983, Diana was wearing almost fuss-free suits and dresses which majored in bright colours and uncluttered lines. In January of that year, wearing a wool suit in bright pink, with a full swing skirt and double-breasted jacket, and high stand-up collar, Diana even managed to make her beloved frilled-neck blouse look part of the team.

The following month, February, Diana's blue wool coat dress with generous, but not too full skirt and sash tie belt in black to match the piping on the collar, showed even more fashion progress.

Fashion disasters

There were, of course, some disasters even in this new, more elegant format. One was the striped blue, pink and white suit she wore in Bunbury, Australia during her first overseas tour with Charles in April 1983. The vertically striped jacket argued with the horizontally striped skirt. The large jagged

1 In Vienna, Austria, in 1986, Diana wears a red Catherine Walker coat dress and a Graham Smith hat. **2** Diana steps out in smart casuals with Charles at a polo match, in 1988. Her shoes echo her white top and black belt. **3** A red coat dress by Catherine Walker, topped by a hat with a nautical feel, worn to Dartmouth Naval College in 1989. **4** Black and white were the order of the day at Royal Ascot in June 1988, with a Philip Somerville hat complementing a Catherine Walker coat dress.

I A red two-piece suit with one of the younger Diana's favourite frilled collar blouses. She wore this on a tour of Australia in October 1985. **2** Diana, in Berlin in 1985, wears an emerald green jacket with a white striped blouse and matching tie above a dark skirt. **Right** Navy blue and white stripes were Diana's choice on this visit to Royal Ascot in 1987.

white collar which dominated the cherry-red silk suit Diana wore at Port Pirie, Australia, also that April, put her fashion rating back a few notches.

But then, at Perth, in the same month, Diana appeared in a sophisticated fuschia and white spotted dress with wrap-over skirt and puff-shouldered sleeves. It was the acme of youthful elegance. The sophistication of this dress, by Donald Campbell,

> "*The Princess of Wales has such elegance and grace. She does not want to be dressed to look English or French, but to be suitable for her own life.*"
> CATHERINE WALKER, DESIGNER, ON DIANA

was confirmed when Diana wore it again in 1985 during her visit to the Vatican with Charles.

Diana's wardrobe generally was much more carefully prepared by this time, and she had also smartened up her hairstyle, making it less girlish. Yet this dress, two years old, did not look like yesterday's fashion, but part of the growing elegance taking place in Diana's clothes.

Diana had now reached the watershed. From 1985 onward, she graduated fast towards the fashion pinnacle she attained in the second half of the

decade. There was the smart black and white silk dress with high neckline and tight belt, which showed off her figure so beautifully at the Guards' Polo Club in July 1985; the double-breasted suit with short, puff-sleeved jacket and slender skirt, which Diana chose to visit West Byfleet in March 1986, and the dark green woollen suit with stepped lapels and velvet collar worn in Portugal in February 1987, which featured a shorter skirt in tune with that season's new fashion. Later, Diana's skirt lengths went up and up.

They ended well above the knee in the plainer but still smart suits she wore after her royal days were over and she was operating, after 1993, as a separated and then divorced princess.

By then the schoolgirlish style of Diana's first years as Princess of Wales had faded so completely that it was almost impossible to equate the Diana of 1981 with the chic princess of a decade later.

Sheer perfection

If just one of Diana's outfits justified the high praise and admiration which the fashion world lavished on the Princess of Wales, it was the tomato-red and bright pink silk dress and jacket by Catherine Walker, which Diana wore in Dubai, the United Arab Emirates, in March 1989.

Now a much more mature 28, Diana looked

simply superb in the plain V-necked short jacket. She wore it without a necklace, where previously she would have worn a pearl choker. There was not a single unnecessary extra. Three large gold buttons marched down from the jacket onto the skirt of the dress. The sleeves flowed straight and stylish from padded shoulders. The colour combination, unlikely at first sight, was a masterpiece of colour cueing.

Together with the broad-brimmed hat in tomato red with pink band, this stunning dress and jacket showed what a fashion icon was all about.

3 On her 1986 tour of Canada with Prince Charles, Diana wore this smart white jacket with a black collar.

4 Polo again and that turquoise pleated skirt reappears (see page 141), this time with a flowery blouse. Once more the effect is smart casual, the right note when off-duty.

IN THE NEWS

Always an easy target for the press

With Diana, the press, especially the fashion pages, liked to have their cake and eat it. One week they would be running a series of stunning fashion shots and claiming that Diana had wowed the crowds and heads of state on a royal tour abroad. And next week they would be doing their best to rubbish her hairstyle or her choice of hats or clothes. Here the Daily Express of November 1984 is disparaging about her change of hairstyle and some of the clothes she has chosen, and suggests she might be undergoing an 'image crisis' after the birth of Harry.

Why Diana got it WRONG (She said so herself)

And how she got it RIGHT

Charitable Concerns

HIV, AIDS and leprosy sufferers were regarded with dread before Diana highlighted their plight. She saw they needed help, and broke down the barriers between them and the sympathy they deserved

After Diana became Princess of Wales and embarked on the charity work which royals have made their own, the scope of her various patronages covered predictable areas. This attitude resembled, though it did not subscribe to, the Victorian idea that some poor people were 'deserving' of help and sympathy while others – the drunkards, the drug addicts, those who suffered from unsocial diseases like syphilis, and anyone else whose plight was self-inflicted – were 'undeserving'

and were, therefore, not due any real compassion.

The Royal Family, like all genuine philanthropists, never thought this way, but the span of their work nevertheless ran along more or less traditional lines. Royal charities helped the blind, the deaf, deprived children, the disabled, sufferers from cancer or meningitis, the elderly and the underprivileged of all sorts, conditions and age groups.

Diana, naturally, followed the same path, at the start. Her early patronages included, for instance,

Above Princess Diana accompanied by a Red Cross worker at a child-feeding scheme at Nemazuva Primary School in Zimbabwe, in July 1993.
Right Talking to a young handicapped patient on a visit to Kuwait with Prince Charles, in March 1989.

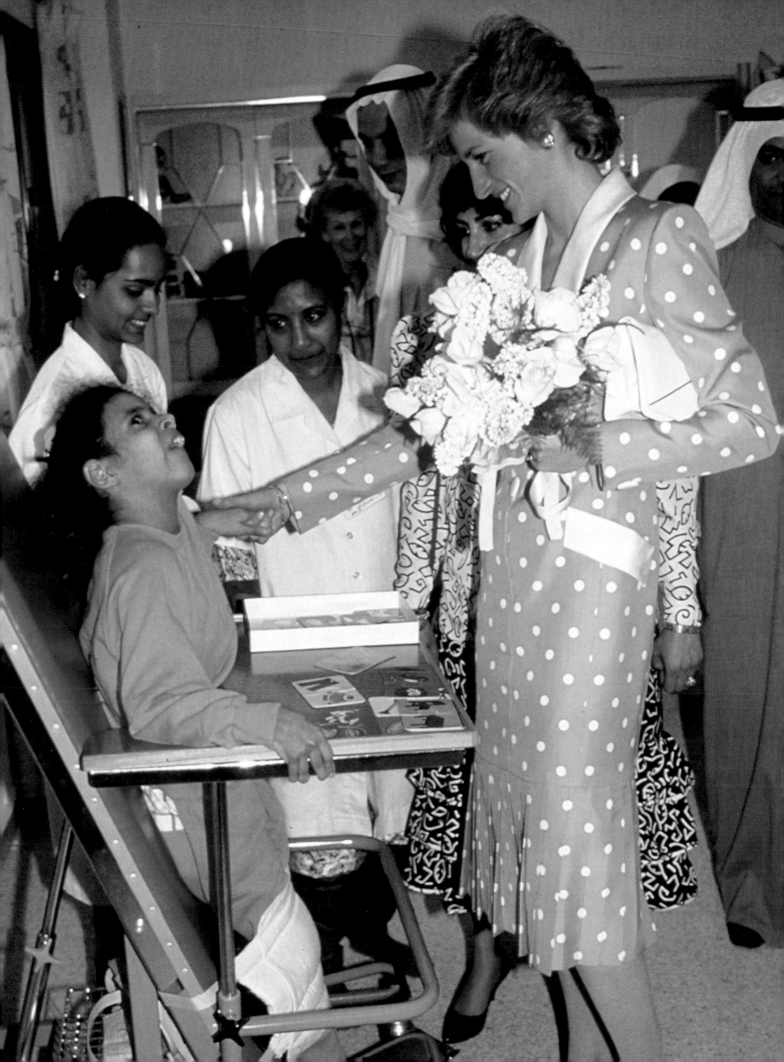

Above Over tea and biscuits at Milestone House, a hospice in Edinburgh, Princess Diana shares a joke with AIDS patients and staff as she learns about their problems at first hand. The visit took place in October 1991. Diana had earlier helped raise the funds to build the hospice.

Dr Barnardo's famous orphanages, the Malcolm Sargent Cancer Fund for Children and the Royal School for the Blind, all of them recognized mainstream royal interests. Diana continued this kind of much-needed charity work and ultimately amassed a list of more than one hundred causes for which she was either patron or president or, if neither, a participant in fund-raising and publicity activities.

Unfashionable charities

It was not long, however, before Diana realized that there was such a thing as an unfashionable charity, the sort where groups and organizations were struggling to gain recognition against barriers of prejudice and fear. Lepers, sufferers from HIV (Human Immunodeficiency Virus) or AIDS (Acquired Immune Deficiency Syndrome) and drug addicts all came into this category. AIDS and HIV had a particular notoriety after they were first diagnosed, in the United States, among homosexu-

als, another pariah group. Drug addicts, who were also at risk from AIDS, were doubly shunned.

Diana's sister-in-law Princess Anne had long been working in the field (away from the charity lunch circuit) as an active president of the Save the

> **"The Princess helped so much. She has shown that lepers are not a risk to anybody."**
> KATE DAWSON, DOCTOR AT A NIGERIAN LEPER HOSPITAL

Children Fund. But even this workaholic princess was only one person and the gap in compassion for those who had brought their tragedies upon themselves was still wide open for royal intervention.

Diana resolved to use her phenomenal popularity to achieve a turnaround in attitude, not an easy task even for the world's most famous and admired

Above On a visit to Great Ormond Street Children's Hospital, of which she was patron, Diana meets Father Christmas as he prepares to tour the wards. **Above right** Meeting some mentally handicapped children in Luxembourg, in September 1993, Diana gets involved in the board games they are playing. **Right** As patron of the British Lung Foundation, Diana takes part in a photocall with a group wearing BLF sweatshirts. She was later seen wearing a Foundation sweatshirt of her own with a pair of jeans — see issue 2, page 42.

princess. Diana, however, had a magic touch few others possessed. If she endowed a charity or spoke up in favour of a new initiative or called for attention and compassion, people automatically sat up and took notice. When she became president or patron of a charity, it suddenly became more popular and the level of its fundraising would soar. This was power of a sort which, probably, only a member of the British Royal Family was able to exercise.

A daunting task

The enterprise was, nevertheless, a daunting one, for both fear and prejudice ran deep. Leprosy, for instance, had been regarded with terror and disgust since Biblical times. It is an horrifically disfiguring disease which, if unchecked, gradually eats up the human body. In challenging attitudes to leprosy, Diana was taking on thousands of years of prejudice, during which lepers were once isolated in special colonies or, if they lived in society, had to carry

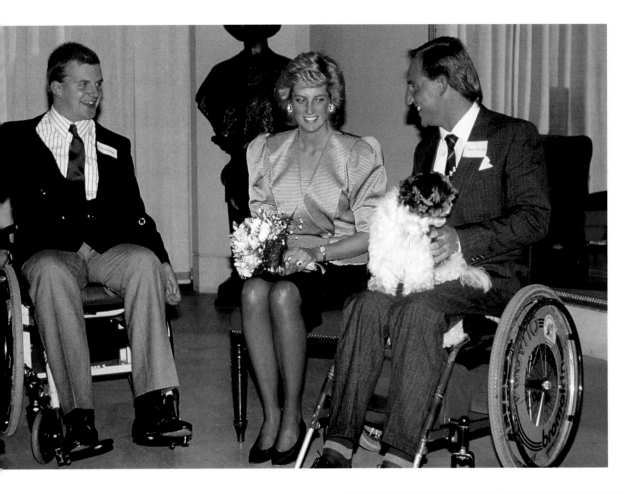

Left Diana chats with two wheelchair users during a reception for the International Spinal Research Trust, held at Grocers Hall in London, in autumn 1987. **Right** In Lahore, Diana sits with a young girl during a hospital visit, while on a trip to Pakistan in May 1997.

a bell which they rang to warn of their approach while crying 'Unclean! Unclean!'.

The notion that this sort of procedure had been left behind in the ignorance and cruelty of medieval times was dissipated by reactions to the modern 'plagues' of HIV and AIDS. After they were first identified in 1981, medieval reactions revived almost at once. In some places, AIDS victims had to be buried in double lead-lined coffins on the premise that their diseased corpses could somehow contaminate the earth. To be HIV positive was to be universally shunned, thrown out of a job and home and treated like an untouchable.

Addicts shunned

Drug addicts were condemned to a similar life of degradation and despair. The parents and families of young addicts suffered alongside them as drugs destroyed their lives, too, and burdened them with unbearable shame.

Though her own life was so privileged, Diana understood perfectly the dreadful mixture of pain,

☙ Protocol ❧

MUGGING UP

*Like other members of the Royal Family, Diana had a lot of studying to do before she embarked on public engagements both in the UK and abroad, such as this visit to Pakistan, **right**. She would be informed about who and what she was going to see, what the work, and problems, of — say — an AIDS unit or a leper hospital were and what the prognosis was for patients there. She spent a lot of time on this preparation and learned quickly. When fully briefed like this, Diana was able to talk knowledgeably as well as sympathetically to patients and staff, and leave them assured that any help she could give was going to be worthwhile.*

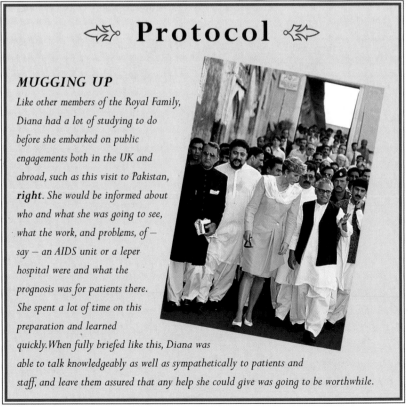

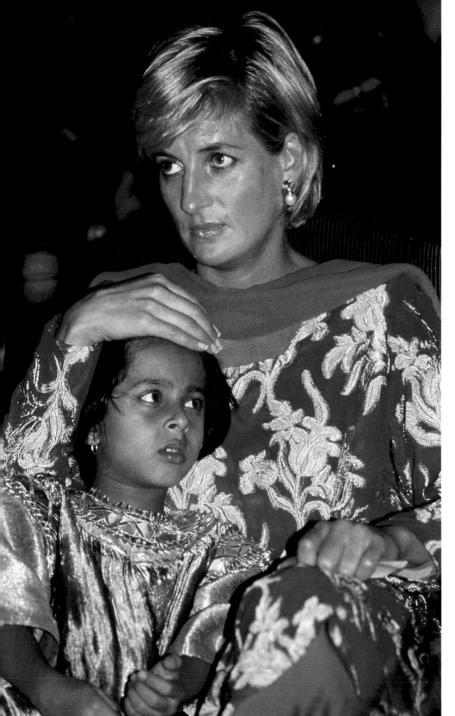

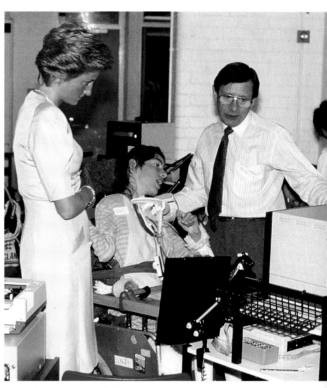

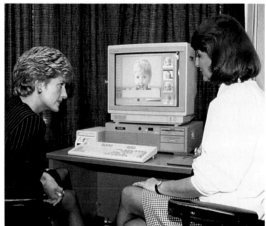

disgrace and hopelessness. She was not one of those 'hothouse flowers' playing at charity for the approval of her friends but a serious combatant in the war against human suffering.

The first of these controversial concerns Diana tackled was drugs. She had a particular concern here, connected to her deep interest in young people. In 1985, the First Lady of America, Nancy Reagan, took Diana to see Straight, the drug rehabilitation programme at Springfield, Virginia. Diana was impressed and, after returning home, she appeared on British television in the Sir Jimmy Savile programme *Drugwatch* – a 'special' devoted to

the drug problem. Diana was the first to sign her name to the 'Just Say No' anti-drugs initiative and she did so in front of millions of viewers.

After that, Diana went into action, mustering her own anti-drug forces. She elicited help from pop and rock stars, whose business was plagued by drugs. In 1989, she had become patron of the Institute for the Study of Drug Dependence. She was patron, too, of the Freshfield drug counselling service at Truro, Cornwall. In 1990, she opened the annual drugs conference of the Association of Chief Police Officers of England, Wales and Northern Ireland.

The way Diana addressed the problem of HIV

Top and above Royal visitors are usually shown the latest technology. In July 1990, a doctor (**top**) at Halliwick College explains how this handicapped child can use a computer for speech therapy, while (**above**) the work of the Missing Persons Bureau and its computer database is shown to Diana in October 1993, at East Sheen, London.

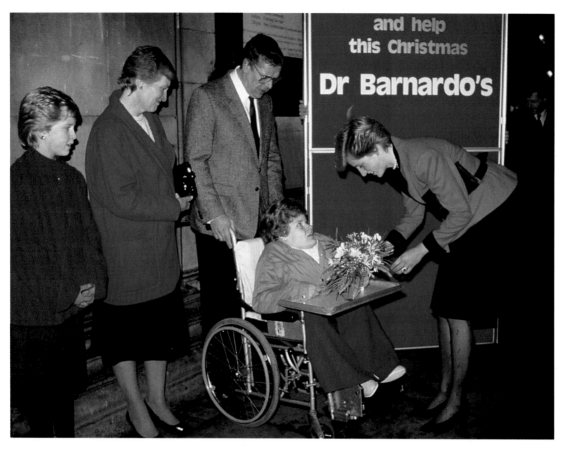

and AIDS involved no less effort, but here considerable courage was required. AIDS was commonly believed to be transmitted by casual contact. Diana set out to prove the notion wrong. In 1987, she opened an AIDS unit at Middlesex Hospital, London and shook hands with the patients. She was not wearing gloves and that was deliberate.

> ## "It meant more to me than anything."
>
> AIDS PATIENT, AFTER DIANA SHOOK HANDS WITHOUT WEARING GLOVES

She repeated the gesture at Mildmays Missions Hospital in East London in 1989, and she publicly cuddled children dying of AIDS when she went to the USA in 1989 and visited the Harlem Hospital.

Back in London the same year, Diana sat in on a counselling session with an AIDS patient and learned about the difficulties of female sufferers who contracted the disease from normal heterosexual sex. This was true groundbreaking on Diana's

part. Not too long before, delicate royal ears were not supposed to listen to such controversial tales.

She did not, however, neglect the fashionable side of charity work, the sort where people pay large sums for the privilege of rubbing shoulders with a celebrity in a good cause. This was what Diana was doing in 1989 at a charity lunch at the Savoy Hotel, London – tickets £175 each – which was staged for the benefit of the AIDS Crisis Trust. The result was a large donation towards the £100,000 needed to build a hospice for AIDS sufferers – Milestone House in Edinburgh.

Angel of mercy

Before long, Diana's work with controversial charities had, in some people's minds, placed her on a par as an angel of mercy with the famous Mother Teresa of Calcutta, the Albanian nun whose work with abandoned children, the sick and the dying was renowned throughout the world and earned her the Nobel Peace Prize in 1979.

Diana met Mother Teresa in 1992 when she flew specially to Rome after illness had prevented the

Above left Attending a carol service at St. Martin-in-the-Fields, London, to raise money for Barnardo's, one of the charities she supported as patron, Diana is presented with a bunch of flowers by a wheelchair-bound admirer. The service was on 15 December 1986.

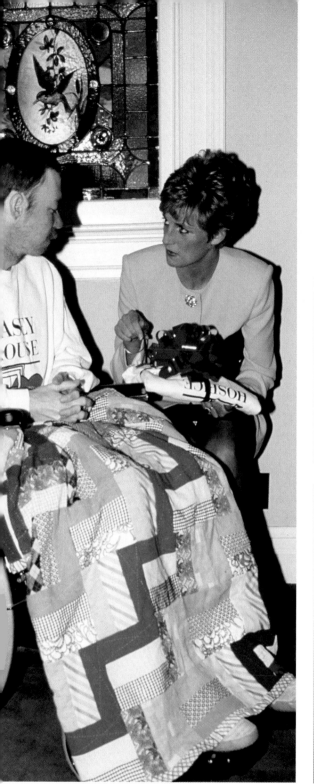

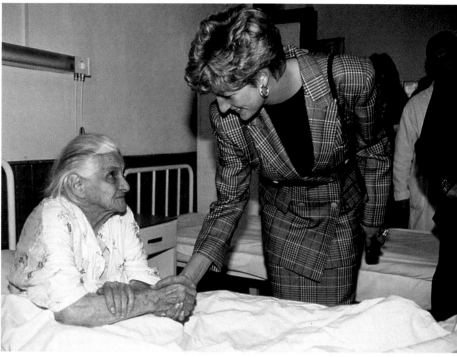

IN THE NEWS

Making time for sick children

Princess Diana is likely to be remembered this way more than any other: bending over, talking, and listening, to children, especially those suffering from HIV, AIDS or any other disease that might cut their lives short. During a royal visit to North America in February 1989, New York's Daily News picked up on this heartwarming aspect of Diana and took her seriously when she said she wanted to be Queen of People's Hearts. More than any other royal, she talked with children, no matter where she was in the world.

nun returning to Calcutta in time to greet Charles and Diana on their tour of India. Diana had already visited the mission hospice in Calcutta, where she sat by the bedside of incurables, dropping boiled sweets, their only comfort, into their mouths. In Rome, Mother Teresa quickly recognized in Diana a fellow zealot in the cause of humanity, though the two of them could hardly have been more different. They seemed to come from worlds far apart – the tall, glamorous young Diana and the diminutive,

wizened lady, who was nearly 50 years her senior.

Diana was not conventionally religious, and the nun had dedicated her life to her faith, but she and Mother Teresa prayed together. Mother Teresa prayed, too, for Diana's happiness.

Despite their differences there was no doubt that the two women had their hearts in the same place, both full of compassion and both courageous in the cause of the sick and suffering.

However, even greater courage than before was

Above left At Casey House, an AIDS hospice in Canada, Diana chats to a patient confined to a wheelchair. **Top** In March 1992, Diana visited Croatia. Here she talks to an elderly, bed-ridden refugee.

Above Diana was a reluctant public speaker but she would always overcome her nerves to stand up and present the case for those charities she supported. Here she heads up a telethon for a children's charity in March 1993.

Right Diana has a laugh with pupils at the Northern County School for the Deaf in Newcastle, on a visit in 1988. She supported several charities for the deaf.

required when Diana came face-to-face with leprosy. Lepers were so changed by their disease that, to many, they seemed like fearful mutants too sickening to touch or even look at. Diana rejected this approach outright. When she went to Jakarta in Indonesia in 1989 and Nigeria in 1990, she visited leper settlements where she shook hands with sufferers, even when the disease had robbed them of their fingers and parts of their palms.

Prince Charles, who was with Diana in Nigeria, though not in Indonesia, promptly followed suit. The sight of these two precious royals, who were destined to become King and Queen Consort of England, crossing the barriers of prejudice and fear in this fashion sent out shock waves of amazement.

Morale-boosting handshakes

Charles and Diana had been advised that leprosy could not be transmitted by handshake, although in some forms it was considered mildly infectious. In other cases, it was contagious. This was, therefore, courage of the highest order on Charles and Diana's part, and the effect on the lepers was extraordinary. In Nigeria, Bulama Duna, chief of the leper colony and his wife Botul, who had no fingers, were almost overcome with emotion as the prince and princess from far away came to smile and chat and be friends. Later, as a result of this encounter, Diana became patron of the Leprosy Mission in Britain.

In all this, Diana was deploying her full battery of ammunition for her chosen causes – her sympathy with sufferers, the mother's touch with children, her celebrity status, and her own words in speeches of no great oratory, but of total sincerity in aid of those whose plight had touched her heart.

KEEPING FIT

Diana's superb figure and generally glowing appearance did not come from nowhere. It required much effort, careful eating and a lot of self-denial and willpower. But the royal look she wanted demanded no less

By 1985, when she was 24, Diana had virtually remade herself in a new, svelte and much more elegant image. Five years earlier, when she became Prince Charles' fiancée, no one could reasonably have called Diana fat.

A little plump maybe, but then she seemed to be still at the 'puppy fat' stage. Size 14 for a girl of her height was not out of the ordinary. Had Diana remained just another pretty girl, size 14 would probably have done very well. But as soon as she

became the fiancée of the next king, Diana was set to be a public figure who would be putting herself on constant show.

Royals were scrutinized and photographed like no other celebrities. Film and television stars were known mainly from their screen appearances, and these were controlled by make-up, lighting and camera angles. Stage actresses and rock stars had the advantage of distance from their audiences. Famous models, too, operated in carefully set up photo-

sessions and only the best pictures were published. Royals, though, were seen close to, in all lighting conditions, from all angles, with a variety of facial expressions and body language. What was more, those who came to see them at public engagements had a licence to stare long and hard, while the camera recorded everything and sought out every flaw.

A NEW CAMPAIGN

Diana, therefore, began a campaign to get herself into shape for the job that awaited her. By the time she married, she had fortunately shed her favourite schoolgirl foods – four bowls of cereal for breakfast, shepherd's pie and baked beans: all of them stuffed with calories. Later, Diana graduated to a more discriminating diet: quiches, soufflés, jacket potatoes, sorbets and salads. Though not

strictly vegetarian, as was supposed at one time, Diana avoided red meat and pork, preferring chicken, seafood or fish. Fruit and vegetables were always on the table and she liked pasta.

There were many stories about Diana chasing food round her plate with a fork and not eating at official luncheons or dinners. Diana, it appears, disliked being watched or photographed eating. At official meals, of course, people constantly stared at her, so there seemed to be no escape.

Diana had to talk to her neighbours and others at the dining table and the double act of eating and speaking was difficult for her. She found a way out

> ## "I'm never on what's called a diet. Maybe I'm so scrawny because I take so much exercise."
> ### DIANA, ON DIETING

of both these problems, though. She ate beforehand at home, in private, before attending formal meals. This lone meal would be light, but filling and enabled her to watch her intake. She also avoided the fattening perils of lavish state dinners. Alcohol served at such meals was not a problem, though. Diana rarely drank, preferring natural mineral water. A lot of calories were saved that way.

There is a great deal more to a good figure than dieting. Exercise is its handmaiden and Diana was

Opening page Diana was a keen swimmer, here seen in the surf off Nevis in the Caribbean. **Opposite page** White-water rafting with the boys in Colorado, July 1995. **Left** A barefoot dash in the mother's race at Wetherby School in June 1989. **Above** Diana on the ski slopes. An avid skier, she went every winter, initially with Charles and joined by The Duchess of York, but in later years Diana skied alone with William and Harry.

IN THE NEWS

Photographer pushes Princess too far

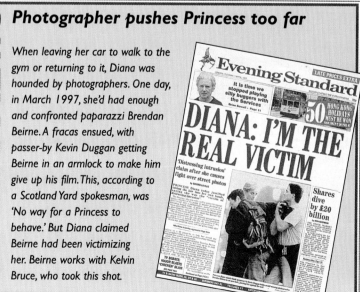

When leaving her car to walk to the gym or returning to it, Diana was hounded by photographers. One day, in March 1997, she'd had enough and confronted paparazzi Brendan Beirne. A fracas ensued, with passer-by Kevin Duggan getting Beirne in an armlock to make him give up his film. This, according to a Scotland Yard spokesman, was 'No way for a Princess to behave.' But Diana claimed Beirne had been victimizing her. Beirne works with Kelvin Bruce, who took this shot.

the first royal to go in for regular workouts. Time off at the gym had another benefit, too. It was a chance for Diana to unwind from the stress of public engagements. This is probably why she herself called her exercise routines 'pamper Diana days'.

The routine was hardly a soft option. Normally, Diana took three 30-minute sessions a week of vigorous exercise. At home, she was said to keep a treadmill for 'walking' two miles a day.

Aerobics played an important part in Diana's exercise agenda, as did jogging. When in London, she was fortunate to have the big expanse of Kensington Gardens close to her home in

> "*She was very good. She surprised me. She has a good serve and forehand, but perhaps her backhand needs a little work.*"
> STEFFI GRAF, TENNIS STAR, ON DIANA

Kensington Palace. She could frequently be seen, though she often went unrecognized, jogging along the paths at a good steady pace at around nine in the morning. She did not jog alone. One or other of her bodyguards used to go with her and he had to jog, too, in order to keep up. Like all good fitness fans, Diana had a substitute for jogging if rain spoiled her outing: an extra two mile 'walk' on her treadmill. Jogging was also part of her day when she was in the country, at Highgrove House, where the grounds offered her privacy and her bodyguards could rest.

DIVING IN

Highgrove had its own swimming pool and provided Diana with more valuable all-over exercise. In London, she used the pool at Buckingham Palace. When at Sandringham, she used to slip away for a swim at the local leisure club.

When abroad, she was known to use any suitable pool which had sufficient security. Majorca, where Diana holidayed with the Spanish royal family, afforded her plenty of opportunity. So did Necker, Richard Branson's private island in the Caribbean. The royal yacht *Britannia* had its own swimming pool, too. Wherever she was, Diana would swim 20 or 30 lengths, of both breaststroke and back-

stroke. As if all this were not enough, Diana added dancing and sports to her regime. She had been fond of dancing since childhood and admitted that it was almost an 'obsession' with her. That included tap and jazz dancing and ballet. Until she grew too tall for it, Diana had wanted to be a ballet dancer, but even then, her interest did not wane.

In 1983, she was said to have taken six weeks of lessons under the aegis of Dame Merle Park, Principal of the Royal Ballet and director of the Royal Ballet School. Ballet training, of course, did wonders for muscle control, deportment and grace and may also have helped Diana cope with the strain on her back from lifting children at the Young England Kindergarten, where she had worked.

FAMOUS PARTNERS

Dancing, though, was the one exercise Diana had to cut down. Her public commitments were so many that time did not allow for it. But she took every opportunity to dance whenever evening engagements, for instance, afforded it. She once jitterbugged with Robert Kilroy Silk, former MP and television personality.

Dancing gave her the chance, too, for another of her reported enthusiasms: meeting film and rock stars. It seemed particularly touching that such a world-famous young woman should get a thrill out of meeting the stars she admired but, according to those who met her, that is precisely how it was. Dancing with partners such as Neil Diamond, Clint Eastwood, Gregory Peck and, before his accident

Opposite page Diana went for regular workouts at a private gym, the Harbour Club in Chelsea. **Above** With former US Secretary of State, Henry Kissinger, at a formal dinner. Such meals were an occupational hazard of being a public figure. **Left** With Steffi Graf after a friendly game of tennis.

IN CONTEXT 1985
RAINBOW WARRIOR SUNK

- Spain ends its siege of Gibraltar
- Mikhail Gorbachev becomes new Soviet leader
- Miners in Britain vote to end year-long strike
- Pop duo Wham! give concerts in China
- Greenpeace ship *Rainbow Warrior*, **right**, is sunk in a French attack in Auckland harbour, New Zealand
- 'Live Aid' appeal in aid of African poor and starving raises some £50 million
- German Boris Becker becomes the youngest ever Wimbledon men's singles tennis champion

Near right Diana is seen here in January 1983, riding at Sandringham. If it came to a choice of exercise, she would put swimming, tennis, skiing, jogging and gymnasium workouts before horse riding. **Far right** Her favourite form of exercise, however, was undoubtedly dancing; she is seen here dancing with Prince Charles in Australia in 1988. She liked nothing better than to take the floor. In her time, she danced with some of the top male dancers of the day: John Travolta at the White House, and Wayne Sleep in a pre-rehearsed routine for a surprise appearance on stage. With her training in ballet and other forms of dance, such as tap, she was certainly a good enough dancer to hold her own in the best company.

⊱ Protocol ⊰

BEING DISCREET

In 1985, Diana's former flatmate Carolyn Pride (now Carolyn Bartholomew), **right**, told an interviewer on Australian television that she thought all Charles and Diana had in common was their children. In this, Carolyn was breaking a golden rule: the understanding that friends of royals and anyone else who met them in private never revealed anything they knew. They were certainly barred from speaking to the media. Contravening this rule meant being crossed off the royal guest lists, usually never to return to favour. Carolyn, though, apparently went unpunished, as a new and more candid attitude to royal matters got under way.

paralysed him, Christopher 'Superman' Reeve, achieved a double purpose for Diana – exercise her favourite way and meeting her idols as well.

Other stars came within Diana's orbit, too. At school, she excelled at sports such as netball and hockey in the winter, swimming and tennis in the summer. Tennis, like swimming, proved an enduring interest. A week or two before her wedding in 1981, Diana was seen jumping up and down and clapping her hands with excitement as John

---

"She told me she doesn't have time to dance any more, and that's sad because the Princess loved her dancing."
HAROLD KING OF THE LONDON CITY BALLET

McEnroe won the first of his three singles titles at the Wimbledon tennis championships. McEnroe, apparently, was one of Diana's tennis heroes, despite his sometimes disruptive manners on court.

Diana was no armchair fan. She played tennis regularly herself and according to tennis star, Steffi Graf, asked her several times to give Prince William lessons. Steffi had quite a high opinion of Diana's tennis skills, which must have been very pleasing coming from one of the most brilliant and successful women players of all time.

BEAUTY ROUTINE

'Pampering Diana', as she called it, included visits to health clubs and health farms, massages using aromatherapy oils, facials and a skin care routine from the USA, which apparently involved splashing her face with water sixty times a day.

All this amounted to an intensive health and beauty agenda, which would have left most women gasping and all crammed into a life much busier than the majority of people ever have. But if every picture tells a story, the many photographs of Diana tell a marvellous one. Her beauty, slenderness, shapeliness and grace often drew gasps from those who saw her in the flesh in public. Considering, however, the time and very real effort that she put into it, she deserved every single one.

The Private Princess
Playing the royal part

I n 1985, rumours were circulating of serious trouble within Charles and Diana's marriage. Claiming the public's right to know, which some called 'the public's right to nose', the media gave mass coverage to the couple's reputed disaffection.

The fact that Diana began carrying out more lone engagements than seemed necessary was another factor in the press argument. In the autumn of 1985, Diana was said to have left Balmoral early, after the annual Royal Family gathering. Charles, it appears, made no attempt to follow her back to Kensington Palace. He stayed on at Balmoral.

Whatever truth or otherwise was gleaned from these rumours

Above Charles and Diana, in Australia in 1985, appeared very much a couple, in spite of the growing rumours to the contrary.

at the time, Charles and Diana got their royal act together and dutifully completed a second tour of Australia in 1985, to attend the celebrations for the 150th anniversary of the State of Victoria. For two people supposedly at loggerheads, according to the media, they performed their engagements 'down under' with great aplomb. Those who did not already know what was being said about them would not have guessed there was a problem.

The Australian tour was a success, but the rumours continued to dog the royal couple.

Glittering Jewels

Diana had very little jewellery of her own when she became engaged to Charles. Elaborate pieces of the royal kind did not fit her pre-marriage lifestyle. But within a short while that was to change completely

Jewels and royalty might have been made for each other. Jewels were evidence of the power and magnificence of monarchy and the badges of its status at the head of society. A royal crown would be nothing without them and a monarch would be incomplete without a jewelled crown.

Such ideas, deeply rooted in the royal mystique, represented yet another change for Diana when she married into the Royal Family. Before then, all she had in the way of jewellery was a pendant necklace with her initial and a pearl choker, which started a fashion after she became a public figure. Her easygoing lifestyle required little more and jewels seemed to mean little to her.

Engagement ring

The first substantial piece of jewellery that Diana owned was her beautiful oval sapphire engagement ring with its corona of fourteen diamonds. On her wedding day, however, most jewellery that she wore was borrowed – the Spencer tiara and pearl and diamond earrings from her mother, and the pearl choker, worn with her going-away outfit, from her sister, Lady Sarah.

Already, though, a start had been made on equipping Diana with the jewellery appropriate for so important a royal as the Princess of Wales,

GLITTERING JEWELS 🌹

Far left Diana is seen as a young princess wearing the Spencer family tiara, along with a set of earrings, pendant and bracelet given to her by the Saudi royals as a wedding present. **Main picture** In 1995, the night her *Panorama* interview was broadcast, Diana looks her glamorous best wearing the giant sapphire – a brooch given to her by the Queen Mother – which Diana had chosen to set on a pearl choker.

QUEEN MARY'S CHOKER

An emerald choker that once belonged to the starchy Queen Mary was pressed into service as a headband by Princess Diana when she attended a dance with Prince Charles in Melbourne, Australia, in 1985. Her tiara had apparently been left behind. Diana delighted in using old pieces of jewellery in imaginative ways — brooches as chokers, necklaces as headbands.

1 Diana wears a diamond choker with a large sapphire at its centre, mounted on velvet, to accompany a star-spangled Murray Arbeid dress. 2 Earlier in 1986, in Japan, the piece is worn as a headband with matching earrings and a Yuki dress.

Two imaginative uses of a long string of pearls. 3 In 1985, attending the London première of Stephen Spielberg's *Back to the Future*, Diana picked up the title in this Catherine Walker dress which had a crew neck at the front with a low V-back, emphasized by the pearls worn back-to-front. 4 At London's Festival Hall, in 1987, Diana, in a Victor Edelstein gown, wears them knotted below her bust.

5 On a visit to Garrard, the crown jewellers who have supplied the world's rich and titled people for many years, Diana wears a diamond and amethyst late 19th-century cross hung on a long faux pearl necklace. With it she wears long pearl drop earrings above a high standing velvet collar of a Catherine Walker Elizabeth I-style gown. She wore the dress in 1987 at a charity function. Garrard was where Prince Charles bought Diana's engagement ring. It later appeared in Garrard's catalogue, priced at £28,500, and Charles was said to be furious at the blunder.

future Queen Consort and future mother of heirs to the throne. The Queen's wedding present to Diana was the glorious lover's knot tiara with tear-drop pearls, which had once belonged to the Queen's grandmother, Queen Mary. This tiara was a weighty item, the sort which gave the wearer headaches if left on for too long. Tiaras, though, were an expression of grandeur unique to royalty and the aristocracy and despite their perils, Diana dutifully wore them. Normally, this was only on grand official occasions.

One of these was her appearance at La Scala opera house in Milan, during the Italian tour of 1985, when she complemented Queen Mary's tiara with a simple pearl necklace and pearl drop ear-

> ## "People keep on trying to make me, but I won't."
> DIANA, ON NOT WANTING TO WEAR BROOCHES

rings. Diana had some difficulty, though, suiting her hairstyle to the ornate tiara. In Milan, there were too many fronds of hair sticking out and too much fringe to do the piece justice.

A smoother, unfussy hairstyle would have been more appropriate, as Diana showed later, in Bonn in 1987, when she wore the Spencer tiara and the suite of matching jewellery in sapphire and diamonds – bracelet, necklace and crescent earrings – given her the previous year by the Sultan of Oman. In Bonn, Diana clearly meant the suite to be the star of her show: her dress was a plain, though stylish, black off-the-shoulder gown by Victor Edelstein.

Tasteful restraint

As her own jewellery collection grew, Diana showed a lot more restraint than most young women who had leapt, as it were, from a couple of modest items to priceless pieces, featuring historic gems and pearls. Diana was also able, like most female members of the Royal Family, to borrow from the Queen's collection, which is not the sovereign's personal property, but heirlooms to be passed on to her successor.

Even with all this to choose from, Diana did not care to load herself with jewels. The Queen and her

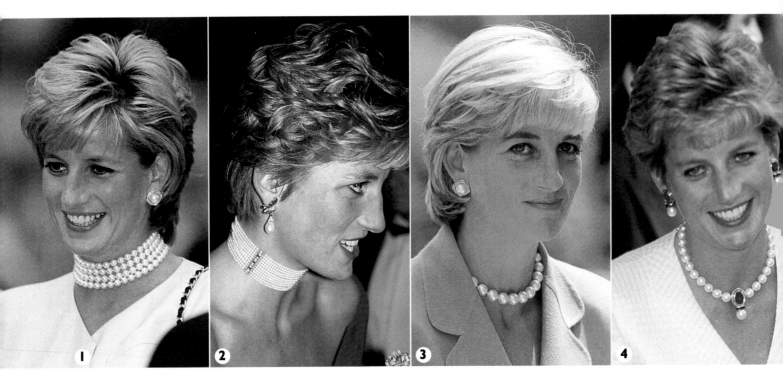

Princess Diana was very fond of pearls and wore the real thing as well as fun fake jewellery bought from Butler and Wilson in London. **1** On a trip to America, Diana wears a four-string pearl choker with a large pair of fake gold and pearl button earrings. **2** At London's Royal Opera House, in 1991, Diana wears an 11-string baby pearl choker with a diamond and ruby inset. Her pearl drop earrings are heavily decorated with rubies and diamonds. **3** With those favourite large fake pearl earrings again, Diana wears a fun faux pearl necklace, on a trip to Washington DC in June 1997. **4** In June 1993, Diana wears another fun set of fake jewellery, this time matching pearl and ruby earrings and necklace.

sister, Princess Margaret, could wear considerable amounts of jewellery – tiara, necklace, earrings, bracelets, brooches, all at once – without looking like Christmas trees. Diana was differently made – too tall, too blonde and too casual in her general look to emulate them.

She went in for the full show on occasion; for instance, the necklace and earrings worn with the Spencer tiara and the Queen's Family Order brooch on a yellow ribbon, all worn with a sparkling red dress in Hobart, Tasmania in 1983. It is significant, though, that the necklace was a small pendant which graced Diana's neck without making a big splash, and the earrings were equally modest drop types with a diamond-shaped clasp. This way, the potentially overpowering effect of all that jewellery was minimized to create a much more elegant look.

This was typical of Diana's personal taste. In the main, her jewellery tended to be understated and was all the more effective for that.

Mistakes

Diana made her mistakes, of course. In 1987, for example, she wore a gold and diamanté necklace to a Lionel Ritchie concert in London, which argued with the high collar of her crimson pink dress. Her casually flicked back hair with sloppy fringe was not

what the matching half-hoop earrings called for, either. This almost recalled Diana's early days when she mistakenly wore pearl chokers with frilled collars in a way that greatly overcrowded her neck.

Nevertheless, Diana certainly knew how to make a striking statement with her jewellery, even when the accent was on restraint rather than show. In 1986, at the America's Cup Ball in London, she

> **"It's like walking around with three books on your head."**
>
> DENISE MCADAM, HAIRDRESSER, ON HOW TO WEAR A TIARA

looked sophistication personified, with a black ribbon round her throat to which she had pinned a small, elegant brooch. The matching black and crystal drop earrings were doubtless taken for real, but they were in fact from Diana's paste collection of fake fun jewellery, which cost about £4500 in all.

Diana's favourite form of jewellery seemed to be earrings, but wisely she realized she was not the sort of woman who could sport big, elaborate 'chandeliers'. Her earrings were mainly quite modest-looking, but they came in almost every form: large and small rounds, half-hoops, heart-shaped, pearl

QUEEN MARY'S TIARA

Probably Diana's most beautiful tiara was the one given to her as a wedding present by the Queen. It was Queen Mary's lovers' knot tiara, set with 19 teardrop pearls that had been given to Mary as a wedding present. It was made by Garrard in 1914. Diana wore it **(above)** in Hong Kong to accompany the superb Catherine Walker cropped jacket and evening dress, with its Elizabethan ruff collar and simulated pearl embroidery.

drop, horseshoes, plain gold rings, small pearl or diamond-studded. In virtually every picture taken of Diana, earrings were usually present, even when she was on the beach sunbathing.

Conversely, Diana rarely wore rings, apart from her engagement and wedding rings, and she disliked some brooches as 'too old'. The Queen Mother gave Diana a beautiful brooch as a wedding present, but she cleverly turned it into a necklace by mounting it on a pearl choker. This was a tactful way of displaying an important gift and her own

> ## "It is beautiful. How generous everyone is!"
>
> DIANA, ON BEING GIVEN A JEWELLED REGIMENTAL BROOCH

style in jewellery at the same time. The choker drew gasps and gazes when Diana wore it to the White House dinner in Washington in 1986.

This was only one example of Diana's creative use of jewellery. Another of her wedding presents was a stunning suite of jewels from the royal family of Saudi Arabia: sapphire and diamond pendant, necklace, bracelet, earrings, ring and watch.

From this, Diana produced a splendid jewelled headband to wear in Japan in 1986. She did a similar conversion on an emerald and diamond necklace which had once belonged to Queen Mary, wearing it round her head during her second visit to Australia in 1985 (see page 162).

Firm favourites

It was unusual, though, for Diana to wear green jewellery. Sapphires were her favourite stone, matching the colour of her eyes. Pearls were a top choice, too, not only in the ubiquitous three-strand choker, but in several other forms.

Diana wore a two-strand twisted pearl necklace more than once, accompanying it with different sets of pearl earrings. She wore single strands as short necklaces, and did inventive things with a long strand of pearls wound twice round her neck and extending to her waist (see page 163 for two pictures of uses of this long strand of pearls).

An important lesson Diana learned was when

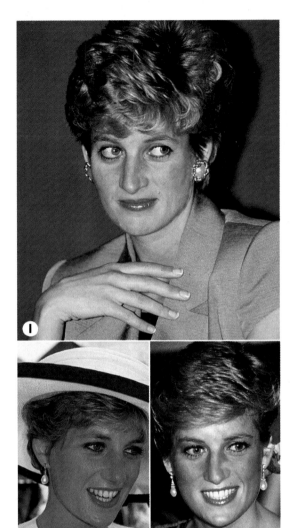

1 Diana on a visit to Kathmandu, Nepal, in March 1993, wears no jewellery, beyond her rings and a pair of large fake pearl earrings in a gold setting. **Opposite page** On 2 June 1997, at the London launch of her charity dress auction, Diana shows her minimalist approach to jewellery again, wearing only pearl drop earrings with a diamond cluster around the clasp and letting nothing detract from the dress and eyecatching cleavage it reveals.

2 Diana had pierced ears and here she wears pearl drop earrings with a gold clasp. 3 Diana had a number of diamond and pearl drop earrings for glamorous occasions. These large pearl drop earrings, worn for an evening out, are supported by two simple diamond studs in a silver setting.

IN THE NEWS

£2million heirloom as squaw's headband

Diana was much more than a clothes horse. She was an innovator, setting fashion by wearing clothes or jewels in her own individual way. Her rather saucy use of a choker as a headband (see page 162), while on a 12-day tour of Australia with Prince Charles, in autumn 1985, caused controversy and made headlines.

This report, from the News of the World, 3 November 1985, by Andrew Morton, suggests that the decision to wear the choker and the dress was a last-minute one, taken in defiance of Charles, who took a more traditional approach to fashion.

GLITTERING JEWELS 🌷

PEARL AND DIAMOND DROP EARRINGS

Right and below These magnificent earrings were a favourite of Diana's. They feature a leaf design of diamonds set in silver with large sea pearl drops. She wore them (**right**) at a gala dinner in Washington DC, on 17 June 1997.

not to wear jewellery. Many of her dresses had necklines which seemed to beg for a necklace, but Diana wisely left them to speak for themselves. There was, for example, the stunning gold lamé dress by Bruce Oldfield, which Diana wore to a film première in Melbourne in 1985. Diana chose pretty gold earrings but that was all. She realized that this dramatic gown resembled a piece of jewellery in itself.

Diana's style with jewellery was as much part of her fashion icon image as her clothes. She saw jewels not as accessories but as part of her whole look. This was always marked by a display of superb taste.

Anne Beckwith-Smith was Diana's first full-time lady-in-waiting and her longest serving. She became a confidante whom Diana would drop in on for a snack and a chat. Apart from organizing the logistics of Diana's day – the timetable of events, how to get there and so on – Miss Beckwith-Smith would often end up with an armful of flowers as she followed Diana around.

The Support Team

Solitude was rare for royals. Ladies-in-waiting were in constant attendance. Diana had detectives and bodyguards to protect her. She found this irksome at times, yet made many friends this way

O ne of the hardest lessons Diana had to swallow when she became a member of the Royal Family was that she would be constantly watched, constantly accompanied and very rarely left alone. Given the threats and dangers facing public celebrities and royals most of all, it could not be any other way. Royals were a target. Royals had to be protected. This was an occupational hazard of the royal job.

The loss of her freedom often irked Diana, which is why she was said to break the rules from time to time, to go driving or shopping on her own.

By rights, she should have had a detective with her in her car, with a back-up vehicle following. By rights, too, a bodyguard should always have gone to the shops with her, to check them for security and keep guard the whole time she was there. Strictly speaking, Diana was not officially allowed to keep possession of her own car keys.

Diana found things much easier when it came to her ladies-in-waiting. This was a royal tradition she understood well. Her own family, the Spencers, had provided royal aides, including ladies-in-waiting for many years. Ladies-in-waiting were well-born

Previous page Inspector Alan Peters, Diana's personal bodyguard, had to keep an eye out for any potential trouble when the princess was in a crowd. **Above** A lady-in-waiting was always in the back seat, discreetly with her royal charge but keeping out of the limelight. Here, at the Glasgow Garden Festival, it is Alexandra Loyd who sits behind the princess.

ladies, well placed in society, capable, good organizers, pleasant and tactful; the sort of women Diana could trust to look after her, not only in public but also as secretaries and companions in private.

Diana's first batch of ladies-in-waiting were appointed some three months after her marriage, in October 1981. Anne Beckwith-Smith, then 39 and the daughter of the Clerk to the Course at Lingfield racecourse, was to be full-time in the job. The other two, Mrs Lavinia Baring, 30, who was a friend of Anne's and Mrs Hazel West, 36, daughter of the Assistant Comptroller of the Lord Chamberlain's Office, would work part-time.

All three fitted well the description of the best ladies-in-waiting. They were pleasant-looking and attractive, but not too attractive and certainly not glamorous. They dressed well, but not too well.

They could fade into the background, yet remain alert for signs of trouble. Ladies-in-waiting were not supposed to rival the royal star of the show, but they should not be frumps or awkward. Diana's ladies-in-waiting passed on all these counts.

> **"I just couldn't have done without you."**
>
> DIANA TO ANNE BECKWITH-SMITH AFTER THE AUSTRALIAN TOUR OF _1983_

Some concern was voiced that they were so much older than the youthful Princess but this was, in fact, a bonus. A lady-in-waiting had to be mature, self-possessed and cool-headed, none of which were normally attributes of youth. Miss

Above left As Diana disembarks from a helicopter, the lady-in-waiting dogging her footsteps is Laura Lonsdale. **Top** Diana with her sister Sarah and the headmistress of West Heath, Ruth Rudge, who rusticated Sarah for a term. Behind them all is Anne Beckwith-Smith. **Above** The diamond-encrusted 'D' Diana gave to Anne Beckwith-Smith. **Left** In the rain, Anne Beckwith-Smith was often there to hold an umbrella over Diana.

Beckwith-Smith, Mrs Baring and Mrs West were, however, as new to their jobs as Diana was to hers. They were assigned initially to Lady Susan Hussey, an experienced lady-in-waiting. Lady Susan had been at Balmoral during the last part of Charles and Diana's honeymoon, standing in for the yet-to-be-appointed trio and assisting Princess Diana.

ALWAYS CINDERELLAS

Ladies-in-waiting, as Lady Susan understood very well, were Cinderellas in a way. They got to go to the ball, but there were no handsome princes waiting for them. Instead, they acted as backstops for 'their' royals, standing by, preferably unnoticed, until they were needed. Ladies-in-waiting were the ones who had to carry the excess bouquets.

Their voluminous handbag contained an emergency sewing kit and cosmetics for royals to touch up their faces during pauses in a public engagement. Spare tights were also stashed in its depths, together with headache pills, tissues and a copy of the royal speech typed in extra large print. Because royals did not carry money, the handbag could also contain cash and a card for spontaneous purchases.

Eventually, as Diana's workload grew, she acquired four more ladies-in-waiting, including Alexandra Loyd, a school friend, Laura Lonsdale, a fluent French speaker useful on foreign tours and

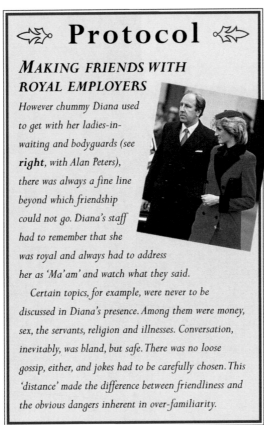

Above Just occasionally, detectives, drivers and bodyguards were called into action. They were quick to react to this anti-royalty protester who had decided to take his protest up to the window of Diana's limousine. **Top centre** Inspector Ken Wharfe prepares to open the car door for Diana. **Opposite page** In Lech, Austria, when Diana and the princes were on a skiing holiday, Ken Wharfe (in red) argues with two Italian paparazzi whose cameras might be concealing guns. **Far right** The more mundane part of the job came when an officer had to guard Prince William on the regular nursery run.

Protocol

MAKING FRIENDS WITH ROYAL EMPLOYERS

However chummy Diana used to get with her ladies-in-waiting and bodyguards (see right, with Alan Peters), there was always a fine line beyond which friendship could not go. Diana's staff had to remember that she was royal and always had to address her as 'Ma'am' and watch what they said.

Certain topics, for example, were never to be discussed in Diana's presence. Among them were money, sex, the servants, religion and illnesses. Conversation, inevitably, was bland, but safe. There was no loose gossip, either, and jokes had to be carefully chosen. This 'distance' made the difference between friendliness and the obvious dangers inherent in over-familiarity.

Jean Pike, daughter of General Lord Michael Fitzalan Howard and Viscountess Hampden.

It was, of course, a great coup for Diana's original ladies to be appointed to such a prominent royal on their first assignment. This ensured them of some exciting experiences, sometimes a glamorous environment like a film première and the chance to see other celebrities and famous names.

On occasion, ladies-in-waiting stepped forward nearer the limelight when their royal forgot a name or became stuck for something to say. Diana tended to be shy and before she became as self-assured as years of experience later made her, one or other of her ladies had to be ready to step in and smooth the conversation through.

It was more likely, though, that they would have to curb Diana's enthusiasm and gently move her on if she stayed too long to talk or shake hands. At the start of her job in 1981, Diana was so friendly that this happened fairly often. Later, she was better at pacing a walkabout or a handshaking session with a line of people waiting to be presented to her.

Considering the many hours and experiences

they shared, it was inevitable that Diana and her ladies should become friends. This applied especially to Anne Beckwith-Smith, who stayed with the Princess for nearly nine years and was eventually promoted to act as her Assistant Private Secretary.

> "*The one good thing about guarding a woman is that, if the worst happens, you can pick her up and run for it.*"
>
> INSPECTOR ALAN PETERS, DIANA'S
> PERSONAL BODYGUARD

Anne's family was well known to the Queen and the Queen Mother, who had an avid interest in horses and racing. It was the Queen Mother who had suggested the friendly, capable Anne for the royal job. She had studied History and Art in Florence and before she became a lady-in-waiting, had worked in a Mayfair art gallery.

Diana found Anne a loyal confidante, another virtue in a good lady-in-waiting. The two became

such close friends that Diana would often be seen driving to Anne's flat in Knightsbridge, close to Kensington Palace, for a chat and a snack, usually scrambled eggs. Diana became so fond of Anne that at the end of the Australian tour of 1983 – the first overseas tour for both of them – she was seen giving her lady-in-waiting a spontaneous hug. Anne also received a splendid present for her efforts in Australia, a large diamond clip decorated with a 'D' and a set of diamond earrings to match.

TOUGH POLICE OFFICERS

Diana's detectives and bodyguards, being professionals from the Metropolitan Police Force, did not have the prior connections with her that her ladies-in-waiting enjoyed. Diana and her ladies came from similar social backgrounds, but detectives and bodyguards had to be tough guys always prepared for trouble. Trained by the SAS, they carried arms and were always prepared to use them.

A young girl like Diana could feel quite daunted by the presence of these formidable men. One of them, Inspector Kenneth Wharfe, was a crack

shot with the rapid-firing Smith and Wesson .38 revolver. Another, Inspector Alan Peters, Diana's personal bodyguard, was another top-class marksman and a big, imposing figure. At 17 stones in weight and a height of 6ft 4ins, he was tall enough to tower over Diana – and that was not a common experience for a girl who was only an inch and a half off six feet herself.

Peters was, inevitably, known as Big Al or The Hulk and when out on engagements with Diana produced a path for her by shouting 'Get out of the way!' The tone was one of such authority that a path normally cleared quickly.

By the very nature of their jobs, bodyguards had a licence to manhandle royals for the sake of their safety. Once, in 1985, Diana was visiting the later notorious Broadwater Farm Estate in north London, when Peters apparently sensed trouble, grabbed her by the arm and told her 'Come on, we're getting out of here!'

There was a natural tendency for bodyguards to be over-protective. Diana, who reportedly disliked the restrictions inherent in having them around, was said to feel nervous when attended by another of

IN THE NEWS

The rumour mill starts

After the engagement and especially after the wedding, there was much speculation as to who would be working with Diana in her role as Princess of Wales. This report in the Daily Express on 12 August 1981, suggesting that Lady Romsey would be working with Diana as a lady-in-waiting, appeared two weeks after the wedding. The paper got it wrong, but that hardly mattered. Everyone wanted to get into print on the subject of Diana and it was the gossip that counted. Unlike other rumours that were to appear later on, this one was at least harmless.

Opposite page, far left
On a visit to *HMS Tamar* in Hong Kong, Diana talks to her bodyguard Graham Smith. Later, when he was taken ill with cancer, Diana invited him and his wife to holiday with her on Richard Branson's private island, Necker in the Caribbean.
Opposite page, near left
Ken Wharfe shadows the royals on a shopping trip in Cirencester. **Above**
Walkabouts always made bodyguards nervous.

her bodyguards, Detective Inspector David Robinson. He later left Diana's service and became a bodyguard to other royals.

Another risk was too much closeness. A man and a woman who spent time together in potentially dangerous situations, an assumption all bodyguards had to make, could theoretically form a relationship not in keeping with their positions in life.

This is what was supposed to have happened with another of Diana's protectors, Sergeant Barry Mannakee. There was talk that Mannakee became 'over familiar' with the Princess and was transferred away as a result. A few weeks later, Mannakee was killed in a car accident, which the ever-fertile minds of gossipmongers interpreted as a 'kill' by MI5. Mannakee himself named 'domestic reasons, the

long hours spent away from home' as the reason for leaving Diana's service, so underlining the unfortunate fact that those who protect the Royal Family have to give a large part of their own lives to it.

LIFE-SAVING ROLE

Bodyguards were, of course, known to save the lives of the royals they were protecting. Chief Inspector Paul Officer, Diana's first bodyguard after her marriage, did just that in 1974 at the Portland Naval Barracks in Dorset, after a sailor broke into Prince Charles' quarters wielding a knife. After he left the Navy, Charles remembered the valiant Officer and in 1981 assigned him to the new Princess.

Bodyguards could, of course, find themselves performing less exciting duties than rescuing the heir to the throne from violent death. When Diana went shopping with one of her protectors, she would ask him to judge the dresses she was trying on. Bodyguards found themselves carrying bags, playing with the children, building sandcastles for them on the beach, or teaching them how to swim. It would not have been surprising if they found all

> ## "It's never boring working for the Waleses."
> ### A SENIOR COURTIER, ON CHARLES AND DIANA

this not in accord with the generally macho image of the Royal Protection Department, as the royal bodyguards and detectives were called. Maybe it was for reasons like this that the doughty Chief Inspector Officer requested a transfer from royal service after less than six months of guarding Diana.

Despite her own reservations about being forever shadowed and watched for her own good, Diana seemed to appreciate the devotion of her

detectives and the difficulties and long hours their work involved for them. She had an unusual insight into their work, gleaned from her own and Prince Charles' training by the SAS in anti-terrorist techniques and unarmed combat. Diana also learned how to drive herself out of trouble.

CLOSE WORKING RELATIONSHIP

This was the more sombre side of royal life not usually apparent to the public, but absolutely essential for such sensitive targets as Diana and the other royals. But if the watchfulness of both bodyguards and ladies-in-waiting was the price which had to be paid for royal celebrity, it also enabled Diana to get close to the public, to talk and interact with them, something she liked doing and did well. She was able to do it knowing she was as safe in such close encounters as human endeavour could make her.

Above For bodyguards, shopping was not only confined to an outing with their wives. If Diana took it into her head to go shopping, either as part of an organized visit, as here in Liverpool, or an impromptu clothes-buying trip to Harrods, then her bodyguard had to accompany her. **Left** Patrick Jephson, the Princess' private secretary, holds open the door as Diana leaves a doctor's surgery.

NATURAL ALLIES

By 1986, when Sarah Ferguson married Prince Andrew, the press was speculating about trouble in the Wales relationship, even predicting its breakdown. The cheery, breezy Sarah seemed just the tonic the troubled Diana needed to deflect the media spotlight

It would be difficult to imagine two more different young women than Sarah Ferguson and the Princess of Wales. Diana was the cool, tall, shapely blonde beauty who might have been a supermodel had she not been a princess. She still had a certain shyness about her. She was friendly and obviously warm-hearted, but seemed highly strung and nervous at times. 'Fergie', as the press immediately labelled Sarah, appeared much more flamboyant, with her glorious red hair, big grin and tomboyish manner. In public, Diana appeared controlled, even a little diffident. Sarah seemed to leap at her public appearances, full of sparky enthusiasm, with the gait of a school hockey team captain.

When the engagement of Prince Andrew and Miss Sarah Ferguson was announced on 19 March 1986, press interest naturally beamed in on the bouncy newcomer. Soon, there were stories that this self-confident young woman, who had lived in the 'real' world and knew what it was to work for

Previous page In spite of their very different personalities, Sarah Ferguson and Diana, here at Royal Ascot in 1991, were natural allies. Sarah clearly brought out a playful streak in Diana. **Near right** Sarah (extreme left) aged 10, and Andrew (second left) with the Queen, at Smith's Lawn, Windsor in 1969. **Far right** Sarah's father, Ronald Ferguson, at a polo match with Prince Charles at Windsor in 1988. **Below right** Diana and Sarah at Cowdray Park Polo in July 1981. **Opposite page** Sarah and Diana, heavily pregnant with Prince William, share a chat in June 1982.

a living, would banish the cobwebs from the 'stuffy' royal set-up and smarten up the royal act.

Comparisons with Diana were inevitable, of course. But despite the 'mover and shaker' press image of Sarah, it was assumed that Diana, who now had five years' royal experience behind her, would be the one to lead her new sister-in-law by the hand through the labyrinth of protocol and the logistics of the public engagement scene.

AN UNUSUAL PAST

It did not work out that way at all. Sarah Ferguson came into the Royal Family at a more mature stage in life than Diana. In 1986, she was 26, the same age as Prince Andrew, though she had been born five months before him on 15 October 1959. Her father, Major Ronald Ferguson, was Prince Charles' polo manager and Sarah was used to being around the Royal Family from her early teens.

Later, like Diana, Sarah joined the 'Sloane Ranger' set of well-born girls, whose main aim was having fun. Sarah was one of the Sloanes who worked for a living, in her case at jobs in public relations and publishing, but work, for her, usually took second place to the hectic Sloane brand of social life.

This far, Sarah's life was a predictable one for an upper-class girl with good connections. However, when she became engaged to Prince Andrew and the media starting digging back into her past, they discovered something else: Sarah's years on the loose as a single girl (she had had six more than Diana at the time of her marriage) revealed a background that was unusual for a potential member of the Royal Family.

In 1980, with a friend, Sarah had travelled rough in America, sleeping in bus shelters and raising funds by doing odd jobs like making chocolate-

> ## "You don't need me anymore now you've got Fergie."
> DIANA, TO JOURNALISTS

covered apple strudel in a factory. Later that year, after her American trip was over, Sarah met the motor racing driver Paddy McNally while skiing in Switzerland. McNally was 20 years older than Sarah and a widower with a marriage and two sons already behind him. Sarah fell rapidly in love and longed to marry him, but McNally was not keen. For five years, Sarah hung on, hoping he would change his mind and meanwhile enduring, without fighting back, the insults and humiliations he dealt her. On the face of it, the jolly Sarah she let the outside world see would never have put up with such cavalier treatment.

BROKEN HOME

The fun girl image was a front. Beneath it, as Sarah revealed in her autobiography *My Story*, published in 1996, she was an insecure, fearful character who was, like Diana, the victim of a broken home.

At 13, Sarah was older than Diana had been when her parents' marriage ended, but other dismal details were similar. Like Diana's mother, Sarah's, too, had left her family to marry another man, in

---

⇒ Protocol ⇐

ARISTOCRACY AND GENTRY

Sarah Ferguson was a commoner like Diana, but there was a difference between them. Diana was an aristocrat, while Sarah and her father, Ronald, **right**, *came from the gentry, the rank below the aristocracy.*

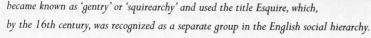

Members of the gentry had no distinct titles, but originally 'gentlemen' were those with the right to bear arms. Later on, in the 14th and 15th centuries, younger sons from aristocratic families, who inherited no titles in their own right, attached themselves to great noble houses or courts, as aides or servants to dukes, earls and other peers. Their descendants became known as 'gentry' or 'squirearchy' and used the title Esquire, which, by the 16th century, was recognized as a separate group in the English social hierarchy.

Left The Royal Family pose for an official photograph on the occasion of Sarah and Andrew's wedding, in July 1986. **Below** Diana, Charles and the Queen Mother in Westminster Abbey. **Bottom** Diana and Charles ride in an open carriage after the wedding. **Opposite page** Diana and Sarah in February 1988 in Klosters, Switzerland.

this case the Argentine polo player Hector Barrantes. Barrantes and the former Mrs Susan Ferguson had married in 1974. Like Diana, too, Sarah and her elder sister Jane were left behind with a father so shocked by his wife's desertion that he became a near-recluse. Ronald Ferguson, like Earl Spencer, married again and in his case began a second family. Like Diana, friends have suggested that Sarah never quite forgave her mother and came out of the trauma of her teenage years craving love, attention and security.

In 1986, it seemed that Sarah was rescued from her sad start in life by the handsome, courtly Prince Andrew. Already acquainted as children, they had met again when Sarah was invited to Charles and Diana's wedding in 1981. Later, Sarah was asked to dances at Windsor Castle and, in 1985, she was invited to spend Ascot Week with the Royal Family.

DIARY DATES

1986

2 March
In Canberra, the Queen signs the Australia Bill, severing Australia's last constitutional links with Britain

19 March
Announcement of the engagement of Prince Andrew and Sarah Ferguson

22-25 April
King Juan Carlos of Spain on first state visit to Britain by a Spanish monarch since 1905

11 June
Prince Andrew opens the Imperial War Museum's new 'superhangar' at Duxford

11 June
Prince and Princess of Wales attend a concert at the Barbican Centre in aid of the Royal College of Music Development Fund and the Musicians' Benevolent Fund

12 June
Princess of Wales presents prizes for the Whitbread Round the World Yacht Race in London

14 July
Princess of Wales attends gala performance of *Onegin* at the London Coliseum

23 July
Wedding of Prince Andrew and Sarah Ferguson

30 July
Prince and Princess of Wales attend the British première of Woody Allen's *Hannah and Her Sisters* in Edinburgh

Diana is said to have played matchmaker, but however that may be, Sarah and Andrew started to take an interest in each other during an Ascot Week dinner at Windsor. At the time, Sarah was still bruised by her hopeless, though not yet ended, romance with Paddy McNally. For her to find a Prince Charming seemed, then, miraculous.

That winter, Sarah became a closer part of the royal scene. She went skiing with Charles and Diana and said 'Yes' when Andrew asked her to marry him at Floors Castle, in Scotland, the home of the Duke and Duchess of Roxburghe.

The wedding of Andrew and Sarah took place at Westminster Abbey on 23 July 1986 and, like

> ## "I'd much rather talk to the Princess of Wales than be nudged in the ribs by Fergie."
>
> A FRIEND OF THE ROYAL FAMILY, ON DIANA AND SARAH

Charles and Diana's wedding five years before, it was treated like a full state occasion. There was the carriage procession, the streets crammed with cheering people, the Royal Family on display in official photographs at Buckingham Palace and the public kiss on the Palace balcony watched by yet more excited crowds.

A DREAM COME TRUE

That morning, it was announced that the Queen had created Andrew 'Duke of York', a traditional title for a monarch's second son, so that when Sarah emerged from the Abbey after the ceremony, she had been transformed into Her Royal Highness the Duchess of York. If it occurred to her then that her nightmares were over and her dreams had come true, it would be hard to blame her.

It had been generally assumed by both the press and public that the new Duchess would be a natural companion for the established Princess. This was not unreasonable. Diana and Sarah were not far apart in age. There was only a 20-month difference between them. They were married to brothers. They would be doing the same sort of public engagements and charity work. They were the chief

Above Sarah gains her pilot's licence at Oxford Airport in February 1987. **Right** An uninhibited kiss for Diana from Sarah as she takes her seat for the Wimbledon Tennis Championships of 1988. **Opposite page** Sarah and Diana discuss the form during a day at the races, the Ever Ready Derby at Epsom in 1987.

female representatives of the younger royals. Consequently, friendship between them seemed logical and Sarah was expected to prove an ally for Diana in 'modernizing' the monarchy...or so the media argument went.

These expectations vastly inflated the power of two young women, however highly placed by marriage they might be, to shift the axis of a long-established monarchy. Its image was rooted not in speculative hopes but in the solid rock of history and tradition. It was never certain that 'modernizing' was what either Diana or Sarah had in mind, or ever dreamed of attempting on the scale being suggested. It was, however, what the media had in mind and what the public, led by the media, seemed to require of them.

THE ROCK OF TRADITION

Apart from being unrealistic in themselves, these notions about the future roles Diana and Sarah would play took no account of factors which stood in the way of such fundamental change. Here, the media appeared amazingly unaware of the effect they were having on Charles and Diana through press speculation about the five-year royal marriage.

In 1986, Charles and Diana were the subjects of intense, and intensely intrusive, gossip about their relationship. The word seemed to be out that their

The Private Princess The holiday that went wrong

When Charles, Diana and their sons holidayed with the Spanish royal family in August 1986, a posse of journalists was shadowing the royal yacht *Fortuna* as it sailed to Cabrera, a small group of islands some 60 miles from Majorca.

There, from a distance, the press watched the royals through field glasses and, according to them, observed some worrying behaviour from Charles and Diana.

They were seen sitting apart, not speaking to each other. If they looked like meeting, one or other of them veered off in another direction. With everyone else on board, Charles and Diana were friendly and relaxed. With each other, they were cold and distant.

This was snooping, of course, but to the press it was indicative: the royal marriage, they concluded, was finished. Press opinion seemed confirmed shortly afterwards when Charles left to

travel back to Scotland, while Diana and their sons remained behind for another two days.

Charles, it was rumoured, was not only returning to his beloved Scotland, but to his beloved

Left *On board the Spanish royal yacht* Fortuna, *in August 1986, Diana tries to get a clearer view of the snooping press pack.*

Camilla. Most startling of all, some might call it most impudent, the press got hold of a story that sexual relations between Charles and Diana came to an end after this Spanish holiday.

Above Diana and Sarah at the family celebrations for the Queen Mother's 86th birthday on 4 August 1986. **Right** Diana and Sarah enjoy each other's company on a skiing holiday at Klosters, the traditional royal winter haunt, in March 1988.

marriage was in deep trouble. Consequently, journalists and photographers who accompanied them on public engagements and holidays kept them under close scrutiny for clues and, apparently, found their suspicions confirmed (see The Private Princess, page 183). The accuracy of the stories was not the only point here. The speculation had the effect of putting Charles and Diana under increasing pressure, whenever they stepped out. Anything they said or did, or were supposed to have said or done, was being constantly raked over. Prisoners being grilled for confessions under a naked light bulb could hardly have been more vulnerable.

Charles, as always, seemed better than Diana at handling it all. He had had far more years than she

IN CONTEXT
THE ROYAL WEDDING YEAR
1986

• US space shuttle *Challenger* explodes on take off

• Three Sikhs sentenced to death in New Delhi for the murder of Prime Minister Indira Gandhi in 1984

• Swedish prime minister, Olaf Palme, assassinated

• Britain and France sign treaty to build the Channel Tunnel

• Royal yacht *Britannia* rescues foreigners stranded in civil war-torn Aden

• Mrs Corazon Aquino sworn in as President of the Philippines

• The Duchess of Windsor, **right,** the wife of the former King Edward VIII, who abdicated the British throne, dies in Paris

IN THE NEWS

A wife for the Duke of York

Royal weddings and press bonanzas have always gone together and the wedding of the Duke and Duchess of York – Andrew and Fergie to the media – produced a mass of enthusiastic coverage. A lot of it was, predictably, over the top, but that was the elated mood of the occasion. With a handsome prince as bridegroom and a sparky, striking-looking redhead as bride, the newspapers could hardly go wrong.

as a focus of press interest and was able to ride the storm of press intrusion. But Diana, always uncomfortable in the media spotlight, appeared to be reacting badly. This was the time when she was reported to be starving herself and running for help to astrologers and alternative therapists.

DISAPPOINTMENT FOR SARAH

However if, by 1986, Diana was as unhappy in her marriage as the media was supposing, the new Duchess of York was not in a position to stage a rescue. Despite the dazzle of her romance, engagement and wedding, Sarah had her own problems and, according to her autobiography, they were deeply worrying. Royal marriage was not turning out as she had expected. On her honeymoon, Sarah wrote, she was much put out when her new husband followed custom on board the royal yacht *Britannia* and invited the ship's officers to dinner every night. Sarah, naturally enough, had expected intimate candlelit evenings. She was also in need of constant reassurance from the man she loved, as she faced new royal duties which she found daunting.

By the autumn of 1986, therefore, when all the excitement was over and the Royal Family went back to business as usual, neither Sarah nor Diana appeared to be in a fit state to rejig the image of the monarchy or give it the youthful pizazz which press and public seemed to expect of them. All they appeared able to think of was how to survive.

Above Diana, Sarah and the two-year-old Prince William enjoy a tour of *HMS Brazen* in February 1986.

Below On a visit to Shetland in July 1986, Diana wears a sensible two-piece with a pleated skirt. **Right** In Scotland again, this time in the Western Isles in 1985, Charles wears a kilt as usual and Diana wears a full-length coat in waxed cotton. **Right, inset** With William and Harry in tweed jackets, Diana wears a double-breasted check two-piece.

Diana looked great in any number of different styles and almost any colour. But one style she did not wear with ease, or indeed very often, was traditional country wear. It was not her fashion scene and she knew it. However, country life, or at least time spent in the country, was a part of the royal social round.

When she was a new young royal, Diana naturally followed the accepted rules for dressing in the country, just as she accepted many things before she began to innovate.

In September 1981, during the last part of their honeymoon at Balmoral, Charles and Diana met the press for a photo call by the River Dee (see page 189). Diana arrived wearing a tweedy skirt and jacket in houndstooth check, with a white blouse underneath. The jacket was a blouson, which Diana wore open at the neck and the skirt had a front pleat. It did absolutely noth-

> **"I was expecting Scottish weather, so I'm wearing thermal underwear."**
> DIANA, ON DRESSING FOR SCOTLAND

ing, though, for her slender figure and not much more for her youth.

Looking too young for some of the clothes she wore was a problem for Diana in her early royal days and traditional country wear was not always made with youth in mind. The colours seemed dreary and Diana never looked entirely at ease in them.

A picture taken by Lord Snowdon ten years after the photo call by the River Dee confirmed this shortfall in Diana's fashion capabilities. The photograph (see Issue 3, page 77) demonstrated Snowdon's great artistry at its best. It showed Charles and Diana with their sons and a horse, in an archetypal country life setting: a picnic beneath a tree. Diana wore tight beige cord trousers, with white open-neck shirt, dark pin-striped jacket and tall, knee-high shiny black boots. Though she appeared elegant, Diana still looked like

Country Wear

Diana in traditional tweedy country wear was not a familiar fashion figure. But 'country wear' could be interpreted in several ways and Diana, who could make fashion whenever she wanted, was not afraid to experiment

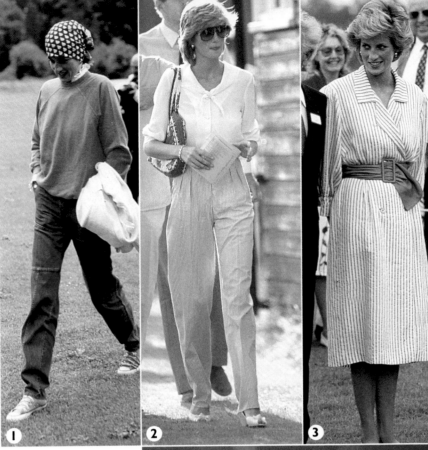

a 'townie' dressing 'country' for the camera.

However, in the decade between the River Dee and the Snowdon sitting, Diana managed to find her own style in country wear. Her idea was to wear colourful, casual and even semi-formal clothes that would challenge the country tweed tradition. It was a daring idea. Royals and aristocrats had donned tweeds for the country for decades, but if anyone could break this habit, Diana could.

At the Braemar Games

Even so, not every country setting had the potential for innovation. This was particularly true of the clothes Diana wore to attend the Braemar Games, a regular September outing for the Royal Family during their summer break at Balmoral. The rule at the Games was tartan, and as September out of doors in Scotland could be chilly, Diana normally appeared well covered up in her tartan outfits. This, however, was limiting.

For her first Braemar Games in 1981, she wore a rust, brown and black tartan dress with a high neck,

> **"Seeing her wear Capri pants when they weren't the most fashionable thing, one realises just how right they were for her."**
>
> JOSEPH ETTEDGUI, FASHION DESIGNER, ON DIANA

long sleeves and a black velvet beret to set it off. Every other part of Diana's wardrobe underwent fundamental change by 1986 and 1987, yet at that stage Braemar was still the odd one out. In 1986, Diana came to the Games in a pleated tartan skirt banded in blue and pink with a white blouse under a warm pink jacket, which had long black lapels and a beret to match. Beside other, high fashion, outfits she wore that year, it looked less than stylish. In fact, the bulkiness of the outfit was somewhat messy.

The following year, Diana seemed to take a fashion step backwards when she appeared in a not very remarkable plum and navy tartan double-breasted suit with a pleated skirt, long revers and matching beret which sported a long feather. It was six years on, yet Diana looked not very different from the

1 Casually dressed at a polo match in pink and white plimsolls, jeans and a pink sweatshirt, Diana hides her hair under a patterned headscarf. 2 Polo at Cowdray Park, Sussex, in July 1983 and Diana wears cool blue and white striped trousers and a light cream blouse. She is carrying a casual quilted floral bag from Souleiado. 3 Diana presents the prizes at a polo match in Melbourne in 1985, wearing a green and white striped dress with a green sash belt. 4 On a visit to the polo field once again, this time with Prince William in 1987, Diana opts for the casual look with white sneakers, pale blue dungarees and a white T-shirt.

BILL PASHLEY SUIT

On honeymoon at Balmoral in 1981, the 20-year-old Diana looked casual and comfortable while on a walk beside the River Dee. She wore this brown and white checked suit by Bill Pashley. Under the blouson-style jacket she wore a white blouse with a mandarin neckline.

RED WOOLLEN COAT AND HAT

Suitably attired for the English weather, Diana was seven months pregnant when she accompanied Prince Charles to the Grand National at Aintree in April 1982. To keep warm, Diana wore this loose-fitting woollen coat in a deep, wine red with a matching hat worn stylishly to one side.

20-year-old in the tartan dress of 1981.

Generally speaking, Scotland put paid to any ideas Diana might have had for making fashion statements with her country wear. This part of the British Isles, though considered by many people to be the most beautiful in the whole country, rarely offered the right kind of weather for anything but the business of keeping warm and dry.

This was brought home to Diana when she visited the Hebrides with Charles in 1985. For a trip across grey choppy waters to Lochmaddy, Diana wrapped herself up in a hefty raincoat with the hood up and a red lifejacket. No chance to show off the wardrobe there, at least not until dry land was reached and Diana was able to reveal a loose-jacketed tartan suit with big blue and pink checks on a black background. With it, Diana wore a bright pink blouse with long ties at the neck. Though it was

eyecatching, this outfit was clearly intended more for warmth than for style. The skirt was full, the jacket rather baggy and to compound matters, the wind blew round both of them, robbing the outfit of any elegance.

At Stornoway, on the Isle of Lewis and Harris, later in the Hebrides tour, Diana wore the plum and navy check suit which appeared again at the 1987 Braemar Games, this time dressed up, not very appropriately, with one of her pearl necklaces.

Other country outings

The Braemar Games was one of three main locales where Diana had to dress for the country life. Another was at home, at Highgrove House in Gloucestershire. The third was Smith's Lawn, near Windsor Castle, where she often went to watch Prince Charles play his beloved chukkas of

1 Accompanied by Sarah Ferguson to polo at Windsor in 1987, Diana wears a jacket and striped trousers. 2 Downdraught from helicopters could be a problem for a princess who wanted to arrive with her hair-do intact. Here Diana tackles the problem with a large headscarf. 3 On a private visit to see a friend at Balmoral in 1988, Diana wears a tweed jacket, cricket pullover and a dark skirt. 4 Visiting the polo at Windsor in 1985, Diana wears jeans and a quilted blue jacket.

polo. The Braemar Games was a semi-official part of the Royal Family calendar. At Highgrove, though, Diana could dress to please herself and please herself she did. There, she was happy to laze around looking like a pretty suburban mum in pink check cropped trousers with a matching pink cardigan and white blouse. She wore rose-spattered trousers with a white shirt, which had rolled up sleeves and one of her favourite frilled collars open at the neck; a white pinafore suit, worn with a white and

> **"She knew what she liked and she could be difficult to sway."**
> ANNA HARVEY, *DEPUTY EDITOR OF* **VOGUE** *MAGAZINE*

peach-striped shirt; and, a little more formally, a cream sweater embroidered in blue and pink with a pleated skirt in kingfisher blue.

Outfits like these provided the vivid colours in which Diana generally looked at her best, something which was not a feature of the muted, rather autumnal, traditional country clothes.

However, it was at Smith's Lawn, Windsor that Diana really let herself go in a series of outfits which showed that any style suited the occasion if she wore it. They were so varied that she pulled surprise after surprise and kept the spectators constantly guessing about what she would wear next.

Polo fashion parade

In 1984, for example, Diana wore a pink and white sailor-style dress and top by Catherine Walker. The following year, 1985, she appeared in more casual gear – a white cotton skirt and blouse with a red cardigan matched by red shoes. The same year, Diana was pictured in 1950s' rock 'n' roll style, with big 'sloppy Joe' sweater, skirt and white ankle socks with polka dots. In 1986, she altered her look to something a bit more 'regulation' for this classy sports event, but not in the least countryfied – pink quilted jacket, white blouse and white skirt with front 'kick' pleats.

In May 1987, Diana watched the polo at Smith's Lawn wearing a lemon double-breasted cotton suit by Bruce Oldfield, with the striking contrast of a

Far left Diana wore this Catherine Walker navy and white jacket with a long pleated skirt when she started the Windsor Pentathlon in July 1988. **1** In 1985, the off-duty Princess looks casual in a red cardigan over a simple white blouse and skirt. **2** At a polo match at Smith's Lawn in July 1986, Diana wears a pretty pink, white and grey quilted jacket with a white shirt and a white skirt with front 'kick' pleats. **3** In a relaxed mood, leaning back against a van as she watches polo at Smith's Lawn, Windsor in June 1987, Diana wears a lemon cotton suit by Bruce Oldfield over a turquoise and mauve spotted silk blouse by Jasper Conran. Her outfit is accompanied by heart-shaped golden earrings.

kingfisher shirt underneath. Then, in July of the same season, she went more casual with a mid-calf length beige pleated skirt and cream blouse with neck ties. A black belt with a big buckle emphasized Diana's slender waist.

It was like a one-woman fashion show of an unusual variety, but a bigger surprise was to come, in May 1988. That month, Diana appeared at her devil-may-care sloppiest, in drainpipe jeans with brown mid-calf boots, baseball cap and her British Lung Foundation sweatshirt (see Issue 2, page 42).

Two months after that, in June 1988, she had switched emphasis yet again. She looked the acme of chic in a vivid red, yellow and blue Bellville Sassoon dress with matching blue shoes. This dress, a favourite of Diana's, made several public appearances, including Diana's attendance at church in Sydney, Australia, during a tour in 1988.

Successes and failures

Scotland was a fashion blind spot for Diana and seemed to trap her in tartans which never quite made it in the fashion stakes. But she certainly showed at Smith's Lawn how almost any type of daywear could look good at a country sports event where more traditional tweedy gear usually had a monopoly. In doing so, Diana moved the parameters of country wear into realms where few others had gone before. But then, that was what a fashion trendsetter was for and what she was very good at.

IN THE NEWS

Dressing traditionally in the early days

Diana the demure appeared with Charles by the River Dee for a date with the press during their honeymoon. This resulting spread from The Sun of 20 August 1981 showed Diana dressed in tweeds to complement the country setting and kilt that Charles always wore when in Scotland. Fishing was a country pursuit that Diana enjoyed, though not with the same passion as Charles. Diana was not a tweedy girl, however, and later, when she shone fashion-wise, it was in very different and much more glamorous outfits.

Spanish

Charles and Diana's four-day tour of Spain in 1987 was more like one of the holidays they had spent previously with their close friends, the Spanish Royal Family

Splendour

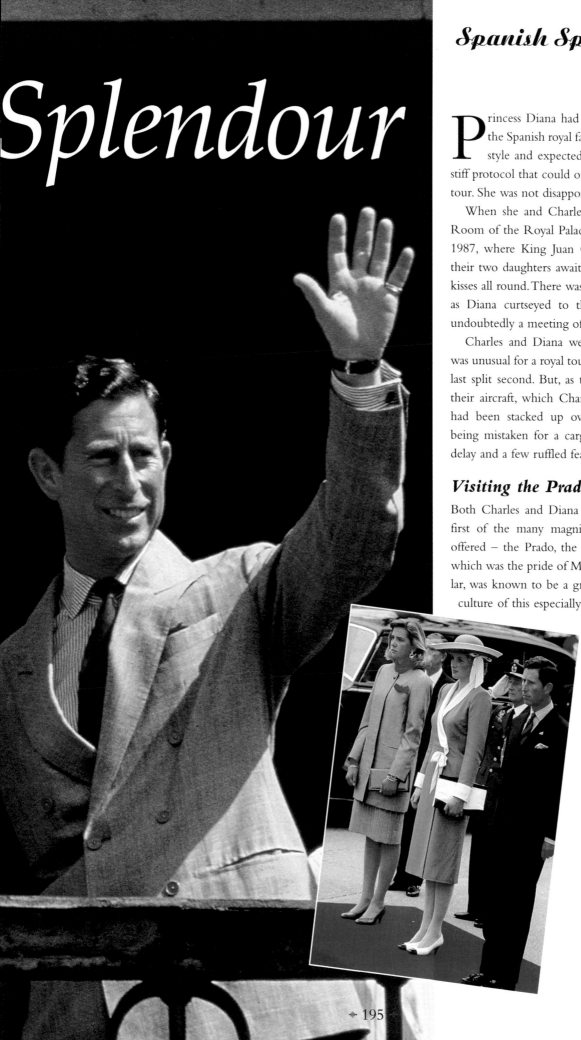

P rincess Diana had long been an admirer of the Spanish royal family's informal easygoing style and expected none of the red tape or stiff protocol that could often mark an official royal tour. She was not disappointed.

When she and Charles arrived in the Tapestry Room of the Royal Palace in Madrid on 21 April 1987, where King Juan Carlos, Queen Sofia and their two daughters awaited them, it was hugs and kisses all round. There was just a touch of formality as Diana curtseyed to the Queen, but this was undoubtedly a meeting of old friends.

Charles and Diana were 15 minutes late. That was unusual for a royal tour which was timed to the last split second. But, as they hastened to explain, their aircraft, which Charles was piloting himself, had been stacked up over Madrid Airport after being mistaken for a cargo plane. It had meant a delay and a few ruffled feathers all round.

Visiting the Prado

Both Charles and Diana were anxious to see the first of the many magnificent experiences Spain offered – the Prado, the world famous art gallery which was the pride of Madrid. Charles, in particular, was known to be a great enthusiast for art and culture of this especially exalted kind. Diana, too, was fascinated by the exhibits at the Prado and proved no slouch, either, when it came to being well informed about them. She showed especial interest in the

Opposite page Charles and Diana and their guide, Doña Cristina, the younger daughter of King Juan Carlos of Spain, wave to a crowd in Salamanca on 22 April. **Left** The royal couple, accompanied by Doña Cristina once more, are welcomed on a visit to the Prado Museum in Madrid on 21 April.

two pictures known as the *Majas*, painted between 1800 and 1805, which were two paintings of the same woman by one of Spain's premier artists, Francisco Goya. One of the Majas was clothed. The other was nude and Diana was amused to learn that Goya had concealed the nude painting beneath the clothed one in the same frame, hiding it from Spanish government officials on the lookout for pornography.

King Juan Carlos had assigned his daughters Doña Elena, 23, a teacher, and Doña Cristina, 21, a political science student, to act as Charles and Diana's guides. Unfortunately, their brother, Don Felipe,

Juan Carlos' heir, was on the other side of the Atlantic on a foreign tour of his own. Felipe was in the Spanish Navy and his ship was paying a courtesy call to Rio de Janeiro in Brazil.

Gibraltar dispute

Six years earlier, there had been some disappointment when the Spanish King and Queen had been unable to accept an invitation to Charles and Diana's wedding. The reason had been Gibraltar, the subject of a longstanding dispute between Britain and Spain and the controversial departure point for Charles and Diana's honeymoon cruise. Fortunately, the Gibraltar problem had cooled off

in the intervening years and in 1987 there were no political embarrassments to get in the way.

The accent of the Spanish tour was, of course, on the magnificent artistic and architectural heritage of Spain, which went a great deal further than the paintings in the Prado. Charles had a little business to do: at a meeting with Spanish manufacturers and

> "*The Princess recognized every (painting by) Velasquez and Goya before I could say a word.*"
> GUIDE AT THE PRADO, ON DIANA

exporters, he urged on them the benefits of investing their money through the City of London.

After that, though, nothing stood between Charles and Diana and the wonders they had come to see. Among the first was the most flamboyant entertainment Spain had to offer; a display of flamenco dancing at a Madrid restaurant well known for this traditional Spanish entertainment.

Diana loved dancing and was normally up on her feet and on the dance floor at the first opportunity. But this time, she resisted the temptation to join in. Flamenco is a specialized and complex form of dance, requiring long training and experience to

Charles and Diana savoured the warm, vibrant Spanish culture. **Above** Diana, wearing a traditional cloak, given as a gift by her hosts, is entertained by a Flamenco band in Salamanca. **Inset left** Diana curtseys to King Juan Carlos at the Oriente Palace, Madrid, as she and Charles attend lunch. **Above right** Diana and Charles watched a display of Flamenco dancing in Madrid.

❦ Protocol ❦

ALL IN THE FAMILY

The British and Spanish royal families are related through their ancestry from Queen Victoria (1819-1901).

*In 1906, Princess Victoria Eugenie (Ena), seen **right** aged 71, one of Victoria's granddaughters, married King Alfonso XIII of Spain. Alfonso and Queen Ena became the grandparents of the present King of Spain, Juan Carlos. Juan Carlos' wife, Queen Sofia, is another of Victoria's descendants, through her mother Queen Frederika of Greece. Frederika's maternal grandfather, Kaiser Wilhelm II of Germany, was the old Queen's first grandchild. Queen Elizabeth II and King Juan Carlos are therefore second cousins three times removed. Sofia is Queen Elizabeth's second cousin four times removed and Sofia and her husband are related in the same way.*

Above Charles and Diana accompanied King Juan Carlos, Queen Sofia and their two daughters to visit the cathedral in Salamanca.

Top right Charles and Diana, flanked by both the King's daughters, Doña Elena (left) and Doña Cristina (right), were guests of the Spanish Royal Family at the Ritz Hotel in Madrid.

Bottom right An impressive military parade was laid on for Charles and Diana, during their stay in Madrid.

perform. Diana was content to sit and watch as the dancers, in their elaborate frilled costumes, whirled and stamped their feet in time to the music.

There was another reason for her sitting this one out, though: the heat. Diana always had a tendency to wilt when temperatures rose too high and could suffer quite badly from heat exhaustion. Temperatures in the nineties were not uncommon for Madrid, even as early in the year as April.

Visiting Salamanca

Next day, 22 April, Charles and Diana were driven to Salamanca, a city of great antiquity 130 miles from Madrid, in the Leon province. Crowds were out in force to see them and Charles and Diana received an excited and enthusiastic welcome. Salamanca was full of marvellous sights to see: the bridge built by the Romans when Spain was part of the Roman Empire 2000 years ago, a 12th-century Romanesque cathedral, the 16th-century Casa de las Conchas, which, as its name suggests, has a façade covered in shells.

Once again, though, it was intensely hot and, at

one point, Diana nearly fainted. She leaned against a wall, trying to recover her composure, and though she carried on, she half collapsed into a pew while touring the cathedral. This time, she took a quiet 10-minute break and a glass of water and was afterwards able to go on to pay a visit to the University of Salamanca, the oldest university in Europe.

> *"She is so pale, so thin,*
> *but so elegant."*
> SPANISH SOCIALITE, ON DIANA

There, Diana cheered up considerably when some of the students, dressed in traditional troubadour outfits, complete with cloaks and roses, serenaded her as she ate a long, leisurely lunch. The students gallantly threw down cloaks on the ground for Diana to walk on. Someone had obviously told them about the time when, historically, Sir Walter Raleigh did the same thing for Queen Elizabeth I 400 years ago, to stop her getting her feet wet.

The friendly jollity, the lilting Spanish music and

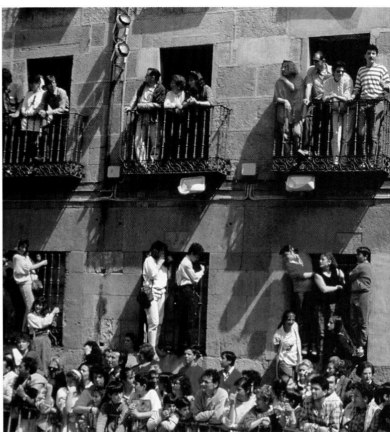

the enthusiasm of the crowds for their English visitors certainly made Diana perk up and she finished the visit to Salamanca looking a lot better.

Afterwards, it was back to Madrid where Diana visited a British Fashion Show. Unfortunately, the heat still seemed to be troubling her, all the more so because she was not wearing her coolest clothes, but mainly suits which did nothing for ventilation.

The drive to Toledo

The 24 April, the last day of the tour, was like a big family outing. King Juan Carlos' gold-painted minibus was made ready and everyone piled in for the drive to Toledo, with the King himself at the wheel. Toledo, lying 40 miles to the southwest of Madrid in the province of New Castille, was a welcome relief for Diana: it was high up in the mountains where the air was a lot cooler. Like Salamanca, Toledo was already a substantial town at the time of the Roman Empire. There was a 13th-century cathedral with colourful and delicate stained glass windows, tapestries and paintings by great artists – Goya again, El Greco, whose house in

Toledo was a museum, and the Dutch painter Rubens. The Moors from North Africa, who ruled Spain for nearly 800 years until the 15th century, had left behind two impressive bridges.

The next day Charles and Diana were in Toledo. There, a lucky group of American tourists joined

Above left Diana chats to models at a fashion show in Madrid. **Above** Enthusiastic Spaniards used every vantage point to catch a glimpse of Charles and Diana.

IN THE NEWS

The press smell a marriage rift

Charles and Diana's visit to Spain in April 1987 had a troubled undercurrent, already detected by journalists. When James Whitaker, royal correspondent of the Daily Mirror, wrote this piece after snooping on the Wales' holiday in Majorca in 1986, he already knew, he said, how discordant relations between Charles and Diana were. In fact, Whitaker believed the royal marriage was already dead. For him, the question in the headline hardly needed asking.

She bops, he mopes.. Royal odd couple go separate ways

ARE CHARLES AND DI STILL IN TUNE?

Above This has the air of a holiday snap on the royals' day out to Toledo. From left, Doña Cristina, Queen Sofia, Prince Charles, Princess Diana, King Juan Carlos and Doña Elena. **Below** The royal couple were swamped by a sea of wellwishers during a walkabout through the historic centre of Salamanca, on 22 April.

an ever-growing crowd of Spaniards who trailed the royal party as they wandered round. Security was tight, but not unusually so in a country where Basque separatist terrorists had been active for nearly 60 years. In one of the many craft shops Prince Charles bought a flowerpot for the garden at Highgrove House and Queen Sofia bought gifts for Charles and Diana, including a traditional Toledo gold inlaid plate, a coffee set and a painting.

Toledo saw the end of the four-day tour, and it was then that Charles and Diana said goodbye to the Spanish royals. As Juan Carlos drove his family back to Madrid, Charles and Diana flew south to the magnificent Moorish city of Granada for a quiet

> **"I wouldn't have thought I was a target, but if your name is on the bullet, there's nothing you can do about it."**
>
> CHARLES, ON THE BASQUE SEPARATIST TERRORISTS IN SPAIN

weekend with their friends, the Marquess of Douro and his wife Antonia. The short break gave Charles a chance for some sketching. When abroad he tried never to miss out on sessions at the easel and intended to go on to Italy for more sketching.

Diana was to return straight home, but not before a couple of days' sunbathing. The 1987 tour of Spain may have been brief, but it was impressive. It gave Charles and Diana plenty to think about and remember as they stored the fascinations of Spain among their other royal memories.

LIFE AT KENSINGTON PALACE

With other royals, Charles, Diana and their sons lived in Kensington Palace when they were in London. 'KP', as they nicknamed it, was much more homely than the word 'palace' suggests

Kensington Palace is probably nobody's idea of a palace. The royal homes inside are called apartments, but no one could compare them to ordinary flats. The Palace complex is more like an enclave, providing London homes for 14 members of the Royal Family.

Charles and Diana moved to Kensington Palace in May 1982, the month before the birth of Prince William. Kensington Palace was home, too, to Princess Margaret, and Prince and Princess Michael of Kent and their two children. Richard, Duke of Gloucester, the Queen's first cousin, and the Duchess, Birgitte, their three children and Princess Alice, the Duke's mother, occupied 35 rooms, ten more than Charles and Diana. Diana's sister Jane and her husband Sir Robert Fellowes,

the Queen's private secretary, lived with their children in the Palace precincts, in a 'grace and favour' house called 'The Old Barracks'.

CINDERELLA AMONG PALACES

KP, the nickname by which residents call it, or the 'Aunt Heap', so-called by King Edward VIII because so many of his elderly royal relatives lived there, is something of a Cinderella among the three central London palaces. St. James' Palace, where Charles and his sons now live, is older and, nominally, the headquarters of the British monarchy. Foreign ambassadors to Britain are accredited to the 'Court of St. James'. Buckingham Palace, formerly Buckingham House, is, of course, the Queen's official London residence and it put Kensington Palace in the shade as long ago as 1762 when King George III began to develop it.

KP, though, was always a favourite with royals. Today, it stands in one of the busiest and most affluent districts of London and is very handy for Knightsbridge, where Diana loved to shop in the many smart boutiques and department stores. The

rebuild KP. It was supposed to be on a modest and intimate scale, rather than a grand one, although another £101,000 had to be spent before the Palace was considered fit for royals to live in.

The Palace was provided with an orangery, gardens, the Round Pond and the Serpentine. Later, King George III gave apartments in Kensington Palace to his brothers. His granddaughter, later Queen Victoria, was born and brought up there, and when she came to the throne, held her first Privy Council of royal advisers at Kensington Palace on the day of her accession, 20 June 1837. She was so fond of the place that it took some hard

> **"It's a royal rabbit warren."**
> CHARLES, ON KENSINGTON PALACE

persuasion on the part of her ministers to get her to move to Buckingham Palace.

By the time Charles and Diana arrived, Kensington Palace already breathed much royal history. But it had a family feel to it as well. The building was of red mellow-stoned brick with a cobbled courtyard. The grounds looked especially lovely in the spring, when hundreds of tulips flowered in the Dutch garden. Roses, honeysuckle and lavender growing in the gardens used to perfume the rooms. There was a chiming clock and, in an old-fashioned but romantic touch, gas lamps, which softly illuminated the buildings and their environs.

PLENTY OF PARKING

One sign of royal business was the line of black official cars, which were parked there ready to whisk royals off on official engagements or private excursions. When friends called, there were plenty of parking spaces for them.

Charles used to park his beloved Aston Martin there, too. Diana was often seen in the parking lot saying goodbye to friends. She usually entertained them to lunch in the Palace if there were no engagements for her to attend. Diana was said to have a habit of sitting on her friends' car bonnets while chatting to them before they parted. Apparently, she did the same to her husband's Aston Martin which had a brilliant shine of which he was

Opening page Diana with the young princes seated at the piano she herself played. **Opposite, top** Diana at her desk. **Left** Princess Diana with the baby Prince William. **Above** Charles and Diana pose for a photo in front of the drawing room's tall marble fireplace.

setting was completely different three centuries ago when William III purchased Kensington Palace for £18,900 in 1689, the year he became King. The building was then known as Nottingham House. Kensington was in the countryside then, and King William chose it because of its fresh air and the fact that London was not too far away

The renowned architect, Sir Christopher Wren, who designed St. Paul's Cathedral, where Charles and Diana were married in 1981, was called in to

very proud. More than once, it appears, he told Diana to get off the bonnet in case she dented it.

Charles and Diana's apartments, Numbers 8 and 9, were spread over three storeys in an L-shaped house and had a relaxed and homely atmosphere much like that of a country mansion, despite the imposing portraits of his royal ancestors which decorated the staircase landings. One of them was of King George III's grandfather, George II, who made his own mark on Kensington: he designed the 275-acre Kensington Gardens. George II and his father, George I, had other uses for the apartments later occupied by Charles and Diana. They kept their mistresses there. Over two centuries later and nine and ten generations on, Prince Charles, direct descendant of the two Georges, had a helicopter pad in the Palace grounds for quick exits when on official business, or when heading for the polo field or sessions of sketching and painting in the country.

BOMB DAMAGE

During the Second World War, the Palace was so badly damaged by fire-bombs during the 'blitz', the German air raid campaign on London, that it was virtually derelict for 30 years after hostilities ended in 1945. Restoration work did not begin until 1975, and was still going on when Charles and Diana married six years later. That explained the ten months they spent living at Buckingham Palace before they were able to move in.

The rebuilt apartments gave Charles and Diana plenty of room for themselves, their family and their

Above Prince William and Prince Harry on rocking horses in the playroom at Kensington Palace. The room is conspicuously neat. **Above right** Diana helps William with some puzzles in the playroom. **Right** Charles, Diana and William in the gardens at KP.

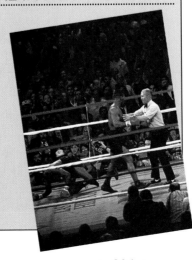

IN CONTEXT 1986 TYSON IS HEAVYWEIGHT CHAMP

• Mike Tyson, 20, becomes youngest world heavyweight boxing champion **(right)**
• Benazir Bhutto jailed in Pakistan
• Arab terrorist bomb explodes in a Paris department store
• Cary Grant, film star, dies aged 77
• Chinese students lead democracy protests in Shanghai
• 'Big Bang' at the London Stock Exchange as computers are introduced on 27 October

of his public activities. Diana had her own sitting room, with wallpaper decorated with Prince of Wales' feathers, where she met with her ladies-in-waiting and other staff and sometimes her dress designers, too.

The sitting room was very much a family place, though. Here, Diana, a keen amateur photographer, kept family pictures which she took herself, as well as some of the souvenirs she and Charles had brought back from their foreign tours. There was a

> "*Diana and I each have such busy schedules that if we shared a room we would only get under each other's feet.*"
>
> CHARLES, ON SEPARATE BEDROOMS

piano which Diana often played and an indispensable piece of equipment to such busy people as the Prince and Princess of Wales: the video recorder they used to make sure they would not miss too many favourite programmes while out on public engagements. Both Charles and Diana were keen film buffs. Charles, in fact, was patron of the British Film Institute. He and Diana frequently watched videos as well as films recorded off the television.

For entertaining at Kensington Palace, Charles and Diana had their yellow-decorated drawing

live-in staff, including aides who worked in offices on the ground floor until the move to St. James' Palace in 1989. As was usual in royal and aristocratic circles, Charles and Diana had separate bedrooms, each with its own bathroom and dressing room. Diana slept in a vast bed, the 7½-foot-wide four-poster that Charles had once used in Buckingham Palace and which he brought over to Kensington Palace specially for her. These private quarters also included large dressing rooms for Diana's extensive wardrobe and a room which housed Charles' numerous service uniforms.

Their apartments provided space, too, for Charles and Diana to do some of their work. Charles had a study on the first floor, where he worked on speeches, conferred with aides and organized much

IN THE NEWS

Charles admits talking to trees

The media have never really understood Prince Charles, or maybe they haven't wanted to. When he talks of intellectual matters, like his love of the countryside and his attachment to Highgrove House, for instance, they tend to treat the heir to the throne as some kind of 'kook'. This article about Charles and Highgrove, published in September 1986, seemed straightforward enough. But what grabbed the headlines in the tabloids was his revelation that he talked to trees.

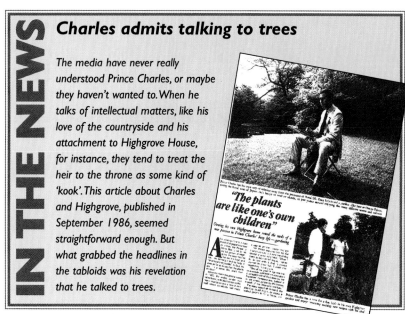

"The plants are like one's own children"

Right inset A statue of
William III in the gardens at
KP, the palace he bought.
Right A planning meeting in
the dining room, attended by
Sir John Riddell and Anne
Beckwith-Smith.
Below right Charles and
the princes at the ceremony
of Beating the Retreat
outside Kensington Palace.

room for receptions, with space for up to 60 people, and a dining room with a 16-place circular table for more intimate suppers with friends or people involved with them in charities and other organizations. Dinners began promptly at 8.30 and usually ended no later than 11 pm.

Charles and Diana were very careful to select menus that would please everyone: big steak meals, for instance, for those with large appetites and no weight problems, but lighter soups, salads, yoghurt and water ices for the more figure-conscious. One

> ### "It's the place where you can hide all your royal skeletons in one cupboard."
> *PRINCE PHILIP, ON KENSINGTON PALACE*

item was never on the menu, though: chips, which both Charles and Diana disliked for health reasons.

The third floor at Kensington Palace provided staff accommodation and the second, a nursery suite and playroom for William and Harry. At Diana's insistence, this was kept much tidier than little boys normally managed, left to themselves. William and Harry had to put their toys away neatly in red racks after a session in the playroom. The boys' rocking horse, sofa and table were, it appears, regularly sponged down after the boys had finished.

Charles and Diana used their roof to provide a private area for relaxation. Charles, a country lover, had a microcosm of the gardens at Highgrove in a special greenhouse on the roof, which also featured a sun terrace and a barbecue. Here, Charles liked to turn chef: he cooked salmon steaks – not barbecued

Protocol

IN ORDER OF IMPORTANCE

Some 22 members of the Royal Family take their places – for example, when receiving foreign heads of state – in a strict order of precedence:
1 The Queen **2** Prince Philip **3** The Queen Mother
4 Prince Charles **5** Princess Diana (when married)
6 The Duke of York **7** The Duchess of York (when married) **8** Prince Edward **9** Princess Anne
10 Prince William **11** Prince Harry **12** Princess Beatrice **13** Princess Eugenie **14** Princess Margaret **15** Princess Alice of Gloucester
16 The Duke of Gloucester **17** The Duchess of Gloucester **18** The Duke of Kent **19** The Duchess of Kent
20 Prince Michael of Kent **21** Princess Michael of Kent **22** Princess Alexandra of Kent.
The children of Princess Anne, Princess Margaret, the Duke and Duchess of Gloucester and the Kent children are not of royal rank and so are not included in the listing.

meat steaks, which he and Diana normally avoided – and jacket potatoes for the boys.

When Prince William was four or five, he loved to explore Kensington Palace, and was often seen hovering in the background when the Wales' butler, Harold Brown, opened the door to visitors.

TIGHT SECURITY

Like all royal residences, Kensington Palace has a tight security net, with all manner of surveillance devices, including laser beams, heat-seeking devices and radio-tracking equipment in all cars, round-the-clock patrols with dogs in the grounds and a manned steel barrier at the end of the long drive.

Despite the bustle of its surroundings, KP retains something of the serenity of the countryside it once possessed for real, before London spread out from the bounds of William III's day and absorbed it into the great conurbation of the capital.

The Private Princess
Diana's Astrologer

Above The astrologer Penny Thornton, who was introduced to Diana by her sister-in-law, Sarah Ferguson.

Royals have always had their aides, advisers and officials. However, the so-called 'gurus' whom Diana consulted, including her astrologer, were in a different category.

A guru is a spiritual guide or mentor in Hinduism, the majority religion of India. Though there was no religious angle to it, Diana's gurus seemed to perform a similar function and, by 1986, she appears to have felt a great need for their services.

At that time, Diana was reportedly an extremely unhappy woman. For comfort and reassurance, it appears, she consulted the astrologer Penny Thornton, who later wrote about her six-year involvement with the Princess in her book *From Diana with Love*, published in 1995.

According to Penny Thornton, Diana was certain she would never be Queen and Charles would never be King. The astrologer warned Diana to be careful whom she trusted and said she foresaw the break-up of Diana's marriage. All this was very far from the usual role of a royal adviser, and the Royal Family were said to see something much more sinister and unsettling in it. Penny Thornton's explanation that Diana simply wanted to get in touch with her future did nothing to calm royal anxieties.

Evening Class

Diana became a fashion icon not only because she dressed beautifully and looked fabulous in anything she wore but also because she created new fashions, especially in evening wear. Some of her outfits were both clever and daring

Left At the première of *Dangerous Liaisons*, in 1989, Diana wears a strapless black velvet dinner dress by Victor Edelstein. **Above** In 1989 the difference in royal style is clear from this shot of Princess Margaret in a ballgown, while Diana sports a cream and salmon pink Catherine Walker dress. **Right** At another première, Diana wears a cream silk chiffon Catherine Walker dress with a Tudor neckline.

Of all the many stunning outfits Diana wore, her evening dresses were the ones which most often typified the beautiful, glamorous fairytale princess. However, not every after-dark engagement lent itself to the grand evening dress treatment. There were cocktail parties, film premières, concerts, some theatre and opera house visits and more informal dinners where the great ball gowns would not only have been inappropriate, but somewhat unmanageable.

It was the less grand occasions which gave Diana the chance to innovate, and so make a fashion mark that was distinctly hers. One example was the long satin, blue and crimson check evening dress, by Bellville Sassoon, which Diana wore to a reception in London in March 1988. The dress raised eyebrows when Diana appeared, and well it might. It looked exactly like a long dressing gown. The material was more fancy and the colours brighter, but a dressing gown it undoubtedly was.

Only a fashion-confident person would have had the nerve to wear such a mundane piece of clothing and turn it into a fashionable outfit, and by 1988 Diana had acquired an assurance which did not exist in her earlier royal years. This is why her most striking experiments with evening wear date from the later years of her time as Princess of Wales. She

> ## "She wanted to wear British because it was something positive she could do for the fashion industry."
> ANNA HARVEY, DEPUTY EDITOR OF VOGUE

had to be mature and self-assured to carry off some of the more adventurous outfits.

At times, Diana achieved a 'grand occasion' look without wearing full-blown evening wear. She managed this on a visit to a Sydney variety show in January 1988, by wearing a short-skirted two-piece suit in lace and satin. Designed by Victor Edelstein, the brilliant gold colour was the key to the glamour. Edged at neckline and hem with lace, and featuring a jacket that looked as smooth as gold leaf, this suit would not have made such an impact in any other colour, even using the same materials.

The demure look

Around this time, Diana, though by now 26 years old, was still capable of appearing demure by night. In 1987 she wore a pink duchess satin gown by Catherine Walker to a ballet performance in Berlin, during her tour of Germany. The dress had a wide white shawl collar, long sleeves with white cuffs and a very full skirt flowing out from the hipline. The next year, in March 1988, Diana seemed to have retreated backwards fashion-wise in a modest little number that looked like mama's idea of how a well-brought-up young lady should dress: at a ballet gala in London, Diana's dress, again by Catherine Walker, was a mid-calf length white silk gown with a shawl collar that made her look as if she had just changed out of her school uniform.

The impression was deceptive. The next time Diana appeared, after wearing these more demure

1 Attending the Newspaper Society Dinner at London's Hilton Hotel, Diana arrives in a Zandra Rhodes pink silk chiffon dress with zigzag hem, first worn in Japan in 1986. 2 In Rio de Janeiro, Brazil in 1991, Diana wears a three-quarter length sari-inspired silk chiffon dress by Gina Frattini.

3 In Paris in 1995, Diana wears a Christian Lacroix bright red cocktail dress, trimmed with a large bow at the bust. The hem finishes just above the knee. 4 At Osterley House in Middlesex, for a charity ball in May 1989, Diana wears a long blue sequinned dinner dress that is split up to the knee and has a plunging neckline. It was created by Catherine Walker and first worn in Vienna in 1986.

5 In June 1989, at the Barbican, London, Diana wears a black and white cocktail dress by Bellville Sassoon and Lorcan Mullany. The black lace bodice is embroidered with black sequins and has a white satin collar trimmed with a central bow. 6 At a dinner in honour of the Australian Prime Minister, Bob Hawke, in London in 1986, Diana wears an unusual blue silk gown with one bare shoulder. She wears it with the Spencer tiara.

CATHERINE WALKER COCKTAIL DRESS

This short, draped cocktail dress in grey silk is embroidered all over with glass beads in a scrolling pattern. It has a halterneck with a plunging V-neckline, and the hem finishes well above the knee. Diana wore it to a reception at the Serpentine Gallery in London in 1995. At the Christie's charity auction in June 1997, the dress was sold for $77,300.

TRADITIONAL SHALWAR KAMEEZ

Diana was given this cream pearl-embroidered shalwar kameez – a traditional Muslim dress – by Jemima Khan, while visiting Lahore in Pakistan to raise money for her husband, Imran's cancer hospital. Here Diana wears it at a fund-raising charity evening at the Dorchester, London, in 1996, in aid of Khan's hospital.

1 Wearing the Spencer family tiara, Diana is dressed in a full-length, 1930s-inspired, fuschia pink silk evening gown by Victor Edelstein in Budapest in 1992. **2** At Sadler's Wells for an evening of ballet, Diana wears a cream satin and lace cocktail suit by Bruce Oldfield.

Left At The Savoy, in London, with Prince Charles, for a gala dinner in March 1989, Diana wears a Catherine Walker dress that was first seen in the Gulf in 1986. Then it had a high neck and long sleeves, in keeping with local Muslim custom, but the designer altered it to create a strapless, low-cut figure-hugging pale blue chiffon and lace evening dress.

dresses, she could look totally different and much more sexy. Diana was infinitely more daring than was usual with royal ladies when it came to revealing parts of the royal anatomy. It went a great deal further than the low-cut, sometimes dangerously low-cut, necklines she wore, showing more cleavage and much more shoulder and leg than royals normally permitted themselves. One outfit of this kind was the black silk, off-the-shoulder dress, with large gold buttons and a very, very short skirt, by Edelstein, with which Diana wowed Parisians in November 1988, soon after appearing so demure.

Slit to the waist

Diana went a lot further, though, when she wore a white, long-sleeved, wide-shouldered top with a long pink skirt that looked quite 'regulation' until she turned round and was seen from the back. The top was slit all the way down to her waist. What was more, the skirt was slit to match. As she walked up the steps into the Royal Opera House, Covent Garden, in 1988, the back seam ended about four inches above her knee. Below that, the skirt parted to give a grandstand view of Diana's legs.

This was not the only daringly split skirt Diana wore. Her burgundy evening gown, embroidered with white and gold flowers, worn in 1986 to the London première of the film *Steel Magnolias*, had a skirt slit up the back to the knee (see page 215). A similar effect, though not quite so dramatic, was

IN THE NEWS

Embarrassing revelations

Diana broke down many barriers in her royal years. But the 'show a leg' incident, reported by Jean Rook in the Daily Express of 18 November 1986, was an unfortunate slip. The usual rule was to observe local customs of dress. Diana did so, but as she stepped from the plane onto the tarmac at Riyadh Airport, to meet her Saudi Arabian hosts, the wind caught her extra long skirt, blowing it up to reveal a flash of leg and underskirt. Diana blushed. The caption notes that this was only the second time King Fahd had been photographed with a woman.

Di's leg show is a real eye-opener for the Saudi stag party

1 In Australia in 1988, Diana wears a double-breasted royal blue jacket and blue chiffon skirt. 2 On an official visit to Brazil in 1991, Diana wears a long evening dress in ivory silk crêpe with pink sequins. This one-sleeved dress was by Catherine Walker. 3 At The Guildhall, London, Diana wears a midnight blue outfit with a velvet top. 4 A Catherine Walker dress, first worn by Diana to a gala dinner in Toronto in 1986. It has an asymmetric bodice of black faille. **Opposite page** The dress, by Catherine Walker, worn to *Steel Magnolias* in 1990. Under a tail coat jacket in burgundy velvet, heavily embroidered with flowers and leaves in simulated pearls, the dress is full length and strapless.

achieved with the blue and cream dress she wore to the London première of *Far and Away* in 1992. This dress had a novel 'tulip' skirt, formed by two overlapping folds in the front which met just below Diana's knees, contrasting with the long back. Nothing too daring there, until the cream halterneck top caught the eye. The top was swathed down over the hips, echoing the tulip shape, and at the neck was cut just about as far as it could reasonably go, revealing bronzed shoulders and cleavage.

Bow ties and tuxedos

These and other revealing dresses were the epitome of femininity. Yet Diana was capable of adopting male dress and turning it into evening suits which looked entirely appropriate on her.

In Portugal, in 1987, Diana wore a brilliant orange satin jacket with wide lapels, and no jewellery apart from her ever-present earrings, to a ballet performance in Lisbon. But around her neck, where any other woman would have worn a necklace, was a large black bow tie. The following year, when she went to the Wembley Greyhound Stadium, Diana went the whole hog, in a tuxedo outfit complete with a black under-the-collar bow tie, white shirt and a brilliant green waistcoat. With

canny fashion sense, Diana resisted wearing her earrings, but the effect was in no way masculine.

This was the latest in a long line of tuxedo outfits which Diana had begun to wear in 1984. In February of that year, she appeared at a rock concert in Birmingham wearing a straightforward 'steal' from the men's outfitters: a suit designed by

> *"Anything the Princess of Wales wears immediately became the height of fashion."*
> JOHN BOYD, HAT DESIGNER, ON DIANA

Margaret Howell, with white jacket, straight-legged trousers, white blouse and a black satin bow tie.

Her most important secret was always to have the unexpected up her sleeve. Demure one evening, she could be outlandish the next. She crossed all accepted barriers for royal evening wear, successfully appropriated male dress, then reverted again to the glamorous, ultra-feminine princess.

It was quite a trick, and Diana achieved something royal ladies had never managed before – she kept the fashion pundits guessing and hit them with one surprise after another, week after week.

The Common Touch

Diana had a remarkable talent for reaching out to people and making them feel she was interested. Though an aristocrat, she seemed like an ordinary girl and the people loved her for it

The British have always liked their royals to have the common touch, the ability to connect with ordinary people and sympathize with their problems, yet at the same time retain royal dignity. The Queen and her family, most especially the Queen Mother, proved very good at being royals of this kind, but Diana brought the royal common touch to a new and different level.

A gift to the press

When she became Princess of Wales, the fuss that was made of her was phenomenal. Her popularity was instant and curiosity about her was unprecedented. The press sensed that here was the new star the Royal Family had not seen for over a century: a very young, beautiful, appealing girl, who had stepped from obscurity into the limelight of a great destiny. She was so sweet and lovely that spinning the story of a fairytale marriage was the easiest task journalists had had for decades.

The royals themselves had seen similar excitement before, at coronations and at royal weddings, where the normally

Opposite page On a visit to Bristol, in May 1989, Diana goes walkabout, chatting to members of a happy, flag-waving crowd. **Below** On a tour of India in February 1992, Diana once again has a child on her lap, this time a young girl who is wearing her finest traditional costume.

Above During a visit to Cornwall, Diana chats to a young mother with a child in her arms. **Above right** At a military ceremony in Portsmouth, in August 1991, Diana talks readily to one of her hosts.

uptight British were fired by emotion and enthusiasm that reached near-hysterical proportions. When the event which had set all this off had ebbed away, the high emotion subsided and normal everyday life resumed once more.

This is what many people, especially court officials, believed would happen once the novelty of Diana had worn off. They expected her to fade eventually into the Royal Family background and perform her duties, support her husband, produce her children and ultimately become Queen Consort without making any undue waves.

Diana-mania

This notion could not have been more wrong. Diana-mania, as the tidal wave of her popularity was called, was no passing phase. The shy, gawky, schoolgirlish Diana seemed an unlikely candidate for it, but she had it in her to become the greatest royal celebrity Britain had ever known.

One reason for this was the unexpectedness of Diana. Here was an aristocratic girl of fine lineage, reared in wealth and comfort. She had led a comparatively sheltered life and despite the misfortune of her parents' divorce, was assured of material

security for as long as she lived. Life had placed her in a protected, privileged position even before she married Prince Charles.

In these circumstances, had Diana turned out to be a well-meaning, dutiful and gracious princess,

> **"She was just like one of the girls. She came in and put her handbag down and chatted to me like an old friend."**
>
> EIRA THOMPSON, 88, PATIENT IN LIVERPOOL WOMEN'S HOSPITAL

no one could reasonably have expected more of her. In the event, they got a great deal more.

Quite unexpectedly, Diana displayed a natural empathy with ordinary people whose lives were quite different from hers. It had been said of the Queen Mother, from the time she was a young girl, that she could talk to someone and make them feel they were the only person in the world in whom she was interested. Diana had the same talent. When people in a crowd looked at Diana, they saw, not a grand young lady with all that money could buy,

Above During the royal tour to India with Prince Charles, in February 1992, Diana squats to talk to a group of children. **Left** While visiting a school for the deaf, Diana inspects some of the things the children have made. **Following page** While on the tour of Canada, in 1991, Diana is snapped as just one of the girls.

but a sweet, charming, vulnerable girl who could have been their daughter, sister or granddaughter. Those who spoke to her got the impression that not only was she interested in them, but she needed something from them: their friendship.

The exigencies of public life were such that the royals could never spend a long time with any one person; conversation, such as it was, was usually bland and brief. Diana, too, had to observe these rules, but in the few minutes when she paused to shake hands or exchange a few words, she got across a warmth that won hearts all round. Very often, people who encountered royals were gripped by stage fright. No one, though, seemed to clam up, tongue-tied, with Diana. She was so friendly that they

Left Diana takes the time to stop and talk to a Chelsea Pensioner who has stood to attention waiting for her.
Above Revisiting one of her old schools, Riddlesworth Hall, near Diss in Norfolk, on 25 April 1989, Diana typically picks up one of the pupils to help her unveil a stained glass window that commemorates her visit.

relaxed and for as long as they could, they chatted to her in a completely natural way. Diana, for her part, helped them along by being unusually candid for a royal and revealing harmless little secrets like the doings and sayings of her children.

When she was pregnant and suffering all-day sickness, she used to share her feelings with the people she met. 'No one told me it would be like this!' she told them ruefully, looking pale, washed out and thoroughly unwell. With that, the emotions of every mother, who knew from experience what Diana was going through, rose up like a tide and engulfed the pregnant young princess.

Very accessible

This was an exceptional way for a royal to behave in public, and those who preferred their princesses more aloof and grand did not approve. In their book, royals did not discuss such things as pregnancy

☙ Protocol ❧

GETTING THERE ON TIME

*Like all royal engagements, Diana's were timed with split-second precision. While an engagement was in progress, everything appeared to be relaxed, but in fact a stopwatch was metaphorically ticking away all the time. Everything was meticulously arranged in advance. Travelling time from home to engagement, see **right**, had already been calculated. The number of minutes needed for Diana to be welcomed by officials was already reckoned. If Diana was to make a speech, the time it would take was known before she opened her mouth. If there was a walkabout, the royal aides had to work out in advance how many people Diana could chat to and shake hands with if the timetable was to be kept.*

in public, or maybe at all. Diana, though, was revealing feelings, thoughts and emotions where dozens of people could hear, and those out of earshot would soon learn what she had said once those who had been closer started talking about it afterwards.

A 19th-century journalist, Walter Bagehot, had once warned that it was dangerous to let light in on the royal mystique, that atmosphere of awe and veneration which sets royals apart from ordinary folk. From this point of view, Diana was not just letting light in, but demolishing the royal mystique. With her confidences, her approachability and joking confessions like 'I'm as thick as a plank!', she was making herself appear so ordinary that she might as well not bother with being Her Royal Highness.

Easy to love

This missed an important point. It was precisely because Diana was a princess that people appreciated just how ordinary she could be. They did not want to be awed by her. They wanted to love her and found that she made loving her easy.

What was more, they responded in kind without any fear of committing *lese majesté*, or presumptuous conduct on the part of inferiors.

Diana, for instance, was a very tactile young woman. She would kiss and cuddle a child, embrace

Left Touring this ballet school would have evoked memories for Diana of her own dancing lessons as a schoolgirl, and she may well have been tempted to join in with the girls. She retained a lifelong interest in dance, especially ballet, from the English National Ballet, of which she was patron, down to classes for the very youngest beginners.

IN THE NEWS

Knifeman at Palace

Where there were royals there was security. It was not too overt, but it was certainly there – as one knifeman discovered in 1987, when he was nabbed in the grounds of Kensington Palace by the police. Headlines were made by the very fact that he got into the grounds, despite blanket surveillance in operation at the Palace, not just for the drama of the event, but for its worrying connotations. The man was carrying a knife and a hammer. In 1985, two girls actually broke into Kensington Palace itself.

Opposite page, far left Diana always seemed to enjoy her visits to the military, readily indulging in banter with the troops.

Opposite page, near left On a visit to a playgroup in Devon, Diana watches the children enjoying water play.

an old woman, hold their hands, even stroke their faces. When they could, people wanted to do the same. Several would reach out from a crowd to touch Diana's face or put a hand on her arm. It was as if she served as some kind of magic talisman. These gestures alarmed Diana's bodyguards, who were always on the lookout for the danger of attack. They soon learned that almost all physical contact with Diana by most people was just an

innocent sign of affection, nothing more.

All the same, Diana was running risks, and from time to time she had to be rescued. Her bodyguard had to extricate her after a man grabbed her arm while she was on a walkabout in Northumberland in April 1989. Two weeks later a man armed with a gas pistol was arrested in a crowd in Cardiff where

> **"The Princess seemed such a good human being."**
> VALENTINO, FASHION DESIGNER, ON DIANA

Diana was due to arrive. Another armed man was apprehended before Diana's walkabout in Inverness and, in the worst case, an Iranian businessman obsessed with Diana had to be removed from the scene on more than one occasion.

Legion of admirers

Fortunately, many more people were fascinated by Diana for the right reasons – her beauty and her flair, as well as her sympathetic nature. Children adored her. Young girls longed to grow up to be like her. Scores of women adopted Diana's hairstyle or exchanged their high heels for the low-heeled

Above On the tour of Nigeria in 1990, with Prince Charles, Diana meets a dance troupe including both children and adults, all dressed in traditional tribal outfits. **Inset right** Visiting Riverpoint Hostel for Single Homeless Women, in March 1993, Diana seems to find time to keep everyone happy in the crowd that has turned out to see her, shaking hands, chatting, laughing and accepting bouquets of flowers.

shoes she wore to compensate for her height.

There was nothing unusual, of course, in royals becoming icons or examples that people wished to emulate. This had long been an important part of the power and prestige of royalty. Where Diana was remarkable was in the range of her influence. She

> **"I just like laughing...
> I'm a normal person,
> hopefully, who loves life."**
> DIANA, ON DIANA

seemed to be several celebrities in one, admired for her charity work, her role in fashion, as a loving mother, a keep-fit buff, an animal lover, a fighter for women's rights, and as a leader of high society. Socialites, especially in America, would pay hundreds or thousands just to be in the same room with Diana at a ball, dinner or reception. It was as if they felt their own prestige was raised by her proximity.

There was no doubt that there had never been a celebrity like Diana, royal or otherwise, and there

may never be another like her again. There was something quite unique about her ability to mix with every sort of person, rich or poor, old or young, of all faiths and all races, sick or dying, with complete lack of affectation.

Previously, the common touch had never been exercised Diana's way and when she died so suddenly and tragically, the outburst of grief and sorrow seemed equally extraordinary. In fact, it was totally predictable, as anyone would know who had seen Diana in action among the people, touching their lives as they had never been touched before.

BEHIND THE SCENES

It took a staff of about forty people to help Charles and Diana
organize their public lives and ensure that everything ran smoothly.
Their jobs were not 'nine-to-five' affairs, but much more demanding

Prince Charles once said about his staff, 'we don't run them, they run us'. That may have sounded like a *bon mot*, a clever, witty saying, but nothing more. Substantially, though, it was true. The roles of Prince and Princess of Wales were so wide-ranging and had so many ramifications that Charles and Diana relied heavily on their staff to keep the royal wheels well oiled and always smoothly up and running.

Staff ranged from private secretaries, aides,

equerries, policy advisers, press and public relations officers to chauffeurs, typists and filing clerks. Diana had her own dresser. Charles had his valet. The ladies-in-waiting doubled as secretaries, and the bodyguards and detectives as child-minders and even messengers.

Whatever function they performed, the most important thing Charles and Diana required from their staff was loyalty, and with that, confidentiality. The aides, secretaries and others were, after all,

working where ever-curious journalists longed to be flies on the wall. They saw Charles and Diana in good moods and bad moods. They heard private remarks and opinions from them that could have been worth thousands if revealed to the media, even if such revelations would have cost them their jobs.

Proximity to royals, especially in confidential

> **"I am a perfectionist with myself, though not necessarily with everyone else."**
>
> DIANA, ON DIANA

day-to-day circumstances, had its own pressures and problems. Royal staff were not dealing with ordinary employers, but with members of the country's premier family, who were used to being regarded with reverence and a fair amount of awe. A 'Sir' or 'Ma'am' omitted, or the slightest hint of over-familiarity, was enough to turn the working relationship cold. Yet, the senior staff, especially the press and policy advisers, were in the tricky position of sometimes telling Charles and Diana what they ought to do, or even where they were going wrong.

These unusual demands meant that Charles and Diana's staff had to be very carefully chosen. Often, they came from social backgrounds which the royals

thought had schooled them in the special qualities they needed to have. The armed services was one of them. Captain Alison Ewan, an equerry to Charles and Diana and the first woman to be appointed to the post, had served in the Women's Royal Army Corps. Her job was to help organize royal engagements, and her colleagues in this were also from the services: Lieutenant-Colonel Brian Anderson, and

Previous page Diana shares a quiet word with her private secretary, Patrick Jephson. **Above left** Diana and her butler, Paul Burrell. **Above** Diana and equerry, Richard Aylard, at a county show in Suffolk.

IN CONTEXT 1988 MICHAEL JACKSON AT WEMBLEY

- Black candidate Jesse Jackson stands for President of the United States
- Prince Charles escapes death in avalanche at Klosters, Switzerland, where his friend, Major Hugh Lindsay, is killed
- Three members of the IRA are killed in Gibraltar by British soldiers
- Hurricane 'Gilbert' wreaks havoc in the Caribbean
- Michael Jackson, **right**, plays to 75,000 fans at Wembley Stadium

Lieutenant-Commander Richard Aylard RN who were, respectively, equerries to Charles and to Diana. Aylard later switched to the post of Charles' press aide. Their service training suited them well to the world of strict timetables and demanding duties in which Charles and Diana lived.

ROYAL RECRUITMENT

Government circles and the aristocracy were other sources of staff suitable for royal service. For example, Sir John Riddell was the 13th Baronet Riddell. David Roycroft, Assistant Private Secretary, was seconded from the Foreign Office. Both Riddell and Roycroft worked to organize Charles' diary and Roycroft handled his public engagements.

The diplomatic service, too, was a good hunting ground for royal recruitment. Oliver Everett came to Charles and Diana's service after leaving his post at the British Embassy in Madrid in July 1981. Everett took charge of the royal correspondence and also helped the new and then inexperienced princess into her public role. He doubled, too, as Comptroller, handling the Household finances.

Diana, however, was a young lady with her own ideas. Anyone who thought of her as a pliable girl who would mutely yield to expert guidance and do everything as it had always been done was in for a

Left Diana's dresser, Evelyn Dagley, whom Diana endearingly called 'Ev'.

⁂ Protocol ⁂

ACQUIRING ROYAL TITLES

The Queen's first two grandchildren, Princess Anne's son Peter Phillips and her daughter, Zara, have no royal titles. Yet Prince Charles' sons are princes and the Duke of York's daughters are princesses. This is because royal titles are passed on through the father, not the mother. Princess Anne's first husband, Captain Mark Phillips, see **right**, had no title, so their children had none, either. The father of Princess Margaret's children, the former Anthony Armstrong-Jones, was made Earl of Snowdon shortly before the birth of his first child in 1961. Because of this, their son is a Viscount and their daughter a Lady. These are titles given to an Earl's children.

Above Diana and Charles pose with the members of their household in Canberra, during their official tour of Australia in May 1985. Diana's dresser, Fay Marshalsea, stands behind Charles. **Opposite page, inset** Royal nanny, Barbara Barnes, carries the baby Prince William on his arrival in Alice Springs, Australia in 1983.

shock. Diana was said to like things to be 'just so' in most departments of her life and she did not appear slow to rap knuckles if she had to. She was not, however, dealing with minions whose function was to obey orders and nothing more. By their very nature and the nature of their jobs, her staff were dynamic types and, as in any important office, a clash of egos was probably inevitable. It was said that by 1986, forty members of Charles and Diana's staff – a hundred per cent turnover – had left their employ in the previous five years. Most appeared to depart between 1983 and 1985 and later analysis was said to point to a number of reasons.

Some left because they were told to go, though this was rumoured to be done in a subtle way.

Either royal displeasure was made apparent and the offending employee eventually got the message and resigned. Or an equerry did the sacking. Others left Charles and Diana because they wanted to retire or, like Anne Beckwith-Smith in 1990, to move on. There were inevitable rumours, which Anne strongly denied, that she had been fired. In fact, Anne returned to her original career in the art world, as Chief Secretary to the Director of British Paintings at Sotheby's auctioneers in London.

MOVING ON

There were also those who left for better-paid jobs – royal salaries are not all that princely – or for jobs that afforded them more time with their own

families. Others departed because they were dissatisfied or bored, like the Wales' butler Alan Fisher, who claimed that the couple were not 'giving proper dinner parties'.

Another reason for leaving was more straightforward: a staffer's period of secondment came to an end. This appears to have occurred with one of Diana's equerries, Lieutenant-Commander Peter Eberle, a former shipmate of Prince Charles when the Prince was in the Royal Navy. Eberle was seconded to Diana in October 1983, but left in 1986 and returned to sea.

Officers like Eberle did not necessarily leave the army or navy when they undertook royal duties.

> ## "She is an exceptionally kind and thoughtful person, but nobody's saying she's a fool."
>
> VISCOUNT ALTHORP (NOW EARL SPENCER), DIANA'S BROTHER, ON DIANA

They were given leave, as it were, for a fixed period of time, normally two years. More than this might not be advantageous for their own careers.

It follows from this that very long service on Charles and Diana's staff was not the norm. Anne Beckwith-Smith, who stayed with Diana as her lady-in-waiting and later her Assistant Private Secretary, for a total of nine years, was one of the exceptions. So was the Hon. Edward Adeane, private secretary to Prince Charles, whose family had served the royals since the reign of Queen Victoria.

LONG SERVICE RECORD

Adeane, whose father had been Queen Elizabeth's private secretary, had been close to the royals since he was a child. The Queen's father, King George VI, was his godfather. While he was still a pupil at Eton, the Queen made him a Page of Honour. Adeane went on to carve out a successful career as a libel lawyer, but gave it up in 1979 to become Prince Charles' private secretary. Adeane doubled as Charles' Treasurer and after the Prince married Diana, he became her Treasurer as well. Although only two years had passed since Adeane had entered royal service, he already seemed to be a fixture, and

DIARY DATES

1988

3-5 February
The Prince and Princess of Wales visit Thailand

16 February
The Prince and Princess of Wales open the 'Suleiman the Magnificent' Exhibition at the British Museum

4-5 March
The Prince of Wales visits Pittsburgh, Pennsylvania, USA

3 May
The Princess of Wales names the British Rail locomotive The Red Cross at Paddington Station, London

11 May
The Princess of Wales opens the new Leisure Pool at Sheringham, Norfolk

1 June
The Princess of Wales visits the Laura Ashley factory in Powys

28 July
The Prince and Princess of Wales attend the Royal Tournament at Earl's Court, London

2 August
The Princess of Wales opens the Barbican Health and Fitness Centre, London

7-11 November
The Prince and Princess of Wales visit France

15 December
The Princess of Wales attends a carol concert in aid of the MacMillan Cancer Relief Fund

20 December
The Prince of Wales visits the Institute of Indian Culture, West Kensington, London

it was expected that he would remain with Charles until he became king and possibly after that, too.

It was, therefore, an enormous shock when Edward Adeane suddenly departed in 1985. The event fired intense speculation. One of the more fanciful rumours concerned 'disagreements' with Diana who, it appears, talked business with Adeane against a background of blaring pop music and surrounded by toys, baby clothes and other nursery paraphernalia. Adeane is supposed to have told a

> **"*I want you to understand that I'm not responsible for any sackings. I just don't sack people.*"**
>
> DIANA TO JAMES WHITAKER, ROYAL CORRESPONDENT, DAILY MIRROR

friend: 'If I see another knitted bootee, I'll go mad!'

It was hardly credible, though, that a man like Adeane would throw up his royal career for reasons like that. A more serious reason, it was alleged, was Prince Charles' reputed tendency to ignore advice.

The advice Charles apparently ignored seems to have concerned his own and Diana's forthcoming meeting with Pope John Paul II, during their Italian tour in the spring of 1985. Charles wanted to join the Pope at a Catholic Mass. Adeane, supposedly, tried to talk him out of it, but Charles was adamant. He and Diana left for Italy with the Mass

IN THE NEWS

Charles Spencer speaks up for his sister

Diana's brother, Charles spoke quite freely to Woman magazine in this interview, revealing many behind-the-scenes facts (and the pain caused by the divorce of his parents in 1969). Always a great champion of his famous royal sister, to whom he was very close, he spoke up for her at a time when she was being criticized for being hard on her staff. According to her brother, Diana was simply trying to get rid of unwanted hangers-on.

still on the agenda. The Queen later vetoed the whole idea, but, by that time, Adeane was no longer in Charles' employ.

For every disgruntled staffer who left, there were many more who were delighted to work for Diana. What was more, they often regarded her as a friend and a good friend at that. The Princess used to lend her car to Evelyn Dagley, her dresser, to enable 'Ev' as Diana called her, to go shopping. When another dresser, Fay Marshalsea, contracted cancer in 1987, Diana was very supportive and even took Fay to hospital for treatment on one occasion.

Diana frequently showed herself thoughtful over the families of her staff who, she knew, were affected by the long hours and absences involved in working for herself and Charles. For instance, she

The Private Princess
The Princess and the valet

When Diana became engaged to Prince Charles, his valet, Stephen Barry, was reportedly very upset. He thought that his master's marriage would endanger his own position.

Barry is supposed to have tried to keep Lady Diana Spencer, as she then was, away from Charles and he also accused her of pursuing and trapping the Prince into marriage.

The antagonism appeared to be mutual. Diana apparently took a very strong dislike to Barry. She seemed to be convinced that Barry, a homosexual, was 'totally infatuated' with her husband. Diana, it appears, resolved to oust the valet and one rumour had it that she confronted Charles with the ultimatum: 'Either he goes, or I do!'

However that may be, it was Barry who went. In 1982, Diana, according to Barry's friends, put so much pressure on Charles that, despite his own regard for him, he had to let his valet go.

Afterwards, Barry tried to save face by saying that he had resigned. He went

Above Charles' valet, Stephen Barry, who fell foul of Diana's displeasure.

to the United States, where he wrote his memoirs. They were a big success there, but were never published in Britain.

In 1986, Stephen Barry died in London, aged 37, as a result of AIDS-related pneumonia. His friends, however, ascribed his premature death to 'a broken heart'.

Above left Diana discusses her schedule with her, then, Assistant Private Secretary, Anne Beckwith-Smith, in the sitting room at Kensington Palace. **Left** Diana's hair stylist, Kevin Shanley, was responsible for the first 'Princess Di' look, copied by women the world over. He is seen at work in his Kensington salon, Headlines.

wrote a special 'Thank you' letter to the wife of her hairdresser, Kevin Shanley, for 'lending' him during overseas tours where he accompanied the Princess.

There were, naturally, many compensations for the demands that had to be made on royal staff. Daily proximity to Charles and Diana was probably the first that would occur to a prospective royal employee. That afforded a feeling of intimacy with these royal stars, whom others could only read about. Fay Marshalsea put it into words for all those delighted to serve Diana when she said: 'She's a lovely person to work for and very special to me.'

Practical Accessories

Diana once said that clothes for her royal job had to be practical. This was particularly true of her accessories, which needed to be neat, convenient and not the kind to get in the way

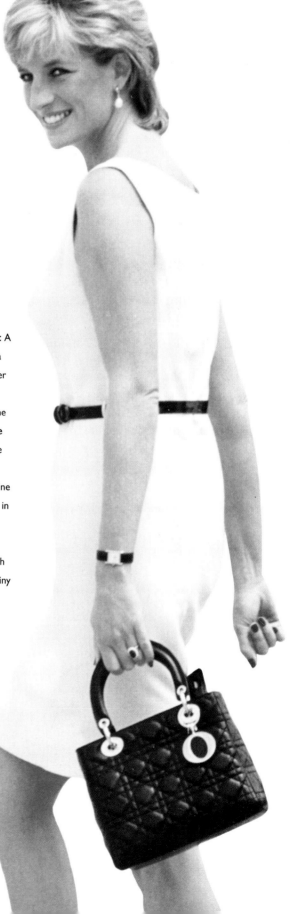

D iana needed to choose accessories that went with the job. However much she wanted to wear them, some accessories had to be turned down if they proved impractical.

A handbag with long handles that swung too much could get entangled while Diana was shaking hands. Out of doors, long scarves could do the same, which is why she hardly ever wore them at public engagements. Belts could not be too tight if Diana had to sit down for any length of time. Shoes had to fit well and have sturdy soles that were not

> *"She made a conscious decision to dispense with formality very early on."*
> ANNA HARVEY, DEPUTY EDITOR OF VOGUE

so thick they made the shoes look 'clumpy' but would still cushion Diana's feet during hours spent standing or walking about on hard surfaces.

In this context, possibly the only accessory Diana could choose simply because she fancied it was hosiery. Even here, though, a certain amount of decorum had to be observed. Emphasizing the royal legs too much could be seen as unladylike. Nevertheless, rather than stick to standard flesh tones all the time, Diana struck out occasionally to

Opposite page, top left A muff was something Diana often wore in cold weather during her early days, and this black embroidered one was a favourite. **Opposite page, bottom left** These long taffeta evening gloves were worn with a Catherine Walker gown in Germany in 1987. **Opposite page, main picture** With this Alistair Blair suit, in Munich in 1987, Diana sports a shiny black belt and clutch bag. **Right** In Argentina, in November 1995, Diana wears a thin black belt and carries a patterned black handbag.

wear coloured or decorated tights. During her Australian tour in 1985, for example, she wore net bows at the heel of her sheer black stockings, in the shape of red polka-dotted butterflies.

On the same tour, Diana arrived at the races to watch the Melbourne Cup wearing black seamed tights with open black bows at the heel (see page 239), to go with her black Bruce Oldfield suit.

Colour wise

Diana appeared in bright red hosiery from time to time, but she wore it less for its own sake than for picking up one of the colours in her outfit or to complete a 'total' look. This is what she was doing when she wore tomato red tights, in Florence in 1985, to go with her Jasper Conran two-piece red suit. She was definitely the lady in red that day. Her shoes and handbag were red, too, and there were even red polka dots on her white blouse.

Belts, like other accessories, had a role to play here and Diana, cleverly, never made the mistake of using them just as extras. In 1985, for instance, in a photo session with Tim Graham at Highgrove House, Diana was pictured wearing muted colours: a cream shirt and grey skirt. Here, she used

> **"She has natural good taste in coordination, which is a great gift."**
> COURTIER, ON DIANA

a belt to enliven what could otherwise have been an understated outfit. The belt in question was warm tan in colour, with a gold buckle.

In time, Diana largely abandoned belts for outfits worn during public appearances and relied more on the tailored lines of jackets and dresses to emphasize her waist. But in 1988 in Australia, she made clever use of a belt on an Alistair Blair outfit. This had a loose, sleeveless patterned top with a straight white skirt. Between them was an integral emerald green cummerbund and at the centre of the cummerbund, a matching green belt with gold buckle (see page 235). Take away the belt, and the outfit would

BOLD CONTRASTS

Left Whatever accessories she wore, from hats down to shoes, Diana always tried to pick up elements of the colour or pattern of her clothes. She was certainly fond of bold contrasts and often wore black with white and, equally, blue with white and sometimes red with white. The pattern might be one of stripes, polka dots or, as in this blouse set off by a belt, a more abstract design.

1 In Thailand in February 1988, Diana sports an emerald green cummerbund and a green belt with a gold buckle.
2 Diana wears a broad black belt to secure the wrap-over top of her outfit, in London in December 1994.
Above In May 1990, at the Badminton Horse Trials, Diana wears a brown leather belt. **Far left** A wide black patent leather belt tops off this black and white check skirt worn in January 1990.

IN THE NEWS

All eyes on Diana's handbag

No detail about Diana was too small for the press. She made news with the slightest gesture or action, even something as seemingly trivial as how she handled a handbag. Better still for picture purposes, she seemed in this instance, in February 1994, to be having some trouble with the shoulder strap. On public engagements Diana often carried clutch bags. This time, she obviously forgot to make the conversion from shoulder bag to clutch bag before she left home.

DAILY Mirror

GREECE FOR £11.50 A DAY

4-PAGE HOLIDAY PLUS INSIDE

DI COMES IN FROM THE COLD

Summer f-f-frock as Britain f-f-freezes

BY JAMES WHITAKER

have lost its chic. It was part of the total Diana look.

That same year, in Thailand, another belt, this time in dark blue, gave the right boost to another Alistair Blair design, which had a cream and navy check top and a straight cream skirt with a dropped waist. The belt divided Diana's figure nicely and echoed the blue of the top while compensating for her height, which could make her look too 'leggy'.

Bags of style

Diana was on the innovation trail once more with her handbags. The standard royal handbag was usually a short-strap number, which hung on the arm and left the hands free. This was practical, but somewhat frumpish. Diana's choice, therefore, was the clutch bag, which she introduced to royal accessorizing in a big way. Clutch bags had the virtue of being small and unobtrusive.

She could afford to carry small bags since, unlike most women, there was not much she had to put in them – maybe just a comb and lipstick. Anything more bulky could be contained in the lady-in-

---

> *"It's a great boost for the firm and exciting for all the staff when we saw our shoes in pictures."*
>
> JOHN GAIRDNER, MANAGER, CHARLES JOURDAN SHOES

---

waiting's handbag. At times, Diana wore a clutch bag with its optional strap, but more often without. The bag could be tucked under her left arm when handshaking.

Clutch bags also lent themselves to clever decorations. The bag she wore with Bruce Oldfield's spectacular silver lamé evening gown, seen at a gala dinner at London's Grosvenor House Hotel in 1985, had inserts in the same material as the dress.

Though usually acting as a complement to her outfits, Diana's handbags sometimes made fashion statements on their own account. In Liverpool in 1987, Diana appeared in a cream dress which was so plain, though

I In Moscow in 1995, Diana has a shoulder bag in cream and blue. **2** On a visit to a school for the blind in Surrey in 1995, the gold chain on Diana's bag matches her buttons. **3** Diana was given a briefcase in Coventry in 1986. **4** At the Dorchester, London, in 1992, Diana carries a clutch bag. **5** At the Falklands Memorial Service, in 1985, the thin stripe in her dress is picked up in navy blue gloves and a clutch bag. **Below** In London, in August 1995, Diana carries a large black sac.

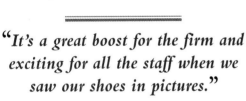

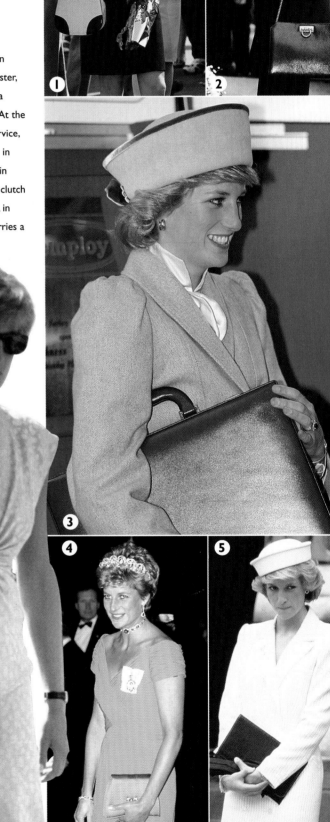

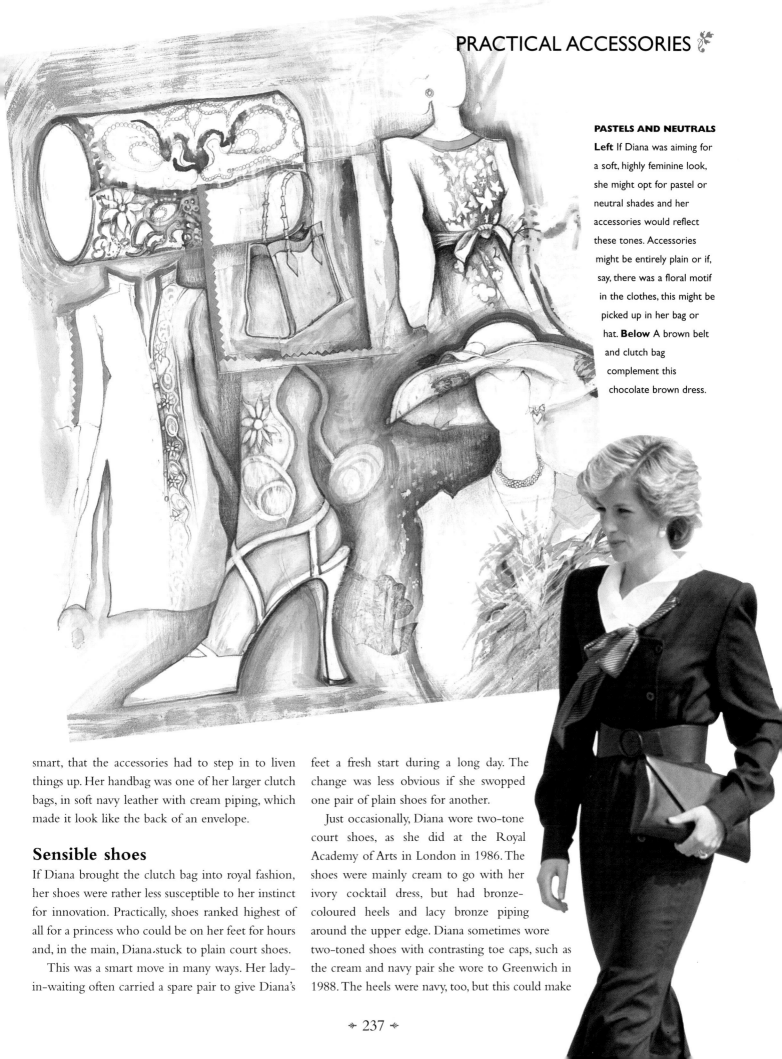

PASTELS AND NEUTRALS

Left If Diana was aiming for a soft, highly feminine look, she might opt for pastel or neutral shades and her accessories would reflect these tones. Accessories might be entirely plain or if, say, there was a floral motif in the clothes, this might be picked up in her bag or hat. **Below** A brown belt and clutch bag complement this chocolate brown dress.

smart, that the accessories had to step in to liven things up. Her handbag was one of her larger clutch bags, in soft navy leather with cream piping, which made it look like the back of an envelope.

Sensible shoes

If Diana brought the clutch bag into royal fashion, her shoes were rather less susceptible to her instinct for innovation. Practically, shoes ranked highest of all for a princess who could be on her feet for hours and, in the main, Diana stuck to plain court shoes.

This was a smart move in many ways. Her lady-in-waiting often carried a spare pair to give Diana's feet a fresh start during a long day. The change was less obvious if she swopped one pair of plain shoes for another.

Just occasionally, Diana wore two-tone court shoes, as she did at the Royal Academy of Arts in London in 1986. The shoes were mainly cream to go with her ivory cocktail dress, but had bronze-coloured heels and lacy bronze piping around the upper edge. Diana sometimes wore two-toned shoes with contrasting toe caps, such as the cream and navy pair she wore to Greenwich in 1988. The heels were navy, too, but this could make

the feet look big and it was neater to have one colour for the foot and a contrast for the heels.

The flat- or low-heeled shoes Diana wore when she first came on the royal scene in 1981 could not continue once she began to step out in smarter outfits that needed the greater elegance of high heels.

Happy medium

She rarely wore very high heels, which would have made her over six feet tall, but kept to a maximum of around two inches. This was a happy medium for several reasons. Diana's height was the obvious one. Any higher and she would be taller than Charles; apparently she didn't like that and neither did he. It also meant a better distribution of her weight, which took the strain off her legs, another bonus. Another was the reduction of wear and tear on Diana's feet, since two-inch heels did not throw her weight too far forward and so produce discomfort.

In the event, Diana never looked anything but comfortable in her clothes, shoes included, and at every appearance gave the lie to the idea that suffering was necessary to achieve beauty.

Opposite page, far left A scarf could be an awkward accessory, but Diana wore this one in Cannes in 1987 because it was designed to go with her evening gown.
Opposite page, near left In Pakistan in September 1991, Diana covered her head with a chiffon scarf as a mark of respect. **1** On the school run, in April 1991, Diana wears black and brown leather boots.
2 Another long skirt and another pair of brown cowboy boots, this time with a leopard-skin insert.
3 At Expo '92 in Seville, Spain, Diana wears these red satin slingbacked high-heeled shoes. **4** At the Melbourne Cup in 1985, Diana wore black seamed tights with a black bow on the heel of each foot. **5** In Cairo, Egypt, in May 1992, Diana wore these pink court shoes with a pink outfit. **6** In May 1991, at Searcy's Luncheon, these red and white striped shoes matched her skirt.

Meeting the Great and Good

When Charles and Diana went on foreign tours as ambassadors for Britain, they were given the full panoply of a state reception by the leaders of their host countries. They also encountered some unfamiliar traditions

As Princess of Wales, Diana acted as an ambassador for Britain, while on foreign visits. Here, celebrity met celebrity. Foreign presidents or prime ministers, and sometimes their wives, were headline-makers themselves. They were, more often than not, a great deal older than Diana and certainly a great deal more experienced.

This was still very much a male-dominated world, as well as a world with far more republics than monarchies. Diana was often cast in a subsidiary role, the normal position for women who were not themselves heads of state, top politicians or, in a monarchy, Queens. The normal procedure was for the men to go off to discuss business and international affairs, while their wives visited hospitals, health projects, schools, nurseries and other places deemed to be of greater interest to women.

This, for instance, was the formula in the USA, when First Lady

Above Princess Diana sits alongside US President George Bush at a banquet in Washington DC, in November 1985.
Left On a later visit to Washington DC, in June 1997, Diana accompanies the Vice President's wife, Elizabeth Dole, to a charity ball.
Right Jacques Chirac, President of France, leans over to talk to Diana at an official function in November 1988.

Diana was a frequent visitor to the United States of America. **Above** In July 1991, Diana accompanies the President's wife, Barbara Bush, on a visit to an AIDS hospital, a typical outing for the wife of a visiting dignitary such as Prince Charles. Fortunately, Diana had a particular interest in AIDS. **Above right** Flanked by former Secretary of State Henry Kissinger and Colin Powell, Chief of the Defence Staff, Diana shakes hands with noted TV sex therapist Dr. Ruth Westheimer, at the Hilton Hotel, in December 1995, during a visit to New York.

Nancy Reagan took Diana off to see a drug rehabilitation centre, during her tour with Charles in 1985. It happened again in 1990, when Maryam, the wife of Nigerian President General Ibrahim Babangida, took Diana to a Rural Women for Better Life fair and a tribal dancing display, during the Prince and Princess's tour.

Charles, meanwhile, would be learning about a country's infrastructure, discussing the environment or promoting opportunities for British business.

Different customs

Diana also had to be something of a chameleon when she was around foreign leaders. As she quickly discovered, the 'Ladies first' ethic, common in the West, did not apply in places where women had a lesser status. It was not an easy situation for either hosts or guest. Here was this beautiful, famous, privileged Princess of Wales, a future Queen Consort, who was used to being treated almost like a goddess wherever she went, arriving, for instance, in an Arab or African country where women were not conspicuous in public life.

Age-old tradition could not change overnight

for Diana's sake and what to do with her sometimes came close to being a diplomatic problem.

King Fahd of Saudi Arabia, for example, was making a big concession when he agreed to be

"I was totally drunk on her charm."

BRIAN PECKFORD, PRIME MINISTER
OF NEWFOUNDLAND, ON CHARLES AND DIANA'S
1983 TOUR OF CANADA

photographed with Diana as well as with Charles, when they were in his country's capital, Riyadh, in 1986. It was only the second time he had been photographed with a woman.

Three years later, in 1989, when Charles and Diana were on tour in Kuwait and the United Arab Emirates, the rules were again stretched when the Kuwaiti Crown Prince Sheikh Sa'ad Abdullah al-Salim al-Sabah gave a banquet for the royal couple. It was a different story when Charles and Diana moved on to Abu Dhabi. There, tradition asserted itself and the segregation of the sexes, common in Muslim countries, came into force. Diana lunched

Above In Italy, in 1985, Charles and Diana met the country's figurehead, President Sandro Pertini. **Left** In Nepal, in March 1993, when visiting a Red Cross project at Panauti, Diana talks with the former Conservative MP Baroness Chalker, the Minister for Overseas Development.

with the ladies, while Charles ate with the men.

In this context, the former French West African colony of Cameroon was the scene of an extraordinary gaffe in 1990. Charles and Diana arrived at Youande on 21 March from Nigeria, to find the usual red carpet laid out for them across the airport tarmac. The Prince and Princess were walking along the carpet, when Cameroonian officials rushed up and shoved Diana off. Charles, apparently, did not notice and strode on, while Diana, recovering herself, walked round behind the guard of honour. In Cameroon, this sort of thing was normal. Society was polygamous and, with so many wives per husband, women occupied a lowly position.

The situation was retrieved by Diana's bodyguard, Kenneth Wharfe, who leapt to her rescue, told off the officials in no uncertain terms, and led Diana back to her place on the carpet. By then,

Diana was blushing deep red with embarrassment.

If Diana had to be careful and prepared for anything in this kind of environment, she could, of course, be more relaxed when meeting Western leaders. Many of them were visibly affected by Diana's charm and beauty, and did not bother to hide it. They were not just susceptible middle-aged or elderly men entranced by a pretty face and a fetching figure. Diana's charm was potent and she knew how to use it. Many leaders had already admired her from afar and seemed anxious to display their gallantry towards her. It was, after all, not very often that state visitors were as glamorous or as youthful as the Princess of Wales.

Winning ways

Kissing a lady's hand, for instance, came naturally to continentals such as Prime Minister Jacques Chirac, when Diana visited France in 1988. Diana, however, scored her greatest coup in this respect when she won over Labour Prime Minister Bob Hawke, during her first tour of Australia in 1983. Hawke, who had only recently been elected, had come to power

⋘ Protocol ⋙

BOWING AND CURTSEYING

When meeting royals, men are required to bow and women have to curtsey. There are occasions when the royals have to do this themselves. A king or queen is of higher rank than a prince or princess. Diana, therefore, curtseyed and Charles bowed to King Juan Carlos and Queen Sofia when they met in Spain in 1987. Diana was also obliged to curtsey to King Constantine of Greece in June 1985, see above. Presidents and their wives, however, being commoners, are ranked below a prince and princess. This is why President Ronald Reagan bowed and his wife Nancy curtseyed when Charles and Diana visited the USA.

The difference between royals and politicians is that politicians come and go with election results, whereas royals are there year-after-year. As a result, Diana met several First Ladies during her time with the Royal Family. **Above** Diana with Hillary Clinton, President Clinton's wife, in Washington DC in 1996. **Opposite page** Diana with Nancy Reagan, US President Ronald Reagan's wife in 1985.

on an anti-monarchist platform. He was committed to shedding the monarchy – Queen Elizabeth II was also Queen of Australia – and declaring his country a republic.

Diana, though, seemed to put a dent in his resolve. When she and Charles arrived in Canberra, the Australian capital, on 24 March 1983, Hawke was there to greet them, but did not give the royal couple the expected bow of respect. Later, though, it was a very different story. After spending some hours with Charles and Diana at Government Lodge, Hawke emerged, apparently a changed man. He was friendly and smiling around the Prince and Princess and said of Diana 'She's a lovely lady'. Bob Hawke remained Prime Minister until 1991 and retired from politics in 1992. Intriguingly, though, Australia has remained a monarchy.

Hawke was only one of Diana's conquests. She was said not to be vain, but she knew how attractive she was, and from time to time, she appeared to turn on the charm deliberately and even, on occasion, became flirtatious. This sort of thing was often

IN THE NEWS

Star-struck at the White House

The stars meet the stars. It was probably difficult to know who was the more thrilled at this meeting of the Reagans and the Waleses in Washington in 1985. Both President Ronald Reagan and his wife Nancy were former film stars, and Diana loved meeting Hollywood stars and other celebrities. On the other hand, she was a major celebrity herself, so the thrill was probably mutual. As, indeed, it probably was when Diana went on to dance with Saturday Night Fever star John Travolta, at a White House reception for the royal couple.

explained as her attempt to liven up a dull official engagement, but Diana would not have been human had she failed to enjoy the effect she created. She was even daring enough to try charming the deeply traditional Gulf leaders in 1986.

'You should have seen some of those Arabs going ga-ga when they saw me on the Gulf Tour,'

"The lady has style."

JOHN TRAVOLTA, FILM STAR, AFTER DANCING WITH DIANA AT A WHITE HOUSE PARTY IN WASHINGTON

---

she was quoted as saying. 'I gave them the full treatment and they were just falling all over themselves. I just turned it on, and mopped them up!'

The following year, during Charles and Diana's tour of Portugal, the Princess sat next to 62-year-old President Mario Soares at a banquet in Lisbon's Ajuda Palace. It was February. The palace was cold and Diana wore an off-the-shoulder evening dress.

'If I get cold, will you warm me up?' Diana teased. Courtly gentleman that he was, the President took off his dinner jacket and offered to place it round Diana's bare shoulders. She reached over and twanged his braces, saying 'You're a socialist, aren't you? You should be wearing red braces.'

Getting flirtatious

According to journalists accompanying the royal tour, Diana went even further than this in Portugal. They reported that she batted her eyelashes at nearly every man, and that it drove Charles nearly frantic with rage. The press inference was that Charles was jealous, but he was also said to be perturbed that his wife was letting the dignified royal mask slip so far with her flirtatious antics.

All the same, the flirting could work both ways. It might be fairly mild, as when Nancy Reagan, a one-time film star, serenaded Charles with one of his favourite songs, *I Concentrate on You*, a loaded title if ever there was one, during a White House

Opposite page Diana with Prime Minister Margaret Thatcher **(far left)** and seated next to her successor, John Major **(near left)** at the 1995 VJ Day celebration. **Above** Prince Charles and Diana pose with their Australian hosts, Prime Minister Bob Hawke and his wife in 1983. **Above, inset** In Thailand, in 1988, with Princess Sirindhorn.

banquet in 1985. Or it could go way over the top, which is what happened in 1986 when Charles and Diana visited Austria.

There, they were guests at a dinner hosted by the Mayor of Vienna, whose wife was the sexy actress Dagmar Koller. Koller evidently took a fancy to

> ## "Well, as long as she doesn't clash with the Pope. He'll be all in white, long dress, long sleeves."
>
> *PAPAL SPOKESMAN WHEN ASKED WHAT DIANA SHOULD WEAR TO MEET POPE JOHN PAUL II IN 1985*

Prince Charles, and put on an extraordinary performance. She tickled Charles with her shawl, raised it to whisper to him unseen by Diana or the other guests, and later, it seemed, during the meal deliberately dropped her lipstick under the table so that Charles, being a gentleman, would have to pick it up for her. Frau Koller was thwarted, however, when a waiter came up and obliged.

Charles, reportedly, hardly knew where to put

As well as meeting the world's top politicians, the royals also often met church leaders. **Above** Diana photographed alongside Pope John Paul II, after she and Charles had a private audience with the Pope at the Vatican, on their Italian tour of 1985. **Left** Diana shakes hands with the Archbishop of Canterbury, George Carey, at Lambeth Palace in London, in October 1993.

himself when subjected to this barefaced display of vamping, but Koller's jokes certainly made him laugh and Diana was said to be looking very frosty. The Mayor's reaction went unrecorded.

An embarrassing toast

Some of Diana's hosts seemed to vie with each other to pay court to her, though the palm probably went to Prime Minister Richard Hatfield of New Brunswick, Canada. During Charles and Diana's tour of 1983, Hatfield abandoned the formal speech normally given after official dinners. Instead, he addressed a fulsome 'toast of love' to Diana, which made her blush.

Incidents like these certainly enlivened Charles and Diana's tours abroad, which had their share of tedium and routine. But when all the flattery and effusiveness was stripped away, Diana still played her part in the prime purpose of these royal excursions: promoting Britain, showing that its monarchy was still a force, and 'flying the flag'.

FRIENDS INDEED

Some were his, some were hers. Others were theirs. Whichever way they came into the orbit of the Prince and Princess of Wales, their friends found the benefits did not always outweigh the disadvantages

When Charles and Diana married, a new royal 'court' naturally gathered around them. This was not a court in the official sense, and was not intended to rival that of the Queen. But the Prince and Princess became the focus around which their friends revolved.

Diana's friends, in particular, acquired a new status that reflected her elevation to royal rank. Being chums with Lady Diana Spencer had been quite different. For a start, friends not previously

known to the Royal Family were investigated by MI5. This most clandestine branch of the secret services 'bugged' the Royal Family in the cause of defending the realm and would certainly not baulk at telling Charles and Diana who they should and should not admit to their circle. Candidates' backgrounds, their families, their previous friendships and associations were put under strict scrutiny.

If they were considered subversive, opportunist or in any other way undesirable, there would be no

more royal invitations. Security also saw to it that Diana's guards had to be informed before friends visited, so that spontaneous get-togethers were all but impossible.

Friends who passed muster and were willing to handle these restrictions, required a discretion and a resistance to pressure never before demanded of them. These were the people, the ones who knew the life of the Prince and Princess from the inside, who were the raw material from which the press hoped to mine secrets and confidences. Big money could be proffered for friends' 'stories' or even a royal quote, though the royal friendship would probably come to an abrupt end if they talked.

RICH AND TITLED

In previous generations, friends of the Royal Family came from the aristocracy or the respectable rich, titled or untitled. Charles and Diana were both born into this exclusive stratum of society, but they also went outside it to choose their friends.

This was how Charles could be friends with the

Previous page Princess Diana with Lulu Blacker, one of the friends that Diana and Fergie prodded with umbrellas at Ascot – the other was Major Hugh Lindsay, who died in a skiing accident. **Above** Diana at a polo match with ex-King Constantine of Greece and his son, who have lived in London and had been friends for many years.

Opposite page, top Diana at the Diamond Ball with the late Lady Dale Tryon, Prince Charles' friend 'Kanga'. **Right** Diana formed a close long-term friendship with the wife of the Brazilian Ambassador in London, Lucia Flecha de Lima.

wife Sarah. Charles had been Hugh Lindsay's Best Man at his wedding in 1987. The Major, an equerry to the Queen, was tragically killed in an avalanche during a skiing holiday with Charles and Diana at Klosters, Switzerland, in 1988. Charles himself narrowly escaped death. Afterwards, the royal couple rallied round the widowed Sarah, who was expecting her first child, and Diana held her hand during her husband's funeral.

DIANA'S GIRLFRIENDS

Many of Diana's own friendships were of very long standing. Some of her school chums remained friends into adult life. One or two, like Alexandra Loyd and Laura Greig, became her ladies-in-waiting. Diana's 'BFs', as she called her best friends, included, too, the girls with whom she was sharing a flat at Coleherne Court in the Earl's Court district of London, when she became engaged to Prince Charles. Ann Bolton, Carolyn Pride and Virginia Pitman knew about Diana's romance long before the engagement was officially announced, and proved to be models of confidentiality. None of them said a word about it, despite the intense press speculation that involved a virtual siege of the flat.

These girls were not all that different from Diana and, except for the royal rank, two of them made similarly 'good' marriages. Ann Bolton, the daughter of a Brigadier, married a wealthy rancher,

> **"Diana is very warm; warmth is a form of intelligence and that draws you to her."**
>
> MILLIE SOAMES, FRIEND OF DIANA AND SISTER OF PHILIP DUNNE

Noel Hill, and moved to a 300,000-acre estate in Australia. Carolyn Pride married the brewery heir, William Bartholomew. Virginia Pitman became an interior decorator. The arts ranked high among girls like Virginia as an acceptable area in which an upper-class girl could work if, indeed, she worked at all. Princess Margaret's daughter, now Lady Sarah Chatto, was another artist friend of Diana's and acted as chief bridesmaid at her wedding. Anne Beckwith-Smith, Diana's first full-time lady-in-

interior designer David Hicks, son-in-law of the Prince's great-uncle and 'honorary grandfather' Lord Louis Mountbatten, but also include in his circle the former 'Goons' Spike Milligan, Harry Secombe and the late Michael Bentine. Similarly, Diana's friends included American-born Queen Noor of Jordan and Natalia, Duchess of Westminster, as well as maths teacher and rugby coach Andrew Widdowson, who met Diana at a ball before her marriage. Widdowson was later crippled in a rugby accident, and Diana, whom he called 'the girl with the golden hair', wrote him get-well letters and invited him to her wedding.

Ex-King Constantine and his wife Queen Anne-Marie of Greece, both distant cousins of Charles, were friends the Prince and Princess had in common. So were Major Hugh Lindsay and his

waiting, who became a close friend, had her own career in the world of fine arts and painting.

Unfortunately, in this world of upper-class friendships, the young men ran particular perils. The press, who were always in close pursuit, usually acted on the premise that platonic relationships between the sexes were unlikely, if not impossible. This was untrue, as was proved, to take one example, by the 30-year friendship between Charles and the late Lady Tryon, or 'Kanga' as he nicknamed her.

> ## "I feel it would be wrong to speak about any of my friends."
>
> KATE MENZIES, FRIEND OF DIANA, ON RUMOURS OF TROUBLE IN THE ROYAL MARRIAGE

'Kanga' acted as Charles' adviser, and lent a ready ear to his troubles and confidences – but no more.

Nevertheless, male friends of Diana's, who were also nothing more, could find themselves cast as love interest. This is what happened to Peter Greenall, a former National Hunt jockey, who danced with Diana at the Casa Antica night club in Klosters, Switzerland during a royal skiing holiday in 1987. Prince Charles had retired to his chalet, but Diana, who never missed a chance to dance, went to the disco. There, she spent an energetic few hours with Greenall. They were, apparently, still dancing in the early hours. The story was spiced up by the disc

IN THE NEWS

Di talks friend out of coma

Diana hit the headlines of the News of the World on 28 May 1989, when her friend, Chloe Teacher, with Diana's help, came out of a coma caused by a riding accident. Chloe had been given a one in twenty chance of survival, but revived after Diana spent hours just talking to her, and made what was rather tentatively called a 'near-total recovery'. The newspaper mentioned two visits by Charles, but credited Diana with the miracle.

DI'S MIRACLE SAVES COMA PAL

NEWS OF THE WORLD, May 28, 1989 33

By CLIVE GOODMAN

PRINCESS Diana has been hailed a miracle worker—after nursing a pal back from the brink of death.

Chloe Teacher had just a ONE IN 20 chance of living, after being kicked in the head by a horse in a riding accident.

But Diana coaxed her out of a coma during a series of secret bedside visits.

Now Chloe, 44, has amazed doctors by making a near-total recovery.

Chloe, wife of Teachers whisky heir James, said "My doctors hadn't thought I'd pull through.

SWEET

"But the Princess's visits helped enormously. "At first she came all the way to Nottingham to see me in hospital, when I was still totally unconscious. Later I'd been twice when I'd been transferred to London," she said.

Prince Charles also visited Chloe twice.

Chloe added: "The Prince and Princess were concerned. I'm so grateful."

Doctors have hailed Diana a healer before—when hospital patients showed an astonishing improvement after an official visit by her.

Consultant by her, Peter Gautier-Smith, of London's National Hospital for Nervous Diseases, said "She seems to have extraordinary healing powers.

"You could almost compare it to the laying-on of hands.

"She has a miraculous effect on people. The uplift which the Princess gives can sometimes do more good than any doctor."

WEIRD

WIDOW Ruby Jones, 85 left more than £70,000 to a model railway club her husband helped set up in Fareham, Hampshire. Members are said to be really chuffed

WORLD

Above Diana with Carolyn Bartholomew, the former Carolyn Pride, a friend from West Heath schooldays, who was also one of her former flatmates. Carolyn is one of Prince Harry's godmothers and was the friend who, in 1988, threatened to reveal all to the press unless Diana sought medical treatment for her bulimia.

jockey's observation that Diana was not wearing a bra underneath her clingy white silk top.

As another friend, financier Charles Carter, had already discovered the previous year, one or two dances with Diana, in his case at the Guards' Polo Club, just before the Duke and Duchess of York's wedding, was enough to get his name and the hint of a scandal in the newspapers.

Stories like these did not arise only from the media's tendency to dig dirt. By 1987, the press was already busy speculating about trouble in the royal marriage, and young men like Greenall and Carter seemed to provide ready fuel for the flames.

THE PRESS TARGET DUNNE

Their brush with the press paled, though, compared to the experience of Philip Dunne, Old Etonian and merchant banker, who seemed to possess every qualification for an extra-marital fling. Dunne was tall, dark, handsome, rich and well-born. His father was Lord-Lieutenant, the Queen's representative, in Hereford and Worcester. Dunne's godmother was Princess Alexandra, the Queen's first cousin. Dunne was also a highly eligible bachelor with a reputation as a lady-charmer. He was in Klosters with Charles and Diana in 1987 and again at Royal Ascot the following June.

The same year, Diana and Dunne were both guests at the wedding of the Marquess and Marchioness of Worcester. So were Charles and

> **"I always have the best fun sitting next to Prince Charles at dinner. You are sure of a good, juicy conversation."**
>
> A WOMAN FRIEND OF CHARLES, ON CHARLES

Camilla Parker-Bowles who, apparently, spent much time in conversation. Diana, meanwhile, was observed dancing several times with Philip Dunne and, allegedly, acted in an extraordinary way for a married woman in her position. She ran her fingers through Dunne's hair, it was reported. She kissed him on the cheek, and she danced until dawn, two or three hours after Charles had departed.

To some, all this seemed like a classic strategy for

Above In an attempt to avoid waiting photographers, Diana steps out along a London street, closely followed by a long-time friend, Catherine Soames, the former wife of Conservative MP Nicholas Soames. **Left** Diana shares a drink with Kate Menzies, daughter of newsagent millionaire John Menzies. Kate runs a catering company and is a friend of Viscount Linley, whose party they were attending. Kate also played tennis with Diana and hosted bridge evenings that the Princess attended.

✦ Protocol ✦

THE DUCHY OF CORNWALL

*Prince Charles derives his income from the Duchy of Cornwall, see **right**, an estate spread over 23 counties, mostly in the south of England. Covering 130,000 acres, and consisting mostly of farmland, only 21,100 acres of the estate are actually in Cornwall. The Duchy dates from 1337, when King Edward III created it for his heir, Edward, the Black Prince. In 1996, Prince Charles' income from the Duchy, which is taxable, was reckoned at around £4.5 million a year. But while the income from the estate is his, Charles cannot touch the capital. That must be preserved for the next Prince of Wales, his son William, who will inherit the Duchy when his father becomes king.*

making a husband jealous, but it was also ideal spice for lurid headlines and, afterwards, the press kept Dunne under regular surveillance. Even so, they managed to get it wrong when they named Dunne as the man who had a *tête-à-tête* with Diana at a David Bowie concert at Wembley in June 1987. As a result, Dunne was obliged to issue strong denials through his solicitor. Philip Dunne married two years later, in 1989, and, doubtless to his relief, put himself out of the running in the press quest for royal scandal.

Gossip had already found other targets, though.

The Private Princess
Diana and the Duchess of York

Fergie, as the press christened the Duchess of York, seemed like a tonic for Diana when she married into the Royal Family in 1986. Fergie was bright, she was breezy, she was irrepressible. She seemed the perfect foil for the quieter, shyer Princess, and the catalyst who would bring out her new sister-in-law.

This was an over-simplification, and ignored the important fact that, despite occasional lapses, Diana was far cannier than Fergie on the subject of acceptable royal behaviour. All the same, Diana seems to have allowed herself to be led into high jinks of the most outrageous kind. It was all giggles and goings-on early in 1987 as Diana and Fergie had a pushing match at Klosters, which ended with Diana losing and sprawling in the snow. Later that year, at Royal Ascot, Fergie egged the Princess on as they jabbed other racegoers in the behind with their umbrellas. But Diana soon appeared to realize the damage this sort of schoolgirlish prank was doing to the sobriety of the royal image. Fergie, it appeared, was a friend she could do without. Within a

Below Fergie and Diana at Ascot, where they indulged in some spirited pranks until Diana realized the bad press this created.

year, by the middle of 1988, Diana was, apparently, starting to distance herself from her sister-in-law – and from the flak which Fergie attracted.

Above On one of her regular visits to the races at Ascot, Diana shares a joke with Viscount Linley, Princess Margaret's son. **Opposite page, top** The Spanish Royal Family were good friends with whom Charles and Diana spent holidays in Majorca and, as here, on board King Juan Carlos' yacht, cruising the islands.

The man in the Wembley *tête-à-tête* was Major David Waterhouse of the Life Guards, bachelor nephew of the Duke of Marlborough and an old friend of the Duchess of York. Waterhouse was also Diana's bridge partner. When, ultimately, he was identified, he, too, forcefully denied a liaison with Diana. It seems they had their heads together because it was the only way they could talk and be heard amid the characteristic noise of pop music.

The strains of royal friendship were, sadly, a common experience among Diana's friends, who out of sheer self-defence tended to adopt a wary attitude. One of them, Kate Menzies, daughter of the millionaire newsagent John Menzies, reacted angrily to press quizzing about Diana's marriage, but not so angrily that she forgot the need for discretion. She clearly understood press tactics.

'It's nonsense,' Kate asserted, 'but it's impossible for me to say anything more in case I'm misinterpreted or misconstrued.'

The speculation and the stories continued, all the same, and became even more insidious when it was reported that Charles and Diana were at odds, not only with each other, but with each

other's friends. The media gossip cast Charles' friends as serious chaps, men of substance and intellect, who were happy to sit for hours discussing weighty subjects like the environment, literature or world affairs. Diana's friends, conversely, were depicted as lightweight, fond of gossip, talk about clothes and television soap operas and social chit-chat. Charles, it was said, could not stand Diana's 'silly' flatmates. The comparison was never fair. Charles' friends were just as capable of small talk. One of Diana's friends once protested: 'Don't think we're all upper-class airheads.'

It was logical, though, that the 13-year age gap between Charles and Diana and the diversity of their interests meant that their friends appeared disparate. When Charles' polo chums got together to

> ## "The stories are a fabrication, and it's appalling the way the Princess is being persecuted."
>
> MAJOR DAVID WATERHOUSE, FRIEND OF DIANA, ON RUMOURS OF A ROMANCE

discuss their sport, Diana would be less than interested. Once, reportedly, she threw down her napkin at the dinner table and stalked out, declaring that she had never been so bored in all her life. Conversely, Charles' friends were not likely to want to be around during sessions of girl talk.

However that may be, part of the difference between their two sets of friends may have been due to the fact that Charles and Diana seemed to have different concepts of social life. Charles, it appears, preferred serious discussion, an exchange of views and the chance to learn about the ordinary world outside the confines that royal status imposed on him. This was why Charles liked talking to people such as Laurens van der Post, the elderly writer, explorer and wartime prisoner of the Japanese.

A CHANCE TO HAVE FUN

Diana, however, had enjoyed more freedom than Charles before their marriage and looked on social life as a chance to have fun, relax, let her hair down and escape, for a time, the demands of her royal status. On such occasions, her friends called her

IN CONTEXT **1989** BERLIN WALL FALLS

- Crown Prince Akihito becomes Emperor of Japan on the death of his father, Hirohito
- Ayatollah Khomeini of Iran pronounces a *fatwa* on Salman Rushdie, author of *The Satanic Verses*
- Soviet troops quit Afghanistan after ten years
- 94 people die in disaster at Hillsborough football stadium in Sheffield
- Massacre of students in Tiananmen Square, Beijing
- Dalai Lama, leader of Tibet, wins Nobel Peace Prize
- Berlin Wall between east and west is dismantled, **right**

Left Charles at a charity polo match with Lord and Lady Romsey. Penelope Romsey was a former girlfriend of Charles. Her husband, Norton Knatchbull, was at Gordonstoun with Charles and is a godfather to Prince William.
Below Diana, in 1991, with Princess Beatrice and the Knatchbulls' daughter Leonora, who was soon to die of leukaemia. **Opposite page** Princess Diana chats with Lord Sam 'Spam' Vestey, the meat tycoon. His wife is a godmother to Harry.

'Duch', a childhood nickname, or just 'Diana' as they had done in her single days. The idea that they invariably curtseyed to her and called her 'Ma'am' was incorrect. But exceptions were those occasions when Diana met her friends in public, or in front of people, like the mothers of William and Harry's school friends, who were not members of the 'Throne Rangers' as Diana's BFs were called.

The girls-together aspect of her social life was therapeutic for Diana. She often took the chance to lunch with them, and go on shopping expeditions or holidays with them. She also played tennis, her favourite sport, with fellow enthusiasts like Catherine Soames, who had married Diana's distant relative, Nicholas Soames, a grandson of Sir Winston Churchill.

The differences between Charles' friends and Diana's inevitably became a rift, though, when the royal marriage started to go wrong and, by 1989, was rumoured to be heading for the rocks. It was then that they ceased to be just company for the Prince or the Princess, and began to resemble groups sharpening their swords for a marital war.

A Real Sport

Diana dressed for sport was as closely watched as Diana the fashion icon. The ski suits, tennis dresses and swimsuits she wore were as influential as her most glamorous gowns

There were factors inherent in sportswear that did not always apply to the outfits Diana wore in her everyday royal life. Ski suits, for instance, had to be warm as well as stylish, but it was important that they didn't look bulky – fashion appeal was a must. Ski boots had to be solid, waterproof and comfortable without being clumpy and inelegant. Tennis dresses required ease of movement and coolness along with their fashion looks. Swimwear had to fit well, yet not be too revealing.

Style on the slopes

Skiing was never just a winter holiday for the royals. The press cameras were always waiting, obliging Charles and Diana to pose for photos. However, when she went skiing with Charles at Lech, in Austria, in 1983, Diana was not as stylish as she later became. Her ski suit was a fairly ordinary red two-piece, with large shoulder flashes in black, lined

Three pictures of Diana skiing in Lech, Austria. **Far left** Diana in a blue and black jacket enlivened by a red starburst motif. She wears sunglasses and black mittens. **Near left** On the same trip Diana rings the changes with a red ski jacket and tight black ski pants. This skiing trip, in 1995, was the last Diana took with her boys. The press intrusion was too disturbing for William and he refused to go skiing again. Instead Diana took them to the Caribbean for a winter break. **Main picture** Diana's fondness for white woollen head coverings helped to create a widely copied trend.

with white (see page 261). Diana's footwear, made by ski boot specialist Nordica, proved to be long-term favourites among her store of twelve pairs of ski boots. They were white with dark blue insets and harmonized with the dark blue leather mittens that completed Diana's outfit.

In 1987, Diana arrived on the slopes, this time at Klosters in Switzerland, in her most chic and stylish ski suit yet. It was an all-in-one jumpsuit, made by Kitex. The purple colour was eye-catching enough, though the focus of the suit was a deep double inverted triangle, which started on each shoulder and met at the waist. Outlined in kingfisher blue, the triangle featured jazzy luminescent pink horizontal stripes, which were echoed by a centrally placed, pink, five-pointed star (see page 261).

With the Kitex all-in-one, Diana wore a knitted white tube which entirely covered her hair, ears,

> ***"Diana's ski wear was sexy. She liked the figure-hugging styles and looked fabulous."***
>
> JAYNE FINCHER, PHOTOGRAPHER, ON DIANA

forehead and neck, enclosing her face in a cocoon of fluffy warmth. On top of that, Diana added an extra knitted white head-covering, creating the look of an Arab 'burnous' head-dress. The Nordica ski-boots were in evidence again, and this time Diana revealed that they stretched up to mid-calf height. Mirror sunglasses completed this outfit, which caused a sensation on the slopes.

Traditional tennis strip

Tennis, Diana's favourite sport, was less of a public royal occasion than her skiing holidays, but her preference in outfits became known when she played the sport's top woman star, Steffi Graf, in 1988. For their mixed doubles match at the exclusive Vanderbilt Club in London, Diana wore a blue and white short tennis dress with a box-pleated skirt. To keep warm after the match, Diana donned a Jasper Conran pink cardigan, but she kept to the traditional tennis colour, plain white, for her shoes and ankle socks.

Tennis may have been her favourite sport but

HEAD SKI SUIT
This red all-in-one jumpsuit by Head has a quilted top for warmth. Diana wore it **(below)** with a plaited woollen headband in plum, pink and white, along with white Nordica ski boots. Underneath the suit she wore a simple white poloneck sweater.

Top Diana in Lech, Austria, in March 1995, wears tight black ski pants with the starburst jacket seen earlier. **Above, inset** On the same trip, with the princes, Diana wears an all-in-one blue padded ski suit. **1** In 1983 Diana was warm in this red two-piece but not highly fashionable. **2** The reverse was true in 1987, in this Kitex jumpsuit with a white burnous-style head-dress.

1 On a beach in Sardinia, in August 1991, Diana wears a jazzy red, purple, black and green bikini. 2 On the same Sardinian holiday, Diana, on board a yacht, wears another bikini, this time a skimpily cut one without shoulder straps. **Main picture** On the Caribbean island of Nevis, in 1993, Diana walks through the gentle surf, wearing a red bikini by Jantzen.

Spy camera in the ceiling

IN THE NEWS

Sneaked pictures of Diana exercising at a private gym produced this sensational 'exclusive' in the Sunday Mirror in November 1993. The report, spiced by 'the most amazing pictures you'll ever see' covered four inside pages and the centre pages, too. Needless to say, it caused a security storm and protests about the invasion of royal privacy, as well as suspicions that the beautifully-coiffed Diana had 'organized' the photo session herself. The pictures had been taken by the gym's manager. Diana sued, making the paper pay a large sum to charity.

from an early age Diana was a keen swimmer and never lost her passion for the water. During her early royal years she often wore bikinis for swimming and sunbathing. A favourite red bikini certainly showed she had the figure for it. She went on wearing bikinis, such as the geometric print number she ordered from the American Jantzen catalogue, but later seemed to prefer one-piece bathing suits. When in London, she used to arrive at Buckingham Palace at around 7.00am, dressed for the swimming pool, wearing her swimsuit underneath her tracksuit.

Diana's swimsuit wardrobe was considerable, and several of her outfits were made of a special material, neoprene, which proved its effectiveness when worn by deep-sea divers. Diana's neoprene one-

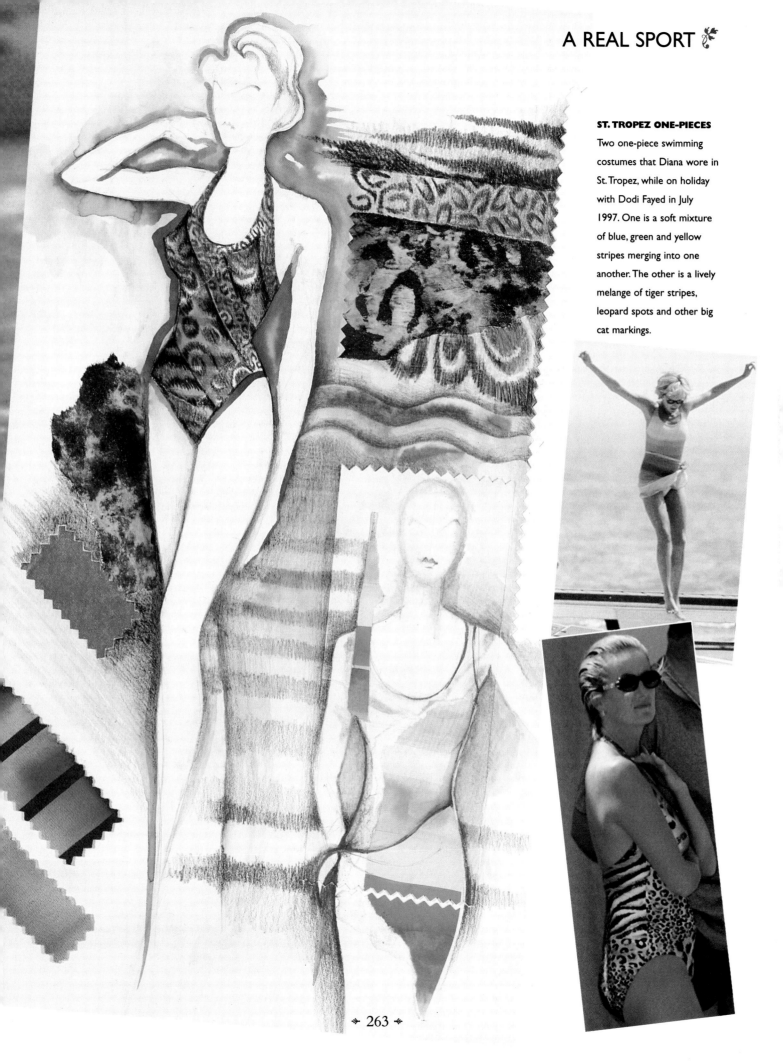

ST. TROPEZ ONE-PIECES

Two one-piece swimming costumes that Diana wore in St. Tropez, while on holiday with Dodi Fayed in July 1997. One is a soft mixture of blue, green and yellow stripes merging into one another. The other is a lively melange of tiger stripes, leopard spots and other big cat markings.

piece in black and shocking pink sent sales of these swimsuits rocketing when pictures of her doing the backstroke in the new outfit hit the front pages. A lot of its popular appeal for women whose figures

> *"Diana was like a sylph. She made the swimwear she wore, not the other way around."*
>
> MARCO HOUSTON, EDITOR OF ROYALTY MAGAZINE, ON DIANA

were not quite as perfect as Diana's lay in the slimming effect achieved by its design, the central panel in black, pink neoprene at the sides, and black piping round the neckline and armholes.

Diana sometimes wore this swimsuit with a matching floaty sarong, which echoed the black and pink colours in its print, combined with yellow on a blue background. The swimsuit and

Above Diana in St. Barthelemy, in February 1995, wearing a one-piece swimsuit which is largely backless. **1** In April 1990, this ocelot print sarong, worn while on holiday on Richard Branson's island Necker, in the Caribbean, instantly set a new trend for beachwear. **2** Diana in a pink one-piece swimsuit on Antigua in 1989. **3** At an indoor court Diana wears a pale blue and white tennis dress. **4** In blue shorts and a stars and stripes top ready for tennis. **Right** Another pink cardigan over a white tennis outfit, worn to keep warm after a game.

③

④

sarong duo became one of her favourites. She was seen wearing a sea green outfit of this kind as well as a striking ocelot (a spotted cat) suit with matching sarong by the Israeli swimwear makers Gottex.

Off limits to the press

A princess in a swimsuit, with or without the cover-up sarong, caused quite a surprise when Diana was photographed baring the royal anatomy for public inspection. A bikini, though normal for most young women on the beach with the figure to justify it, was even more of a shock on a princess.

Though a ski suit was far less revealing, it was still a radical departure, after so many years when royals in sportswear, especially brief sportswear, had been off limits to the press. With Diana, however, all this changed, and press and public were allowed to see a princess as a fashion trendsetter who could rival top models, looking just as good in sportswear as in everything else she wore.

Welcome in the Valleys

Wales was the scene of the first royal tour that Diana made. While she visited again several times, it was the three-day tour of October 1981 that was the biggest test for the new Princess.

It was late October. The skies were slate grey. It rained. It was cold. But the Welsh were out in their smiling, cheering thousands to welcome Diana, then only three months married, as their very own princess. They brought their children, they brought their flags, but above all, they brought a willingness to accept her without reservation.

Welsh nationalists resented the displacement of their own native princes by the heir to the English throne – to them, a foreign throne – and there had been threats. Security guards defused two bombs, and placards along the route read 'Go Home, Diana' and 'Go Home, English Prince'. Nationalist slogans were chanted, Charles and Diana's car was sprayed with paint and, at Bangor, there were student demos, scuffles and stink bombs were thrown.

In spite of these incidents, thousands of friendly faces gathered everywhere Charles and Diana went. Their placards read 'Charles Loves Diana' and 'God

Main picture The Nantgynant Valley in Caernarvonshire. On a lightning three-day tour from city to city in 1981, Diana could only get a flavour of the Welsh countryside.

Above During the 1981 tour, shadowed by detectives and local policemen and trailed by lady-in-waiting Anne Beckwith-Smith, Diana reaches out to shake a proffered hand.

Inset, far left Diana pauses to chat to the crowds on a walkabout during the 1982 tour.

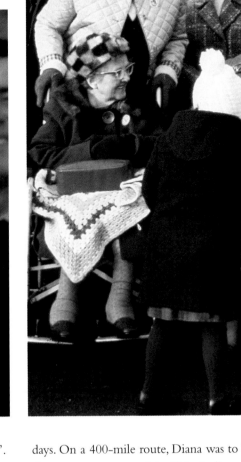

Above Charles and Diana look pleased at another warm welcome. For Diana, her first tour was marked by hats in a similar style, and she was still fond of frilly white collars at this stage.

Above right Accepting carnations from a child to the delight of the crowd, during the tour of Wrexham on 26 November 1982.

Bless the Prince and Princess of Wales'. Shopkeepers had clearly done bumper business in hats and Union Jack flags, which waved in their dozens from the crowds and adorned buildings.

Diana's First Tour

As Charles' own principality, Wales was the first choice for Diana's debut. Even so, many people saw Wales as a tryout, which would show how well, or otherwise, Diana was going to handle the business of public appearances and walkabouts. She was completely inexperienced. Nothing in her previous life as Lady Diana Spencer had approached the demands of the big royal occasion. Confronted by thousands of strangers, a shy young lady like Diana might have taken fright.

What people had overlooked, though, was the generosity of the Welsh towards the royal newcomer who, they realized, still had much to learn. Diana made mistakes, though nothing serious, and the crowds forgave her and warmed to her.

The 1981 tour of Wales, which began on 27 October at Rhyl, in north Wales, had Charles and Diana on the go for 12 hours every day for three days. On a 400-mile route, Diana was to be shown almost every corner of the Principality.

At the start of the tour, Diana was tense and later confessed to being 'scared stiff'. But she soon relaxed after she was welcomed to a Deeside Leisure Centre, where the harpist Ceirwen Stuart serenaded her. This was only the overture to a feast

> *"The people who stood outside for five or six hours, in torrential rain – that's what I remember."*
> DIANA, ON HER 1981 WELSH TOUR

of Welsh music that greeted Diana everywhere.

Wales has long been known for its magnificent choirs, which have basses of a richness and depth known nowhere else. The Welsh pulled out all the musical stops for Diana as she toured the hills and valleys, with their neat chapels and black-smoked collieries. The music and the welcome it indicated banished Diana's initial hesitancy and brought some colour to her pale cheeks.

At this time, Diana was in the early stages of her

Inset below Everywhere Charles and Diana went during their 1981 tour of Wales, they were met by patient crowds, displaying Welsh flags and waving Union Jacks, despite the bad weather. Many were rewarded for their perseverance with a handshake or a brief chat from the royal couple.

of blooms grew to such proportions that Diana had to load them onto her lady-in-waiting, her detective and the good-tempered policemen and women who were accompanying her.

There was a two-way message being exchanged here. Diana was giving notice that, as Princess of Wales, she was not going to be a royal figurehead but an active player in her new role. The response that came back was one of instant affection. The Welsh crowds, who were the first to experience Diana's new approach, were soon calling her 'Di bach' just as they called Charles 'Carlo bach'.

It was unfortunate, though, that the royal timetable gave too little time for the crowds to see both Charles and Diana. The couple's strategy, however, was to split up for each walkabout and to take one side of the street apiece. On Diana's side, she gave the children first pick of her attention, while Charles concentrated on the adults on his side.

There were, however, plenty of views to be had of Charles and Diana together in the big-windowed car, driving slowly past the crowds with its

first pregnancy, though no announcement had yet been made, and Prince Charles was seen hovering around protectively, keeping an eye on his new young wife. However, when he realized that despite her nervy start, Diana was coping and getting into her stride, Charles felt able to go further afield and chat to the crowds on his own. Diana was, in any case, in safe hands – those of her lady-in-waiting, Anne Beckwith-Smith, and of her detectives.

Warm greetings

Diana's technique was to get as close to the people as she could. She frequently stopped to chat face-to-face, gave people gentle pats on the arm and always spent time with small children who were lifted up to get their cheeks 'chucked' or their hair affectionately ruffled. One of the first things onlookers noticed was, that despite the cold, Diana was not wearing gloves. She shook every hand she could reach and, in the unscheduled time it took, the timetable slipped further and further behind.

Another reason for the delay was the vast number of flowers people had brought along to present to Diana. As the walkabouts progressed, the armfuls

Di conquers Wales

This headline in the Daily Mail of 28 October 1981 reflected the fact that there had been no Princess of Wales for over seventy years, ever since the previous Princess became Queen Mary in 1910. The picture of Diana in Wales on her first public tour, surrounded by smiling people extending their hands to be shaken, would be repeated over and over again in succeeding years as Diana evolved into the most popular royal ever.

Daily Mail

Welcome to Wales—by nearly all

AT LAST—OUR OWN PRINCESS

By BRIAN JAMES

red and yellow royal standard streaming in the wind from the roof. The tour of Wales was so concentrated and so short that this distant view of the royal couple was all that many people were able to get.

Had they been close enough, they might have caught a glimpse of the large map of Wales spread out on the armrest between Charles and Diana. As the tour progressed, Charles showed his wife the high spots of their route and, with his considerable knowledge of Wales and its history, enlivened the

> *"Poor you! I feel cold myself. My hands are freezing, and you must be much worse. Thank you for waiting for us!"*
>
> DIANA, TO A WOMAN IN THE CROWD ON HER WELSH TOUR

places they visited with interesting information. Diana could hardly have had a better tour guide.

Charles had much to tell Diana when they reached the imposing stone walls of Caernarvon Castle, where he was to present her to the Welsh people. The Castle, nearly seven centuries old, was a mighty structure with high thick walls and slit windows, from where medieval archers had fired down at enemies. On the cold, damp day when Charles and Diana were there, Caernarvon looked its most impressive and daunting. The sun, when it shone, was pale and autumnal; very different from

the midsummer day 12 years earlier when the 20-year-old Charles was formally invested Prince of Wales within its precincts by the Queen. Later, the Queen stood with Charles on the balcony and presented him to the Welsh people.

On 27 October 1981, when Charles, in his turn, did the presentation, he and Diana waved and smiled to the huge crowd in the courtyard below as the wind whipped at his hair and her skirt. The crowd roared back their greeting and sang 'God Bless the Prince of Wales' with such enthusiasm the cold stone of the castle seemed to warm to it.

Next, it was on to Bangor. This was where the most serious of the nationalist protests were staged but, with remarkable aplomb, Diana seemed not to

⫷ Protocol ⫸

WHY AN ENGLISH PRINCE OF WALES?

*Prince of Wales is a title which has been granted to the eldest surviving son and heir of English monarchs for nearly 700 years. The first was Edward, whose father, King Edward I, presented him to the Welsh people as an infant at Caernarvon Castle in 1284. The child, who later became King Edward II, was meant to replace the Welsh princes, the last of whom, Llewellyn ap Gryffd, died in 1282. The heir to the English throne has usually been Prince of Wales ever since. Prince Charles, seen **above** at his Investiture in 1969, is the twenty-first to hold the title.*

notice. Arrests were being made only yards away, but the Princess, now gaining in confidence, was working her way along the crowds, shaking hands, smiling and chatting – as if nothing untoward was happening. Steady nerves in the face of danger had long been regarded as a royal virtue. Diana, though a new girl, had learned the technique already.

St. David's Cathedral

The following day, 28 October, the royal couple visited the ancient Cathedral of St. David's on the Pembrokeshire coast. The cathedral, a century older than Caernarvon Castle, housed the bones of St. David, the patron saint of Wales, and was for hundreds of years a place of pilgrimage. Charles and Diana's tour coincided with the cathedral's 800th anniversary, and the couple attended a special service to mark the occasion. Charles' personal standard, emblazoned with the Welsh dragon, flew from the vaulted roof in honour of his presence.

Afterwards, Charles and Diana emerged to find larger crowds than ever waiting for them as the

cathedral bells pealed out. Diana seemed anxious to meet the people, who had been waiting for her in freezing, squally conditions as the wind whipped in from the grey, unfriendly sea. Some of them had been standing there since dawn.

Without waiting for Charles, Diana walked smartly through the medieval gateway and was soon handshaking and chatting in her now characteristic style. Watching his wife perform with such grace and charm, Prince Charles was beaming, evidently very proud of her.

When Charles and Diana reached Carmarthen the rain came lashing down, soaking everyone and everything, including the royal couple. The welcome, even so, reached new heights of excitement.

Opposite page, top Diana, wearing a brown chequered coat dress and a large brown beret, stands next to a broadly smiling Prince Charles on the 1982 tour. **Above left** In Rhyl, North Wales, in 1981, the crowd get their first glimpse of Diana's trademark pearl choker. For a 20-year-old, who just months before had been a 'nobody', meeting hordes of people desperate to see her must have been daunting. **Inset** Crowds line the route to glimpse the royal couple. **Above** Charles and Diana arrive for an evening engagement, during the first tour of Wales.

Word had evidently got around that Diana was a handshaker extraordinaire. People were so anxious to claim their share that some even thrust their hands through the legs of press photographers. Remarkably, many of them succeeded. Diana was willing to ignore the awkwardness and bend down for handshakes just the same.

> ## "She sympathizes with us – you can sense it."
> WELSH WOMAN IN THE CROWD, ON DIANA

It was so wet, though, that umbrellas were virtually useless. Diana became more and more sodden. The feathers on her hat drooped, the veil hung limp, and her hairstyle collapsed into damp, clinging strands. No amount of rain could dampen her smile, though, and eventually she slung her umbrella over one shoulder and carried on regardless.

The last day

Diana stopped for even longer than before at a group of a dozen disabled people who were parked by the kerbside in their wheelchairs. Diana held their hands for some time as she talked to them, standing in the gutter so as to get as close to them as possible. Later on, when Charles and Diana had dried out, they donned evening dress and went to a gala concert in Swansea.

The last day of the brief tour, 29 October, was spent in Cardiff, the capital of Wales, where Diana

Above right In the pouring rain at Carmarthen, Diana takes the time to chat to members of the crowd who had waited to see her.
Right Streets were bedecked with bunting and people carried flags, ready to wave them excitedly when the royal couple appeared.

was given a considerable honour: the Freedom of the City. Apart from the Queen, Diana was the only woman to be accorded this honour. In response, she included a few well-rehearsed words of Welsh in her acceptance speech.

After 1981, Diana returned to Wales many times and throughout her royal career took a great deal of interest in the Principality. However widely she travelled the world in later years, she never forgot that Wales was not only the scene of her first royal tour, but also the scene of her first great triumph.

FAVOURITE THINGS

Even if they had never met her, people felt they knew Diana personally. What she liked, what she enjoyed were all part of the picture. These were favourite things she shared with ordinary people

Anything and everything to do with Diana became of enormous interest and curiosity when she burst on to the royal scene in 1981. The public appetite for Diana trivia seemed endless, and the press were soon hard at work digging for it. This was how they came to know about Diana's penchant for wine gums.

In 1981, newsmen staked out the local shop at Tetbury, near Highgrove House, and were there when the newly married Princess slipped down to the village to buy her favourite sweets. The media

coverage added to the furore current at that time about press intrusion into Diana's privacy. All the same, the wine gums became the first in a long list of things Diana liked, a list which grew in time to form a panorama of her personal choices.

In 1981, the press were quick to point out that some of Diana's preferences were distinctly childish. That much could be expected of a girl who was rather young for her 20 years. The wine gums were only the start. It later transpired that Diana had a very sweet tooth. She loved toffees, fruit

pastilles, Creme Eggs, Mars bars, Kit Kat, Yorkie bars and Opal Fruits. Lindt chocolate was a more sophisticated choice, as were Bendick's Bittermints.

Diana made her own sweets, too, using a recipe she learned when she took a ten-week cookery course in 1978. It included a whole pound of sugar

> "*I have an enormous appetite, despite what people say...I would walk miles for a bacon sandwich.*"
> DIANA, ON FOOD

and two ounces of butter, together with a large tin of condensed milk. The number of calories in the finished fudge was not an amount a slimmer would care to contemplate, and Diana, in the popular mind, soon became the ultimate slimmer.

The idea that Diana was eternally dieting, something she herself denied, got around because she never seemed to eat very much at official dinners. Diana was fond of her food but soon realized that if she ate the beautifully prepared and tempting meals laid before her during public engagements, she could say goodbye to her much-prized figure.

FAVOURITE DISHES

Diana took the edge off her appetite with a light meal at home before going out. Sometimes, she chose fast food for this purpose. She liked Chinese take-aways, pasta, pizzas and bacon sandwiches. Shepherd's pie, which she had loved since school-days, was another favourite of hers. So was the savoury snack Twiglets. Diana also went in for less fattening foods such as chicken, plaice, kippers, fruit, vegetables and salads.

Satisfied beforehand with a selection of these favourites, Diana could sally forth and easily resist the temptations of the official dinner table. Alcoholic drinks never bothered her, as she rarely drank any. She preferred mineral water – the still rather than the sparkling variety.

Diana's taste in reading was distinctly romantic. Since her schooldays, she had been an avid reader of novels by Barbara Cartland, who became her step-grandmother when Cartland's daughter,

Previous page Diana and actor John Travolta take the floor at the White House. **Above** Diana, with Wayne Sleep, is introduced to the corps de ballet at the Royal Opera House, Covent Garden. **Inset** Dancing with Wayne Sleep in December 1985 on stage at the Royal Opera. **Above right** A lifelong lover of ballet, Diana watches the dancers go through their paces while on a visit to a ballet school. **Right** On a trip to the Suffolk County Show, Diana has bought some carved wooden figures and is looking at the cosmetics.

Raine, married Diana's father, Earl Spencer, in 1976. Barbara Taylor Bradford, Danielle Steele, Colleen McCullough and the prolific Mary Stewart also wrote books Diana liked to curl up with. Daphne du Maurier was a frequent choice, while Jeffrey Archer's punchy, political and sometimes raunchy novels provided a departure from romance.

POP AND ROCK MUSIC

When she was very young, Diana went through the normal teenage fads for pop and rock music, and the list of her favourite groups was very long. She was certainly a fan of groups such as Dire Straits, Genesis, Spandau Ballet, 10 CC, Kid Creole and the Coconuts and Supertramp. Individual stars who counted among Diana's favourites included Neil Diamond, Barry Manilow, Michael Jackson, Phil Collins, Jean-Michel Jarre and Elton John, who became a personal friend.

Diana always kept herself up to date with what was top of the pops and as Princess of Wales she had unparalleled opportunities to meet her idols.

DIARY DATES
1990
2 March
Princess of Wales visits Metropolitan Police Driving School, London
5 March
Princess of Wales launches the Dump 1990 Campaign for the destruction of unwanted medicines and poisons
18 April
Princess of Wales opens the annual drugs conference of the Association of Chief Police Officers
18 May
Princess of Wales attends the British Sports Association for the Disabled 'Wheelchair Basketball Day' in Brentford, Middlesex
23 May
Prince of Wales attends Jester Ball in aid of Action on Addiction in London
6 June
Princess of Wales lays foundation stone of new clinical block at the Royal Marsden Hospital, London
4 July
Princess of Wales attends graduation ceremony at Royal Academy of Music
11 September
Princess of Wales launches Birthright's healthy eating leaflet for pregnant mothers, at Tesco's in Southport
22 September
Princess of Wales attends Black and White Festival Ball in the Piazza, Covent Garden, London
19 November
Princess of Wales re-opens Spencer House, London

An eternal enthusiast who loved meeting the stars, she was known in her early royal days to forget her exalted status at a public engagement and rush forward to shake a pop, rock or film star's hand. Fortunately, she stopped short of screaming with delight, as fellow fans of her age did when they gathered outside to see the stars arrive.

Diana put her encounters with the stars to a serious purpose, by co-opting them in her efforts to

> ## "I have all your albums at home and I know the words of all your songs."
>
> DIANA TO AUGUST DARNELL, LEADER OF KID CREOLE AND THE COCONUTS

raise money for charity. This was yet another of Diana's innovations. Royals and rock had never met before in joint charitable ventures, and there was a lot of disapproval from traditionalists that the Princess was 'cheapening' the royal image. Diana, though, was in her element and her rock connections justified themselves when huge amounts were raised through their involvement.

Diana's participation meant millions. In 1982, at the suggestion of their royal fan, Status Quo gave the first of a series of concerts in aid of Prince Charles' own charity, The Prince's Trust. Fifteen more concerts followed in the next five years, and one of them, in 1986, raised nearly £1.2 million in ticket sales, television fees, record sales and video rights. Other 'gigs' that year raised £1 million.

Here, Diana was skirting the edge of the acceptable. Royals were not supposed to be involved in active fundraising. Their function was to set the ball rolling for others to do the work of bringing in the cash. That objection lapsed, though, when Prince Charles attended the concerts.

CLASSICAL TASTES

Charles' kind of music was at the other, classical, end of the spectrum. He was an enthusiastic opera fan and seems to have had some influence on Diana. She, too, came to appreciate the operas of Giuseppe Verdi and Wolfgang Amadeus Mozart. She also had other favourite classical composers: Rachmaninov,

Schumann, Grieg and Tchaikovsky, all of them big names in the 19th-century era of romantic music. Diana classed Verdi's eloquent *Requiem* as her top choice among individual compositions and often attended gala performances at London's Royal Opera House.

Diana's favourite tenor, a frequent performer

Above Charles and Diana at a barbecue at Kingsmere Farm, Ottawa, Canada, about to eat some sweet corn. They preferred fish to red meat and would barbecue salmon rather than steaks.

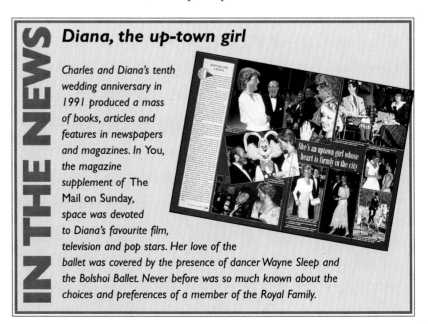

IN THE NEWS

Diana, the up-town girl

Charles and Diana's tenth wedding anniversary in 1991 produced a mass of books, articles and features in newspapers and magazines. In You, the magazine supplement of The Mail on Sunday, space was devoted to Diana's favourite film, television and pop stars. Her love of the ballet was covered by the presence of dancer Wayne Sleep and the Bolshoi Ballet. Never before was so much known about the choices and preferences of a member of the Royal Family.

Right On a tour of Marks and Spencer's store in Paris, Diana casts a look at the Chocolate Chip Cookies. In her younger days she certainly had a liking for chocolate. **Below** While travelling, Diana finds time for a slice of cake. The member of staff behind her holds a glass of champagne but Diana was not a great drinker of alcohol and usually preferred a glass of still mineral water.

there, was the golden-voiced Luciano Pavarotti, who, later on, was so upset at her sudden death that he did not trust himself to sing at her funeral without breaking down. The top female soprano, as far as Diana was concerned, was Kiri Te Kanawa, the lovely New Zealand opera star, who sang at the Royal Wedding in 1981.

The stars of the dance world had a special niche among Diana's favourite performers. Dancing, as she admitted, was almost an obsession with her and she regretted growing too tall to be a ballet dancer. But it was fine compensation for her to dance with two of her favourites in one year, 1985.

The first, in November, was John Travolta, who had shot to fame with his dancing in the films *Saturday Night Fever* in 1977 and *Grease* in 1978. Prince Charles, who watched as he and Diana danced at a White House ball, said Diana 'would have to be crazy not to want to dance with John Travolta'.

The second dance star to partner Diana, in December 1985, was Wayne Sleep, who had been principal dancer with the Royal Ballet between 1973 and 1983. It was said to be a long-standing dream of Diana's to dance with Wayne Sleep, even though he was nearly nine inches shorter than her. Diana achieved her dream with the three-and-a-half-minute performance the two of them gave on the stage of the Royal Opera House, Covent Garden. It was a smash-hit success, and was the result of careful preparation and rehearsal.

SECRET REHEARSALS

Diana had approached Wayne Sleep with a request that he choreograph a short dance for her as a surprise for Charles. The enterprise was kept strictly secret. Sleep came to Kensington Palace for rehearsals. There was no barre, the long rail that dancers use to steady themselves as they go through their exercises. Diana and Sleep used a piece of her Chippendale furniture instead.

Wayne Sleep soon concluded that Diana was a naturally fine mover, very adept at the jazzy dance

> *"We had a lot of laughs. You'd never expect her to be that funny."*
> WAYNE SLEEP, ON DANCING WITH DIANA

steps he planned to include in her performance. Though nervous at first about how to approach her, he treated her like any other student, barking out orders, such as 'Princess, over here!' or 'Arch your back!'. 'What d'you think I am, a forklift truck?' Sleep later revealed he had joked with Diana, as he raised her in his arms during rehearsals.

On the night of the performance, Diana waited backstage while Wayne Sleep went on first. When she followed, the audience gasped with surprise. Charles, it was reported, was 'speechless', though whether this was because of the skill of Diana's dancing or the controversial sight of a future Queen Consort on stage remained unclear.

It was certainly a daring and unprecedented thing for Diana to do. She was skirting the very edge of the acceptable, and there were, inevitably, grumbles from killjoy traditionalists that it was all

Right At a party for the 10th anniversary of the Prince's Trust, Charles and Diana cut the cake, watched by Mark Knopfler, Joan Armatrading and others who helped raise money. **Inset** Diana meets Phil Collins and Genesis after a concert. **Far right** Diana with one of her favourite authors, Jeffrey Archer.

✧ Protocol ✧

THE CIVIL LIST

*Few things about the monarchy are more misunderstood than the Civil List. This exists for the sole purpose of paying the Queen's expenses in performing her public duties, **right**, and presently stands at £7.9 million. However, in exchange for the List, under an arrangement made in 1760, the royal hereditary revenues, which amounted to £88.4 million in 1994/5, are surrendered to Parliament. Other payments are made to members of the Royal Family, but out of the £2,517,000 involved, all but £643,000, to Prince Philip, and £359,000, to the Queen Mother, are repaid by the Queen. Instead of paying for the monarchy, therefore, the country actually makes a profit out of the Royal Family of just under £79 million.*

The Private Princess
Diana and her in-laws

Diana's position within the Royal Family was never an easy one, and when her marriage to Prince Charles started to deteriorate, it became even more difficult.

Below Diana with the Royal Family at the annual gathering in front of Clarence House on the Queen Mother's birthday; her 89th.

As the newest member of a very exclusive club, there was a lot she had to learn. Diana's friendliest in-law relationship was with Princess Margaret, who acted as her guide to the rarefied royal world into which she had married. Margaret doubtless knew how Diana felt, as an outsider. Margaret learned what it was like to be on the outside during her ill-fated romance with Captain Peter Townsend in the early 1950s.

According to friends, the Queen Mother was not particularly fond of Diana, possibly because she did not approve of Diana's mother, Frances. The Queen Mother, of course, had great influence over Prince Charles, and Diana often felt excluded when grandmother and grandson got together.

The Queen proved more cordial, but Diana reportedly came to believe that her mother-in-law blamed her for the difficulties in her marriage to Charles. It seems that, from the Queen's point of view, Diana's bulimia (see Issue 4, page 86) was the cause rather than a symptom of the trouble.

Prince Philip was a difficult ally, partly because Diana apparently believed Charles was intimidated by him. It was evidently the case that Philip wanted Charles to consult him more and may have thought that, potentially, Diana stood in the way. Diana and her sister-in-law, Princess Anne, had their charity work in common, but shared few other interests.

very undignified. Most people, though, seemed to think it was harmless and really rather delightful.

Among other dancers Diana admired were Mikhail Baryshnikov, the spectacular Latvian who had danced with the Bolshoi, and the greatest of English ballerinas, Dame Margot Fonteyn.

Where cinema was concerned, Diana was a fan of the hunkier type of male film star: Clint

> *"You can't help but be entranced by Princess Diana...and I think everyone who has met her personally falls in love with her a little, including myself."*
>
> NEIL DIAMOND, POP STAR, ON DIANA

Eastwood, Robert Redford, Michael Douglas and Tom Selleck, with the suave and sophisticated Roger Moore included as well.

When it came to television, Diana was an avid soap opera-watcher. Her video must have worked overtime to record episodes when she was out on public engagements. Diana followed the most popular home-grown and Australian soaps – *Crossroads, East Enders, Home and Away, Coronation Street* and *Neighbours,* as well as the glitzy American imports

Dynasty and *Dallas.* Among the various comedy programmes, *Bread* ranked tops with Diana.

More became known about her favourite things than had ever been known about any royal before. The details revealed a young woman not all that different from others of her generation, and much closer to the ordinary girl in the street than young aristocrats were normally considered to be. This made it that much easier for people to feel they were close to her and it was heart-warming to know that a royal star of Diana's magnitude, with the world at her feet, could be as anxious to meet the famous as they were to meet her.

Above left Diana with opera singer Luciano Pavarotti at a charity concert for Bosnia, held in Modena, Italy. **Above** Diana with Paul and Linda McCartney in 1992. **Opposite page** Diana alongside pop superstar Michael Jackson backstage at Wembley stadium before his concert in July 1988.

IN CONTEXT 1990   NELSON MANDELA RELEASED

- Mayor of Washington, DC, in the USA is arrested on charges of using 'crack' cocaine
- In South Africa Nelson Mandela, **right,** is released from 27 years' imprisonment
- In New Zealand Richard Hadlee becomes the first cricketer to take 400 Test wickets
- Boris Yeltsin is elected as President of Russia
- Iraq invades and conquers Kuwait
- The former East Germany and West Germany unite
- PM Margaret Thatcher is ousted by the Conservatives

Separate Ways

Diana started many new fashions, and one was for the patterned sweaters she wore in her leisure time. Even that old warhorse, the pleated skirt, acquired a new lease of popularity

Wearing glamorous, expensive designer dresses, as Diana did, with dozens more waiting their turn in her vast wardrobe, may sound like every woman's dream. But constantly dressing up had its tedium and Diana used to kick against it at times by wearing sloppy unco-ordinated leisure clothes. Her skirts and sweaters did not go this far, but created a leisure fashion while still representing time out.

Diana appeared in smarter skirts and sweaters when she knew the press would be present, most often when she took her sons to school. Nothing

> **"Diana always had such style that she elevated the simplest clothes to fashion statements."**
>
> MARCO HOUSTON, EDITOR OF ROYALTY MAGAZINE, ON DIANA

embarrasses little boys more than turning up with an extravagantly dressed mother, unless it is arriving where their school friends can see them with a messily-dressed one. The skirt and sweater served as a halfway house for Diana – neat, but not too glamorous, and not too different from what the other mothers were wearing. They, too, could buy their sweaters at the same shops as Diana. One was the Peruvian craft shop Inca, in Belgravia, where Diana bought sweaters in sky and cloud patterns, among

Opposite page Diana is all in red, wearing culottes, topped by a red pullover with white motifs. **Main picture** Leaving the boys' school, Diana wears a simple black skirt with a white V-necked, cable-stitched pullover. **Above right** In a blue, crew-necked pullover with a strong gold motif, at a tennis tournament. **Right** A long purple and black-trimmed cardigan worn with a white high-necked blouse.

283

other motifs. Inca still receives queries for 'Diana sweaters', even though they no longer stock them.

Warm and Wonderful, which had a shop in Kensington when Diana lived there, was the source of Diana's sheep-patterned sweaters. Jumpers in Cirencester, Diana's local large town when she was staying at Highgrove House, was the place where she purchased elephant- or flower-motif cotton sweaters for the summer.

> **"Sweaters and skirts may have been technically separate with Diana, but they were always beautifully co-ordinated and looked made for each other."**
>
> FIONA SINCLAIR, NEWSPAPER ROYAL CORRESPONDENT

As with virtually everything Diana wore, her sweaters took time to graduate from the ordinary to the eye-catching. Those she wore in early photographs were quite unremarkable. There was a purple sleeveless V-neck worn over a plain pink shirt and accompanied by the filmy polka-dot printed skirt that hit the headlines in 1981 because Diana's legs could be seen through it (see Issue 1, page 11). Another casual outfit of her pre-marriage days, with no pretensions to fashion, was an ill-fitting white V-necked cardigan worn over a kingfisher blue shirt.

Future trends

However, three other sweaters heralded the shape of fashion things to come. Diana was pictured walking back to her Coleherne Court flat wearing a long-sleeved green sweater over a white shirt with a straight navy-check skirt and green tights to match the sweater.

Also in 1981, the fashion she was to set for patterned sweaters was heralded by a purple cardigan decorated with a line of sheep. The cardigan came from Warm and Wonderful and with it she wore a grey pinstripe skirt and a brilliantly coloured, long-sleeved sweater from Inca with green, white, blue and black stripes on a bright pink background.

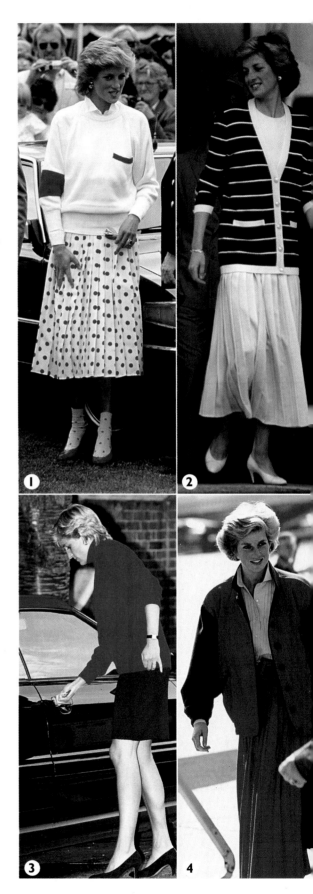

1 Arriving at the polo field, Diana wears a smart white pullover with red flashes that pick up the red of her shoes and the red polka dots of her pleated skirt and bobby socks. She wore this rock 'n' roll look by German designers Mondi in 1986.

2 In September 1989, at Wetherby School, Diana wears a long black and white striped cardigan over a long pleated white skirt. The buttons of the cardigan appear to echo her earrings.

3 Diana as a woman about town is comfortably dressed in a short black skirt and a fetching red polo-necked pullover.

4 Passing through Heathrow Airport, Diana wears a red fabric jacket with black sleeves over a red pleated skirt.

There was a llama, one of the pack-animals of Peru, on each shoulder, and lines of Peruvians in traditional dress across the midriff and on the sleeves.

After her marriage, Diana confined the straight skirt largely to the suits she wore and went more for the pleated variety with her sweaters and cardigans. The easy-move swing of the pleated skirt looked better in longer lengths, and was more suitable for the long-line sweaters Diana later favoured.

Even when she did wear straight skirts with knitwear, ease of movement was incorporated into

them. For instance, the straight black skirt she wore with a blue, black-patterned sweater by Jasper Conran, when taking William to nursery school in 1985, had a long slit at the back to give Diana a full stride as she walked along. Likewise, Diana's straight taupe skirt, seen when she and William arrived at the nursery school in 1987, had kick-pleats on the left-hand side.

Diana went all-pleated, though, at the Braemar Games in 1986. Her skirt featured a pink, blue, gold and black tartan pattern and came down to an inch

JUMPER DESIGNS

A colourful abstract design **(top)** that featured on the back of a jumper Diana wore. The black polo neck pullover is a versatile garment that can be worn effectively with many things, including a black and white dogtooth jacket or a long bright red jacket.

or two below her knees. Later the same year, in August, Diana arrived at Aberdeen Airport (see right) with William and Harry, on the way to their annual summer holiday at Balmoral. She wore a white pleated skirt, white ruffle-necked blouse and, over it, a long-sleeved navy sweater with pink, blue and green stripes at the shoulders and waist. Diana had another version of the sweater with stripes in the same colours at the wrist and along the breast-pockets.

Diana wore pleats again at the school in January 1987 when she delivered William for the Spring term. She wore a red skirt and matching collared

---

> *"Those lambs were really cute. Diana loved animals and had them on her sweaters to show it."*
>
> VICTORIA AUSTIN, ROYAL FEATURES WRITER, ON DIANA

---

red sweater by Jasper Conran. Just over a year later, in February 1988, Diana arrived at Zurich Airport for her annual skiing holiday at fashionable Klosters wearing a full, though unpleated, calf-length skirt in tan suede.

The sweaters Diana was wearing by this time had advanced enormously from the modest numbers of her first tentative royal days. As early as 1983, she appeared for the polo at Smith's Lawn, Windsor, wearing a Warm and Wonderful high-necked red sweater covered in white sheep, with an odd-man-out black sheep among them.

Polo sweaters

Another striking sweater, which Diana wore to Smith's Lawn in 1986, was plain navy, but with a swirling white satin appliquéd motif on the front. This sweater was all the more attractive because its motif was on its own, standing out against a dark background. This principle also characterized two other sweaters which Diana wore.

One was the cream coloured number, which she wore with a turquoise pleated skirt at Highgrove House in 1985. The decoration on this sweater was

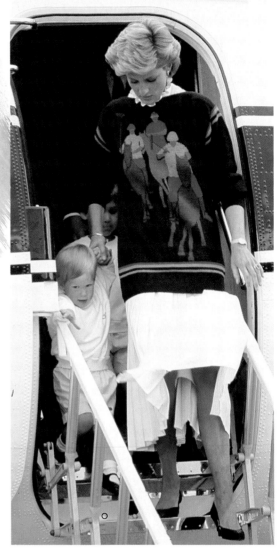

MONDI AT THE RACES
Arriving at Aberdeen Airport with Harry and William, Diana wears a dark blue pullover with a design in four colours, depicting three jockeys on racehorses. The colours of the design are picked up in the stripes at each shoulder and below the waist. It was created by German designers Mondi.

① ②

AZTEC DESIGNS

These figures (left) and the animal (below) are Aztec-style design elements from sweaters that Diana wore around the time of her engagement in February 1981 (see inset below).

confined to a wide band echoing the V-neck and repeated round the sleeves. The ornate 'frame' in navy, edged with light blue touches, featured pretty embroidered deep red and crimson roses. Here, Diana showed how very romantic sweaters could be. The rose-motif would have been just as appropriate decorating a glamorous dress.

The other sweater was more sporty. It was a cream cabled style, which Diana wore to take Prince Harry to school in 1990; it had a band along the V-neck, with diamond shapes in black, a motif echoed around the cuffs of the long sleeves.

Fashionable sweaters

Before Diana appeared in sweaters like these and made the school run into a photo-opportunity, sweaters and cardigans were relatively humble garments, intended for warmth and little else. Sweaters might have had some textural interest, usually cabling or a similar fancy stitch, but cardigans and the once ubiquitous twin-set were more often than not undistinguished.

It took Diana to change all that and raise knitwear and the skirts accompanying them into fashions that required as much care in matching colours and harmonizing styles as was lavished on more formal clothes. When Diana intervened in this area of fashion, the once unconsidered skirt-and-sweater outfit joined the rest of her wardrobe to set yet another fashion example for others to follow.

1 With the princes at Aberdeen Airport once again, Diana is warmly dressed in a pleated wool skirt, a cream hand-knitted sweater and a black bomber jacket and white scarf.
2 A double-breasted plum cardigan covers a high-necked white blouse and a tartan straight skirt. **Right** A red sweater covered with a pattern of white sheep and a single black sheep.

Speaking Out

Public speaking or broadcasting was always an ordeal for Diana. At first, she was terrified, but she worked hard to overcome her nerves and disadvantages and give her speeches more impact

The Princess of Wales was rather like a star of silent films. Like them, she was seen, admired and adored in still photographs or on the screen, smiling, waving, looking beautiful and being gracious, but there was no soundtrack. Only a few people who had heard Diana giving a speech in public knew how she sounded and whether, like some stars of the silent screen, her voice seemed at odds with the way she looked.

Making speeches was quite different from meeting the public face to face. Once she had learned the royal brand of small talk, Diana had no problems coping with that. However, standing up in front of an audience, with all eyes on her, and making a speech lasting some minutes was another game altogether. So was being pinned by the eagle eye of the television camera, with millions waiting to watch and listen at home.

A few words

Initially, Diana was terrified of public life. During her first three years as Princess of Wales, she avoided giving speeches whenever she could and when she could not, she made do with just a few words. In fact, between 1981 and 1984 Diana spoke no more than about five hundred words in public and seemed to prefer remaining a beautiful, smiling, but largely silent figure.

Public speaking, of course, was bound to catch up with her sooner rather than later. Speeches formed an integral part of royal duties and it was unfortunate that Diana was not a natural at it. It

Left Surrounded by American dignitaries, Diana makes an after-dinner speech at the Humanitarian of the Year Awards in New York, in December 1995. **Below** In April 1990, she addresses an audience at the Tenth National Drugs Conference in Preston, Lancashire.

Above Diana speaking, as many practiced speakers do, with the help of notes, to pupils of her old school, West Heath in Sevenoaks, Kent, in November 1987.

did not help that she was thrown in at the deep end when she was required to make her first speech on her very first tour as Princess: in Wales in 1981, when she thanked the Lord Mayor and Council of Cardiff for granting her the Freedom of the city. It was a brave effort, all the more so because it included a sentence or two in the Welsh language, which Diana had to learn phonetically.

Work needed

All the same, it was evident that she would have to work hard at improving her diction and delivery and somehow get her nerves under control. This became all the more vital as her list of presidencies and patronages expanded. She found herself addressing conferences and meetings where she

spoke up for Barnardo's, the Child Accident Prevention Trust and RELATE, among others.

Fortunately, expert help was at hand in the shape of Sir Richard Attenborough, the distinguished film

> *"When I make a speech in public, I'm nervous and when I'm nervous, I giggle."*
> DIANA, ON SPEAKING IN PUBLIC

actor and director, who was Chairman of the Royal Academy of Dramatic Art (RADA). Diana became President of RADA in 1989, but before that, Sir Richard had been giving her the benefit of his considerable skills. He made speech-making easier for

Diana by telling her to include 'stage' instructions in her text, such as: 'Lift your head here... Smile here... Pause... Smile again.' The trick, which she mastered with practice, was to follow the instructions naturally, as if they were not there.

The most important thing for Diana to control, though, was her tendency to gabble out her words in a rush and to breathe in the wrong places, both sure signs of nerves. Gradually, she learned to break sentences into phrases, to pause before starting on a new topic, and to vary the pitch of her voice to avoid sounding stilted and monotonous.

However, like all nervous people with a mountain to climb, there were occasions when Diana forgot her lessons and all the practice she had put in. She sounded far too small-voiced, for instance,

Diana had the opportunity to learn just how to make public speeches at first hand from one of the best teachers: Charles.
Above Diana listens intently as Charles speaks to an audience in Sydney, Australia in April 1983.
Right Watching audience reaction in Brixton, London, in May 1986 at the opening of the Shaftesbury Society housing complex.

during her television interview with Charles, when Sir Alastair Burnet came to Kensington Palace to make a television programme about the couple and their charity work in 1985.

One of Diana's basic problems had nothing to do with speech delivery techniques. The press got the idea that she was intellectually lightweight. They went overboard for her looks, her charm and her grace but came to the patronizing conclusion that a girl with those advantages had no need of brains. Unfortunately, when they dug into it, which they did with their usual diligence, the press managed to discover 'proof' of their presumption in Diana's

Above Diana addresses an audience at a Safety On The Move campaign at Lancaster House in London, in October 1991. The message is clearly aimed at drivers with the campaign slogan 'Kill your speed. Not a child.'.

∾ Protocol ∾

SPEAKING TO THE COUNTRY

*Diana was not the only royal to find public speaking an ordeal. None of the three monarchs who have broadcast to the nation at Christmas found it any easier. The Queen's grandfather, King George V, was probably the most adept, though his enunciation was not all that clear. For his son, King George VI, the broadcasts were hurdles of extraordinary difficulty because of his stammer. The Queen, **above**, the only monarch of the three to broadcast on television at Christmas, is not a natural public speaker and often appears uncomfortable and unsmiling. It can take three sessions for her to complete her 15-minute message.*

education record. Intellect did not seem to be high on her list. At school, Diana failed her GCE examinations in English Language, English Literature, Geography and even Art, and failed them again at her second attempt a while later. Neither did she improve her unintellectual image with jokey, self-deprecating remarks such as, 'I'm as thick as a plank'.

These were simply reflections of the idea, common in her class, that education was not a priority

---

> ## *"It's a typical young aristocratic way of speaking...the stereotype of the stiff upper lip."*
>
> *JEANETTE NELSON, DRAMA EXPERT, ON DIANA'S EARLY SPEECH TECHNIQUE*

---

for the well-born and privileged, who did not need it to make their way in the world. What she probably did not realize was that the press took her comments seriously, and while she won hands down in the contest for beauty and popularity with her sister-in-law the Duchess of York, the Duchess

was streets ahead when it came to making public speeches. Fergie was jaunty, amusing, a dab hand with the clever phrase, spattered her scripts with jokes, and could even make speeches in French.

Armed with conviction

However, the conclusion that serious thought was beyond Diana was not only cruel, but incorrect. She may not have been academic and may have lacked an outgoing personality, but Diana possessed talents perfectly suited to her royal role: sympathy and understanding and the ability to communicate at a personal level, as well as commitment to causes she believed in. These were not skills that could be learned at school, or anywhere else.

Diana possessed a stubbornness and self-discipline that made her determined to succeed and shame her critics into taking her seriously. The days were long gone when Lord Altrincham had been ostracized for daring to say that the young Queen Elizabeth spoke like a schoolgirl. Those privileged days when royals were protected by deference from criticism lay 30 years in the past.

Above left Diana receives the applause of her hosts and the audience as she finishes a speech she made as patron of Headway – the charity for head injury victims – at the London Hilton in December 1993. With obvious difficulty, she had just announced her temporary withdrawal from public life in this televised speech. It was a stressful and painful moment for her. **Above** Speaking to an audience of hearing impaired, Diana uses sign language in July 1990.

Diana had to prove herself, and she knew it. Her first step was to become President or Patron of charities and to work hard for them so that she could not be cynically dismissed as playing at good works. Shrewdly, she avoided opting for the obvious, children's, charities, and chose instead less fashionable causes: child abuse, alcoholism, marriage breakdown, drug addiction, AIDS and HIV.

Careful preparation

Diana also resolved to show that she could learn. As Patron of the British Deaf Association (BDA), she set about mastering sign language in order to communicate with those isolated in their silent world. This was no mean enterprise for a young woman who was not a natural linguist. Because of its very nature, sign language has little use for the nuances of tone and expression which are an important part of communicating by speech. All the same, Diana became sufficiently fluent and confident by 1990 to give a 'speech' replying to a message of welcome at the BDA's centenary congress in Brighton, Sussex.

Left Speaking at the Family of the Year Awards ceremony at the Inn on the Park, London, in February 1990. Diana was patron of Relate – a charity that offers guidance and counselling to families in crisis.

IN THE NEWS

Diana gets the giggles

By 1988, seven years after she had become Princess of Wales, the press was not quite so deferential towards Diana as it had been at the start. Somewhat ungallantly, this edition of the Daily Mirror, published on 3 May, highlighted two of her enduring problems: her awkwardness and lack of charisma as a public speaker and the fact that important people so daunted her that she got totally inappropriate fits of giggles. This made Diana appear frivolous, when, in fact, she was simply nervous.

Opposite page, far left Diana in New York, in January 1995, at the New York Fashion Awards. **Left** Making a speech on presenting a new flag to her regiment, the Light Dragoons, in Bergen-Hohne, Germany, in July 1995.

Diana soon discovered, though, that being taken more seriously involved her in giving more speeches of the conventional kind. Not only that, they were speeches that required detailed information and careful preparation.

What she did not want was to be excused from the high standard of public speaking she wished to attain simply because she was Princess of Wales. She was aware, too, of a certain paradox: she earned sympathy from an audience when she appeared hesitant and vulnerable. It was kind, but it was patronizing and not nearly good enough for Diana.

Resolved instead to succeed on her merits, Diana took to studying the subjects of her speeches in great depth. She collated the relevant facts so that no one could accuse her of not knowing what she was talking about, and combed the draft speech

> **"She has a way of making a request that...not even the hardest business tycoon can turn her down."**
> ONE OF DIANA'S AIDES, ON DIANA

prepared by her staff for words and phrases she felt would sound awkward coming from her. One of the most glaring faults in Diana's early speeches as a royal was the 'mouthpiece' impression she gave when she read out speeches written for her. These said the right things, but not in Diana's way. Her own personal touch was lacking and such speeches came out as performances rather than pieces of genuine self-expression.

To inject this indispensable quality, Diana worked over a text, paraphrasing here, rearranging

Top Speaking to members of the Corf Trust at the Mayfair Hotel, London on 27 May 1992. **Inset, above** Peter Settelen, a former *Coronation Street* actor, helped Diana to train her voice by getting her to recite speeches with marbles in her mouth.

sentences there, adding or subtracting words and phrases, until it acquired her own individual touch. She worked, too, on getting herself out of the habit of playing safe and reading her speeches from notes, a surefire killer when it came to sounding natural and impressing her audience. Instead, she practised using her text an an aide-mémoire, a sort of prompt, which would enable her to lift her eyes from the paper and look her audiences in the eye. This, of course, took great courage.

Two big tests

Of course, working out a speech quietly at home was one thing. Standing and delivering it was another. In the spring of 1986, Diana was confronted with two big tests of her carefully acquired abilities. First, she spoke at the launch of the Help the Aged Silver Jubilee Appeal, in London, before an audience that included several show business personalities. If anyone was expert at timing and

delivery, they were. The experts were out again in force for Diana's second speech, when she addressed the North-east Council on Drug Addiction in Newcastle. Despite her stage fright on both occasions, Diana spoke well and impressed her

> **"My family are my worst critics. Rude royal relations knock my speeches."**
> DIANA, ON SPEAKING IN PUBLIC

audiences with her knowledge and commitment without their having to make allowances for her.

Though Diana was never a renowned orator, her delivery improved dramatically and she began to sound much more authoritative and self-confident. She was certainly a totally different public speaker twelve years on from the shy, faint-voiced Diana of 1981, who used to read whatever was put in front of her, made very little impact and looked visibly, pathetically relieved when the ordeal was over.

THE TENTH ANNIVERSARY

Charles and Diana's tenth wedding anniversary was on 29 July 1991. On 1 July, Diana had turned 30. In ordinary circumstances, these would have been causes for celebration. But circumstances, unfortunately, were far from ordinary and no one felt like celebrating

During the Royal Family's Christmas break at Sandringham in 1990, Diana left the house, got into a Land Rover and drove eight miles to Snettisham on the Norfolk coast. There, bundled up in boots, scarf and warm padded jacket, she walked across the sand for 45 minutes, a sombre figure with her head bent against the cold wind off the grey wintry sea. Back at Sandringham, it appears, members of the Royal

Family were discussing a proposal by the Queen. She had in mind a party at Buckingham Palace to celebrate Charles and Diana's tenth wedding anniversary, due seven months later, in July 1991. The excited plans would have been normal for most marriages which had reached such a notable milestone, but in Charles and Diana's case, things were far from normal. The lone figure on the windy beach reflected the mood of the Prince and

Princess of Wales far more accurately than any talk of celebration. By this time, Charles and Diana appeared to disagree on almost everything, but on this subject, they were in accord. Neither of them wanted to celebrate their tenth anniversary.

Press gossip that all was not well in the royal marriage had started as early as 1982, when Charles had been unable to attend a brunch Diana gave to mark the birth of Prince William on 21 June, due to a prior engagement. As the years went by, the press homed in on the slightest hint to support their thesis. A frown, a slanting look, a glum face, tense body language – any sign, however fleeting or minute, that Charles and Diana were less than blissfully happy, was taken as proof of trouble in the paradise the royal marriage was supposed to be.

Previous page The Prince and Princess of Wales, seen at the Surf Carnival in Sydney, Australia, in January 1988, were skilled at putting on a good public performance, even when all was not well between them.
Above A touching moment as Charles places his hand on Diana's while listening to her make a point during a ceremonial they attended in Australia, while on Diana's first overseas tour in 1983.

This 'ideal' or 'fairytale' marriage was a fabrication, peddled largely by the press and swallowed whole by the public. It was a bubble that had to burst. When it did, sections of the media went into reverse and tried to tear down the idol they had created. The public, for their part, thrived on the gossip and revelled in the headlines that ensued, lapping up every salacious detail about a high-profile marriage which, according to the press, had long been losing its magic.

TRYING TO MAKE IT WORK

Meanwhile, two people who found themselves smothered in fantasy on the one hand and gross intrusion on the other, had the task of trying to make their marriage work. For quite a time, Charles and Diana appeared to be making a good job of it. They received enthusiastic greetings wherever they went. Everyone who saw them seemed to be convinced that they were an ideal royal couple. Yet, Charles and Diana were putting up a façade behind which all was not as it appeared.

Camilla Parker-Bowles, as Diana later remarked, was 'always there', but her presence was not all-pervading. There seemed to be plenty of evidence that Charles and Diana were happy together. They

> *"A princely marriage is the brilliant edition of a universal fact and, as such, it rivets mankind."*
>
> WALTER BAGEHOT, 19TH-CENTURY JOURNALIST AND HISTORIAN

often appeared smiling at each other. They were photographed dancing together, evidently enjoying the experience. They often kissed for the camera.

There were, naturally, differences between Charles and Diana, but not all of them were unbridgeable, given a reasonable degree of mutual tolerance and understanding. A husband who preferred opera and chose to read books on philosophy or religion was not automatically at odds with a wife who chose to listen to pop and rock music and read romantic novels. Such disparities could have been accommodated, given a degree of goodwill between the parties. However, this goodwill

Above On a trip to Australia, in January 1988, the slightly strained look on Diana's face is just the sort of tiny clue the press would take as an indicator that all was not well. It might, of course, have been tiredness or just boredom with the particular event. The fact remained that Charles and Diana were able to go on touring, despite their marital problems. **Left** A pensive Prince Charles with Diana and baby Prince William at the Government House, Auckland, New Zealand, in April 1983.

CHRONICLE

was not really there. The two great stumbling-blocks were Camilla and Diana's expectations of her husband which he was quite unable to fulfil.

Charles' liaison with Camilla, built up over a 20-year relationship, seemed nothing compared to the activities of his predecessors. Some of them, like his great-great grandfather King Edward VII or Diana's ancestors King Charles II and King James II, had

> **"I was young and naïve and I was beginning to feel this was not the way to conduct a romance. Camilla was always there."**
> DIANA, ON HER ROMANCE WITH PRINCE CHARLES

collected mistresses as other men collected postage stamps. Charles might well have asked himself why he was expected to be the only Prince of Wales not to have a mistress. Diana was prepared to tell him why, though the fact that Charles asked the question at all suggests there was much he did not understand about her.

BEHIND THE FAÇADE

Diana was frequently depicted as a romantic young girl who, it was said, had her head filled with fairy-tale dreams of a handsome prince wafting her away to happiness ever after. This, however, seems to have been a superficial view of the Princess of Wales. The truth was far more brutal. The outward glamour of the fashion icon and the sweetness of the caring princess concealed several demons.

Diana was insecure. She craved love, appreciation and approval. She wanted Charles to love her, look after her and protect her. The bitter divorce of her parents when she was only eight years old had inflicted damage that appeared to seriously affect Diana's judgement, leaving her defenceless against blows which a more mature woman with greater self-esteem might have been able to parry.

In her defence, Diana was a young, inexperienced girl thrust by marriage into the gruelling limelight of public life. This, in her case, involved an unrelenting pursuit by the press and the enormous expectations of a nation which had lacked a Princess of Wales for nearly three generations. What

Above Prince Charles playing polo at Cirencester. Throughout his marriage he continued to play regularly. **Right** Diana was a loyal 'polo widow', often turning up with the young princes to watch Charles play. And sometimes, as here, she even presented Charles with the winner's trophy. **Opposite page, top** Charles and Diana, with the young princes, at a happier stage of their marriage, on board the Royal Yacht *Britannia* in Venice in 1985.

☙ Protocol ❧

THE CROWN JEWELS

Contrary to popular opinion, the Crown Jewels are not the Queen's personal property, but national heirlooms for use at ceremonials such as the Queen's coronation in 1952, **right**. The present Crown Jewels date from 1661, and replaced those which were sold off by Parliament during the period of republican rule that followed the execution of King Charles I in 1649. The Jewels include St. Edward's Crown, used at the coronation of King Charles II in 1661, the Imperial State Crown, based on a design made for Queen Victoria's state crown in 1838, and the Imperial Crown of India made for King George V in 1911. Besides other crowns, including the Prince of Wales crown, the Jewels include diadems, sceptres and orbs.

Diana needed most was a husband to back her up one hundred per cent, but with Camilla in the background, she felt she was not getting his full support.

CONTRASTING CAMILLA

Camilla, on the other hand, was a much more mature and strong-minded older woman who knew her place in the world. There were no public pressures, except in the gossip press; these Camilla could and did ignore. She had no contact with the public, nor needed any. She was sure of herself, sure of her purpose and sure of her relationship with Charles. No greater contrast between two women was possible.

Camilla, it appeared, represented a haven of calm and acceptance for Charles, who needed her mature understanding. This was why the Charles-Camilla relationship continued throughout Charles' marriage. In the circumstances, it seemed quite

extraordinary that the union ever got within reach of a tenth anniversary.

That it did was a tribute to both the Prince and the Princess. Behind the united royal front, at which they were both adept, the couple could conceal all their arguments and differences and give near-perfect public performances of amity and togetherness. This, in effect, is what Charles and Diana did for several years and the public, who viewed them from afar, were largely convinced by it. The press read the runes differently and they had the axe of shock-gossip headlines to grind.

The public appearances of Charles and Diana carried their own perils. The problem became apparent at the very beginning, when Diana scored phenomenal success on her first tour, to Wales in 1981. It was clear even then that Diana's runaway popularity vastly exceeded Charles'.

CHARLES COLD SHOULDERED

For a while, Charles appeared to believe that once the novelty of Diana had worn off, things would normalize, but as time passed and this did not look like happening, the Prince grew hurt at getting the cold shoulder from the public.

Left Charles and Diana showing quite different public faces in an open carriage at the Garter ceremony in 1992.
Far left Enjoying a dance together on the Australian tour in October 1985.
Inset left A rather glum Charles poses with a contented-looking Diana and Prince Harry on holiday in Spain, in August 1986.

Some observers claimed that Charles grew jealous of Diana and came to believe that she enjoyed upstaging him. Reportedly, he felt that his own position was being usurped and that the respect which was his due as Prince was being deliberately taken from him. Others saw a certain amount of spite in Charles' objections to his wife's over-familiarity with crowds, which he thought lacked appropriate royal dignity. Maybe it did, but the crowds loved it. Diana's approach forged a closeness and a love for the 'people's princess', which royal dignity was unlikely to accomplish.

CRAVING FOR APPROVAL

However, even public adoration did not seem to assuage Diana's craving for approval, and around 1987 or so, friends reckoned, she stopped trying to get it from Charles and sought it elsewhere. As Charles himself is said to have told Major Ronald Ferguson, his polo manager and the father of the Duchess of York, marital relations had lapsed by 1986. After that, it would appear that the Prince and Princess were held together only by their children and their joint public duty. In the event, the anniversary was greeted with several specially

The Private Princess
Against the royal marriage

Above Diana's grandmother, Ruth, Lady Fermoy, who later expressed grave doubts about the matching of Charles and Diana.

The Royal Family was hiding a dark secret on the day of Charles and Diana's wedding, 29 July 1981. Several people who knew Diana well had told the Queen that they believed she was not up to the pressures and responsibilities of her future role as Princess of Wales.

The most important was her father, Earl Spencer. An emotional and rather effusive man, Earl Spencer appeared to have grave fears for his youngest daughter and was not happy with the idea that, after her marriage, he would only be able to see her when royal duties permitted. The Earl's doubts that Diana could cope were echoed by a formidable family figure, Diana's maternal grandmother, Ruth, Lady Fermoy.

Although initially 'delighted' by the match, Lady Fermoy was reported to have later expressed reservations at Diana's ability to manage. Friends of Charles were also not slow to speak up at the time. Penny Romsey, for example, a Mountbatten relative of Charles, apparently thought that he and Diana were ill-matched. There were several others who concurred with this assessment.

While the public rejoiced and the press sentimentalized about the 'fairytale' marriage and the royal love-match, these doubters viewed the forthcoming royal wedding day with a degree of anxiety.

written books and press articles, which surveyed the 'success' of the first ten years and looked forward to the next. There was, however, to be no big tenth wedding anniversary party at Buckingham Palace. And on 1 July, there was no 30th birthday dance for Diana; Charles was said to have offered her this several times, only to be turned down. The couple spent the weekend of 29 and 30 June 1991 at Highgrove House, and aides, when asked, suggested

> ## "He has simply thrown petrol on the fire and turned a private dispute into front page news.... All quite unnecessary."
>
> COURT OFFICIAL, ON A SUGGESTION, LATER REFUTED, THAT CHARLES HAD 'LEAKED' NEWS OF A RIFT WITH DIANA

there had been a private birthday celebration. No one, though, was known to have been invited. On Monday, 1 July, Diana celebrated her birthday with a quiet tea at Kensington Palace with Prince Harry and her sister, Lady Jane Fellowes. Charles, meanwhile, was in Scotland.

On 29 July, the anniversary of the wedding, Diana spent the morning representing the Queen at the Queen's Review of the Royal Air Force College, Cranwell, at Seaford, Lincolnshire. Later, she set off for Wales, where she had engagements to perform the next day. While she was there, Charles was in London. Meanwhile, earlier that same month, the more sensationalist press had been

Above The Royal Family spends Christmas together at Sandringham. At the 1990 get-together, they discussed plans for celebrating the tenth wedding anniversary.

IN CONTEXT — GULF WAR ERUPTS
1991

- The Gulf War, **right**, codenamed 'Desert Storm', takes place in January and February
- British Prime Minister John Major says Poll Tax will not be abolished
- South African President F.W. de Klerk abolishes last apartheid laws
- British ballerina Margot Fonteyn dies
- Boris Yeltsin elected President of Russia
- The Lazio football club of Rome offers £6 million for Paul 'Gazza' Gascoigne

making great play with the reported rift between the couple. Denials were issued. The Princess was reputedly 'disgusted'. Charles was 'angry'. Diana's friends believed, and so apparently did Diana, that Charles had arranged for details of the rift to be 'leaked'. Charles denied it.

A SHOW OF UNITY

The royal couple's aides, striving desperately to dam the flood of bad publicity, advised that a show of unity was urgently required and, on 8 July, Charles and Diana appeared at a 'special birthday concert' given by the London Symphony Chorus at the Royal Albert Hall in Kensington. There, all the glitz of a full-dress evening occasion went into action. Charles beamed. A smiling Diana was charming.

But those who were in the know refused to be fooled. They saw behind the masks, they said, and realized that the first ten years of Charles and Diana's marriage would not, barring a miraculous turnaround, be followed by another ten.

Below The royal couple in Qatar during their Gulf States tour in 1986. Despite the tensions of touring while all was not well in their marriage, Charles and Diana kept up public engagements very effectively.

Below left The skiing holiday was an annual fixture for Charles and Diana until they separated. But for both of them it was always spoilt by the attendant press pack and the need for a photo call.

High Street Fashion

Diana broke many royal rules to do things her way, and shopping was one of them. Unlike other royals, she did her own, and came home with a variety of off-the-peg purchases

Left Diana in Germany in November 1987, wearing a yellow and black overcoat by German fashion company Escada. The wide black suede belt and hat are by Philip Somerville. **Opposite page** An uncrushable blue and white patterned summer dress from Kanga in Beauchamp Place, London. Diana wore this on several occasions, including a polo match in Palm Beach, Florida, in 1985. **Opposite page, inset** Diana bought this pale pink embroidered lace dress with a zigzag hem and collar trimmed with mock pearls from Zandra Rhodes' shop in Mayfair. It became one of her favourites and she wore it numerous times, including this occasion in Japan, in 1986.

Most members of the Royal Family never see the inside of a shop, unless it is during a public engagement. Diana, however, knew the shops well. She gave up a lot of the freedom of her single days when she married, but not her shopping. Though she hated being called a 'shopaholic', she enjoyed having sprees in her former Sloane Ranger stamping-ground, as well as further afield in London's West End.

In some ways, Diana never stopped being a Sloane. When she became engaged, she lodged her

> **"She used to dive in through the front door for toiletries and tights."**
>
> SPOKESWOMAN AT FENWICK'S
> OF BOND STREET, ON DIANA

wedding present list with the Peter Jones department store in Sloane Square, as all the Sloanes did. After her marriage, the Laura Ashley shop, in Harriet Street (just off Sloane Street), remained the source for Diana's famous frill-necked blouses.

In Sloane Street's smart clothes shops, Diana liked to spend time looking through the latest designs by Christian Lacroix, Chanel, Valentino and Karl Lagerfeld, or surveying the new Moschino outfits at Browns in South Molton Street, just off Oxford Street. She generally wore their clothes in her private life, but one outfit in particular emerged into the public realm when Diana

attended the christening of Princess Eugenie at Sandringham in December 1990.

Diana bought the Moschino suit from Harvey Nichols, the fashionable Knightsbridge store. She 'invented' the suit herself, mixing a red and white check jacket with black inserts, slinky high-necked black sweater, and a straight skirt in black and white check (see page 310). It was a daring idea, but it worked. At Eugenie's christening, Diana wore the suit with a wide-brimmed red hat with black band round the crown, and black shoes with red uppers.

Harvey Nichols was said to be Diana's favourite shop. She used to go from floor to floor, choosing

> ### "She treats the girls in the shop with such respect, and knows all their names."
> JANET REGER, LINGERIE SPECIALIST, ON DIANA

her casual wear from the less expensive ranges, like the DKNY label by Donna Karan, and buying her sportswear. Down on the ground floor, Diana would buy Donna Karan tights, which were subtly shaded to look as if they were not there, so giving Diana the tanned bare-leg look she liked.

Shopping in style

The first floor at Harvey Nichols was a particular favourite with Diana. Its showcases contained a selection of designs by internationally known fashion names, and complete sections or separate shops exclusively given over to clothes by the New York designers Ralph Lauren, Donna Karan and Isaac Mizrahi. Clothes by Sonia Rykiel, Jean-Paul Gaultier and Claude Montana from Paris were there, too, as were designs by Dolce e Gabbana and Moschino from Italy.

Harvey Nichols was an easygoing place. It offered a private suite where Diana could try on clothes, but she often preferred to wander round the departments, picking and choosing. Harrods, though, was much more decorous and formal. Here, there was a strategy for dealing with VIPs. A call from the Palace would alert Harrods staff to the imminent arrival of a royal client – Diana often got her lady-in-waiting to ring. When Diana arrived,

1 Diana wore this Jack Azagurny black velvet top with glittering stars to a ball in Florence in April 1985. It accompanied a drop waist organza skirt.

2 Out shopping as a divorcee, Diana wears a simple black dress with white polka dots, black court shoes and a black pullover knotted around her shoulders.

3 At the polo again, Diana wears a calf-length white pleated skirt with a blue and white cardigan and gold pumps.

4 At the polo, in Cirencester in 1985, Diana wears a turquoise skirt with a bold floral pattern, topped by a white blouse with a sailor collar.

5 A red and white patterned silk dress with a deep V neckline, lace insert and a bow. Diana wore this outfit at a polo match in July 1988.

6 This jumper and skirt outfit was typical of the separates that Diana favoured for trips to and from the boys' schools.

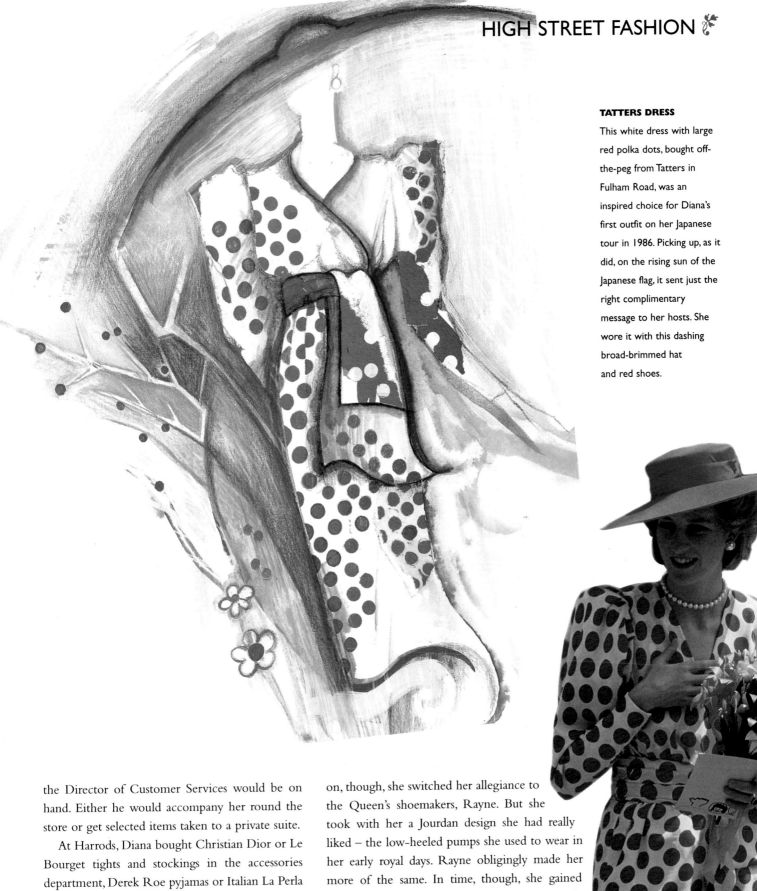

TATTERS DRESS

This white dress with large red polka dots, bought off-the-peg from Tatters in Fulham Road, was an inspired choice for Diana's first outfit on her Japanese tour in 1986. Picking up, as it did, on the rising sun of the Japanese flag, it sent just the right complimentary message to her hosts. She wore it with this dashing broad-brimmed hat and red shoes.

the Director of Customer Services would be on hand. Either he would accompany her round the store or get selected items taken to a private suite.

At Harrods, Diana bought Christian Dior or Le Bourget tights and stockings in the accessories department, Derek Roe pyjamas or Italian La Perla designer lingerie, which included her favourite pleated Fortuny-style items.

Close by Harrods, in Brompton Road, the Charles Jourdan shoe shop was the place where Diana used to buy all her shoes and handbags. Later

on, though, she switched her allegiance to the Queen's shoemakers, Rayne. But she took with her a Jourdan design she had really liked – the low-heeled pumps she used to wear in her early royal days. Rayne obligingly made her more of the same. In time, though, she gained enough confidence to wear higher heels, which she bought from Manolo Blahnik in Old Church Street, Chelsea, not far from Kensington.

Diana went in for less expensive shoes when she found the designs attractive. These often came from

MOSCHINO MIX 'N' MATCH

These were the Moschino-designed clothes that Diana selected off the peg at Harvey Nichols and put together to create an outfit, which she wore to the christening of Princess Eugenie, the Duke and Duchess of York's daughter, in December 1990. The hat is by Philip Somerville.

Pied à Terre in Sloane Street, or the same shop's branch in South Molton Street. The shopping mall of South Molton Street, closed to traffic, also gave Diana the chance to pop in to Browns' boutique, which had a wide range of her favourite designer labels, including the Italians Genny and Romeo Gigli, and Azzedine Alaia from France. Just around the corner, in Bond Street, Fenwick's provided Diana with seamless Gossard Glossy bras and bikini briefs, as well as a brilliant pink gabardine suit by Paul Costelloe, which she bought there in 1991.

Not too far away from Harrods, Beauchamp Place provided more of Diana's favourite shopping. Janet Reger's lingerie boutique was there, offering silk underwear. Diana purchased Reger bras, briefs, cami-knickers, slips and bias-cut bodysuits.

Personal selection

Kanga, the shop owned by Prince Charles' late friend, Lady Tryon, was a short way down the road from Janet Reger. Here, Diana used to buy non-crush printed rayon dresses, which she wore to

1 Visiting Bosnia in 1997, Diana is casually but practically dressed in a pink shirt, black drainpipe jeans and black loafers.

2 This cotton print dress in autumnal colours is by Paul Costelloe. Diana first wore it to Wetherby School in 1989 with a smart tan suede bomber jacket. Here she is at Aberdeen Airport in 1991, wearing it with a dark blazer.

3 A white and black patterned cotton shirt with full, puffed shoulders by Jan van Veldon. Diana wore it with a wide black belt and a plain white skirt to the polo in Cirencester in 1983.

watch polo matches at Smith's Lawn, Windsor, and elsewhere, and tennis matches at Wimbledon.

Beyond Knightsbridge, Diana liked trawling shops in Fulham Road. Butler and Wilson had a shop there and Diana was among the celebrities who bought their high-fashion costume jewellery.

Across the road, the Tatters dress shop was tempting. Diana went for one of the Tatters beaded

> *"She has fabulous feet, it's a very intimate and personal thing fitting feet."*
>
> JOHN GAIRDNER, MANAGER, CHARLES JOURDAN SHOES

short evening dresses. And, on the first day of her 1986 tour of Japan, she turned up wearing a white Tatters dress with large red circles that echoed the Japanese national flag (see page 309).

The padded shoulder bags with matching purses, which Diana often used off duty, came from Souleiado in Fulham Road. Their large capacity was ideal for attending private all-day events.

It was one of the penalties of fame that Diana's favourite shopping haunts became known, and photographers would lie in wait for her. But Diana out shopping was Diana exercising what little freedom her royal role allowed and nothing, not even a lurking lens, could make her give it up.

IN THE NEWS

Fashion correspondent twists the knife

After her divorce in 1996, Diana dressed much more casually than in her royal years. The Sun made the point in its own way on 5 September 1996. Under the heading 'The knives are still out for Charles', it drew attention to the dagger motif on a pair of Diana's jeans. The jeans, designed by Rifat Ozbek, cost £85 a pair, a mere bagatelle, as The Sun rightly pointed out, for a well-heeled divorcee with some £17 million in the bank.

DI IS A JEAN GENIUS

She has 30 pairs in her wardrobe

Persil gives brilliant results every time.

The French Connection

The Princess of Wales earned a reputation in France for being chic, beautiful and elegant. The French fell in love with her and she fell in love with France, becoming a frequent visitor

Left Charles and Diana were captivated by the châteaux of the Loire, like Chenonceau here.
Below Diana is met at Orly by French Prime Minister Michel Rocard.

Diana and France were made for each other, or at least the French appeared to think so once they realized that *la Princesse de Galles* was a jewel among Englishwomen. She had charm, she had style, she was beautiful and she possessed that tasteful chic which the French have always admired.

But the French were no pushovers, even for Diana. There had long been a certain amount of resistance to all things English, the fruit of seven centuries of national rivalry. The French scorned English cooking, believing it to be tasteless, and regarded Englishwomen as 'badly dressed and frumpish'. France, to them, was the epicentre of taste and culture and England, they convinced themselves, could not compete.

Then along came Diana, the epitome of the English Rose and fashion icon *extraordinaire*, to prove them wrong. Not only that, the French attitude towards her, once they had seen her in action and got to know her, took on the proportions of a special relationship. Never mind what Diana's passport said about

her nationality – *la Princesse* was so enchanting, she could have been French.

It was, however, to Diana's advantage that her first official visit to France did not come until 1987, when she went there with Charles to launch an Anglo-French aircraft at Toulouse, on 14 February. By then, Diana was 25 years old, the ideal age for

> **"She has wonderful blue eyes that would inspire a poem."**
>
> JACK LANG, MAYOR OF PARIS, ON DIANA

maximum chic, and she had already been six years in the field, learning her royal trade. The shy, coy, hesitant young princess had been replaced by an outwardly more self-confident young woman, well seasoned in making public appearances and able to carry off her fashions with *élan*, that quality of dash and spirit which the French so appreciated.

Toulouse, though, was just a taster. Down the Riviera coast were ritzier places such as Cannes.

Diana got the chance to sample the high life on 15 May 1987, when she and Charles attended the film festival at Cannes. Famous faces crowded the streets, as film stars, film directors and other glitterati arrived to see and be seen. Diana, however, outclassed them all as the most dazzling celebrity of 1987 and it was not just because she was a princess.

Charles and Diana were, of course, treated as topflight VIPs and, with TV cameras much in evidence, they visited the Hôtel de Ville, the town hall. The crowd outside reached as far as the eye could see when the couple appeared on the balcony to wave

Above left On the Wales' official tour to Paris in November 1988, part of the formal welcome included a reception at the Hôtel de Ville, the town hall. Diana was at her most chic in this Catherine Walker outfit.
Above Jacques Chirac, the Mayor of Paris, gave a welcoming speech full of compliments to his guests.

Left Charles sports a poppy and Diana wears a Catherine Walker ballgown at a British Embassy gala in Paris, in November 1988. **Inset below** On 14 February 1987, on their first joint visit to France, Charles and Diana christen the new Airbus 320 aeroplane with a magnum of fine champagne.

⚜ Protocol ⚜

DIANA'S ROYAL ANCESTORS IN FRANCE

King Charles II (1630-1685) **right** *would have been gratified to see what a big impact Diana, his descendant, made in France. The king's own French adventures were far less pleasant. In 1648, towards the end of the Civil War with Parliament, Charles' mother, Queen Henrietta Maria, fled to her native France with her children, leaving her husband, Charles I, to face trial and execution. The future kings Charles II and his brother James II, also an ancestor of Diana's, became refugees and poor relations living off King Louis XIV of France. This grim period in the life of Charles II came to an end in 1660, when he was eventually restored to his throne.*

to the excited onlookers. In their honour, five Union Jacks were flown on the building, but they were dwarfed by the two huge tricolors, the French flag, which hung all the way down from the roof.

Less than four months after that, Charles and Diana were back in France on a third one-day visit to Caen and Bayeux in northern France, which took place on 9 September 1987.

Battles remembered

Caen was one of the battlegrounds where fierce fighting took place after the D-Day invasion of Normandy on 6 June 1944. Bayeux was of especial interest to Prince Charles, whose sense of history was roused by the famous tapestry recounting the Battle of Hastings in 1066, when the Normans, under William the Conqueror, invaded England.

However, to the frustration of the French – and probably Diana as well – the brief visits of 1987 had not included Paris, the capital not only of France

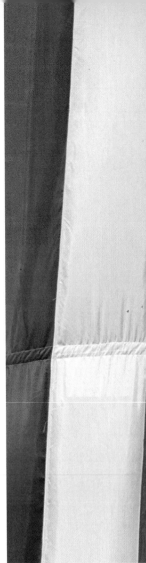

Left Charles and Diana in Cannes, in May 1987, for the film festival. Here they get the red carpet treatment as they make their way to the Hôtel de Ville, the town hall. **Above** Standing on the balcony of the Hôtel de Ville with the Mayoress of Cannes, the couple were able to get a panoramic view of the city and see the crowd which had gathered to greet them. **Inset far right** The royal couple were in Cannes to help boost the British film entries, especially a film called *The Whales of August*. When they turned up for a film show, 4000 people had gathered to see them arrive.

but also, according to the French, of fashion, elegance, art, culture and all that was typical of France at its finest. Frustration ended, though, in 1988 when Charles and Diana made up for the omission with a five-day tour lasting from 7 to 11 November.

Flying in to Paris

The couple flew in to Orly airport outside Paris with Charles piloting the aircraft of the Queen's Flight. Realizing the important role of fashion in Paris, which for decades had sent out its decrees for women the world over to obey, Diana staged a clever piece of flattery by emerging onto the tarmac at Orly dressed in an outfit by Chanel, the doyenne of French design.

When the waiting crowds recognized the compliment, Diana received what amounted to a standing ovation. Further surprises awaited, though. Carefully packed in her luggage were several gowns by Catherine Walker, who, despite her English name and English base of operation, had been born in France. Diana was used to being very closely exam-

ined, of course, but she knew that in Paris the searchlight of scrutiny would be particularly intense. Passing the fashion test the fastidious Parisians set her would not be easy. Diana was well known in Paris from television reports, newspaper coverage and dozens of magazine covers, but there were still enough sceptics who clung to the belief that, being English, she did not know how to dress, be elegant or display that flair which the sophisticates of Paris prized so much.

Sceptics wanted to be convinced that Diana's triumphant appearance at the Cannes Film Festival had not been a flash in the pan. Diana need not have worried, however. Once Parisians saw her in the flesh, all their presumptions and prejudices seemed to vanish and the visit to Paris progressed from one triumph to the next.

The crowd waiting to see Diana at Orly were only the first to buzz with admiration as she came into sight. More crowds were always on hand to

watch Diana arrive for engagements during her visit to Paris and, most of all, for the important state events where no amount of grandeur was spared.

Lavish treatment

President François Mitterrand, for instance, gave a lavish state banquet for the royal couple at the Elysée Palace. There was an elaborate dinner at the British Embassy and a reception at the Hôtel De Ville, where the future Prime Minister and President of France, then Mayor of Paris, Jacques Chirac, made Diana blush with his effusive compliments. The fact that Chirac spoke through an interpreter — Diana's French was by no means fluent — took nothing away from his gallantry.

Prince Charles lost little time sampling the architectural magnificence of Paris, and ventured to the top of the 35-storey Arche de la Défense (Defence Arch), which was some 360 feet high and straddled the entrance to a tower-block complex forming the

Above Accompanied by her sister Lady Sarah, her detective Ken Wharfe and Jack Lang, the French Minister of Culture, Diana waves to the crowd and the waiting press, who have gathered to see her.
Right On the same trip, Diana on a walkabout shakes hands with eager onlookers and exchanges a few words in her elementary French.

Above Diana at a formal banquet in Paris on her visit in November 1992. The dinner was hosted by Bernard Houchner, the French Minister of Health and Humanitarian Aid.

largest business district in Europe. Charles found it 'very remarkable'.

Charles and Diana experienced another, romantic, aspect of Paris on their second day in the capital, 8 November. They boarded a *bateau mouche* and took a trip on the River Seine, which flows through Paris. Dining by candlelight, the couple watched the panorama on the river banks as the

boat floated slowly along. There was a band on board, playing *I Love Paris* among its repertoire.

The Paris tour was not all splendour and romance, however. November was the time of year for remembering the war dead, just as it was in

> **"Normally, your English princesses wear velvet uniforms and terrible Girl Guides hats."**
> FRENCHMAN, ON ENGLISH PRINCESSES

London at the Cenotaph ceremony in Whitehall. Charles and Diana were present at the French National War Memorial to attend the ceremony celebrating the Armistice. The ceasefire, which ended the fighting in the First World War in 1918, came only after France had lost one million men and had many more wounded. It meant a great deal to the ex-servicemen present that the Prince and Princess of Wales had come to share their remembrance of those nightmare days, and were wearing the symbolic poppies.

Amid the dazzle of the Paris visit, Diana did not neglect her charitable concerns. The previous year,

IN THE NEWS

France takes the royal couple to its heart

In November 1988, the French had seen Charles and Diana on separate engagements and as a royal couple, when, according to The Times, they practically conquered Paris. The papers also gave extensive coverage to the tail-end visit of the tour, to the Château de Chambord, which lay in the area where, The Times was not slow to emphasize, King Henry II of England had once ruled.

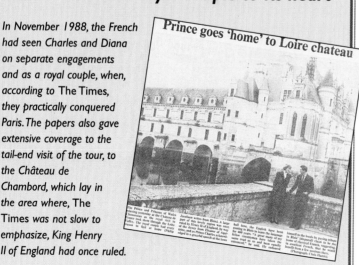

Prince goes 'home' to Loire chateau

Above On a trip to France in 1992, Diana paid a visit to a cancer hospital in Lille, where she met the nursing staff and some of the young cancer patients. **Inset above** France became a favourite destination of Diana's and she is seen here on a visit in 1994 sharing a laugh with UNESCO President Frederico Mayor, at a charity dinner held at Versailles Palace, near Paris.

1987, she had begun her connection with the work against AIDS. Pursuing this interest in the middle of a particularly glamorous tour, Diana visited the laboratory of the world-renowned Pasteur Institute in Paris to meet Professor Luc Montagnier, who had isolated the HIV virus there. Professor and Princess discussed the problems of HIV and AIDS and Montagnier was impressed by Diana's knowledge.

Château in the Loire

The visit to Paris was, necessarily, brief but the thrills of France were not yet over for Charles and Diana. After leaving Paris, they travelled to Blois, 35 miles southwest of Orléans in the Loire Valley. This was the sort of country, steeped in history, which Charles loved. It was from Blois that the famous Joan of Arc set out to raise the siege of Orléans in 1429, towards the end of the Hundred Years War with England. Blois had longstanding royal connections and was in fact known as 'the city of kings'. Not all of them were French. One of the medieval kings of England, Stephen, came from Blois.

Eleven miles to the east lay one of the greatest of Renaissance châteaux, Chambord, which had once been the hunting lodge of the Counts of Blois. The

château, some 500 feet wide and more like a castle stronghold with its mighty cream-coloured walls and round towers, provided a magnificent setting for a dinner attended by Charles, Diana and, among the other guests, Princess Caroline of Monaco. The two princesses kissed on meeting, as was the practice in France, and spent quite some time happily chatting across the dinner table.

Diana sat next to a former Prime Minister, Raymond Barre. On learning that Barre was on a

> "*The charm and elegance of the Princess of Wales has already seduced the French people.*"
>
> JACQUES CHIRAC, MAYOR OF PARIS, ON DIANA

diet, Diana helped him out by eating his portion of pâté de fois gras as well as her own. It was not, perhaps, what the Frenchman expected of an elegant princess, but Barre seemed to find Diana's behaviour perfectly charming.

The host at the Château de Chambord was the French Minister of Culture, Jack Lang, who was much taken with Diana and, in a lyrical after-dinner speech, paid her yet more Gallic compliments.

Charles and Diana returned home on 11 November, having scored what had clearly been a triumph for Anglo-French relations, but above all a triumph for Diana. She left behind a dazzling impression among Parisians, who had seen for themselves the calibre of Diana as a fashion icon, and clearly fell in love with what they saw.

DEATH OF EARL SPENCER

Although she often appeared an ordinary woman, Diana came from
an aristocratic family of great distinction. The Spencers enjoyed all the
trappings, wealth and social eminence of their class. But when their
mother left there was a vital omission from the children's life: happiness

When the searchlight of fame and publicity was beamed on Diana in 1981,
it also fell on her family, the Spencers
of Althorp. Because of Diana, everything the
Spencers said or did and everything that happened
to them became news. When Diana's father, the 8th
Earl Spencer, died in 1992, the newspapers and
television were out in force to report his funeral.
The divorce of Diana's brother, Charles, 9th Earl
Spencer, from his wife Victoria in 1997, was a
media feast of scandalous allegations in Britain and
in South Africa where the court case was heard.

Though this newfound interest was not always
welcome, the Spencers were no strangers to the

headlines. In 1978, for example, Diana's eldest sister, Lady Sarah, was being widely touted as a future bride for the Prince of Wales. The gossip subsided only when Sarah announced that, though she thought him 'a fabulous person', she was not in love with the heir to the throne.

Later, after Diana's marriage to Charles brought the Spencers to public notice again, Sarah's own unhappy past was dug out of the family closet. The press discovered that, during a troubled childhood, Sarah had behaved so riotously at school that she

> **"It was a dreadful time for my parents, and probably the root of their divorce because I don't think they ever got over it."**
>
> THE 9TH EARL SPENCER, ON THE DEATH OF HIS ELDER BROTHER JOHN

was told to leave and that she had suffered from the eating disorder, anorexia nervosa.

Sarah's problems, like Diana's bulimia, were ascribed to the stress and insecurity caused by the divorce of their parents in 1969. This had been the sombre sequel to the most brilliant society marriage of 1954, when Edward John, then Viscount Althorp and heir to the Spencer earldom, wed an 18-year-old debutante, the Hon. Frances Roche, daughter of Maurice Roche, 4th Baron Fermoy.

'Johnnie' Althorp, as Diana's father was then known, was classed as a 'deb's delight' – the press name for the more eligible young men who went fishing for brides, or were netted by them, in the course of the 'Season'. Some twelve years older than Frances, he was genial, good-looking, rich, well-connected and 'in' with the royals, whom his own family had served for generations.

SOCIETY WEDDING

The couple were married in Westminster Abbey on 1 June 1954 and the Queen, Prince Philip and Princess Margaret were among the 1700 guests. The reception, for 900 guests, was held at St. James' Palace. Their first child, Sarah, was born nine months later, followed in 1957 by another daughter, Jane. Johnnie, needless to say, longed for the

⋙ Protocol ⋘

THE DUCHY OF LANCASTER

*The Duchy of Lancaster, comprising some 50,000 acres of land in Cheshire, Shropshire, Derbyshire, Northamptonshire, Lincolnshire, South Wales, Staffordshire, Lancashire and Yorkshire, is a royal estate which has passed to each successive monarch in turn since 1399, when Henry IV, **right**, came to the throne. It is the Queen's equivalent of Prince Charles' Duchy of Cornwall, providing her with an income, but allowing her no access to the estate's capital. In 1760, when King George III surrendered the revenues from the rest of the Crown estates in exchange for the Civil List, the Duchy of Lancaster was retained. As well as areas of land, the Duchy owns commercial properties in London and has an investment portfolio.*

male heir which every titled father requires, but when, in 1960, a son, John, was born, every parent's worst nightmare came true. The child was badly deformed and died within ten hours. The Spencer family, it appears, began to question Frances' fitness to produce heirs. She had to undergo the deeply humiliating experience of medical examinations designed to discover why she had given birth to two living girls and a son who died.

The wormwood of resentment over John's death and its shaming sequel, had already begun to corrode the marriage when a third girl, Diana, was born in 1961. Later on, it did Diana's self-esteem no good to learn that she 'should have been a boy' and that her parents were so sure before her birth that she was, they did not bother to choose any girls'

Opening page Gathered for the funeral of the 8th Earl Spencer are his widow Raine, his daughter Diana and his son and heir Charles, the 9th Earl Spencer.
Top centre Johnnie Althorp and his second wife, Raine, in front of Althorp House.
Above The proudest day of Earl Spencer's life was when he gave away his daughter Diana to Prince Charles at St. Paul's Cathedral in 1981, just over three years after recovering from a near-fatal brain haemorrhage.
Left The young Diana Spencer with a pram at Park House, Sandringham, where she spent her childhood.

DIARY DATES

Jan-May 1992

1 February
The Princess of Wales attends Wales v France rugby match at Cardiff Arms Park

4 February
The Princess of Wales visits Myton Hospice, Warwick

10-15 February
The Prince and Princess of Wales tour India

25 February
The Princess of Wales lays foundation stone of the new wing of the National Hospital for Neurology and Neurosurgery, London

3 March
The Princess of Wales attends première of film *Hear My Song* at the Marble Arch Odeon, London

11 March
The Princess of Wales opens the Daily Mail's 'Ideal Home Exhibition' at Earl's Court, London

19 March
The Princess of Wales attends performance of *Romeo and Juliet* by the London City Ballet at The Hawth, Crawley, Sussex

7 April
The Princess of Wales visits the Hospital for Sick Children, Great Ormond Street, London

28 April
The Princess of Wales opens the Red Cross Centre at Baghington Hospital, Derby

5 May
The Prince of Wales opens the 1992 National Garden Festival at Ebbw Vale, Wales

names for her. Three years later, in 1964, the family was completed with the birth of a healthy son, Charles, the present Earl Spencer.

ALTHORPS SEPARATE

In September 1967, the Althorps decided to separate. One of the reasons for their separation was the millionaire sheep farmer and wallpaper manufacturer Peter Shand Kydd who, with his artist wife Janet Munro, had become friends with the Althorps after they met at a London dinner party. Soon afterwards, the Shand Kydds and the Althorps went on a Swiss skiing holiday together where, it appears, Peter and Frances became closer than they should have been. Peter seemed to be everything the 'dull' Johnnie was not: lively, artistic and amusing.

The holiday was no sooner over than Peter left his wife and three children and began seeing Frances in secret. She moved out of Park House and took an apartment in Cadogan Place, London, having made arrangements, or so she thought, for her children and their nanny to join her. There were feeble attempts at a reconciliation, but the marriage foundered when Johnnie demanded the children be returned to Park House for Christmas 1967 and refused to return them to London in the new year.

In June 1968, the Althorps' divorce case came to court. It was a long and damaging wrangle. Frances,

already cited as 'the other woman' in the Shand Kydds' divorce, was branded the villain of the breakdown, and her own mother, Ruth, Lady Fermoy, testified against her. As a result, Frances lost custody of the children.

Diana, her brother and sisters were virtually torn apart. Young Charles, only five, sometimes cried for his mother all night and all the children grossly misbehaved. They locked their nannies in the bathroom, spiked their chairs with pins and threw their

> **"I remember Mummy crying. Daddy never spoke to us about it. We could never ask questions...the whole thing was very unstable."**
> *DIANA, ON HER PARENTS' BROKEN MARRIAGE*

clothes out of the window. Little wonder that several nannies concluded that these were children from hell and departed in a constant exodus.

Johnnie, meanwhile, had sunk into deep depression over the divorce and took to sitting in his study all day. Frances routinely burst into tears at the thought of having to part with the children after their weekend visits. Diana and the others ended up confused and miserable, emotions that could not be assuaged by the piles of expensive presents they received from both parents at Christmas.

SUCCESS AT SCHOOL

Fortunately, school life provided some sort of stability. Sarah and Jane proved to be clever, did well at examinations and excelled at sports. Diana, less academic, proved a fine athlete, swimmer and tennis player. She was also a good dancer and a creditable pianist. Schooldays provided, too, a chance for Diana to show a talent the whole world later came to recognize: her ability to connect with the sick. She formed an unusual rapport with handicapped teenagers on regular school visits to a mental hospital near Dartford, Kent. It was an achievement to get these severely depressed youngsters to smile, but Diana managed it.

New upheavals awaited, however. First, in 1975, Johnnie's irascible father, the 7th Earl Spencer, died and he inherited the title. The family moved to

Opposite page, top At the Althorp Horse Trials, before their divorce, Charles and Victoria Spencer, with their children Amelia, Eliza and Kitty. **Opposite page, left** Diana and her mother, Frances Shand Kydd, pictured together at a wedding at Althorp. **Above** Diana with her mother, Frances, and Prince Harry attend a church service at Brington, Northamptonshire. **Right** Diana with her eldest sister, Lady Sarah, who became one of her ladies-in-waiting.

Althorp House, the Spencer family seat in Northamptonshire, which included 13,000 acres of land. Next, on 14 July 1977, after figuring as co-respondent in her divorce, the new Earl Spencer married Raine, Countess of Dartmouth, the exotic, larger-than-life daughter of romantic novelist Barbara Cartland.

Raine had been on the Spencer scene for some five years by that time, and had made a spectacular appearance at Lady Sarah Spencer's 18th birthday in 1973. She was a formidable woman who gushed charm and steely determination in equal measure and set about dealing with her new husband's problems – crippling death duties and escalating running costs – like a chainsaw felling a forest of oaks.

HATED STEPMOTHER

Diana and the other children, it was reliably reported, disliked Raine (whom they called 'Acid Raine') from the first. Their hatred of her deepened further when in a savage economy drive, she cut down on staff, opened Althorp to the public and sold off family valuables at rock-bottom prices.

Before long, Raine became the epitome of the wicked stepmother, but in 1978, she did her husband the greatest service a wife can offer: she saved his life. The Earl collapsed with a cerebral haemorrhage in the courtyard of Althorp that September and was rushed to hospital. The prognosis was very

> *"How many of those 14 years were happy? I thought all of them, until the day we parted."*
>
> THE 8TH EARL SPENCER,
> ON HIS FIRST MARRIAGE

bad, but Raine resolved, against all medical opinion, that Johnnie would live. For months, he lay in a coma. For months, Raine sat by his bed, willing him, according to her own account, to hold on.

Eventually, she obtained a 'miracle' drug from Germany, Aslocillin. It was not licensed in Britain, but Raine insisted that it be administered. Miraculously, or so it seemed, Johnnie regained consciousness, and in January 1979, after four months, he left hospital. Though he never recovered

The Private Princess
Taking William to school

On 10 September 1990, in full view of a horde of press reporters and cameramen, Prince William, 8, was taken by his parents to his first day at boarding school – Ludgrove Preparatory School, near Wokingham, Berkshire.

However, according to observers who saw what really happened, Charles and Diana concocted a performance, both for William's sake and to scotch speculation about their marriage.

Parents and new boy drove up to the school together in their Bentley, but out of sight, behind some laurel bushes at the back of the school, another car was parked. It was Diana's Jaguar, in which she had driven William to Wokingham from Kensington Palace. Charles and the Bentley were waiting for them. The family went through the usual performance on such occasions, shaking hands with the two headmasters, chatting for a while, then saying goodbye to William, whereupon Diana cried. Charles and Diana then drove off in the Bentley.

Above *Charles and Diana with Prince William meet the headmaster on William's first day at Ludgrove Preparatory School.*

Behind the bushes, Diana got back into her Jaguar and drove off to Kensington Palace, while Charles headed for Highgrove House. The couple had spent half an hour together. They would not see each other again for 39 days. Press rumours that the Wales' marriage was tottering were fuelled by the royal ploy.

Left At a ceremony, in July 1987, at which Diana was presented with the Freedom of the City of London, are Raine and Earl Spencer, the Earl's heir Charles, Frances Shand Kydd and her mother, Ruth, Lady Fermoy. **Right** In April 1992, at the funeral of Diana's father, Earl Spencer, Prince Charles commiserates with Lady Sarah McCorquodale, Diana's eldest sister. Sarah, a one-time girlfriend of Charles, had married Neil McCorquodale, an ex-Guards officer and heir to a millionaire. **Below** Diana has a word with her brother Charles at a Birthright Ball.

IN THE NEWS

Who gets Earl Spencer's fortune?

In royal circles it was impolite to talk about money, but the press simply could not resist it when Diana's father, Earl Spencer, died in 1992. Other people's money, especially when they are aristocrats, has an ongoing fascination and The Sun made the most of it in this rundown of bequests. Diana, reportedly, inherited between £1 million and £3 million from her father.

fully, Raine had helped save her husband's life.

Warfare between Raine and her stepchildren had, however, continued unabated and there were furious exchanges in the hospital corridors as she tried to prevent the children from seeing their father. Johnnie himself was convinced, though, that without Raine, he would never have lived to see Diana married three years later. Even so, Diana's hatred for her stepmother endured. As late as 1989, when Raine emerged from the nursery at Althorp after a wary encounter with Diana's mother, the Princess of Wales pushed her stepmother, then aged 58, down the stairs. Sue Ingram, Raine's personal

> ## "He was really miserable after the divorce, basically shell-shocked."
> ### CHARLES, 9TH EARL SPENCER,
> ON HIS FATHER AFTER THE DIVORCE

assistant, watched as she tumbled all the way to the next landing. Raine was shaken, but unhurt.

Whatever Diana thought of her, Raine achieved another 14 years of life for her father, who eventually died of a heart attack on 29 March 1992. Johnnie had foreseen what would happen at this juncture and left instructions in his will that Raine should be given six months to move out of Althorp to make way for Charles, the new Earl.

OUSTING RAINE

Charles Spencer, however, had a much more rapid timetable in mind and had never made a secret of it. Backed up by his sisters, he obstructed Raine at every turn and refused to allow her to remove anything from Althorp without proof of purchase. Raine was not even allowed to take her clothes away in suitcases, which, Diana and her brother claimed, did not belong to her. The clothes were stuffed into plastic bags normally used for carrying away rubbish.

As the ultimate humiliation, Raine was not invited to the ceremony on 1 April, at which her husband's ashes were placed in the Spencer family vault. The same day, only three days after his death, Raine was forbidden to set foot in Althorp again. The revenge of the Spencers was complete.

IN CONTEXT   COMEDIAN BENNY HILL DIES

1992

- Comic Benny Hill, **right**, dies of a heart attack
- Heavyweight boxing champion Mike Tyson is imprisoned for six years for rape
- Humorous magazine *Punch* closes after 150 years
- Albert Reynolds becomes Prime Minister of Eire
- NASA confirms Big Bang theory of the creation of the Universe
- Former Wimbledon tennis champion Arthur Ashe confirms he has AIDS
- Anti-Mafia judge Giovanni Falcone is killed in Sicily

Opposite page Raine Spencer with her mother, the celebrated romantic novelist Barbara Cartland, at a Memorial Service for the 8th Earl Spencer. **Above** Sarah and Diana with the casket containing their father's ashes. **Right** The note Diana wrote on the flowers for her father.

I miss you dreadfully. Darling daddy, but will love you forever...

Diana.

An Eye for Design

The Emanuels, Catherine Walker and Victor Edelstein were some of the leading designers who created clothes for Diana. For them, it was the ultimate accolade. For Diana, it was a chance to display some great British fashions from designers with vision

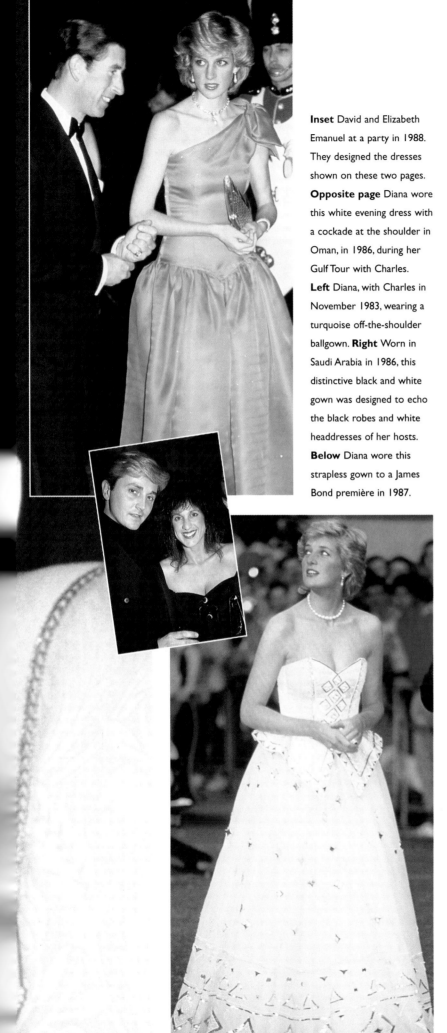

Inset David and Elizabeth Emanuel at a party in 1988. They designed the dresses shown on these two pages. **Opposite page** Diana wore this white evening dress with a cockade at the shoulder in Oman, in 1986, during her Gulf Tour with Charles. **Left** Diana, with Charles in November 1983, wearing a turquoise off-the-shoulder ballgown. **Right** Worn in Saudi Arabia in 1986, this distinctive black and white gown was designed to echo the black robes and white headdresses of her hosts. **Below** Diana wore this strapless gown to a James Bond première in 1987.

David and Elizabeth Emanuel started something big when they designed the Princess of Wales' wedding dress in 1981. They gave notice that the royal star the fashion world had been waiting for had arrived, and that catering for her needs was the accolade to aim for.

The Emanuels, who have since split up, were barely known outside fashion circles when the young Lady Diana Spencer sought them out in 1981. The romantic Emanuel style was bound to attract the starry-eyed young bride.

David and Elizabeth met as students at the Harrow School of Art, near London. David, born in Bridgend, Wales in 1952, and Elizabeth, born in London in 1953, married in 1975 and together enrolled at the prestigious Royal College of Art. There, they created a sensation with a graduation fashion show, made up entirely of all-white outfits.

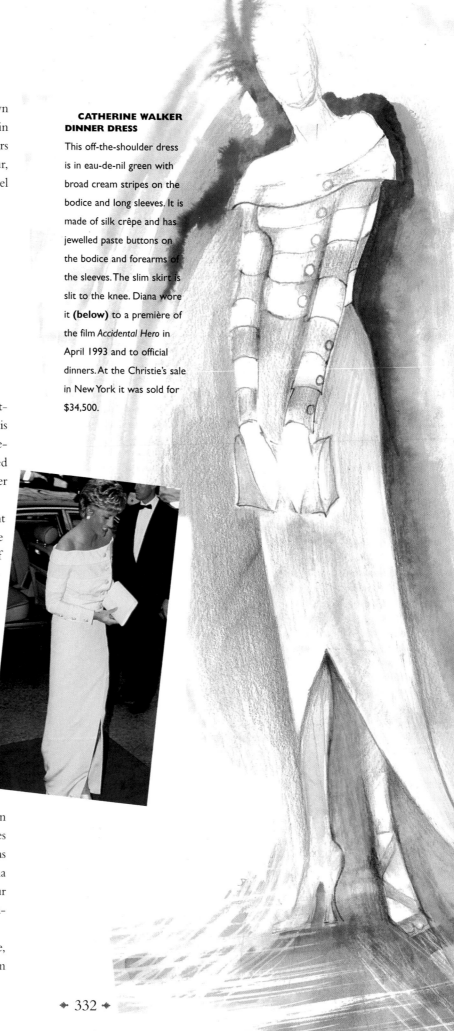

Subsequently, the Emanuels opened their own
fashion salon and showed their first collection in
1977. The big-name clients included such film stars
as Elizabeth Taylor, Joan Collins and Jane Seymour,
as well as Shakira Caine, wife of film star Michael
Caine, Bianca Jagger and Jerry Hall.

> *"As she matures, her clothes
> are becoming simpler and more
> sophisticated. She seems to be
> relying heavily on people like
> Catherine Walker."*
>
> JAYNE FINCHER, PHOTOGRAPHER, ON DIANA

Diana's wedding dress was, of course, the greatest challenge for the Emanuels. They felt that this
marriage was so special, they had to outdo all previous wedding gowns. The Emanuels researched
the longest royal wedding train, and made a longer
one, measuring 25 feet.

One commission that was almost as important
as the wedding dress was the wardrobe the
Emanuels were asked to design for Diana's Gulf
Tour with Charles, in November 1986. The
Emanuels came up with a range of beautiful out-
fits, including an ivory beaded evening gown.

Catherine Walker

It was not the Emanuels, however, who came to
dominate Diana's wardrobe, but French-born
Catherine Walker. She was ready and waiting
with her simple and colourful, yet sophisticated designs just when Diana was prepared to
move on and adopt more mature fashions.

From that point, Walker was responsible
for some of Diana's most showstopping outfits. The puffball-skirted dress and fine silk chiffon
gown in pastel blue that Diana wore at the Cannes
Film Festival in 1987 were Walker creations. So was
the fuchsia pink and purple evening dress Diana
wore, with silk flowers in her hair, during the tour
of Thailand in 1988. Yet, remarkably, this imaginative designer had no formal training.

Catherine Walker was born near Boulogne,
France and at first took a path as different from

fashion design as it was possible to contemplate. She took university degrees in philosophy and aesthetics. In 1970 she married an English lawyer, John Walker, but he died five years later. With two young daughters to care for, Catherine Walker converted the wine shop below her Sydney Street, London flat into a dress shop. There, she sold maternity dresses and children's clothes which were based on late Victorian and Edwardian styles.

The leading British fashion magazine *Vogue* soon noticed Walker's talents and, after one of her dresses first appeared in its pages, in January 1982, her fame grew. Before long, she had left children's smocks behind and was designing the sleek and stylish daywear with beautiful tailoring, and the evening gowns hallmarked with decorative beading which eventually made her what many considered to be Diana's favourite designer.

Walker, who, at just over 5ft 10ins, was as tall as Diana, specialized in the long look which maximized the elegance of good height by showing it off.

Catherine Walker's expertise brought not only a

sheaf of eminent clients but also awards as Designer of the Year for British Couture in 1990/1 and Designer of the Year for Glamour in 1991/2.

Victor Edelstein

Unlike Catherine Walker, Victor Edelstein came into Diana's fashion orbit after long training. Born in London, he joined Alexon in 1962 then, in 1967, became assistant designer and pattern cutter at the famous Biba fashion house which helped promote the youth styles of the time. In 1975 he moved on, and up, to Christian Dior in London. Edelstein left Dior in 1978 to set up his own ready-to-wear fashion house. Before long, though, this highly innovative designer found ready-to-wear too limiting and he returned to haute couture, creating special outfits for individual clients.

Edelstein's speciality was evening dress grandeur, achieved by lavish use of the finest satins and velvets, though in complete contrast, he became a top exponent of the 'little black dress', that modest but essential item in every smart wardrobe.

Four designs by Catherine Walker (**inset above**).
1 A full-skirted evening gown in pink satin, with cuffs and off-the-shoulder collar in white raw silk. Diana wore it in Germany in 1987.
2 This was described as 'a dressing gown with style'. It is certainly stylish, with its white lace embroidered with flowers in blue silk and white sequins. Diana first wore it in France in 1988.
3 A black and jade evening dress which Diana wore on the 1991 Canada tour.
4 Diana at the Garrick Club, Covent Garden, in 1990, wearing a cream silk chiffon evening dress.

His first design for Diana was a high-waisted pink taffeta maternity evening dress, made for her when she was expecting Prince William in 1982. Edelstein's most spectacular contributions to her wardrobe were such dazzling evening dresses as the midnight blue velvet ballgown she wore at the White House when she danced with John Travolta in 1985. Another stunning Edelstein gown was the

> ## "It was the first time I didn't look at other women and think 'Grr!'."
> GAYLE HUNNICUTT, ACTRESS,
> ON WEARING AN EDELSTEIN DRESS

off-the-shoulder cocktail dress Diana wore in Hamburg, Germany in November 1987. It featured delicately patterned black lace on a pink silk lining.

Edelstein also designed eyecatching daywear for Diana, notably the fluorescent pink jacket with black wool kick-pleated skirt she wore on a visit to Littlehampton, Sussex in November 1986 and another suit, in green wool, worn in Portugal in February 1987, with a straight skirt and a jacket featuring stepped lapels and a velvet collar.

Like the Emanuels and Catherine Walker, Victor Edelstein played an important part in creating the elegance combined with an almost theatrical impact which lay at the heart of Diana's image as a glittering and glamorous princess.

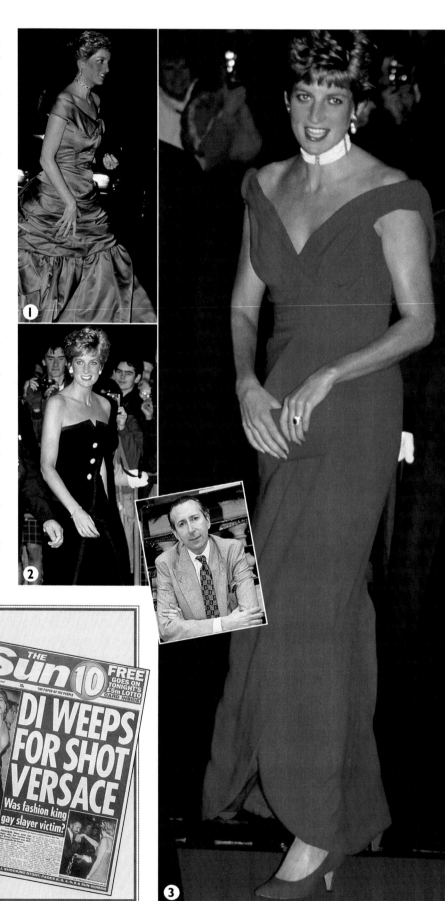

IN THE NEWS

Gianni Versace murdered

On 15 July 1997, the fashion world was severely shaken by the savage murder in Miami of the brilliant and unorthodox Italian designer Gianni Versace. The killing captured world headlines for several days. Versace had not been one of Diana's most frequent designers, but his death horrified her and the publicity went up a notch when press pictures showed her attending a memorial mass in his honour on 22 July in one of his dresses.

THE Sun 10

DI WEEPS FOR SHOT VERSACE

Was fashion king gay slayer victim?

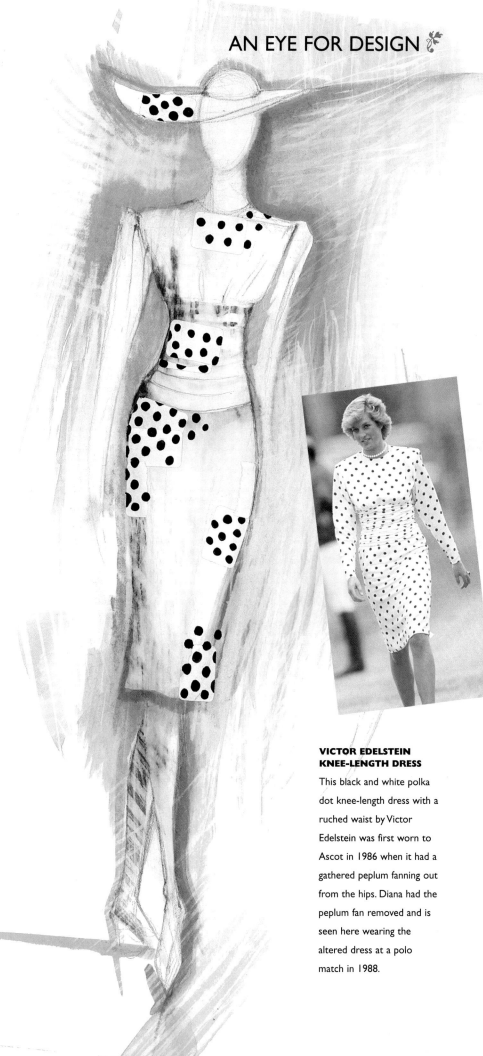

All designs on these two pages are by Victor Edelstein **(inset left)**.

1 This satin ballgown was inspired by late Victorian fashions and has a bustle. Diana wore it in November 1987 at Syon House, Isleworth, for a ball.

2 A long, strapless, black velvet evening dress, which takes its inspiration from a man's tailcoat. She wore it to several film premières.

3 This vivid scarlet silk dress has a draped cowl at the neck and was inspired by 1930s' styles.

4 Diana at the Elysée Palace, Paris, in 1988, wearing an embroidered dinner dress with a short bolero jacket.

VICTOR EDELSTEIN KNEE-LENGTH DRESS

This black and white polka dot knee-length dress with a ruched waist by Victor Edelstein was first worn to Ascot in 1986 when it had a gathered peplum fanning out from the hips. Diana had the peplum fan removed and is seen here wearing the altered dress at a polo match in 1988.

Stressed Out

The demands made by fame and the intense press interest and curiosity that went with it caused Diana considerable stress and put time alone, to relax and be herself, at a premium

Diana, like all members of the Royal Family, had to be a performer. Her public was adoring and thrilled at the excitement of seeing her, even more so if they were lucky enough to shake her hand or talk to her. The very act of putting a posy of flowers in Diana's royal hand was an experience to be cherished. It was likely that everyone she met would never forget their encounter with the dazzling and beautiful Princess of Wales.

The price of all this exposure was a lot of stress and much physical exhaustion. As Diana soon discovered, an unusual amount of energy, self-discipline and patience was required if she was to get through and leave her public satisfied and happy. Their scrutiny was so great and the slightest flicker of impatience or boredom was at once noted and discussed at length by fans who expected her to appear nothing less than perfect.

The press monster

Shadowing all this was the endless and intrusive press coverage. To Diana the press seemed a monster, with batteries of lenses like open mouths waiting to gobble her up. This was the fact behind every picture of Diana meeting the people, smiling, chatting, receiving flowers and presents. Out of sight, but not out of mind, were the massed ranks of cameras.

Diana was not the first member of the Royal Family to run this particular gauntlet. All of them

Inset above Diana expressing frustration with photographers while on holiday in St. Barts, West Indies in February 1995.
Right Diana pursued by a photographer while out shopping in Knightsbridge, London, in July 1994.

Above Snapped while kissing a friend, William van Straubenzee, in a London restaurant in April 1994, Diana turns round to glare with annoyance at the intruding photographer.
Above right A doorman at The Ritz, London attempts to shield Diana from harassment in June 1994.
Opposite page A posse of cameramen snap Diana after a meal in one of her favourite restaurants, San Lorenzo, in London in March 1994.

had faced it and most had learned, in time, to at least tolerate it. None of them, however, had provoked such a furore of interest as the Princess of Wales. Nor had they ever sought, as Diana did, to get within kissing and hugging distance of the public. From the first, Diana's spontaneous, tactile approach had been two-edged. The public were delighted, and loved her for it, but very few understood the price Diana paid for the thrill she gave them.

As one of her staff observed early on in her royal career, Diana would come home after an engagement, throw off her shoes and collapse into a chair utterly played out. If the adrenaline kept her going while she was on show, it soon drained away into exhaustion once the show was over.

The stresses on Diana were all the greater because being an object of public curiosity went against the grain of her shy and diffident nature. Crowds, she herself admitted, terrified her. Even the almost tangible power of their love was frightening.

This was Diana's experience from day one. She called her first public tour, to Wales in 1981, a 'baptism of fire' and, as friends later revealed, she felt completely unable to cope.

The fact that she was in the early stages of her

> "*When the wolf-pack-like British tabloid press...write something horrible, I get a horrible feeling...and I don't want to go outside.*"
> DIANA, ON THE PRESS

first, as yet unannounced, pregnancy with William, made matters even worse. Diana's morning sickness was especially severe and she was constantly in tears. As she and Charles travelled by car from one Welsh venue to the next in a hectic three-day tour, Diana

⤜ **Protocol** ⤛

NEVER COMPLAIN, NEVER EXPLAIN

*Press intrusions into Royal Family life were extraordinary during Diana's time as Princess of Wales, but they were not unprecedented. Over a century ago, Queen Victoria, too, had to run the gauntlet of press comment and criticism. The main cause was her virtual withdrawal from public duty and into perpetual mourning for her adored husband, Prince Albert, who died prematurely in 1861. However, one of Victoria's prime ministers, Benjamin Disraeli, **right**, advised her never to complain about press behaviour, and never to explain herself to the public. This, Disraeli felt, would better preserve the dignity of the Crown and avoid controversies. The Royal Family has largely followed his advice ever since.*

kept telling her husband that she was unable to face the crowds. Diana's friends also revealed that she wished herself back at Coleherne Court, where she had lived before her marriage, when life with her friends was care- and stress-free.

Charles sympathized, Diana's friends recounted, but as he knew only too well from his years of experience, there was no escape. The royal show had to go on. The tour of Wales, as it turned out, was a huge success, as Diana managed to set aside her doubts and give a tremendous performance. This did much for Diana's self-esteem in public, but she did not become fully accustomed to the pressures for some time.

There were private pressures as well. The Royal Family ran on devotion to duty, and, as a young wife, it seems that Diana was determined to keep up with the Windsors. She refused to make allowances for her pregnancy problems, spurred on by what the Duchess of York later called the 'you are never ill'

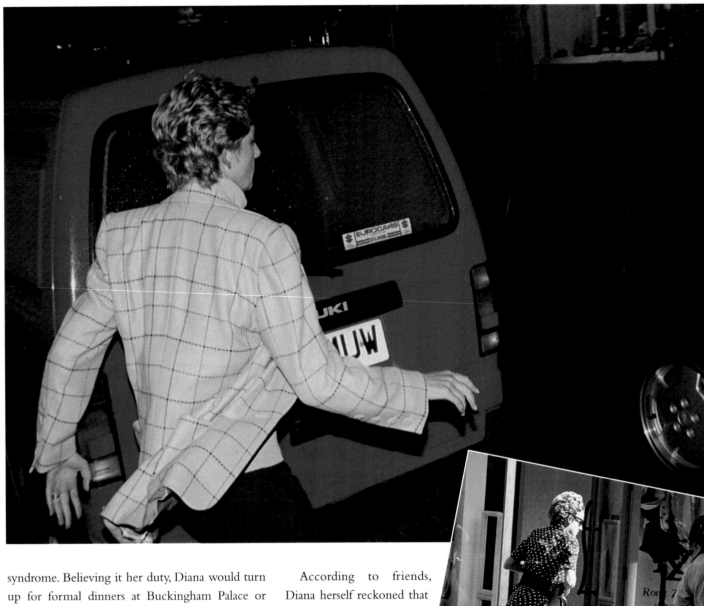

syndrome. Believing it her duty, Diana would turn up for formal dinners at Buckingham Palace or Windsor when she knew she should have been resting in bed.

Diana refused, too, to turn down an important public engagement even when she was feeling quite ill. But, if Charles was also there, she took to standing as close to him as possible, as if drawing comfort from his proximity. Friends revealed, however, that she used to tremble at the very thought of her first solo engagement, which turned out to be switching on the lights in London's Regent Street for Christmas 1981. On that occasion, she later told friends, she was paralysed by nerves; she gabbled out the words to her speech in a quiet monotone. Afterwards, Diana admitted, Buckingham Palace was a haven to which she gladly fled.

According to friends, Diana herself reckoned that it took her all of six years to control her nerves, put aside her fear of crowds and settle down calmly to the royal routine. That was a long apprenticeship and made her appearances at 835 engagements in Britain and 282 abroad, between 1981 and 1987, into great acts of courage.

A big factor in that courage was the way Diana managed to hide almost completely the pressure she was suffering. The smile, the charm, the concern were always up front, on show, and few guessed at the turmoil beneath.

When Charles and Diana visited Australia and New Zealand in 1983, on the most extensive tour 'down under' for 30 years, a member of the Queen's

Sometimes, when the pressure was great, Diana simply turned tail and fled. **Above** Running from photographers after a meal at Fedo, a smart Knightsbridge restaurant, in January 1993. **Inset** Haring down Beauchamp Place, Knightsbridge, to avoid photographers, in June 1994.

interest was very different from crowd interest, where the huge numbers rather than the nature of the scrutiny was the factor she found daunting. The press wanted something from her for themselves – pictures to boost circulation, a scoop to outdo rivals

> *"You think: Oh gosh, I don't want to go out and do my engagement this morning...but you've got to push yourself out."*
> DIANA, ON PUBLIC ENGAGEMENTS

– and Diana often felt, with reason, that she was simply being used. Her aversion to press presence, and the great efforts she made to preserve her two sons from their intrusions, began even before she became Princess of Wales.

Late in 1980, when media speculation was rife, an army of cameramen descended on the Young England Kindergarten where Diana worked and

Household said it would take ten years before the new princess learned how to be royal. In fact, Diana learned how to be royal on that very same tour, which involved a punishing schedule lasting over six weeks, from 17 March to 30 April. When the six weeks were up, it was evident that Diana had learned her lessons very well but the hidden cost was considerable and Diana got through by emulating her mother, Frances. Frances, her daughter revealed, was an expert at covering up negative feelings with a sunny front.

Where Diana's carefully nurtured front slipped, though, was in her contact with the press. Press

Above Diana remonstrates with a photographer after leaving Daphne's restaurant, another favourite London haunt, in February 1994.

Above right A miserable-looking Diana walks past a horde of photographers in December 1994, after attending a function for Headway, the National Head Injuries Association, a charity of which she was patron.

took pictures of her with her young charges. The photograph which became famous was the one which showed her legs through the filmy material of her skirt. Afterwards, she told friends, she believed she had been manoeuvred into posing for that picture against the light, and burst into tears when she saw it.

The experience served to sour Diana's approach to the press, though it was many years before she made her most direct and savage protest against their intrusions. That came in 1993 when Diana and her sons came out of a Leicester Square, London, cinema to find a photographer, Keith Butler, waiting for them. Observers of the scene were startled when Diana rushed up to Butler with clenched fists, and yelled at him: 'You make my life hell!', before marching off in tears.

Long before she reached that breaking point, Diana seemed to handle the stress of the ever-present lens rather more calmly and with a certain amount of impishness. She seemed to play games with the press, one moment charming and co-operative, the next grouchy and reluctant.

Diana once said: 'I simply treat the press as though they were children,' but that inferred a degree of control over them which she did not really possess. Instead, Diana used tricks seemingly

> **"She can be very truculent
> and that's a polite word. She can
> be a cow, actually. Other times,
> she's charming."**
>
> HARRY ARNOLD, ROYAL CORRESPONDENT OF
> THE SUN, ON DIANA

designed to off-balance reporters and photographers. She told a *Financial Times* reporter, for instance, that she lined her budgie's cage with his newspaper. On another occasion, Diana insulted *The Sun* when she told a man she saw reading it during one of her walkabouts: 'I use it as bedding for my children's hamsters.'

The Sun, demonstrating an admirable sense of humour, exploited Diana's remark by getting a group of veterinary surgeons to expound on the

warm, soft, happy comfort hamsters derived from sleeping on its pages. The newspaper took the joke a step further by getting 20 hamsters to sleep on 20 different papers. The rodents, it appears, 'voted' *The Sun* tops for a good night's rest.

Of course, not all Diana's brushes with the press

Above Diana is mobbed by a crowd at the Royal Opera House, Covent Garden, in January 1994. **Inset** Diana returning from Lech, Austria, on the death of her father.

were that good-natured. At times, the Princess proved perfectly capable of turning her back on the cameras to prevent anyone getting a good picture. If she could not help herself, she would put on a glum face to spoil a photograph and make it, in effect, unpublishable.

Paparazzi

If Diana handed out this treatment to accredited photographers from respectable newspapers, her attitude towards the freelance paparazzi was a great deal darker. These opportunists used to sneak up on her, hide behind bushes or openly chase her through the streets in order to snatch pictures of Diana off duty, or in private moments while on holiday. This was the major drawback Diana faced

IN THE NEWS

The Press and the Abdication

This headline of 3 December 1936 was a complete shock to the British public. Through voluntary press silence, they remained ignorant of King Edward VIII's wish to marry the divorcee Mrs. Simpson. This was in total contrast to the ongoing coverage of more recent royal scandals. In 1936, the cataclysmic event was announced and concluded in only eight days, from the first news to the abdication on 11 December.

ABDICATION OF EDWARD VIII:

Daily Mail

THE KING HAS CHOSEN

"I Have Determined To Renounce The Throne"

The Text Issued Last Night of THE BILL OF

Top Totally distraught, Diana is flanked by a senior policeman while on a visit to the Ashworth Hospice in Southport, Merseyside, in June 1992. **Inset** The press pack was an unending fact of life for Diana. Here the massed ranks of photographers gathered at the London Hilton Hotel on 3 December 1996 to record her 'resignation' speech.

through her desire to lead as normal a life as possible, especially when it came to shopping or taking William and Harry out for treats. The imposition was no more tolerable to Diana because of that and, though she often took precautions not to be recognized, by wearing sunglasses or casual outfits, the eagle eyes of the paparazzi often saw through her disguise. All they got for their pains, sometimes, was a photograph of Diana haring along the street, moving away at speed, trying to get away from them, but the irony was that even this served their purpose. A picture of Diana, any picture, was worth many thousands, sometimes millions, to the paparazzi.

The first big outrage of this kind occurred in 1982 when paparazzi took photographs of the five-months' pregnant princess on a beach on Eleuthera, in the Bahama Islands. The penultimate intrusion took place in Sardinia where Diana was on holiday with Dodi Fayed, and the pressure then was so great that the couple fled the Mediterranean island and

headed for Paris. There, of course, the car chase awaited them which culminated in their deaths.

At that juncture, Diana's brother, Earl Spencer, said he 'always knew the press would kill Diana one day', but if death was the ultimate price of fame, life

> **"However bloody you are feeling, you can put on the most amazing show of happiness. My mother is an expert at that, and I've picked it up."**
> DIANA, ON APPEARING IN PUBLIC

was no joy ride. The pressure of mass love by adoring crowds, like the rabid attentions of the media, was both wearing and unnerving. It is not hard to imagine the extent of Diana's relief when the public show was over for a while, the front door at Kensington Palace closed and the world's most famous woman could relax, out of the public gaze.

THE BUBBLE BURSTS

Andrew Morton's book Diana: Her True Story *caused an uproar when it appeared in June 1992. It told Diana's story of a marriage which, according to Morton, was not a fairytale but a nightmare*

It is extremely rare for a single book, even a book about Diana, to make worldwide headlines, set off a furore of angry debate and put a formerly revered institution such as the Royal Family into the firing line. Yet this is precisely what occurred on 7 June 1992, the day *Diana: Her True Story* by Andrew Morton was published.

Written by a skilful journalist who was no rumour-mongering hack, the book was dynamite. Appetites were whetted in the usual way, through pre-publication serialization in a national newspaper. Even the title of the book was provocative, implying that the truth about Charles and Diana had not, until then, been told.

Morton's book revealed what some had long suspected, others had energetically denied and many had feared: that the marriage of the Prince and Princess of Wales was a sham. Morton claimed there was no great love-match, no wedded bliss, not even a measure of rub-along contentment. The

DIARY DATES

Previous page Taken at the Gulf Parade in London, in June 1991, this was a picture that a number of newspapers chose to interpret as indicating that all was not well in the royal marriage. **Right** Princess Diana and the Queen Mother at Ascot in June 1992, shortly after the publication of Andrew Morton's book. **Below right** Prince Charles and his two sons walk to church at Sandringham on Christmas Day 1992; Diana was not with them. **Opposite page** Another picture, taken in 1987, which sections of the press interpreted as showing Diana's unhappiness.

outward happiness and accord that Charles and Diana had shown to the world for nearly 11 years was said to be a camouflage. Behind the façade, Morton asserted, Diana was miserable; Charles did not love her, but was besotted by a long-standing mistress, Camilla Parker-Bowles.

Morton painted a picture of a cold, arrogant prince, jealous of Diana's success and contemptuous of her supposed lack of intellect and 'trivial' interests. In the background, wrote Morton, the unfeeling, hidebound Royal Family saw Diana as a 'problem' and sought to sideline her and stifle her individuality. Behind them lay the courtiers whose job it was to whip Diana into line.

SHOCKING DETAILS

If the general message of *Diana: Her True Story* was shocking, the details were nothing short of appalling. Diana, Morton wrote, had attempted suicide five times and on one occasion, had thrown herself down the stairs while pregnant. Charles, the book revealed, teased Diana with a story, actually not true, that his previous girlfriends had been married

seemed that every time Diana pressed the 'last number re-dial' button on Charles' telephone, it rang in Camilla's home, and sometimes Camilla answered.

Before long, Morton's book claimed, the infection of the Waleses' troubled marriage spread to other members of the Royal Family. In 1991, the nine-year-old Prince William pushed tissues under the bathroom door at Kensington Palace where Diana was crying bitterly after a row with Charles.

> *"Marriage…is rather more than falling in love with somebody and having a love affair for the rest of your life."*
> PRINCE CHARLES, ON MARRIAGE

The Queen Mother, it was alleged, came out against Diana to become 'the fount of all negative comment'. The Queen hinted in a Christmas broadcast that she would not abdicate and privately blamed the rocky state of her heir's marriage for the decision. In his turn, Charles apparently refused to talk to his mother for days and put the blame on Diana.

What is more, Morton wrote, Diana never received one word of thanks from her in-laws for her devotion to royal duty and was given no help to ease her into her royal role. They just left her to flounder, said Morton, until she found her own feet.

DEMONIZING CHARLES

One-sided though the book obviously was, its effect was to iconize the princess and demonize Charles. In addition, it up-ended all previous notions of the Royal Family as exemplars of dignity, probity and even honour. The speed with which so many readers appeared willing to ditch their regard for the royals was one of the most shocking results of Morton's book.

Diana was seen as much more than an unhappy wife. While people sympathized because she was going through a rough patch not uncommon in a ten-year-old marriage, many were also ready to believe she was a martyr to her royal destiny and a sacrifice on the altar of the cruel Windsor dynasty.

This popular conclusion was not entirely a surprise. The public had already been primed for it; the

women as they were always more discreet.

The book told how, on the very day she and Charles were married, Diana discovered a bracelet inscribed 'Fred to Gladys', Fred supposedly being Charles and Gladys, Camilla. On their honeymoon, photographs of Camilla were said to have fallen out of Charles' diary and Diana noticed her new husband was wearing cufflinks inscribed with two intertwined Cs, for Charles and Camilla.

The terrible revelations, it appears, carried on into 1982. Shortly after the birth of Prince William, Diana apparently overheard a conversation, presumably with Camilla, in which Charles said: 'Whatever happens, I will always love you.' Later, it

press had banged this drum for years. The most minute sign of anything less than bliss had been interpreted as trouble in the Waleses' marriage, and even where some rumours had been proved ill-founded or quite clearly invented, the ideas they had peddled left behind a trail of doubt.

In this atmosphere of suspicion and unrest, the steadfast, often monotonous denials that came out

Above One scenario was that Charles and Diana would lead separate lives, meeting only at set pieces, such as Trooping the Colour. **Right** Diana with William at London's Natural History Museum in April 1992.

IN CONTEXT
1992
AGASSI WINS WIMBLEDON

• US player Andre Agassi, **right**, wins the men's singles title at Wimbledon

• President Mohammed Boudiaf of Algeria is assassinated

• Marjorie Robb, last known survivor of the *Titanic* disaster in 1912, dies, aged 103

• Denmark wins the European Football Championship with a 2-0 victory over Germany

• John Smith is elected leader of the Labour Party

• The summer Olympics take place in Barcelona, Spain

The Private Princess
How Morton's book came about

If Andrew Morton had not been able to authenticate the details contained in *Diana: Her True Story*, it could never have been published. Authentication was vital because his book did not, and could not, have the sanction of Buckingham Palace.

In 1991, a crop of books appeared celebrating Charles and Diana's tenth wedding anniversary in glowing terms. Some of Diana's friends, it appears, decided that these were such travesties of the truth that it was time to tell Morton the 'real' story of Diana's royal life.

This, apparently, was how the book contained information from informants who could be identified. In this way, Morton achieved his authenticity. What no

Above *At the time of publication, Andrew Morton poses with a copy of his book against the backdrop of Windsor Castle.*

one, not even Morton, was willing to disclose at the time was that Diana had been directly involved. After her death, when the book was republished as *Diana: Her True Story – In Her Own Words*, Morton revealed that not only had she supplied information, she had part-edited the book, writing comments in the margins of the original manuscript.

Her friends and relations acted as go-betweens, so that if Diana was ever asked by members of the Royal Family whether or not she had dealt with Morton, she could truthfully deny it.

of Buckingham Palace soon acquired the air of a cover-up. Sceptics made the point, not without some justification, that official explanations of events were frequently untrue. The individual popularity of the two contestants, as Charles and Diana were now seen, also had its influence.

Since 1981, Diana had built up an image of sweetness, compassion, motherly devotion and beauty, which held the public in thrall. She was not

> "*The marital squabbles of the spoilt young Windsors...are opening a potential hole in the royal ozone layer.*"
>
> ANTHONY HOLDEN, ROYAL AUTHOR, ON THE ROYAL FAMILY

just popular, she was adored. She was not just admired, she was, in many quarters, practically worshipped. However excessive this devotion may have appeared, it was a predictable reaction. The public face of royalty was all that people were permitted to see and the royals were judged by it.

Diana's public face was so dazzling that, blinded by it, the millions who believed Morton's book told the truth were unable to imagine that Diana was in any way at fault, or that Morton had misrepresented Charles and his family. *Diana: Her True Story*, millions were convinced, must be true.

NO-WIN SITUATION

Prince Charles, the apparent villain of the piece, found himself outmanoeuvred. There was, in fact, no easy or practical defence against such an onslaught. Striking back from his weaker position was out of the question. 'Putting the record straight' was not an option since that would involve the unseemly spectacle of Charles and Diana disagreeing in public, and through a hostile press at that. For Charles, it was a no-win situation.

His standing – as a prince, a man, a husband and a father – was seriously undermined. Never before in the history of the British monarchy had the anatomy of a royal marriage been so brutally exposed for public inspection and judgement. The limited royal publicity machine had never been

⋙ Protocol ⋘

ROYAL PRESS PACK

*Despite clashes between the Royal Family and the press, there is a body of reporters and photographers who are officially accredited to Buckingham Palace. This press pack, sometimes termed the 'Rat Pack', often accompanied Charles and Diana on their tours, **right**. Andrew Morton, later the author of* Diana: Her True Story, *was one of them, and this is how Diana got to know him. The press pack regularly attend briefings by royal press aides. Since they are all travelling around together, the royals and the accompanying press can become friends. In fact, Charles and Diana used to give a special reception for the accompanying press whenever they were abroad and, at one time, gave them off-the-record briefings at the start of a trip.*

geared to cope with this kind of situation. It was largely confined to court circulars, carefully worded official statements and 'No comment', or rather silence, in the face of any rumour or speculation. This had been long-standing practice at the palace, and was designed to distance the Royal Family from controversy. The system also served to put the Royal Family in a position where any criticism seemed unfair because they were 'unable' to respond to it.

Diana: Her True Story exposed the weakness in this procedure. Total silence was now taken as arrogance or lofty contempt for public opinion. Alternatively, it appeared as an admission of guilt. Charles was hamstrung, too, because his own popularity was nowhere near as high as Diana's.

For decades, the popular press had revelled in celebrities, including the royals, who lived glamorously. There were a lot of column inches in a buccaneering royal like Charles' predecessor as

At times the strain of the marriage and the difficulty caused by relationships outside it, particularly that of Charles and Camilla Parker-Bowles, showed on the faces of the three parties involved. Speculation in the press contributed to the strain. **Left** Diana and Charles on a visit to Germany in 1987. **Right** Diana in Glasgow on a 1991 visit. **Below** Camilla Parker-Bowles snapped in her garden in 1993.

Prince of Wales. Though he later abdicated as King, he was known as 'a bit of a lad' in his youth and was often seen in nightclubs surrounded by pretty girls.

NOT A PHILANDERER

Prince Charles was a different kind of man. His pleasures were more cerebral and solitary: he often went off alone to paint or croft in Scotland, and became actively interested in such things as farming and conservation. The most shocking thing Charles had ever done was to get caught, at age 15, drinking cherry brandy in a pub. That, and a picture of him dancing with a scantily clad carnival dancer in Brazil in 1978, was the extent of his gallivanting.

For the rest, though, Charles was regularly mocked in the press for his 'oddball' interests, such as alternative medicine and mystic religions. The Prince's Trust, which he founded to help the disadvantaged and the homeless, never received the same flamboyant 'press' as Diana's charity work did.

All this meant that Prince Charles was ill-equipped to fend off the frontal assault of *Diana: Her True Story*. And in 1992 this was not the first body blow the Royal Family suffered (nor would it be the last). On 19 March, the Duke and Duchess of York separated. More quietly, Princess Anne and her husband Captain Mark Phillips, separated since

> "*...a tabloid-flavoured rendering of the Princess of Wales' bulimia, suicide attempts and marital problems with Prince Charles.*"
>
> THE DUCHESS OF YORK,
> ON DIANA: HER TRUE STORY

1989, began divorce proceedings on 13 April. What the Queen later described as her *annus horribilis* had got under way, and when *Diana: Her True Story* provided the third royal crisis in three months, it fell to Charles and Diana to reassure the nation that all was well, and so keep the royal flag flying.

It was an impossible task to ask of them. Diana's misery, as described by Andrew Morton, was far too intense. The sense of fury and betrayal felt by Charles' friends and supporters, and probably Charles himself, was too deep for any outward

show of amity to paper over the cracks. As the Duchess of York wrote in her 1996 autobiography, there are some things for which no apology can be adequate and no recompense can be made. In this context, *Diana: Her True Story* was a point of no return. If, for Diana, the truth was out in the open at last, there was no going back on it. If, for Charles, the book seemed the worst sort of betrayal, it was impossible it could be forgotten, still less forgiven.

THE RING OF TRUTH

Even this, though, was not the end of it. *Diana: Her True Story* had an air of authenticity, which for many readers meant it could not be dismissed as grubby gossip. Andrew Morton was a journalist with a well-deserved reputation for thoroughness. He wrote well and his research had been meticulous.

He had spoken at length to Diana's friends and relations, and they made no attempt to hide their involvement. Had this not been the case, Morton's book would not have exerted so much power. But questions soon arose: who had spoken to those informants, and in such intimate detail? Who knew the anatomy of the marriage so well?

The obvious answer was that Diana must have co-operated with Morton, or at the very least sanctioned the book. However, as the author revealed five years later, a few weeks after Diana's death, the Princess of Wales did a great deal more than that.

Above The book painted Charles in a bad light but there was little he could do.
Right Shortly before publication, Diana, seen here in Egypt, looked tense.
Opposite page The Waleses always came together for family events. On this occasion it was the memorial service for Earl Spencer, in May 1992.

IN THE NEWS

Diana's suicide attempts revealed

Diana: Her True Story, serialized in The Sunday Times, was sensational fodder for the rest of the press. One of the most startling revelations, as detailed by the New York Post on 8 June, was that Diana had attempted to take her life on six occasions. As reported on the front page, she had thrown herself down the stairs, slit her wrists, hurled herself at glass, taken sleeping pills, cut herself on the chest and slashed herself again. The Post promised 'the full story on the desperate royal'.

NEW YORK POST
SPORTS EXTRA
PRINCESS DIE
Books: She tried suicide 6 times...
- Threw self down stairs
- Slit wrists with razor
- Hurled self at glass
- Took overdose of pills
- Cut herself on chest
- Slashed herself again

PEROT FEVER!
BEWARE OF VIDEO SCAM
YANKS WIN, METS LOSE

Necklines and Hemlines

Diana's necklines and hemlines needed careful choosing. They could not be too revealing, but had to stop short of being frumpish, or playing so safe that chances were missed for a touch of innovation

When it came to necklines and hemlines, Diana's task as a royal trendsetter was to be decorous but stylish and to avoid the impression that she was playing safe.

The modest-length straight skirts and full or pleated skirts Diana wore in her early days as Princess of Wales served the royal purpose very well. So did her favourite ruffle-necked blouses, which covered her up to the chin. But the greater sophistication that followed meant she had to take greater chances, especially with evening wear which, by its very nature, revealed more rather than less.

Daring approach

An early sign of a more daring approach came in 1982, when Diana wore a low-necked midnight blue evening gown by Bellville Sassoon to a dinner with Margaret Thatcher at 10 Downing Street. Diana, pregnant with Prince William, allowed herself just a hint of cleavage at the base of the plunging neckline. The main interest, though, was a lavish white lace collar which reached across her shoulders in generous folds and was echoed by matching lace at the wrists. This was very much a young princess' evening gown, pretty rather than

Above For the charity auction of her dresses, held in New York in June 1997, Diana wore this Catherine Walker sequinned dress with a low-cut neckline.

Main picture In Cornwall, in 1990, Diana wears a warm jacket and a high-necked silk blouse. **Left** In Nepal in 1993, Diana is colourful but restrained in a jacket and a long matching dress. **Below** At a charity concert, in jazzy primary colours and a short skirt by designer Tomas Starzewski, in 1991.

chic. But, there were signs of greater chic even in 1982, when Diana appeared at a reception at Grocer's Hall, London, in a turquoise cowboy-style neck scarf with a matching printed shirt and bolero by Donald Campbell.

By 1984, though, Diana's growing fashion confidence enabled her to strike out and wear a stunning strapless red evening gown with red lace overdress

> "*We used to rehearse necklines, making sure they weren't too low, thinking about how she'd have to decorously get out of a car.*"
>
> CAROLINE CHARLES, DESIGNER,
> ON DIANA'S NECKLINES

by Jan van Velden to a ballet gala in Oslo, Norway, in February of that year. The double interest – low-cut gown combined with high-necked lace – was quite an advance for Diana at the time.

One of the most beautiful necklines Diana ever wore, again in a fetching combination of daring and demure, was the star-shaped, wide and deep neckline cleverly filled in with black lace, on a black Catherine Walker dress. Diana wore it to a concert in Swansea in November 1985.

The following year, David and Elizabeth Emanuel were responsible for a most ingenious neckline to a long-sleeved black dress that Diana wore for a dinner at the Mansion House in December 1986. It had a cut-out neckline, but with an extra twist: a silver satin collar that extended from shoulder to shoulder, while leaving the front of the cut-out uncovered. This catered for an important factor in royal fashion: when Diana would be seen for a long period from the waist up only, seated at dinner, for instance, the top half of a dress was designed to be particularly interesting.

Top interest

The logistics of royal appearances in public were a feature Diana's designers always had to bear in mind. A dress for a theatre visit had to focus interest on the bodice – providing 'top interest' – since only the top half of Diana would be seen from outside the royal box. An example of an ideal dress for

1 A wide-shouldered jacket with a V-neck decorated with two golden buttons that mirror her earrings. Designed by Rifat Ozbek, Diana wore it in 1987.

2 A 1984 outfit by Jan van Velden, worn while Diana was pregnant. The blouse has a large square collar.

3 The scalloped neckline of this 1991 red velvet top by Catherine Walker is attractive, eyecatching and feminine without being revealing – neatly fitting the demands for royal dress.

4 An off-the-shoulder tunic top in shrimp pink silk by Catherine Walker, decorated with bands of flowers in simulated pearls and paste jewels. The neckline is lightly scalloped with a small V.

5 This blue evening dress, by Donald Campbell, stayed well within the royal dress code, achieving the difficult feat of being both demure and revealing. The transparent top layer, made of blue silk chiffon embroidered with a leaf pattern, has a ruffled collar and a pleated yoke. Beneath this Diana wore a simple blue dress with a plunging neckline. The dress was first worn in Wales in 1981.

VARIED NECKLINES

Above This 1988 neckline by Catherine Walker is like an elegantly draped scarf. Its black and white pattern is echoed on the hat, thus framing the face and throat. **Centre and photo** A sari-style ballgown by Catherine Walker. The purple sash forms a single shoulder strap for the strapless silk chiffon bodice. Diana wore it in Thailand in 1988. **Far right and photo** A chocolate-tin-soldier outfit by Catherine Walker, worn to a passing-out parade at Sandhurst in 1987. The V of the neckline is mirrored by the hemline.

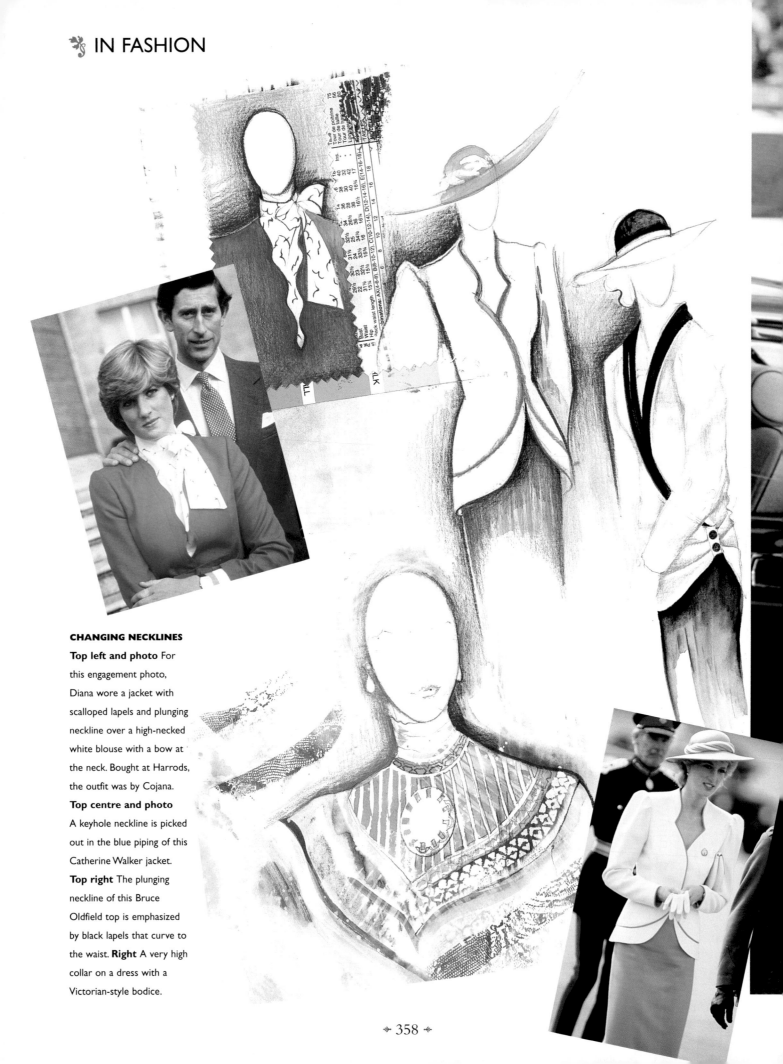

CHANGING NECKLINES

Top left and photo For this engagement photo, Diana wore a jacket with scalloped lapels and plunging neckline over a high-necked white blouse with a bow at the neck. Bought at Harrods, the outfit was by Cojana.

Top centre and photo A keyhole neckline is picked out in the blue piping of this Catherine Walker jacket.

Top right The plunging neckline of this Bruce Oldfield top is emphasized by black lapels that curve to the waist. **Right** A very high collar on a dress with a Victorian-style bodice.

Left A bright Diana steps out in Manchester, in 1993, in a shocking pink Catherine Walker two-piece, where the hemline of the long drape jacket almost touches that of the short skirt.

1 In June 1993, at the Café Royal, London, Diana wears a coffee-coloured Catherine Walker suit with a round neckline and no collar.

2 In Ealing in 1992, Diana wears a deep burgundy suit with a mid-calf pleated skirt.

this purpose was a Catherine Walker white silk gown with wide shawl collar, otherwise fairly plain, which Diana chose for a ballet gala in London in 1988. Surprisingly demure for Diana at that stage, it framed her shoulders like a pretty picture.

Practical hemlines

The logistics of hemlines were even more demanding. Designers had to reckon with the big test for royal ladies – getting out of a car. Doing that decorously could be imperilled by a hemline that was too short or gave no relief, like a set of kick-pleats, for easy movement.

Diana solved the short skirt problem at times by the simplest method: she capitulated and wore a lower hemline, often stretching to mid-calf. This, though, had its own drawbacks. With her height, longer hemlines looked awkward because they divided her figure unevenly. She tried several times, but the long hemline for daywear was not one that Diana could wear without looking swamped by her own clothes, and she usually settled, more happily, for hemlines just below the knee.

The problems of revealing too much came with this territory, of course, and to afford the shorter hemline, as it were, many of Diana's skirts were 'relaxed' so that they would not ride up too far when she got out of cars. There was ample room for

> *"She got away with a lot. Some of those necklines were pretty borderline, but she always managed to keep within the royal bounds."*
> VICTORIA AUSTIN, ROYAL WRITER, ON DIANA

this purpose in the figure-hugging bright pink dress by Victor Edelstein in which Diana appeared at a Lionel Richie concert in London in April 1987. The skirt was gathered across the hips and the hemline was notched at one side, so giving ease of movement but without undue revelations.

Another way round the short hemline problem was a fringe of lace along the hem. This enabled the hemline to be shorter than usual, at the knee or above, while the lace obscured the view. Diana chose a cream satin and lace Victor Edelstein suit with this type of hemline for a variety show in Sydney, Australia, in January 1988. The previous year, she tried something similar in day wear with an Arabella Pollen cream-coloured suit with scalloped hemline. The scallops obscured the fact that Diana was showing rather more knee than usual.

Sometimes, the hemline became the whole point of an outfit. This was certainly so with the

> **"Her hemlines and necklines could go up and down like yoyos, though always in good taste, but she could wear practically anything and look terrific."**
>
> FIONA SINCLAIR, ROYAL CORRESPONDENT, ON DIANA

proscenium arch-shaped hemline of a velvet and taffeta evening gown by Catherine Walker, which Diana wore on a visit to the Munich opera in 1985.

The taffeta skirt, deeply ruched below the hips, fell in generous freeform pleating to just below the knee at the front, trailing down the side to ground level at the back. This framed Diana's long, slender legs against a dark backdrop, and it was stunning.

When choosing necklines and hemlines, Diana knew exactly how to balance her desire for innovation with the restrictions of her royal role.

IN THE NEWS

Daring to be different

The rather demure Diana who visited Venice with Charles during their Italian tour of 1985 returned ten years later, a much more svelte and sophisticated woman. This fashion report in the Daily Mail of 15 June 1995 underlined the difference, with a photograph of the Princess in a skirt below the knee and the 1995 version, in short, tight, above-the-knee skirts. Diana's wardrobe was certainly more daring after her separation from Charles, and the sight of a royal thigh proved it. Necklines, too, were more revealing, and press and public were quick to notice.

Two little black numbers. **Above** This well-known 1993 dress by Christina Stambolian catches the eye both top and bottom, being as off-the-shoulder as possible and having an asymmetrical hem, with a sash that falls from the waist far down the legs. **Right** A simply cut black Versace cocktail dress with shoulder straps and a hem that finishes well above the knees, worn to a London cinema in 1995.

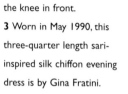

1 Designed by Catherine Walker in 1992, this dinner dress in cream pleated silk was worn in Nepal in 1993. Floral designs in paste jewels and simulated pearls decorate the upper bodice, sleeves and the medallion on the wide leather belt.

2 This 1986 long dinner dress by Catherine Walker is covered in sequins, has a wide V neckline and is slit to the knee in front.

3 Worn in May 1990, this three-quarter length sari-inspired silk chiffon evening dress is by Gina Fratini.

A Taste of Hungary

Charles and Diana's four-day tour of Hungary in 1990 was special. A year earlier, when the Communists still ruled, it would have been impossible. But then, the democratic Hungary, with new freedoms, was born

A real-life prince and princess arriving in Hungary to be welcomed by a genuine democratic head of state was something most Hungarians never thought they would see. Yet when Charles and Diana arrived at Ferighey Airport, Budapest, for a four-day visit on 7 May 1990, just over six months after Hungary threw out its Communist rulers, the impossible came true.

The Prince and Princess of Wales were the first British royals to make an official visit to Hungary, which had fallen into the Communist orbit in 1948, before either Charles or Diana were born. Their host, the recently elected President Arpad Goncz, had spent six years in prison after the abortive bid to win back Hungary's freedom in 1956. The emotion of the moment was all the greater because the

A Taste of Hungary

Opposite page Diana receives a rose from a well-wisher during her visit with Charles to the Plains region of Hungary on 9 May. **Main picture** Diana admires the view from the Budapest Citadel on the first day of the Hungarian tour.

royal visitors were greeted on arrival by the Hungarian national anthem, which was being played for the first time since Communist rule had been brought to an end the previous October. The significance of it proved too much for Zsuzsa Goncz, the 64-year-old wife of the President. As the music began, she burst into tears. Diana, with ready sympathy, held Zsuzsa's hand until her tears dried.

Economic mission

As often happens on a royal tour, Charles had a brief to fulfil – promoting opportunities for British investment in Hungary. Charles was there partly as Patron of Business in the Community, and he checked on progress at the Ganz Hunslet Vehicle Factory, which British investment had rescued from the brink of bankruptcy in 1988. He also visited the computer software firm Microsystems, where he met Dr. Rubik, the inventor of the famous cube.

Charles was given a warm reception everywhere he went. He was treated by Hungarians almost as

Above Diana is a guest at a fashion show in Budapest. **Right** On her arrival at Budapest Airport on 7 May, Diana is presented with a small bouquet by a young boy. **Above right** Diana and Charles are welcomed to Hungary by their hosts, President Arpad Goncz and his wife Zsuzsa.

ceilings, the ornately decorated restaurants, and the sounds of gypsy violins playing sweet melodies.

Hungary was, nevertheless, depressingly poor, a fact not lost on Charles and Diana. As they drove from the airport to the Government Guest House in Budapest, their gleaming Bentley was in stark contrast to the generally run-down air of the Hungarian capital. Most Hungarians could survive

> **"I am immensely proud of the Hungarian blood which courses somewhere in my veins."**
> CHARLES, ON HIS HUNGARIAN ANCESTRY

only by doing three jobs, and rows of seedy houses betrayed a lack of funds even for essential repairs.

It is a truism in royal circles that the poorer the country, the grander the welcome, and the banquet staged by President Goncz at the Parliament building on the evening of 7 May amply demonstrated this belief. The building itself was magnificent, painted in gold and decorated with statues, carved gold figures and palms. The banquet was also a big dress occasion, including diamond-studded skullcaps worn by some of the male guests. Next day, 8

one of their own, on the basis of his descent from the Count and Countess Kir-Rhedey (see Protocol). He was given a portrait of the Countess as a memento. Charles showed that he understood the sufferings of the country under Communism. In a speech that he gave at the Budapest Institute of Economics on 8 May, he complimented his audience on their courage, stressing that the re-emerging democracies of eastern Europe owed a great debt to Hungary, which had been the first to break free in 1989. 'We remember who cut the first wire of the Iron Curtain,' Charles said.

Savouring the atmosphere

The visit was not all business, of course, and Charles and Diana had plenty of opportunity to savour the characteristic atmosphere of Hungary. A great deal of it had survived the long, drab Communist years. The cosy Budapest cafés were still there, as were the elegant neo-classical houses with their frescoed

⟫ Protocol ⟪

CHARLES' HUNGARIAN RELATIVES

Prince Charles has little-known Hungarian ancestry. His great-great-great-great grandmother Claudine, born in 1812, was a member of the Hungarian family of Rhedey. She was created Countess of Hohenstein by the Emperor of Austria and subsequently married Alexander, Duke of Württemberg. They had a son, Francis, who was created Duke of Teck. He married Princess Mary Adelaide of Cambridge, a granddaughter of King George III, and their daughter became Queen Mary, consort of George V. They, **right**, *were Prince Charles' great grandparents.*

May, the royal couple toured the Dimitrov Ter covered market. The market was a colourful treasure house of all kinds of goods, from food to flowers, trinkets to T-shirts, with the red, yellow and blue flowered drawstring blouses peculiar to Hungary very much in evidence.

The welcome Diana received was exceptional, even in her experience. There were cries of 'Viva

> ## "Hungarians are elated to be free. I can feel the excitement among the people here, it's almost spiritual."
> ### DIANA ON THE NEW DEMOCRATIC HUNGARY

Diana!' Men stepped forward to bow and kiss her hand in gestures of old-fashioned gallantry. Stallholders handed her roses. Others gave her jars of honey. At intervals, children's voices piped up: 'Diana! Diana!' and she turned to see groups of youngsters peering at her through balustrades or lining a wall.

The following day Charles and Diana were given a complete change of scene. They drove out into the broad plains of the countryside to savour the excitements of traditional Hungary. The country roads were rough and unmade, and the royal Bentley had to jolt along to Bugac on a 90-minute journey. Diana arrived feeling rather queasy, but there was soon much to distract her. A folk dancing

IN THE NEWS

Diana in tears

If anything showed how different Diana's approach was to that favoured by the rest of the Royal Family, it was her reaction when confronted with suffering. As reported in the Daily Mail on 11 May, when Diana visited the Peto Institute during her tour of Hungary with Charles, the suffering there was just too much for her. She was visibly upset at the ravages that cerebral palsy wreaked on the young patients.

Touched by true courage

FROM GEOFFREY LEVY

'It's heartbreaking, but it is wonderful work they do'

'I'm not a baby machine, says Princess'

display awaited, with performers in white lace costumes and a musician playing a hurdy-gurdy. Next, Charles and Diana climbed into an open carriage which set off down lanes flanked by meadows scarlet with poppies. Reacting badly, as always, to the heat, Diana tried to keep cool with a peacock fan.

Al fresco lunch

When the Prince and Princess stopped at a farm, they were offered freshly baked bread and lunched in the open air as butterflies fluttered among the springtime lilac. Charles and Diana noticed a wreath of corn attached to a tree and were told that this was a talisman to ensure a good harvest.

The day in the countryside ended with the thrill of watching dashing Hungarian wild horse-riders

On 9 May Charles and Diana visited the Plains region of Hungary to see the traditional side of the country. **Opposite page** They watched a display of folk dancing in the town of Bugac. **Above** From Bugac Charles and Diana were treated to a carriage ride, then lunched in the open air at a farm. **Left** Hungarian wild horse-riders performed daring feats for the royal couple.

performing daring feats, such as standing upright in the saddle as their exotic greys galloped past at speed. The riders prided themselves on being warrior nomads, flamboyant and free, showing off the skills that had been handed down to them through the generations. It was a stimulating show, full of thundering hooves, daredevil deeds, cracking whips and gaudy, colourful costumes.

Back in Budapest that same evening, Charles and Diana went to the theatre to see a performance of William Shakespeare's great, though gory, tragedy *King Lear*, performed by the Renaissance Theatre Company. The British actor Richard Briers for once shed his TV comedy image to play the old king who is betrayed and driven out by his own daughters. Diana looked away during the scene where one of the characters, the Duke of Gloucester, had his eyes gouged out on stage, but next day, 10 May, she did not shrink from an equally distressing experience. She visited film studios outside Budapest where a picture, *Hungarian Requiem*, about the failed uprising of 1956, was being shot. Diana was clearly upset as she watched

---

> ### "*You know, Daddy, it was one of the best trips ever. We really felt needed.*"
>
> DIANA TO HER FATHER, ON RETURNING FROM HUNGARY

---

the actors perform a scene in which a rebel student was executed on his 18th birthday.

That same morning, Diana trod ground more familiar to her when she visited the world-famous Peto Institute, sited on a hill above Budapest. The Institute treats children with cerebral palsy, and for many of them it provides the only hope of improvement for this deeply disabling condition. Diana had a duty to perform on behalf of the Queen. She presented Dr. Maria Hari, the physiotherapist running the Institute, with an honorary Order of the British Empire.

The Princess' time, however, was mostly occupied with the children, some of whom could barely stand and many of whom could hardly control their limbs or their features. Tears soon sprang to Diana's eyes as she heard what she described as 'absolutely heartbreaking' accounts of the children's sufferings and of their slow recovery.

Riding the tram

The Hungarian tour was almost over, but before flying home, Charles and Diana treated themselves to a pleasure not easily available at home in England. They hopped on a tram and rode to Vigado Square, the main square in Budapest, where they went on a brief impromptu walkabout. Surprised and delighted Hungarians crowded round them. Some kissed the tips of Diana's fingers in the continental fashion, or shook her hand and beamed

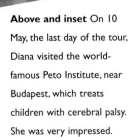

Above and inset On 10 May, the last day of the tour, Diana visited the world-famous Peto Institute, near Budapest, which treats children with cerebral palsy. She was very impressed.

as she responded with the word '*Koszonom*', Hungarian for 'Thanks'.

Before Charles and Diana finally departed, President Goncz told them that he hoped they had 'felt the love of the Hungarian people'. They certainly had. The royal visit, surprisingly, was not widely publicized, even in Budapest, so most Hungarians had no chance to make preparations. Most could never have spared a day off work, or the precious money it earned them, in order to spend time on the streets waiting for the royal visitors. But it was better this way. The Hungarians' greetings were natural and spontaneous.

Their new freedom might be heady, but things were still drab, and getting back on their feet was going to be a long haul. But the few days in springtime when Charles and Diana were in their midst was a bright spot they would never forget.

DARK DAYS FOR CHARLES

The 40th anniversary of the Queen's accession was in 1992 and the year should have been joyous. Instead, there was bitterness in the palace and throughout the nation at Morton's book about Diana

A storm of violent emotions was unleashed on 7 June 1992, the day *Diana: Her True Story* by Andrew Morton was published. There was outrage and an upsurge of sympathy for the beautiful, compassionate Diana, presented by Morton as cruelly betrayed and misused by Prince Charles. There was fury on the part of those who refused to believe the allegations against the Prince.

There was distress and confusion that the long-revered Royal Family, the bastion of respectability and unity, should have been pictured as cold, uncaring and, worst of all, fallible. There was hatred for Camilla Parker-Bowles, Prince Charles' mistress, who many felt had lit the fuse for this explosion of scandal and revelation. Perhaps most potent of all, there was grief that the 'fairytale

marriage', which, in 1981, had enlivened a time of economic hardship and misery, had turned sour. Millions who had celebrated then felt cheated now.

In the welter of media coverage that ensued, it was as if Andrew Morton's book had unleashed a volcano that would not stop erupting. The lava of the headlines that poured out was red-hot from the very start. 'Diana, The Cry For Help That's Gone So Terribly Wrong,' proclaimed the *People*. 'Di Hurled Herself Down The Stairs,' trumpeted the *News of the World*. 'The Royals: A Family At War,' announced the *Evening Standard*, though the article continued more even-handedly, with 'Despairing Di tried to kill herself over loveless marriage' balanced by

---

> **"It is obvious that, whether directly or through friends, the Princess was talking to the newspapers."**
>
> LADY ELIZABETH CAVENDISH, MEMBER OF THE PRESS COMPLAINTS COMMISSION, ON DIANA'S INVOLVEMENT WITH MORTON

'Hurt Charles feels betrayed by his wife over public claims'.

The *Sun*, commenting on 5 June about the serialization of Morton's book, came out for Charles with 'Diana Has Betrayed Me'. However, just a week later, on 12 June, the same newspaper gave its entire front page to a picture of the Princess, face crumpled and weeping, with a small headline 'The Love That Moved Diana To Tears'. It was a photograph of a princess unable, for once, to retain her composure as she visited a hospice on Merseyside on 11 June. One of the elderly patients touched her face and Diana burst into tears.

AN OFFICIAL RESPONSE

The heat generated by all this soon reached the Press Complaints Commission, the body that was supposed to prevent the media from going too far. Since 1990, Sir Robert Fellowes, the Queen's Private Secretary and Diana's brother-in-law, had been urging the Commission to do something to stem the tide of tabloid innuendo about the 'failing' royal marriage. Nothing effective had yet been done, but once *Diana: Her True Story* was published,

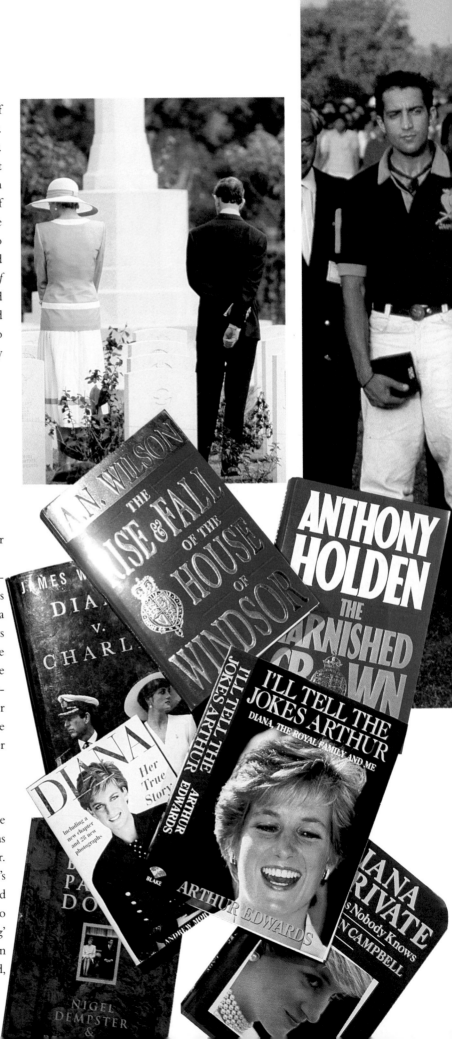

the Commission's Chairman, Lord McGregor of Durris, was at last moved to act.

Lord McGregor sought assurances from Sir Robert Fellowes that Diana and her friends had had nothing to do with Morton's book. When Sir Robert gave him these assurances, Lord McGregor issued a forthright statement slamming Fleet Street, and the wider press, for 'dabbling in the stuff of people's souls'.

The next day, however, it was revealed that several journalists had already guessed at Diana's involvement in the book. Andrew Knight, Chief Executive of the News International Group – publishers of the *Sunday Times*, which had carried the serialization – presented the guesswork as fact when he spoke to Lord McGregor, who was shocked. Lord McGregor remonstrated with Sir Robert but was told that the assurances had been given in good faith.

DIANA'S APPROVAL

It was Sir Robert's turn to be shocked next. On 10 June, Diana called on Carolyn Bartholomew – formerly her flatmate friend, Carolyn Pride – at her

Opening page and opposite page, top The stress of appearing together began to show for Charles and Diana during a visit to Delhi, India, in early 1992. **Left** Andrew Morton's book on Diana was part of an avalanche on the Windsors' troubles. **Above and right** At a polo match in Jaipur, India, 1992, Diana turns away from Charles' kiss.

DIARY DATES
July 1992
30 June – 2 July
The Queen visits Canada
7 July
The Prince of Wales opens the National Organic Education Centre in Coventry, Warwickshire
7 July
The Prince of Wales visits the Prince's Youth Business Trust 1992 trade fair at the NEC, Birmingham
8 July
The Queen opens The King's Apartments at Hampton Court Palace, Middlesex
17 July
The Princess of Wales attends the first night of the Proms at the Royal Albert Hall, London
18 July
The Prince of Wales officiates at the Honorary Degree Ceremony at University of Wales College, Cardiff
24 July
The Prince of Wales attends a Gala Concert at the Glyndebourne Festival Opera, Lewes, East Sussex
28 July
The Princess of Wales opens the British Deaf Association 1992 Triennial Congress at the Winter Gardens, Blackpool
28 July
The Princess of Wales visits the Blackpool RELATE centre
30 July
The Princess of Wales attends the film première of *Far and Away* at the Empire Cinema, Leicester Square, London

home in Fulham, west London. Carolyn had been one of Morton's named sources for *Diana: Her True Story*. When Diana was photographed exchanging kisses as she left the Bartholomew home, this was taken as proof that she approved of her friend's participation and, by inference, had sanctioned Morton's book. Sir Robert, enraged, realized he had been duped. Mortified, he offered his resignation but the Queen refused to accept it.

By this time, the controversy had penetrated government circles. Prime Minister John Major was

> *"One of the biggest changes over the years has been that women are not prepared to put up with a bad marriage for any longer than they need to."*
>
> ZELDA WEST MEADES, FORMER SPOKESPERSON FOR RELATE, ON MARRIAGE

informed of Diana's 'involvement', as was the Lord Chancellor, Lord Mackay, and Lord Wakeham, the leader of the House of Lords. At this juncture Diana's cooperation with Morton was still only a suspicion, on the verge of becoming fact, but unconfirmed nonetheless. Confirmation, from Morton himself, did not come until five years later.

All the same, the suspicion that the Princess of Wales had manipulated the press against her husband seemed enough to qualify as a constitutional crisis. It created the horrifying prospect of royals brawling in public over private differences.

A WAR OF WORDS

Diana, though, was not the only one to exploit the media for her own ends. Charles' friends resolved to put the Prince's side of the story. Penny Junor, biographer of Charles, Diana and former Prime Minister Margaret Thatcher, was asked to write an article for *Today* magazine in support of the Prince. Junor's article had the appearance of propaganda and painted a damning picture of Diana. The Princess was accused of being 'paranoid' over Charles' friendship with Camilla Parker-Bowles, a friendship described as 'innocuous'. Diana was jealous of Charles, wrote Junor. She threw tantrums, thwarted

IN THE NEWS

Fact replaces rumour

When The Sunday Times Review published this article, Diana: Her True Story, published a month earlier, was still a heated talking point with press and public. The book's revelations replaced the speculation and gossip of previous years, and newspapers, quoting Andrew Morton, examined the royal marriage in detail. Articles like these were a more sober, more incisive assessment than either the rumour-mongering or the eulogistic coverage that marked Diana's early days.

his efforts to be a loving father and was a disturbed woman working every dirty trick known in the annals of discontented wives.

Charles' friends described their own version of the episode in Morton's book where the pregnant Diana threw herself down the stairs at Sandringham

> "*It was all very unfair. Diana had breached confidentiality yet Charles was getting all the flak.*"
>
> FIONA SINCLAIR, ROYAL CORRESPONDENT, ON MEDIA REACTION

at Christmas 1981. Diana's account, as told by Morton, was that Charles coldly ignored her as she lay at the bottom of the stairs. As Charles' supporters recounted it, however, the fall occurred after a flaming row with Charles, but Diana and her unborn child were unhurt. She was, it seems, fit enough to get to her feet and swear at her husband as he stalked off to go riding in an effort to get away from his shrewish young wife.

SYMPATHY FOR DIANA

The public, pummelled by claim and counter-claim, accusation and denial, insult and justification, ended up not knowing who was lying, who was exaggerating or even what the truth was likely to be. This did not prevent general conclusions being drawn and public sympathy appeared to be largely with Diana as the wronged wife of a cruel husband.

Meanwhile, as Andrew Morton later reported, his sources, Diana's friends, were receiving nuisance telephone calls and early morning knocks on the door and had their own reputations shredded by insults and smears in the press. The Morton affair was fast assuming the proportions of a propaganda war, with no quarter given and no prisoners taken.

Prince Charles, it was understood, did not approve of the assaults on his wife. His then private secretary, Commander Richard Aylard, told journalists: 'The Prince is worried by (Diana's) volatile and emotional state and therefore he thinks it is totally unfair to attack her.' Charles, however, had made no comment on Penny Junor's article in *Today*, and the

Opposite page Diana presents a polo trophy to her horseriding instructor, Major James Hewitt, with whom she was romantically involved. **Above** Charles and Hewitt ride close in the heat of a polo match. **Left** In spite of the obvious strain, the Prince and Princess show a united front during their tour of India in early 1992.

Right Anne, the Princess Royal, with her husband Captain Mark Phillips at a dinner in London. She was granted a decree nisi to end their marriage on 23 April 1992. Anne's divorce, coming just over a month after Prince Andrew's separation from the Duchess of York, added to the Queen's sorrows in a distressing year.

❧ Protocol ❧

BUCKINGHAM PALACE

In the past, courts moved from palace to palace every few weeks in order to maintain 'sweet' living conditions. By the 18th century, though, hygiene had improved and palaces were cleaner and healthier. This is what enabled King George III to establish Buckingham House, later called Buckingham Palace, as a permanent royal home. The house, built in 1702-5, was purchased by King George in 1760. Much modified, Buckingham Palace remains the monarch's official London residence today.

Top left James Gilbey, who became a close friend and confidant of Princess Diana, with friends at a party for Louis Vuitton at the Hurlingham Club in June 1993. **Above** Oliver Hoare, another of Diana's intimate friends, accompanies the Princess at the Royal Ascot horse race meeting in 1986.

subsequent impression was that Charles' seeming gallantry towards a lady in distress was two-edged.

Charles' own silence in the midst of furore also appeared to some like impotence under fire. That was untrue. On 7 June, the day *Diana: Her True Story* was published, Charles saw the Queen at Windsor.

> **"I'm delighted to be going on holiday. It's like a snake pit in there."**
>
> ROYAL OFFICIAL, ABOUT KENSINGTON PALACE, DURING THE SUMMER OF 1992

They discussed divorce and, after much agonizing, agreed that the legal machinery should be set in motion. The Queen, however, urged Charles to speak to Diana to see if an accommodation could be reached. The couple met next day, 8 June, in Kensington Palace. A diary kept by one of Diana's friends tells what happened. The talk was quiet and reasonable. Charles and Diana agreed they were incompatible and 'decided on a parting of the ways'. There were no tears and afterwards Diana 'slept through the night without sleeping pills'.

PUBLIC APPEARANCES

Diana's sense of relief, however, did not last long. She still had to face the Royal Family and, with them, the public. June was the month when the royals made high-profile public appearances together, on the balcony at Buckingham Palace after the Trooping the Colour ceremony and later, at Royal Ascot, during the third week of the month. In between there was the private Garter ceremony for members of the Order of the Garter, which included Charles.

Though tired, tearful and apprehensive, according to her friend's diary, Diana managed to get through the balcony appearance on 12 June, standing at a distance from Charles, but close to the Queen. Royal Ascot was more testing. The crowds were closer and the exposure was far longer. For all her trepidation, though, Diana scored a triumph. As the royals drove along the racecourse in their horse-drawn carriages, the punters cheered her vociferously. The Queen and her family, by

The Private Princess
Royal wives in league

Above *Sarah Ferguson presenting prizes at the Berkshire Polo Club in July 1992, just two months after she separated from Prince Andrew.*

On 19 March 1992 the Duke and Duchess of York separated – and the collapse of their marriage was apparently the result of a plot brewed by the Duchess herself with Princess Diana.

It appears that the pair planned to leave their husbands and the Royal Family together. The Queen was even said to know of it and told them: 'You egg each other on!' Perhaps they did, but when the separation of the Duke and Duchess was announced, Diana made no move to follow suit.

According to the Duchess, who recounted the episode in her autobiography, Diana just sat back to see what would happen.

What happened was fearful. Almost overnight, the Duchess was stripped of her bodyguards, her status, her privileges and everything that made her royal.

At Royal Ascot, three months later, she was relegated to standing in the crowd with her daughters where, once, she would have been by rights in the royal enclosure. As the press had it, the 'knives were out for Fergie', and she was cut off completely.

The Duchess was beside herself with rage and distress at what she saw as Diana's perfidy. But Diana had been wise. She saw in the harsh treatment meted out to Fergie the fate that would befall her should she leave Prince Charles precipitately.

contrast, received only a minimum of polite applause. The Queen Mother, with whom Diana shared a carriage, was described as 'stone cold' by an observer. Later, in the royal box, Prince Philip pointedly ignored his daughter-in-law.

This behaviour was partly due to the upsetting scenes at Windsor before the excursion to Ascot. Face to face with a visibly pained Queen and an

> "*His friends know Charles to be kind, dutiful, sympathetic and intelligent and we had to try to get across our fundamental belief that he was married to an unstable, moody, irrational woman who was out of control.*"
>
> CHARLES' FRIEND, ON PRO-CHARLES PRESS ARTICLES

enraged Prince Philip, Diana, according to her friend, had been brutally grilled. She was accused of bringing the Royal Family into disrepute, colluding with Andrew Morton and of speaking directly to Andrew Knight about the serialization of the book. As evidence, Diana was told, there was a tape of the conversation. Diana denied it and wept.

Prince Charles, meanwhile, was silent. Even when Diana asked him to tell his parents of their discussion at Kensington Palace, he appeared so daunted by confronting them that he said not a word. 'It was as if our conversation had never taken place,' Diana explained to friends.

UNDER ATTACK

Diana, it seems, was back to square one, but with a new worry: the tape of her supposed discussion with Andrew Knight, a discussion she knew had never taken place. At first, Diana thought the tape was a bluff to force some confession out of her. Then, she began to fret that her telephone had been tapped. Sir Robert Fellowes confirmed that a tape existed, but would not tell her what it contained. He advised Diana to do nothing about it.

Four letters to Diana, worded as strongly as only an enraged Prince Philip knew how, arrived within

the next few weeks. Diana found she was living in an atmosphere of vicious court intrigue as rumour, hearsay and conspiracy electrified the palace. Really frightened now, according to her friends, she resorted to scrambler telephones, the paper shredder and the coded conversation to protect herself from

Diana's support network was selective. **Above** In mourning for Adrian Ward-Jackson. **Above right** Rugby star Will Carling. **Right** With bachelor David Waterhouse.

IN CONTEXT   DRUG LORD ESCAPES PRISON
1992

- Nick Faldo of Great Britain wins his third UK Golf Open Championship
- General Manuel Noriega of Panama is given a 40-year prison sentence in Miami for drug trafficking
- Women in Afghanistan are barred from appearing on television
- Drug 'lord' Pablo Escobar, **right**, escapes from prison at Medellin, Columbia
- Vaclav Havel resigns as President of Czechoslovakia before the Czech Republic and Slovakia separate

unseen spies. When Stephen Twigg, Diana's masseur and confidant, publicly warned that pressure on Diana could cause a 'tragedy', the Princess of Wales was forced by courtiers to dismiss him for breaching confidentiality.

If the palaces of London were dens of intrigue, as Diana told her friends, then Highgrove House was infinitely worse. Charles' supporters, it seems, advised him to 'kick your wife out'. 'Megalomaniac', 'clinically mad', and 'manipulative' were only some of the epithets they lobbed at Diana.

NEWSPAPER HOLDS TAPE

Diana, understandably, began to wilt under the savagery of this onslaught. But there was even worse to come. Two months into the increasingly vicious dispute, Diana learned that the *Sun* had a tape – not the Andrew Knight tape, which had never existed, but a recording of her conversation with another man whose secret talk with her would soon prove the most damning testament yet.

Expecting in Style

Pregnancy is hardly a woman's most elegant time, but Diana was still obliged to appear in public and make a stylish job of it. There were, though, major fashion contrasts between her two pregnancies

At one time royal mothers-to-be did not have to worry about how they should dress in public. As soon as a pregnancy began to 'show', they would cancel all their engagements and vanish from public view until after the happy event. This practice, a relic of Victorian prudery, was abandoned by Princess Margaret in 1961, and from then on royal ladies carried out their duties regardless of expanding waistlines.

When Diana became pregnant only two months after her wedding in 1981, the new rule pioneered by Margaret 20 years earlier was hard to live with. Quite apart from the fact that Diana was one of

> **"Other pregnant mothers looked to Diana for fashion guidance. She did not disappoint them."**
>
> FIONA SINCLAIR, ROYAL CORRESPONDENT

those unfortunate young women who felt ill most of the time, an early pregnancy stunted her fashion development. She had not, in fact, advanced very far from the fussy, girlish styles that marked her first appearances as Charles' fiancée and bride before the figure she had so painstakingly wrested from her puppy fat began to disappear.

By January 1982, Diana had to put away her fitted clothes and turn to her maternity wardrobe. Bellville Sassoon designed a beautiful gown in a shimmering red taffeta empire-line style decorated with a long-tailed bow at the front for Diana to wear at a gala evening in aid of the St. John's Ambulance at London's Barbican Centre in January

Left In her ninth month of pregnancy with her eldest son, William, Diana wears a simple pink smock for a visit to the Windsor polo field in June 1982. **Above** A deep pink hat and matching coat with a high collar keep Diana warm as she arrives by train on a visit to Liverpool in April 1982. **Right** The young Diana was fond of ruffled collars and frilled cuffs. This lightly patterned blue maternity smock has both. Diana wore it over a white blouse in the Scilly Isles in April 1982.

1982 (see page 381). In keeping with the wise rule that neck and shoulders should serve as a focus of interest, the square-cut neckline was fringed with white lace, which also frothed out from the bell-shaped wrists of the long sleeves, distracting the eye.

Polka dots

By wearing completely loose dresses it was relatively easy to hide what Queen Victoria, who had nine pregnancies and hated them all, once called 'the hideous bulge'. Catherine Walker provided a blue spotted frill-necked number that Diana wore on a short tour to the Scilly Isles with Charles in April 1982. Seven months pregnant by this time, Diana benefited from the optical illusion created by the white polka dots, which tended to break up the outline of a burgeoning figure. The frill, too, distracted attention as it spilled over from the neck.

Catherine Walker opted for a green background and blue polka dots for a dress with yoked shoulders that Diana wore to a weekend polo match at Smith's Lawn, Windsor in May 1982. In June 1982, with less than three weeks to go, Diana went to tea with Charles at the Guards Polo Club wearing a delightful soft peach smock in pastel silk, with a low round neckline decorated by a bow.

A week or so later, Diana appeared on the balcony at Buckingham Palace after the Trooping the

> *"Diana showed that you needn't feel fat and frumpy while pregnant. She opened up new opportunities in maternity fashion."*
>
> VICTORIA AUSTIN, ROYAL WRITER

Colour ceremony, wearing a dark green dress with four buttons down the front, an open mandarin collar, smocking on the shoulders and long, full sleeves.

Prince William was born on 21 June 1982. After the birth, Diana set out in earnest on the odyssey that made her a fashion trendsetter. The frills and furbelows, the fussy necklines and the overlarge collars began to give way to slinkier silhouettes, more understated and therefore more elegant designing and better colour coordination. Then, in late 1983, she became pregnant again. This time, though, preg-

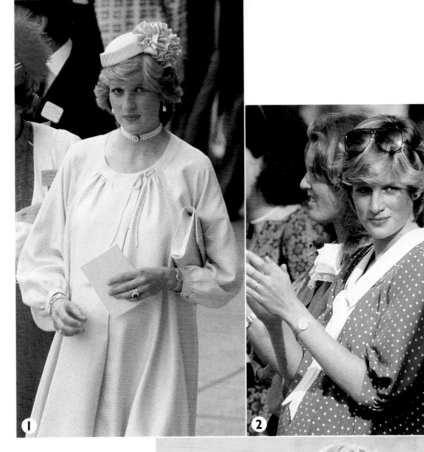

1 Attending Ascot in June 1982, Diana contrived to look as smartly dressed as other women on the day. She wore a simple pale peach silk dress but the attractive little hat and pearl choker set it off nicely.

2 Seen here with Sarah Ferguson at a polo match in June 1982, Diana wears a dark green Catherine Walker dress with fine white polka dots and white collar.

3 With the mayor on a visit to Tulse Hill in January 1982, Diana wears a loosely fitting blue woollen coat decorated with green piping and leaves and flowers.

4 Another polka dot dress by Catherine Walker. This one has a ruffled collar and cuffs with puffed sleeves, and is cut to fall from the bust. Diana wore it on a trip to the Scilly Isles with Prince Charles in April 1982.

BELLVILLE SASSOON GOWN

Right and photo In February 1982 Diana attended a gala concert with her husband at the Barbican Centre, London in this deep red taffeta and lace empire-line gown. It is trimmed with lace at the cuffs and around the square neckline. The taffeta falls in a ruffled frill around the neckline, while at the bust there are two bows for added decoration.

BELLVILLE SASSOON DRESS

Above An off-the-shoulder ballgown with a bow at the bust and a belted waist, which Diana wore in November 1981. **Above right** Diana at the Royal Academy in May 1984. She is wearing a cream chiffon empire-line evening dress with a silver chequered pattern and a decoration of silver feathers. Around her neck is a diamond Prince of Wales' feathers pendant.

nancy did not bring a halt to her fashion progress. If anything, it enhanced the new image Diana had begun to create with an improved standard of chic and a heightened sense of style.

Daring dresses

It was clear this second time around that Diana was to make no concessions to 'suitable' materials for her maternity dresses – and the emphasis on polka dots was largely abandoned. Her second mother-to-be wardrobe was much more adventurous than her first. Her designer and friend Bruce Oldfield told her to be more daring this time, and she obliged.

While two months pregnant, a stage not always proof against the first hints of 'the hideous bulge', Diana wore a red duchess satin gown with lace

bolero jacket sparkling with sequins by Jan van Velden to a ballet gala in Oslo, Norway, in February 1984. There was a bright red, black-collared, double-breasted coat by Catherine Walker for a visit to Birmingham in the same month, and during this visit Diana ventured out in her first tuxedo suit.

Three months later, in May 1984, nature had asserted itself and Diana was back in smocks. But they were certainly much smarter smocks, like the pale blue and white striped dress with a white sailor collar by Catherine Walker. Diana chose to wear this dress when watching polo at Windsor.

Clever collar interest was the secret of several of Diana's 1984 maternity outfits, serving to balance out a figure that risked looking ungainly as the pregnancy progressed. In May 1984, for a visit to

1 Pregnant with Harry in June 1984, Diana wears a maroon Catherine Walker dress and a white cardigan. **2** At the Wimbledon tennis in July 1984, Diana wears a red and white striped dress. **3** In Chester in 1984, her hat sets off a Jan van Velden woollen coat and blouse.

Odstock Hospital, Salisbury, the bulge was ingeniously camouflaged by Jan van Velden with a lilac wool crêpe dress, with pleated skirt and matching jacket that Diana wore buttoned at the top so that the edge opened in a generous triangular shape.

> "*The first time around, Diana was a little girl surprised fashion-wise to be pregnant. The second time, she was to set a new standard.*"
>
> MARCO HOUSTON, EDITOR OF ROYALTY MAGAZINE, ON DIANA

Underneath, she wore a white blouse with a wide white stencil-cut square collar that naturally drew the eye. The daring that Bruce Oldfield had urged on Diana was certainly evident when she chose an apricot façonné silk suit, again designed by Jan van Velden, to attend Royal Ascot in June 1984. The suit had a full skirt and loose top with long ties and long, deeply cuffed sleeves.

A blow for pregnancy

Prince Harry was born on 15 September 1984 and with his birth Diana said goodbye to her maternity wardrobe. But she had shown that in the fashion battle of the bulge, shapeless smocks were not the only answer. Diana had proved that even when heavily pregnant, mums could still look a treat.

IN THE NEWS

The Princess is pregnant again

In May 1984, the press was still enjoying its love affair with the Princess of Wales. Although, as was later revealed, the strains in her marriage were already beginning to emerge when she was pregnant with Prince Harry, in 1984, a sentimental tone was still common in reports. Diana was five months pregnant when this report appeared and the Daily Mirror was, apparently, celebrating the fact that she was doing nothing to hide it. Diana's decision to carry on as normal, coupled with the flair of her designers, meant she was the most photographed pregnant princess.

Lighting up the Third World

Seven out of ten people experience a grim reality of poverty and hopelessness in the Third World. But Diana, like Mother Teresa of Calcutta, was resolved to make a difference to their lives

Mother Teresa of Calcutta and Diana, Princess of Wales, seemed to belong to worlds far apart – a nun who forswore earthly comforts to embrace poverty, and a princess with all the wealth and privilege her status conferred. Yet when their worlds met, their common ground was at once apparent. They were both there to help, cheer and comfort the poor, the underprivileged and others who knew little but hopelessness and despair.

Mother Teresa chose to live in Third World conditions in Calcutta, eastern India, an ancient city which could well be termed the destitution capital of the world. Diana, the aristocrat who became royal – and in terms of her lifestyle, never wanted for anything – chose to enter the Third World on a quest for knowledge. What the Princess saw there aroused all her compassion.

A world of poverty

The term 'Third World', when it was first coined in 1961, was not meant to describe the appalling living conditions that have become associated with the expression. At that time, during the Cold War between the 'First' and the 'Second' Worlds – the United States and the Soviet Union – a group of countries declared themselves 'non-aligned', that is siding politically with neither of the two other

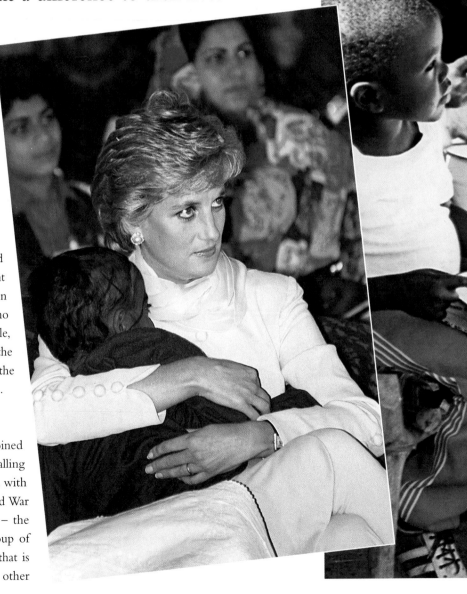

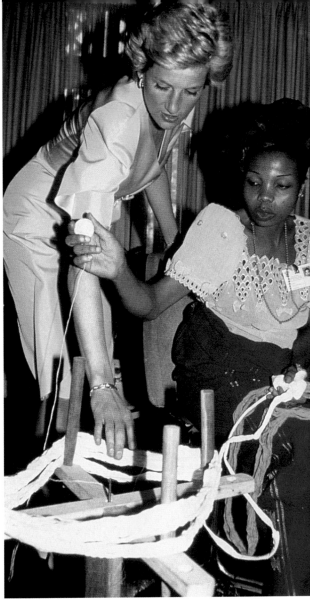

Worlds. The term 'Third World' caught on after it was used in a speech by Pandit Jawaharlal Nehru, then Prime Minister of India. Unfortunately, the poverty-stricken image of the Third World arose as

---

> "*She did so much more than she had to. She need only have shaken their hands and moved on, but she sat on their beds and listened.*"

DOCTOR AT THE SITANALA LEPROSY MISSION, JAKARTA, ON DIANA

---

many countries in this group were either small or were former colonies, newly independent but lacking the infrastructure or technology to forge a secure life for their peoples.

Facilities taken for granted in Europe or America – clean water, public health systems, electric power, even a proper food supply – were all too often

almost non-existent in the Third World. As a result, millions went hungry or died before their time from diseases that were curable in the West.

When Diana, who was born in the same year that the Third World came into being, arrived on the royal scene 20 years later, she was already aware of areas of suffering, such as blindness, disability, mental problems or infirm old age. As her early patronages indicated, she was anxious not only to give her royal name to organizations such as the Royal School for the Blind or the British Deaf Association, but to be active in their service as well. However, royal and family duties saw to it that for several years she was unable to start exploring in person the wider, grimmer panorama of poverty and want that disfigured more than half the world.

Diana had a first long look at Third World conditions in 1989 in Indonesia, when she went there with Charles and visited a leper hospital outside the capital, Jakarta. The following year, she went to

The Prince and Princess of Wales' visit to Nigeria in March 1990 was one of Diana's first experiences of the underprivileged Third World. **Above left** Diana is shown how nuts are husked by hand. **Above** The Princess takes a close interest in a loom during a demonstration of weaving.

 Protocol

THE COMPASSIONATE ROYALS

*With her compassion for suffering and her willingness to face its most ghastly effects, Diana followed in some distinguished royal footsteps. Princess Marina, Duchess of Kent, Princess Alexandra and the present Duchess of Kent, Catherine Worsley, all worked in a medical capacity in children's hospitals. So did the Queen Mother, **right**, who was a teenager when her mother, the Countess of Strathmore, turned her family home into a hospital for soldiers wounded in the First World War.*

Nigeria and Cameroon in West Africa, and the year after to Brazil, where the gap between the very rich and the hopelessly poor was a chasm.

Poverty in India

A visit to India followed in 1992, and though the contrasts there were not so great, the abject poverty that existed in this vast subcontinent was so overwhelming that 45 years of democratic government and technological advance had been unable to make an appreciable change. It was a task too monumental for a quick solution, and sprang as much from social and medical factors as from economic want. Even the dedicated Mother Teresa of Calcutta could do no more than help those who came within her immediate area, while setting an example that others, hopefully, might follow.

Mother Teresa, who was absent in Rome when Charles and Diana arrived in India for six days in February 1992, had founded the Order of the

Left Diana with the diminutive Mother Teresa of Calcutta in New York in June 1997. The Princess, inspired by Mother Teresa's work with the needy in India, became a devoted admirer of the Roman Catholic nun. **Right** Diana appears as relaxed as ever during a signing ceremony on a visit to Nepal – one of the poorest countries in the world – in 1993. **Inset, far right** Garlanded with flowers, the Princess performs a traditional greeting during the same visit to Nepal.

Missionaries in Calcutta in 1948, the year after India gained its independence from Britain. Born Agnes Gonxha Bejaxhui at Skopje in Yugoslavia in 1910, she was Albanian in origin. Calcutta was not chosen lightly as her base of operations. She deliberately went for the worst environment. In Calcutta, filth and squalor stalked the streets. People died on the pavements as crowds passed by, not noticing because the sight was so common. To a westerner, the suffering was appalling.

Strong nerves

The aims of Mother Teresa's Mission show the extent of the problems she faced and which Diana, in her turn, later worked to combat. The Mission's aims are to help lepers, cripples, the homeless and the dying, not only in Calcutta or India but throughout the world. Diana's ambitions in this area were no less wide-ranging, but the task demanded strong nerves, a strong stomach and a

great deal of self-control. The notion that royals live in some kind of fairyland, pampered and spoiled, with everything money can buy and with plenty of it left over, appeared true when the royals were seen at film premières, grand state occasions or dressed

"*I will never complain again.*"

DIANA, AFTER VISITING A FAMILY'S ONE-ROOM HUT IN NEPAL

up in gowns costing thousands at galas and balls. But strip all that away, and place royals in the Third World on the charity trail, and the picture is very different. Diana and her doughty sister-in-law Princess Anne, President of the Save the Children Fund, knew that difference very well.

There, before them, were the terminally ill, the hideously crippled, lepers eaten away by this most cruel of afflictions, abandoned children or homeless

people cast adrift without roots, without a future and often without hope. It was a hard school for royals and for all her dedication, Diana found it difficult. But once there, she knew she could not flinch, switch off or shirk her duty. She had to stay, smile and be gracious, caring, cheering and comforting, no matter how ghastly the human wreckage before her.

Diana earned her spurs on her first encounter with Third World suffering, when she visited the Sitanala Leprosy Mission outside Jakarta, Indonesia, in 1989. There were half a million lepers in Indonesia, 15 million world wide, and those at Sitanala were the lucky ones. Diana never flinched, but her distress was barely contained, especially on the children's ward. It was here that Diana demonstrated real courage, shaking the hands of lepers,

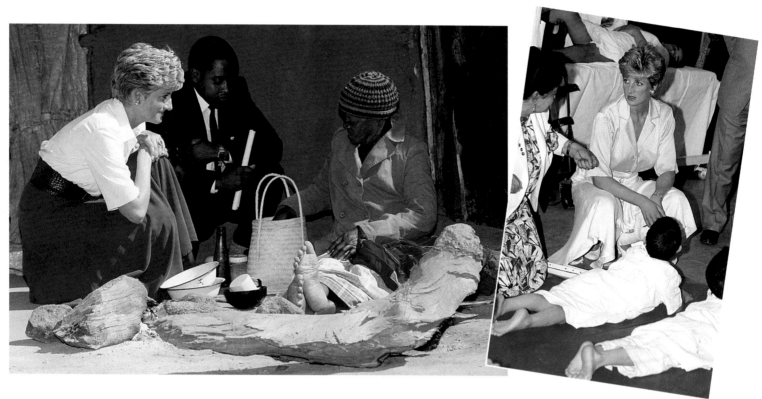

Left Diana meets Brazilian children in 1991. She was distressed by the plight of homeless children in Brazil, many of whom had AIDS. **Above** The Princess tours a refugee camp in Zimbabwe in 1993. **Inset, above right** Diana is touched by youthful suffering in Egypt, in 1992.

something from which most people would have recoiled in horror and disgust.

Both she and Charles had been assured that there was no risk of contracting leprosy this way, but that was not the only problem. Lepers' hands were often fingerless and horribly distorted, their faces, attempting a smile, frequently had no lips or noses. Yet Charles and Diana had to behave as if shaking hands with such people was perfectly normal. For some members of the media teams on the tour it

was too much to be in the same room as lepers. It was enough to make strong men blanch and several strong men did. But the Prince and Princess just went ahead and did their duty.

The handshakes were repeated in Nigeria in 1990, when Charles and Diana visited a leper colony there. Diana became visibly upset, though, when she learned that beggars and cripples had been cleared out of one town to avoid 'offending' her. The second half of the West African tour, to the former French colony of Cameroon, followed. Here, Diana visited a Special School for Children with Deficient Hearing, but was saddened to learn that in this country of some ten million people, this was the one and only school of its kind.

Confronting AIDS

Brazil, which Charles and Diana toured in 1991, brought the Princess face to face with a different problem: the modern plague of AIDS and, what was most upsetting for her, children with AIDS. As Diana quickly learned, Brazil, a spectacular country full of beautiful tourist sights and enormous personal wealth, had a horrifying secret — a mass of homeless children, many abandoned, who lived by their wits. It was even rumoured that the children were sometimes killed off by death squads

IN THE NEWS

Diana in Zimbabwe

When royals, whose hands are normally unacquainted with hard domestic work, take on roles their servants usually perform for them, the newspapers like to publish pictures and reports like this one in the Daily Mirror. Here, Diana is seen dishing out food to hungry children in Zimbabwe, in July 1993.

By this date Diana was separated from Charles and was doing things on overseas visits which were quite different from the run-of-the-mill routine on the more traditional royal tours that she and Charles had undertaken together.

as if they were garbage littering the streets. If they survived to their teens, they were very lucky.

When Diana arrived, she saw only the tiniest remnant of these human cast-offs: ten children aged from five months to five years left in the streets by mothers who were drug addicts or prostitutes and retrieved only by the mercy of the Foundation for the Welfare of Miners. All of them were HIV-positive, some had full-blown AIDS. Experiences like

> "You are not just a fairytale princess locked up in a palace, you help the handicapped and other helpless people."
>
> TAMANA CHONA, DISABLED INDIAN GIRL, TO DIANA

this, with which Diana was already familiar from her visits to AIDS hospitals in the USA, helped inspire her to tackle the problem of AIDS.

Through her influence, the sufferings of AIDS victims became better known throughout the world. Photographs of the Princess kissing, cuddling and playing with young AIDS victims in Brazil and elsewhere had a powerful effect in moving others to set aside the prejudice and fear the disease had created and perhaps to join in the fight against it. If the Princess of Wales could treat children with HIV or AIDS like ordinary youngsters rather than pathetic pariahs, that gave a potent lead to others less venturesome or brave.

Meeting Mother Teresa

In her first two years in the Third World, Diana had seen enough to know what she was talking about when she first met Mother Teresa after her Indian tour in 1992. Diana's visit to the dying incurables at the Calcutta Mission was still fresh in her mind when she flew specially to Rome, where Mother Teresa was recovering from illness.

At this time, Diana's marriage problems were acute, but her meeting with Mother Teresa renewed her resolve to set aside her own difficulties and concentrate on the plight of those who were worse afflicted. Diana and Mother Teresa met again, in

The Princess was always a welcome visitor. **Top** Diana walks over a carpet of freshly strewn petals, during a tour of Pakistan in 1991. **Inset, above** A child in Delhi, India, proudly clutches Diana's hand in 1992.

London in September 1992 and 1993, and early in 1997 in Washington, DC, where doctors were treating the nun for a heart condition. Diana was in the USA prior to the auction of her evening gowns. By that time, the Princess' work among the world's deprived had been expanded by the civil wars in Angola and Yugoslavia, where thousands had been dispossessed. Diana had turned her attention to the victims of landmines in Angola and Bosnia, once part of Yugoslavia, as well as to the thousands of homeless refugees displaced by the brutal fighting of the civil wars.

Mother Teresa and Diana died within days of each other only a few months later. But they left behind an eloquent image: the tiny, wizened old lady and the tall, beautiful princess – age and youth, poverty and privilege, bound together by compassion – standing hand in hand for photographers.

CAPTURED ON TAPE

Andrew Morton's book on Diana, published in June 1992, was only the start of a long summer of controversy for her. The next big drama broke in August, when the Sun *leaked the so-called 'Squidgy' tape*

In the summer of 1992 Diana was in a very difficult position. She had scored a significant pre-emptive strike against Prince Charles with the publication of *Diana: Her True Story* on 7 June, but the backlash had been little short of ferocious.

Charles' friends, enraged at her allegations of the Prince's cruelty, insulted Diana to her face and planted terrible stories about her in the press. She was called 'mad', 'paranoid' or, at best, 'disturbed'. Members of the Royal Family ostracized her. She suspected dark conspiracies against her at court,

and clandestine operations worthy of a James Bond movie: telephone tapping, hidden surveillance, 'agents' inside Kensington Palace trawling her wastebasket or reading her correspondence.

At this time, too, the *News of the World* received a stream of anonymous letters about meetings between Charles and Camilla Parker-Bowles. Fortunately, newspaper editors were too hard-nosed to fall for every titbit offered them, and as far as the *Sun* was concerned, they suspected they already had the real thing in their possession. For

nearly two years, the tabloid had been holding a tape of a telephone conversation which ostensibly took place between Diana and a man tentatively identified as James Gilbey, a friend of hers from pre-marriage days.

Gilbey, it seems, had spoken to Diana on his mobile phone from a roadside in Abingdon, Oxfordshire. Neither of them realized, though, that their conversation was being recorded by an Abingdon radio enthusiast. She was Jane Norgrove, who later revealed that her recording had been

> **"If this is the price of public life, then it is too high a price to pay."**
> DIANA TO FRIENDS, ABOUT THE SQUIDGY TAPE

made on 31 December 1989. At that time, Diana and the rest of the Royal Family were at Sandringham, where they had assembled to celebrate Christmas. Norgrove's recording came to light several months after Cyril Reenan, a second radio enthusiast with a recording, had sold his copy to the press (see In The News).

At first the *Sun* was reluctant to publish what might turn out to be a fake, and January 1990 was not, in any case, the right time. Diana was then riding high and the tape, if revealed, might have looked like another piece of rumour-mongering.

In August 1992, however, when Andrew Morton's book, *Diana: Her True Story*, had already set the pace for revelations about Diana, the appropriate time had clearly arrived.

BREAKING THE STORY

That fired the starting pistol, and on 24 August 1992, the *Sun* published a transcript of the tape. 'My Life Is Torture' was the front page headline. It was a scoop but the rest of the press soon leapt into battle with 'Love Tapes Upset Diana' from the *Daily Express* on 25 August and, three days later, 'I Just Called To Say I Love You' from *Today*, which had a smiling James Gilbey on the front page.

The *Sun* soon went one better than the rest of the pack. The paper set up a telephone line so that the public, already titillated into a fever of interest, could listen in to the tape. It was dubbed

'Dianagate' after the 'Watergate' political scandal in the USA. The Watergate affair had ended with the downfall of Republican president Richard Nixon. Charles' friends, who were elated at the weapon against the Princess which Dianagate gave them, doubtless hoped it would do the same for her. The name of the recording was soon changed, though,

Previous page Princess Diana in Glasgow in June 1992, 12 days after Morton's book appeared. **Above** Carrying on as normal at Thorpe Water Park with Princes William and Harry.

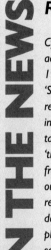

Radio ham is famous for a day

Cyril Reenan, a retired bank manager, achieved brief tabloid fame in August 1992 when he was revealed as the 'Squidgy' tape source. Analysis of his recording by a Sony engineer, though, indicated it was made using a wire-tapping device and had later been 'treated' to sound as if it had come from a mobile phone. It later turned out that Reenan had made his recording on 4 January 1990, four days after the conversation took place. It was suspected that the secret services had 'broadcast' the version that Reenan taped.

Above James Gilbey (right) with a motor racing colleague, pictured in November 1992 when the press were still making wild guesses about his relationship with Diana.
Left Prince Harry with Diana as both try to relax at a polo match. Diana sought what comfort she could from her close family during this period.

CHRONICLE

DIARY DATES

August 1992

6 August
The Prince and Princess of Wales leave on a cruise accompanied by Princess Alexandra, Angus Ogilvy and Lord and Lady Ramsey

8 August
Princess Beatrice celebrates her fourth birthday

14 August
The Duke of York attends a concert in support of the Grand Columbus Regatta, in Liverpool

15 August
Princess Anne celebrates her 42nd birthday

16 August
The Prince and Princess of Wales return from their 10-day cruise

16 August
The Queen, Prince Philip and Prince Edward disembark from *Britannia* at Aberdeen and drive to Balmoral for the summer

16 August
The Queen Mother attends a service at St. Peter's Church, Thurso, to mark the 75th anniversary of the Scottish Women's Rural Institutes

21 August
Princess Margaret celebrates her 62nd birthday

24 August
The Prince of Wales takes the salute at the Edinburgh Tattoo

30 August
At Balmoral, the Queen receives a gift from the City of Aberdeen to mark the 40th anniversary of her accession to the throne

to the 'Squidgy' tape when Gilbey was heard to use 'Squidgy' as a pet name for Diana. The Independent Committee for the Supervision of Standards of Telephone Information Services stepped in quickly to ban the tape as 'an unreasonable invasion of privacy', but by that time 40,000 people had each paid 48 pence a minute to eavesdrop on the recorded conversation. They doubtless expected the tape's revelations to be even juicier than the topless photographs of the Duchess of York, which had been the front page sensation on 20 August.

REVELATIONS

The hotline to the Squidgy tape was not quite as steamy as the listeners had been led to expect. Most of it was just social chit-chat about friends but there was enough there to indicate first, that the talk was surprisingly intimate, second, that Gilbey appeared to be in love with Diana and, last but not least, that Diana was in a state of considerable distress.

Charles, Diana told Gilbey, 'makes my life real, real torture'. Diana confessed to crying at the dinner table in front of the royals. 'I just felt sad and empty,' she said. 'I thought, "Bloody hell, after all I've done for this f★★★★★g family".'

The tirade continued as she went on to complain of the innuendo directed against her, and threatened, 'I'm going to do something dramatic because I can't stand the confines of this marriage.' Next, Diana appeared to perk up and

> **"He has a very maternal quality which appeals to women. He is not particularly intelligent, but pragmatic, the kind of person who can be relied on."**
>
> A FRIEND OF JAMES GILBEY, ON JAMES GILBEY

turn defiant: 'I'll go out and conquer the world...do my bit in the way I know how, and leave him (Charles) behind.'

Diana had some hard words for the now deeply disgraced Duchess of York, and for the Queen Mother who, she told Gilbey, gave her a 'strange look...it's not hatred, it's sort of interest and pity'. James Gilbey proved a good, patient listener and he

Opposite page Diana, Harry and Prince Charles with the Queen Mother at Clarence House on the occasion of her 92nd birthday in August 1992. **Above** Diana and Harry ride with the Queen Mother at the Trooping the Colour in June 1992, shortly after Morton's book appeared. The atmosphere between the two women was said to have been strained.

Above Talking to one of the young bridesmaids at a friend's wedding reception at the Mayfair Hotel, London. **Left** Diana chats with members of the crowd during a walkabout while on a visit to Manchester Infirmary.

CHRONICLE

was undoubtedly devoted to Diana. He called her Squidgy or Squidge no less than 67 times and kept whispering, 'I love you, I love you, I love you!'

Further on in the tape, amid more small talk about fashions and astrology, Diana mentioned another man, James Hewitt, whom, she told Gilbey, she had 'dressed from head to foot'. 'Cost me quite a bit,' Diana concluded ruefully. This was really amazing news. It indicated that Hewitt was, in

> *"She is at her lowest ebb for years. Her self-confidence is destroyed. In fact, she is on the verge of packing her bags."*
> A FRIEND OF DIANA, ON DIANA

effect, a 'kept man' and a kept man to many eagerly listening ears meant a lover.

Hewitt was not unknown to the press. In 1991, his girlfriend, Emma Stewardson, had told the *News of the World* that he had a crush on Diana and had visited the Princess several times at Highgrove and Kensington Palace. There, apparently, he regaled her with accounts of the Gulf War of January and February 1991, in which he had served as a tank commander. Later, in July, Diana reportedly invited Hewitt to spend the evening of her 30th birthday with her at Kensington Palace.

CASHING IN

James Hewitt's valet, Lance Corporal Malcolm Leete, knew all about his master's 'liaison' with Diana, so he had a story of his own to tell. It was published in the *News of the World* in the wake of the Squidgy tape. Hewitt threatened to sue for libel, but afterwards had to withdraw because, it seems, the cost of the suit was too great.

At around this time, rumours reached Diana that Hewitt himself was going into print. He denied it and no memoirs appeared. Neither did that part of the Squidgy tape in which Diana expressed fears of becoming pregnant, only to be assured by James Gilbey that this would not happen. A transcript of this part of the tape emerged seven months later, in March 1993, but according to her friends, Diana became frantic with worry over the news breaking.

Despite press speculation and antagonism from the Palace, life had to carry on. **Right** Throughout this period Diana continued with her public engagements. She is seen here on a visit to Hull. **Below** Diana, accompanied by Prince William, takes Prince Harry to school in September 1992. Charles was not with them. **Below right** James Gilbey at the Hurlingham Club in London, at a *Concours d'Elégance* for cars.

The Private Princess
No second honeymoon

Above *Greek tycoon John Latsis owned the yacht* Alexander, *which the royals borrowed on several occasions. He owned ten other luxury yachts.*

On 6 August 1992, royal officials seeking to limit the damage done by the publication of *Diana: Her True Story* organized a cruise for Charles, Diana and their sons on the luxury yacht *Alexander*, belonging to the billionaire John Latsis.

Charles' cousins, Princess Alexandra and her husband Angus Ogilvy, and Lord and Lady Romsey went, too. The cruise, lasting ten days, was unwisely touted as a 'second honeymoon' for Charles and Diana, but it was nothing of the sort.

As Diana's friends later revealed, the couple had separate cabins. Diana shunned the adult company at mealtimes and spent most of the cruise playing with the children. Charles, it appears, telephoned Camilla Parker-Bowles from the yacht.

Diana, who overheard, was said to have told him: 'Why don't you go off with your lady and have an end to it!'

This was not Diana's first time cruising on the *Alexander* and she told friends it had very bad memories for her. This was where Charles had once initiated a discussion about the worth of mistresses. On that occasion, as well, Charles had apparently telephoned Camilla.

The bad blood between Charles and Diana, it seems, was worse at the end of the cruise on 16 August than at the start.

She took to raking over each day's papers, wondering if this most damning statement was going to appear. Doubtless to her relief, there was no sign of it, but what had been revealed was devastating enough.

Diana, her friends later recounted, swung between despondency and bravado, despair and defiance. Either way, it seemed clear that she was severely shaken by the publication of the tape and feared that her position had been undermined in the talks about her separation from Charles.

James Gilbey, meanwhile, was being hunted as only a prurient press knew how. He became a fugitive and went into hiding for a fortnight after the

> ❝*I haven't got a single supporter in this family, but they are not going to break me.*❞
> DIANA, ON THE ROYAL FAMILY

tape became public. When he moved from place to place, it was in the boot of a friend's car.

Gilbey was already known as one of Andrew Morton's sources for *Diana: Her True Story*. But despite the impression given on the tape, Gilbey and Diana were never romantically linked. He was more the sort of friend common in aristocratic circles, one of a crowd who met socially. Gilbey had known Diana in her Coleherne Court days before her marriage and escorted her to the theatre with her flatmates, but he sought romance elsewhere. At the time of the Squidgy revelations, Gilbey, who

IN CONTEXT 1992 — SERBIAN DEATH CAMPS FOUND

- Wave of terrorist attacks in Haiti kills ten
- 3000th victim of sectarian violence killed in Northern Ireland
- Serbian death camps discovered in Bosnia, **right**
- Nigel Mansell of Britain wins the Hungarian Grand Prix and becomes Formula One Champion of the World
- Hurricane Andrew sweeps through the city of Miami in Florida
- John Sirica, judge at the Watergate hearings, dies

Above Diana on a visit to an orthopaedic hospital in Stanmore in July 1992.
Oppposite, top Diana, on a visit to a hospital in Glamorgan, talks to a patient in a wheelchair.
Right Diana seen on 2 June 1992 with John Latsis at a charity luncheon for Birthright. Five days later, on 7 June, the storm broke about Morton's book.

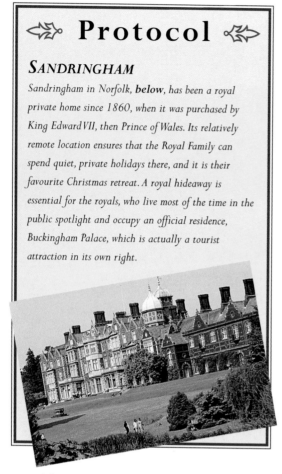

Protocol

SANDRINGHAM

*Sandringham in Norfolk, **below**, has been a royal private home since 1860, when it was purchased by King Edward VII, then Prince of Wales. Its relatively remote location ensures that the Royal Family can spend quiet, private holidays there, and it is their favourite Christmas retreat. A royal hideaway is essential for the royals, who live most of the time in the public spotlight and occupy an official residence, Buckingham Palace, which is actually a tourist attraction in its own right.*

worked in the motor industry and was involved in motor racing, was romantically involved with Lady Althea Saville, the daughter of the Duke of Mexborough. Both Althea and Diana frequently dined at Gilbey's flat in Lennox Gardens, Knightsbridge, where Gilbey, a first-class chef, cooked for them. According to Gilbey's business colleagues, Diana and the Duchess of York used to call on him at work from time to time, and he was seen dining out with Diana and her friends.

James Gilbey has a very sympathetic nature and friends, both male and female, regard him as a 'good shoulder to cry on'. This, it was suggested, is what Diana was doing in October 1989 when she spent several hours at Gilbey's flat while her personal detective waited outside. Diana left at one o'clock in the morning. Rather defensively, Gilbey claimed that other guests had been present as well, but no one else, apparently, was seen to leave the flat. The Squidgy telephone call was made two months later, and Gilbey, for all his explanations, found himself cast by the press as Diana's illicit lover.

SYMPATHY FOR 'WRONGED' WIFE

However true or untrue that was, the fallout from *Diana: Her True Story*, which had won the Princess great sympathy as a wronged wife, tended to blunt the edge of blame for the Squidgy revelations. The idea that Diana had been justified in seeking solace to compensate for her 'miserable' marriage was a pretty potent one, and went far to exonerate the Princess with a large section of the public.

The order of events had been fortunate, though. Morton's book appeared first, establishing the extent of Diana's misery. Had Squidgy preceded it, public opinion might have been far less tolerant.

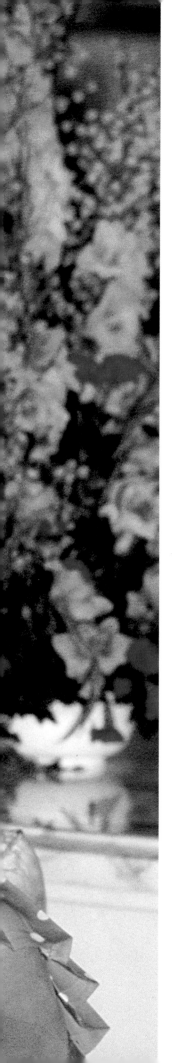

Material Girl

The materials, textures, colours and patterns of Diana's clothes had to be carefully chosen if she was going to maintain her chic appearance right the way through a lengthy engagement

Like everything else about her royal life, the materials that went to make Diana's clothes for public engagements and tours had their own rule book. The rules were especially strict for all-day engagements, when Diana was under scrutiny for hours on end and had to look uncrumpled from start to finish.

Her first lesson in how *not* to achieve this all-day smartness was learned on her wedding day. When Diana emerged from the Glass Coach outside St. Paul's Cathedral, the much-heralded gown in silk taffeta by David and Elizabeth Emanuel emerged with her in scores of tiny creases.

Taffeta and velvet

This did not mean that taffeta, a beautiful material with a subtle shine, was necessarily exiled from Diana's wardrobe. Properly used, it could look splendid. A Rifat Ozbek suit in turquoise moiré taffeta with gold decorations, which Diana wore in Spain in 1987, observed the non-crumple code by being made from a heavier material and having a straight skirt better able to defy the creases.

Velvet, the warm-looking, peach-textured material which was one of Diana's favourites, served her well in this regard. The material looked very smart and smooth in, for example, the deep plum off-the-peg suit by Jaeger that she wore in Wales in 1981, with a matching hat by John Boyd.

Silk and satin made many appearances during Diana's public life. One example was the green and white spotted dress in silk that Catherine Walker made for Diana to wear on the royal visit to Saudi

Opposite page, far left In a Catherine Walker red and pink silk coat dress in the UAE in 1989. **Opposite page, main picture** Another Catherine Walker outfit, worn in Kuwait in 1989. Polka dots look good close to.
Right A metallic blue-grey evening gown in shiny satin, in Japan in 1986. **Below** At Ascot in 1987 in lively yellow and turquoise.

Arabia in 1986. There was also the luxurious ivory satin evening gown with lace bodice by the Emanuels, worn in Oman on the same tour. Satin was a good material for keeping an unblemished sheen throughout a long public appearance.

The Gulf Tour highlighted Diana's greatest problem: she reacted badly to the heat. Even the best materials for keeping cool – cotton or silk – did not always serve her needs in this area. Whenever the mercury soared, Diana was likely to bake.

Naturally, she was better off when in England, and looked nice and comfortable in the white cotton dress with generous navy collar, revers and cuffs

---

"You never knew what colour Diana was going to wear next, but she looked terrific in all of them."
FIONA SINCLAIR, ROYAL CORRESPONDENT

---

which she chose to wear for the Queen Mother's 87th birthday lunch in August 1987. This dress was so good, that Diana wore it again, in a much hotter climate – midsummer in Australia in January 1988.

However, cotton had its disadvantages when compared to silk, another choice in which Diana strove to keep reasonably cool. Cotton could crease very heavily and lacked the elegant suppleness of silk. Flax brought similar problems, even though Paul Costello's cleverly styled yellow and white hand–painted dress with a pleated skirt, which Diana also wore in January 1988 in Australia, would have made it in the elegance stakes but for its rather thick-looking, dropped-waist bodice.

Wool for warmth

When it came to winter wear, Diana was able to combat the cold with her renowned thermal under-wear. Wool was her most frequent choice for winter, not only for warmth but also for another imperative of the royal public appearance: the brilliant colours it was able to take, which enabled royals to be easily seen. The need for royals to be visible in crowds was the most basic of the wardrobe rules. This accounted for some of Diana's brightest outfits – a Donald Campbell jacket in brilliant red, which she wore with a green pleated skirt in Wales

1 A bright pink two-piece linen suit, worn in Australia in 1988. It is teamed with a pink and white, patterned, silk blouse with a sash at the waist.

2 A subtler pink is combined with pale yellow in this two-piece, where the buttons and yoke of the top pick up the colour of the hat, which has elements of a pith helmet. Diana wore this Catherine Walker silk suit in the Cameroons on a visit with Charles in 1990.

3 Royal blue and white combine with great elegance in this fetching two-piece with a matching hat set off by two feathers. Diana wore this Catherine Walker outfit in Dubai in March 1989.

4 The polka dots on the jacket, this time in black, are picked up by the smaller dots on the satin blouse. Diana wore this two-piece Jan van Velden suit in Canada in 1986.

5 In Thailand in 1989, Diana wears a gingham short-sleeved blouse with a white, belted, linen skirt designed by Alistair Blair.

6 In Jakarta, Indonesia, in 1989, Diana wears a turquoise, two-piece evening suit in silk by Catherine Walker with diamanté buttons. The wide V of the neckline is mirrored by the high-cut V of the hemline.

Above left A sarong-style
evening dress in pale pink
chiffon. The bodice is
embroidered with an overall
Paisley design in pearls and
gold beads. Diana wore it on
a visit to Pakistan in 1991.
Above This bright blue
taffeta peplum suit has an
attractive rippled pattern
within the material that gives
depth and a sense of
texture. This does not in any
way detract from the
embroidered, swirling gold
scrolls. Diana wore this two-
piece, designed by Rifat
Ozbek, to a fashion show in
Spain in April 1987.

on her first tour in 1981, for example, and pretty
tartan dresses for the Highland Games in Scotland.

The royal visibility rule meant that Diana could
not often choose complex patterned material for
her outfits, even where the colours were bright
enough. From a distance, an overpatterned outfit
could look messy and obscure the figure. Polka dots
were a frequent choice of Diana's when plain

material, however pretty, palled. They had the
advantage of blending into the main colour when
viewed from afar. So did white patterns on pastel
dresses, like the yellow and white crêpe-de-chine
number by Jan van Velden, which Diana wore in
Alice Springs, Australia, in 1983.

Stripes, though, qualified as an acceptable pattern,
if they were vertical, as in the yellow and

BRILLIANT SURFACES

Above This red evening gown in duchess satin was worn with a separate lace bolero jacket embroidered with sequins. It was designed by Jan van Velden and worn by Diana in Norway in 1984.

Above right A star-spangled, strapless, midnight-blue evening gown made of silk tulle embroidered with diamanté brilliants. The top layer of the tulle skirt is embroidered with diamanté stars. The gown was designed by Murray Arbeid and first worn by Diana to a private dinner held at Claridge's in 1986 for King Constantine of Greece.

1 Diana in Portugal in 1987 in an orange-red satin jacket with a black silk bow tie.

2 This Catherine Walker evening gown, worn in Kuwait in March 1989, has a brocaded floral top and a long skirt in lilac silk with a gathered waist.

3 A diaphanous, pale lilac evening gown with a white snowflake pattern. Diana wore this silk chiffon dress by Zandra Rhodes in 1989.

white-striped Arabella Pollen suit Diana chose to wear in Adelaide, Australia, also in 1983. Verticals enhanced the figure, horizontals expanded it and blurred its outline. Consequently, Diana's most successful striped outfits featured the former.

Figured fabrics, with surface interest that could look almost three-dimensional, appeared in Diana's working wardrobe from time to time. One of her early favourites was a pink quilted suit. The quilting looked interesting close to and the pink caught the eye from afar.

The same went for the crushed silk used by Bruce Oldfield for the peach suit Diana wore in Japan in 1986, which had an intriguing self-pattern like rivulets of water on glass.

Adventurous evening wear

In the evening, Diana's dresses could have really adventurous surface textures. The slinky white single-sleeved evening gown by Hachi, which she wore to a dinner at the National Gallery in Washington in 1985, was spattered with gold and silver bugle beads. That gave Diana a shimmering appearance, while still emphasizing her slenderness.

The trick with materials, colours, textures and patterns was to follow the royal dressing rules without making them obvious or letting them get in the way of innovation and creativity. What the crowds saw was a supremely elegant princess, setting trends and looking chic as only a leader of fashion could.

IN THE NEWS

Party nightie by Galliano for Christian Dior

When Diana attended a charity function in New York in December 1996, the fashion pundits went wild about her midnight-blue 'nightie-style' evening dress by John Galliano. Some 900 high-society figures, including many celebrities, paid £600 a head to sit down to dinner with the Princess. Supermodel Iman talked of Diana's 'tremendous style'. She was also called 'drop-dead sexy'. The consensus of opinion had it that in her sensational evening gown, she completely outclassed beauties such as Linda Evangelista, Christy Turlington and Bianca Jagger.

Arabian Nights

Charles and Diana's 1986 tour of four states in the Persian Gulf was the grand, glittery occasion to be expected when royalty met royalty – hosted by some of the richest men in the world

The Arab states of the Persian Gulf have a romantic image. Sand, sun, travel-brochure colour and glamour, rulers so oil-rich that zeros worked overtime to express their wealth, nomads riding free over mile upon mile of heat-baked desert – all this was an exotic scenario.

Unlike most idealized concepts, much of it was true. There were many fascinating cultural experiences to be savoured in Oman, Qatar, Bahrain and Saudi Arabia. However, where two cultures meet, they can also clash, and the royal couple had to undergo some careful preparation and briefing.

Male-dominated culture

The most important difference was the male-dominated nature of the Gulf States. Men and women led essentially separate lives, with women protected and subordinate, and certainly playing no great part in state or any other public business. This was why many Arabs in the Gulf states were puzzled when the press corps seemed far more interested in following Diana than Charles. To them, Charles, being a man, was the more important of the two.

The moral code of Islam was just as strict. Charles and Diana caused quite a stir when they exchanged a post-match kiss on a polo field in Oman. The incident so alarmed the television authorities that the footage was cut from newscasts in case viewers became offended.

Islamic morality also explained why Diana had to cover herself up in high necks, long sleeves and long hemlines or trousers. The only concession to her Western origins was that she was allowed to reveal her face. Many women in the Gulf States have to

Above In Oman, Diana visited Qaboos University and talked with female students. **Right** Camels and traditional flowing robes were still much in evidence.

Top Beneath this castle commanding the maritime approaches, Charles and Diana were given the red carpet treatment as they were greeted by a line of dignitaries in Oman.
Inset, above Charles and Diana at the Royal Palace in Oman with the country's absolute ruler, Sultan Qaboos bin Said.

wear veils because it is believed that only their husbands have the right to see their faces. In England, some newspapers later floated the idea that Diana had been 'humiliated' by the restrictions. Charles, for instance, was supposed to take the lead with Diana walking far behind. Her main problem in the Gulf States, however, was less likely to be her reduced status as a woman than the extreme heat, which never suited her.

Charles and Diana's visit began in Oman, which lies between the Indian Ocean and the Gulf of Oman, on 10 November 1986. The day was very hot and the shade of large umbrellas on the tarmac was only slightly less fiery, but though drained and suffering from jet lag, Diana refused to wilt.

Sultan Qaboos bin Said of Oman was so impressed with the Princess that he took an unprecedented step: he opened up his guest palace to the press and was pictured with the Princess and her husband amid its stunning opulence. Sultan Qaboos was an absolute ruler with a hold on power Prince Charles would never achieve. Head of State, prime minister and minister for foreign affairs, defence and finance, he could do as he pleased.

A different world

The Sultan gave a splendid banquet for the royal visitors at which guests were plied with the richest of rich food. During the stay in Oman, which lasted four days, Diana met female students at Qaboos University and sat chatting with them for some time. Diana, emancipated, privileged and a

Left In Qatar, the second state on their tour, Charles and Diana were the guests of Emir Sheikh Khalifa bin Hamaid al-Thani. Diana is seen here with the Emir, watching a camel display in the desert. One of the riders upset the royal couple with the rough way he handled his camel.

❧ **Protocol** ❧

ARAB ROYAL TITLES

Although the rulers of Arab Islamic countries in the Gulf or the Middle East, such as Fahd of Saudi Arabia, **right**, *or Hussein of Jordan, call themselves kings, this is a Western-style title. The Islamic name for 'king' or 'sovereign' is sultan, a title last held by the Sultan of Ottoman Turkey, who was forced to abdicate in 1921. An emir is not so highly placed. Emirs were princes or governors, but they had the distinction of being descendants of Mohammed, the prophet who founded the Islamic religion in the early 7th century. Sheikh is a title that recalls the Arabs' nomadic past. It denotes a chief or head of an Islamic tribe, family or village.*

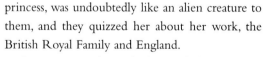

princess, was undoubtedly like an alien creature to them, and they quizzed her about her work, the British Royal Family and England.

On 14 November, Charles' 38th birthday, the royal couple moved on to Qatar, a peninsular country bounded on the west by the Gulf of Bahrain

> "*Super, nice, intelligent and a lady all Arabian men and women admire.*"
>
> PRINCE SULTAN BIN SALMAN OF SAUDI ARABIA, ON DIANA

and on the east by the Persian Gulf. It is a small country, only five per cent the size of Oman, with about a third of its population, but Charles and Diana paid a three-day visit. They received a lavish welcome from Emir Sheikh Khalifa bin Hamaid al-Thani. The Emir found an ingenious way around

WELCOME

Top On their brief visit to Bahrain Charles and Diana were taken to the Hope Institute for Handicapped Children. **Inset, above** In the evening there was yet another formal state banquet to attend; Diana wore a tiara for the meal.

the traditional segregation of the sexes. Diana was made an 'honorary man' for an evening, enabling her to get round the Islamic law which forbade social mixing between men and women. Thus 'transformed', Diana attended the birthday dinner given for Charles by the Emir, but was the only woman there.

The Emir did not pay quite the same attention to his visitors' humanitarian sensibilities. Qatar, like the other Gulf states, is a settled country descended from nomadic tribes, who once rode the desert on camels. The old days in the desert were not forgotten, though, and in Qatar, Charles and Diana were treated to an exhibition of the desert lifestyle.

Unfortunately, one rider handled his camel too roughly and kept pulling hard on the ring slotted through the animal's nose. The camel was clearly in pain and both Charles and Diana were seen to

wince at the animal's frequent groans of protest. The desert environment was evoked more pleasantly when Charles and Diana were entertained on their arrival in spectacular surroundings modelled on a traditional Arab tent. Beautiful figured archways enclosed luxurious curtains. A centrepiece set in the marble floor was adorned with a multi-

> **"She must have left the (male) dinner guests...totting up how many camels they would have to give to woo such a woman."**
>
> VICTORIA AUSTIN, ROYAL CORRESPONDENT, ON DIANA

coloured flower bouquet. Charles, Diana and their hosts, who were wearing flowing robes and head-dresses, sat in gilt-edged chairs.

Charles spent part of his birthday visiting the BBC's Eastern Relay Station at Mbirah before the

royal tour moved on to Bahrain on 16 November. Bahrain is even smaller than Qatar, about half its size, but with a comparable population of half a million. Here, Charles and Diana met Sheikh Isa bin Sujlman al-Khalifa, another autocratic ruler, but one with liberal leanings. The royal visitors were treated to the by-now regulation grand banquet, where Diana sat next to the Emir, who was

Above Diana sits cross-legged, at ease in a tent in the Saudi desert.

Top right Part of the entertainment arranged for the royal couple in Saudi Arabia was a stirring display of falconry.

resplendent in his black robes and head-dress decorated in gold.

The visit to Bahrain was brief, little more than two nights' stay, but Diana was able to visit the Hope Institute for Handicapped Children, where she was given a fine red-and-gold traditional Bahraini dress.

Surprise encounter

While in Bahrain, Diana met her gynaecologist, George Pinker, who was in the Gulf state to attend a wedding. The press corps jumped to the conclusion that she was pregnant for a third time, but they were disappointed. Diana was amazed to encounter Pinker. 'George! What are you doing here?' she wanted to know and the hoped-for press scoop bit the desert sand.

On 17 November, having spent only one complete day in Bahrain, Charles and Diana departed for the major visit of the tour, to Saudi Arabia. This oil-rich kingdom of some 16 million people is so

vast that its northern border, deep into the trackless desert, has never been precisely mapped.

So far, the sensitive diplomatic niceties, apart from the kiss on the Omani polo field, had been smoothly observed. In Saudi Arabia, though, Charles and Diana flew into controversy. Their host, King Fahd's brother, Crown Prince Abdullah, was nowhere to be seen. Charles and Diana were told he had left the country for health reasons.

Abdullah had left the country all right, but turned up in the Canary Isles, 60 miles off the north-west coast of Africa, fit as a flea and basking in the pleasures of a luxury hotel. It appears that the Crown Prince had refused to meet Charles and Diana because of a row between Britain and Syria. Three Syrian diplomats had been expelled from

IN THE NEWS

Uneasy contrasts

During the Gulf Tour of the Arab states in 1986, the British press made a meal of the contrast between Diana, the emancipated Western woman, and the apparently inferior position of Muslim women. Concentrating on Diana's assumed reactions to male oppression and the 'indignities' heaped on women, the Star of 17 November paraded what they depicted as Muslim women's second-class status. It also published a picture of the polo match kiss, which got the royal couple into trouble with the 'prudish' Omanis.

Britain over alleged terrorist activities and, in retaliation, three British diplomats were ordered to leave Syria. That had been the previous May, but the quarrel still rankled and the Crown Prince had clearly snubbed the royals.

Fortunately, King Fahd ibn Abd al-Aziz as Sa'ud, a man of charm and tact who had ruled Saudi Arabia since 1982, was there to smooth over the incident. He took personal charge of the tour and quickly organized the state banquet at his magnificent palace in Riyadh, the capital.

In Saudi Arabia, the royal couple were again treated to traditional entertainments that only the Arabs could stage. From carpets laid out on the sand, Charles and Diana were able to watch Saudi dancers leaping and whirling to the rhythm of desert drums. Warriors mounted on camels and white horses performed in a colourful swirl of exotic costumes, their long swords catching the brilliant sunlight.

Traditional Bedouin tent

Charles and Diana dined in a traditional Bedouin nomad tent where a whole roast sheep, complete with head and eyes, was on the menu. In Arab society, the eyes are a great delicacy traditionally offered to guests, but Charles and Diana escaped this honour. Fortunately for them, plenty of vegetable dishes and yoghurt were also being served.

Arab hospitality is legendary and King Fahd spared no effort to lay on a superb show for his guests. Another of the Saudi royals, Prince Sultan

Opposite page Diana visits a home for handicapped children in Riyadh. **Above left** Diana was a guest at the horse racing in Riyadh. **Top** Diana and Charles were later presented with a portrait of themselves in a desert setting. **Inset, above** The royal couple with Prince Sultan bin Abdul Aziz, the Saudi Minister of Defence, at his guest palace in Riyadh.

Top Diana with King Fahd (far left), the ruler of Saudi Arabia who hosted the visit in the absence of the Crown Prince. **Inset, above** Charles and Diana on the escalators with their Saudi Arabian hosts in the Royal Terminal at Riyadh Airport.

bin Salman, a nephew of the absent Crown Prince, paid Diana lavish compliments and entertained her and Prince Charles with his experiences as a major in the Saudi Air Force and his adventures as a member of a space shuttle crew.

Despite the absent Saudi Crown Prince, the kiss in Oman and the cruelty to the Qatari camel, the Gulf Tour of 1986 proved to be one of Charles and Diana's greatest triumphs. Charles took full advantage of opportunities to promote British business in all four states. Diana beat the heat, the bans on women and the problems of modest dressing required by Islam to sparkle and to charm her hosts.

The Gulf Tour, which ended on 19 November, was nevertheless very demanding, and a welcome 35 hours' cruising in the Red Sea on the Royal Yacht *Britannia* afforded a brief period of relaxation.

Charles sailed on *Britannia* to Cyprus, where he was to visit troops of the Parachute Regiment stationed there, and to do a little painting. Diana, meanwhile, flew home from Hurghada Airport in Egypt on 21 November, carrying a mass of gifts for

> **"She had to remember to keep her elbows, chest and legs modestly covered to avoid insulting Islam."**
> SALLY MOORE, ROYAL CORRESPONDENT

William and Harry. Charles had been presented with an £80,000 convertible Aston Martin and Diana with a superb collection of jewels – a sapphire and diamond necklace, bracelet and matching earrings made in a crescent shape. This was not a coincidence, but cleverly designed to remind her of ten exciting days in the desert.

THE SEPARATION

The end of a marriage is the failure of hope and the defeat of endeavour. Charles and Diana suffered this profound sadness in the last half of 1992 as their marriage finally crumbled

As the dramatic summer of 1992 moved into autumn, the leaves were falling fast from Charles and Diana's marriage. There was so much hurt and anger on both sides, so many terrible things had been said and so many cruel accusations made that, to friends of the couple and many others, their relationship seemed past mending. In fact, a member of Charles' circle laid a wager in January that the couple would part by the following December. The intensity of press and public interest, embellished as it was with rumour, speculation and moralizing, must have exerted unbearable pressures on the couple.

Although they presented a gracious, smiling exterior, the public, they realized, wanted a resolution to the situation that was evidently becoming intolerable. Separation seemed the obvious and only answer. Although Charles and Diana had

already discussed a separation the day after Andrew Morton's *Diana: Her True Story* appeared on 7 June, the practical negotiations did not start in earnest until the autumn. As they and their advisers soon discovered, picking apart the seams of a marriage was extraordinarily painful.

For Diana it was also a time of great anxiety. She was up against the most powerful family in the land and, as one adviser revealed, 'she was terrified that (they) were going to take the children away and drive her into exile. It was her greatest anxiety. She was prepared to give up everything, do anything, to keep the boys.'

FUTURE OF THE BOYS

It never came to that, of course, but as witnesses attested, the children's future was the most highly emotional theme of the negotiations. The public impression that, at this stage, Charles and Diana agreed about their future was wide of the mark. At one point during the ongoing negotiations, Diana

Previous page There was an awkward atmosphere between Charles and Diana throughout their tour of South Korea in November 1992. **Above** Diana and Charles dutifully visited the Korean National Cemetery in Seoul. **Right** Diana at the Sejong Cultural Centre in Seoul. **Opposite page, top** Charles and Diana receive welcoming bouquets at Seoul Airport. **Opposite page, bottom** At times, such as during a speech at this presidential banquet, Diana's thoughts seemed to be elsewhere.

threatened to take William and Harry to live abroad, in Australia. It was a big mistake. Charles' answer had the force of tradition and law behind it. The boys were not 'hers', he was said to have told Diana; they were not even 'his'. They were heirs to the throne, the sons of a future King of England. They could not be taken out of the country. They had to remain at court and become accustomed to their future royal responsibilities.

There was no argument here. The Queen, as sovereign, had the right to decide and control the lives and fate of her grandchildren and other close

> ## "We are glad to have got rid of Diana."
> #### PRINCESS MARGARET, ON DIANA

relatives under a precedent set as long ago as 1717. At that time, King George I, an ancestor of the Queen and Charles, had disputed the education of his grandson, Prince Frederick, with the boy's father, who later became King George II. The judgement came down on George I's side and the supremacy of the sovereign has remained common law ever since.

Diana had done her cause no good by making this threat. All that happened was that Charles' advisers, who were already at daggers drawn with her, recommended that, as a woman 'out of control' and a 'danger' to the monarchy – which was apparently the view of the Royal Family, too – she should go to Australia and live there on her own.

EXILE IN AUSTRALIA

The Princess' lawyers, alarmed at this nasty turn of events, urged Diana to be more discreet and trust to negotiations rather than confrontation to get at least something of what she wanted. She took their advice, turning to less controversial issues such as the homes and administrative offices she shared with Charles. There she could fight her corner with less peril, but even so, the fire in the arguments still blazed fiercely.

Whenever Charles, Diana and their advisers met, discussion could rapidly degenerate into warfare. Doors were slammed. There was shouting and

tears. 'They yelled at each other, as is the way in messy divorces,' remarked one adviser.

This sort of thing was agony for Prince Charles. As one of his advisers told Andrew Morton, Charles was a man who liked 'a quiet, ordered existence. He went through mental anguish every time he met (Diana) because he experienced at first hand the slamming of doors, the shouting, the stamping of feet, the sheer unreasonableness of her behaviour.'

Now, confronting the wasteland his marriage had become, Charles still seemed wary of Diana. 'All I

> "*The separation was a dreadful admission of failure, all the worse for having to be performed in public.*"
> FIONA SINCLAIR, ROYAL CORRESPONDENT

want is for Charles to leave Kensington Palace,' she had insisted, but, in fact, she wanted more. She wanted her staff to be split from his and for them to move from St. James' Palace to Buckingham Palace. Charles proved reluctant, not necessarily due to any great inconvenience involved, but because he did not really want to separate from Diana at all.

'The prince was reluctant to go down the road of separation and divorce,' one of Charles' advisers later remembered, '…he wanted things to continue as they were, but for them to live apart.' There were

IN THE NEWS

The saddest of endings

The feeling of disappointment was intense when Charles and Diana's separation was announced. This Daily Mail headline of 10 December 1992 said what a lot of people felt. A 'fairytale' marriage, royal or otherwise, might be an illogical concept, but the public's sadness at its failure was real enough. The pictures were appropriate – the couple were shown looking reflective and downcast – and the text of the report was printed between their photos, so emphasizing their parting.

Opposite page, top At times even Charles appeared to reveal his inner feelings in public. **Opposite page, bottom** On their individual engagements, such as this visit by Diana to construction workers on Teesside, the royal couple were able to rediscover their sense of humour. **Left** On a visit to RAF Wittering, in November 1992, Diana enjoyed being shown an aircraft's controls by a pilot. **Below** Diana did her best in Korea to put on a brave face. The infectious enthusiasm of the people during walkabouts made her task an easier one.

precedents for such an arrangement. Royalty and aristocracy often maintained a front of unity, which preserved a marriage, while in reality leading separate lives. This, however, was never going to be acceptable to Diana who, as Andrew Morton revealed in *Diana: Her True Story*, fought vigorously to expel the 'third person', Camilla Parker-Bowles, from her 'crowded' marriage.

PROPAGANDA WAR

As the months dragged on and the negotiations – despite all the difficulties – continued, the advantage seemed to swing from Charles to Diana and back again. At first Charles had refused to attack Diana in public, despite the urgings of his friends. Some of them saw this as indecision, some, more positively, as the behaviour of a gentleman. However that may be, these friends took it upon themselves to go on feeding the press with pro-Charles, anti-Diana stories, which built up his image as a popular employer of staff and a caring, attentive father. The staff at Highgrove House, for instance, were pictured warmly greeting their royal master at a party from which Diana, of course, was absent. The message was obvious, and deliberate.

Diana was also said to have prevented William and Harry from accompanying Charles to a children's museum – an indication, apparently, of her

> **"** *Were we going to stay together or were we going to separate? The words separation and divorce kept coming up in the media on a daily basis.* **"**
> DIANA, ON HER SEPARATION FROM CHARLES

spitefulness and obstructive nature. Other rumours said that she was demanding her own palace and huge sums of money, and wanted her own court.

Diana, for her part, was pleased to be told a story that Camilla had berated Charles for not making up his mind whether to stay with his wife or part from her. 'You never do anything you say,' Camilla was said to have told the Prince. Diana, happy to believe the tale, told her friends: 'I didn't realize she was pushing for exactly the same thing as me.' Diana also passed on to friends a rumour that Camilla's

long-suffering husband, Andrew Parker-Bowles, who had so far accepted his wife's relationship with the Prince, had lost patience and was going to sue for divorce. Furthermore, the story went, Parker-Bowles intended to cite Charles as co-respondent. True or untrue, it never happened. Diana was soon telling friends that the palace had pressurized Parker-Bowles into dropping the idea.

While scandalous tales like this were told and gossip was spreading them, the normal royal reaction, which was not to react or comment, was observed as usual. Throughout this fraught time, Charles and Diana had not neglected their duties. They still appeared in public, singly or together, or, as Diana later expressed it, they 'struggled on'.

TOGETHERNESS TOUR

Their public front was, as usual, impeccable. They appeared gracious, smiling, even serene, while, in private, their life was in turmoil. Charles and Diana had a long-standing date to visit South Korea between 2 and 5 November 1992 and the Prince's private secretary, Richard Aylard, presented it to the press as a 'togetherness tour'.

The Prince and Princess were to visit three locations: the South Korean capital, Seoul, Kyongju and Ulsan. On 5 November, Charles would go on to Hong Kong while Diana returned to England. This post-tour practice was not unusual for the couple. They had frequently returned home separately from abroad. Now that reconciliation

The Private Princess A Mother's Woes

A few hours before Diana's separation from Charles was officially announced, her mother Frances rang her in a highly emotional state.

Now divorced from her second husband, Peter Shand Kydd, Frances was more than depressed. She was distraught at what she saw as yet another personal failure. Diana, however, was a skilled counsellor.

Above *Diana's mother, Frances Shand Kydd, had problems of her own.*

As patron of RELATE, she had often sat in on sessions with people whose marriages had broken down. Now, she used her knowledge to calm Frances down and bring her out of her melancholy. When the conversation ended, Frances, still shocked at her own ill luck, was a great deal less distressed. Diana, however, was about to face the public trauma of her own separation.

had been touted as a possibility, the *Sunday Times*, briefed by Richard Aylard, published articles on 28 October, which put forward the idea that Charles and Diana were 'back together' and were 'putting their differences behind them'. Some other newspapers jumped on this hopeful bandwagon, the *Daily Mail* headlining a picture of Diana with 'From Diana, the look as hopes rise of a marriage on the mend'.

These hopes were quickly deflated. When Charles and Diana emerged from their aircraft at

> "*They never smile, laugh or do anything together.*"
>
> ANDREW JACQUES, OF THE ROYAL POLICE, ON CHARLES AND DIANA

Seoul Airport on 2 November, James Whitaker of the *Daily Mirror*, one of the journalists waiting for them, detected signs of a violent argument only minutes old. The residual rage barely contained, Charles and Diana stood on the tarmac and fumed their way through the official welcome.

As it began, so it went on. Under the sharp gaze of the press, which recorded and reported home every flicker of fury, and every whiff of 'bad' atmosphere, Charles and Diana gritted their way through their duties. They refused to look at each other, relaxed only when on separate engagements and set out on what seemed to the media to be two separate tours. The couple appeared to be not speaking by the time the tour ended, ironically, with a visit to the Great Lovers' Temple at Ulsan.

PRESS CLAIMS

Official explanations that the couple were tired out and jet-lagged failed to wash with newsmen, who speculated that a reluctant Diana had been ordered to Korea by the Queen. From this followed press claims of a rift with her mother-in-law, which Diana vigorously denied.

What no one could deny, though, was that the 'togetherness' tour had been a disaster. Some headlines described Charles and Diana as 'the Glums' and the situation was made even worse by the appearance in paperback of *Diana: Her True Story*,

Opposite page, top Princess Diana on a solo visit to Earl's Court in London in September 1992 is welcomed by the mayoress. **Above** The Princess of Wales arrives at The Coliseum in London in July 1992 to attend a performance by an Australian ballet company. **Left** The Queen at the re-opening of Leicester Square in London in June 1992. She was anxious that Charles and Diana should either patch up their differences or formalize the breakdown by agreeing to a trial separation.

which set off a fresh furore at home, amplified and embroidered by speculative press reports.

At this time, Charles wrote to a close friend that he dreaded the future, and after he returned from Hong Kong on 8 November, it was clear that he had been right to do so. Diana refused to attend a

> **"I have been acting the biggest role of my career for ten years. I should be in movies. I'm going. So are the boys. It's an impossible situation."**
>
> DIANA, ON HER MARRIAGE

party for friends at Sandringham, formerly a regular feature of their social life, in the third week of November. She would not allow William and Harry to go, either. Charles urged her to change her mind. She remained adamant. Suddenly, it seems, Charles could not stand it any more. He asked Diana for a legal separation. She agreed.

The young princes had to be told the news and on 2 December, Diana drove down to their boarding school, Ludgrove in Berkshire, where William burst into tears on hearing his parents' decision. Harry appeared more stoical. Diana made no mention of Camilla Parker-Bowles, but before she left, she asked headmaster Gerald Barber and his wife to ensure that her sons did not see the newspapers.

ANNOUNCED TO THE NATION

A week later, on 9 December, Prime Minister John Major got to his feet in the House of Commons: 'It is announced from Buckingham Palace,' he said, 'that, with regret, the Prince and Princess of Wales have decided to separate. Their Royal Highnesses have no plans to divorce and their constitutional positions are unaffected. This decision has been reached amicably and they will both continue to participate fully in the upbringing of their children.'

With that, the last hammer blow of the *annus horribilis* was struck. The only bright spark was Princess Anne's second marriage, to the admirable Commander Timothy Laurence, on 12 December.

But Charles' friend had won his wager. The fairytale which had begun in such hope and excitement, only 11 years before, was all but over.

Above Princess Diana, after the film première of *Just like a Woman,* meets the stars, Adrian Pasdar and Julie Walters. **Right** Individual engagements continued throughout the negotiations about a separation. Here, Diana is seen on a visit to the Cleveland Alzheimer's Centre in Kirkdale.

IN CONTEXT   CLINTON BECOMES PRESIDENT
1992

- Bill Clinton, **right**, defeats US President George Bush and becomes President of the USA
- Diplomatic relations between the Vatican and Mexico are restored after 130 years
- The Royal Mint introduces the new, smaller ten pence coin
- In the USA, the first patient to receive a baboon liver transplant dies soon after the operation
- British Heritage Secretary David Mellor resigns over a sex scandal involving actress Antonia de Sancha

Protocol

HEIRS TO THE THRONE

There are two kinds of heir to the throne. Prince Charles is heir apparent because, as the Queen's eldest son, no one can supersede him. The Queen, though, **right,** was heir presumptive to her father, King George VI. As a female, she could have been superseded if her parents had had a son during her father's reign. As next in line after his bachelor brother King Edward VIII, George VI was himself 'presumed' to be heir unless and until Edward had children of his own.

Main picture Diana in South Korea, the tour that the Queen hoped would bring about a reconciliation in the royal marriage.
Right Charles at Westminster Abbey in October 1992 for a ceremony to mark the 50th anniversary of El Alamein.

Designs on You

Bruce Oldfield, Jasper Conran and Caroline Charles were three designers who eased Diana out of her early, fussy phase and set her on the road to elegance and world fame as a fashion icon

Three designs by Bruce Oldfield. **Main picture** In Tasmania in 1983, Oldfield's dramatic touch is evident in the lavish frilling of the deep ruffled neckline of this red silk gown speckled with gold. **Left** An ultra-feminine evening gown with a bodice decorated with lace. **Below** A red and white two-piece, worn in Washington in 1985.

Bruce Oldfield, Diana's adviser and friend, as well as the creator of some truly stunning and imaginative outfits for her, was party to Diana's fashion development almost from the start. So were Caroline Charles and Jasper Conran.

Oldfield's most spectacular design was the shimmering silver lamé evening gown with built-up shoulders (see page 429) that Diana wore in Melbourne in 1985. Drama and adventure in his use of colours and materials was typical of Oldfield. As early as December 1981, Diana wore his rich blue velvet, full-skirted suit, with a pale pink crêpe-de-chine blouse, for her first solo engagement, switching on the Regent Street lights, in the heart of London's West End.

Bruce Oldfield was a Barnardo's boy, arriving at the children's home in 1951, the year after his birth in London. He was fostered by the dressmaker and tailor Violet Masters, and her line of work appears to have rubbed off on him. After school in Yorkshire, Oldfield began studying to be a teacher, but in 1971 he switched to a fashion and textile course. The following year, he moved on to the prestigious St. Martin's School of Art in London and soon began to attract attention in the fashion world. He was noticed by executives at the New York store Henri Bendell, and they invited him to the United States. There, Oldfield gave his first solo fashion show in the splendid setting of the New York Plaza.

Dramatic evening wear

The young designer set up his own company in London in 1975 and was soon in demand. He specialized in striking, glamorous evening gowns that only a rich, international clientele could afford.

Oldfield almost always managed to provide some striking feature to give his designs an extra impact. The shimmering material of the famous silver lamé gown parted to create a wide triangle, which

> *"She was aware that even in some far-flung part of the world she was representing Britain and couldn't be just a clothes-horse."*
> BRUCE OLDFIELD, ON DIANA

revealed Diana's back from the foldover shoulder-line right down to her waist. The electric blue crêpe-de-chine gown, one of Oldfield's firsts for the Princess, in 1982, satisfied her love of frills in an unusual way: there was a deep frill running diagonally along the top of the one-shouldered style.

The satin suit and camisole top Diana chose for a rock concert in Melbourne, in 1985, was smoother and simpler. But the Oldfield touch was still there in the innovative colour contrast: the suit was a rich mauve, the top a brilliant crimson pink.

Caroline Charles

If Bruce Oldfield's evening wear did most to establish the fairytale image of a beautiful princess by night, Caroline Charles and Jasper Conran helped establish her as a sweet but stylish figure by day. Caroline Charles' speciality was turning lavish

All designs on these two pages are by Bruce Oldfield **(inset below)**.

1 A frothy evening gown in turquoise blue, shot through with a shimmering silver thread that is echoed by the wide belt and matching handbag. Diana wore it in Sydney, Australia, in 1983 on her first foreign tour.

2 An example of a strong daywear design by Oldfield. Diana wore this black and white creation in Rome on the Italian tour of 1985. The wrap-over top, with extended black lapels, fastens at the hip.

3 Just the sort of slinky, dramatic evening dress that would make any woman feel like a million dollars. It is made of spangled silk chiffon. Diana wore it in London to a première of the film *When Harry Met Sally*.

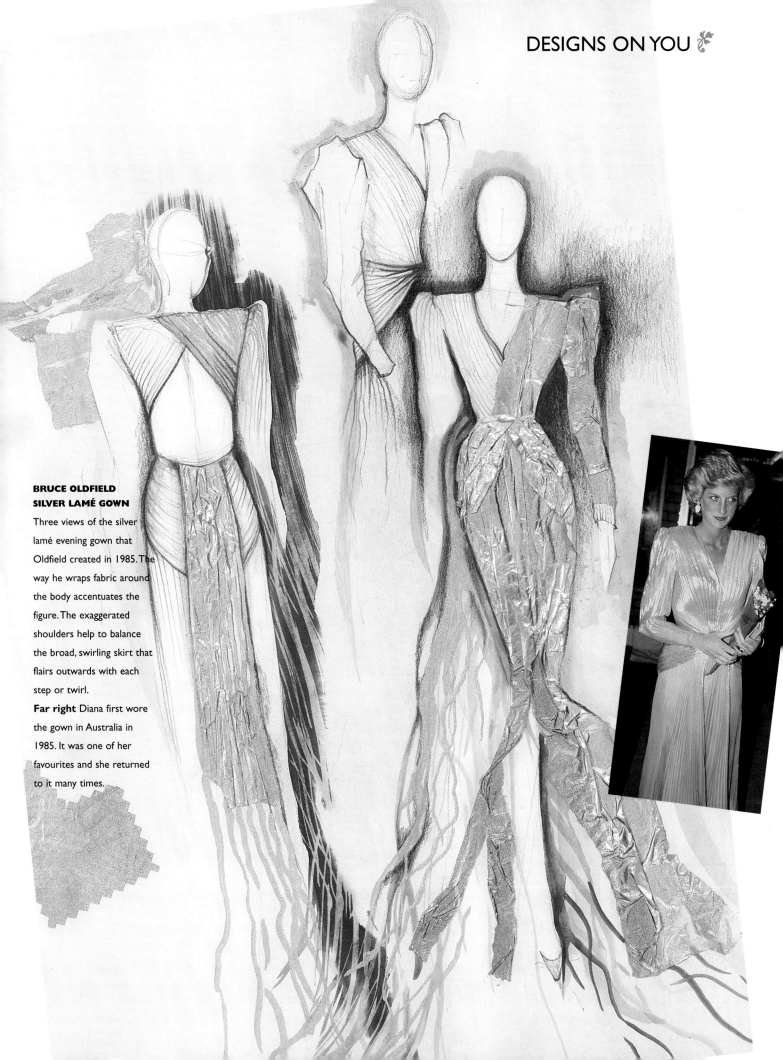

BRUCE OLDFIELD SILVER LAMÉ GOWN

Three views of the silver lamé evening gown that Oldfield created in 1985. The way he wraps fabric around the body accentuates the figure. The exaggerated shoulders help to balance the broad, swirling skirt that flairs outwards with each step or twirl.

Far right Diana first wore the gown in Australia in 1985. It was one of her favourites and she returned to it many times.

1 Diana wore this green velvet suit and hat at the Guards Chapel in November 1983. The jacket is fastened with a line of small buttons and secured with a cummerbund.
2 Diana at St. David's in Wales in 1981, wearing a beige coat with ruched shoulders and a toning hat with a plume.

CAROLINE CHARLES BLUE TWO-PIECE

All designs on this page are by Caroline Charles (inset above). The two-piece suit above has a mid calf-length skirt and is decorated with a leaf pattern. The jacket has puffed sleeves, is nipped at the waist and flares over the hips. As a final touch there is a smart blue hat with a cockade in front.

materials, patterns and prints into wearable clothes. Born in 1942 in Cairo, Egypt, Caroline Charles became an apprentice to Michael Sherard when she was 18 and had just left the Swindon School of Art. In 1961, she went to work for Mary Quant, one of the most prominent fashion gurus of 'Swinging Sixties' London, then set up on her own in 1963.

For Diana's first Braemar Games, in September 1981, Charles created a delightful long-sleeved tartan dress with tiny black buttons down the front. It was made in a muted, autumnal red and ochre plaid. From there, Diana went on to the beige tweed coat with long revers and ruched shoulders in which she, unfortunately, got drenched by rain, but still looked smart, in Wales at the end of October 1981. When the Braemar Games came

round again in September 1982, Caroline Charles produced another tartan dress, this time in black and brown. Three months later, for the visit to University College Hospital in London, Diana chose a deep blue Caroline Charles dress with very full skirt, three-quarter sleeves and cummerbund in her favourite material, velvet.

Jasper Conran

Jasper Conran, is the whizz-kid designer son of Sir Terence Conran, interior designer/businessman and authoress Shirley Conran. Jasper was dressing Diana even before she married. In March 1981, at Tetbury, she wore a Conran suit in red with white polka dots on the jacket, and a plain red skirt. The jacket, which had long revers, divided at the front

Two designs by Jasper Conran **(inset above)**.
1 A white two-piece worn in Cornwall, in March 1983, with a veiled hat.
2 Diana at Tetbury in March 1981, in a blouse, red polka dot jacket and red skirt.

in a deep V, giving a pleasing view of the buttons on the blouse. The outfit was youthful and pretty and it was fun, which was typical of Conran designs.

Jasper Conran was only 16 in 1975, when he won a place at Pearson's, the world-famous design

> "*When the Princess of Wales came to my show-room, she knew that by going around and saying 'Hello' she could brighten someone's day.*"
> JASPER CONRAN, ON DIANA

school in New York. After finishing there in 1977, he was snapped up by the house of Fiorucci and then moved on to Wallis. In 1978, still only 19, he designed a collection of his own and put on his first fashion show. With his unusual, even quirky fashion, he won instant approval from the young.

Diana wore another suit of his on a visit to the Royal College of Music, London, in 1983. The frill-necked blouse was still there – Diana did not shed this favourite fashion for some time – but the suit was already leading her along a less fussy path. Made in a vibrant pink, it featured a generous swinging full skirt and a double-breasted jacket with a high mandarin collar and turned-back cuffs. The frill-necked blouse tended to crowd the suit collar, but the general effect was pretty and elegant.

Sophisticated tastes

In the same year, 1983, Jasper Conran got Diana into a more grown-up pillbox red suit, which she wore on a visit to Brixton, London, in October. The jacket had long revers and was three-quarter length, and the skirt was straight. When the suit appeared in Florence, Italy, on the tour of 1985, Diana did the jacket justice by wearing a high-necked red and white polka dot blouse beneath it.

The young Princess of Wales, still dressing girlishly at 20, had been like a canvas waiting to be painted with style, colour and a fashion trademark that was distinctly hers and hers alone. Oldfield, Charles and Conran were foremost among the artists who saw to it that the finished picture was as pretty as could be.

Designing for Diana brings fame

Diana was a goldmine of publicity for the designers whose clothes she wore. She ensured that their names became widely known, even when only a few women were able to afford their clothes.

This fashion report, in the Daily Mirror of 5 February 1991, was typical of those in which Diana featured in newspapers and magazines over the years. No other royal ever had complete articles devoted, on a regular basis, to their fashions. Diana was, in fact, the ultimate fashion model, and she received more coverage than all the leading supermodels of the day.

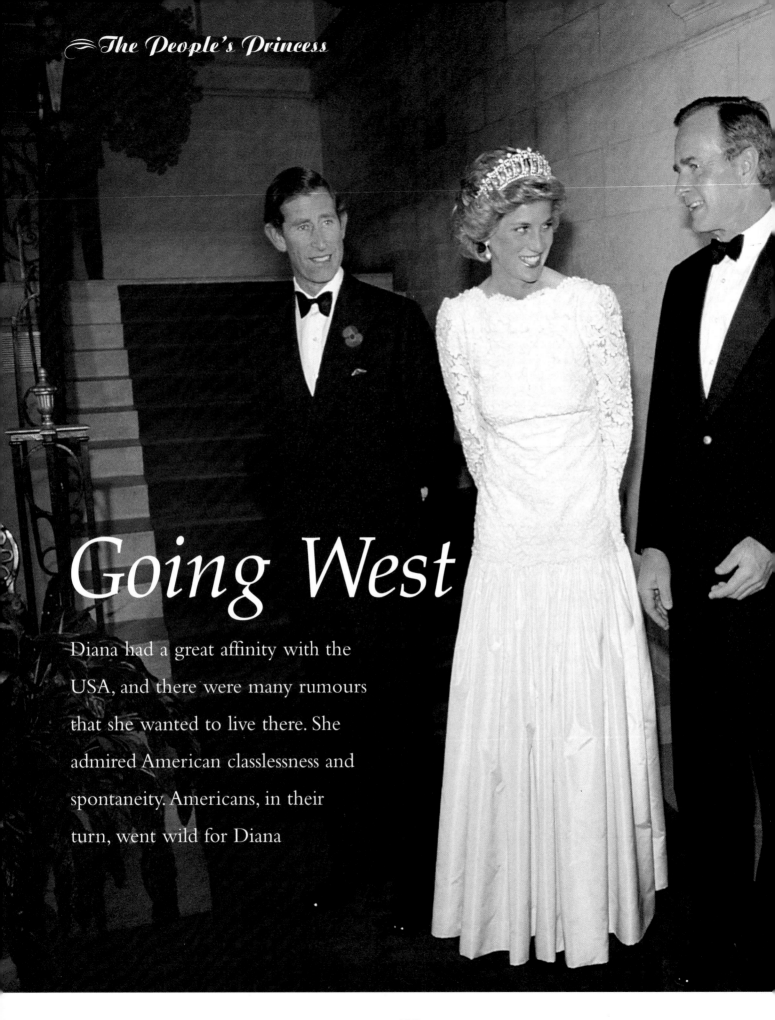

Going West

Diana had a great affinity with the
USA, and there were many rumours
that she wanted to live there. She
admired American classlessness and
spontaneity. Americans, in their
turn, went wild for Diana

Left On a 1985 visit to Washington DC, Charles and Diana pose for a picture with Vice President George Bush and his wife Barbara.
Above Chaperoned by the police, Diana meets admirers in New York.
Below Shaking hands in Chicago in 1996.

Diana was a multi-faceted princess. She seemed to fit in anywhere and everywhere, whether it was in the Third World of poverty and deprivation, the sophisticated culture of the European Old World or the go-getting pizzazz of the New World.

To the Americans, it appears, Diana was an ideal: beautiful, chic, rich, approachable, warm, titled in her own right but classless and, to cap all that, royal. For a people who had shed their English king, George III, with such vigour in the War of Independence (1776-1783), Americans had an unusual fascination with royalty. But they admired achievers, and the story of Diana, the 'ordinary' girl who was marrying the world's most eligible prince and acquiring a future as a queen, was the stuff of the American Dream.

One of their own

Diana, of course, was not at all ordinary, as her aristocratic lineage attested. However, the fact that she never stood on her royal dignity, was never haughty or deliberately grand, went a long way towards explaining her close and lasting rapport with Americans. Many of them had no time for airs and graces. Neither had Diana. She also had family links with the United States,

which tempted her many American admirers to claim her as one of their own.

Diana's American connection came about through her mother's great grandmother, Frances Work. The daughter of a Manhattan millionaire, Fanny, as she was known, crossed the Atlantic in 1880 and married James Boothby Burke Roche, the future 3rd Baron Fermoy. Fanny's father, Frank Work, had an intense dislike of foreigners, but, after her marriage ended in 1891, he re-embraced her and her three children when they returned to New York. This did not prevent Fanny marrying another European, a Hungarian racehorse trainer called Aurel Batoryi in 1905, whom she divorced in 1909.

Diana's American cousins

Fanny's first husband died in 1920. Their son Maurice succeeded him as 4th Baron Fermoy and settled in England, at Dersingham, Norfolk. In 1931 he married pianist Ruth Gill and went to live in Park House on the Sandringham estate at the invitation of King George V. Their daughter, Diana's mother Frances, was born there in 1936.

Maurice Fermoy's sister Cynthia remained in the USA and, through her, Diana acquired several distant American cousins. In 1984, three years after Diana became Princess of Wales, the Genealogical Publishing Company of Baltimore brought out a book entitled *American Ancestors and Cousins of the Princess of Wales*. The authors, Gary Boyd Robert and W.A. Reitweisner, delved back into the Work family line to discover distant relationships between

Above left The US President's wife, Nancy Reagan, took Diana to a drug rehabilitation centre in Springfield, Virginia, during Diana's visit in 1985.
Above The Prince and Princess of Wales standing to attention at Arlington National Cemetery, Washington DC, on Remembrance Day.

Left Closely attended by plain-clothes agents, Diana, on a February 1989 solo visit to New York, is taken to the Henry Street Settlement Center, which provides temporary accommodation for the city's homeless. **Below** Diana met and talked to some of the children and their parents, who were housed in the Henry Street shelter.

☙ Protocol ❧

NO TITLES FOR AMERICANS

*Members of the British Royal Family have long been personally popular with Americans, but this does not mean that, officially, the United States approves of monarchy or aristocracy. In fact, Article One, Section Nine of the US Constitution states that '…no title of nobility shall be granted by the United States and no government official can accept any gift or position from any king, prince or foreign state without permission from Congress'. This antipathy arose out of the War of Independence, when the American colonies won their freedom from Britain. In this conflict, King George III, **right**, and the aristocratic, hardline British prime minister Lord North were portrayed as the principal villains.*

Diana and George Washington, first president of the United States, and two more presidents, Calvin Coolidge and Franklin Delano Roosevelt.

By the time this book appeared, Americans were eagerly anticipating a visit from the Princess. For

> **"You are a wonderful caring person and we are lucky to have you here."**
>
> SAMUEL SKINNER, US TRANSPORT SECRETARY, TO DIANA

Charles and Diana's overseas tours, countries of the Commonwealth had first pick, since the Queen, as Head of the Commonwealth, was their monarch, too. The Americans' turn did not come until 1985, when the USA became the second foreign country, after Italy, to welcome Diana.

It was a relatively short tour, lasting four days in November. Charles and Diana flew in to

Above In October 1990 at Grandma's House, a home for abused and HIV-positive children in Washington DC, Diana was greeted by the Terrific Peers, a network of volunteer helpers. They presented her with a set of their all-black strip.

Left Diana cut the ribbon to formally open the home.

Washington, to be greeted by President Ronald Reagan and his wife, the First Lady, Nancy. Both were former film stars, which greatly pleased Diana, who was somewhat star-struck and enjoyed meeting show-business personalities.

At the presidential banquet given for the couple on 9 November, Diana had wanted to meet the film

> "*New York is marvellous, quite dramatic.*"
> DIANA, ON THE BIG APPLE

star Robert Redford and had asked that he be invited. Redford, however, was filming in New York and could not be there, but he made amends by sending two bottles of champagne to Charles and three dozen red roses to Diana. Both Charles and Diana were big fans of the singer Diana Ross, but she, too, was absent filming and preparing for her wedding.

The banquet was, nevertheless, a star-studded affair. The ballet dancer Mikhail Baryshnikov was there, and so were actors Tom Selleck, Clint

Above Diana found time in February 1989 for some shopping. She is seen here at Dawson's International Reception, a knitwear company specializing in cashmere. **Above right** Dressed for an evening event in New York in February 1989, Diana looks every inch the glamorous princess as she holds a bouquet that has just been presented to her.

Eastwood and John Travolta, and singer Neil Diamond. The last four each danced with Diana, and the few minutes Travolta spent on the dance floor at the White House did wonders for his faltering film career. Afterwards, he confessed that, as a dance partner, Diana was not only top class, but also 'made me feel I was somebody again'.

Rather charmingly, Diana reacted like an excited young fan, utterly thrilled at the chance of meeting her heroes. She gave Baryshnikov her autograph when he asked for it and told him: 'I've got yours, you know. It was at Covent Garden years ago. I was one of the girls who were waiting for you for hours and hours after the performance.'

With a cast of this calibre, the banquet was one of the great social events of the year. Charles and

Diana were entertained by Neil Diamond, the opera star Leontyne Price and by Nancy Reagan. Everyone who was anyone wanted to meet the Princess. Charles and Diana dined with Vice President George Bush and his wife Barbara and lunched with the billionaire philanthropist and connoisseur of art Paul Mellon before leaving for Palm Beach, Florida, the playground of American high-society. Among the Florida set was the glamorous *Dynasty* star Joan Collins, newly married to her fourth husband, who came to a banquet given by Dr. Armand Hammer, the entrepreneur, art expert and philanthropist. Film stars Gregory Peck, Bob Hope and Cary Grant were also there.

Star-studded tour

Although Diana did not forget her charity interests, and visited a drug rehabilitation centre with Nancy Reagan, her first American tour was the sort of high-powered event, studded with big names and awash with displays of wealth, that only Americans could stage. They pulled out all the stops and Diana's effect was such that famous stars seemed as

excited to meet her as she was to meet them. However, the riches so blatantly flaunted during the tour did not go down well in Britain.

There was criticism that the whole business had been a 'rent-a-royal' jaunt, which debased the monarchy. In February 1989, when Diana returned to the States, this time on her own, her schedule showed that the charges had hit home. There was more substance than glitter this time, with tours of New York's Lower East Side, where homelessness and alcoholism were rife.

Visiting the homeless

There, in typically spontaneous style, the Princess tied a little boy's shoelace after spotting that it was undone. Here, too, she saw the other, sombre side of the American Dream, as she talked to the boy's homeless mother, who was at a settlement centre with her three children. It was on this trip, too, that Diana spent over an hour at Harlem Hospital with seven children who were dying of AIDS.

There was also a cultural side to her visit – attending a production of Verdi's *Falstaff* by the Welsh National Opera, at the Brooklyn Academy of Music, and a reception at the British Consul General's for the friends of the American Foundation for the Royal Academy of Music.

Even so, the emphasis was strongly on Diana the royal celebrity and all the glitz and glamour that

Above During a visit to the States in 1996 Diana visited Northwestern University in Chicago. She's seen here in the college grounds with principal, Henry Bienen.

Wowing the American people

Diana's arrival in the USA with Prince Charles was featured as the great event of 1985. The excitement that the Princess generated among Americans was reflected in effusive newspaper coverage shortly afterwards. The Sunday Express reported every aspect of Diana's impact – her own star status among the stars at the White House, her philanthropic work and her encounter with disabled children. To sum up her impact, the paper's cartoonist superimposed her face on the Statue of Liberty, one of the most revered of American symbols.

SUNDAY EXPRESS

NOW THE U.S. FALLS TO DI

Will you watch the sky for the comet tonight?

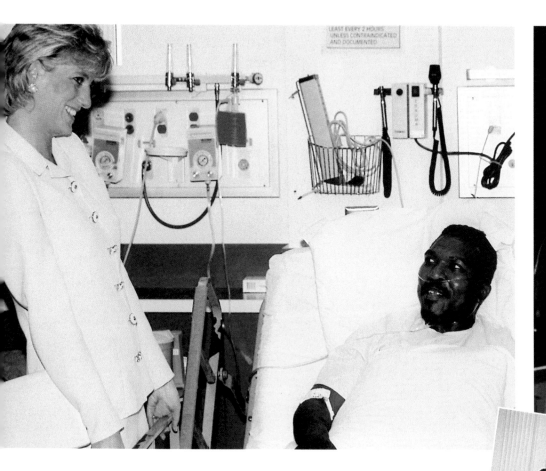

went with her. Thousands of New Yorkers crammed the wet, windswept streets for a glimpse of her. The lucky ones were treated to a handshake and few cared that *Newsday* groused that New York workers should have had better things to do.

Newsday was not alone. There was a virtual contest between pundits who disliked all the fuss a

> ## "It's an egalitarian society. They accept you for what you are, not who you are."
> ### *DIANA, ON AMERICA*

fiercely republican country was making over a member of the Royal Family, and the gushing enthusiasts who reached for every over-the-top adjective to describe the 'wonderful', 'elegant', 'enchanting', 'amazing', 'dazzling' Princess Di. 'Dia-mania' was definitely in the air and, before the Princess had arrived, some newspapers were warning New Yorkers not to fall for it. One political columnist protested against the 'pro-monarchist

yearnings' of Americans who had obviously forgotten that their country was free only because their ancestors had rebelled against the British. A more personal barb came from the socialist Pete Hamill of the *New York Post*, who called Diana 'the most famous welfare mother in the world, a permanent recipient of the British dole'. Hamill conceded that Diana seemed 'a decent person', but added: 'She doesn't work, has no known talents and derives her celebrity from the man she married.' There were also pro-IRA, anti-Diana demonstrations and much chat-show gossip about the rumours surrounding the Waleses' marriage.

Well protected

Though these sour voices were drowned out by a huge tide of excitement and admiration for Diana, the New York Police Department was unwilling to take any risks and, to protect their royal visitor, drafted in 400 extra police officers armed with

Above left Diana at Cook County Hospital during her trip to Chicago in 1996. **Top** In January 1995 Princess Diana is pictured at the New York fashion awards. **Inset, above** At the Washington White House in 1996 Diana is seen alongside *Washington Post* proprietor Kathleen Graham, the President's wife, Hillary Clinton, fashion designer Ralph Lauren and *Vogue's* Anna Wintour.

Above In New York in December 1995, Diana, alongside former Secretary of State Henry Kissinger, says hello to a young admirer. She was the guest of honour at the Humanitarian of the Year awards, held at the Hilton Hotel. At the right of the picture is General Colin Powell, a member of the Administration.

machine-guns and wearing bullet-proof vests and flak jackets. Diana was chauffeured in a bullet-proof Cadillac, which moved her through the streets in a 12-car motorcade with police motorcycles driving both in front and behind her.

Despite the more serious nature of the 1989 visit, showbiz gloss and socialite rivalry could not be entirely avoided. *Falstaff* in Brooklyn was attended by 800 people who had fought to pay £500 a seat to sit in the same theatre as Diana and afterwards attend a high-society banquet at the Wintergarden. *Superman* star Christopher Reeve was there, as were the billionaire publisher Malcolm Forbes, the subsequently disgraced Donald Trump and members of the wealthy Astor and Rockefeller families.

Expensive meetings

When Diana returned for a short, 22-hour visit to the USA in October 1990, the price of proximity to her had rocketed. At the fund-raising function in Washington DC that she attended, tickets were priced at £1325 for a distant view of the Princess and £1850 for a face-to-face meeting. The event raised £418,271 for the Washington Ballet, London

City Ballet and a Washington home for abused and HIV-positive children, called Grandma's House, but that was less than was anticipated. Diana was in the USA again in 1992, 1994, 1995 and 1996. She went five times within one year, 1994-5, and rumour had it that she was house-hunting in the Big Apple.

> **"She's stunning. The people of New York are charmed by her."**
> BIANCA JAGGER, ON DIANA

When she appeared at the Lincoln Center in 1995, a man in the audience shouted: 'Move to New York!', but the rumours never came to anything.

Even so, the magnetic draw Diana exerted on Americans remained. They treated her as a cross between a social icon, a fairytale princess, a star of the first magnitude, a lady of mercy and a fantasy figure who radiated magic. The British press took to wondering if Diana was having 'a love affair' with America in general, and New York in particular. Whether she was or not, in their own brash fashion, the Americans were surely in love with her.

FURTHER REVELATIONS

The year 1992 – the Queen's annus horribilis *– saw appalling shocks for the Royal Family. But Charles and Diana's separation on 9 December was by no means the last of the royal upheavals. Only five weeks later, 1993 delivered another major scandal: Camillagate*

The day her separation from Charles was announced in Parliament, the Princess was in Tyne and Wear, northeast England. It was a routine day of royal engagements – until, that is, Diana heard the news on the radio. 'It was just very sad,' she said later, 'really sad.' Sadness, though, was mixed with relief that she and Charles had at last made up their minds what to do with a marriage that both of them had found intolerable. But, for the moment, grief at their failure intervened as Diana contemplated an unknown future outside, yet still attached to, the Royal Family.

Diana was not the first Princess of Wales to separate from her husband: that sombre honour went

CHRONICLE

to Caroline of Brunswick, who parted from Prince George, later to become King George IV, in 1796, barely a year after their marriage. But Caroline had never been the royal celebrity Diana was. Royals were less actively involved in public life in her day, and Caroline never had Diana's obligations, her world-wide fame and, above all, her exposure to the all-probing eye of an intrusive media. These were the factors that would ultimately affect Diana's plans for the rest of her life. First, though, the dismal practicalities had to be addressed.

ESTABLISHING SEPARATE HOMES

After some initial resistance, Charles had agreed to move out of the family home at Apartments 8 and 9, Kensington Palace. His paintings and prints, his desk, his books, his clothes and uniforms were all transferred to his new quarters at St. James' Palace. While this was going on, Diana was on holiday with William and Harry. When she returned, a reminder of Charles' presence was the silver model of HMS *Bronington*, the coastal minehunter he had commanded in his Royal Navy days. Though that remained in a downstairs waiting room, Diana ordered the removal of the big mahogany bed Charles had brought over from Buckingham Palace for her in 1982. The bedroom was repainted. The apartment door locks were changed.

Diana, in her turn, was being expunged from Highgrove House. Her clothes and cosmetics, her photographs, her menagerie of stuffed and pottery

> ## "He does not want to go down in history as Charles the Divorced."
> ### AN ADVISOR, ON CHARLES AND DIVORCE

animals, her paintings and prints, all went to Kensington Palace. Charles then brought in a local designer and had Highgrove redecorated. Unwanted items were piled on a big bonfire and burned. They included some of the gifts Charles and Diana had received while they were married.

The removals were conducted like a secret mission. Charles' wardrobe, for instance, was taken to St. James' Palace by night, and when the New Year of 1993 dawned, the Prince and Princess of Wales

IN CONTEXT
1993
CULT HQ TURNS INTO INFERNO

• End of the 51-day siege, **right**, of the Branch Davidian religious cult at Waco, Texas; over 80 die

• Czechoslovakia is split into the Czech Republic and Slovakia in a friendly, 'velvet' divorce

• Death of Cyril Northcote Parkinson, historian and proponent of 'Parkinson's Law'

• Five people are killed in a bomb blast at the World Trade Centre, New York

• Eight Picasso and Braque paintings, worth £40 million, are stolen from an art gallery in Stockholm, Sweden

were ready to step out into their new, separate lives. Diana had briefly toyed with the idea of leaving Kensington and finding a home in the country. That had the appeal of a fresh start, since the Palace, she told friends, felt like 'a prison'. Partly this was due to the security, partly to unhappy memories.

An alternative, offered by her brother Earl Spencer, was a house on the family's estate, Althorp. That fell through when the Earl backed off because of the extra police, security cameras and other surveillance Diana's presence would require. Because the expense of a new home would expose her to charges of extravagance, Diana decided to stay on at

Opening page Diana enjoyed the sunshine while holidaying on the Isle of St. Kitts with William and Harry. At the same time, Charles was having his possessions moved to St. James' Palace.

Opposite page The royal show continued as normal during 1993 despite the personal ructions. In March, Diana visited Nepal.

Right The 'Camillagate' scandal as it broke in the press. Rumours of what the taped call between Charles and Camilla, **top**, contained were substantiated by a printed transcript.

Kensington Palace. There had, naturally, been enormous interest in Charles and Diana's first public engagements in their new solo roles. After the separation in December, both of them performed as usual, the smiling fronts in evidence as they went about their royal duties. However, before business could resume in 1993, yet another earthquake burst through the crust of royal normality and put Charles back on the rack of public disapproval.

Two weeks into the new year, the papers were full of details of a tape, purporting to be a telephone conversation between Charles and Camilla Parker-Bowles, supposedly recorded by the secret services on 18 December 1989. The six minutes of taped material included, together with some social chit-chat and a few jokey exchanges, sexually explicit references to knickers, tampons and foreplay.

THE SCANDAL BREAKS

On 13 January 1993 Britain woke up to what might be the most serious royal scandal of recent times, when reports about the 'Camillagate' tape appeared on virtually every front page. In the Church of England, the military and in Parliament, the reaction went beyond shock, and questions were asked about Charles' fitness as a future king. A Cabinet minister remarked that Charles should break off with Camilla 'and start off with a clean slate'. According to Andrew Morton's *Diana: Her New Life* Army officers discussed replacing the Prince as colonel-in-chief of six regiments.

Neither Charles nor Camilla denied, or indeed affirmed, that the Camillagate tape, 1574 words long, was genuine. The tape did not contain the

---

> **"I think that tape was really shattering in the sense that somebody got hold of it."**
>
> DR SIDNEY CROWN, PSYCHIATRIST,
> CONSULTANT TO THE BOOK
> DIANA ON THE EDGE

---

whole of the conversation – the recorder had been switched on when it was already in progress – but transcripts were soon available for anyone to read. Diana, like everyone else, read the transcript and, to

IN THE NEWS

Andrew Parker-Bowles speaks out

Brigadier Andrew Parker-Bowles, Camilla's husband, was treated by the press as a fairly minor player in the 'triangle' which included Prince Charles. On 17 January 1993, however, he took centre stage for this dramatic headline in which he denied rumours that he was about to divorce his wife. This was in the aftermath of the Camillagate tape. It proved, however, to be a sad case of 'famous last words'. Andrew and Camilla Parker-Bowles divorced two years later.

NEWS OF THE WORLD
BRITAIN'S MOST POPULAR NEWSPAPER
Royal exclusive
Charles calls in the Bug Busters
MY CAMILLA STAYS WITH ME!
Says her husband
FREE FOOTBALL TICKETS FOR YOUR KIDS ONLY IN

her, friends reported, it appeared that all her years of suspicion about Camilla and Charles were confirmed. What shocked Diana most, though, were the names of friends and acquaintances who, according to the tape, had obscured the trail of the love affair, made up cover stories, connived at meetings in 'safe'

> **"I can't find anyone inside the Palace with a good word to say for her."**
> VISITOR TO BUCKINGHAM PALACE, ON DIANA

houses and covered up for Charles and the woman Camillagate now revealed to be his mistress.

If Camillagate did not elicit quite the same frenzied public response as previous revelations, the reason, it was suggested, was that people now felt a certain amount of 'scandal fatigue'. Diana retained her popularity and seemed to be assured of popular sympathy as a wronged, betrayed wife, but this was not a comfort for long. The royal establishment had different ideas. Their prime concern was the preservation of the monarchy. Whatever Charles had said or done, he was the heir to the throne. That, maintaining the royal status quo, and retrieving Charles' good name, were all that mattered to the Palace.

MAKING LIFE DIFFICULT

It soon became clear that, in this context, Diana was expendable. Diana was carpeted by the Press Complaints Commission for conniving with the media to get her side of the story into print during the months before the separation. Charles' friends, of course, had done exactly the same thing and two tabloid newspapers vouched for their involvement. Yet it was Diana who suffered the consequences – a public dressing down.

In addition, reports appeared in print labelling Diana as an 'unstable' woman. Briefings from the Queen's private secretary, Sir Robert Fellowes, Diana's brother-in-law, were used in newspaper articles and in one of them, a courtier accused Diana of being 'headstrong' and warned that she might become 'bitter and twisted' unless carefully handled. An enraged Diana complained to Sir Robert at this clear implication that she was no

Opposite page Diana in July 1993 at the funeral of her grandmother, Ruth, Lady Fermoy. The service was also attended by Charles and the Queen Mother.
Above Diana talked to Omah Hunter, aged 8, on a visit to Great Ormond Street Hospital in May 1993.

Above On her one-day trip to Luxembourg in September, Diana had a friendly chat with this Down's Syndrome boy.
Right In her capacity as patron of the Chicken Shed Theatre Company, Diana attended a charity performance at the Equinox Playhouse, Leicester Square, London, on 1 November and was the guest of honour at a fund-raising dinner.

Above On 6 July, on a visit to the Broadwater Primary School in London, Diana was entertained by the children. Later she opened a new Early Years Unit. **Left** At the première of *Jurassic Park*, Diana met the film's director, Steven Spielberg. **Right** Diana visited Enniskillen in Northern Ireland in November 1993.

❧ Protocol ❧

WINDSOR CASTLE

Damage caused by the fire at Windsor Castle, which broke out on 20 November 1992, was the penultimate blow in the annus horribilis and took five years to restore. Windsor Castle, the largest and most prestigious castle in England and one of the Queen's homes, stands on the edge of Windsor Great Park in Berkshire, close to the one-time hunting grounds of former kings. The original was built by William the Conqueror. King Henry II replaced his wooden structure with stone in 1165-1176, in the first of many alterations over the centuries. The grounds contain the Royal Family mausoleum at Frogmore and St. George's Chapel, where the royals regularly worship.

better than an undisciplined child, but the damage had already been done.

As if this was not discomfiting enough, Diana found, too, that her activities were being curtailed. When she proposed to visit British troops and refugees in war-torn Bosnia, on behalf of the Red Cross, of which she was patron, Diana was told that, since Charles had similar plans, she could not go. In September 1993, Diana was informed that

> "*I will make mistakes, but that won't stop me from doing what I think is right.*"
> DIANA, AFTER HER SEPARATION

'security reasons' barred her from meeting the Irish president Mary Robinson. It was Charles who went to Eire to meet the charismatic head of state.

Then, when Diana suggested to Prime Minister John Major that she be appointed a 'roving ambassador' he, duty-bound, informed Buckingham Palace, and was told that this was a role for the Prince, not the Princess of Wales. Less directly, Diana discovered that invitations she would have formerly received mysteriously failed to materialize. Messages went undelivered, letters were 'lost'. In this atmosphere, it was not surprising that Diana believed there was a Palace conspiracy.

In March, at her own request, she went to Nepal, though that was somewhat spoiled by new Squidgy tape transcripts published in Australia, which at last revealed the fear she had voiced of becoming pregnant. In April, Diana attended a conference on eating disorders. In May she even attended a service with Charles in Liverpool.

TAKING TIME OUT

But what Diana wanted most was time and space to rebuild her private life. On 3 December she announced she was withdrawing from public life (see The Private Princess). The shock and dismay were intense. It was obvious that if Diana left the stage, there was no one else to fill her place. That seemed true enough but, in saying farewell, Diana gave her admirers a gleam of hope. She was disappearing now, but, she pledged, she would be back.

The Private Princess
Withdrawing from public life

Diana, who was not the most fluent or confident of public speakers, prepared herself carefully for her 'retirement' speech of 3 December 1993. She was afraid, at first, that the emotion of the moment would overcome her, but, as she told the novelist and politician Lord Archer, she was determined there would be no tears.

At 10.30am on 3 December, Archer sat with the Princess in her drawing room at Kensington Palace. The day before, he had been called to 10 Downing Street. There he was told that the Princess was altering her speech to

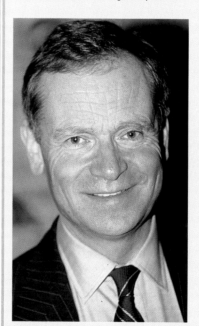

Above Looking tense but determined, Diana makes her withdrawal speech before a battery of pressmen. **Left** Jeffrey Archer, who cast an eye over her script.

include a statement about her future – and was asked to read over, but not alter, the speech.

Already agreed by the Queen and the Prime Minister, it was three pages long. There had been a lot of rewriting. Archer at first doubted that the Princess

could cope with such a momentous address, but he was wrong. As the luncheon progressed, Diana was certainly nervous. In fact, her hands were shaking. But when the crunch came, she walked to the podium, surveyed her audience and began to speak without hesitation. Her voice was not always steady in the five minutes the speech lasted, but, as she had wanted, it was done with calm and dignity.

A Wealth In Store

The cost of Diana's wardrobe provoked much speculation during her years as a member of the Royal Family. But to be fit for a princess, it had to be extensive, and therefore expensive

O n her marriage, Diana took on fashion as well as charity, social and other obligations. She was expected to be a showcase for British designers. Youthful, tall, slim and beautiful, Diana was a gift to young innovative designers who had waited years for their royal chance. Once she was there, they made the most of her.

Costly talent

Their attentions, which eventually made Diana a fashion icon, did not, however, come cheap. And that was not surprising, considering the brilliant talent that went into clothing the Princess. All the same, Diana knew that she could not afford to be seen spending money too freely on clothes. It was bad enough that the press dubbed her a 'shopaholic', a term she hated, and that there were stories of her running amok in Knightsbridge with the Duchy of Cornwall credit card.

But if 'Spend! Spend! Spend!' was not to be her motto, Diana had to find other ways of fulfilling her fashion obligations. This, possibly, is the reason why she rarely went in for 'high-fashion outfits'. Something smart, colourful, versatile and classic,

Main picture In the Shetlands in a brown check two-piece suit with a toning hat. **Far left** In Hatton Garden, London, in May 1997 in a pale blue Chanel two-piece, holding a bouquet of the Princess of Wales rose created for her.

**BELLVILLE SASSOON
DAY DRESS**

A simple blue day dress with a strong floral pattern. The dress has a rounded neck, puffed shoulders, short sleeves, a ruched waist and a tapering skirt. An ideal garment for any location on a warm day, Diana wore it (**right**) on a trip to Brazil in 1991. On that occasion she matched it with a blue handbag and blue shoes.

rather than off-beat, was a much more practical proposition. Clothes like this could be dressed up, dressed down, matched with different accessories and shoes, and still come up looking good.

One example was a pretty crimson polka dot Donald Campbell dress with tie neck, long sleeves

> ## "Diana couldn't afford to do it on the cheap."
> FIONA SINCLAIR, ROYAL CORRESPONDENT

and built-up shoulders; Diana wore it in Perth during the 1983 tour of Australia, along with a cream handbag and shoes and a crimson hat. She wore it again with crimson shoes but no hat to visit the Vatican on the 1985 tour of Italy. Even evening dresses, which were more individual and difficult to vary, were worn several times. For instance, David and Elizabeth Emanuel's shoulderless white chiffon dress adorned with gold decoration doubled nicely

for a banquet in London in 1986, with tiara, and without one at a film première in 1987.

There was, however, a limit to this re-use, and Diana learned an awkward lesson on her tour of Spain in 1987. She wore one old outfit after another, disappointing the Spanish fashion pundits and society women, who hoped to see something new.

The need to spend

In this situation, Diana had to keep spending on top-quality outfits commensurate with her royal status and her stylish reputation. Sometimes she got away with off-the-peg clothes which, though not cheap, circumvented the sky-high prices attached to one-off designs. But it was no secret that Diana's expenditure on her wardrobe was considerable.

In 1990, at the request of Andrew Morton, *Royalty* magazine assessed Diana's expenditure on her working wardrobe at £833,750 in the ten years since her engagement in 1981. Another £200,000 went on her off-duty wardrobe. The greatest

1 A neat black two-piece with white piping, matching shoes and a black clutch bag, worn in Chicago in 1996.
2 A blue, yellow and pale pink two-piece, worn with pink accessories to Great Ormond Street in May 1993.
3 A turquoise two-piece suit with a navy blue trim, worn with navy blue accessories in April 1993.
4 A pink linen Catherine Walker two-piece worn in Egypt in May 1993.
5 A powder-blue Catherine Walker two-piece with pale blue trim, worn on a visit to Lincoln in 1992.

After her divorce Diana was seen carrying designer bags and liked Hermès, Versace and Chanel.

1 A Hermès cream leather shoulder bag worth around £1000.

2 A black leather Chanel bag with a gold chain and clasp, retailing at £300-500.

3 A two-tone stone and coffee-coloured clutch bag worth about £250.

expense was her evening gowns. She owned 95, all but four assessed at an average of £2000 each. The others cost twice as much. This may seem excessive, but Diana was moving in mega-rich circles and had to match up. In the company of billionaires and super-wealthy pop and film stars, a royal had to be a step or two ahead of the pack.

Other items were also pricey – jeans at £85 a time, for instance, or dry cleaning bills at £70 a gown. Even an outfit as modest as Diana's blue two-piece engagement suit had a £310 price tag.

Daywear prices

Diana's daywear was of much the same order. She had 178 suits, which cost an average of £1250 each, and 176 day dresses at £1000 each. Like the dresses, Diana's coats – 54 of them – also cost £1000 each, her 141 hats £200 apiece, her 71 blouses and shirts £250 each and her 29 skirts another £200 a time.

The skirt count was relatively low; so were Diana's 25 pairs of trousers and culottes at £250 each, her 28 sweaters at £100 each and 20 jackets at £150 each. However, these clothes rarely suited the formal dressing-up requirements of royal public life.

The figures shot up again, though, when it came to Diana's shoes. She owned no less than 350 pairs, which cost an average of £100 a pair and reflected, more than anything, her ability to wear virtually any

colour outfit. Diana was meticulous about colour cueing, and here, literally, she hardly ever put a foot wrong. Part of her standard kit on tour was an extra pair of shoes to give her feet a fresh start on a long, often hot day. Since she performed an average of nearly 143 engagements every year – 238 in the specially busy year of 1989 – keeping her feet happy was a must. To go with her shoes, Diana had 200 handbags, which cost around £125 a time.

Boots, though, made fewer public appearances. Diana's tour of Oslo, Norway, in February 1984, was

> **"I just couldn't win. They either accused me of spending too much on my clothes, or wearing the same outfit all the time."**
> *DIANA, ON CHARGES OF EXTRAVAGANCE*

one engagement where she wore them; another was the windblown visit to Hull in 1986 when Diana wore shiny black patent, knee-high boots. Generally speaking, though, boots lacked the elegance of shoes and were only suitable for outdoors. Even so, she had 12 pairs of boots at £150 each, including ski boots. Skiwear and sportswear together cost Diana a modest £1350 over the 1981-1990 period.

In the wrapping-up-warm stakes, furs hardly figured. She relied much more on wool suits, coats and

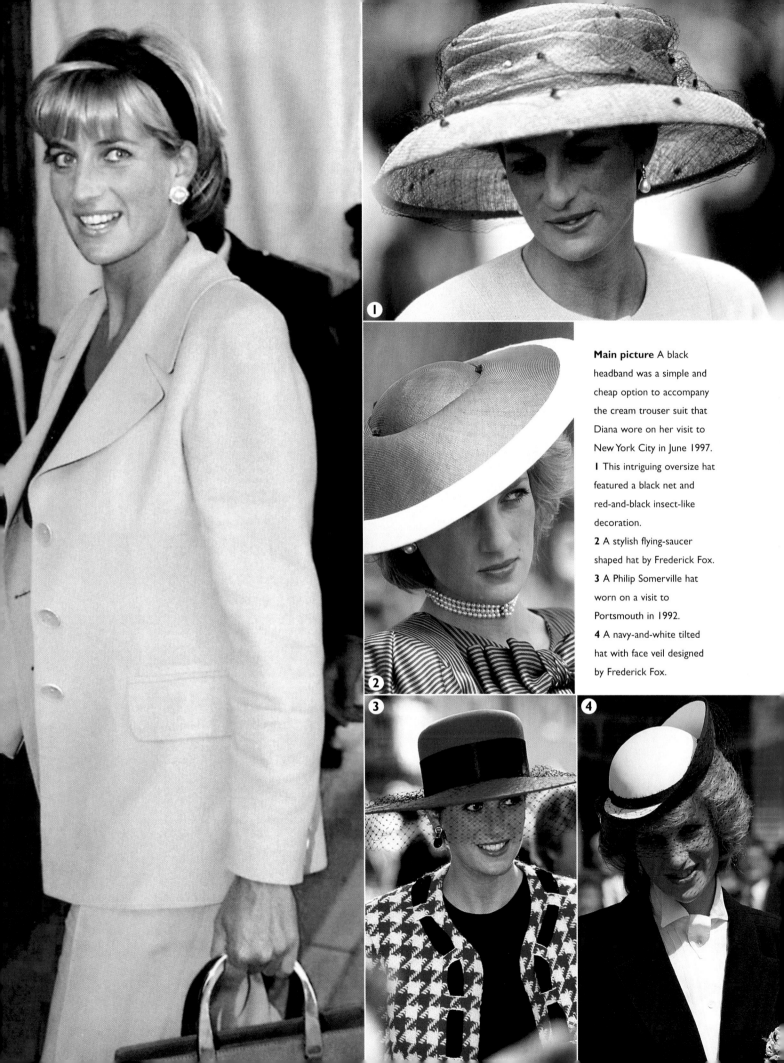

Main picture A black headband was a simple and cheap option to accompany the cream trouser suit that Diana wore on her visit to New York City in June 1997.

1 This intriguing oversize hat featured a black net and red-and-black insect-like decoration.

2 A stylish flying-saucer shaped hat by Frederick Fox.

3 A Philip Somerville hat worn on a visit to Portsmouth in 1992.

4 A navy-and-white tilted hat with face veil designed by Frederick Fox.

dresses, and her famous thermals. She had just one fur jacket, price £5000. She spent the same amount on her collection of gloves, muffs and belts.

In the underwear department, Diana spent a total of £13,000 in ten years; much of this was on Janet Reger's superb but pricey lingerie. Tights totted up to £6750, which was a lot, perhaps, for a princess who liked to go barelegged whenever she could and often 'cheated' by tanning her legs to look as if she was wearing hosiery.

Those formal occasions that required robes or uniforms, such as her uniform from the Red Cross, set Diana back £3500, although she also had the use of another £50,000-worth that were gifts.

Average spending

Averaged out over the ten years and including her £30,000 wedding outfit, Diana spent £10,354 a month or £2389 per week on her working and personal wardrobes. It helped that she had an allowance from the Foreign Office for overseas tours. These sums may have been vast and were certainly beyond the scope of average women, but they were, nevertheless, well spent.

Because of Diana's range of outfits, British design acquired a new international reputation, and royalty gained a new glamour. Diana put the royals at the heart of the glamour business and no one can deny the dazzle of those days when the Princess of Wales was the fashion pride of Britain.

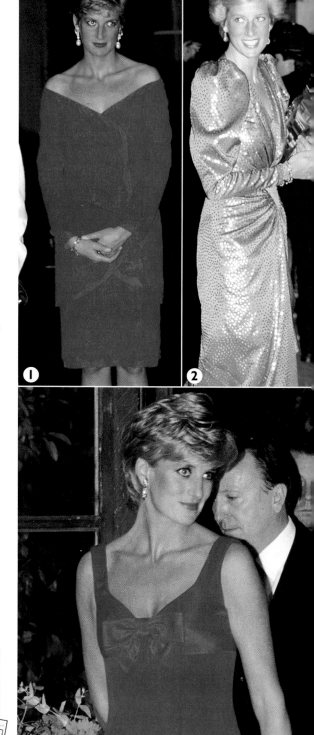

1 An elaborate two-piece in pink with red floral decoration that gives the effect of embossing. Diana wore it with red accessories in Rio de Janeiro, Brazil, in April 1991.

2 Film premières were glamorous occasions that called for flamboyant clothes like this shimmering green Bruce Oldfield evening dress worn with green shoes. Diana wore it in 1990 to see *The Hunt for Red October*.

3 A simple but effective Christian Lacroix red cocktail dress, embellished only with a red bow at the bust, worn with a red clutch bag and red stilettos. Diana wore it in Paris in September 1995 to a gala dinner at the Grand Palais.

IN THE NEWS

Making her clothes work

Although Diana spent lavishly on clothes, she felt bound to assure the public that she was not being too extravagant, and this report in the Daily Mirror of 13 October 1993 revealed how she was doing it. The illustrations show three outfits, each of which she wore twice. Doubling up on clothes had its perils, though. As the newspaper reveals, she made the mistake of wearing the same suit twice to the same place, Birmingham, in May and October 1993. Whatever Diana wore she couldn't please everybody, but it always gave the newspapers a story.

Who it's a fashion repeat for the penny-wise Princess of Wales

Second-hand Di

I'M GOING ON AN ECONOMY DRIVE, SHE SAYS

JUNE 93   MAR 93   MAY 93

EMANUEL EVENING GOWN

An off-the-shoulder evening gown with a strongly-shaped bodice, a full skirt and a pattern of diamonds and triangles. The bodice is in white silk and the skirt is of sheer white organza. Diana wore it **(right)** to a reception at the German Ambassador's Residence, London, in July 1986.

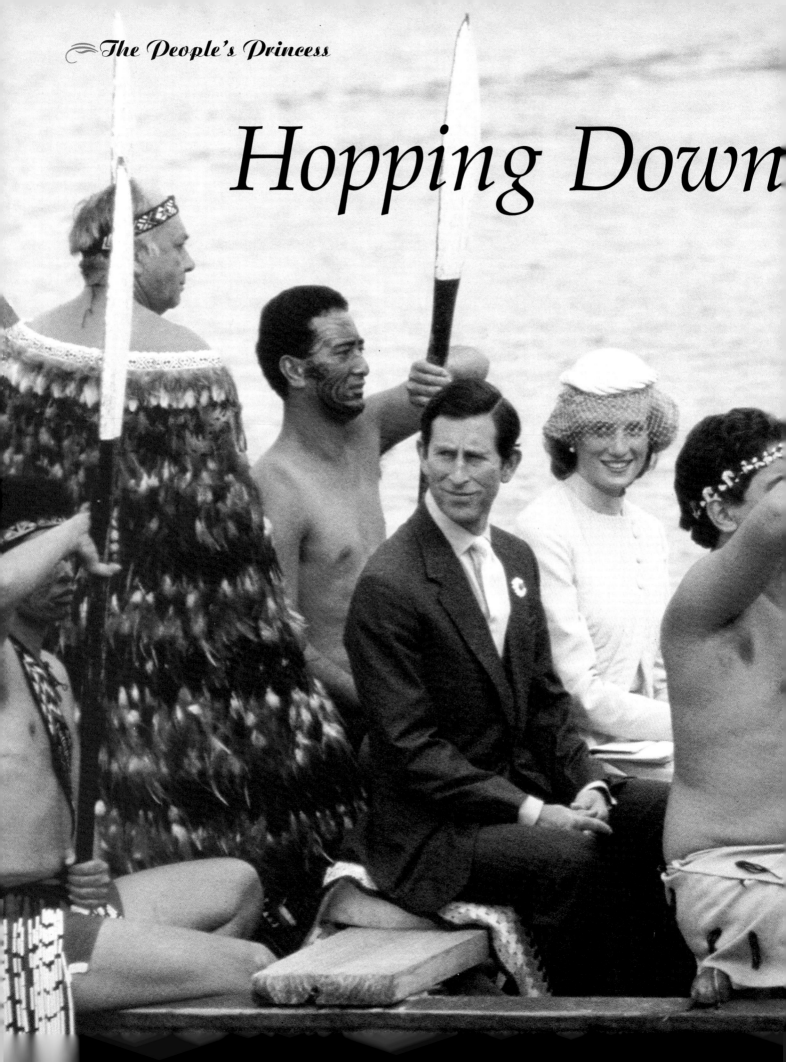

Hopping Down

Under

Diana's first overseas tour with Charles, to Australia and New Zealand in 1983, was the greatest test she could have had. This was the deep end, sink or swim. Despite nerves, though, Diana swam beautifully

Left Charles and Diana in a Maori war canoe in the Bay of Islands in New Zealand. **Below** The royal couple at sunset in front of Ayers Rock in central Australia.

The tour of Wales in October 1981, Diana's first ever as Princess, might have served as a mini-rehearsal for the major effort to come: her visit, with Charles, to Australia and New Zealand in the early autumn, antipodean time, of 1983. But in fact, nothing could have prepared Diana for the terrifying magnitude of this, the longest and most ambitious royal tour since 1953-4, when the Queen made her own Coronation visit 'Down Under'.

Six-week trip

Charles and Diana's stay lasted six weeks – four in Australia, from 20 March to 17 April, the rest, from 17 to 30 April, in New Zealand. It was a tremendous challenge for the largely untried Diana, who had never yet faced crowds so vast, or so emotional. Australians and New Zealanders did not simply welcome Diana, they over-whelmed her. They were not just delighted to see her, they were frenzied. Even Charles, with all his experience, had never seen anything quite like it.

Fortunately, there was a safety valve. The usual royal practice on overseas tours was to leave the children at home. But because of the great length of the Australasian visit, Diana became pro-foundly upset when she was told that nine-month-old Prince William would have to be left behind. The Queen, however, kindly bent the rules for Diana, and so William became the youngest touring royal of

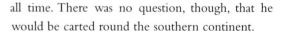

all time. There was no question, though, that he would be carted round the southern continent.

Instead, he and his nanny, Barbara Barnes, were based on a 400-acre sheep farm at Woomergama in New South Wales. In between visits round Australia, his parents flew down to spend short breaks with their son and get in some relaxation. Relaxation was certainly needed. The itinerary was a marathon. Charles and Diana were going to cover 45,000 miles, visiting every possible corner of Australia, from the Northern Territory to New South Wales, the island of Tasmania, South Australia, Western Australia, Queensland and Victoria. After that, they would travel round New Zealand, fortunately a smaller country, but extensive enough. The Wales family and their 20-strong

retinue flew in to Alice Springs, in the centre of Australia, in a Royal Australian Air Force Boeing 707 on Sunday, 20 March. Prince William, carried off the aircraft by Barbara Barnes, was the main

---

"Who's the little superstar, then?"
DIANA, TO PRINCE WILLIAM IN NEW ZEALAND

---

focus of attention, as someone in the waiting crowd yelled: 'Here's Billy the Kid!' It was soon goodbye, though, as William and his nanny headed for Woomergama, while his parents settled into a nearby motel. Charles and Diana had two suites, one for themselves and one for their luggage.

Alice Springs provided the sort of situation where royal sympathy was a great comfort. Some

300 people had recently been drowned in floods, following torrential rain. Bridges and trees were carried away and a hundred people had to leave their homes. It was a bonus to have Charles and Diana there, inspecting the damage, listening to survivors' stories and giving reassurance.

Sunset at Ayers Rock

Soon, though, the royal couple were on the move. They started out at the famous Ayers Rock, the largest single stone in the world, and a holy place of great significance to the Australian Aborigines. Charles and Diana climbed the lower slopes and were later taken to the best viewing point to watch the spectacular sunset, a parade of brilliant orange-yellow, fading to scarlet to purple to black. Next came a visit to Tennant Creek, a gold-rush town in

Above The royal couple were greeted by a large crowd when they arrived in Canberra. **Opposite page, top left** Diana rode in a stagecoach and Charles rode shotgun at Sovereign Hill near Ballarat. **Opposite page, top right** Charles and Diana were happy to pose for the press with young Prince William at Eden Park in New Zealand. **Opposite page, bottom** Charles and Diana at Port Pirie, New Adelaide, in South Australia.

Protocol ❦

QUEEN AND COMMONWEALTH

*The British Commonwealth is an association of 50 independent countries, which once belonged to the British Empire (**below** members at the annual Commonwealth Service). The Queen is Head of the Commonwealth, even though it contains several republics, such as India, and countries such as Tonga in the Pacific, which have their own monarchs. Although they do not feature specifically in the Queen's official title, she is also Queen of Australia, Queen of Canada and Queen of New Zealand. Moves have been made in Australia to declare the country a republic, but the monarchy still has supporters and, often, all it has taken to push back the tide of republican sentiment is a visit from members of the*

1851, where they visited Karaguru School and encountered the blast-furnace temperatures of the Australian autumn. After the first brief reunion with William at Woomergama, Charles and Diana arrived in Canberra on 24 March.

The walkabout in Canberra was a stunning success as Diana showed her talent for communicating with the huge crowds. As she smiled, shook hands, chatted and joked, no one guessed that she was still jet-lagged, had caught a cold in Woomergama or felt sore from some unwise sunbathing at Alice Springs. Later, she confessed that the crowds were a 'shock' and facing them required all her self-discipline. But she was learning to be a consummate royal.

Costly bushfires

She was royal again, and dazzlingly so, at the state banquet at Government House, Canberra, that evening. But a sobering note was sounded by the presence of Kim Bonython, a millionaire art dealer, and his wife. They had just lost everything in one of the bushfires that plague South Australia.

Charles and Diana were so affected by the tragedy that they cut short their stay in Canberra and headed for Cockatoo, near Melbourne, where the bushfires had been especially costly. More

Above left Diana and Charles in the studio of the School of the Air in Alice Springs, Australia. This is a radio service designed to teach children on remote farms who are unable to get to a school. **Above** Diana on a walkabout during the visit to the Australian island of Tasmania. The welcome here was just as rapturous as every other the royal couple received during the Australasian tour.

victims awaited at Stirling Oval in the Adelaide Hills, and more fearful stories of fire, destruction and loss. Diana shook the hand of one 18-year-old who had survived after being trapped by a ferocious wall of 90-foot flames.

Returning to their timetable in Sydney, Charles and Diana were virtually mobbed by wildly excited crowds as they drove to the Opera House in their open-topped Rolls Royce. A few anti-royalists made their protests, but they were drowned out in

> ## "My wife has been enveloped in warmth and affection."
> CHARLES, ON DIANA'S RECEPTION IN AUSTRALIA

the welter of cheers and excited yelling coming from the ranks of onlookers. One valiant old lady, evidently a staunch monarchist, took it upon herself to snatch placards straight out of protesters' hands and trample them underfoot.

Diana dazzled again at the ball that evening at Sydney's luxurious Wentworth Hotel and there were smiles, waves of admiration and roars of delight for her all the way from Newcastle on the Pacific coast, across to Hobart in Tasmania and back to the mainland to Adelaide, Renmark, Port Pirie, Fremantle and Perth. Some lucky fans of Charles and Diana got close enough to claim royal kisses. There were 13,000 children waiting for the couple at Bunbury, and Diana was almost mobbed, again, at Brisbane. In Melbourne, a massive 200,000 people came to see the Prince and Princess.

Wanted couple

In Ballarat, the centre of the Australian Gold Rush of 1851, Charles and Diana had fun on a stagecoach run, with the Prince riding shotgun Wild West style, and a police trooper, in mid-19th century costume, pretending to arrest the royal visitors as a 'wanted couple'.

The Australian tour, on which about one million of the country's 17 million population turned out to see the royals, ended with a grand ball at the

Top Meeting the Australian comedian Paul Hogan, who went on to make the *Crocodile Dundee* films, at a Melbourne concert hall. **Above** On day 20 of the tour in Perth, Diana was met by a forest of hands from an enthusiastic crowd who had turned out to greet her.

Above Having been shown how to do the 'hongi', the traditional Maori greeting, Diana greeted a Maori lady in the old way. **Left** In Auckland, New Zealand, a group of Maori women, dressed in their colourful, traditional costumes, shared a laugh with Diana.

Melbourne Hilton. It had been a triumphal tour, especially for Diana, by the time the royal couple flew on to Auckland, the capital city of New Zealand, on 17 April.

On to New Zealand

The welcome in New Zealand, a country often taken to evoke an England of the southern hemisphere, was just as warm and excited, though maybe a little less frantic, than it had been in Australia. The weather, however, was inclement. There was a deluge at Pupuke while Charles and Diana were watching children canoeing, but the band raised a royal laugh or two when they played 'Raindrops keep falling on my head'. The planned walkabout at Pupuke barely escaped being rained off. Next, the royal car failed to start in the soaking conditions.

Diana was learning fast the truth of the royal dictum that when things go wrong on tour, they go wrong in a big way. A 117-foot war canoe nearly capsized while Charles and Diana were aboard, when too many Maori warriors, dressed in their traditional finery and plumage and complete with fearsomely-tattooed faces, tried to get in with

them. Fortunately, the canoe just managed to stay afloat. The Maoris took it skimming across the Bay of Islands to the Waitangi Treaty Ground.

Here, the royal couple were on tricky territory. The Treaty of Waitangi, concluded between the British government and 46 Maori chiefs in 1840, had long been a sore point with the Maoris, after its terms were cynically broken and they lost the full rights to their land, which the agreement was supposed to ensure.

Protesters condemning Waitangi as a 'fraud' awaited Charles and Diana at the Treaty Ground. The protests, and the evident fury behind them, were not entirely a revelation. Already, in Auckland, a Maori had been arrested for insulting the royal couple in the traditional fashion of his people – baring his bottom. Anti-monarchists and IRA sympathizers also made their own voices heard.

Maori greeting

The normal business of the royal tour continued all the same, with Maoris in more friendly guise. At Eden Park in Auckland, Diana got her first experience of the 'hongi', the traditional Maori greeting,

which involves rubbing noses. A huge crowd of 45,000 children were there to watch Diana as, giggling, she soon got the hang of it.

The children put on displays of singing and dancing and a demonstration of Maori war techniques. A boy, dressed as a chief, issued a 'challenge' and stuck his tongue out, the traditional Maori way

Above In New Zealand, Prince Charles and Princess Diana were presented with a carved wooden gift by a Maori elder.

IN THE NEWS

Billy the Kid

It was somehow typical of forthright Australians to give Prince William the nickname of a Wild West outlaw, Billy the Kid. William was certainly a major star of his parents' tour of Australia and New Zealand in 1983, as the Daily Express reported on 1 March 1983. Part of his royal charm was complete ignorance of protocol. When greeted by the crowds in Australia, he blinked and yawned. The Aussies loved it.

When the tour moved on to New Zealand the press in both hemispheres made much of Prince Edward's job as a tutor.

of frightening off strangers. Things appeared to get serious, though, when the 'chief' lunged at Diana with his spear and, as she later confessed, she thought for a moment he was going to stab her.

There was a Royal Family reunion in New Zealand when Charles' youngest brother, Prince Edward, appeared while the couple were on a visit to Banganui Collegiate boarding school, where Edward, 19, was working as a tutor and house-master. The young prince had obviously got into the spirit of the place: he was wearing the cere-monial feathered cloak of a Ngati Awe chieftain, given to him by the Maoris.

Prince William and Barbara Barnes, meanwhile, were staying at Government House in Auckland.

> **"She looks much prettier in the flesh than she does in pictures."**
> AUSTRALIAN ONLOOKER, ON DIANA

William, inevitably, stole the show when he went 'crawlabout' for the cameras on the lawn. This was when journalists discovered his parents' nickname for him. Charles was heard to whisper 'Wills' to the 10-month-old as he explored the grass.

Charles appeared to get a particular thrill from another engagement, an impressive display of aerial acrobatics by pilots of the Royal New Zealand Air Force at Wigram airfield. Charles, who is himself a competent pilot, excitedly told Diana: 'I'd love to have a go at that!'

Gallipoli veterans

On 25 April, five days before the end of this most challenging of royal tours, ANZAC day was com-memorated, recalling the landing at Gallipoli, Turkey, by Australian and New Zealand forces in 1915, during the First World War. Gallipoli was a disastrous failure, where 5000 men, trapped on a narrow beachhead, were killed by Turks com-manding the rocky heights above.

Even after nearly 70 years, the impact of that tragic waste of life was still fresh, and Charles, grim-faced, stood in full naval uniform to take the salute as the surviving veterans of Gallipoli marched past. A state banquet in Auckland rounded off the tour

and on 30 April, as Prince William and his nanny flew back to England, an exhausted Charles and Diana headed for Bermuda and a well-earned 10-day rest. The break was important, for another big tour – 18 days in Canada – would start soon.

But as she sunned herself in the Bermudan warmth, Diana could look back on several lessons well learned. The Australasian tour had shown her the extent of her unprecedented personal popula-rity. She had learned, too, how to keep going in spite of weather, heat and her own nerves, to make a tour a job royally done. But Australia and New Zealand had also shown Diana at first hand that, behind the gloss and gaiety of a royal visit, there was suffering, resentment and even enmity to be con-fronted. And that, as her later royal career amply demonstrated, was the most vital lesson of all.

Above At Eden Park, the rugby stadium in Auckland, New Zealand, a Maori boy, dressed as a chief, issued a challenge to Charles and Diana and, having stuck his tongue out to frighten them, really scared them by lunging convincingly at them with his spear.

NEW CONFIDANTS

Diana took two giant steps within 12 months. She separated from Charles, then withdrew from the public life she had known for 12 hardworking years. Adjusting to all this was very difficult

Diana's retirement from public life was not exactly a leap in the dark, but it came close to that. The crowded, sometimes overcrowded, royal life she had known for the last 12 years was about to change – and radically.

With the separation, the glamour days were on the wane. There were fewer glittering galas and film premières, and no overseas tours where heads of state waited on red carpets to greet their royal visitors while bands played national anthems.

Diana might well have been glad to leave all that behind at the start of 1993, but at the year's end she faced an even more trimmed-down future: no more public engagements, except for a few long-standing commitments; no more huge crowds waiting hours to get a glimpse of her; and no more waves of the adulation that had once reassured her that she was loved by millions.

At 32, Diana was still comparatively young; she was also beautiful, desirable and charismatic, but it all seemed to be going to waste. And, as friends often testified, Diana, a rejected wife and the sometimes dejected child of a broken home, needed love, attention and appreciation like she needed air.

SEEKING MALE COMPANY

Inevitably, in these lonely circumstances, Diana began to seek male company. Or rather, she perhaps felt freer to seek it than she had done before the break-up of her marriage. As a result, 1994 opened with the makings of yet another first-class scandal, when nuisance calls to the millionaire antiques

Previous page Diana on a skiing trip with friends in Austria in March 1994, a trip on which the paparazzi's intrusion brought her to tears. **Right** Attending the D-Day anniversary in June 1994 in Portsmouth. **Top right** With Kate Menzies and Viscount Linley at a party in May 1994. **Bottom right** Leaving hospital after visiting her brother's new-born son in March 1994. **Below** Antiques dealer Oliver Hoare in August 1994.

dealer Oliver Hoare were traced to Diana's phone. Oliver Hoare, 39, dark, handsome, debonair and married with three young children, had first met Diana nine years earlier at a reception in Windsor Castle for Royal Ascot racegoers. Before long, the two couples – Charles and Diana, Hoare and his

---

> ## "*Oliver was frightened of her obsessive behaviour.*"
>
> ### BARRY HODGE, OLIVER HOARE'S FORMER CHAUFFEUR, ON DIANA

---

attractive wife Diane – had become friends and the Hoares were invited to dinners at Kensington Palace. For Diana, the Hoares were fun company: witty, sophisticated, intelligent and sympathetic.

Unfortunately, however, Oliver Hoare proved too sympathetic for his own good. At this time, Charles and Diana's marriage was already starting

to fracture, and Hoare provided a ready ear for Diana's woes. He was also, allegedly, a line of information on Camilla Parker-Bowles.

According to Andrew Morton's *Diana: Her New Life* and Nicholas Davies' *The Princess Who Changed The World,* Diana grew increasingly desperate and came to rely on Oliver Hoare's sympathetic ear far more than she should have done. If she could not see Hoare personally, she would keep him on the phone for half an hour or more, telling him how unhappy she was, how she feared the future and generally how terrible life could be. At weekends, it appeared, the phone at Hoare's home rang constantly, in addition to Oliver Hoare meeting Diana once or twice each week.

AN OBSESSION

This pattern continued for some years, and by 1992 the Hoare marriage was starting to suffer. Diane Hoare even went so far as to accuse her husband of having an affair with the Princess but, in fact, Oliver's relationship with Diana was much more complicated than that. Diana had, it seems, become obsessed with Hoare and imagined that she had fallen head-over-heels in love with him.

Like many soft-hearted, decent men before him, Oliver Hoare had no idea of how to handle the situation in which he found himself. In the cool, sophisticated circles where he and Diana moved, emotions, especially violent emotions, were not

Di's nuisance calls revealed

As with the 'Squidgy' and 'Camillagate' calls, the nuisance calls to Oliver Hoare went unrevealed for several months after they were made. When the story broke in the News of The World on 21 August 1994, the headline carried hidden meanings. At the time, press rumours were still circulating that suggested Diana was 'mad', so accounting for the word 'cranky'. The description of Hoare as 'married' reflected gossip that Diana liked men, such as Will Carling, who already had wives.

IN THE NEWS

Above A keen rugby fan, Diana watches the France versus Wales clash in January 1995. **Above right** England rugby captain, Will Carling, became linked with Diana. **Right** In spite of the press rumours, life went on. Here Diana goes on a shopping trip to buy party balloons. **Far right** At Silverstone racing circuit in July 1994, Diana presents Britain's Damon Hill with the winner's trophy.

normally put on such dramatic display, if they were displayed at all. Hoare, therefore, shrank from hurting Diana by telling her that their relationship had to end. However, like many resolute wives with pestered but indecisive husbands, Diane Hoare insisted that this was precisely what he must do.

In the summer of 1993, Hoare told the Princess that the phone calls had to cease. They did not. Instead, they became 'silent'. The phone would ring. One or other of the Hoares would answer, but no one, it appeared, was on the line. Diane Hoare calculated that 300 such calls were received, a num-

> **"I now realize there is a pattern in the way there's always an unavailability about the men I go for."**
> DIANA TO HER ASTROLOGER, DEBBIE FRANK

ber the Princess later termed impossible, considering how busy her life was.

Eventually, the Hoares had to seek help. They contacted British Telecom, who agreed to set up their call tracing service. There was a brief rest, then, after two months, early in 1994, the calls resumed, but this time there was a 'trace' on them. Their sources, it was revealed, were Kensington Palace, the home of Diana's sister Sarah, and other locations to which Diana had access.

This information found its way to Sir Robert Fellowes, Diana's brother-in-law and the Queen's private secretary, via the Royal Protection Squad and the Home Office. Sir Robert Fellowes contacted Diana. The silent calls ceased.

TABLOID ATTACK

The story was picked up by the *News of the World*, which, on 21 August 1994, blazoned 'Di's Cranky Phone Calls To Married Tycoon' (see In The News) across its front page. The rest of the tabloid press, predictably, leapt into action. Reporters and photographers descended on the Chelsea Harbour Club, where Diana worked out and played tennis. As it happened, it had been Oliver Hoare who had introduced Diana to the expensive and exclusive Harbour Club, by the Thames at Chelsea, southwest

The Private Princess
The dominant partner

The position of estranged husbands and wives is always an invidious one. They are free but not free, married but not married. They can be a worry to other married couples, who may view separated partners as a threat to their own relationships.

The same problems applied to Diana, but as a semi-detached royal as well as an estranged wife, she had added difficulties to bear. Separated or not, she remained the wife of the heir to the throne, and technically at least, she was still the next Queen Consort. As such, she could look very much like forbidden territory to any man in whom she became interested. Beneath all her charisma as one of the world's most famous women, she was a very unhappy person whose life had been destabilized. Although this had the effect of lowering her self-esteem, she still had to take the initiative when it came to forming friendships with potential male suitors. Needless to say, men such as Christopher Whalley and Will Carling, who had never before mixed with royalty on a personal basis, were immensely flattered, but their own much more ordinary position in life meant that Diana was always the major

Christopher Whalley (above) leaves the Harbour Club, Chelsea, and is seen (left) with Princess Diana.

player. Since she appeared to like masculine, dominant and self-possessed men, it was discomforting for them to have to play second fiddle. They were also in the awkward position of being involved with someone on the fringes of the Royal Family, the most powerful and influential family in the land.

Although Diana remarked to Debbie Frank, her astrologer, that there was a certain unavailability about the men she met after her separation, she, in fact, was the one who was unavailable because of her high-profile position.

London, early in 1993, as a promising place to make new friends. It was also a place for the rich, beautiful and famous. It was here that Diana encountered Christopher Whalley, a wealthy property developer, and Will Carling, the England rugby captain and one of the country's best-known sportsmen.

As friends and journalists had often noticed, Diana could be something of a flirt, but she normally played the teasing game for fun rather than for real. According to Chris Hutchins and Dominic

> *"She chose the most exclusive health club in the country, and the one in which she is likely to meet the right set of people."*
>
> MARY SPILLANE, IMAGE CONSULTANT, ON DIANA AND THE HARBOUR CLUB

Midgley's *Inside The Mind Of The Princess of Wales*, it was in this flirty way that she introduced herself to Christopher Whalley, who was, like Diana, a fitness fanatic.

'What does a girl have to do to get a guy to buy her a cup of coffee round here?' she was heard to ask, as she stood at the bottom of the Harbour Club staircase and Whalley stood at the top. He was apparently so surprised that he turned round to check if Diana was talking to someone else, but there was no one there.

FLOODED WITH CALLS

Soon, they met regularly over coffee – cappuccinos for her and espressos for him. She offered him her private telephone number. He reciprocated and found his line flooded with calls. She invited him to dinner at Kensington Palace and took him to her favourite London restaurants. He took her to his family's Yorkshire farmhouse at weekends.

Gradually, though, Whalley found himself edged into the same position as Oliver Hoare. Diana made him her confidant and emotional support. Even so, her relationship with him never became as obsessive as the one with Hoare. As recounted in *Inside the Mind…* Whalley continued to see other women, including a former fiancée. Diana, it

Main picture and below left Despite everything else that was going on in her life, and whatever scandal the newspapers were using to boost circulation, Diana always found time for her boys. She is seen here during a trip to Alton Towers, in April 1994, with Princes William and Harry and their friends.

❧ Protocol ☙

TROOPING THE COLOUR

The ceremony of Trooping the Colour, **right,** is one of the big tourist attractions in London in the summer, complete with marching troops in full ceremonial dress, military bands and the Queen taking the salute. The ceremony takes place on or near the sovereign's official birthday, 10 June, and is held on Horseguards Parade, near Buckingham Palace. Traditionally, the flag 'trooped' is that of the monarch, which was displayed in battle to enable foreign troops or mercenaries to recognize where their commanders were situated. After the ceremony, the Queen and her family appear on the balcony at Buckingham Palace, to acknowledge the cheers of the crowds outside and review an RAF flypast.

appears, became interested in Will Carling, even though he was on the verge of marriage.

Diana was already distantly acquainted with Carling, whom she had encountered at rugby international matches. She met him again at the Harbour Club in the spring of 1994. Like Christopher Whalley before him, Diana invited Carling to Kensington Palace, where William and Harry, both

> "*...we take turns...Whenever I am getting it (from the press) I just think 'It will be his turn next'.*"
>
> DIANA TO ASTROLOGER,
> DEBBIE FRANK, ON CHARLES

rugby fans, were delighted to meet their hero. Carling's wife Julia, however, was not so happy with her new husband's friendship with Diana and told the press so. That sparked off rumours of daggers drawn between the two women, with a helpless Carling in the middle. By then this controversy had already been upstaged by Charles, who shocked the nation with a revelation of his own.

The stage was a two-and-a-half-hour BBC television documentary in which the Prince of Wales talked in detail to Jonathan Dimbleby about his life and works. But in a tiny three-minute section, all the good intentions were blown away when Charles made a highly personal confession that made Diana's 'cranky phone calls' appear tame.

Above With Mme. Giscard d'Estaing in Paris in 1994. **Right** Diana and Princess Margaret, in June 1994, at the Canada Memorial in Green Park, London.

IN CONTEXT   KILLER QUAKE IN LOS ANGELES
1994

• A major earthquake in Los Angeles, California, **right**, kills 34 people

• The Eurofighter 2000, built by Britain, Germany, Italy and Spain, makes its first successful test flight

• Former US President Richard Nixon dies

• Nelson Mandela is sworn in as South Africa's first black president

• Former football star Bobby Charlton is knighted

• In the civil war in the former Yugoslavia, 68 people are killed by artillery fire in a Sarajevo market

Diana with
Prince Edward and Lady Sarah
Armstrong-Jones at Lord
Linley's wedding, at
St. Margaret's Church,
Westminster, London, in
October 1993.

Dressing the Family

As a wife and mother, Diana had a major say in what her husband and sons wore. She encouraged Charles to be more stylish and ensured that their sons wore fun clothes like ordinary boys

When Diana married Charles, she quickly decided that his wardrobe required a thorough rejigging. Charles had never shown much interest in cutting a stylish figure. Unlike his predecessor as Prince of Wales, who became King Edward VIII in 1936, Charles was not known as a snappy dresser.

His tailors were in Savile Row, the top-drawer venue for menswear, but he often managed to look unpressed and ill-at-ease in his clothes. His suits were far too conservative, his shirts were too city-styled, and, last but not least, his lace-up shoes, though practical, were far from elegant.

However, as soon became plain, Charles was hard to budge. Early on in her campaign, Diana bought Charles a stylish pair of trousers. He put them away and never wore them. She bought him snazzy ties. They met the same fate.

Miniature adults

Later on, when it came to dressing their two young sons, it was always easy to see which of their parents had been in charge. When it was Diana, they dressed brightly and casually. When it was Charles, the boys looked like smaller versions of himself — tweed jackets, plain shirts, tightly knotted ties,

Main picture The young princes wear bright anoraks on a sleigh in Lech, Austria, in March 1994. **Inset** The boys in matching outfits in June 1986 at Highgrove.

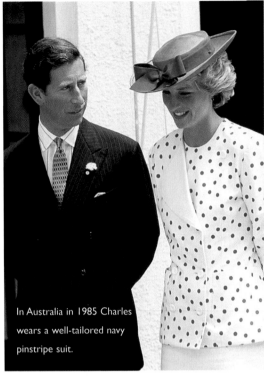

In Australia in 1985 Charles wears a well-tailored navy pinstripe suit.

SAVILE ROW SUIT
Charles wearing a double-breasted, lightweight summer suit in grey check with a pink tie, made by his Savile Row tailors; Diana is in a Catherine Walker dress. They wore these clothes in August 1987 at the Queen Mother's 87th birthday **(inset right)**.

Left On a visit to Lisbon, Portugal, in 1987, Diana is wearing a Catherine Walker skirt and white zipped coat with matching hat. Charles has made an effort in a French-style raincoat but looks a little uncomfortable.

formal shoes. It was as if the habit of dressing children as though they were miniature adults, something which died out over a century ago, had been revived for an afternoon.

Despite resistance, though, Diana made some progress. Charles cut a fine figure, well-muscled, of a good height, and never overweight, but he did tend to be rather unadventurous when it came to colours. Except for the kilted outfits he wore when

> "She has weaned (Charles) away from his 'young fogey' image."
>
> ANN CHUBB, FASHION WRITER,
> ON DIANA'S SARTORIAL INFLUENCE

on holiday in Scotland, navy, grey and white were usually as far as he would go.

The 'smarten up Charles' initiative, when he responded to it, produced some pleasing results. His suits were still made in Savile Row, where the tailoring was without equal, but Diana persuaded him to change to one of the less conservative outfitters, Anderson and Shepherd. Now, for the first time, Charles' clothes began to attract attention. In 1985, in Australia, the Prince appeared in a classic navy

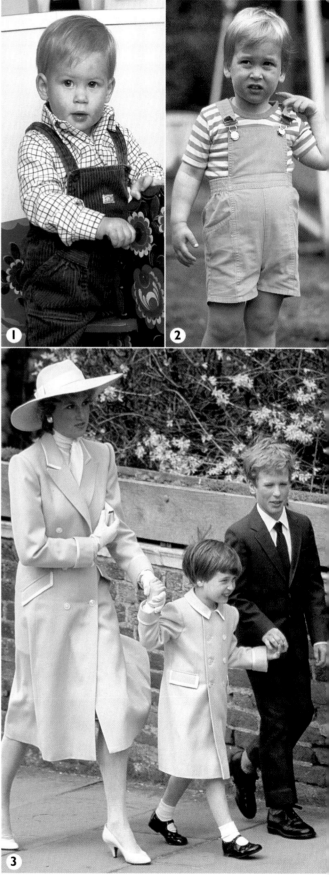

pinstripe suit (see page 476), a white shirt with a blue stripe and a blue-and-white patterned tie – still a fairly conservative mix, but much better cut and styled than before. The same year, for a family lunch at Clarence House to celebrate the Queen Mother's birthday, Charles appeared in a grey suit with a large self-check and a pink tie.

Fashionable Charles

Quite evidently, progress had been made, and it continued. In 1987, on Charles' tour of Portugal with Diana, he wore a cream tie with a blue shirt, as well as a beige, French-style raincoat (see page 476). The following year, for the official photograph to mark his 40th birthday, Charles really pushed the fashion boat out. His suit was a smart, shiny beige, his tie was lemon yellow and his shirt was a pale blue-and-white check. The detail of

Above Stripes for Diana and Harry on a holiday trip to Palma, Majorca, in 1986.
1 Prince Harry, aged one, in a Viyella shirt and blue cord dungarees at Kensington Palace in November 1985.
2 Prince William in blue dungaree shorts with a stripy T-shirt in June 1984 at Kensington Palace.
3 Diana and William in matching Catherine Walker coats accompany Peter Phillips on the way to a 1987 Easter service in Windsor.

Charles' wardrobe had also stepped up a notch. The handkerchiefs which peeped out of his breast-pocket were no longer uniformly white. They became multicoloured, sometimes patterned, and were designed to match his now more daring taste in ties. The materials, too, were much more fun –

> ***"William and Harry can choose whatever they want, which she feels gives them a degree of personal freedom in their restricted lives."***
>
> FIONA FLORENCE, ROYAL CORRESPONDENT, ON WILLIAM AND HARRY

sheeny silk, interestingly textured wool and tweed and the Prince of Wales check.

In addition, Charles became more adventurous in his footwear, opting sometimes for brogues, slip-ons or black patent evening shoes in place of his sensible lace-ups. He also exchanged sober crombie-style overcoats for a version of the 'baggy' look, pioneered by his great-uncle Edward VIII.

However, the one thing Diana never managed to do was to get her husband into jeans. Charles stuck firmly to his favourite soft cords, tweeds and cotton trousers for summer and off-duty wear.

William and Harry, by contrast, were introduced to jeans as soon as they were old enough to wear them. This was the sartorial slant to her determined

Above Red sweatshirts with black and white shorts on a windy August day in 1989. **1** William in Bermuda shorts at a 1989 polo match. **2** Denim shirts, jeans and ship's caps on a 1991 visit to *HMCS Ottawa* in Canada. **3** William in a bomber jacket at Thorpe Park, 1993. **4** William leaves school in a polo-shirt and trainers in 1990. **Right** The princes at Balmoral in August 1997, wearing casual clothes their father would endorse.

campaign to make sure that the young princes were able to live as 'normal' a life as possible.

As soon as the boys emerged from baby clothes, Diana made it clear that she would have no truck with the 'miniature adult' approach. It was to be jeans, sweatshirts, open-necked shirts, anoraks, striped sweaters, baseball caps, trainers and other with-it gear, the sort of clothes young royals had never worn. These clothes also acted as 'camouflage': the princes and their mother could go shopping and few people would recognize them.

Two of everything

Diana used to shop for her sons' clothes herself, always buying two of everything to avoid arguments. But as they got older, the boys refused to go out as a matching pair. Prince William, for instance, might be seen in a dark blue sweatshirt with a prominent multicoloured 'Tramliners' motif on the front. Prince Harry, by contrast, and over two years younger, was meanwhile wearing a Batman sweatshirt. Together with Diana it was, invariably, jeans all round to complete the outfits.

Diana's approach to her sons' clothes was relaxed and contemporary. She aimed for comfort, colour, informality and gear which did not make the boys look like fashion throwbacks next to their friends. Her attitude to the family's clothes was yet another example of the innovations that Diana made to the long-established royal way of doing things.

FLYING THE FLAG

On holiday in Majorca in 1987 **(inset)** the boys' beachwear is in red, white and blue. Harry's dungaree shorts are by Circus and his shoes have Snoopy motifs.

IN THE NEWS

Matching up to expectations

With a fashion icon for a mother, the media spotlight was turned on William and Harry and the clothes they wore. This prompted articles like the 1989 Daily Mirror piece **(right)** about their short trousers and visible knees. At this age they were still wearing matching outfits.

This piece was not just about boyish fashion, though. It reflected a favourite press image of Diana as a caring mother who took the trouble to make sure her sons' style of dressing did not overemphasize their special position and so isolate them from ordinary boys and their friends.

Princess Courageous

In 1997, Diana embarked on a true
mission of mercy on behalf of the
Red Cross and others – the
campaign to ban the use of
landmines. It was her last but most
crucial initiative for charity

One of Diana's enduring desires was to use her worldwide fame and popularity to improve the lives of others. Whatever Diana did, the world noticed. Whatever she said, people listened. This was real power and, early in 1997, the cause illuminated by it was the scandal of anti-personnel landmines, which killed and maimed long after their use in war was over. They blew off feet and legs. They blinded. They ruined lives, especially the lives of children in places such as Angola or Bosnia, where surviving was hard enough for the able-bodied, let alone the crippled.

In 1995, when the issue first came to Diana's attention, some 26,000 men, women and children were being killed or horrifically maimed every year by devastating landmine

Main picture Princess Diana visits a minefield being cleared by a landmine charity, The Halo Trust, in Angola in January 1997.
Right At Nevef Bendinha, an orthopaedic workshop in Luanda, Angola, Diana talks to a landmine victim, 13-year-old Sandra Thijika.

Pictures on these two pages are from Diana's trip to Angola in January 1997.

Above Attending an International Red Cross briefing in the capital, Luanda, on her first day.

Right A member of The Halo Trust shows Diana the type of landmine in use in Angola and how it works.

Top centre and top right Diana meets some of the landmine victims being helped with artificial limbs and crutches at a centre run by the International Red Cross in Luanda.

explosions. Several voluntary organizations had sprung up to handle the problem. The Cambodia Trust, The Halo Trust, the Mines Advisory Group and the Red Cross had all sent volunteers and officials abroad to clear minefields, and care for victims in places recently scarred either by war or civil war. They travelled to Afghanistan, Angola, Bosnia, Cambodia, Chechnya in the former Soviet Union, Mozambique, Sri Lanka and Sudan, all poor countries where the basic necessities of life were often minimal. Meanwhile, the small but determined International Campaign to Ban Landmines took the field to protest, lobby and demonstrate in order to draw public attention to these weapons and their hideous consequences.

Of all these organizations, the Red Cross had the greatest resources and worldwide influence. The global nature of the Red Cross, with over 150 societies in different countries, made the

⇒ **Protocol** ⇔

ROYAL HANDS OFF POLITICS

*The Queen has no open political say in the
government of her realm and neither she nor
her relations are allowed to touch on sensitive
political issues. This is because past kings
abused their political powers. In 1689 a
long contest between the monarchy and
Parliament ended in a Parliamentary
victory. Constitutional monarchy, in which
the sovereign reigns but does not rule, was
introduced as a condition of the
accession of William III **(right)** and
Mary II, in 1689. Since then, royal
involvement in politics has been
severely limited by unspoken agreement and tradition.*

landmines issue an obvious cause for action. The
organization's trump card in publicizing the problem was, of course, Diana, who had been their
patron and was made vice-president in 1994.
Diana, who had already indicated her interest,
began to receive photographs, articles and videos,
which were, necessarily, of the most horrific nature.

Damning statistics

In her usual thorough fashion, Diana made a close
study of the subject, absorbed the statistics and
acquainted herself with the mechanics of mines and
the logistics of a problem that seemed to grow
more awesome the more she learned. The most
damning of these statistics came from the
International Red Cross. Over the previous six
years, the organization had produced 100,000 artificial limbs for 80,000 victims in 22 countries, with
the majority going to Cambodia, Afghanistan and

Above Before flying out of Sarajevo, the capital of Bosnia, in August 1997, Diana posed for a photo with French soldiers from the UN Peacekeeping Force. **Left** Diana with Ken Rutherford, who lost both his legs clearing mines in Somalia. His organization, Landmine Survivors Network, helped coordinate Diana's Bosnia trip. Here they are visiting Bujakov Potek, a village near Sarajevo.

Angola, all of which had been involved in civil wars. Afghanistan alone had taken delivery of 600 wheel-chairs and 6000 pairs of crutches, but that had been enough to help only a fraction of the victims.

Diana came out in the open against landmines on 12 February 1996, when she was the star guest at the première of Sir Richard Attenborough's film *In Love and War*, which was raising funds for the Red Cross appeal. For Diana, however, it was not enough for the glamorous Princess of Wales to draw attention to a cause by gracing yet another film première, then going home. Diana resolved to see the problem for herself and, early in 1997, she volunteered to travel to Angola to meet landmine victims and force the world to take notice.

Angola, a former Portuguese colony in south-west Africa, had been transformed by a recent long and brutal civil war into the world's most heavily

landmined country. As in other similar countries where the landmine problem was acute, the weapons had been laid haphazardly, with no maps and no records to tell where they were.

Some countries, such as Canada and Norway, were already agitating for a ban. Others, such as

> ## "*Landmines kill children, don't they Mummy?*"
> ### Prince Harry, to Diana

Russia and China, wanted to retain landmines, while Britain, like the United States, preferred to wait for a general agreement before acting.

Whatever their position, the vested interests of various countries turned landmines into a political issue and, as Diana knew very well, this made the

whole question a minefield in itself. Members of the Royal Family were not supposed to go near politics. Although her own motives were wholly humanitarian, she was open to criticism.

'A loose cannon'

One Conservative minister labelled Diana 'a loose cannon'. Another called her 'uninformed', which was totally untrue. In reply to these criticisms, Diana later called the Conservative government 'hopeless' and welcomed the Labour Party's land-slide election victory of 1 May 1997 as a sign that here, at last, was a government which was altogeth-er more likely to heed the moral and ethical factors that underlay the use of landmines.

On 12 January 1997, when Labour's general election triumph was still four months away, Diana travelled to Angola, complete with press corps, to

Above In the village of Bujakov Potek, outside Sarajevo, Diana stopped to talk to Mirzeta Gabeliz, a 15-year-old girl who had lost her right leg below the knee when she stepped on a landmine. Diana was close to tears as they talked.

Left Diana on her way to a Landmine Survivors Network conference in Tuzla, Bosnia. **Above** Diana near Zenica, Bosnia, with the Bradoric family, whose 14-year-old son lost his left foot in a landmine explosion.

begin her own campaign on the ground. She had seen some appalling sights in her time as a royal, but the scenes she witnessed in Angola were harrowing. One small Angolan girl she saw had had her intestines blown out. In one photograph in which she posed with four victims, Diana was the only one who still had both legs. Equipped with protective visor and body armour, Diana ventured into a cleared minefield. As the TV cameras rolled, she walked past notices placed every few metres which read, in Portuguese, '*Perigo minas!*' - 'Danger, mines!' – above a skull and crossbones.

Back in Britain, extensive newspaper coverage along with TV footage of her visit and in-depth

> **"I hope...we shall focus world attention on this vital but, until now, largely neglected issue."**
> DIANA, TALKING TO THE PRESS

background reports alerted people to the issue and the horrors that were going on. A groundswell of disgust and fury began to reach politicians and governments, who were now being told to do something, and do it as fast as possible.

Eight months later, on 8 August 1997, Diana was on the landmines trail again, this time in Bosnia where civil war had resulted in indiscriminate laying of landmines after 1992. Once again, Diana was seen amid the horrors, this time listening to the grisly accounts of several victims whose stories were no less harrowing for being told through an

IN THE NEWS

Diana and politics

Diana's royal status was an invaluable boost to the campaign to ban anti-personnel landmines. But the landmines were a political issue, and Diana's involvement brought charges that she was meddling in matters that were more properly the preserve of governments. The quote from Diana which provided this headline showed where she herself believed she stood: on the side of humanitarianism pure and simple. It was not as easy as that, and politicians remained convinced that here was undue royal meddling. Criticism of her continued until she died.

Above On her trip to Bosnia in August 1997, Diana visited the city of Zenica, where she watched a volleyball match between two teams of landmine victims, posing with them afterwards for a photograph.

interpreter. Diana sat long and patiently as she heard of husbands killed and children asking over and over again where their fathers were as their mothers wept. Diana would hold their hands until they were able to go on. Some of the newsmen, hard-bitten by years of seeing tragedy, disaster and suffering, were themselves in tears at the pitiful scenes.

The courage of victims

However, the courage of some victims was, in its way, the most moving of all. Two 12-year-old boys, each of whom had lost a leg, told Diana they intended to become footballers. The youngsters laughed and joked as they told Diana what had happened to them. One lost his leg while walking through the woods. The other stepped on a mine as he was carrying bricks to help rebuild his home.

Once again, pictures relayed around the world stirred consciences and when, just over three weeks later, Diana was killed in Paris, the tragedy seemed to serve as a final impetus to the ban she had been working for with such dedication. A fortnight after Diana's death, a preliminary treaty banning the

future use of landmines was signed by 100 nations in Oslo, Norway. The final draft of the document was signed in December 1997, in Ottawa, Canada, the country which had led the campaign.

A few weeks prior to that, in October 1997, the International Campaign to Ban Landmines

> **"You read the statistics, but actually going into the centres and seeing them struggling to gain a life again after they have had something ripped off – that is shocking."**
> DIANA, ON LANDMINE VICTIMS

received the highest accolade. Together with its co-ordinator, Jody Williams, the organization was chosen as recipient of the Nobel Prize for Peace.

Jody Williams, interviewed on television after receiving the prize, had no doubts as to how the dream had come true. Without Diana, she asserted, the landmine ban might never have happened.

THE SCANDALS CONTINUE

In 1994, the juggernaut of royal scandal rolled relentlessly on. By the middle of the year, it was once again Charles' turn to be in the spotlight, but Diana's next bout with the headlines was not far behind

Diana's advantage over Charles after their separation was that, whereas she was able to drop out of public life, this was not an option for him. He was still heir to the throne and remained an essential royal figure – it was imperative that he take action to repair the image that had taken so severe a beating in the last few years.

This was the main purpose of a television documentary *Charles: the Private Man, the Public Role*, in which the Prince was interviewed by the broadcaster and author Jonathan Dimbleby, who had written a full-scale biography of Charles to be published later in the year. The programme, which was screened on Wednesday 29 June 1994, aimed to give a rounded picture of the Prince – his activities, his interests, his hopes and plans for the future – and was intended to present the heir to the throne as a caring, committed king-in-waiting. The

plan misfired badly, however, when three minutes of the two-and-a-half-hour documentary dominated newspaper coverage the next day.

There was a great deal of solid content in the programme, including Charles' views on the environment, architecture and religion. But all that faded dramatically into the background when, in front of 14 million viewers, the Prince of Wales confessed to adultery. When Dimbleby asked Charles if he had been faithful to Diana, the Prince

> **"*I admired the honesty....
> To be honest about a relationship
> with someone else, in his position,
> that's quite something.*"**
> DIANA, ON CHARLES' TV APPEARANCE

said: 'Yes, absolutely'. Pressed further, Charles said 'Yes' again, but then he added 'until it became irretrievably broken down, us both having tried'.

The press pack leapt back into the saddle, and ignored virtually everything Charles and Dimbleby had so carefully prepared. A trail of red-hot headlines scorched across the front pages. Predictably, less publicity was given to a positive response to the programme – the Buckingham Palace switchboard, for example, was jammed with calls from viewers who said they welcomed the opportunity to see what the Prince was like, and liked what they saw.

HUSBAND UNDER ATTACK

The tabloids continued where the uproar over 'Camillagate' had left off. Once again, Charles was cast as a bounder who had betrayed and misused the lovely Diana. The fuss overshadowed what would have been a happy celebration: the 25th anniversary, on 1 July, of Charles' investiture as Prince of Wales. To mark the occasion, Charles gave a party, which included a pageant at Caernarvon Castle, where the investiture had taken place in 1969. Diana was not invited. However, on the same day, her 33rd birthday, pictures of her, taken by celebrity photographer, Patrick Demarchelier, appeared on the cover and inside *Vogue* magazine.

Diana's public appearances, whether in print or in person, were still comparatively few. At the

Opening page Diana presents a polo trophy to James Hewitt in 1989, at the height of her romantic involvement with him. Prince William looks on. **Opposite page, top** Charles with British Prime Minister John Major, in March 1994 at St. James' Palace, just three months before the screening of the controversial documentary TV programme. **Opposite page, bottom** Dimbleby's biography of Charles was another part of the attempt to remake the Prince's public image. **Left** The news of Diana's involvement with Hewitt was still not public knowledge when she attended the 1994 Wimbledon ladies' singles tennis final with Prince William in June. **Bottom left** A smiling James Hewitt drives away from the pursuing press pack.

IN THE NEWS

Popular press look for scandal

The publication of Jonathan Dimbleby's biography of Charles in 1994 sparked media anticipation that the Prince was about to spell out his love for Camilla Parker-Bowles. The Sun of 22 October went to town, saying that their relationship had lasted almost 25 years because of Charles and Camilla's shared love of zany humour. In the 573-page book itself, however, Camilla was mentioned on just 20 pages, and with never a whisper of sleaze. The rest dealt with much more solid issues.

DIARY DATES
1994
5–16 August
The Prince of Wales, Prince William and Prince Harry visit Crete for a holiday cruise

1–2 September
The Prince of Wales visits the Institute of Architecture Summer School at Viterbo, Italy

17–18 September
The Prince of Wales attends a ceremony commemorating the 50th anniversary of the Second World War Battle of Arnhem in the Netherlands

19 September
The Princess of Wales attends the Voice for Hospices Concert in London

1–4 November
The Prince of Wales visits Los Angeles

17 November
The Queen visits the Eastchurch Church of England Primary School at Kelmsley, Kent

30 November
The Queen receives the Governor-General of the Solomon Islands at Buckingham Palace

1 December
The Princess of Wales opens Mortimer Market Centre, London

6 December
The Prince of Wales gives a luncheon for members of the board of The Prince of Wales Business Leaders' Forum

16 December
The Princess of Wales attends a Head Injuries Association luncheon at the Hilton Hotel, London

Queen's invitation, she joined Prince Charles at the official commemoration on 6 June of the 50th anniversary of the D-Day landings in Normandy, France, during the Second World War, and on 14 July attended the wedding of Lady Sarah Armstrong-Jones, Princess Margaret's daughter.

But her public exposure was severely reduced compared to the busy years that had gone before – until, that is, an incident occurred that rocketed her

> "*I daren't get too close to him, but he's so stable and earthy. I can read his mind and we both like the same things. It's incredible!*"
>
> DIANA, ON JAMES HEWITT

back into the headlines. On 27 September 1994, Anna Pasternak's book *Princess in Love* was published, revealing that during her marriage Diana had conducted a long relationship with an army officer in the Guards, James Hewitt. It emerged that Hewitt had hired Pasternak to write the book.

The Princess had suspected that Hewitt was going into print when, in 1992, a friend warned her that he planned to sell his story to a tabloid newspaper. That proved a false alarm, but in the autumn of 1994, to a fanfare of tabloid comment, the tale of Hewitt's 'three-year affair with Di', as the *News of the World* headlined it, was out in the open.

Diana restricted her official appearances in 1994. **Opposite page** At the Royal College of Nursing, London, in September. **Left** With Prince Harry and friends on a visit to the musical *Oliver!* in December. **Above** Diana chats to Robbie Williams of the pop group Take That at a charity concert in December.

PRESS OUTRAGE

Princess in Love was critically slammed as syrupy tosh written in the style of a romantic novel, but this did nothing to cool the furore it created. In the aftermath, Hewitt took all the flak, even though Emma Stewardson, his girlfriend at the time he met Diana in 1986, claimed that the Princess had chased him relentlessly. Hewitt was ostracized by his regiment. Elsewhere he was called a 'love-rat', a 'cad', a 'bounder', even 'vermin'. He was, of course, charged with 'revolting greed' for 'ratting' on Diana in a book which, it was reckoned, would make him richer by some £3 million.

The name James Hewitt was not entirely unknown before *Princess in Love* appeared. In the 'Squidgy' tapes of 1992, Diana had told James

Protocol

THE BRAEMAR GAMES

Attending the Highland Games at Braemar, Scotland, **right**, is an annual tradition for the Royal Family during their summer holiday at Balmoral. It is also a tradition for the royals to wear tartan as a compliment to their Scots subjects. At the Games, the men dress in kilts and the women wear plaids. The Highland Games were originally meetings of the Scots clans, but developed into more formal gatherings in the early part of the 19th century. The Games include feats of strength and brawn such as tossing the caber, throwing the hammer, wrestling and running. Queen Victoria, who with Prince Albert purchased the manor house of Balmoral as a royal holiday home, made a visit to the Games a regular family tradition after 1850.

Gilbey that she spent a fortune on Hewitt, dressing him from head to foot. According to Emma Stewardson, Diana bought Hewitt £1500 Savile Row suits, £75 made-to-measure shirts, £700 pairs of shoes and much else, which he could never have afforded on his army salary of £24,000 a year.

Diana met Hewitt after he had been engaged to teach the young princes, William and Harry, how to ride – and to attempt to cure Diana of her own fear of the saddle while he was about it. Hewitt, then 28, was handsome, dashing, kind and attentive, and it seems that Diana rediscovered her sense of fun with him and, Pasternak claimed, a level of passion she had simply never known before.

A LONG-DISTANCE LOVE AFFAIR

Diana later admitted that she had been 'very much in love' with Hewitt. Even so, she had doubts about him. As a serving officer, Hewitt had to be away for months at a time, first in Germany in 1990, next, in 1991, in Saudi Arabia during the Gulf War with Iraq. Even though Emma Stewardson claimed that

> "The overall impression given by the film…is that here is a man of sincerity who has thought long and hard about the duties that lie ahead of him."
>
> BOB HOUSTON, ROYALTY MAGAZINE FOUNDER, ON CHARLES' TV APPEARANCE

Diana pestered Hewitt with phone calls when he was in Germany, by that time the Princess' ardour was apparently cooling. Diana, friends revealed, began to suspect that Hewitt was not in love with her and what he really wanted was the kudos of an affair with the Princess of Wales.

In addition, Hewitt was less than discreet. Once, during the Gulf War, he borrowed a reporter's mobile phone and talked to Diana for three minutes while the press stood around listening. The news reached the tabloids at home, and Diana was said to be both amazed and alarmed at the man's tactlessness. Instead of acknowledging his mistake, though, Hewitt compounded it by revealing to his

The many faces of a Princess. **Left** Trying out a state-of-the-art telephone at the Ideal Home Exhibition in London, in March 1992. **Opposite page, bottom left** Resigned to press attention, leaving Harvey Nichols, in Knightsbridge, in September 1994. **Opposite page, right** After the separation from Charles, on holiday in the French West Indies in February 1995.

The Private Princess
Deciding Diana's future

During 1994, behind the royal scenes, constitutionalists, courtiers and advisers were hard at work discussing the problem of Diana, Her Royal Highness the Princess of Wales, the estranged wife of the heir to the throne.

The discussions centred on what Andrew Morton called the 'If the Queen falls under a bus tomorrow' syndrome. If the Queen had suddenly died, Charles would have become King and Diana would have become his Queen Consort. However, the prospect of an estranged couple occupying the throne of England was not one that could be contemplated with any degree of equanimity.

There would be, to start with, the practical difficulties of a couple who lived apart and led separate lives having to come together on state occasions and act in unison. There would also be the problems of King Charles and Queen Diana having to undertake overseas tours, when being in each other's company for long periods of time in a

Above Sir Robert Fellowes, the Queen's Private Secretary, is one of Her Majesty's closest advisers. His proposals regarding Diana would have carried much weight.

foreign country might well be the last thing they wanted. The element of charade that would be involved could well demean the monarchy, something officials were anxious to avoid.

One solution that was put forward was that Diana should be persuaded to renounce her rights to be Queen while her mother-in-law was still alive. This would have been unprecedented, but the only logical alternative, divorce, was not being contemplated at the time.

friends intimate details about Diana and her life with Charles. As Diana told her friends, she finally came to realize how unwise she had been to become involved with a character like Hewitt.

The relationship foundered on what she saw as his 'betrayal' in selling his story, but she was at least gratified that *Princess in Love* had no effect on her popularity. The general tabloid consensus was that with a 'cold, unfeeling husband', as they called

> **"*Charles did not want her, James Hewitt let her down – it was Diana's sad fate to make mistakes in her choice of men.*"**
>
> FIONA SINCLAIR, ROYAL CORRESPONDENT

Charles, Diana had been justified in seeking love elsewhere. In a *Daily Mirror* poll, in fact, 73 per cent of readers subscribed to this view.

CHARLES' COMPLAINTS

But this new year of scandal had not yet finished with the royals. On 3 November, Jonathan Dimbleby's biography of Prince Charles appeared and ructions were reported at the Palace over its claims about Charles' 'miserable' and 'lonely' child-hood. The biography even implied that the Queen had been a largely absent mother, preoccupied with duty and with her workload as sovereign. All in all, if the royals were to choose an *annus horribilis II*, then 1994 would be a prime contender.

IN CONTEXT
ESTONIA FERRY DISASTER
1994

- The ferry *Estonia* sinks in the Baltic, **right,** with 912 reported deaths
- Syd Dernley, Britain's last hangman, dies
- Peace is signed in the Angolan civil war
- The last Allied soldiers leave Berlin after 50 years of guarding the city
- The notorious terrorist Carlos the Jackal is captured
- At her last Wimbledon tournament, nine-times champion Martina Navratilova is runner-up for the title
- Norwegians vote not to join the European Union

Sale of the

Diana's separation and divorce from Prince Charles also separated her from her previous royal public life. Auctioning 80 of her evening dresses in New York in 1997 symbolized a new start and a new life

Century

It was Prince William who thought of it. For some time before his parents' marriage finally ended in divorce in 1996, it was evident that the high-profile celebrity functions they attended together had come to an end. Fashion-wise and in many other ways, it was the end of an era in Diana's life and of all the many clothes in her wardrobe, her showpiece evening gowns were the most redundant. With no place to go, these dresses would remain on their hangers, mute witnesses to a glitzy past. Rather than leave them there, or give them away, William suggested to his mother, why not auction them for charity? William was only 14, not

Left At the reception held in Christie's New York salerooms, the night before the sale, Diana stands next to one of her glamorous Catherine Walker evening gowns. **Above** Diana in the same gown, at a formal reception in the Palace of Versailles, France, on 28 November 1994.

TOP-PRICED VICTOR EDELSTEIN GOWN
An exquisite off-the-shoulder midnight-blue gown, designed by Victor Edelstein. This fetched the highest price – $222,500 (£133,500) – at the auction.
Inset Diana's beauty graces this dress on a visit to the Austrian capital, Vienna, in April 1986.

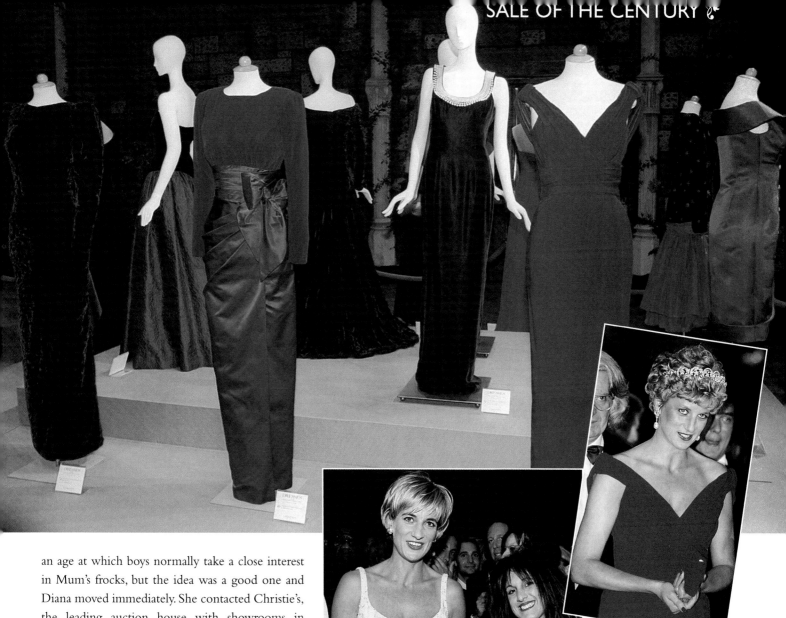

an age at which boys normally take a close interest in Mum's frocks, but the idea was a good one and Diana moved immediately. She contacted Christie's, the leading auction house with showrooms in London and New York, and the deal was on.

The news hit the headlines on 29 January 1997 and in some papers was illustrated by pictures of Diana wearing her John Galliano 'petticoat' dress. For simplicity and sophistication, this dress could not have been more different from some of those which were to go under the hammer on 25 June at Christie's in Park Avenue, New York.

Roll call of top designers

Christie's produced a magnificent catalogue which later became a collector's piece in its own right. A copy signed by Diana fetched some £15,000 after her death. The catalogue's contents read like a roster of her glamorous royal life. Most of the famous designers who had furnished her with evening wear were there – Catherine Walker, Bellville Sassoon (who had 'dressed' Diana since her earliest days as a

princess), Bruce Oldfield, Victor Edelstein, the Japanese designer Yuki and several more. The auction became one of the most talked about and eagerly anticipated events of the New York summer season. The results were anticipated in the same vein by the AIDS and cancer charities that were to benefit, and a figure of 'well over £1 million' was touted as the likely sale proceeds.

For Diana's admirers, though, there was a certain sadness in the undertaking. Among the dresses to be auctioned were some of the most beautiful she had ever worn, and it was obvious that in the future she

Top Diana's gowns on display in Christie's, including, front right, a Victor Edelstein design. **Inset, above** Diana wears this Edelstein gown with the Spencer family tiara to a performance by the English National Ballet in Budapest, Hungary, in March 1992. **Inset, above left** At the sale reception, with Elizabeth Emanuel, designer of the Princess' wedding gown.

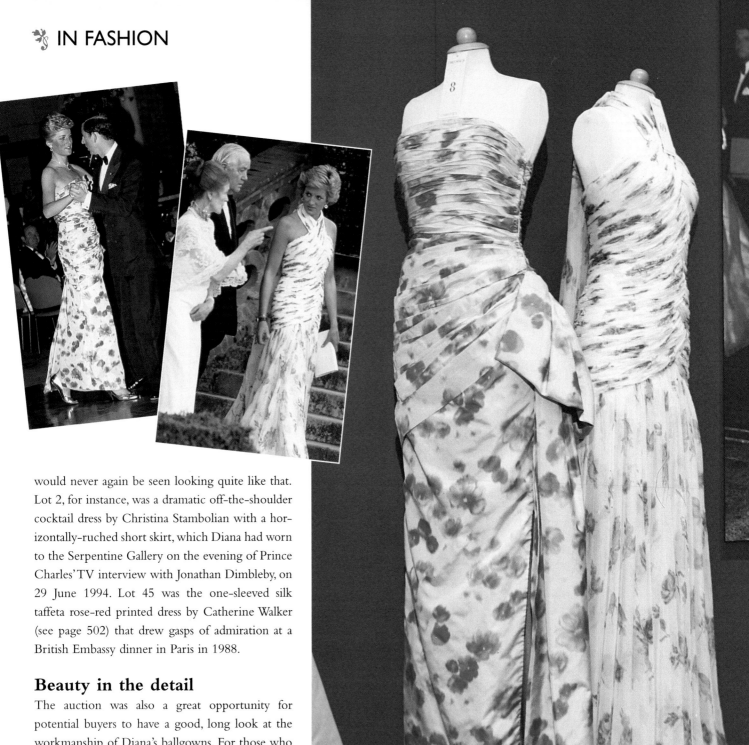

would never again be seen looking quite like that. Lot 2, for instance, was a dramatic off-the-shoulder cocktail dress by Christina Stambolian with a horizontally-ruched short skirt, which Diana had worn to the Serpentine Gallery on the evening of Prince Charles' TV interview with Jonathan Dimbleby, on 29 June 1994. Lot 45 was the one-sleeved silk taffeta rose-red printed dress by Catherine Walker (see page 502) that drew gasps of admiration at a British Embassy dinner in Paris in 1988.

Beauty in the detail

The auction was also a great opportunity for potential buyers to have a good, long look at the workmanship of Diana's ballgowns. For those who could not attend in person, the catalogue provided close-ups of details that it would have been impossible to see when Diana was wearing the dresses. One of Catherine Walker's most stunning gowns, Lot 43, which had an asymmetrical bodice of white ribbon lace edged with pearls, was by this means revealed in all the marvellous intricacy of its rose-like profusion. Diana wore the dress, which had a skirt of black silk, during a visit to Pakistan in 1992.

Another stunning detail showed the star-and-flower embroidery on the bodice of Jacques Azagury's 'flapper' dance dress in black rayon and blue organza, which came in at Lot 22. Diana wore

this ballerina-length dress in Florence in 1985 and again in Toronto the following year.

The evening before the auction, Diana was in New York to attend a reception at Christie's for the sale of tickets. She was greeted by the auctioneer, Lord Hindlip, a former officer in the Coldstream Guards, and by a highly excited crowd of New York socialites. Hindlip found himself hard pressed to steer a path for Diana through the packed show-room and made the next day's tabloid headlines by

Above Catherine Walker dresses: on the left, a silk taffeta evening dress with blue flowers; on the right, a dance dress of printed silk chiffon. **Insets above left** Diana shines in the blue-flower gown in Australia in 1988 and in the chiffon dress in England in 1990.

**CATHERINE WALKER
EVENING DRESS WITH
EMBROIDERED BOLERO**

The bodice of the dress and
the bolero are embroidered
and decorated with sequins
in floral patterns reminiscent
of Mughal designs. The
bolero sleeves and skirt are
in pink wild silk. **Inset** The
dress on a mannequin. Diana
wore the dress to a private
function on the India tour in
1992, but was never
photographed in it.

CHRISTIE'S

Misguided speculation

Even Diana, the darling of the media for most of the time, was not invulnerable to press barbs. This report in the Express of 23 February 1997, some four months before the auction, suggested that the Princess was profiteering and that the sale of her gowns was being staged only partly for the sake of charity.

In the event, the auction was a non-profitmaking effort on Christie's part. Aside from their proper expenses, all the money went to UK and USA charities chosen by Diana, including the AIDS Crisis Trust and the Royal Marsden Hospital.

gently placing a hand on the royal rear. He explained that he was trying to protect Diana and, it would seem, with some justification, as her admirers crushed so close to her that they might have been forming a rugby scrum.

Cocktail dress

Diana's outfit on this occasion was in sharp contrast to the lavish gowns that had been placed on display on dress models, alongside the occasional life-size picture of the Princess in one or other of them. She was wearing an above-the-knee cocktail dress with a short slit at the back of the skirt, a wide neckline, with narrow shoulder straps and red roses clustered on a white background. Its cost was said to be £2500, a mere

after the reception. She arranged to be kept informed at Kensington Palace of the progress made in New York. It was going to be virtually an all-night vigil. The auction was due to begin at 11.30pm London time on 25 June.

In the event, the sum raised by the auction fell far short of the most inflated estimates, but still reached an appreciable figure of £1,955,250. Naturally, every one of the gowns was sold and even the lowest price was notable: the £21,850 paid for Lot 72, a Catherine Walker pleated tunic

> **"I hope they don't deter buyers. What I'd say to people is, please do try, I'm sure there'll be some reasonably priced dresses."**
>
> DIANA, ON THE HIGH AUCTION PRICES

dinner dress in shrimp pink silk, which Diana wore at an English National Ballet gala evening in 1993.

The highest price, £133,500, was claimed by Lot 79, which was Victor Edelstein's inky blue off-the-shoulder gown in silk velvet, inspired by late-Edwardian – around 1910 – dinner dresses (see page 498). Appropriately enough, this dress had specific American connotations. Diana wore it in 1985 at a state dinner given by US President Ronald Reagan, at the White House in Washington DC, when she danced with John Travolta.

bagatelle compared to the vast prices that her ball-gowns were going to fetch.

It was infinitesimal compared to the ancillary sales that went with the auction. On the eve of the sale, the January estimates of £1 million had risen to £1 million for the catalogue sales, and £2 million for the picture syndication rights, before the auctioneer even raised his gavel. Other statistics were hardly less newsworthy. Some 1500 socialites had registered to bid, £125,000 was raised in two minutes at the ticket sale reception and the sale itself was now expected to raise £6 million. Diana herself was said to be 'amazed and concerned' at the huge prices being quoted for individual dresses.

She elected, however, not to attend the sale itself and flew back to London on the evening of 24 June,

Main picture and insets Each gown held memories. **Inset, top left** Diana wore this dramatic Catherine Walker creation on a visit to France in November 1988. **Inset, bottom left** Diana in a Bruce Oldfield gown at the première of the film *Hot Shots* in November 1991. **Inset, above** Diana in a Murray Arbeid dress, in London in 1986. **Top** At the Christie's reception, Diana shares a joke with fashion designer Zandra Rhodes.

Flying down to Rio

Charles and Diana had toured rich countries and poor countries. They had seen fabulous wealth and abject poverty and want. But the contrasts they encountered on their visit to Brazil in 1991 were uniquely harrowing

S easoned royal travellers like Charles and Diana were not easily shocked when they toured foreign countries. However, the Prince and Princess were taken by surprise when they went to Brazil, the only Portuguese-speaking country among the otherwise Spanish-dominated nations of South America, in April 1991.

The country had long been somewhat romantically listed in the travel brochures as 'a land of stark contrasts', but the royal couple found that the contrasts were so stark, the state of the rich and the poor so far apart, that Brazil came as a series of revelations – many unpleasant. As they quickly discovered, Brazil was a country where it was possible to look out from the windows of a luxury hotel and see, only yards away, a shanty town of squalid 'houses' made from bits of cardboard, metal and rubbish. Abandoned children lived on the streets, many

Main picture Charles and Diana's busy itinerary did leave them time to take in the breathtaking views over the great coastal city of Rio de Janeiro. **Above left** Enthusiastic crowds waving Union Jack flags welcome Diana to Rio de Janeiro.

Top Diana watches a display of gymnastics at a São Paolo school. **Inset, above** In Carajas Botanical Gardens, the royal couple planted a Brazil nut tree. **Opposite page, left** Diana visited a home for AIDS sufferers in São Paolo. **Opposite page, right** Attending the ballet in São Paolo.

thieving to survive, while beggars of all ages scrabbled a living. Yet the rich had more money than they knew what to do with and turned their homes into fortresses to keep out the poor.

Both Charles and Diana had acute social consciences. There could be little doubt that they were shocked, not only by the scenes of want and squalor they witnessed in Brazil, but also by the lack of compassion shown by better-off Brazilians who had it in their power to help.

In the jungle capital

The tour began in Brasilia, a beautiful purpose-built city, 3000 feet above sea level, which became the country's capital in 1960. The location of Brasilia, in the middle of the jungle, means that it is accessible to travellers only by air. Charles and Diana flew in on 22 April – autumn in the southern hemisphere – and were at once confronted by a problem which disturbed them. Charles, with his interest in the environment, was concerned to learn that millions of trees in the Brazilian rainforest, a vital resource for the whole world, had been hacked down to

> **"What really bothered her was the hopelessness she saw there. If no one cares, nothing will be done."**
> A FRIEND OF DIANA, ON THE BRAZILIAN TOUR

create not only Brasilia, but also the gigantic open-cast mine at Roseane, 1000 miles to the northwest, the largest mine of its kind in the world.

The Brazilian government, however, was mindful of the dangers to the world's oxygen supply that the destruction of the rainforest implied. Charles and Diana made their own contribution to the state afforestation programme by planting a Brazil nut

tree. A special plaque was erected at the Carajas Botanical Gardens which read, in Portuguese: 'Tree planted by their high royals Prince Charles and Princess Diana on the occasion of their visit to the Botanical Park of Carajas on 23 April of 1991'.

High-society banquet

Royal tours always required Charles and Diana to play a mixture of roles, and on the evening of 23 April, back in Brasilia, they wore their high-society hats for a dinner hosted by President Collor. The 350 guests were the cream of Brazilian society, and Diana drew gasps of admiration for her ballgown. There was a diversion, though: a crank known locally as 'the Kisser'. This man, 53 years old, had earned some notoriety for gatecrashing state occasions and planting kisses on the men. Pope John Paul II, Frank Sinatra and Julio Iglesias had been among his 'victims' and the Brazilians were determined that Prince Charles was not going to be

❧ Protocol ☙

BRAZIL'S ONLY ROYALS

*Brazil is the only modern country in South America to have had a recognized royal family. Emperor Pedro I (1798-1834), who made Brazil independent of Portugal in 1822, had the misfortune to fall foul of republicans, who forced him to abdicate in 1831. His son, Emperor Pedro II (1825-1891), **right**, was not much luckier. An opponent of slavery, he came up against plantation owners who relied on slave labour. Pedro left the country, after being forced to abdicate in 1889, and the slaves remained. A lover of gadgets, Pedro was Emperor long enough to become one of the first crowned heads to try out the new Bell telephone, in 1876. 'My God!' Pedro exclaimed, 'It works!'*

next. Although 'the Kisser' dodged armed guards, he was caught and locked away. Charles was safe.

On the next day, the scene changed again. The royal couple flew to Rio de Janeiro, the former cap-

> ## "Charles and Diana had never before done a tour which offered so much excitement, but also so much pain."
>
> FIONA SINCLAIR, ROYAL CORRESPONDENT, ON THE BRAZILIAN TOUR

ital, well known to tourists for its carnival, its Copacabana and Ipanema beaches, Sugar Loaf mountain and the statue of *Cristo Redentor* (Christ the Redeemer) on Mount Corcovado.

Diana's first interest was not, however, in the tourist sites. She visited a city refuge, which housed

destitute children rescued from the streets, and presented equipment worth £8000 to the AIDS research laboratory of the University Hospital. She also toured the hospital wards and was visibly affected when she was told that the AIDS victim whose hand she was stroking had only a few weeks to live. Diana chatted, too, with four other patients, showing her usual compassionate concern and friendliness towards people who were more used to being treated as pariahs.

Cristo Redentor, one of the greatest tourist sights in the whole of South America, was not to be missed, though. As always, the statue was crowded round with tourists as well as *cariocas*, as the inhabitants of Rio are called. Diana mingled freely with the crowds, who, when they recognized her, crushed about her to view the most famous, most photographed woman in the world. From Mount Corcovado, Diana was able to see the great spread

Above Diana at Iguaçu Falls, one of many sites of astonishing natural beauty in Brazil. **Opposite page** High above Rio, the great statue of Christ the Redeemer on Mount Corcovado looms behind Princess Diana like a protecting presence.

Opposite page At the thundering Iguaçu Falls on 26 July. **Far right** Diana watches the work at an open-cast copper mine in Carajas. **Right and inset below** Charles and Diana were guests of the state governor and his wife at an official dinner at the Palacio de Cidade.

of Rio de Janeiro laid out before her, as it curved around the bay, with the famous Sugar Loaf mountain looming above the city's tall white skyscrapers and lush shores.

Samba beat

The face of Brazil changed again that same evening when Charles and Diana attended a dinner at Rio's city palace, hosted by the governor, Lionel Brizma.

Afterwards, there was an exhibition of samba dancing, which Charles and Diana watched from a balcony. The couple had missed the famed carnival by two months, but this was a sort of consolation prize as they were treated to a special display of the rhythmic, foot-tapping samba by a group of carnival girls.

Thirteen years earlier, in 1978, a carnival girl had achieved brief eminence when Charles, then a bachelor, danced with her on an occasion that was remembered for the girl's extremely brief, if elaborate, costume. Charles, in fact, had not forgotten her and had enquired about her this time. He learned that she was now married, with a baby on the way, and he referred to her in a speech he made at the presidential banquet in Brasilia.

In 1991, the samba-dancing carnival girls obviously hoped to repeat their predecessor's success and kept asking Charles to come down from the balcony and join them. He resisted, but Diana, who loved dancing, staged her own response, swaying to the seductive samba beat of the drums.

The colourful glamour of Brazil, as represented by its carnival and infectious dance rhythms, did not sideline Charles' and Diana's concern for the distressing problems they had observed during their five-day tour. Diana had witnessed a most appalling situation when she visited, at her own request, a

Above Diana talks with an AIDS sufferer in the University Hospital, Rio de Janeiro. Her natural manner and genuine warmth were a great comfort to patients.

small hostel for abandoned children in São Paulo, Brazil's leading industrial city. There, lying on threadbare bedding in iron cots, she saw the abandoned children of prostitutes and drug addicts. Some of them were HIV-positive, one was only five months old, and Diana was told that they would be fortunate if they lived beyond the age of 12. Diana kissed and cuddled them in her usual spontaneous way, but she was deeply affected by these sad cast-offs of a largely uncaring society.

Before they left Brazil on 27 April, Charles and Diana took the opportunity to make their feelings known about what was in many ways Brazil's biggest problem: the apparent lack of a social conscience among those with the power, wealth and influence to make life better for the poor. Diana told Brazilians that it was imperative for them to reach out to the victims of society, to help those too ground down by poverty to help themselves. Charles, for his part, tackled the big businessmen, urging them to adopt a more responsible role in the

community. Companies, Charles said, should devote more energy to good and deserving causes, and formulate a new business ethic which would recognize the complex web of modern economic and social relations. The tour ended with Charles

> *"My hair is sparser, but I'm still wearing the same suits."*
> PRINCE CHARLES, RECALLING HIS VISIT TO BRAZIL IN 1978

and President Collor co-hosting an environmental seminar on the royal yacht *Britannia*, which was moored at the mouth of the mighty Amazon river.

Just how much Charles and Diana succeeded in getting across their humanitarian message was not something either of them could quantify. But it was certainly true that the kind-hearted, compassionate Prince and Princess of Wales gave the Brazilian people a great deal to think about.

Diana, pale and drawn during her *Panorama* interview with Martin Bashir, revealed intimate details of her marriage breakdown and revelations about royal life.

NO GOING BACK

In 1995, more salvoes were fired in what the press commonly called 'the war of the Waleses'. Neither Prince Charles nor Diana wanted a divorce, it appears, but clearly there would be no ceasefire without it

The popularity of the Princess of Wales was a phenomenon unique in the annals of celebrity. Nothing she did or said, no scandal in which she was involved and, most important of all, nothing the Palace could do seemed able to shake it. Despite the 'Squidgy' revelations, the phone calls to Oliver Hoare and the affair with James Hewitt, the British people forgave Diana everything, and she survived with their love and adoration intact. But, as the second year of her separation from Charles began, Diana put this extraordinary public regard under yet more strain.

In 1994, she had ended her relationship with Hewitt, and been warned off Hoare, but the ruggedly handsome England rugby captain, Will Carling, remained close to Diana, despite his

marriage in July to the dynamic Julia Smith. As a celebrity, Carling was newsworthy. His attractive wife, too, was a news bonus. Julia Carling objected to what she saw as her husband's undue closeness to Diana. Princess or no Princess, she was the 'other woman'. Although Carling insisted that the friendship was 'harmless', Julia publicly accused Diana of trying to ruin her marriage.

'She picked the wrong couple...this time,' Julia asserted. 'But it does make you stronger no matter how much someone is trying to destroy you.'

CARLING OUTFLANKED

This was fighting talk, and the press depicted the Carling-Diana triangle as a tussle for possession, with the bemused rugby star being pulled this way

and that between two women equally resolved to triumph. The beleaguered Carling came to the conclusion that he had been 'stupid' to imagine that even an innocent friendship with someone as celebrated as Diana would be taken as that, and only that. He was made to realize how right he was in September 1995, when he arrived at Kensington Palace with a couple of rugby jerseys. Diana was out at the time. But when Carling told newsmen staking out the palace that the jerseys were gifts for William and Harry, he was greeted with jibes. Quite possibly, Will Carling, a man who had risen to sports stardom because of his talent rather than

Above Carling – seen here leaving his London home on 25 September 1995 – was swamped by media attention amid speculation about his relationship with Diana.
Top At the Five Nations rugby match – Wales v England – at Cardiff Arms Park on 6 February 1993, Diana was introduced to the England team by their captain, Will Carling.

his social connections, was flattered by Diana's interest. And maybe this was the reason he stuck his neck out over the Princess in so many unwise ways.

According to his one-time personal assistant, Hillary Ryan, Carling met Diana for breakfast and

Above Diana leaves the Harbour Club gym, Chelsea, after a daily workout, five days before her *Panorama* interview was broadcast.
Top right Newly-weds Will and Julia Carling visited Smith's Lawn Polo, Windsor, in July 1994.
Left Julia Carling and co-presenter Mark Little discuss the news with actress Nerys Hughes, on Channel 4's *Big Breakfast*. The headlines reveal details of Charles and Diana's divorce settlement.

> "*This has happened to her before, and you would hope she won't do these things again, but she obviously does.*"
> JULIA CARLING, ON DIANA'S RELATIONSHIPS

a fitness workout two or three times a week in the early part of 1995. Carling often told Ryan that he would be 'away' from the office and she later discovered he had gone to Kensington Palace with Diana. The rugby star had a special direct phone link installed between his office and Diana's apartment, which no one but he was supposed to use. Ryan revealed that Carling and Diana talked on

this phone 'for an hour or more, laughing and giggling. At other times, they seemed to be having quite intimate conversations.'

CONTRADICTIONS

Little wonder, then, that scandal-mongers in the media concluded there was an affair going on. Julia Carling, meanwhile, was still on the rampage and, in the late summer of 1995, she appeared to have prevailed when she told the press that her husband's involvement with Diana was over. She denied, though, that she had given Carling an ultimatum.

The decision, Julia said, was 'Will's alone'. The triumph, if it was one, proved shortlived. Only two days afterwards, Diana and Carling were seen together at the Chelsea Harbour Club. After a second meeting, even the feisty Julia retired from the fray. The Carlings separated on 28 September 1995, after only 14 months of marriage. On 29 August the following year, they divorced.

By that time, Will Carling's royal friendship had also ended. The rugby hero had wilted, it appears, under the pressure his involvement with Diana had created. He was said to have told Diana that he felt 'like a cork bobbing about in an ocean rather than taking control of the situation'. With that, the relationship was clearly at an end, and Diana was alone again. Alone, but still plagued by her own demons.

Above In Venice for a biennial arts competition, Diana travels to the Palazzo Grassi in a motor boat.
Right Diana, Prince Harry and Kate Menzies on a skiing holiday in Lech, Austria, in March 1995.

CURBING DIANA

Diana had been aware for a long time, even before her separation from Charles, that the royal advisers at Buckingham Palace – 'the grey men' as she called them – were anxious to lower the profile that her huge popularity had given her. What alarmed them, it seems, was the way in which Diana consistently outperformed and upstaged Charles and even the Queen. She had become more of a showbiz-type celebrity than was considered seemly for a royal.

With Charles and Diana's estrangement, some subtle but powerful interventions began to be made in the Princess' affairs. A charity, for instance, asked

> **"It was a perfectly harmless friendship. Maybe I was just stupid."**
>
> WILL CARLING, ON HIS RELATIONSHIP WITH DIANA

Diana to visit one of its projects abroad. She accepted, but the enterprise foundered because Buckingham Palace or Foreign Office officials let charities know that such proposals were 'unacceptable'. This is what happened in 1995, when the Red Cross asked Diana to lend her royal flair to the worldwide celebrations of their 125th anniversary. It occurred again when the British Red Cross invited

Opposite page, top Talking to medical students in the obstetrics unit at Tushinskaya Hospital, Moscow, June 1995. **Above** In February 1995, Diana escapes the stresses of public life on the Caribbean island of St. Barthélémy. **Left** Reviewing the Light Dragoons in Germany.

IN THE NEWS

Diana speaks out

The Sun's banner headline in this issue, printed five days before Diana's sensational Panorama interview was screened, got it exactly right. The revelations she made on TV were indeed dynamite. No royal secrets of this kind had ever been so brutally revealed in public before. No Prince of Wales had ever been so reviled. Front pages like this naturally created an enormous public appetite to know more and, on 20 November, millions were glued to their TV sets the world over.

The Private Princess
Diana at war with Tiggy

Diana took a deep dislike to Alexandra 'Tiggy' Legge-Bourke, who was assistant to Prince Charles' press aide, Commander Richard Aylard. Tiggy had been seconded to look after William and Harry while they were on holiday with their father and was soon being called their 'surrogate mum' by members of the press.

Diana felt Tiggy was supplanting her, all the more so because the young princes became extremely fond of their stand-in carer. According to authors Chris Hutchins and Dominic Midgley in their 1996 book *Diana on the Edge: Inside the Mind of the Princess of Wales*, the Princess appears to have decided to get at Tiggy during a Christmas party for royal staff at the Lanesborough Hotel, Hyde Park Corner, London, on 14 December 1995. The Princess walked up to Tiggy and said, without ceremony: 'Sorry to hear about the baby.' Tiggy was so shocked, she collapsed into a chair.

Later, she told friends that she was 'stunned and amazed', especially when

Above 'Tiggy' Legge-Bourke with Prince William and Prince Harry, fording the River Dee during a summer stay at Balmoral.

Diana went on to hint that Prince Charles was the father of this non-existent infant. The 'pregnancy', Diana implied, had been dealt with when Tiggy went abroad for a quiet abortion.

Tiggy considered suing Diana for slander but was dissuaded by her lawyer, Peter Carter-Ruck. The matter did not end there, though. The allegation came to the notice of the press. They, too, were warned off reporting the story. They published nonetheless, although it was some six weeks later and the passage of time had taken some of the sting out of the unsavoury incident.

It is uncertain whether or not Diana believed the pregnancy story to be true, but she was, reportedly, unwise enough to repeat it to the Queen. From this arose the suggestion, picked up by the media, that Diana's extraordinary behaviour helped persuade the Queen to press Charles to divorce her.

Diana to become their ambassador overseas. The powers that be quashed that notion, and Diana soon came to believe the decision was made right at the top. She reached the conclusion that those pulling the strings were resolved to exclude her, as far as possible, from the public spotlight.

They did not, however, have a monopoly of determination. Towards the end of 1995, Diana prepared what turned out to be the coup to end all coups, virtually a public declaration of war against all those she suspected of conspiring against her. On 4 November, Martin Bashir, a relatively unknown BBC interviewer, arrived at Kensington Palace with a film crew, and there taped an hour-long interview. The enterprise remained a closely

> *"Because I know the character, I would think the top job...would bring enormous limitations on him and I don't know whether he could adapt to that."*
> DIANA, ON CHARLES AS KING

guarded secret. Not even Diana's press aide, Geoffrey Crawford, knew of it and, when he found out, he was so outraged that he resigned.

News of the forthcoming TV interview, tantalizingly trailed as an exposé of the royal marriage, broke on Charles' birthday, 14 November. Through mysterious press leaks, the general tenor of the programme was either known or suspected in royal circles and, as the *Daily Mirror* noted, there was 'Palace fury at [the] secret TV deal'. The tabloid was unable to resist the opportunity of trading on past comments on Diana's state of mind. On 14 November, the day that Diana visited Broadmoor, the secure psychiatric hospital in Berkshire, the *Mirror* headed its front page 'Has She Gone Mad?'

Just under a week later, on 20 November, the interview was broadcast on the BBC's *Panorama* programme. Millions the world over were riveted to their screens in a mood of high expectation, and they were not disappointed. Diana appeared as no one had ever seen her before – pale, drawn, her hair barely brushed and wearing a dreary black suit. It

Left Diana as she was seen by millions during her interview with Martin Bashir on the BBC's prestigious *Panorama* programme, on 20 November 1995. Shown on the Queen and Prince Philip's wedding anniversary, for Her Majesty it was the last straw; she told Prince Charles that he must divorce Diana as soon as possible.

Left Conservative minister Nicholas Soames, a friend of Prince Charles, called the Princess 'unstable'.
Right Geoffrey Crawford, Diana's press aide, resigned in the wake of the *Panorama* interview, which he had known nothing about.

⋙ Protocol ⋘

CEREMONY AT THE CENOTAPH

*Every year on Remembrance Sunday, the Sunday closest to 11 November, the anniversary of the armistice that ended the First World War in 1918, the Royal Family attends a ceremony honouring those who died in both World Wars and in other conflicts. The ceremony takes place at the Cenotaph in Whitehall, London, completed in 1920. 'Cenotaph' means 'empty tomb' in Greek. The Queen and other members of the Royal Family lay wreaths on the Cenotaph steps and afterwards stand for a two-minute silence. Royals not actually taking part in the ceremony, such as the Queen Mother or the Princess Royal, watch, black-clad, from a nearby balcony as political, military and royal representatives (such as Prince Philip, **right**) honour the war dead.*

was, some commentators later claimed, the uniform of a victim, and deliberately worn.

ASTOUNDING REVELATIONS

Gently prodded by the tactful, quiet-voiced Martin Bashir, who was asking pre-arranged questions, Diana revealed the most astounding inside details of royal life that viewers had ever heard, or were likely to hear. She spoke of the insidious activities of 'the grey men' and her doubts that Prince Charles was fit to become king. She criticized the monarchy – and, by implication, her parents-in-law, as well as their advisers – and the remote, stuffy royal ways which put up barriers against the people. She emphasized her desire to be of service to the victims of society worldwide as 'Queen of People's Hearts'.

Once she had finished exposing these details, though, Diana did not spare herself. Speaking quietly but fluently, she told of her eating disorders, her

> **"I think the British people need someone in public life to give affection, to make them feel important…to give them light in their dark tunnels."**
> DIANA, IN PANORAMA INTERVIEW

self-mutilation and her inability to cope with the pressures of royal life. She even went so far as to admit adultery with James Hewitt, though she said nothing about any suicide attempts. She affirmed that she did not want a divorce, but acknowledged that she would have to go. She promised, however, that she was not going to go quietly.

The candour of it all was quite breathtaking and, if Diana had gambled on that to win her the day, victory, it appeared, was hers. Almost universally, the next day's press praised her 'gut-wrenching honesty'. The Kensington Palace switchboard was overwhelmed with calls applauding her 'brave', 'fearless' and 'wonderful' performance. The public came out yet again in Diana's favour as a poll taken after the programme showed a big majority believed Diana had been right to speak out as she did. Charles' ratings, conversely, slumped to a new low.

ANTI-DIANA LOBBY

Some voices were raised against Diana. Nicholas Soames, a government minister, hammered the Princess as 'unstable'. There were mutterings, too, of 'betrayal' and scorn for Diana's 'psychobabble', which, it was suggested, she had picked up from her therapists. Nevertheless, Diana's critics were vastly outnumbered and she doubtless hoped that she had won the battle for public acclaim. But then the one voice that mattered most spoke up. This was when the Queen told Charles that he now had only one choice: though neither he nor Diana wanted it, they must divorce, and the sooner the better.

Above Charles and James Hewitt in action at the Royal Berkshire Polo Club in 1991, prior to the revelations of the 'Squidgy' tape. **Opposite page, top** Showing a united front, the Waleses meet Dr. Andrew Gailey, on William's first day at Eton. **Right** The Queen, with princes Philip, Charles and William, attend the VJ day celebrations on 19 August 1995.

1995

- Earthquake devastates Kobe, Japan
- US space shuttle *Discovery* and Russian space station *Mir* rendezvous in space
- Collapse of Barings Bank after fraudulent dealing
- Terrorist bombing of the federal building, **right**, in Oklahoma City, USA
- France announces nuclear tests in the Pacific
- British boxer Frank Bruno wins WBC World Heavyweight title
- Assassination of Israeli Prime Minister, Yitzhak Rabin

The Pattern of Change

After her estrangement from Charles, Diana's fashions changed. The grand occasions, which had seen her at her most stylish, were fewer, but she was less restricted by the royal rules

Long before Diana's evening dress auction at Christie's, New York, in 1997, gave notice that her glitziest royal days were past, she had chosen a new fashion direction. For some time Diana had longed for freedom from 'establishment' outfits and for the opportunity to be herself.

Her chance came with the semi-detachment from the Royal Family and their rules that followed her separation from Charles. This was Diana's cue to put an end to formality, and she lost no time. Very quickly, she became much more daring in her choice of fashion houses, and no longer concentrated on British designers.

Continental flair

She now went in for Chanel, Yves Saint Laurent, Armani and Valentino – all of them adventurous, highly imaginative designers at the high, and sometimes controversial, peak of fashion, and all of them foreign. She also began to patronize a designer who was far too avant-garde to provide clothes for traditional royal ladies: Gianni Versace.

For Diana, of course, Versace never went to the lengths available to actress

Main picture In Chicago in June 1996, Diana is wearing a white belted shift dress by Gianni Versace. **Far left** In Washington in 1997, she wears a red evening dress by Jacques Azagury.

🌿 523 🌿

Elizabeth Hurley, who once appeared in a hardly there evening dress held together by safety pins. Nevertheless, Versace's simple but stylish above-the-knee shifts, and his slinky, clingy evening gowns, were very much part of Diana's new look. She wore his classic black shift to the memorial service held following the designer's murder in Miami on 15 July 1997. The previous year Diana was seen more than once in what was clearly a favourite outfit – Versace's asymmetrical, electric-blue evening gown, which revealed her glorious figure as no evening gown had ever done before.

Understatement, with more emphasis on line and shape than on the splendid decoration that had often characterized Diana's royal appearances of previous years, went well with the new freedom of the separated Diana. This was evident in a series of pictures taken in 1994 and 1995 by photographer

> ## "*Will the real Diana please sit down and dress like a princess?*"
> TATLER, ON *DIANA'S REVEALING FASHIONS*

Patrick Demarchalier, which showed Diana at her most alluring and contravened virtually every concept of acceptable royal dressing. No future Queen Consort, which Diana remained as long as she was still married, had ever looked like this.

In one Demarchalier photograph, she wore a simple black evening gown with a black net insert, which showed her cleavage, and a split running far up one side. Another dress, in black sparkled with silver, had a halter neckline, a long slit in the skirt, and revealed even more of her cleavage. A third dress covered up more, but the shimmering red material emphasized every curve as Diana posed with one hand on her fetchingly extended hip.

Split skirts by day

The change in Diana's fashions was just as apparent in other sections of her wardrobe. The split skirts appeared daily when she wore them in 1994 to collect her sons from school, and she caused quite a stir when she wore one to church that Christmas. Diana was criticized by fashion pundits for turning herself into an 'Essex girl' or 'TV soap star' and for

1 In Washington in June 1997, Diana gave a speech to the American Red Cross on the landmines issue. She wore a lilac two-piece suit with a belted jacket – a simple but pretty suit for a working princess. The skirt was in the style she had come to favour since her separation and divorce, with a hem several inches above the knee. Around her neck she wore a pearl necklace.

2 On a visit to Liverpool on a cold November day in 1995, Diana keeps warm by wearing a black polo neck and warm black tights with this bright orange two-piece suit by Gianni Versace.
3 At Heathrow Airport in November 1995, en route to Argentina, Diana wears a red figure-hugging jacket with a short straight black skirt. This practical suit was a favourite with the Princess and she wore it on several occasions in 1995.

4 In Leatherhead, Surrey, in January 1995, Diana wears a bottle-green two-piece with a black Chanel handbag. The drape jacket has a velvet collar and is worn over a short skirt.
5 In March 1996 Diana visits the National Hospital for Neurology in London. She wears a simple pale pink two-piece with a black patent Kelly Bag by Hermès.

THE PATTERN OF CHANGE

CATHERINE WALKER PLAIN PATTERNED DRESS

Diana caused a stir when she arrived at the London première of *In Love And War*, in February 1997, **inset right**, wearing this stunning full length dark blue lace dress by Catherine Walker. The dress was low-cut with thin satin straps and a suggestive cream lace panel at the back. The film, directed by Diana's friend Sir Richard Attenborough, was preceded by a showing of the TV documentary *Diary Of A Princess*, about Diana's experiences in Angola.

525

chasing her 'supermodel' image too frantically. Diana, however, seemed to care little or nothing for such judgements and went her own way regardless. One way or another, her splendid legs were on view almost every time she left home.

The photographers who stalked her so persistently recorded her leaving the gym after a workout still dressed in her tight bicycle shorts, as well as her casual sneakers, baseball caps and sweatshirts. For her

> *"Diana's true style only began to come into its own over the past four years, since the separation from Charles."*
>
> TASMIN BLANCHARD, THE INDEPENDENT
> FASHION EDITOR, ON DIANA

official engagements, she so frequently wore suits featuring above-the-knee skirts that they began to achieve the status of a uniform.

When she visited Broadmoor Hospital on 14 November 1995, the day her forthcoming *Panorama* interview was announced, Diana wore a figure-hugging black suit with tulip-shaped jacket and velvet collar, cuffs and pocket flaps. In 1996 and 1997, there was the red suit with flared jacket and black bow tie; the powder-blue suit with white outlined jacket hem, rolled collar and pocket flaps, the green suit with shirt-style belted jacket and short sleeves; the lilac suit with wide lapels; and the white suit with polo-style jacket – every one of them accompanied by a straight skirt with a hem a few inches above the knee.

Relaxed and dynamic

Dressed like this, there was undoubtedly a big difference in Diana. The new-style princess looked a lot happier and more relaxed in photographs taken after the separation. The smile was more spontaneous, the head was up, the body language much more confident. The whole impression was one of dynamism. Traditionalists tut-tutted and fashion pundits were unsure, but the new, more daring Princess of Wales, it seemed, was the real Diana at last.

CATHERINE WALKER DINNER DRESS

This red and black dinner dress was said to be militarily inspired. The sleeveless bodice with a high neck is in a Hussar style, trimmed with black braid. The three-quarter-length skirt, made of scarlet silk crêpe, is also trimmed with scarlet silk braid. Diana wore it to the Red Cross' 125th birthday appeal, **inset below**, on the evening of the VE celebrations, in London, in May 1995.

1 **2**

3

THE PATTERN OF CHANGE

4

1 In December 1996 Diana attended a ball celebrating the opening of the Christian Dior exhibition at the Metropolitan Museum of Art in New York City. She wore this stunning midnight-blue lace-trimmed petticoat dress by John Galliano. It was said to have cost £10,000.

2 In Sydney, Australia, in October 1996, Diana wore this slinky, electric blue Versace evening dress, with matching clutch bag and shoes, to a charity ball.

3 For a reception at the White House, Washington DC, in September 1996, Diana returned to a trusted designer, Catherine Walker, who created this diamanté and lace halter dress.

4 Diana arrives at the Bolshoi Ballet in Moscow, in June 1995, wearing a white and gold brocade dress by Catherine Walker with a silver clutch bag.

IN THE NEWS

Conservative press bemoan the changes

Certain elements of the press, particularly the more conservative end, took the moral high ground when it came to discussing Diana's changing taste in fashion after her separation. As they saw it, she was once the demure little girl and dressed like it. Next she was the dutiful mother, wearing modest fashions. Finally, Diana turned into a 'got it, flaunt it' Essex girl, with short, tight slit skirts, low necklines and other similar provocations. This article from the Daily Mail of 17 March 1994 charts her fashion progress from virginal to vampish.

Main picture Soaked to the skin by a downpour, Diana and Luciano Pavarotti meet backstage after a concert in Hyde Park, London, in July 1991. **Inset** Backstage with Elton John after a concert in May 1993.

Stars in Her Eyes

As a royal and a celebrity, Diana had unparalleled opportunities to meet the stars of the rock, film, theatre, opera and ballet worlds. Nothing could have been more thrilling for Diana, the lifelong fan and autograph hunter

Film star Elizabeth Taylor once said, 'The Princess of Wales was always a fan'. This was an astute observation that saw beneath the glamour of Diana the princess and went straight to the heart of the matter. Diana was more celebrated, more photographed, more adored, more admired, more lauded and more frequently in the newspapers than any other star. Yet she was still touchingly capable of showing the joyous thrill which all fans feel when confronted with their favourites.

A lasting thrill

At an engagement in 1982, as a very young princess barely versed in royal ways, Diana ran to greet the Status Quo pop group in an evident froth of excitement. There was much shaking of traditionalist heads at the sight of a future Queen of England letting her guard down in this somewhat undignified fashion, but many others found her enthusiasm rather charming. However, this was not a part of Diana that vanished, as it so often does, with maturity. She never got over that thrill and relished meeting the stars whenever she could.

Diana's new position in the public eye yielded one big star even before she married Prince

Above At a première of the film *Stepping Out*, in 1991, Diana chats to stars Liza Minelli and Julie Walters.

ᘐ Protocol ᘑ

HONOURING POP STARS

The idea of royal awards going to pop stars provoked horror during the 1960s, the decade of the 'generation gap' and long-haired youthful rebellion against established values. This was evident in 1965, when the Beatles — John Lennon, Paul McCartney, George Harrison and Ringo Starr — were each awarded an MBE for services to pop music. Several existing holders of this honour were so outraged, they returned their medals to Buckingham Palace in protest. More recently, though, there was little fuss when knighthoods were awarded to Boomtown Rat and Band Aid organizer Bob Geldof (right), to singer Cliff Richard and to pop musicians Paul McCartney and Elton John.

Charles. On her first public engagement in March 1981, when Charles took his new fiancée to the Royal Opera House, Covent Garden, London, Diana met the beautiful, stately Princess Grace of Monaco, the one-time film star Grace Kelly. Grace, who was as kindhearted as she was beautiful, lent the 19-year-old Diana her shoulder to cry on when the unfortunate young lady found her strapless evening gown was cut far too low for modesty.

Grace also took the tearful young girl to the powder room, helped her dry her eyes and adjust her make-up and gave her some good advice about coping with the pressures of being a princess. Sadly, in September of the following year, when Princess Grace died after a car crash, Diana had to represent the Royal Family at her funeral in Monaco.

By then, Diana had thought of a way to put her love of the stars to practical use. The glitterati, the big stars, found themselves roped in to further the cause of royal charity. At that time, the principle

outlet for Charles' and Diana's good works was the Prince's Trust, which Charles had founded in 1974. The Trust had long outgrown the Royal Navy pay with which Charles had initially financed it. Money

> **"I wanted to see you seven years ago [1977] at Woburn Abbey, but my father wouldn't let me. Well, he can't stop me tonight, can he?"**
> DIANA, TO SINGER NEIL DIAMOND

was now required on a vast scale to aid the young people, the unemployed, the homeless and the numerous others the Trust aimed to help.

Fund-raising, though a big innovation for royals with its whiff of commercialism, was the logical answer. This was where Diana's fondness of pop music and rock stars came in useful. She was familiar with the big chart successes of the pop world

Opposite page, top left Diana, Phil Collins and the other members of Genesis after a 1984 Birmingham concert. **Top centre** Sharing a joke with film star Tom Hanks at the London première of *Apollo 13* in 1995. Beside him is his wife Rita, director Ron Howard and Kathleen Quinlan. **Above** With Paul and Linda McCartney, in Paris in November 1992. **Left** With dancer Wayne Sleep at the Royalty Theatre, London, in June 1989, after the show *Bits And Pieces*.

Above Diana meets with Tom Cruise and his co-star and wife Nicole Kidman at the London première of *Far And Away*, in July 1992.
Above right Diana talks with pop singer Alison Moyet backstage at Wembley Arena after a Prince's Trust Concert in June 1987.
Right Diana with singer Neil Diamond, after a concert he gave at Wembley Arena in November 1989.

and the groups who scored them. The stars themselves, when approached, were eager to give their help and the first concert in aid of the Prince's Trust was given by Status Quo in 1982. Within five years, 15 fund-raising concerts had taken place, one of which, held in the summer of 1986, raised nearly £1.2 million in ticket sales, television fees, record sales and video rights. Others held the same year produced nearly £1 million more, and, though less highly advertised than in the early days, this form of fund-raising continued into the 1990s.

It was, of course, almost unprecedented for members of royalty and pop music stars to unite in this fashion. Despite the fine cause the concerts served, such an unusual juxtaposition raised many traditionalists' eyebrows. There was more shock when Bob Geldof, the pioneer of 'Band Aid', the method of using pop music to fund famine relief, turned up

to see Charles in his normal state of disarray – three-day stubble, long uncombed locks, worn-out jeans and crumpled T-shirt. Prince William apparently came into his father's study and, with the candour of three-year-olds, wanted to know what this 'dirty man' was doing there.

Band Aid concert

The same question was asked for more snobbish reasons by a variety of critics. Snobbery, however, was never in Charles' or Diana's vocabulary and on 13 July 1985, they sat with Bob Geldof at Wembley Stadium, watching his brainchild, the Band Aid concert raise money for famine-blighted Africa. Charles and Diana were there again on 25 May 1986 when Geldof organized his 'Race Against Time' initiative for Sportaid in Africa.

The pop and rock world connection had its problems, though. Concern was voiced that the

Prince and Princess were consorting with stars, such as Boy George, who were known drug users. Boy George also raised eyebrows because he was an outlandishly dressed homosexual. Traditionally,

> "*The Princess gave John a real run for his money. She was every bit as good as him. It was real Hollywood tinsel-town stuff.*"
>
> CHARLES PRICE, US AMBASSADOR TO BRITAIN, ON DIANA'S DANCE WITH JOHN TRAVOLTA

royals were meant to keep well away from the edges of society. What critics failed to realize, however, was that Charles and Diana were not only showing that they were a Prince and Princess for all the people, but were gaining valuable information about problems that they would embrace in the

Above Princess Diana with singer Chris de Burgh and Richard Branson, the founder of Virgin. She is admiring a golden disc marking hit sales of Chris de Burgh's record *Lady in Red*. The occasion was the launch of a Virgin Airlines aircraft, which was itself named *Lady in Red*.

Top left At the London première of the film *The Haunted*, in October 1995, Diana is seen with the film's star Anthony Andrews. **Top centre** Diana shakes hands with Cliff Richard at a charity concert at the Royal College of Music in January 1992. On his right is actress Hannah Gordon. **Inset above** At a fund-raising concert held in London in 1985, Diana talks to pop star Tina Turner. Also on the bill was Rod Stewart.

future. 'Mixing' with drug users never prevented Diana from speaking out strongly against drugs, and her acquaintance with homosexuals enlightened her future campaigns to help AIDS victims. Never a snob, Diana had no truck with those people who believed that only the most squeaky clean were fit to touch the hand of a princess.

At the same time, Diana herself came as a surprise to the stars she met. If any of them expected a rather grand, aloof lady, they were soon disabused. When she first met singer Neil Diamond, he found her far from formidable. In her still youthful way, Diana bubbled with excitement and told him: 'I've always wanted to see you!' She showed the same natural, unaffected approach when she met August Darnell, leader of chart-toppers Kid Creole and the Coconuts. Instead of offering a few, stilted words of royal small talk, Diana stood there talking effusively about the group's albums. The stars, naturally enough, were flattered by all this royal attention

and, in 1987, singer Lionel Ritchie was among several leading artists who gave Diana a complete set of his albums. Soul star Mica Paris was just as delighted when the Princess wanted her latest release to play on her portable CD player.

> **"*I thought the Princess would stay half an hour, but she was there chatting to Margot for an hour and a half. It really made Margot's day...*"**
>
> HAROLD KING, OPERA AND BALLET PRODUCER, ON DIANA AND MARGOT FONTEYN

Prince Charles, though not as keen on pop music as his wife, joined forces with Diana to give parties in the drawing room of Kensington Palace for performers who had given concerts for the Prince's Trust. Diana would dance on these occasions, while Elton John played the piano. Film stars received the same enthusiastic reaction from Diana,

Above right In 1983, at the Royal Festival Hall, London, Diana chats to Barry Manilow, one of her favourite pop singers, after a charity concert there.

who appeared completely unaware of her own celebrity when confronted with them. In 1982, she met the glamorous Elizabeth Taylor, one of the great beauties of the silver screen, and at once copied the film star's make-up trick of outlining the lower rim of her eyelids in blue. Three years later,

when Charles and Diana visited the USA, Diana was too shy to ask for a dance with fellow guest John Travolta and enlisted her hostess, First Lady Nancy Reagan, to intercede for her. Nancy duly went up to John Travolta and told him: 'The Princess is hoping you will ask her to dance.' Travolta, whose dance with Diana became the big event of the evening, was not the first one to find her honest approach unusual and refreshing.

Opera singers

Diana's love of opera, less well known than her attachment to pop, led to a famous friendship with Italian tenor Luciano Pavarotti, and another with the lovely New Zealand soprano Kiri Te Kanawa, who sang at her wedding in St. Paul's Cathedral in 1981. Pavarotti and Te Kanawa, needless to say, became Diana's favourite opera singers.

Television, too, was a prize source of star-gazing for Diana. She was thrilled, for instance, when the ultra-glamorous Joan Collins, star of *Dynasty*, one of Diana's favourite 'soaps', offered to get her a part in the show when she came to Los Angeles. Diana

IN THE NEWS

Two stars dine out

The combination of two world-famous stars – in this case Princess Diana and Clint Eastwood – was something that the press found irresistible. In September 1993, the Sun made the most of this meeting, featuring it on the front page. Diana and the film star dined with movie executives at the Savoy Hotel in London after Clint Eastwood had escorted Diana to a première of Harrison Ford's thriller The Fugitive. Diana recognized the value of stars such as Eastwood in publicizing her charitable work, and loved meeting them anyway.

Top Diana shakes hands with singer David Bowie at the Concert of Hope at Wembley Arena, held in 1993 to raise money for the AIDS charity Crusaid. Also in the line-up are pop stars Mick Hucknall and George Michael, along with film producer David Puttnam.

Inset above Diana shares a joke with pop megastar Michael Jackson in July 1988, before a concert he gave at Wembley Stadium, London.

could not, of course, take up such an offer. Even a princess who introduced so many innovations into her royal role could not go that far. But she was always delighted when the opportunity arose to meet TV personalities.

Diana met Michael Aspel, danced with Robert Kilroy-Silk, twice sat next to Jonathan Ross at functions – 'I think he's wonderful!' she said – and herself appeared on the small screen when she took part in *Drugwatch* with the irrepressible Jimmy Savile. In Savile, Diana encountered a philanthropist and worker for good causes as keen and dedicated as herself. She became the first person to sign her name to Savile's 'Just Say No' anti-drugs campaign.

Diana's royal status and her work heading charities allowed her, in addition, to mine the ballet world for big names. She was deeply impressed to stand on the same stage with prima ballerina Alicia Markova in 1990, told Mikhail Baryshnikov that she

treasured his autograph obtained many years before, and was over the moon when Dame Margot Fonteyn, widely considered to be the greatest ballerina Britain ever produced, came to

> *"Lady Diana...touched my life in an extraordinary way. I'll always remember her with deep love and joy."*
> LUCIANO PAVAROTTI, OPERA TENOR

tea at Claridges in London in 1990. The meeting was set up by the opera and ballet producer Harold King, who discovered that each of these celebrities was longing to meet the other. Tea at Claridges turned into something of a mutual admiration society. For Diana, who had wanted to be a ballet dancer but was too tall, talking to a legendary ballerina was a fan's greatest dream come true.

DIVORCE MADE FINAL

The end of Charles and Diana's marriage came neither quickly nor easily. The road to divorce, accompanied by rumour and speculation, was an uncomfortable one. Diana, gossip had it, made all the running

Rumour, speculation and half-truths had stalked Charles and Diana throughout their marriage, and even before. The press, relentless in pursuit, had poked and pried into the most private moments of their lives.

Their divorce in 1996 was no exception, all the more so because a blanket of silence from official sources stifled all information about it. Since legal procedures were involved and solicitors are, as they should be, the most tight-lipped of confidantes, very little news emerged from the negotiations. Those facts that were known were pretty basic. On 20 December 1995, a month after Diana's contro-versial appearance on the BBC's *Panorama*, Buckingham Palace had taken the unusual step of putting out a statement on the royal marriage.

'After considering the present situation,' it read, 'the Queen wrote to both the Prince and Princess…and gave them her view, supported by the Duke of Edinburgh, that an early divorce is

desirable. The Prince of Wales also takes this view and has made this known to the Princess of Wales.'

Christmas came and went. The new year of 1996 dawned, but Diana remained silent. The end of February arrived before things started to happen. Charles, it became known, had written to his wife suggesting, politely but firmly, that she was dragging her feet. On 28 February, Diana responded. She asked for a meeting at 4.30 that afternoon in

> **"Diana was becoming so much of an irritant to the whole monarchical system that it was being brought into disrepute."**
>
> DR. DENNIS FRIEDMAN, PSYCHIATRIST AND CONSULTANT TO THE BOOK DIANA ON THE EDGE

Charles' apartments at St. James' Palace. The late hour was significant. Earlier that day, Diana had driven to William's school, Eton College, and then contacted Harry at Ludgrove School in Berkshire. In the light of Diana's initiative later that day, it was presumed she had told her sons that an announcement about the divorce was going to be made.

GETTING IN FIRST

No one knew, though many tried to guess, precisely what Charles and Diana said to each other at St. James' Palace. Diana had indicated her concern that the details would be leaked, yet only an hour after the meeting ended, the Princess instructed her press aide, Jane Atkinson, to issue an announcement. This was, in effect, a pre-emptive strike.

Diana's statement, put out through the Press Association, let it be known that she had agreed to a divorce and to the loss of her title HRH – Her Royal Highness. She would in future wish to be known simply as Diana, Princess of Wales. In addition, Diana would participate fully in any decisions concerning William and Harry, and she would continue to live at Kensington Palace.

The Queen's press office was caught completely on the hop, but staff jumped to it and responded promptly with a counter-statement that spoke of Diana's 'claims' and let it be known that Her Majesty was 'most interested' in them. This, in

Previous page On the day her divorce was finalized, Diana visited the English National Ballet, in Kensington. **Above** With the ENB's Deputy Director, Richard Shaw. **Right** Diana's solicitor, Anthony Julius, of the law firm Mishcon de Reya. **Opposite page, top** Diana at Harefield Hospital in April 1996, viewing open-heart surgery. In London, the delicate divorce negotiations were under way.

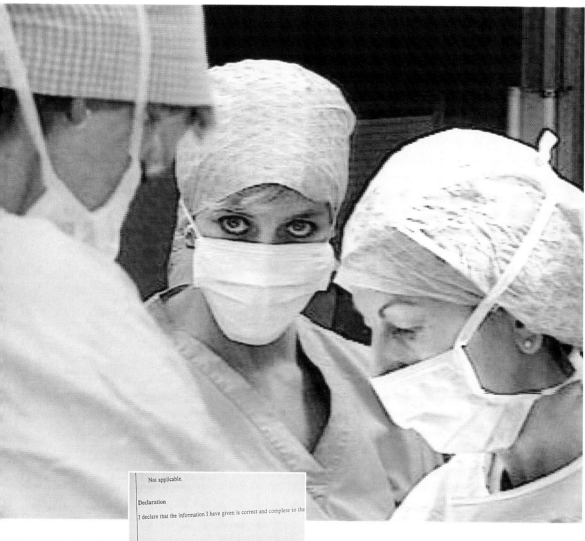

Above The decree nisi, signed by Charles and Diana, was granted on 15 July 1996. **Right** Prince Charles at the Order of the Garter ceremony at Windsor Castle in June 1996.

DIARY DATES
1996
8-9 February
The Prince of Wales visits British troops in Croatia, then flies to Bosnia
23-27 February
The Prince of Wales visits Morocco
22 February
The Princess of Wales visits Pakistan
17 March
The Queen visits the site of the Dunblane massacre, Scotland
22 March
The Prince of Wales opens the Urban Renaissance Exhibition in Bologna, Italy
22 April
The Princess of Wales observes a heart operation at Harefield Hospital, Middlesex
23-29 April
The Prince of Wales visits Canada
3 May
Artist Antony Williams' new portrait of the Queen is unveiled
5 June
The Princess of Wales visits Chicago to raise funds for cancer research
12 July
The Queen receives South African President Nelson Mandela for a state visit
13-16 July
The Prince of Wales visits Brunei
17-18 July
The Prince of Wales visits the USA
28 August
The Princess of Wales attends a luncheon at the English National Ballet, Kensington, London

royal-speak, was a put-down. In terms of proper procedure, a matter of such gravity as the divorce of the heir to the throne was not supposed to be revealed by a press release from one of the parties. It was a matter the Queen should have first discussed with the prime minister, the members of her Privy Council and possibly Commonwealth leaders.

The Queen's frosty reaction cast doubt on any agreement reached so far and also plunged the whole matter into a vast fogbank of secrecy, which

> ### "It was the saddest day of my life."
> DIANA, ON THE DAY DIVORCE
> NEGOTIATIONS STARTED

was to obscure it for several months. This, naturally enough, set off a public guessing game, with members of the press scrabbling around for information on which to hang their theories.

A promising titbit seemed to offer itself when photographers staking out the north London home of Susie Orbach, Diana's psychotherapist, caught the Princess as she was leaving after a session. Obviously close to tears, Diana raced for her car, but before she could even open the door, she broke down completely and, standing there in the street with a dozen lenses staring at her, sobbed uncontrollably. From this was spun a story that Diana was under enormous pressure and the presumption was that the divorce negotiations were not going her way.

DIANA BOUNCES BACK

No sooner had this idea been floated than Diana began to appear on public engagements – in Pakistan, London and Chicago – as her usual smiling, spontaneously forthcoming self, happily greeting the eager, excited crowds that gathered to see her. Far from retiring from the limelight, Diana was in fact exploring new avenues of public life and, on the evidence of these appearances, seemed perfectly able to handle it, press presence and all.

At this, speculation shifted its emphasis. Diana was now seen as an aggressive prime mover instead of a tearful victim. Stories based on nothing except fevered imagination, as far as anyone could tell, had it that she was demanding a country home and a house abroad in addition to the apartments in

IN THE NEWS

The end of all the dreams

The mundane nature of the divorce that ended the most glittering of royal marriages was the sad theme of newspaper reports when the decree nisi was reported on 15 July 1996. The Evening Standard explained, without frills, the formal procedure and regulation pronouncements by the judge which applied to all divorces. This seemed to emphasize how ordinary it all was. In fact, the divorce was far from ordinary: no heir to the British throne had ever been divorced before.

Opposite page Diana with Jemima Khan, wife of the Pakistani sportsman-turned-politician Imran Khan, during a February trip to Lahore. **Left** Diana offers comfort to a patient in a children's hospital funded by Imran.

Above Charles was in Southeast Asia when the decree nisi ending his marriage to Diana was granted in July 1996. He represented Britain at the splendid 50th birthday celebrations of the Sultan of Brunei. **Right** In January 1996 Diana leaves the offices of Associated Newspapers, Kensington, after meeting Max Hastings, editor of the London *Evening Standard*, and lunching with executives of the newspaper group.

Kensington Palace. The Queen and the government, it was rumoured, were prepared to give in to Diana all along the line and let her have the high-profile public role she wanted.

There was much talk about the 'court' Diana would create to rival that of the Queen. And if she did not get what she wanted, she would menace Charles with a court contest when he wanted a

> "*The negotiations…were greatly assisted by both the fairness of His Royal Highness the Prince of Wales' proposals and by Her Royal Highness'… ready acceptance of them.*"
>
> A JOINT STATEMENT ISSUED BY SOLICITORS ACTING FOR CHARLES AND FOR DIANA

quiet divorce. Diana would also threaten to spill yet more beans about Camilla and might even resort to television again to publicize her demands. As for the money, fantastic sums of up to £50 million were rumoured. The picture created by this orgy of speculation cast Diana as a guerrilla fighter harassing the Royal Family and driving them to surrender.

POWER OF THE PALACE

It could not possibly have been true. The truth was that all the big guns were on the royals' side, not Diana's. Not only was the financial settlement in their gift, but they would be the ones to decide the most important aspects of Diana's future.

The Queen was empowered by law to say what happened to Prince William and Prince Harry, and it was only because of her compassion and, as far as her advisers were concerned, the bad publicity that would result, that Her Majesty declined to exert those rights and exclude Diana. Diana had acquired the honorific HRH only because she had married Charles, and what the royals had given, they could also take away.

As far as was known, and not much was, the diligent Anthony Julius of Mishcon de Reya, Diana's solicitors, fought his royal client's corner assiduously. But the fact remained that as one who was confronting the most powerful family in the

Throughout the difficult period of the divorce negotiations, Diana was relentlessly pursued by the paparazzi, who took pictures such as this one of her clambering out of the pool during a break at a Majorca hotel in May 1996, and, **right**, leaving her gym in Chelsea in the same month.

❧ Protocol ❧

DIVORCE, ROYAL STYLE

*In the 16th century, King Henry VIII (**right**) divorced two of his six wives and had another marriage annulled, but that was when royals could do as they pleased. It was very different for more recent royal divorcees. With Lord Snowdon (1978), Princess Margaret's former husband, Captain Mark Phillips (1992), Princess Anne's first husband, and the Duchess of York (1996), the Royal Family called all the shots. After the divorces, which the royals arranged, all three spouses were sidelined, though the photographer Lord Snowdon still gets calls from the Palace to take royal pictures. The Duchess of York was virtually expelled from the royal circle and left to fend for herself.*

land and was soon to be an outsider, the Princess of Wales was in royal hands, not the other way round.

In the event, the settlement looked remarkably generous after a statement was issued by Buckingham Palace on 12 July 1996, announcing that the terms of the divorce had been agreed. Like the Duchess of York, who had been divorced six weeks earlier, Diana was to lose the title HRH and would be known as Diana, Princess of Wales. Unlike the Duchess, though, Diana was in a special position as the mother of Prince William, the second in line to the throne, and because of this would be regarded by the Queen and Prince Charles as

> *"The wedding...cost millions and was watched...by millions. The divorce today cost £80 and was watched by 29 journalists."*
> LONDON'S EVENING STANDARD, 15 JULY 1996

still a member of the Royal Family. On certain state or family occasions where the order of precedence was involved, Diana was to retain the same, fifth, place she had occupied when she was married. She would also remain at Kensington Palace.

The question of Diana's future role was left open: the form it would take was up to her, but the Queen and her ministers retained the right to be consulted. The financial settlement was deemed 'a private matter' but a sum of £15 million was mentioned in the press. This was very much less than the wildly speculative figures that had been bandied about. There was also talk that both Charles and Diana had been handed a 'gagging order', preventing them from making the full terms known.

PRESS CAMPAIGN

Three days later, on 15 July, Charles was granted a decree nisi, with the decree absolute due to follow within six weeks. In these dying weeks of the marriage, controversy still raged. The *Daily Mirror* mounted a campaign to prevent Diana losing the title HRH. This was an entirely legitimate move: objections could be lodged by anyone in such circumstances. The paper claimed a massive response, with 10,000 readers apparently supporting the

The Private Princess
Giving up Charities

On 16 July 1996, the day after her divorce became absolute and the title HRH was taken from her, Diana made the shock announcement that she was giving up her work for 101 of her charities.

Her reason, she explained, was that since she was now no longer Her Royal Highness, the charities would lose some of the lustre her name had once brought them. Apparently without any warning, Diana pared down her charitable work to six organizations in Britain and one, the American Red Cross, in the USA. The remaining charities were Centrepoint, the English National Ballet, the Leprosy Mission, the National Aids Trust, and the Royal Marsden and Great Ormond Street hospitals. Though Diana ceased to be a patron of the British Red Cross, she retained her links with the organization's landmines campaign.

These were the charities on which Diana wished to concentrate more of her efforts in future. She told friends that some of those she had abandoned involved too many mundane activities.

There was, predictably, an enormous outcry from the charities left off Diana's shortlist. With Diana as patron or president, they had acquired a high profile and contributions to their cause had risen. Without Diana, they would lose a large slice of the publicity she had once brought them. 'She's Broken Our Hearts' was how the *Daily Express* headlined the

Above *Diana in happier times, at a carol concert for the Young Red Cross in Bristol Cathedral in 1984.*

development, describing Diana sarcastically as 'the bitter self-styled Queen of Hearts'.

Columnist Marjorie Proops berated Diana for her 'selfishness' and said just giving the royal name to a charity was enough to bring them kudos. This, though, was to misunderstand Diana's motives. She had never been content to be just a figurehead. She wanted personal involvement and an active role.

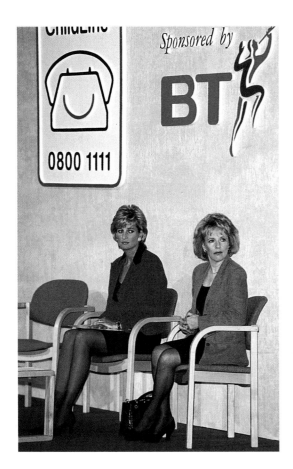

move to save Diana from humiliation. On 25 July,
the *Daily Mirror* published its readers' opinion. Two
to one said 'No' to depriving Diana of her title, and
while they were about it, a majority expressed the
conviction that Charles was not fit to be king.

EMBARRASSING PROTOCOL

In a blatant dig at HRH Princess Michael of Kent,
long regarded by the tabloids as the Aunt Sally of
the Royal Family, the *Mirror* announced that 69 per
cent of its readers did not want to see Diana curt-
seying to her. Theoretically, this could happen, and
the *Mirror* manufactured a provocative picture of
this unpopular turn of events. It was also true, again
theoretically, that Diana would have to curtsey to
Prince Charles and her own sons, all of whom, like
Princess Michael, still had the title HRH.

But the sound and fury of this campaign was all
for nothing. On 28 August 1996, a civil servant put
his stamp on the decree absolute and by that simple,
sombre act ended the marriage of Prince Charles
and Princess Diana. The Princess' title of HRH was
banished and would never return.

Crowning Glory

When the mousy-haired Lady Diana Spencer turned into the golden girl Princess of Wales, her hairstyles became the subject of intense scrutiny. Long, short, waved or straight, Diana's hair was always a talking point

Above The pre-Royal look. Diana in September 1980 at work in the Young England kindergarten. She wore her hair in a short, unfussy style. **Centre right** Now a young mother, at home in Kensington Palace in February 1983, Diana models a longer swept-back cut, created by Kevin Shanley. **Bottom right** By 1991, Diana has moved on to a shorter, lightly waved cut.

When it came to Diana's hair, the wind blowing out of doors during public engagements was her chief enemy. Lacquer was her fail-safe precaution and a good cut was a true ally.

On becoming Princess of Wales, she had been unwilling to abandon the casual, shortish style of her late teens. Not for Diana the safety of Princess Anne's long hair which could be pleated or pinned up to look neat. Not for Diana, either, the tight curls favoured by the Queen, which had a stay-in-place solidity.

Shanley's sweep

Kevin Shanley, Diana's first hairdresser, was a willing ally, despite an early mishap. Shanley aimed to create a new look for Diana's wedding day in 1981, but she spoiled his sweeping fringe by taking out the rollers too soon. As the pictures showed, her fringe flopped over her forehead.

Later in 1981, Shanley persuaded Diana to grow the sides of her hair longer to increase its fullness. He drew his fingers through the finished style, creating interesting ridge-lines before applying lacquer. In its final form, Shanley's creation featured a gently curving fringe, long flicked-up sides and a neat tucked-in back. By now, with the help of highlights and, later, all-over hair colouring, Diana's

On a 1995 visit to Argentina, Diana appears with the informal hair she favoured for much of the 1990s. This style of long layers tapering down the neck was soft and flattering and very fashionable at the time.

once light brown locks were decidedly blonde. But the Princess soon began to tire of the 'little girl' look, which at 21 or 22 still made her seem too young. Diana's solution was to grow her hair even longer than Shanley suggested.

In 1984 it reached shoulder-length and at that point Diana went in for a complete change of style, which Shanley disliked. The hairdo harked back to the 1940s and wartime (see page 549). It was not a success. That same year, Diana had her long hair gathered up into a chignon for the State Opening

> **"I loved working for the Princess, but it was twice a day, sometimes seven times a week. For eight years, I never went away for a weekend."**
> RICHARD DALTON, HAIRDRESSER, ON DIANA

of Parliament. For that, she was criticized for making too much of a fashion splash on a state occasion. Never popular, the long hairstyle soon went.

In 1985, Diana reached a half-way house with the slightly shorter style which became known as 'Dynasty Di' after the glossy American TV drama. Here, Diana's fringe made a comeback, though this time it covered only half of her forehead. The other half of the fringe was flicked up over her hairline. The sides were full and swept outwards to cover her ears while the back skimmed clear of her collar. This, many considered, was Diana's perfect style – elegant but youthful, freewheeling but controlled.

Dalton ducks in

Diana did not stop experimenting. Some of the changes made with her new hairdresser, Shanley's successor Richard Dalton, who had a salon at Claridges Hotel, London, arose out of necessity. Too much hair worn too long was a liability when touring hot countries, so the surplus was trimmed.

In its place, Diana adopted the hairstyle she sported during her visit to the Gulf States in 1986: the top sideswept off the face, short sides brushed back to expose most of her ears and a short straight back combed to the centre – a 1950s' teddy boy style known as a 'duck's bottom' – allowing any breeze to play round her neck. Though practical, it

Above Diana's longer hair, shoulder length by 1984, created a range of new possibilities, including (**main picture**) the 1940s' style with which she experimented briefly that year. Here she visits a family centre run by SENSE (The National Deaf, Blind and Rubella Association) in west London in August 1984.
1 The glamorous swept-back 1985 hair with a lifted fringe that was nicknamed 'Dynasty Di'.
2 Another full, longer style falls victim to outdoor conditions in 1983.

3 Diana wore this striking French pleat in 1989.

4 The 1986 image. Richard Dalton encouraged Diana to try a shorter style.

5 Practical and relaxed – the hallmarks of most of the 1990s' styles. This image is from July 1997.

6 From February 1992, one of the shorter, waved cuts created by Sam McKnight to create more body.

had its limitations, however. Diana's hair tended to disappear under anything but the tiniest of hats and the 'duck's bottom' was far too casual for tiaras and formal evening occasions.

These considerations led to Diana's second attempt at growing her hair in 1987. Unfortunately, it was no more successful than her first. Diana was soon faced with the fact that, now she was 25, long hair was ageing rather than 'grown up'. What was more, longer styles, being rather severe, emphasized her large nose. Attempts to soften the look by having it done loosely were not a good compromise.

In 1987, Diana wore her hair up with a long loose pony-tail pinned forward across her head, the

> **"Over the years, the Princess' changing hairstyles have been copied the world over."**
> ANN CHUBB, BEAUTY WRITER

front rolled backwards to blend with her tiara and the back sagging just enough to counterbalance that nose. Many thought it a mess and, by 1988, Diana's hair was short, simple and fringed once again.

Layer it again, Sam

By 1989, she had settled into one of her most attractive styles, a layered look, longish at the back but flicked up all over. This time, the nose was well served and it seemed at last that Diana's hairstyle exactly reflected her age. But then came the heatwave of 1990 and Diana, as always, had problems coping. With that, her hair reached its final cut.

Her hairdresser, now Sam McKnight of the London salon Daniel Galvin, trimmed it very short at the neck, short and off her ears at the sides, with the top lightly waved and a short segmented fringe to balance the severity of the cropped back.

This style was ideal for Diana's daily swimming session. Later on, with her separation and divorce from Charles, the practicality of the style, which she could maintain herself, came to suit her new, pared-down image. Out went the glamour and the extravagant wardrobe. In came the serious, dedicated worker for charity and her simple, unfussy hair became a symbol of the new-style Princess.

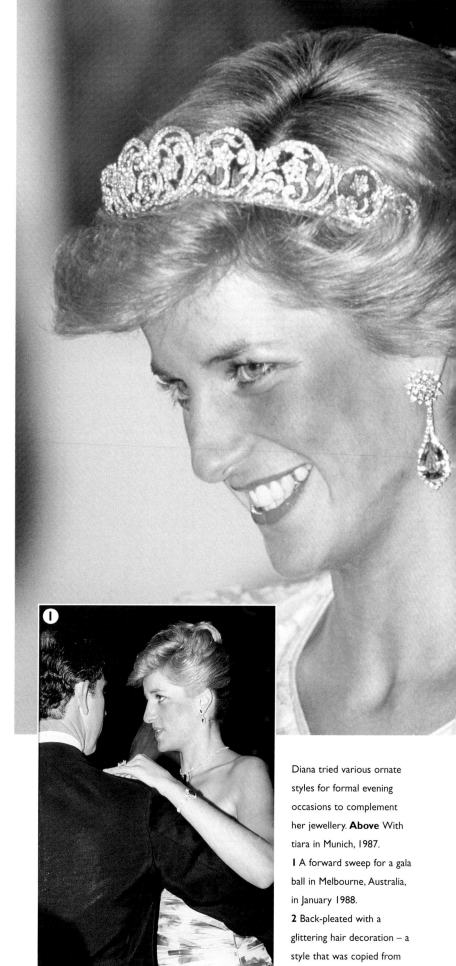

Diana tried various ornate styles for formal evening occasions to complement her jewellery. **Above** With tiara in Munich, 1987.
1 A forward sweep for a gala ball in Melbourne, Australia, in January 1988.
2 Back-pleated with a glittering hair decoration – a style that was copied from the Duchess of York.

Illustrations and photo
Elegant, swept-back styles complement Diana's pendant earrings. This picture was taken in November 1988 at the Elysée Palace, Paris.

IN THE NEWS

Slick it to us, Di

Diana's new slicked-down hairstyle, the Flip, rapidly created by Sam McKnight and seen in New York in 1995, did not meet with universal approval. Onlookers gasped, said the Daily Star of 1 February, when they saw Diana's flattened locks, though whether with admiration or dismay was not reported. At first, the paper suggested Diana was following a New York fashion. By the end, the news was that thousands of women would want their hair 'flipped' now that Diana had shown the way. In any event, the radical departure for a royal hair-do warranted three pages of coverage.

Passage to India

Charles and Diana's tour of India in 1992 was one of their last joint visits abroad, but it was also among the most exotic. India, they found, featured great beauty, much magnificence but also great suffering

Left Diana pauses for reflection during her solo visit to the Taj Mahal at Agra. **Above** The Princess' image adorns the cover of a magazine grasped by one of a crowd of well-wishers in Rajasthan. **Below** Diana makes a young friend.

India has long held a sentimental fascination for the British. Eastern, exotic, mystical and spiritual, India retains the familiarity it possessed one and two centuries ago when the Raj ruled it as the 'Jewel in the Crown' of the British Empire. Of all the countries Charles and Diana visited during their marriage, India was the one most likely to have a familiar, home-from-home feeling – especially for the Prince, with his interest in the spiritual.

The royal couple flew in to Delhi, India's capital city, on 10 February 1992. Sadly, it was a time when their marriage was fast faltering, and this unhappy fact explained why they undertook largely separate tours.

A couple apart

Charles visited Bangalore on his own, while Diana made solo trips to Calcutta and to Agra, the latter being home to a prime tourist attraction, the Taj Mahal. Even when they were both in Delhi, Charles and Diana kept different appointments, though they were together in Jaipur and Hyderabad.

The couple were received soon after their arrival by Dr. Chankar

Dayal Sharma, the Indian Vice-President, at the official presidential residence in Delhi, Rashtrapati Bhavan. They came there in style, escorted by the cavalry of the President's bodyguard, to find an all-services guard of honour awaiting Charles' inspection. Excited crowds crammed into Delhi, and Diana's outfit – in India's national colours of orange, green and white – gained instant approval.

Paying royal respects

The very first stop on the royal tour was the memorial to Mahatma Gandhi beside the River Jumna. The vast black marbled platform at the Raj Ghat was the spot where, in keeping with Hindu custom, Gandhi's body was cremated after he was murdered in Delhi in 1948. Going barefoot in the shrines and temples of India was a long-standing mark of respect, which Charles and Diana naturally observed. Both removed their shoes to walk to the memorial,

where they laid a wreath for remembrance. Princely India – those states once ruled by their own potentates throughout the British Raj – left behind the country's most opulent palaces, sumptuously decorated and, until the thieves got in, superbly

> "It was obvious what was going on in India. Charles and Diana opened up and smiled when they were apart. Together, they seemed tense and pensive."
>
> FIONA SINCLAIR, ROYAL CORRESPONDENT, ON THE TOUR OF INDIA

bejewelled. One of these palaces, formerly the property of the Nizam of Hyderabad, was the setting for a splendid banquet held in Charles and Diana's honour. The toasts were made in apple juice, since alcohol is never served on official occasions in India. This let Diana off the hook: she rarely drank

Above left After an enthusiastic welcome, Charles and Diana struggle to hold their floral tributes at the Mianpur Old Age Welfare Centre. **Above** The Prince attempts a traditional Indian greeting at Nalu Village. **Far right** Diana's easy manner and approachability once again won her many admirers, including this devoted young guide, on the Indian tour.

⫷ **Protocol** ⫸

EMPERORS OF INDIA

In 1876, Queen Victoria became the first, and only,
sovereign Empress of India. The British had dominated
India since 1757 and in time it became the most
dazzling possession of the British Empire. The Queen's
elevation to Empress confirmed its glory, and the title of
Emperor was inherited by
Edward VII, George V,
Edward VIII and George VI.
Queen Elizabeth II,
however, was never
Empress. India became
independent in 1947,
nearly five years before she came
to the throne. The splendour of this imperial title was
illustrated by the Durbar of 1911, **above left**, when
the newly crowned King George V and Queen Mary
received the homage of their Indian subjects in Delhi.

alcohol on state or any other occasions. Next day, 11 February, Charles and Diana parted company.

He remained in Delhi to tour a school for architects and also addressed a business forum. This was Charles' normal procedure when abroad: he always took advantage of the opportunity to promote trade between Britain and the host country. Meanwhile, Diana travelled the 100 miles southeast of Delhi to see the Taj Mahal, the stunningly beautiful 'poem in stone' and 'dream in marble', as it has been called, which the Mogul Emperor Shah Jahan built between 1630 and 1648 to house the remains of his beloved wife, Mumtaz.

The Taj was the very stuff of love and romance and some Indians, knowing the parlous state of the royal marriage, apparently hoped it would work some sort of magic. There was, sadly, no real chance of that, but Diana at least felt the spell of the Taj and described being there as 'a healing experience'. On

12 February Charles went off on his own again. He visited the workshop of 84-year-old Dr. Abdul Hameed, known in Delhi as the 'Guru', whose speciality was diagnosing illnesses by taking a patient's

> ## *"I am sure you can tell just by looking at me that I'm all right."*
>
> *CHARLES TO GURU ABDUL HAMEED, AFTER DECLINING TO HAVE HIS PULSE TAKEN*

pulse. Charles was about to offer his wrist to the Guru, but was warned off by one of his aides who pointed out how unwise it was for the heir to the English throne to be diagnosed while the world's press was watching, cameras at the ready.

While Charles was at Dr. Hameed's, Diana was elsewhere in Delhi visiting a nursery school for disabled children, founded among the slums by

Left Diana, who sometimes struggled to cope with the heat, wears an elegant wide-brimmed hat while touring the Mogul Gardens of the Presidential Palace in Delhi. **Above and inset right** The Princess fulfilled a dearly held ambition by visiting Mother Teresa's mission in Calcutta and meeting the nuns. Mother Teresa herself was away receiving medical treatment. **Above right** As a souvenir of their tour, the royal couple were given an embroidered print of their engagement portrait.

Shayma Chona, whose own daughter Tamana was disabled. Mrs. Chona inadvertently let slip how the nursery came to be built: Diana had donated £5000 for the purpose from her own charities trust. In keeping with Indian traditions for greeting guests, the young Tamana presented Diana with a garland of flowers.

A young admirer

As Diana was touring the school, one of those unscheduled, impulsive gestures occurred which always served to lighten an official timetable. A nine-year-old girl named Kulbir Soni ran up to the Princess to offer her a biscuit and an apple. Diana smiled and accepted the gift, but then Kulbir, with a young child's complete disregard for the niceties of protocol, grasped Diana's hands and simply refused to let go. The little girl was still

hanging on when the time came for Diana to unveil a commemorative plaque.

Later that day, in a total change of scene, Charles and Diana got together for a stroll in the perfumed gardens of the Rashtrapati Bhavan palace. They were accompanied by President Ramaswami Venkataraman and his wife Janaki.

Traditional greeting

When the tour moved on to Hyderabad in southern India, Charles and Diana were treated to another old custom: both of them had their foreheads marked with 'Tilak', a smudge of red paint which denotes a greeting and is commonly worn as an ornament throughout India. Afterwards, they visited the Andra Mahila Sabha family clinic where Charles was presented with a puppet bearing the slogan 'Healthy Individuals, Healthy Nation'.

Family planning was, as it still is, a matter of urgency in overpopulated India, which in 1992 had a phenomenal birthrate of 70,000 infants an hour. The royal couple toured the clinic, and Diana later went on her own to a similar establishment, the

Parivar Seva Sanstha Clinic, to see the work being done there to promote the use of contraceptives.

Charles and Diana were given a colourful display of traditional Indian dancing, in which another girl made an impromptu appearance. She decided to show the royal visitors how it was done and was ready-dressed for the occasion, in a brilliantly coloured costume and elaborate jewellery. Diana looked on indulgently and was quite clearly

Although they wanted to be apart, the royal couple gamely came together for official duties. **Top** The Prince and Princess lay a wreath at the Delhi memorial to Mahatma Gandhi. **Above** At a sumptuous dinner held on the first night of the tour.

Above Side by side once more at a polo match in Jaipur, the occasion of the notorious 'missed kiss' – when Diana turned away as Charles moved to kiss her.

enchanted. Another of India's many experiences, which Charles in particular was eager to enjoy, was offered by the game of polo.

The sport had once been played by Indian princes in the days, three and four hundred years earlier, when the Mogul Emperors ruled northern India. The royal tour had now reached Jaipur, the capital of Rajasthan province in northwest India, and the penultimate day of the visit had arrived. The date – as the 20,000 Indian spectators did not fail to notice – was St. Valentine's Day, 14 February, and a highly appropriate time, they believed, for the long-awaited

IN THE NEWS

Putting her best foot forward

This report in the Daily Mirror of 15 February cheered the unflappable nature of the Princess of Wales when she became an object of near worship by the poorest of the Indian poor on a visit to Hyderabad. Men and women of the 'Untouchables' reached out to touch and caress her feet and shoes. According to custom it would have been offensive to these people if Diana had tried to prevent them touching her, but, as the Mirror crowed, even 'if they were "untouchable", she certainly was not'.

> "*I watched one of the cruellest, most public put-downs of any man by his wife.*"
>
> JAMES WHITAKER, ROYAL CORRESPONDENT,
> ON THE 'MISSED KISS'

royal kiss. The polo match went well for Charles, whose team triumphed. Diana was there to hand out the medals and, as he had often done in England over the years, Charles stepped forward to plant a kiss on her cheek. But as he did so, Diana turned her head away and Charles was left awkwardly kissing the empty air (see Issue 16, page 371).

This 'missed kiss' became notorious in the British tabloids, which took it as a sign that all was finished

Above In Agra, Diana visited the Marie Stopes Clinic, named after the British campaigner for family planning. Both Diana and Charles showed an interest in India's population problems and in possible solutions, and both also visited clinics elsewhere in the country.

with the royal marriage. The spectators in Jaipur saw it quite differently. Believing, it seems, that here at last was a gesture of affection that proved all was well between Charles and Diana, they rose to their feet and surged forward, clapping and cheering at what they took to be a loving gesture. Such was the crowd's excitement that the police had to use batons to keep order.

The royal tour of India ended the following day, 15 February, when Charles flew off to neighbouring Nepal, leaving Diana behind. He spent four days in this small kingdom high in the Himalayas, visiting Gurkha regiments and trekking with them in the mountains. In the capital, Kathmandu, Charles was given a royal audience by the Nepalese monarch, 47-year-old King Birendra.

The nuns of Calcutta

Diana stayed on in India and travelled to Calcutta, where she hoped to meet the renowned Mother Teresa and visit her mission. However, when Diana arrived on 18 February, Mother Teresa, 82, was away in Rome receiving medical treatment for heart and lung problems. Nevertheless, Diana was able to tour the mission, where the nuns cared for the destitute and dying. The Princess was warmly welcomed but she emerged from her visit visibly affected by the suffering of those for whom death was the only release from a squalid existence.

The tour of India was a success. It impressed and excited Charles and Diana's hosts, and the royal

> "*The Taj...is within more measurable distance of perfection than any other work of man.*"
>
> H. R. NEVILL, 1920S' WRITER,
> ON THE TAJ MAHAL

couple, as usual, played their roles impeccably. Yet the unhappy state of the royal marriage was plain from their many separate engagements and the fact that they were seen to look much more relaxed when apart. India did undoubtedly have magic, but sadly it did not work for Charles and Diana. By 19 February, both were back in England, with the beauties, excitements and problems of India half a world away and only a fading memory.

BLUE DAYS

Divorce counts among the most stressful of life's experiences. Diana discovered how true this was after her marriage to Charles ended and she was once again a free woman – for freedom made her vulnerable

There is no such thing as an easy divorce. The legal technicalities may have been simplified, but that does not soften the dislocation, the bruised self-esteem and the regret at a failure that cannot be retrieved. Charles and Diana had to suffer the most painful kind of divorce: an all-too-public break-up on which the world could express an opinion or take sides. Charles, whose royal position was unchanged, was less badly affected than his ex-wife. Diana, on the other hand, was thrown off course and found herself back at square one.

For her, it was not just a case of no husband, but also no job, no direction and a difficult future as a semi-royal. Any concessions to her post-divorce status were largely due to her position as mother of a future king. For the rest, she would be left on her own to sink, swim or flounder. For some time

before her marriage ended, Diana had been seeking a recognized public role as a roving ambassador for Britain or, as she herself had put it, 'Queen of People's Hearts'. But nothing had transpired.

Political leaders might have been sympathetic and realized the great asset they had in this particular Princess of Wales, but they did not have the

> *"She needs to take on something new to fill her life with. She needs to learn something...rather than being a Florence Nightingale figure or a clothes horse."*
> MARY SPILLANE, IMAGE CONSULTANT, ON DIANA

final word. That belonged to Buckingham Palace, which vetoed any such role. This did not mean that Diana ceased to perform charity engagements. It did not stop her attending gala dinners or fundraising functions. What it did mean was that her activities lacked their former pattern and she lost the protection her full royal status had provided.

Previous page Diana attends the funeral, in 1996, of Yannis Kaliviotis, a student she had befriended, who had died in London of cystic fibrosis and had been flown for burial on the Greek island of Evia. **Above** Trying to leave a café in Rome, in 1996, Diana is surrounded by hundreds of sightseers and photographers, making it impossible for her to move around normally.

Above During a visit to Sydney, Australia, in October 1996, to attend a charity fund-raising ball for research into heart diseases, Diana was jostled and stared at while dancing. **Left** At a fashion sale for breast cancer research in Washington DC, Diana and designer Ralph Lauren admire a silver casket.

Only six weeks after the divorce became final, a new Diana scandal appeared in the press when the *Sun* headlined a 'secret' 80-second video, which purported to show the Princess cavorting with James Hewitt at Highgrove House. The video was quickly revealed as a hoax, perpetrated by a film maker called Nick Hedges in order to 'fool a newspaper'. The people in the video were look-alikes.

On 8 October, the *Sun* had to admit that the hoax had fooled it all too well, and offered its profuse apologies. But the damage had been done, nonetheless. The hoax had shown that a semi-royal Diana was up for grabs by anyone who cared to use her name and image for fun or profit.

RUDELY MOBBED

Diana's new vulnerability was underlined again that same month. At the end of October, she travelled to Australia, where she was to be guest of honour on 31 October at a £500-a-head Grand Ball in Sydney, staged to raise funds for research into heart diseases on behalf of the Victor Chang Institute.

The event produced £500,000 for the Institute, but only after Diana was involved in scenes that would never have occurred had she been guarded, as she once was, by regular royal security personnel. She was virtually mobbed by admirers. As she danced after dinner with Neville Wran, former Prime Minister of New South Wales, other couples on the floor came too close and, according to one onlooker, 'stared at her as if she was in a zoo'.

Some 45 minutes before she was due to leave, Diana had had enough. She managed to find a privately hired security guard to escort her away. But it was another discomfiting lesson on what it meant to be outside the Royal Family, while still having the curiosity value of her royal celebrity status.

> *"We had broken from powerful families and...lost our protection. Both were considered 'hysterical, unbalanced, paranoid and foolish'."*
>
> LADY COSIMA VANE-TEMPEST STEWART, ON HER FRIENDSHIP WITH DIANA

Meanwhile, back in Britain on the same day, another drawback to royal divorce was in the headlines.

Diana's name had been removed from the Parliamentary prayers for the Royal Family; instead of being specifically named, as before, she was included anonymously along with the other minor royals. Diana's staunch supporter Lord Archer – Jeffrey Archer, the novelist – went on record with a protest and this somehow became linked with a supposed campaign to get Diana's HRH title restored. Nothing, bar embarrassment, came of it.

Before long, the strain resulting from these changes began to show. In photographs, Diana looked tight-faced and her eyes seemed lack-lustre. Her hair often appeared as if she had barely brushed it. She seemed not to bother, either, with her make-up. She was no longer the dazzling, every-hair-in-place princess that people had come to expect. Even worse, Diana seemed to be shedding relationships.

Her staff, it was said, were having a hard time. Some of them found Diana impossibly demanding,

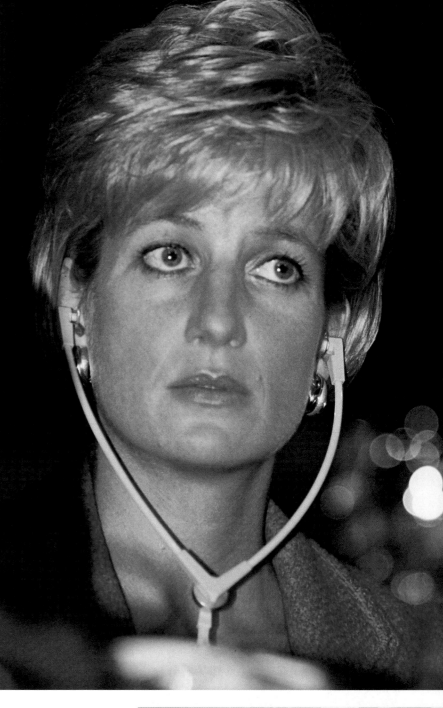

Above At a Humanitarian Awards ceremony in Rimini, Italy, in October 1996, Diana listens as an interpreter translates the speeches. **Right** In December 1996, when Diana visited the Wellcome Trust for a 30th anniversary celebration of an anti-leprosy federation, she was greeted by a fan, Colin Edwards, who gave her a card and chocolates.

and employees were said to be leaving fast. Much of this was sheer gossip, but there were at least two well-documented exits in late 1996 and early 1997.

LOSING MEMBERS OF STAFF

One story concerned Jane Atkinson, Diana's press secretary. Mrs. Atkinson was not told beforehand, as she should have been, that Diana was going to resign from over 100 charities the day after her decree nisi was granted on 15 July 1996. The announcement caused dismay in the press and among the abandoned charities and, Mrs. Atkinson claimed, Diana blamed her for it. A short time later, she resigned, after only seven months in the job.

The other exit, on 24 January 1997, involved Victoria Medham, Diana's assistant and holiday companion, who suddenly quit with no explanation, no comment and no new job. The press speculated on whether there had been a disagreement or whether work pressure had taken its toll.

There were several open quarrels, too, and more embarrassing incidents. On 8 February 1997, it

Above Diana listens to renowned South African heart surgeon Dr. Christiaan Barnard at a Humanitarian Awards dinner held at the Grand Hotel in Rimini, Italy, in October 1996.
Right Jane Atkinson, who was Diana's press secretary for just seven months, leaves Kensington Palace in the back of a limousine.

> ## "People think that, at the end of the day, a man is the only answer. Actually, a fulfilling job is better for me."
> DIANA, ON MEN

became known that Diana had fallen out with Gianni Versace, the celebrated Italian fashion designer, after he had persuaded the Princess to contribute a foreword to a book published to support singer Elton John's AIDS Foundation. Unknown to Diana, the book included several explicit photographs with homosexual overtones.

This was a very different matter from the inoffensive pictures Diana had been assured it contained. The potential for embarrassing the Royal Family was considerable and the row with Versace was cited as yet another example of how easily the unprotected semi-royal Princess could be exploited. It was not, sadly, the only example.

On 1 April 1997, Diana was involved in a set-to with a photographer, Brendan Beirne, when she found him waiting for her outside the Earl's Court

IN THE NEWS

Royal writers dredge up shocking news

On 15 July 1997, a year after the divorce, the tabloids were still working hard to get Diana on the front page. Here the Mirror's correspondent, James Whitaker, pursuing Diana in a boat on the Mediterranean, revealed that William and Harry wanted their mother to quit Britain and live abroad. That way, the boys believed, she could avoid the hot pursuit by the press which had long plagued her. An impossible idea, of course, as the press would follow her across the globe in search of a story.

⚜ Protocol ⚜

HER ROYAL HIGHNESS

Despite public protests, Diana had no right to retain the title Her Royal Highness after the divorce. The title belonged solely to wives of princes in line of succession to the throne, such as the Duchess of Gloucester (below). But new ground in royal protocol was broken when the divorced Diana and Duchess of York were deprived of the HRH. On the only previous occasion the title was in dispute, the Duchess of Windsor was denied an HRH on her marriage to the former King Edward VIII in 1937. This was because it was thought that the union would not last, and that, once given, an HRH could not be taken away.

gymnasium where she had been working out. Diana demanded that Beirne hand over his film, and enlisted the support of a burly young passer-by, Kevin Duggan. Duggan got Beirne in an armlock, wrested the film from him and gave it to Diana, who walked off with it. The police were placed in an awkward position when Beirne reported the incident. They took no action, but asserted 'this is no way for a Princess to behave'.

EMBARRASSING INTERVIEW

A month later, on 30 May, Diana, it seems, became enraged when an interview with her mother, Frances Shand Kydd, appeared in *Hello!* magazine. Frances had talked about Diana's bulimia and other matters, which the Princess told friends she would prefer were forgotten. Diana at once put a stop to the magazine's privileged access to her activities.

> "*I think she will become a greater and greater irritant…an oddity. This 'Queen of Hearts' thing will just come to look more and more ridiculous.*"
>
> GEORGE AUSTIN, ARCHDEACON OF YORK, ON DIANA

Only a few weeks later, on 2 July, the front pages featured an eight-month-old quarrel between Diana and the Duchess of York over a reference in Fergie's autobiography, published on 14 November 1996, in which she claimed that a pair of shoes the Princess had lent her gave her verrucas. The former sisters-in-laws were not speaking and Diana, according to the Duchess, was refusing to make up.

A while before this sorry tale of arguments and anger, there were reports in which friends claimed to have been cold-shouldered by Diana after failing to accompany her on holiday at short notice. In June, Ingrid Seward, editor of *Majesty* magazine and

Left *Hello!* magazine's interview with Diana's mother, Frances Shand Kydd, was the lead in two consecutive issues of the magazine. **Right** In June 1996, at the Mortimer Market Centre, an AIDS hospice in London, Diana accepts a bouquet of flowers from Aileen Getty, who is HIV positive. She is the daughter of the legendary billionaire and philanthropist John Paul Getty.

Above Diana with Sir Richard Attenborough at the première of *In Love And War*. **Right** On a 1996 trip to Australia, Diana talks to wellwishers who had waited to see her arrive at a medical research institute.

The Private Princess
Diana's secret missions

Diana was often accused of manipulating the press for her own advantage. The media, of course, had a function in publicizing Diana's charities and so helping to raise funds.

But what most people never knew – and that included the press – was that Diana often made secret visits to comfort the sick and dying when there was not a reporter, a photographer or a television crew in sight. She knew that heavy press presence could be disconcerting to the sick and often stopped her from contacting them. Diana preferred to drive herself to a hospital like an ordinary visitor, slip unnoticed into a ward and sit with patients, talking with them.

On one occasion, at St. Mary's in London, she persuaded a young AIDS sufferer, Bonnie Hendel, to eat a meal where everyone else had failed. Diana wrote letters to Bonnie and sent a photograph of herself which the child would keep by her bed and kiss before she went to sleep. Diana became a familiar figure at St. Mary's.

When 12-year-old Bonnie was dying, staff rang Kensington Palace. Sadly, Bonnie died before Diana could get there, but she sat with her parents, crying with them and sharing their grief. 'You were a heroine to Bonnie,' the child's mother told Diana.

Bonnie was only one of many sick children Diana helped in this

Above *Diana, in August 1991, on one of her many visits to friends and members of the public at St. Mary's Hospital, London.*

way during the last ten years of her life. Her approach was simple and disarmingly modest: 'Just tell me if I can be of particular help,' the Princess told doctors, 'and I will do whatever you think is best.'

a reputable journalist well acquainted with the Princess, wrote that Diana's behaviour was causing concern. According to Seward, when Charles gave Diana 40 places for her own guests at Prince

> "*I'd like to represent this country abroad. As I have all this media interest, let's not just sit...and be battered by it....Let's use it in a productive way to help this country.*"
>
> DIANA, ON WHY SHE WANTED TO BE AN AMBASSADOR

Above In Vienna to publicize the German edition of her autobiography, Sarah Ferguson holds up two copies of her book.
Right In Bosnia, on 9 August 1997, Diana poses for a photo with landmine victims in the village of Tuzla.

William's confirmation on 9 March 1997, she invited no one. Instead, Diana came alone and stood apart, barely talking. Seward even went on to claim that Diana had taken to wandering round her Kensington Palace apartment in the dark, drawing curtains so that no one could see in.

Whatever the truth behind all this, Diana was clearly far from happy. Divorce had given her freedom, but it had also made her vulnerable and easy to exploit. Fortunately, though, the direction and fulfillment she was seeking was already at hand, in

IN CONTEXT 1996/7 — DAMON HILL WINS TITLE

- The American TV show *Frasier* wins four Emmy awards and its third award for best comedy
- British mother-to-be Mandy Allwood loses last five of the octuplets she was carrying
- Britain's Damon Hill, **right**, becomes Formula One world champion at the Japanese Grand Prix.
- Auction in Vienna of art treasures stolen from Jews by the Nazis
- A Labour Government is swept to power in Britain in a landslide general election victory
- Tim Henman and Greg Rusedski become first British men to reach Wimbledon quarter-finals since 1961

Left The polo-playing Dodi Fayed, the 41-year-old son of Egyptian billionaire businessman, Mohamed Al Fayed, had a reputation as a playboy, but friends described him as kind-hearted and romantic. Diana and Dodi had met previously, but it was not until a holiday at Mohamed Al Fayed's St. Tropez villa that romance appeared to blossom between them.

the Red Cross anti-personnel landmines campaign and in a completely unexpected place: a villa in St. Tropez, owned by a friend of her late father, Mohamed Al Fayed, the Egyptian billionaire businessman and owner of Harrods.

After months of asking, Al Fayed eventually persuaded Diana, with her two sons, to holiday at the villa, which had the virtue of security from press intrusions. The invitation included the use of Al Fayed's yacht *Jonikal*.

But a pleasant break was not all St. Tropez had to offer. For Mohamed Al Fayed had a 41-year-old son, the eldest of his five children. He was handsome, attentive, and compulsively generous. In Arabic, his name, Emad, meant 'one you can depend on'. But he was better known as Dodi.

Made by Design

Bellville Sassoon and Donald Campbell worked with the young Diana when she was a woman of great fashion promise. Milliner Philip Somerville came later and underlined Diana's growing sophistication

Bellville Sassoon and Donald Campbell first came to public attention as Diana's designers within days of each other. Bellville Sassoon – the design duo of Belinda Bellville and David Sassoon – created the lovely crimson-pink suit with deep V-neck frilled collar that she wore on 29 July 1981 to travel from Buckingham Palace to Broadlands for the first stage of her honeymoon. For the second stage, where Diana sailed from Gibraltar for a cruise on the royal yacht *Britannia*, Donald Campbell provided a beautiful white façonné silk printed suit with tied bolero.

Both outfits were typical of their designers. Donald Campbell's speciality was beautiful fabrics; Bellville Sassoon majored in romantic glamour, framed in luxurious and eye-catching materials. Milliner Philip Somerville was also keen on fine fabrics, but he began to design for Diana some years later, when the Princess had become stylish enough to show off his elegant hats at their best.

Bellville Sassoon

Belinda Bellville founded her own design company in 1953. Five years later, the talented 26-year-old David Sassoon caught her attention. Romantic femininity with a touch of drama were his fashion signatures and, in 1958, not long after he left the Royal College of Art design school, he joined Bellville in a partnership which lasted until she retired in 1983. By that time, Bellville Sassoon had set Diana well and truly on the high fashion trail.

Their famous red and white striped 'Andy Pandy' suit, with its straight red skirt and long

Two Bellville Sassoon outfits. **Above** Diana at the Royal Albert Hall, London, in May 1983. **Right** In a typically romantic evening dress at Stanmore in March 1984.

sleeveless coat, attracted much attention at Ascot in June 1981, before her marriage. Later that year, in November, Diana positively dazzled in a full-skirted Bellville Sassoon evening dress in filmy blue and white with a blue waistbelt (see page 571). The next day, on 5 November 1981, when Diana's first pregnancy was announced, she was at the Guildhall in London, wrapped up against the autumn chill in a Bellville Sassoon coat with fringed collar and hem and a ribbon effect in yellow and turquoise.

Bellville Sassoon coats figured prominently in Diana's wardrobe, and they came in a striking range

> **"What I remember most is that she was great fun and didn't take her clothes that seriously."**
>
> DAVID SASSOON, ON DIANA

of colours. There was a fluffy pink coat with a wide fringe-edged collar (see picture 6), and a dark green coat with mandarin-type velvet collar, appliquéd velvet pattern down the front, and velvet cuffs; she wore both in March 1982. The following month, in Liverpool, Diana chose a Bellville Sassoon coat in bright pink velour with a wide frilled collar. Two years later, in February 1984, Diana travelled to Oslo, Norway and wore a royal blue three-quarter-length Bellville Sassoon coat with striped blue and white floppy tie (see picture 5).

Donald Campbell

Donald Campbell, meanwhile, had been shadowing Bellville Sassoon with his own distinctive designs. Born in Canada, Campbell came to England to design ready-to-wear ranges for John Cavanagh, before opening his own London showrooms, first in Chelsea in 1972, and afterwards in Knightsbridge in 1977. One of his clients was Lady Jane Fellowes, who in 1980 asked Campbell if he had anything that might suit her younger sister. The younger sister, Diana, soon cottoned on to Donald Campbell's easy-to-wear and tastefully understated styling.

The façonné silk 'going away' outfit of 1981 was only the start. One of Diana's early favourites was Campbell's striking black, red and white print dress with big white frilled collar (see picture 1, page

Designs on these two pages are by Bellville Sassoon. **Inset below** David Sassoon.
1 Diana at the Barbican, London, in 1982, wearing a crimson evening dress.
2 At Sadler's Wells, in October 1990, Diana wears an off-the-shoulder evening dress decorated with a bow.

3 Diana arriving for a performance of *Romeo and Juliet* at the London Coliseum in 1993, wearing a décolleté evening gown with an asymmetric hem.
4 Diana in June 1981 at a James Bond première at the Odeon, Leicester Square, London. She is wearing a red and gold chiffon gown, which has a boned top, pleated full skirt and tiny shoe-string straps. She carries a silver clutch bag.

5 In Cardiff, in March 1984, Diana wears a blue three-quarter length coat. She had worn it previously in Oslo in February that year.
6 In March 1982, on a visit to Huddersfield, Diana wears a pink mohair coat with a large fringed collar.

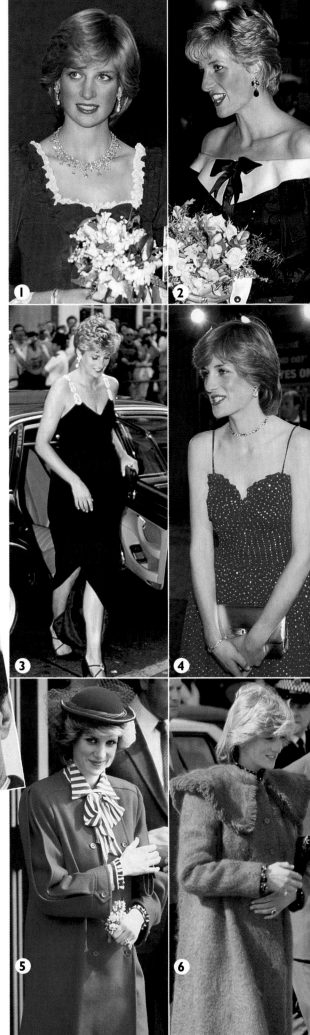

**BELLVILLE SASSOON
DRESS**

Diana wore this eye-
catching, dressing-gown-style
dress to a reception in
London **(above)** at the
beginning of British Fashion
Week in March 1988.
Bellville Sassoon designed
this multi-coloured coat
dress in vivid satin. It has a
rope-tie belt characteristic
of dressing-gowns, and
quilted lapels and cuffs of
the type found on dressing-
gowns or smoking jackets.

Diana wore this Donald Campbell white-spotted fuchsia dress in Perth, during her Australasian tour with Prince Charles in March and April 1983. It has a gathered neckline, puffed shoulders and a nipped-in waistline. The matching fuchsia hat, made in organza, is by John Boyd.

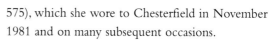

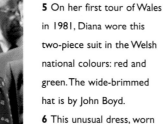

All designs are by Donald Campbell **(inset below)**.
1 On a visit to an adventure playground in Cheltenham, Gloucestershire, in May 1983, Diana wears a favourite print dress.
2 In 1982, at London's Royal Marsden Hospital, Diana wears a printed silk suit.

3 For an evening at the Queen's Theatre in October 1983, Diana wears an off-the-shoulder lilac evening dress which, for modesty, has had a neck band added.
4 Diana wore this blue dress to a reception at the Hyde Park Hotel, London, in November 1982.

5 On her first tour of Wales in 1981, Diana wore this two-piece suit in the Welsh national colours: red and green. The wide-brimmed hat is by John Boyd.
6 This unusual dress, worn in Brisbane, Australia, in April 1983, is an early example of Diana's love of innovative designs. A conventional print dress becomes memorable thanks to its asymmetric cut and contrasting bodice.

575), which she wore to Chesterfield in November 1981 and on many subsequent occasions.

In December 1982, when Diana was becoming more mature in her choice of fashion, Campbell proved thoroughly equal to the task with the printed suit – dominant colour turquoise (see picture 2) – which Diana chose for a visit to London's Royal Marsden Hospital. Campbell's white-spotted fuchsia dress with long sleeves, puff shoulders and wrap-over skirt (see page 574), which Diana wore in Perth during her Australasian tour of 1983,

> *"She had sparkle. It was simply magnetic and in the end it transcended her clothes."*
> ANNA HARVEY, DEPUTY EDITOR OF VOGUE, ON DIANA

marked her transition into more svelte, sophisticated styling. The dress was another long-term favourite. Diana wore it again to visit the Vatican during her tour of Italy with Charles in 1985.

One particularly striking Donald Campbell design first appeared on the Australian tour of 1983. It was his appealing and distinctive blue-on-white patterned dress with a white-on-blue pattern over half the bodice and one sleeve (see picture 6).

Auckland, New Zealand, was the setting for a lovely lilac evening dress in raw silk, by Donald Campbell, which Diana chose for a ballet gala in April 1983. It had a full skirt and was worn off the shoulder. The dress was probably considered a bit too low-cut for royal purposes and, when it was seen again in London in late 1983, a lilac neck band had been added to support the front (see picture 3).

Philip Somerville

Throughout these early Diana years, John Boyd was providing the small, curly-brimmed hats which became the Princess' trademark. The symbiosis between hat and dress design was vital for Diana's 'total look' and, in subsequent years, Diana went to a milliner, Philip Somerville, who specialized in hats matched to specific collections.

Philip Somerville came to London on a visit from his native New Zealand in 1962, and decided to stay. Somerville became sales manager and personal assistant to the renowned doyen of millinery, Otto Lucas. Somerville took over the business on Lucas' death, building a thriving company with ready-to-wear and couture collections appearing every year. Complementing the latest fashions became the Somerville forte, as was evident when, in France in 1987, Diana wore his red boater with

> ## "What I remember most about going to Kensington Palace for fittings is the room we'd work in – a small drawing-room with bowls of wonderful flowers. This terrific smell would hit you as you walked in."
> #### PHILIP SOMERVILLE, ON DIANA

black-edged brim and deep black band round the crown, which perfectly matched her black-trimmed red suit by Rifat Ozbek. A particularly sophisticated detail was the black snood she wore underneath the hat (see page 577).

Somerville's flair extended to the broad-brimmed hat, which was not normally a royal choice because it tended to conceal the face. Diana, however, was never one to follow royal rules regardless and, with Somerville to provide the designs, she frequently got away with it.

Risking a wide brim

Diana wore Somerville's quite saucy cream broad-brimmer at Ascot in June 1986, and his emerald green number with a slightly curled white brim and a long tie over her left ear on a visit to Madrid during the Spanish tour of April 1987. Photographers and crowds had no trouble seeing Diana's face, and the Madrid headwear showed quite strikingly the marriage of hat and outfit which Somerville aimed to achieve.

Philip Somerville, Bellville Sassoon and Donald Campbell were highly influential in their own right. But they represent just some of the designers whose talents transformed Diana in a very few years from a fairly ordinary, not very clothes-conscious 20-year-old into a fashion megastar.

All hats are by Philip Somerville **(inset below)**.
1 This hat with a nautical feel was worn at Dartmouth Naval College in 1989.
2 Diana wore this broad-brimmed cream hat in May 1991 to a military service in Hyde Park, London.

3 A touch of the Mad Hatter: at Sandringham on Christmas Day 1992, Diana peeks out from beneath an elaborate black hat with a large bow and a veil.
4 In May 1985, Diana's Philip Somerville hat tops off a Jan van Velden coat and Catherine Walker dress.

IN THE NEWS

Cheap and cheerful

In January 1992, the Sun filled a page with this cheap-to-research piece. Reporting on a survey by Hello! magazine, in which 12 European designers had voted for their favourite outfit worn by Diana the previous year, the Sun was happy to illustrate the dress that came top and six other contenders.

The dress voted top by Paco Rabanne, Karl Lagerfeld, Hubert de Givenchy and others was a supremely stylish shocking-pink ballgown created by Victor Edelstein, one of Diana's favourite designers. It was valued by the Sun at £5000.

TWO SOMERVILLE HATS

Left This yellow and black turban was designed to accompany a coat **(below)** from the German fashion house Escada, on a visit to Germany in 1987. **Below left** Diana wore this striking red and black hat on a 1987 visit to Normandy, France, to accompany a Rifat Ozbek suit **(bottom)**.

On the Rhine

Diana made four visits to Germany. There was one official tour, in 1987, but the rest of her visits centred on a special interest of hers – the British soldiers and members of their families stationed there

One of the official duties which Diana enjoyed a great deal came her way through the practice of inviting members of the Royal Family to become colonels-in-chief of army regiments. Diana performed this role in Britain for the 13th/18th Hussars and the Royal Hampshire Regiment, while abroad she was colonel of the Royal Australian Survey Corps and the Canadian Princess of Wales' Own Regiment. A colonelcy mainly involved attending social occasions, such as dinners in the mess, presenting new colours and inspecting parades. A colonel-in-chief was also expected to take an interest in the welfare of the soldiers and their families.

British Army presence worldwide had shrunk considerably after the colonies attained independence in the years after 1947, but one posting that persisted was Germany. Regiments had been stationed there since the end of the Second World War in 1945.

Top Tiger

In 1985, when Diana became their colonel-in-chief, the Royal Hampshires, or Tigers as they were known, were on a tour of duty in West Berlin. Diana lost no time in paying the Tigers' 1st Battalion a visit and, in October 1985, she made her first official trip to what was then West Germany. For the soldiers, who had just acquired the youngest, prettiest and already most famous colonel-in-chief they could have wished for, the prospect of meeting Diana was an exciting

Left Diana and Charles in 1987 at the City Hall in Bonn. **Above** Diana in January 1991, meeting the families of British troops serving in the Gulf War.

Above Diana talks to German Chancellor Helmut Kohl during her 1987 tour of Germany with Prince Charles. **Right and inset** Two years earlier, when Diana visited the Royal Hampshire Regiment, she had the chance to drive an armoured personnel carrier. She is seen receiving instructions before starting.

one, and they made careful preparations. Before she arrived at their camp, Wavell Barracks, the battalion prepared a special ladies' room which was in total contrast to the normal spartan grimness of a military installation. Next door, in fact, is Spandau Prison, where Hitler's deputy, Rudolf Hess, was still serving a life sentence for war crimes. Diana's room, with its pink wallpaper and brass fittings, would not have disgraced a top-class hotel, but home-from-home luxuries were not of prime interest to the royal colonel. Her visit was a prize opportunity to indulge her great love of driving.

The Tigers offered Diana a thrilling driving opportunity: taking the wheel of a 15-ton FV432 armoured personnel carrier that was armed with a 30mm cannon. Donning a black and yellow tracksuit and plimsolls, she climbed into the carrier and, after basic training, began driving around the parade ground. She performed a reversing manoeuvre and took the carrier round a corner. The heavy vehicle

☙ Protocol ❧

ROYALS AS WARRIORS

Once, the kings of England had a duty to lead armies against the country's foes. Richard the Lionheart (1157-1199), **right, centre**, was a notable warrior who led the Christian forces in the Third Crusade of 1191. Other prominent royal war leaders were King Edward III (1312-1377) and his heir, Edward, the Black Prince (1330-1376), who won the famous Battle of Crecy against the French in 1346. The last king to lead his soldiers into battle was George II (1683-1760) in 1743. After that, royal military connections became largely ceremonial and continue today in the colonelcies-in-chief of regiments held by members of the Royal Family.

was not all that easy to control. At one stage, her instructor had to leap out of the way as his colonel came haring towards him. Nevertheless, he gallantly gave Diana ten out of ten.

There was a lot more gallantry on display. Ten soldiers came abseiling down ropes suspended from

> **"It was thrilling! I enjoyed it...**
> **I would love to do it again."**
> *DIANA, ON DRIVING A PERSONNEL CARRIER*

two helicopters and handed a blushing Diana a box of chocolates and a single red rose. When the visit was over, the Princess took away with her a memento, a regimental brooch made from diamonds, emeralds, rubies and pearls set in gold, purchased from contributions by Tigers past and present.

Two years later, Diana was back in Germany, this time with Charles, for a six-day official visit, in

November 1987. The royal couple flew in to Berlin, with Charles at the controls of the BAe146 of the Queen's Flight, on 2 November. Charles landed the plane at RAF Gatow close to the controversial Berlin Wall, which separated communist East Berlin from the democratic West. Waiting to greet them was a big crowd of servicemen from the 3300-strong British garrison, together with their families. The Berliners themselves had to wait until the evening, when Charles and Diana arrived at the Rathaus Schoenberg, the West Berlin Parliament. Hundreds of Union Jacks were in evidence and the Berliners' reception was enthusiastic.

Bonn and Cologne

The next day, on 3 November, the royal couple were in Bonn, the West German capital, for a meeting with President Richard von Weizsacker.

They went on to Cologne, where Charles inspected the restoration work being carried out on

Above Diana reviewing the Royal Hampshire Regiment, of which she was Colonel-in-Chief, during a visit to Berlin in October 1985.

Charles ended up with a lipsticked cheek. Diana was once more her glamorous and sophisticated self at a subsequent state banquet in Bonn, where her jewellery, a present from the Sultan of Oman, became a big talking point. Later, Diana, with Charles, attended a charity fashion show, which featured the work of British designers.

Cultural delights

Germany's cultural heritage could not be neglected, and a visit to Munich, the Bavarian capital, allowed Charles and Diana to see a performance of Mozart's *The Marriage Of Figaro* at the world-famous Munich Opera House. While in Bavaria, in the south of the country, Charles and Diana were entertained by Prince Franz, head of the royal

the city's ancient cathedral, and Diana tasted 'kolch', the local beer. Never fond of alcohol, she found the experience broke her normal polite composure; she grimaced. The incident, although unpleasant, had no effect on her sense of humour. When a young woman in the crowd asked if she could kiss her, Diana declined, but suggested Charles instead. The young woman took her at her word and

Above On a January 1991 visit to the RAF Bruggen air force base in Germany, Diana is shown the workings of a plane's cockpit by one of the pilots. **Inset left** In Berlin, on the 1987 official visit with Charles, Diana talks with one of a troupe of art body painters.

Far left In June 1991, after the Gulf War, Charles and Diana are introduced to service chiefs at a thanksgiving service. **Above** On a visit during the build-up to the Gulf War, in December 1990, Diana saw *Joseph And The Amazing Technicolor Dreamcoat.* **Near left** In February 1991, Diana visited troops and their families at Sennelager.

IN THE NEWS

A united front in Berlin

In this front page report of 2 November 1987, the Daily Mail's Richard Kay, covering the arrival of Charles and Diana in Germany at the start of their official tour, jumps to the conclusion, like many other members of the press, that Charles and Diana were still 'in love'. What reporters and photographers were really seeing was a pair of professionals well schooled in the art of putting up a convincing front in public. The royal marriage was already in a perilous state and had been subject to intense speculation in the media at home and abroad.

Daily Mail

Charles and Diana so glad to be together again

HAPPINESS IN BERLIN

Wittelsbach family, at the magnificent Nymphenberg Palace. Afterwards, the attentive Prince Franz gave Diana a personal tour of the portraits hanging in the Palace's Gallery of Beauties.

Family relations

Two other German cities which the royal couple saw, Celle and Hanover, were virtually visits to ancestral homes for Charles. His direct ancestor nine generations before had been the Elector of Hanover, who became King George I of England in 1714. George left behind a divorced wife, Sophia Dorothea, who was imprisoned in Ahlden Castle in 1694 and died there in 1726. Sophia, also Charles' ancestor, was the daughter of the Duke of Brunswick-Luneberg-Celle. The scandal-thirsty

Above Diana sits down to dinner with the Colonel of the Royal Hampshire Regiment, and his officers and their wives, during a visit to West Berlin in October 1985.

German press was not slow to compare the divorced George with Prince Charles, whose divorce they were already predicting.

Press tittle-tattle about the marriage shadowed Charles and Diana throughout their German tour. Fortunately, it had no effect on the tour's success, or the couple's view of Germany.

Later visits

Charles was in Germany again, in fact, in 1988, when he attended the Schleswig-Holstein Music Festival. Diana returned in December 1990, when army families were facing a Christmas without husbands and fathers who had been sent to the Gulf in preparation for war against Iraq. Hostilities were due to commence on 16 January 1991 if, that is, Saddam Hussein did not back down first.

When Diana arrived, no one knew which way the tense situation would go, and the families were fearful. But they could hardly have had a more

comforting visitor than Diana to chat to, listen to their worries and impart some good cheer.

Fortunately, Operation Desert Storm, the campaign in the Gulf, proved brief and successful. And in June 1991, Charles and Diana were back in Germany, to attend a dinner in Munster for British army units that had served in the war. This was

> **"I love a man in uniform."**
> DIANA, ON SOLDIERS

their last joint visit to Germany, though Charles returned several times in subsequent years.

Diana's many visits had shown the breadth of her appeal – from the daredevil driver who enjoyed being 'one of the boys' to the compassionate royal. Her military role may have been purely ceremonial but Diana was a great morale booster for the soldiers of the Rhine and their families.

TRUE LOVE WAYS

Diana's supposed romance with Dodi Fayed was sudden and sweet, but brief. The Princess who longed for love had, it seemed, found happiness at last. But fate lurked nearby, and would strike a cruel blow

In July 1997, for the first and last time in her life as Princess of Wales, Diana was able to take for granted a privacy from prying eyes and lenses more complete than any she had ever known. This seeming miracle had been worked by the Egyptian billionaire owner of Harrods, Mohamed Al Fayed. He lent Diana his villa, Castel St. Thérèse, at St. Tropez, for a holiday with her sons. He also made available his 195-foot yacht *Jonikal* and a posse of personal bodyguards to fend off the press. Al Fayed also asked his eldest son, Dodi, to provide company for the Princess.

Dodi, who arrived four days after Diana, on 16 July, was to stay at the fisherman's cottage on the villa estate, some 200 yards from the main house. He was discreet, considerate, willing to play with William and Harry in the private swimming pool or take them to the local amusement park, but courteous enough to address Diana as 'Ma'm', at least at first. It was inevitable, though, that Diana

would get to know him as more than the slight acquaintance who had crossed her path several times before. They had met in 1986, when Dodi and Prince Charles played polo at Windsor; in 1992 at the London première of the film *Hook*, for which Dodi, a lifelong film enthusiast, had been an executive producer; and earlier in 1997, when he came to a dinner given by Diana's stepmother, Raine.

Though he was more substantial and sensitive than the playboy he was often depicted to be, Dodi certainly indulged in a carefree jet-setting life of fast cars, beautiful girls, private yachts, private planes, homes across the world, including a Scots

> ## "I need another marriage like I need a bad rash on my face."
>
> *DIANA TO HER FRIEND ROSA MONCKTON, ON MARRIAGE*

castle, and year-round holidays. He had once been married, in 1986, for eight months, to American model Susan Gregard. Remarkably for an ex-wife, Gregard had only fond words for Dodi.

Diana, it seems, soon discovered why: Dodi was kind-hearted and romantic. There was, besides, the empathy of a shared sadness. Dodi's mother, like Diana's, had left his father when he was very young and, like Diana, he had never entirely got over it.

FALLING IN LOVE

Above all, Dodi was willing to be supportive of Diana – and someone happy to do this was what she most dearly wanted. The pair talked for hours over lunch or dinner or during peaceful walks along the beach and, the press later speculated, it was then that they fell in love. Later, this translated into claims that Dodi and Diana intended to marry.

Three weeks after the St. Tropez holiday, the pair flew out in a private jet for a cruise in *Jonikal* around the Mediterranean islands of Corsica and Sardinia. The press came after them in full cry. Diana and Dodi managed to elude the cameras during a visit to Monte Carlo and while they were staying at the more remote Corsican resorts. But they were still on the run from the papparazzi, one of whom, Maro Brenna, made a fortune with an

out-of-focus shot of them kissing on *Jonikal's* deck. With that, the Dodi and Diana 'romance' hit the headlines and their privacy was at an end.

On 21 August, after Diana had travelled to Bosnia on behalf of the anti-landmines campaign – in the Harrods private jet – and another cruise, with Rosa Monckton, to the Greek islands, she and

Previous page Diana and Dodi sharing a joke in a small motor boat on the Mediterranean off the South of France in July 1997. They are being ferried out to the luxury yacht *Jonikal*.

IN CONTEXT   MONTSERRAT EVACUATED
1997

- Labour Government sweeps to power in landslide general election victory
- Summit of G7 countries convenes at Denver, USA
- Tim Henman and Greg Rusedski become first Britons to reach Wimbledon quarter-finals since 1961
- 67 dead in Venezuelan earthquake measuring 6.9 on the Richter scale
- Evacuation of inhabitants on the Caribbean island of Montserrat because of volcanic eruptions, **right**

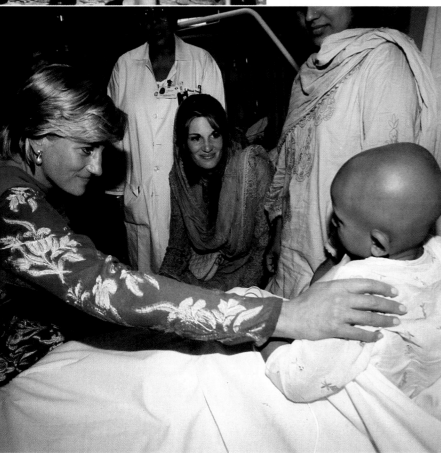

Above left Family and godparents pose for a group photograph after Prince William's confirmation in March. Among the godparents were ex-King Constantine of Greece (back left), Princess Alexandra (back centre) and Lord Romsey (back right). **Above** Diana, Sting, his wife and Elton John at the funeral service of Gianni Versace, in Milan, on 22 July. Sitting behind Sting's wife is designer Karl Lagerfeld. This was the occasion on which Diana and Elton John patched up their friendship after an earlier quarrel. **Left** Diana in Lahore, Pakistan, in May. She is with her friend Jemima Khan on a visit to the Khans' hospital.

DIARY DATES
1997
12-13 May
The Prince of Wales visits Hesse, Germany
30 June
The Prince of Wales attends ceremonies for handing over the colony of Hong Kong to China
3 July
The Prince of Wales visits Manila, the capital of the Philippines
7-10 July
State visit of President Nelson Mandela of South Africa
14 July
The Prince of Wales attends a Farewell Gala Concert at the Royal Opera House, Covent Garden, to mark its closure for redevelopment
15 July
The Prince of Wales opens the new Romano Gallery at the British Museum, London
15 July
The Queen and Prince Philip give a Golden Wedding garden party for other couples married in 1947, at Buckingham Palace
17 July
Prince Charles gives a 50th birthday party for Camilla Parker-Bowles
18 July
The Queen visits the Royal School for the Deaf
21 July
The Prince of Wales visits the Tate Gallery, London
22 July
The Princess of Wales attends the funeral of the murdered Italian fashion designer, Gianni Versace, in Milan, Italy

CHRONICLE

Below Diana and Prince Harry enjoy sun and sea during their holiday arranged by Mohamed Al Fayed with Dodi in St. Tropez, France, in July. **Right** Before news of the romance with Dodi has broken, Diana, accompanied by bodyguards, tries to negotiate some privacy with a motor launch containing the press, including the *Daily Mirror's* royal correspondent, James Whitaker (in green).

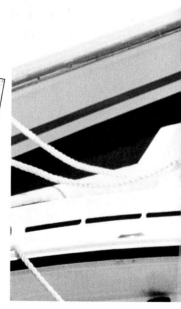

Top Dodi Fayed was a lifelong film enthusiast and had come into contact with the royal family on several occasions in his role as executive producer. Here he meets the Queen Mother at the première of *Chariots Of Fire* in March 1981.
Above Dodi and his father, Mohamed Al Fayed, in April 1989, at a party thrown at the Harrods store in Knightsbridge that Al Fayed owns.

IN THE NEWS

Blessed by Mohamed

The media did not fail to pick up on Mohamed Al Fayed's delight at the 'romance' between his son Dodi and Princess Diana, and blazoned it across the front page of the Evening Standard on 8 August 1997. The story was expanded on two inside pages, but at that juncture, the press had very little to go on. The love story was unconfirmed by either of the two people involved. They had, in fact, known each other for only four weeks when this report appeared.

Dodi tried again. They flew to Portofino in Italy where *Jonikal* was moored. It appears that Dodi's aides informed the press. Subsequently, the media claimed that Diana wanted them to let the world know that she had found the love of her life.

However, Diana and Dodi did not behave as if they welcomed the press when a boat-load of paparazzi intruded on them while they were taking an early morning swim in a Sardinian cove. Fayed's bodyguards told them to go away.

Paparazzi presence effectively imprisoned the couple on *Jonikal*, where they tried to keep out of sight, but they finally concluded that this was no way to enjoy a holiday. Instead, in an impromptu

> ## "*That was the best holiday I ever had in my life.*"
> ### DIANA, ON HER ST. TROPEZ HOLIDAY

change of plan, they flew to Paris. There, Diana planned to buy presents for William and Harry. Dodi wanted to look at two 'Tell Me Yes' engagement rings at the exclusive Paris jewellers, Repossi.

The French paparazzi had, however, been alerted by their colleagues in Sardinia, and when Dodi and Diana disembarked at Le Bourget airport at 3.20pm on the afternoon of Saturday 30 August, they found six photographers waiting for them. They pursued Dodi and Diana's Mercedes all the way to the Ritz Hotel, which Dodi's father owns. Dodi and Diana remained in the privacy of the hotel's luxury suite, the Imperial, for the next two hours, though Dodi made a brief excursion to Repossi the jewellers. Later, a ring was delivered to him at the Ritz.

DINNER AT THE RITZ

As Diana and Dodi left the Ritz by the service entrance at the rear at 7.00pm, the photographers were waiting for them. They were staked out, too, in front of Dodi's apartment on the Champs Elysées, and that led Dodi to abandon all thoughts of taking Diana out to dine at the top-class Le Benoit restaurant. There, a big window overlooking the street promised the prospect of a posse of photographers ranging over the pavement outside. Instead, Dodi and Diana decided to return to the better security

of the Ritz. They left the apartment at about 9.30pm, ran the gauntlet of the waiting paparazzi, and drove back to the hotel, with 15 photographers trailing them all the way.

During dinner at the hotel's Espadon Restaurant, couples at other tables who continually stared at Diana made her feel very ill-at-ease. By 10.15pm, she and Dodi had gone upstairs to dine in private in the Imperial Suite.

Outside the Ritz, in the Place Vendôme, the paparazzi were still hanging around, accompanied by some 300 onlookers. There was a ripple of excitement at a rumour that Diana and Dodi would be leaving at around 10.40pm, but it was

> ## "We were immediately surrounded by about a dozen photographers who jostled us. Some were aggressive, others were OK."
>
> KES WINGFIELD, FAYED BODYGUARD, ON ESCORTING DODI AND DIANA INTO THE RITZ

nearly midnight before they came downstairs. One look confirmed that the photographers were still outside, so Dodi arranged that two decoy cars should leave the Ritz, inviting a pursuit that would enable his own Mercedes to drive off unnoticed.

Diana and Dodi waited at the back door of the hotel. With them were Henri Paul, the hotel's security officer, who was to drive the couple back to Dodi's apartment, and Trevor Rees-Jones, one of the Fayed bodyguards. At 12.20am they walked out to their waiting Mercedes, only to discover that the ruse had failed. Three paparazzi were stationed there. Using mobile phones, they flashed the news that Dodi and Diana were leaving to the photographers at the front entrance, and the chase to pick up the couple's trail began once again.

THE CHASE WAS ON

One of the paparazzi, Romauld Rat, spotted the Mercedes, with Dodi and Diana in the back, at the intersection of the Place de la Concorde and the Champs Elysées. As he approached on his motorbike, the Mercedes shot away and gathered pace, racing along beside the River Seine at a speed Rat

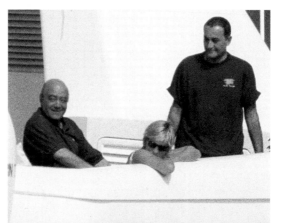

Top Diana, Harry and Dodi in St. Tropez in July. **Above, left and right** Al Fayed's yacht *Jonikal*, and the company of Mohamed and Dodi, provided a welcome relief from intense press intrusion in July and August.

The Private Princess
The Doctor's story

Dr. Frederic Maillez, 35, of SOS Medicins, an emergency call-out service, reached the scene of the crash barely a minute after it had occurred.

He found Diana, whom he did not recognize, half kneeling with her legs buckled under her and her head resting in the gap between the two front seats. Dr. Maillez sprinted back to his car to fetch oxygen and returned to find Diana crying out in pain.

As he tried to reassure her, Diana kept on telling him how much she was hurting. Maillez put a resuscitation mask over her mouth but at that stage did not think she was mortally injured. However, she lost consciousness as Dr. Maillez waited by the Mercedes for the emergency services to arrive. He waited six minutes, the longest minutes of his life, he said afterwards. It was some hours before he saw a TV newsflash about the crash and was astonished to discover he had been treating the famous Princess of Wales.

Afterwards, he agonized over whether he could have done more to save Diana, but his colleagues assured him that no one could have survived the grave internal injuries she suffered. Dr. Maillez' story did not appear in the press until late November, when he also revealed how 'hundreds of journalists' had pursued him with huge offers of money to tell what he knew. 'I could not go anywhere without being

Above *Dr. Frederic Maillez, of SOS Medicins, attended Diana as she lay injured in the crashed Mercedes.*

followed or pestered,' he said. 'I think I know a little of how she must have felt.'

Six months later, in February 1998, a book about the crash, *Death of a Princess* by Thomas Sancton and Scott McLeod, criticized the French practice of stabilizing victims at the scene of a crash. Dr. Maillez was one of those who protested that French procedures had been emulated worldwide and had saved hundreds of lives.

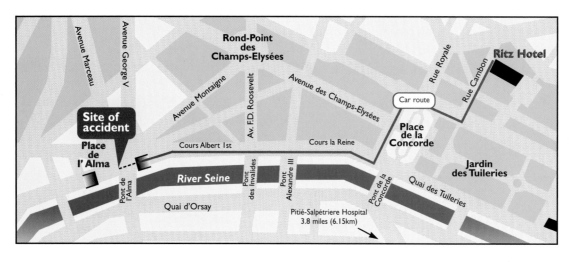

Opposite page, top The scene of the accident, at the entrance to the Alma Tunnel, Paris. Opposite page, bottom The wrecked Mercedes S-220 being loaded onto a truck. The front bears the shape of the tunnel's 13th pillar, which it initially struck. The roof has collapsed after the car overturned.

reckoned to be 80 mph, heading for the underpass next to the Pont de l'Alma. The paparazzi were unable to keep up and soon fell behind.

What happened next is not, and may well never be, clear. It appears, though, that Henri Paul put his foot down hard and the Mercedes, an S-220 model capable of 135 mph but probably going at 120 mph, shot towards the underpass. There, at the entrance, it collided with or clipped a white Fiat Uno, leaving shattered glass on the roadway and a skid mark 62

> *"I tried to take her pulse and, when I touched her, the Princess moved…she was breathing."*
>
> ROMAULD RAT, PAPARAZZO, ON ARRIVING AT THE CRASH SCENE

feet long before Henri Paul regained control and raced down the right-hand lane.

The lane was blocked by a Citroen BX. Paul swung to the left, maybe to overtake, and stamped on the brakes. It was a fatal mistake. The Mercedes skidded for 105 feet and smashed into the 13th support pillar inside the tunnel. Recoiling from the impact, the car swivelled in a semicircle and careered across the road to smash into the opposite wall in a tangle of mangled metal and broken glass.

Henri Paul died instantly. Dodi, too, was killed at once. Trevor Rees-Jones, sitting in the front of the car, was badly but not fatally injured, though unconscious. Diana, who had been thrown around the car and onto the floor between the front and back seats, was seriously hurt, but still alive.

Above The route taken by the couple's Mercedes from the Ritz Hotel to evade press photographers in the early hours of Sunday morning, 31 August. Right and below Stills from the security video at the servants' entrance of the Ritz Hotel show Diana and Dodi entering for dinner at 9.50pm, then leaving with driver Henri Paul (in front of them) at 12.20am.

Right In 1986, on the Gulf Tour with Charles, Diana visited a home for handicapped children in Riyadh, Saudi Arabia. Setting off her lively red-and-white dress, she wore a simple gold band around her neck and large gold earrings.

Below In Birmingham, in October 1995, Diana wears pearl earrings in a simple, circular gold setting.

All that Glistens

In public, Diana wore gold jewellery less frequently than diamonds or pearls. But when she did, she wore it with her usual impeccable taste – not too much, not too little and always teamed with suitable clothes

Diana's unerring taste in choosing the right jewellery for the right clothes and the right occasion never let her down. Whether it was pearls, diamonds, coloured stones or gold jewellery, it always blended beautifully with her 'total look'. This was rather unexpected in a young girl who, before she made a royal marriage, had very little jewellery of her own. The then Lady Diana Spencer had a modest little necklace with her initial hanging from a gold chain, and a Russian wedding ring made traditionally from three inter-linked rings in white, yellow and red gold.

Gold charm bracelet

Soon after they married, Prince Charles gave Diana a gold charm bracelet and added charms to it for special occasions, such as birthdays or other special events. The milestone of Diana's first overseas tour, to Australia in 1983, was marked by a solid gold charm in the shape of a koala bear. With her second tour, to Canada the same year, the bracelet acquired a gold wombat, which Charles gave her on her 22nd birthday on 1 July. In 1982, to mark the birth of Prince William, Charles gave her a heart-shaped necklet in gold and pearls.

Gold, though, was not Diana's first choice in jewellery. Her preference was for pearls, which not

Above On the Spanish tour, in April 1987, Diana attended a fashion show in Madrid with members of the Spanish royal family. For the occasion, she wore this turquoise taffeta peplum suit with gold embroidery echoed by her large dangling gold earrings. **Right** Visiting a Red Cross project in Zimbabwe in July 1993, Diana wore these broad gold hooped earrings.

1 On the Canadian tour, in May 1986, Diana wears a faux gold necklace enlivened by a butterfly with a black and white pattern picked out in jet and diamanté.

2 In November 1985, Diana watches Charles play polo at Werribee Park, Melbourne, Australia. She wears double-hooped gold earrings and, around her neck, a simple gold chain with the pendant letter 'D'.

3 At the National Theatre, London, for an awards ceremony, in December 1993, Diana wears a plum velvet suit by Amanda Wakely, set off by a three-strand gold-link necklace and chunky gold earrings.

only suited her fair colouring, but matched her perennially fresh and youthful air. The same went for the dazzling whiteness of diamonds or the coolness of silver. Gold, however, was harder and more flashy in appearance. Gold also lacked the delicacy offered by pearl or diamond jewellery.

A challenge

Gold was therefore something of a challenge. One approach was to wear only part-gold jewellery. At a film première in 1981, for instance, she wore a beautiful choker of gold, rubies and diamonds with matching bracelet and earrings.

Three years later, in Toronto, Canada, during her tour of 1986, Diana chose a gold necklace with a gold bow edged in blue stones to complement her blue-and-white outfit by Catherine Walker. The wider, segmented necklace Diana wore to a Lionel Ritchie concert in 1987 looked more substantially gold than it really was: the necklace and matching hoop earrings were part-diamanté, and that gave them a silvery sparkle which enlivened the gold. Diana's other approach to gold was to wear it in

only small quantities. Apart from tiaras, necklaces were the most up-front pieces of jewellery a woman could wear. Bracelets, on the other hand, were a lot less conspicuous and Diana chose to wear two – a gold bracelet and a gold watch – when she visited King's Lynn in 1983. They successfully enlivened her somewhat muted Catherine Walker dress in grey silk with pink edging.

Diana's way with modest shows of gold came in useful, too, to complement Catherine Walker's dark

> "*Diana was a beauty, but not an exotic one. The discreet way she wore gold shows that she knew it, and knew how to handle it.*"
> JEAN ST. CLAIR, ROYAL WRITER, ON DIANA

green sequinned evening gown, in Vienna in 1986. Diana wore a thin gold necklace with a Prince of Wales pendant which, unobtrusively but perfectly, emphasized the scooped neckline. Diana rarely went anywhere, even on the beach, without a pair

ALL THAT GLISTENS

DIAMOND AND AMETHYST NECKLACE AND EARRINGS

The necklace has twin strings of amethysts with three large amethysts in oval diamond settings. Each drop earring has two amethysts surrounded by diamonds. Diana wore them **left** on a visit to the Munich Opera House, Germany, with Charles, in November 1987.

of earrings and here, too, gold could be used modestly and tastefully, and sometimes cleverly.

When she wore Bruce Oldfield's spectacular silver lamé evening gown to a dinner in London in March 1985 and again in Melbourne that November, Diana opted not to wear silver jewellery to match. Instead, she chose a pair of delicate gold

> **"Charles continued a romantic royal custom when he added charms to the gold bracelet he gave Diana – the custom was started by Queen Victoria's consort, Prince Albert."**
>
> MARCO HOUSTON, EDITOR OF
> ROYALTY, ON CHARLES

drop earrings, wearing no other jewellery, apart from her engagement and wedding rings.

In 1987, gold teamed up with diamanté and sapphire in heart-shaped earrings which Diana wore during her tour of Spain. Her mid-blue white-striped outfit was somewhat muted, and the earrings gave a necessary touch of sparkle. However, the gold was confined to the clasp, the heart-shaped surround and the outer edge only. Gold was part of the supporting cast again when Diana had to wear black for a war memorial service in Paris in 1988: her round earrings with pearl centre and gold surround (see right) provided a flash of colour.

Suiting her clothes

A further use for gold was as an echo of another feature on Diana's outfits. This is what her pearl 'blob' earrings with gold surround were doing when she wore Catherine Walker's tomato-and-pink dress in Dubai, during the Gulf Tour of 1989. The dress had three gold buttons down one side, echoed by the similarly shaped gold and pearl earrings and complemented by a simple gold bracelet.

As with everything else to do with fashions, Diana knew how to wear splendid jewellery, gold or otherwise, and still look tastefully decorated. It was a knack she possessed from the start, and the way she 'tamed' gold, which can look very brassy if not worn with discretion, was an object lesson to the millions of women who followed her lead.

GOLD EARRINGS

Clockwise from top: Star earrings in diamanté and pearl in a gold setting; a small central heart amid paste diamonds in a heart-shaped gold setting; gold leaf-shaped drop earrings, worn **right** in Melbourne in 1985; gold bauble earrings worn in Caën in 1987; and (bottom) pearl and gold stud earrings, worn in Paris, 1988.

Above and below As Colonel-in-Chief of the Royal Hampshire Regiment, Diana was entitled to wear the regimental badge, featuring a crown above a lion and a rose. **Left** Sydney, 1988: blue-and-gold earrings pick up the tones of Diana's Bellville Sassoon dress.

IN THE NEWS

Diana made jewellery fun

For the media, Diana was a window on many royal subjects. There was no problem filling whole pages – like this one in a 1992 edition of *Woman* magazine – with big Diana coverage. This page featured her jewellery, together with a portrait of the Princess wearing one of her tiaras. It makes great play of her innovative approach to jewellery, with headlines like 'Ears a new look'. Diana was the ultimate model, not just for clothes but for jewels as well, and chose gold jewellery with impeccable taste, as her display of earrings, watches and other pieces shows.

Art to Art

Diana once called herself 'thick as a plank' and that spread the idea that she was lowbrow. But there was nothing lowbrow about her appreciation of the arts, or the enthusiasm she showed for them

When Diana first came on the royal scene in 1981, a great deal was made of her interests in rock and pop music, romantic novels and TV 'soaps' and the general idea that she was not intellectual. The young Diana encouraged these notions, probably without realizing how it would make her task that much more difficult when it came to convincing people that she could be serious about weightier matters. Ultimately, she managed to dissipate this 'airhead' picture, and one way in which she did it was through her work in supporting the arts.

The list of organizations of which she was president or patron was a long one, and it was both unfair and inaccurate when it was presumed that she was doing no more than performing her royal duty while being thoroughly bored by it all. Her arts

Above Princess Diana talks to New Zealand opera star Kiri te Kanawa at the Royal Opera House, Covent Garden, in November 1991. **Left** At the Queen Elizabeth Hall, London, in December 1992, Diana chats with members of the National Children's Orchestra, of which she was patron. **Right** Diana talks to a pupil at a ballet class in Cardigan, Wales, in October 1985.

patronages, in fact, represented many of her own personal interests, such as classical music, opera, ballet, painting and some of the crafts. The patronages connected with music made a particularly prestigious list: the Royal Academy of Music, London Symphony Chorus, Scottish Chamber Orchestra and Welsh National Opera, to name only a few. She was, in addition, patron of the London City Ballet and the English National Ballet, as well as president of the Royal Academy of Dramatic Art (RADA).

A musical background

There was, in fact, a strong musical strain in Diana's background. Her maternal grandmother, Lady Fermoy, was a professional concert pianist until she married the 4th Baron Fermoy. As girls, Diana and her two sisters all had music lessons. Diana came to the piano rather late, at the age of 14 in 1975, but 13 years later, while on tour in Australia with Prince Charles, she played briefly at an arts college in Melbourne and received much praise – and a kiss – from Professor Henri Touzeau, who had once taught Charles to play the cello.

The music Diana played on that occasion came from Rachmaninov's *Piano Concerto No. 2*, a very challenging piece that was one of her favourites. Another was Verdi's *Requiem*. Diana also appreciated the music of Grieg, Schumann, Tchaikovsky and Mozart – wide-ranging tastes that were never as widely publicized as her fondness for pop.

Over-emphasis in the tabloids on those interests she did not share with Prince Charles effectively hid the fact that both of them were great opera fans, and Diana's friendship with the great Italian tenor Luciano Pavarotti was not just another instance of her being star-struck. She adored his beautiful voice and was willing, with Prince Charles and thousands of others, to get well and truly soaked in Hyde Park in 1991 when Pavarotti gave an open-air concert in the rain (see In The News). Hairstyle completely wrecked and flattened and eye make-up starting to run, Diana's excited smile revealed that she thought the ducking was well worth it.

Realizing what a problem funding for the arts could be, Diana personally promoted business sponsorship and, in 1989, presented awards from the

Top This beautifully posed picture of Diana with the corps de ballet of the Royal Ballet graphically makes the point that Diana was central to the well-being of ballet in Britain. **Inset, above** Following a performance of *Carnival For The Birds*, a ballet gala in aid of the Royal Society for the Protection of Birds, performed at the Royal Opera House, Covent Garden, Diana talks to prima ballerina Natalia Makarova.

Association of Business Sponsorship of the Arts (ABSA) to 12 of that year's winners.

Diana's link with Wales, as its Princess, gave her plenty of opportunities to encourage the arts, especially the performing arts. One of Diana's first patronages, in 1982, was the Welsh National Opera, which had been a professional company for only six years, after decades as an amateur group. In March 1984, Diana opened the WNO's new rehearsal rooms and restaurant in Cardiff and frequently attended the company's performances, both in Cardiff and London. While in New York on her first big solo trip overseas in 1989, Diana made a point of attending a gala performance of Verdi's *Falstaff*, at the Brooklyn Academy of Music.

Orchestral manoeuvres

Diana was known for taking a personal interest in individuals who came to her sympathetic attention, and one of the lucky youngsters she noticed was a Welsh boy, Philip Boyden from Gwent. Philip was just 14 and still at school when he won a prize in a competition to write a soothing lullaby for Prince Harry in 1986. He was then a member of the National Children's Orchestra, of which Diana was

patron, and he had the thrill of seeing Diana presented with a keepsake version of his lullaby.

As always, Diana was an active and enthusiastic patron for the Children's Orchestra. From 1982 onwards, she regularly attended rehearsals and con-

> "It was wonderful. Thank you for writing it."
>
> DIANA TO PHILIP BOYDEN, COMPOSER OF A LULLABY FOR PRINCE HARRY

certs at Queen Elizabeth Hall in London's South Bank art complex, or during the Edinburgh Festival, where the Orchestra played each August.

Knowing Diana was keen that her sons should learn music, the Orchestra presented her with a violin, reduced four times in size, for the then infant Prince William. A 10-year-old violinist played the instrument for her and Diana was, reportedly, utterly delighted. Teaching her sons to appreciate music became part of Diana's campaign to give them a taste of the lives open to ordinary boys. She later booked both William and Harry on special 'Fun with Music' cruises down the River

Above left Diana with photographer Richard Avedon at an exhibition of his pictures in London in March 1995. **Above** On an official visit to Tokyo, Japan, in November 1990, Charles and Diana are guests of honour at a performance of Richard Strauss' opera *Salome*, given by the Welsh National Opera, who were on tour. Afterwards the royal couple chat with members of the cast.

Above At the Barbican, London, in November 1990, Diana shakes hands with the jazz violinist, Stefan Grapelli. **Inset, near right** Diana poses with the Kirov Ballet at the Coliseum, London, in June 1993. **Far right** Diana adds a final touch to a mural at a hospital in Melbourne, Australia in 1985.

Thames in London. Works by Handel, the 18th-century composer who once wrote music for Charles' ancestor King George I, were played, and a music teacher explained the composer's work.

In 1986, Diana was in Cardiff to attend a gala concert given at St. David's Hall by the Children's Orchestra and paid them a special compliment by wearing a cherry-red dress, which matched the red uniforms worn by the young players. This was the sort of touch which endeared Diana to the organizations she helped. Diana's personal interest meant a great deal to the arts companies she supported, especially when the arts were having a hard time surviving in difficult economic conditions.

Supporting ballet

This was particularly true of ballet which, like opera, was a specialized art, considered by many to be 'elitist'. Diana, however, was one hundred per cent in favour of ballet, and serving as patron of two

❧ Protocol ❧

ARTISTS OF THE ROYAL FAMILY

Until recently, protocol did not permit royals to use their artistic talents professionally. Prince Charles, a fine painter and storyteller, came close with the publication of his book The Old Man of Lochnagar, *written for his brothers in 1968. Princess Alexandra,* **right**, *whose father, the late Duke of Kent, reached near-professional standard as a pianist and Princess Margaret — an excellent mimic, pianist, singer and dancer — had to reserve their gifts for family and friends. It was only with the younger generation of royals that protocol relaxed to enable talents and careers to go together — Prince Edward with his work in the theatre and television, Viscount Linley with his furniture designs, and Lady Sarah Chatto with her paintings.*

Diana bursts into giggles while talking to violinist Nigel Kennedy at the Variety Club Awards, which were held at the Metropole Hotel, Birmingham, in 1991.

Above A young and obviously star-struck Diana talks to the renowned ballet dancer Rudolf Nureyev, after a gala performance in aid of charity at the Royal Opera House, Covent Garden, in December 1982.

ballet companies proved to be fine compensation for a girl who had grown at least five inches too tall to contemplate following a career as a ballet dancer. 'I overshot the height by a long way,' she once remarked ruefully. 'I couldn't imagine some man trying to lift me up.'

Diana was a veteran ballet-watcher long before she became Princess of Wales. While she was still at school, she could not get enough of ballets such as *Swan Lake*, *Giselle* or *Coppelia* and often spent hours, along with other enthusiastic fans, waiting at the stage door hoping to get the dancers' autographs when they emerged after the performance.

This was how she managed to get the famous Russian dancer Mikhail Baryshnikov to autograph her programme after a performance at the Royal

Opera House in London's Covent Garden. Many years later, in 1985, when the once unknown girl had become one of the most famous women in the

> *"She is a...talented player... very accomplished. She shows great musical ability and she is very sensitive."*
>
> PROFESSOR HENRI TOUZEAU, MUSIC TEACHER, ON DIANA

world, Diana reminded Baryshnikov of her long-ago triumph and gave him her autograph in return.

Diana's ballet patronages therefore gave her special pleasure. In order to help her keep fit enough

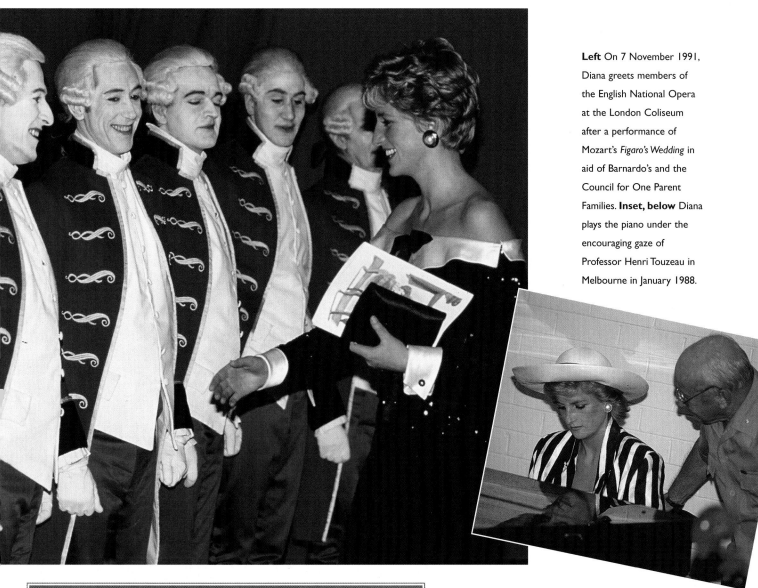

Left On 7 November 1991, Diana greets members of the English National Opera at the London Coliseum after a performance of Mozart's *Figaro's Wedding* in aid of Barnardo's and the Council for One Parent Families. **Inset, below** Diana plays the piano under the encouraging gaze of Professor Henri Touzeau in Melbourne in January 1988.

IN THE NEWS

The heavens open

The British weather was at its drenching worst on the night that Luciano Pavarotti gave an open-air concert in London's Hyde Park on 30 July 1991. Charles and Diana were there and got soaked to the skin along with the rest of the audience.

No other royal lady ever had her hairstyle so thoroughly obliterated, but Diana revelled in the music and the weather, smiling the broadest of her smiles on the front pages reporting the event next day. Drenched Di, in fact, got more publicity than the famous Italian tenor.

for her job and to indulge her passion for dancing, Diana used to take hour-long ballet lessons in the Throne Room at Buckingham Palace. Diana had more lessons from Dame Merle Park, the renowned ballerina who became Principal of the Royal Ballet and Director of the Royal Ballet School. She also had regular private tuition at the studios of the English National Ballet near the Royal Albert Hall, which was not far from Kensington Palace.

These efforts put Diana in a good position to understand the hard work and devotion which ballet dancers had to put in to maintain high standards, and enabled her to be the sort of patron she most wanted to be: knowledgeable, sympathetic and active. The first ballet company of which she became patron, in 1983, was the London City

Above Diana at *Accademia Italiana*, an exhibition of Italian art and antiques, which she opened in London in December 1990.

Ballet and her involvement virtually rescued the company from oblivion. She worked hard to publicize the company and attract business sponsorship, regularly attending business meetings with the

> "*She just lived for ballet and was completely dedicated. Her lessons helped her get away from the pressures of being a member of the Royal Family.*"
>
> LILY SNIPP, DIANA'S BALLET TEACHER, ON DIANA

board of directors and personally writing a foreword to the City Ballet's brochure for 1989-90.

Diana became patron of a second ballet company in 1989, when she took over from Princess Margaret as patron of the English National Ballet. The next year, she attended a glamorous ball following the company's 40th anniversary gala at the Royal Albert Hall. There, she was swept onto the

dance floor by the Hungarian-born artistic director Ivan Nagy, who was not in the least concerned that his royal partner was nearly six inches taller than he was. Nagy pronounced Diana 'a natural' and the Princess took it as a great compliment to be so described by a former ballet star who had once danced with the prima ballerina Margot Fonteyn. 'She is the most light-footed dancer I have ever partnered,' Mr. Nagy later enthused.

Magical world

Diana's involvement in the arts may not have hit the headlines with quite the same splash as the pop concerts or the fashion shows she attended. Yet it was in the arts world that the public life she often found so taxing met long-standing passions of her own, especially for the ballet. At ballet performances, too, she could become absorbed, if only for a while, in the magical make-believe world which might have been hers had she not outgrown it or gone on to become a princess.

GOODBYE, ENGLAND'S ROSE

When Diana died in 1997, millions went into shock. As a royal celebrity, she had always seemed larger than life. In the aftermath of the crash, she also became an enduring symbol of compassion

It seemed like an ordinary summer Sunday morning. There were lawns to be mown, lunch to prepare, church to attend, dogs to be walked. Ordinary, that is, until the newspapers arrived. The headlines were a violent slap across the face of a leisurely day off. A car crash, they said. Dodi was dead. Diana was 'seriously injured'.

But the television and radio were more definite. Newsreaders had barely materialized on screen,

together with world leaders paying tribute, before the watching millions realized the appalling fact that Diana was dead. Her injuries, which included a torn left pulmonary vein (a major blood vessel of the heart), had been too severe for her to survive.

The shock that shivered through Britain and around the world was like an emotional earthquake. There was incredulity, anguish, regret, remorse, an almost paralysing sense of loss. There

DIARY DATES
1997
31 August
The Princess of Wales dies in Paris following a car crash, and the Prince of Wales and her sisters, Sarah and Jane, go to Paris to identify the body, returning with it to RAF Northolt, Middlesex

1 September
Dodi Fayed is buried at Woking, Surrey

5 September
The Queen makes a broadcast to the nation about Diana's death

6 September
A memorial service is held at Westminster Abbey for the Princess of Wales, followed by a private burial at Althorp

8 September
It is announced that contributions to the Diana, Princess of Wales Memorial Fund have come in at the rate of £160,000 a day

6 – 18 October
The Queen and Prince Philip embark on a tour of Pakistan and India

29 October – 5 November
The Prince of Wales visits Swaziland, Lesotho and South Africa

20 November
The Queen and Prince Philip celebrate their Golden Wedding anniversary

4 December
The Prince of Wales visits the offices of *The Big Issue*, the magazine for the homeless

11 December
The royal yacht *Britannia* is decommissioned

Previous page A sea of flowers covers the parkland outside Kensington Palace. **Above** On its return from Paris, Diana's coffin is unloaded by servicemen at RAF Northolt in north-west London, at 7.00pm on 31 August 1997. **Right** Countless thousands of people queued for 10–12 hours or more to sign books of condolence. **Far right** Outside Buckingham Palace, the Queen talks to people who have been waiting to pay their respects and are anxious for news from the Palace.

Above Princes Charles, William and Harry examine some of the tributes left for Diana at Kensington Palace. **Left** The very personal tributes made much of Diana being 'Queen of Hearts' to the people.

were those who felt guilty at the part they had played in this tragedy. If they had not pried deep into Diana's private life, lapping up the scandals and gossiping – would the papers have been stuffed so full of revelations and have ultimately hounded Diana to her death? Too late now. Diana was gone and only the guilt, real or imagined, remained.

Within hours, crowds had already started to drift up to central London, to gather outside the royal

> **"I thank God for the gift of Diana and for all her loving and giving. I give her back to Him with my love."**
>
> FRANCES SHAND KYDD, DIANA'S MOTHER

palaces as if seeking solace in proximity to places Diana had known. Some just stood staring into space, numbed and speechless. Others wept. Others gave vent to fury – against the media, the paparazzi, the security services who should have kept her safe, the doctors who should have saved her, and against the Royal Family who remained at Balmoral, where they spend their annual summer holiday.

BREAKING THE NEWS

At Balmoral, however, the royals had already absorbed the first tremor of the tragedy in Paris. Prince Charles learned of it at 2.00am after a call came through from Buckingham Palace. Diana was still alive then, but an hour later, the Prince was informed that, despite frantic efforts to save her, she been pronounced dead at 4.00am, Paris time. At 7.30am, after the young princes awoke, Charles had the painful task of telling William and Harry.

By then, the news had been flashed halfway across the world to Diana's brother, Earl Spencer, in South Africa, and closer to home, to her mother Frances in Scotland. Diana's sisters Sarah and Jane were told and they arranged to go with Charles to bring Diana home from France.

Even now, controversy, never very far from Diana in life, was dogging her in death. A supposed row about the funeral arrangements hit the headlines; the media claimed the Queen wanted Diana, who was no longer a member of the Royal Family, to have a private burial. A strongly worded denial

from Buckingham Palace was soon forthcoming. But there was also a reported clash between Prince Charles and his father, who, it was rumoured, sought to downgrade the funeral to less than royal status. Charles, it seems, insisted that at least some of the honours due a royal should be accorded his former wife. He got his way. Arrangements were made for Diana to be flown home in an aircraft of the Royal

---

"*I want to do it for Mummy.*"

PRINCE HARRY, ON WHY HE WANTED TO WALK BEHIND DIANA'S COFFIN

Squadron and to lie in the chapel at St. James' Palace with the royal standard draped over her coffin.

All day long, the grim saga unfolded across the television screens. William and Harry, dignified but pale, were seen being driven to Crathie Church near Balmoral. Later, Charles and Diana's sisters, all of them gaunt and red-eyed with grief, arrived at RAF Northolt with Diana's coffin.

The mangled wreckage of the Mercedes repeatedly flashed across the screen. Reports came through of the French paparazzi photographing Diana as she lay huddled between the seats. To widespread disgust in Britain, five of the crash-scene pictures were published in Germany.

SEA OF FLOWERS

Meanwhile, in London, makeshift shrines appeared around trees outside Kensington Palace, their candles flickering in the late summer breeze. At the gates outside, at St. James' Palace and Buckingham Palace, carpets of flowers were beginning to smother the pavements and spill over into the roads. Eventually, a flood of lilies, carnations, sunflowers and roses was washing up against the palace gates like high tide. Here and there, people were leaving small gifts, money, children's toys and messages that revealed an overwhelming sense of heartbreak.

Television crews were soon out and about, filming and interviewing. A passing motorist, spotting one crew outside Buckingham Palace, shouted 'Are you happy now, press scum?' as he drove by. He reflected the dominant mood.

'She's been taken from us by those bastard photographers,' said one woman. 'The press killed

IN THE NEWS

Pressure builds for the Queen to speak out

Newspapers spearheaded public demand that members of the Royal Family express grief at Diana's death. The royals believed that it was more important to comfort William and Harry on the untimely death of their young mother and remained at Balmoral for that purpose. Public anger was too vociferous, though. The Evening Standard of 4 September broke the news that the Queen had bowed to the pressure and was to make a special television broadcast on the following day.

Diana!' a man shouted outside Buckingham Palace. Another marched through Hyde Park, declaring: 'Ban all landmines – we love you Diana!' Onlookers clapped, cheered and wept, not caring who saw them, as the renowned British reserve broke down.

But all this anger and anguish came with a demand, which seemed to grow increasingly threatening, that the Royal Family show themselves and join in the public sorrow. The first focus of this fury was the empty flagstaff at Buckingham Place, where according to protocol, flags never flew unless the Queen was in residence. But the public was in a mood to smash through protocol and, eventually, the Union Jack was raised to half mast, even though the Queen remained in Scotland.

WHIPPING UP HYSTERIA

The next target of furious complaint was the very fact that the Queen stayed at Balmoral. The press whipped up anti-Windsor sentiments with headlines such as 'Your People Are Suffering, Speak To Us, Ma'am' or 'Show Us You Care' and 'Where Is Our Queen?'. The Queen was forced to respond and by Friday, 5 September, the day before Diana's funeral, she was on television speaking of her grief

Left Among the mourners at the Abbey was Dodi's father, Mohamed Al Fayed (left), the owner of Harrods and the Paris Ritz, who only days before had buried his son. At his side is his spokesman Michael Cole.
Right From the pulpit, Earl Spencer paid tribute to his sister in moving terms.

Right Celebrities present included Tom Cruise, Nicole Kidman, Phil Collins and, here, Prime Minister Tony Blair and his wife, Cherie.
Below right Singer and friend Elton John at the piano in Westminster Abbey, waiting to deliver his song *Candle In The Wind* in tribute to Diana. Within weeks his recording of the song had sold 30 million copies.

☙ Protocol ❧

DIANA'S WILL IS MADE PUBLIC

Normally, royal wills are never made public, but Diana's was the exception. Her will, below, made in June 1993, was published on 3 March 1998 — and naturally made big headlines. The unsurprising part was the news that the bulk of her fortune — £13 million after £8 million inheritance tax was paid — was put in trust for William and Harry, who will share it equally. Among other bequests, Diana's butler, Paul Burrell, received £50,000. Somewhat controversially, though, Diana requested that Prince Charles consult her mother Frances about her sons' 'upbringing, education and welfare', something which is normally the preserve of the Royal Family. Diana went further, though. She requested that if Charles were also to die before William and Harry come of age, then her mother and brother, Earl Spencer, should become their legal guardians. By inference, this excluded members of the Royal Family.

as her subjects required of her. For her pains, she was accused of not showing sufficient emotion.

Meanwhile, the Duke of York and Prince Edward appeared in the Mall, talking to the thousands who were queuing for hours to sign books of condolence at Buckingham Palace. William and Harry, composed despite a tear or two, were moving among the crowds outside Kensington Palace.

The crowds stood grim-faced but calm when, on Saturday, 6 September at 9.08am, Diana's cortège began its journey to Westminster Abbey for a memorial service. Many people had slept rough all night so that they could pay their last respects.

> ## "This is the most tragic and senseless death."
>
> ### SINGER ELTON JOHN, DIANA'S FRIEND

Charles, William, Harry, Earl Spencer and Prince Philip joined the procession in the Mall. When the cortège passed Buckingham Palace, the Queen and her family, all clad in black, were outside the gates.

All the way to the Abbey, where a bell tolled at one-minute intervals, the route was lined with onlookers who wept, choked back tears, or gazed sadly after the coffin as it passed by on its gun carriage. The scene was eerie in its silence, with only the clatter of horses' hooves to break it.

At the Abbey, where 2000 mourners waited and loudspeakers were to relay the service to the crowds outside, Diana's friend, Elton John, sang his tribute *Candle In The Wind*. As he neared the end with the words: 'Goodbye, England's rose, from a country lost without your compassion…' several of the distinguished congregation cast aside decorum and unashamedly cried in public.

EARL'S TRIBUTE

Afterwards, Earl Spencer delivered his own tribute, in which he flayed the 'guilty' press and skirted controversy as he spoke of Diana's wish that her sons should not be 'immersed by duty and tradition'. Few doubted that this was a dig at the Royal Family. Few doubted, either, the strain on the young Earl whose voice broke several times. As the echoes of the Earl's final words faded, television

The Private Princess
Remembering Diana

Above *Within days the shops were full of Diana memorabilia, not all of it in the best possible taste.*

Just as there was bound to be an avalanche of souvenirs of Diana, there were bound to be numerous attempts to exploit her memory.

This seems to have been a first thought for Buckingham Palace officials, who set up the Princess Diana Memorial Fund within 24 hours of her death. The Fund's function was to vet souvenirs for suitability. It was also meant to ensure that a percentage of the proceeds went to the Fund for use by charities Diana had favoured.

Fears of commercial exploitation proved well founded and the safeguard of a special logo containing Diana's signature was a wise move. Not all proposals were as tasteful as the beautiful candleholder that was the first memento approved by Buckingham Palace.

Some extraordinary, and what Prime Minister Tony Blair called 'tacky', ideas surfaced all too quickly. Products proposed included household cleaners, hair lacquer, a Diana pizza, and a Diana chamberpot.

Much more acceptable was the concept of a Diana memorial garden in Kensington Gardens, the Diana museum Earl Spencer planned to create at Althorp and a 'people's promenade', inspired by the crowds which thronged the Mall after Diana's death.

Beyond the reach of palace permissions, in the USA, for instance, a porcelain Diana doll was speedily on sale, as was a heart-shaped gold and diamanté pendant containing a single rose. The Americans produced, too, a crown-shaped tribute ring with three pearls and ten white sapphires on a solid silver frame.

The first commemorative stamp issue came from the Marshall Islands in the Pacific. Great Britain issued five Diana stamps on 3 February 1998.

audiences were stunned to hear a ripple of applause from those outside the Abbey. It grew into a roaring sea of heartfelt approval that swept through the silent mourners, including the Royal Family, inside.

When it was over, Britain was hushed as a minute's silence was observed. Then, Diana's last journey, the 77 miles to Althorp, began. The hearse carrying her lily-strewn coffin moved slowly through central London, heading north for the M1 motorway. As it passed by, bunches of flowers were thrown onto the bonnet and rose so high up the

> "*A wonderful place, it's beautiful and quiet and peaceful. A perfect place for Diana.*"
>
> BETTY ANDREW, FORMER ALTHORP HOUSEKEEPER, ON DIANA'S ISLAND GRAVE

windscreen that the windscreen wipers were unable to clear them from the driver's view.

More mourners massed at Brent Cross, the start of the M1. After the hearse and its outriders left the motorway, the narrow country lanes that led to Althorp were crammed with another 250,000 people who had waited hours to decorate it with yet more flowers flung from the roadside.

Finally, the hearse drove past the flowers specially cleared to the sides to fringe the entrance to Althorp, and turned right up the narrow drive that led to the house. Then it disappeared from view.

A FINAL RESTING PLACE

Later, England's rose, as Elton John had called Diana, was buried in a specially consecrated grave on an island in the centre of a small lake in the grounds. Only her former husband, her sons and her family were present in this beautiful place where she had once loved to play as a child.

In time, the greatest tragedies become history. The dazzle of celebrity fades. But, despite her flaws and faults, Diana's star is set to shimmer for a long while yet. She was so many different people in one: the loving mother; the compassionate campaigner; the stylish beauty; the wronged wife; and the Queen who never was. An extraordinary woman. An extraordinary royal. An extraordinary life.

Above As the coffin is moved from the gun carriage to the shoulders of pall bearers, Earl Spencer and the Princes stand in silence. **Right** In Knightsbridge, in the window of Mohamed Al Fayed's department store, Harrods, was this tribute to a loving couple – photos of Diana and Dodi alongside a wreath of lilies.

IN CONTEXT   NANNY FOUND GUILTY
1997

- Mother Teresa of Calcutta dies
- British nanny Louise Woodward, **right**, is found guilty of murdering US baby; the charge is reduced to manslaughter
- Scots and Welsh vote in favour of devolution
- In Saudi Arabia, British nurse Lucille McLauchlan is found guilty of murder and sentenced to eight years in prison and 500 lashes
- International Committee to Ban Landmines wins Nobel Peace Prize

Top Her Majesty the Queen
and other members of the
Royal Family wait outside
Buckingham Palace for the
cortège to pass by on its
way to Westminster Abbey.
Above Flowers covered the
hearse on its journey from
Westminster Abbey to
Althorp House in
Northamptonshire.
Left Diana is buried on this
tranquil island in the man-
made lake at the Spencer
family estate of Althorp.

The Fashion Icon

Once, all the Royal Family – men and women – had been the focus of the fashion-conscious. After years in which royalty had few links with fashion, Diana put them back on the map

Above At a film première in 1991, Diana wears a Catherine Walker gown in ivory silk crêpe.

The day that Diana entered public life – her engagement day, 24 February 1981 – British fashion designers knew she was the answer to their dreams. Royals had once been the fashion trendsetters – for example, Queen Mary, the Queen's grandmother, with her toque hats, and Queen Elizabeth, now the Queen Mother, with her pastel-coloured outfits – but over 50 years had passed. Then Lady Diana Spencer appeared – shy, slightly gawky, schoolgirlish, but promising.

Unsophisticated

However, it took professionals who knew what could be done with raw material to guess, correctly, that Diana had the makings of a fashion icon. On her first public appearance as Charles' fiancée, in her blue Cojana suit, bought for £310 from Harrods, Diana looked as if she had just stepped out of her school uniform. She was a total innocent in the ways of style and chic. Diana did all the obvious, but non-stylish things. She was very tall, close on six feet, so she tried to minimize her height by wearing low-heeled shoes.

Her shoes became an instant craze and so did her youthful floppy-fringed hairstyle. Shoe shops and hairdressers were, by all accounts, besieged by girls and women demanding that they be instantly turned into Diana lookalikes. This, though, resulted only in more women looking like overgrown schoolgirls. It had nothing to do with real style or meaningful fashion.

While the fashion designers laid plans to give Diana much more chic than she possessed on her

Main picture Diana at Westminster Abbey in December 1985 for the Children of Courage Awards. She is wearing a Caroline Charles waisted two-piece with puffed sleeves, topped by a matching cockaded hat.

Top left Diana wears a strapless evening dress and cropped bolero jacket by Catherine Walker to the British Fashion Awards in October 1989. **Bottom left** After opening the first Covent Garden International Festival, in September 1990, Diana leaves with baseball caps for the boys. She is wearing a pink two-piece by Paul Costelloe, which has a long collarless jacket with large gold buttons.

**CATHERINE WALKER
TWO-PIECE SUIT**

A pale yellow suit with a
long drape jacket, pleated
skirt and a navy hem,
reflected by the navy blue
hat with yellow ribbon.
Diana wore this Catherine
Walker suit on several
occasions including, **inset
above**, Easter Sunday in
April 1992, when the Royal
Family gathered at Windsor.

1 In October 1990, to greet Italian President Francesco Cossiga, Diana wears a natty green Moschino two-piece with a Somerville hat.

2 At Westminster Abbey in October 1992, Diana wears a pale blue-and-cream suit by Catherine Walker.

3 In Southgate, London, to attend a conference on mental health in June 1993, Diana wears a pale blue double-breasted jacket and a pleated skirt.

4 On a visit to St. James' Anglican Cathedral, Toronto, Canada, in October 1991, Diana wears a Catherine Walker white two-piece suit trimmed with red on the jacket and a matching red-and-white pillbox hat created by Philip Somerville.

5 On a visit to Birmingham in May 1993, Diana wears this shocking-pink two-piece. The outfit by Catherine Walker has a long jacket and a straight skirt that finishes above the knee.

6 On St. David's Day 1991, Diana accompanies Prince William on a walkabout in Cardiff. She sports a daffodil and the yellow of the flower is picked up by the band of the hat. The blue two-piece suit is by Catherine Walker.

own, there were some factors they could take for granted. Unlike fashion models or film and television stars, a Princess of Wales was regularly on show in public. There were, of course, actresses and models who were more beautiful than Diana. Many were more shapely, more striking and better proportioned. But as far as the public was concerned,

> ## "She has single-handedly revitalized the British fashion industry."
> SALLY MOORE, ROYAL AUTHOR, ON DIANA

they were not real, live women, in the sense that they existed only in pictures or as moving images on a cinema or television screen. The Princess of Wales, on the other hand, was very real. She would be there, in the flesh, during public appearances. People could, and did, touch her, see her up close, watch her walking, talking, smiling and laughing.

Clothes in action

In these circumstances, the clothes she wore were going to be seen in action, not carefully posed for effect like a model's. Onlookers could see how the clothes coped with natural body actions like extending arms and shaking hands, sitting down, getting into cars, walking along a street, or even picking up the children and carrying them around.

Though Diana's wardrobe cost thousands, wearing it in public put her on a par with other women who had to wear clothes suited to the demands of everyday living. In this context, it helped that Diana had an amazing capacity to persuade people that she was just an ordinary woman, instead of an aristocrat who had become a princess. With her modest manner, Diana, who was regularly on show, managed to put across the idea that ordinary women could dress just like her and look just as good.

Even her imperfections and drawbacks were assets in setting her up, eventually, as a fashion icon women would be happy to emulate. She did a lot for tall women, who might feel out of place among others who, on average, could be six inches shorter, or more. Plenty of women with large, prominent noses felt cheered by the fact that the future Queen Consort had one, too, and what is more, refused to have it 'fixed'. Women with small eyes learned from Diana how to make them look large and luscious. Those who became red in the face when overheated saw how Diana, who suffered in this way, managed to make herself look cool. A fashion icon, after all, should not be a goddess, perfect in face and form and out of reach, suitable only for other women to envy and wish 'if only....' Rather, she should be a woman who can overcome her disadvantages and set a high standard of elegance. And that is precisely what Diana and her designers did.

Before this happened, though, Diana had several fashion habits to shed. The frilled collars of which

---

> ## "As a style icon of the late 20th century, Diana will have no equal."
>
> MIMI SPENCER OF THE LONDON EVENING STANDARD, ON DIANA

---

she was so fond were unsophisticated and little-girlish. So was her early tendency to overdo her necklines with frilled collars and pearl chokers worn together. Those low-heeled shoes had to go, because they tended to make her stomp around rather than glide. She also had to stop belting up her suit jackets and making herself look dumpy on top.

Diana's designers, wisely, played the waiting game. In her early days as Princess of Wales, they conceded the frilled collars, belted jackets and

1 In Paris, in 1992, Diana wears this eye-catching black dress with a red design that looks like a bell pull hanging down the left-hand side.

2 Attending Sadler's Wells for a gala, in June 1990, she wears a Bruce Oldfield cream satin jacket with a lacy skirt. Its scalloped hem matches the bustline.

3 At Spencer House, London, in May 1992, Diana wears a Catherine Walker dress in blue-grey chiffon.

4 At a banquet at the Dorchester, in November 1993, Diana wears an emerald green dance dress by Catherine Walker.

5 In an evening coat dress by Catherine Walker, Diana arrives at the Royal Opera House, Covent Garden, in June 1989.

6 Diana arrives for *La Favorita*, at the Royal Opera House, in a cream silk chiffon dress by Catherine Walker.

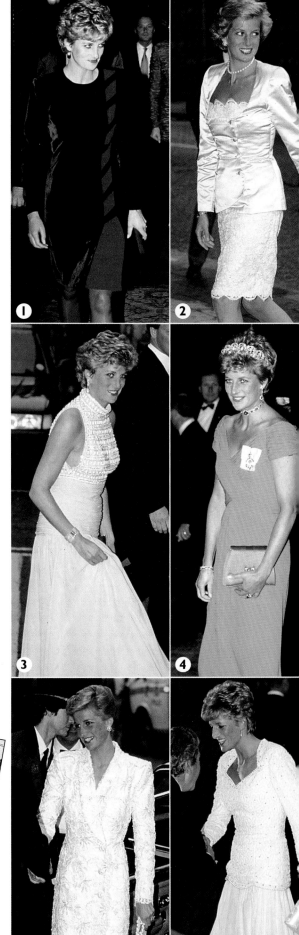

IN THE NEWS

Forever in fashion, always in Vogue

Diana had a special relationship with Vogue magazine and posed for pictures, by Patrick Demarchelier, which featured both on the cover and inside pages of their issues. For Diana, the magazine was a valuable source of fashion advice. For Vogue, the exclusive pictures the Princess gave them were a priceless boost to circulation, since a picture of Diana on the cover of any magazine made sales rocket. In all, Vogue played an important part in helping Diana to become a fashion icon. This is the cover from the retrospective October 1997 issue.

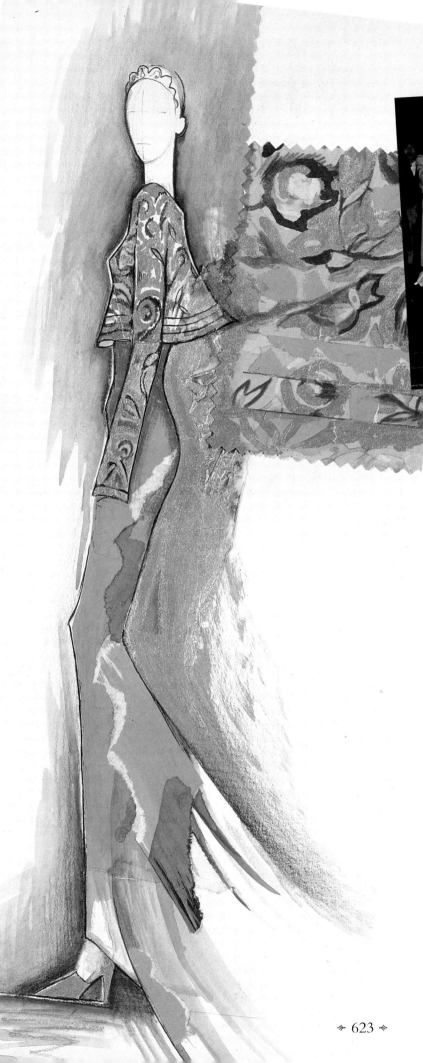

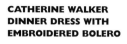

CATHERINE WALKER DINNER DRESS WITH EMBROIDERED BOLERO

The bolero jacket is beautifully embroidered with mauve violets and pink roses in silk and chenille on lilac silk. The skirt is in silk crêpe. Diana wore it to a state dinner, **left**, on the South Korean tour in 1992. At the 1997 Christie's auction it realized $51,750/£31,000.

low-heeled shoes, but gradually moved her along towards the greater elegance of the simple line and the uncluttered silhouette. They experimented with unusual colour combinations, carefully keyed to her blonde looks. By 1985, four years after her marriage, Diana had been transformed. In the hands of

> *"A lot of international press and buyers came to London in the Eighties because of her....She brought some international glamour to British public life...."*
>
> CAROLINE CHARLES, DESIGNER

Catherine Walker, Victor Edelstein, Bruce Oldfield and the rest, her outfits had become the epitome of wearable but sophisticated style. Diana's ballgowns were marvels of glamour, yet could be copied by ordinary women. Her carefully nurtured 'total look' was a wonder of clever co-ordination.

Hard work

It took time and effort, especially from Diana, who crafted her figure by regular exercise and careful food intake. It took imagination and very real talent on the part of the designers. It deserved to work, and it did so brilliantly. Diana may have largely retired from the role of fashion icon at the end of 1992, when she separated from Charles, but her elegant example lived on. Fashions may change with the years, but their icons are enduring.

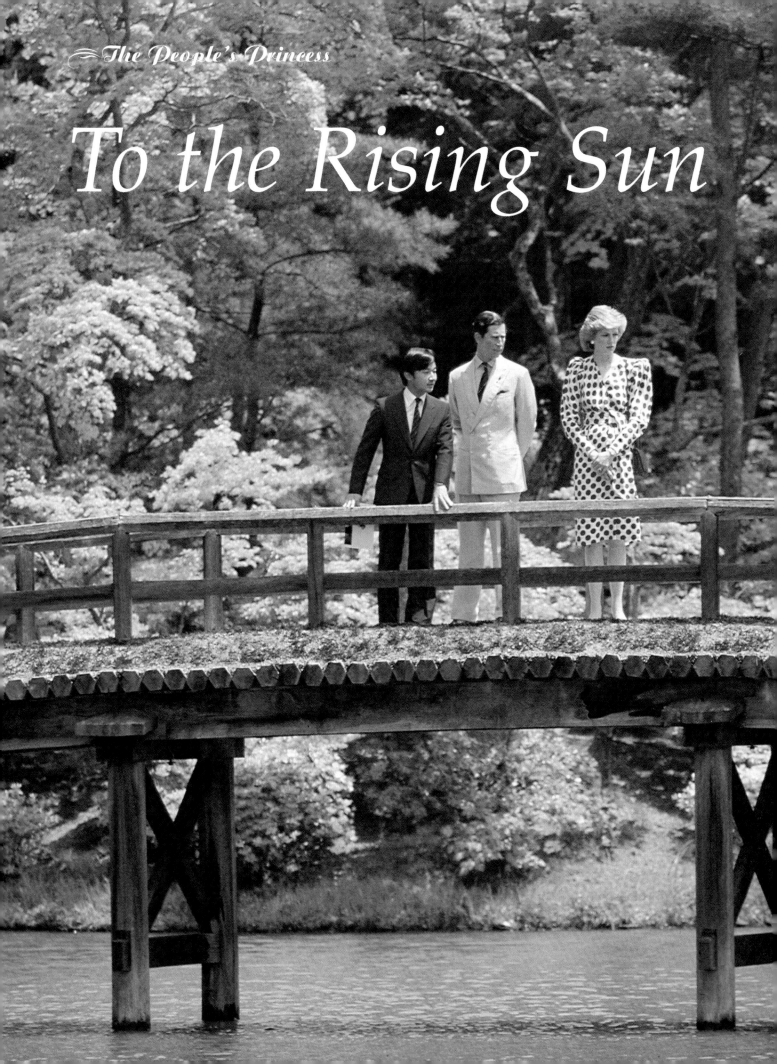

To the Rising Sun

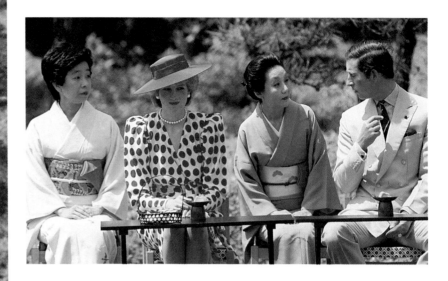

Excited anticipation was the norm before Diana arrived on a tour overseas, but the Japanese went in for unrivalled displays of 'Di-mania', both before her arrival and during her stay

Main picture A guide in Kyoto points out the beauties of a Japanese garden to Charles and Diana. **Top right** Charles and Diana experience the Tea Ceremony in Kyoto. **Right** Visiting St. Alban's Church in Tokyo, Diana receives a bouquet from a young Japanese girl.

B efore Charles and Diana arrived in Japan on 8 May 1986 for a six-day tour, royal fervour gripped the country. There were Charles and Diana dolls, which walked when wound up, porcelain figures of Diana, and copies of her jewellery, which ranged from a 'D' initial pendant, price £40, to copies of her favourite pearl necklaces for £800. Special phonecards were issued that allowed people to dial a recorded commentary of the royal wedding of 1981.

Copying Diana

Pictures of Diana took over the front covers of magazines. Articles instructed diminutive Japanese brunettes on how they could turn themselves into copies of the tall, blue-eyed English royal blonde. Japanese television was swamped with Diana programmes – documentaries, quiz shows, even a cartoon Diana starring as the heroine of a royal love story.

It was, of course, all dignity and decorum, complete with a smartly uniformed guard of honour, when Charles and Diana landed in

Osaka. They were greeted by the young Prince Hiro, grandson of the reigning Emperor Hirohito, and the Japanese Prime Minister Yasuhiro Nakasone.

At the palace in Kyoto, the ancient capital of Japan, where they were to stay, Charles and Diana found a huge crowd of 10,000 people waiting. This

> **"No woman could have a more caring...husband, but even the Prince cannot paper over all the cracks that have begun to appear in his wife's persona."**
>
> JAMES WHITAKER, ON THE JAPANESE TOUR

was a foretaste of what was to come, as Diana performed no less than 29 engagements in six days.

Part of this enthusiasm was down to the thrill of seeing the future King and Queen of England in the flesh. The Japanese royal family was far less accessible than the Windsors and, despite renouncing his

traditional divinity in 1945, Emperor Hirohito was still regarded by many of his subjects as a god. By contrast, Charles and Diana were very informal.

Sampling Sumo

Diana, in her turn, was fascinated by Japan. She was specially interested in the Sumo wrestlers, those mighty mountains of flesh and power whom the Japanese regard as heroes. She watched a series of energetic bouts from the imperial box normally reserved for the Emperor and the royal family. The wrestlers themselves had been rather concerned that the Princess might consider it indelicate to see their vast bulk clad only in a minimal loincloth but when they asked the British Embassy, officials assured them that Diana would not mind one bit.

After the match, Diana met the mighty Salevaa Konishiki, who was 6ft 4ins tall and, at 36 stones, weighed almost five times as much as Diana. This, Diana said later, was the highlight of the whole tour

Above At a Japanese Foreign Ministry banquet in Kyoto, Diana, wearing a Zandra Rhodes dress, sits on a padded seat at the low-level table. In the foreground is a geisha girl, waiting to serve the next course of the 12 that were on offer.

Above right In Tokyo, on 13 May, Charles and Diana talk to the actors after watching a show at a Kabuki theatre. **Far left** During her stay in Tokyo, Diana found the time to visit a workshop where craftsmen made dolls that were perfectly dressed in varieties of traditional Japanese costumes.

❧ Protocol ☙

THE ROYAL FAMILY OF JAPAN

The Japanese idea of monarchy is somewhat different from the British one. In Britain, the constitutional monarch is an honoured figure, but is subject to the will of Parliament. In Japan, the monarchy has been constitutional since 1947, two years after the Second World War, but many ancient traditions still persist. The Imperial family, once headed by a divine Emperor, would never have to endure the press gossip and speculation that have hounded the British royals. Instead, Emperor Akihito (who succeeded in 1989 on the death of Hirohito) and Empress Michiko, **right***, are treated with an awed reverence. Yet it is possible for Japanese royals to renounce their titles and become commoners, something unthinkable in Britain.*

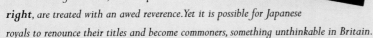

for her. But she skated a bit close to the diplomatic wind when she prodded Konishiki in his massive stomach, apparently to check whether the bulky expanse was muscle or flab. Since sumo wrestlers have the status of heroes in Japan, this looked rather like a bit of royal impudence.

At Kyoto Palace, Charles took the opportunity to do some sketching as Diana relaxed by strolling round the gardens. The first full day of their tour, 9 May, was punishing, and Diana was on her feet for up to 12 hours in temperatures of 75°F. It was reckoned that some 100,000 Japanese squeezed into the narrow streets of the old Japanese capital, chanting 'Diana! Diana!', as she toured a museum and three temples. Later, she and Charles were treated to a cut-down version of the Tea Ceremony where they were served bitter green tea.

Afterwards, the couple visited the ancient castle of Nijo. There, ten young kimono-clad girls used 13-stringed lyres called 'kotos', which normally

played traditional Japanese music, to give an unusual rendering of the Beatles' hit *Hey Jude*.

Onlookers were again packed tight in the streets when Charles and Diana attended a Japanese Foreign Ministry banquet in the evening where no less than 12 courses were served. In traditional Japanese style, the guests sat close to floor level, eating from low tables. Diana proved deft with the chopsticks and enjoyed the raw fish.

Crowds in Tokyo

Next, in Tokyo, the royal couple visited a department store and drove in an open car to the Akasaka Palace. The biggest single crowd they had ever seen in a foreign country – 150,000 people – turned out to watch, and their excitement came so close to hysteria that 7000 police guards were barely able to hold the crush barriers. When Charles and Diana reached the palace, demonstrations in the traditional Japanese arts of doll-making and *ikebana*, flower arranging, were waiting for them. More traditional Japanese culture followed on 13 May, the last day of

IN THE NEWS

A Japanese speciality

When Charles and Diana went to Japan in 1986, the photo opportunity afforded by the Princess' meeting with sumo wrestlers was probably the best of the tour. There could hardly have been a greater contrast between the tall, willowy English blonde and the mountainous Japanese sumo giants. The wrestlers were greatly flattered that Diana had especially asked to see them. Sumo is quintessentially Japanese and its rituals and laws are not widely understood in Britain.

Above left After watching the sumo wrestling, Diana takes the chance to chat to one of the combatants and find out what he eats. **Above** At Nijo Castle in Kyoto, Diana is presented with a hand-made kimono which, to the delight of photographers, she tries on then and there. **Above right** In Tokyo, on 10 May, Charles and Diana in animated conversation with Crown Prince Akihito and the Crown Princess.

the tour, with a visit to a Kabuki theatre. In a more high-tech setting, a Tokyo television studio, Diana watched the filming of an episode of a 12th-century drama *The Legend of Benkei*, which had the ingredients of love, jealousy and rivalry usually found in ancient and medieval Japanese tales.

Diana was certainly getting her fill of the exotic fascinations of Japan, but the pace was taking its toll. That evening, the last of the tour, when the 84-year-old Emperor Hirohito received Charles and Diana at the Imperial Palace in Tokyo, the Princess told him she was feeling tired out.

However, with her usual self-discipline, Diana sparkled at the grand banquet which the Emperor gave for his royal visitors. Diana sat next to the aged Emperor, who found her charm so irresistible that

the age difference of nearly 60 years did not matter. The Emperor, who had come to the throne ten years before the Princess' mother was born, quite clearly enjoyed the company of the beautiful royal blonde from faraway England. This was all the more remarkable because Hirohito had to communicate through an interpreter. Even so, the Princess and the Emperor managed a few laughs and the aged ruler seemed more animated than his family and court officials had ever seen him.

Valuable gifts

When Charles and Diana flew home next day, they took a vast number of gifts with them. They were given a car, a £5000 motorcycle and video equipment, all samples of the industrial power of modern Japan. The most meaningful mementoes, though, were their memories of this fascinating country.

For Diana there was one particular incident during a temple tour, when she had hand-fed a giant golden carp that inhabited the temple pond. It had been a peaceful moment, in the company of a fish which was unaware that the hand that fed him was royal and did not realize what it meant to have a few quiet moments on a really hectic tour.

INDEX

This index is a complete alphabetical guide to *Diana: An Extraordinary Life.*

Page numbers in *italic* refer to pictures.

Prince Charles and
Lady Diana Spencer
after their engagement.

Charles and
Diana leave St.
Paul's on their
wedding day,
29 July 1981.

The royal couple show off baby Prince William, a future King of England.

Glamorous as ever, Diana at a film première in 1991.

On holiday in Majorca in 1988 with Prince Harry and the family.

Diana and the young Princes enjoying a good soaking in April 1993 at Thorpe Water Park.

PICTURE CREDITS AND ACKNOWLEDGEMENTS

Allsport Picture Library: 204bl, **Alpha Picture Library:** 5, 6t, 8b, 9b, 10b, 18(4), 19, 22(6), 34, 35t, 37c, 37b, 43tr, 44br, 45, 46, 46, 47bl, 50tl, 51b, 53, 54l, 66(4), 67, 69b, 81, 94, 95(3), 95b, 98r, 101t, 104, 111b, 113b, 122l, 126tl, 127, 128t, 134l, 138(2), 144, 145, 146, 147tr, 149cr, 153, 154, 154, 158tl, 158bl, 163(1), 166(1), 168, 169, 171, 171, 171, 171, 172tr, 173t, 174tr, 176tr, 177, 181, 183t, 186l, 188b, 191(1), 220, 224cr, 235tl, 235bl, 239(1), 239(2), 239(3), 239(5), 239(6), 240b, 243b, 248b, 249, 254tr, 254tl, 255, 256t, 263br, 264tr, 265(3), 282, 282, 284(2), 287bl, 296t, 303, 324tl, 326t, 331tr, 334(2), 334in, 339t, 341, 341, 344l, 345, 347, 350t, 351b, 354l, 358tl, 360r, 361(3), 371b, 373t, 374tl, 374r, 376t, 377b, 384c, 393, 395tr, 397t, 399bl, 400br, 405tl, 406tc, 451(2), 451(3), 451(4), 451(5), 453(1), 453(3), 469t, 502cl, 514br, 516br, 519t, 519cr, 519bl, 521t, 548, 548, 549(3), 549(5), 562br, 564t, 565t, 567r, 572(3), 573, 576(1), 576(3), 576(4), 594l, 595br, 618l, 621(3), 621(5), 622(1), **Bridgeman Art Library:** 14tl, 14tr, 15tl, 59b, 315b, 322b, 339b, 365b, 435b, 483b, 542bl, 580br, **Camera Press:** 22(4), 34(b), 37(t), 40(cr), 55, 89 (c), 95(cr), 99(tr), 132(c), 133(t), 134(b), 144(tr), 151(tr), 21(br), 218(tr), 222(tl), 248(t), 270(b), 292(br), 326(c), 348(bl), 398(b), 412(t), 415(tr), 446(cl), 494(t), 521(bl), 568(tl), 602(cl), 610(b), 614(br)./Peter Abbey: 77(b), 89(tl), 92(tl), 98(tl), 99(br);M. Anthony: 325(t);Barlow: 96(cl); Baron: 184(bl); Bassano 14(cl); Beaton: 75(c); Jim Bennet: 60(t), 90(tl), 270(t), 380(b); Bronco 7(tr); Joe Bulaitis: 84(t), 572(tl); Burns: 372(t), 489(t); David Cairns: 374(b); Lionel Cherruault: 82, 247(t), 266(b), 267(r), 431(tl), 458(b), 460(tl), 461(cr), 575(tr); Alan Clifton: 266; Bryn Colton 18(2), 86, 189(cr), 268; Charles de la Court: 7(cl); Alan Davidson: 85(c), 285(tr), 535(tr); Djukanovic: 187(br); Tony Drabble: 287(cl), 431(tr); Richard Gillard: 101(bl), 211(tl), 261(cr), 444(t), 472(t) Ken Goff 16, 75(t), 120, 121(br), 122(tr), 128(bl), 404(tr), 445(c), 450(r), 504(tl), 507(tl), 508, 510(t), 554(t), 557(tr), 558(c); Peter Grugeon 14(bl); Benoit Gysembergh: 400(bl); Glenn Harvey 18(3), 49(br), 61(t), 92(bl), 182(b), 184, 186, 188(tc), 191(tc, tr), 193(tc, bc), 219(t), 244, 260(l), 286(br), 307, 366(t), 375(tr), 428(tc), 531(tr); 543(r), 553(b); Chris Hewitt: 428(c); Nigel Hinkes: 500(tc); Hussein: 148(br); David Hutchinson: 493(b); ILN: 387(b); Patrick Lichfield: 33, 114(cl), 116(bc), 118(tr); LNS 17(bc), 323(tr, br); Stewart Mark: 63(tr);212(tr), 221(br), 242(tl), 418(t), 431(c), 473, 513(t), 538(t), 539(c), 544(b), 606(t), 617(t); B. Morton: 413(l), 551(tr); G Dalla Pozza 9(t); 14(br); Rota 15(br); G. Shakerley: 443(t); John Shelly: 433(tr), 435(tr), 500(tl); Sirman: 197(b); Slade: 83(br); Terry Smith: 231(b); Snowdon: 77(tl), 129(c); Albert Watson: 180(tl). **Demarchelier** © Conde Nast PL - British Vogue: 72 **Daily Mail:** 26 (br) **John Frost:** 11br, 23br, 36br, 47br, 55b, 60br, 71bc, 78tr, 79tr, 79b, 80b, 84b, 95b, 103b, 109b, 118b, 123b, 130b, 143b, 151br, 155br, 166br, 174br, 185br, 193br, 199br, 213br, 223br, 230br, 235br, 246br, 252br, 262b, 269br, 276b, 287br, 295c, 302bl, 327br, 334bl, 343bl, 352br, 360b, 372b, 383br, 391b, 394br, 407br, 414b, 420bl, 431b, 438b, 443c, 444b, 454bl, 463br, 468bl, 479br, 487b, 491br, 502b, 510b, 517br, 527br, 535b, 540b, 551br, 559b, 565b, 566tl, 576br, 583b, 588b, 599bl, 607b, 612b, 622bl, 628b, **Tim Graham:** 42, 49, 57, 58b, 61b, 62c, 62br, 66(6), 73b, 74, 78r, 82l, 82br, 85b, 87b, 90r, 93r, 95(2), 103t, 105, 106, 107t, 108, 109tl, 109tr, 110, 111tr, 111tl, 112, 117tr, 117tr, 124, 131, 150tr, 159, 160, 162, 163(3), 164(1), 164(3), 165, 166(3), 167, 170, 172br, 174tl, 178tr, 180br, 184tl, 188(3), 190, 193(2), 193(3), 194, 196bl, 198l, 200b, 201, 202, 204tl, 204br, 204tr, 206, 225, 226tr, 227bl, 228, 229, 230t, 232, 233, 235(2), 236(1), 236(2), 236(3), 236(4), 238, 239(4), 240, 254cr, 258, 271l, 273, 274b, 276t, 277, 278r, 279, 280tr, 286tr, 290, 291t, 292tr, 294r, 295t, 297, 299, 300t, 304t, 308c, 308(3), 308(4), 308(6), 311bl, 316, 317, 318br, 319t, 322t, 324br, 325b, 327bl, 329b, 330, 331tl, 332, 333, 335r, 346b, 348br, 349, 350b, 352tl, 353, 355tc, 356(2), 356(5), 357tc, 359, 361tc, 364b, 369, 370tc, 373b, 378bc, 380(1), 382l, 387t, 392b,

413tr, 396, 401r, 403, 404(1), 404(3), 404(5), 404(6), 407(2), 407(3), 408r, 410cl, 411, 414t, 415l, 416, 419b, 420br, 422, 423, 424c, 425l, 425br, 428(3), 430c, 430(2), 432, 434r, 436, 437, 439tr, 442t, 446(inset), 448, 452(2), 453(2), 453(4), 454(1), 454(2), 456, 458tl, 459, 461tr, 462t, 474, 476, 477(1), 477(3), 478tr, 478(2), 478(4), 479lc, 479bl, 480, 481, 482, 494rc, 496, 498, 499, 501, 503tr, 510lc, 511, 512, 522r, 524(2), 524(5), 526, 528, 534tr, 536t, 538b, 539br, 546r, 546cr, 546cl, 548r, 549(4), 550, 555r, 556t, 558t, 559t, 560, 566b, 572(4), 572(6), 575(4), 575(6), 577cr, 578, 579, 580c, 581, 583tl, 584, 594r, 596(2), 597, 599tr, 599br, 600r, 600b, 603tr, 606, 610t, 611t, 611c, 613, 614tl, 614c, 616t, 618tr, 621(4), 622(2), 622(3), 622(4), 622(5), 62296), 625b, 626t, 627t, 628l, 629r, 631, 632, 633tl, **JS Library:** 7b, 22(5), 28c, 58tr, 60c, 95(1), 132r, 142r, 164(2), 164(4), 166(2), 235tr, 298t, 426, 503c, 519br, 534cl, 546cb, 604b, 628tr, **Network:** 29br, **Hulton Getty:** 4, 7tl, 8t, 8c, 9c, 10cr, 12cr, 12r, 41, 555bl, **PA News:** 12b, 107b, 520, 612t, **Photographers International / Jayne Fincher:** 18(5), 18(6), 21, 43c, 6692), 71(1), 92(3), 131b, 137, 139, 140, 141, **Popperfoto:** 38b, 592cr, 592br, 593br, **Rex Features:** 3, 10tl, 10tr, 11t, 12t, 18(1), 22(1), 22(3), 23, 25, 27, 28t, 29t, 29l, 30, 31, 32t, 36t, 38tl, 38r, 39, 40t, 40t, 51t, 52, 54r, 56b, 58tp, 62tl, 62tr, 62bl, 64, 65, 66(1), 66(3), 66(5), 68, 69(1), 70, 71br, 79tl, 80t, 83c, 85t, 86t, 88tc, 90c, 92(1), 92(4), 96r, 97b, 100, 102, 117cr, 123t, 125, 126tr, 126b, 130t, 132t, 133cr, 135b, 136, 138(1), 138(3), 138(4), 142(1), 142(2), 143(3), 143(4), 147tl, 147b, 148t, 150tl, 152c, 155t, 156, 157, 158r, 163(2), 163(4), 163(5), 172, 175, 176b, 178tr, 178tc, 179, 180cr, 182tc, 183b, 185cr, 191(2), 192, 195, 196t, 197t, 198tr, 198cr, 199tr, 199tl, 200t, 207r, 208, 209, 210, 213(1), 213(2), 213(3), 214, 215, 216, 218tr, 219bl, 221tr, 221tl, 222r, 223t, 224t, 226tl, 226b, 227br, 236cb, 236(5), 237, 242tr, 243t, 245, 246tr, 246tl, 247cr, 250, 251, 252, 253, 256b, 257, 261t, 261bl, 261bc, 262t, 263cr, 264cr, 265l, 265tr, 268t, 269c, 271tr, 271c, 272, 274t, 274cr, 275t, 278tc, 278b, 280tl, 280b, 281, 283tr, 283br, 284(1), 284(3), 284(4), 285cr, 286(1), 288, 289, 291br, 292tl, 294tl, 296cl, 300b, 301, 302tl, 302cl, 302tr, 304bl, 304br, 305, 306, 307cl, 308(1), 308(2), 309, 310, 311(1), 311(2), 312, 313, 314, 315tr, 315tl, 318t, 320, 321, 327t, 328, 329t, 331cl, 331b, 334(1), 334(3), 335(4), 336, 338, 340, 342, 343t, 343cr, 344t, 346t, 348t, 351t, 352tr, 354r, 355cr, 356(1), 356(3), 356(4), 357tr, 358br, 361(2), 362, 264tr, 364tl, 367, 368, 370tr, 370b, 373cl, 376b, 377t, 378tr, 379, 380(2), 381(3), 381tr, 382tr, 383(1), 383(2), 383(3), 384r, 386, 388, 389, 390, 391tr, 391tl, 392t, 394t, 395b, 397c, 397bc, 398t, 399r, 400t, 401tl, 402, 404(4), 405r, 406tl, 407(1), 408l, 410t, 412t, 415cr, 417, 418br, 419t, 420t, 421, 424tr, 424br, 425tr, 427, 428(2), 429, 430l, 430l, 433b, 434l, 435tl, 438t, 439tl, 439cr, 440, 441, 442b, 445tl, 445b, 446tl, 446r, 447, 451(1), 452(1), 452(3), 452r, 454br, 455, 457, 458tl, 460tl, 460tr, 462b, 463t, 464, 465, 466, 467, 468, 469b, 470, 471, 472bl, 472br, 477(2), 477l, 478(1), 478(3), 484, 485, 486, 487t, 488, 490, 491t, 492, 493tl, 493tc, 495, 497, 500r, 502tl, 502tr, 504r, 506, 507tr, 509, 510tc, 514tr, 515tr, 516tr, 516cl, 517tl, 517bl, 518, 521br, 522c, 524(1), 524(3&5), 525. **FSP:** 17br, 24, 26t, 32cl, 40br, 44tr, 50tr, 56tr, 76, 77tr, 134t, 149, 262tl, 262tr, 264bl, 483tr, 568tr, 586t,587b, 588lr, 591bl, 593bl, 609,624, 625tr, 626bl. **Sunday Magazine:** 205br. **Times Newspapers Ltd.**/Peter Nicholls: 602 (tr). **Topham:** 6b, 507br, 514c, 515tl

Packaged by De Agostini Rights/meb.dap